ABORIGINAL PEOPLES IN CANADA

Ninth Edition

D1284012

JAMES S. FRIDERES
University of Calgary

RENÉ R. GADACZ
Grand Prairie Regional College

Toronto

Vice-President, Editorial Director: Gary Bennett
Editor-in-Chief: Michelle Sartor
Editor, Humanities and Social Sciences:
Joel Gladstone
Marketing Manager: Lisa Gillis
Supervising Developmental Editor: Madhu Ranadive
Developmental Editor: Cheryl Finch
Project Manager: Lesley Deugo
Manufacturing Coordinator: Susan Johnson

Production Editor:
Misbah (MPS Limited, a Macmillan Company)
Copy Editor: Susan Adlam
Proofreader: Sally Glover
Compositor: MPS Limited, a Macmillan Company
Art Director: Julia Hall
Cover Designer: Miguel Acevedo
Cover Image: Getty Images / Altrendo

Credits and acknowledgments borrowed from other sources and reproduced, with permission, in this textbook appear on the appropriate page within text.

Statistics Canada information is used with the permission of Statistics Canada. Users are forbidden to copy the data and redisseminate them, in an original or modified form, for commercial purposes, without permission from Statistics Canada. Information on the availability of the wide range of data from Statistics Canada can be obtained from Statistics Canada's Regional Offices, its World Wide Web site at **www.statcan.gc.ca**, and its toll-free access number 1-800-263-1136.

If you purchased this book outside the United States or Canada, you should be aware that it has been imported without the approval of the publisher or the author.

Library and Archives Canada Cataloguing in Publication
Frideres, James S., 1943–
    Aboriginal peoples in Canada / James S. Frideres, René R. Gadacz. — 9th ed.

Includes bibliographical references and index.
ISBN 978-0-13-216197-8

    1. Native peoples—Canada. 2. Native peoples—Canada—Social conditions. 3. Native peoples—Canada—Politics and government. 4. Native peoples—Canada—Government relations. I. Gadacz, René R. II. Title.

E78.C2F7 2011   971.004'97   C2011-903372-0

ISBN 978-0-13-216197-8

Brief Contents

Contents

Preface

When the first edition of this book was published more than three decades ago, little did we know that today it would still make an important scholarly contribution to the discipline. Since then, the global environment has changed substantially and new people have come to occupy positions of power. Old political figures are no longer recognized by young Canadians, and new institutions and new ways of operating have been created. At the same time, while the process of devolution has continued, many of the attributes of colonialism still remain. This new edition chronicles the changes that have taken place over the past century and explores how they have affected Canadians and Aboriginal peoples alike. Presented in a more reader-friendly framework, this new edition will allow the reader to follow the process by which Aboriginal people have come to find themselves in the margins of Canadian society. The use of "boxes" throughout the text offers examples, reinforces key concepts, and provides a focus for the reader. We also introduce the concept of identity and examine how it has come to affect Aboriginal people and their relationship with government. In addition, new evidence is presented with regard to the effects of *Bill C-31* and the McIvor decision.

Utilizing the 2006 Census and recent information from the Department of Aboriginal Affairs and Northern Development, this new edition incorporates up-to-date statistics regarding the demographic, social, and economic position of Aboriginal people in Canadian society. Statistical data presented also allows the reader to compare the different Aboriginal groups as well as compare Aboriginal people with the non-Aboriginal population. In addition, whenever possible, this new edition allows the reader a historical perspective, a view of how things have changed over time. In the end, the reader will be able to create a social profile for Aboriginal people in Canada.

A new chapter called "Great Strides and New Challenges: City Life and Gender Issues" addresses issues of urbanization and outlines how this process differentially impacts Aboriginal men and women. In addition, this chapter provides a chronicle of how the "sex wars" have emerged in Aboriginal communities across Canada. Our examination of the role of women and their effect on the Aboriginal way of life allows for a more nuanced understanding of the tension evident in many Aboriginal communities.

As Aboriginal Affairs and Northern Development continues to undergo changes in both their mandate and operations, this new edition identifies and comments on those changes. Moreover, this edition looks at how the Auditor General has evaluated the Department over the past decade. Finally, current information reveals that Aboriginal Affairs continues to unilaterally engage in policy development and implementation without consultation with Aboriginal peoples. Issues such as Aboriginal residential schools, the apologies for Inuit and First Nations, and the creation of the Truth and Reconciliation Commission are addressed. New information reveals that some First Nation communities have opted out of the *Indian Act* and are exploring alternative modes of operating in Canadian society.

This new edition sees separate chapters on Métis and Inuit. In both chapters, current, up-to-date statistical information is presented as well as an examination of how these groups have adapted to their inclusion in the Canadian Constitution. The material traces their historical origins and their struggle for cultural, political, and legal recognition in Canada. As a result, the reader will understand the place of Métis and Inuit in Canadian Confederation and the challenges they face in the future.

Numerous court decisions have been rendered in the past decade, and this edition of *Aboriginal Peoples in Canada* provides the reader with a current understanding of Aboriginal rights within the context of the Canadian Constitution. For example, the "need to consult" condition now placed on various development projects has forced both the private sector and government to rethink their relationship with Aboriginal peoples. We begin with a historical discussion of Aboriginal–non-Aboriginal relations and then trace the evolution of these relations over time. We provide this through a number of lenses. For example, the Supreme Court of Canada has addressed Aboriginal rights and their links to British property law, and has clearly acknowledged that there is a new constitutional meaning and role for Aboriginal people. We also show how Aboriginal issues are viewed by politicians and representative Canadians.

Updates on court decisions regarding land claims and treaties are presented, which allow the reader to see trends in legal thinking regarding the various claims being brought forward by Aboriginal people across Canada. The linkage between the judiciary and policy makers is discussed, and implications for the future are addressed. In addition, we identify new directions that the Government of Canada is taking with regard to Aboriginal economic development. Examples of how some First Nation communities have undertaken their quest for self-determination and economic self-sufficiency are presented. These new directions emerge out of the Harvard Project, and the reader will be apprised of the core of these new solutions.

A new concluding chapter serves as a capstone to the book by familiarizing the reader with the ways Aboriginal people in Canada share their struggle with Indigenous peoples around the world. Through the support of international organizations, Aboriginal people have pursued the goals of social justice and cultural legitimacy.

For the first half of the 20th century, Canadians showed little interest in the concerns of Aboriginal people. However, by the 1950s, government had become embarrassed by international incidents that placed Canada and its treatment of Aboriginals on the global map. Through the commissioning of government reports, a small body of evidence emerged that suggested Aboriginal people were not benefiting from the growing economy. In the 1960s, academics began to write on the subject and add to the expanding knowledge base. However, it was not until the 1970s that an explosion of books, articles, movies, and other popular cultural and media representations occurred as a renaissance in Aboriginal identity began. By the mid-1980s and beyond, Aboriginal issues were addressed by the mass media on a regular basis. Academics, including First Nation, Métis, and Inuit scholars, now routinely teach in Native Studies programs or courses concerned with Aboriginal people. In the past several decades, a growing literature on Aboriginal people has been published in scholarly journals and in the popular media by both Aboriginal and non-Aboriginal authors. These and other publications have a diversity of foci—legal, land claims, justice, deviance, health, housing, language, media and communication—from a variety of theoretical perspectives, including Eurocentric,

Aboriginal, feminist, Marxist, and structural-functional. Aboriginal Studies is now a burgeoning area of study, regardless of its lack of boundaries and central focus, and 12 different universities across Canada now offer academic programs with advanced degrees in the area. Also in this edition, the voices of Aboriginal scholars are prominent in the discussion of various issues. A quick look at the bibliography will reveal that over the past five years, an increasing number of Aboriginal scholars have entered the discussion on Aboriginal–non-Aboriginal relations.

The ninth edition follows the general format of the original and previous editions. Nevertheless, the present volume comprises a considerable updating and revision of the last edition. While there have been many specific changes over the past five years, the overall position of Aboriginal people in our society has not appreciably changed. It is said that if one works on an enterprise long enough, one will eventually gain some perspective on it. But as noted elsewhere, failing eyesight sometimes offsets the gain in perspective. We have no doubt that as we write the ninth edition, both statements have proven to be true. Nevertheless, we are convinced that the perspective offered to the reader will illuminate his or her intellectual world and provide for a better understanding of Aboriginal people in Canadian society. We hope we are able to give the reader a lens through which to view our complex and diverse society and the ability to develop a better appreciation of how historical events influence contemporary issues; in the end, we hope the reader will have the intellectual tools necessary to better analyze Aboriginal–Euro-Canadian relations.

Our goal has been to write a book that provides a critical interpretation of the events that have shaped Aboriginal–Euro-Canadian relations and that thus have formed the structure of Canadian society. As we note in the text, many of the original works on Aboriginal people were written from the point of view of the dominant group. The material offered in this book tries to present ethnic relations from the position of "outsider," identifying both the majority and minority perspectives.

Acknowledgments

Those who know the subject area will recognize that we owe a large debt to those who have already worked on and written about Aboriginal people. As such, regardless of what the copyright law says, this book is not the sole product of the co-authors. We have drawn heavily on the works of our colleagues across Canada and they have shared their thoughts and ideas with us. Their understanding and criticism of old ideas made us search constantly for new conceptualizations and, hopefully, new solutions. We thank them for their insightful and analytical comments. We would also like to thank those Aboriginal people who have, over the years, shared with us their views and interpretations of Aboriginal–Euro-Canadian relations in this country.

At Pearson Education, we are grateful to our Acquisitions Editor, Joel Gladstone, and Marketing Manager Lisa Gillis, for the strong support they have given this project. We owe special thanks to our Developmental Editor, Cheryl Finch, for her endless good humour, patience, careful guidance, and outstanding contribution in preparing the manuscript for publication. Susan Adlam deserves accolades for her very fine copyediting. We also thank MPS Ltd for shepherding the text through production, as well as the team in Creative Services for their skilful design of the text. We would like to thank Sally Glover for her exceptional ability to see errors and omissions in the text. Lastly, we acknowledge Carole Blackburn, Laurie Milne, and Zahra Montazer, whose critical review comments helped shape this edition of *Aboriginal Peoples in Canada*.

We would like to thank our students and co-learners, past and present, for participating in the often difficult task of nation-building by questioning (and sometimes revising!) their personal assumptions and philosophies regarding Aboriginal issues. Thanks to Heather Luhtala for her initial suggestions for revising and improving the previous edition and a spirited "high five" to Jennifer Schulze for her meticulous and always excellent research assistance on the ninth edition. We also are grateful to Michael I. Asch, Betty Bastien, the late Bruce G. Trigger, and many others for opportunities and encouragement over several decades of scholarship.

J. S. Frideres
Calgary, Alberta

René R. Gadacz
Grande Prairie, Alberta

Supplements

All instructor's supplements can be downloaded by instructors from a password-protected location on Pearson Canada's online catalogue (**www.pearsoncanada.ca**). Navigate to your book's catalogue page to view a list of those supplements that are available. See your local sales representative for details and access.

Instructor's Manual (978-0-13-287968-2)

The Instructor's Manual introduces each chapter with the learning objectives and chapter overview. The manual also provides suggested lecture outlines, additional discussion questions, easy-to-administer classroom assignments and a list of additional resources available from other sources.

Test Item File (978-0-13-279154-0)

The Test Item File is a new supplement created for this edition of *Aboriginal Peoples in Canada*. This test bank in Microsoft Word includes over 600 questions. There are approximately 55 questions per chapter, including multiple choice, true/false, and short answer, and essay questions. Each question is accompanied by the correct answer, a page reference where the answer can be found in the book, and a classification of difficulty level (easy, moderate, challenging).

PowerPoint Presentations (978-0-13-279155-7)

The PowerPoint offers over 20 slides per chapter and includes selected figures and tables from the textbook This supplement provides a comprehensive selection of slides highlighting key concepts featured in the text to assist instructors.

CourseSmart for Instructors (978-0-13-218125-9)

CourseSmart goes beyond traditional expectations–providing instant, online access to the textbooks and course materials you need at a lower cost for students. And even as students save money, you can save time and hassle with a digital eTextbook that allows you to search for the most relevant content at the very moment you need it. Whether it's evaluating textbooks or creating lecture notes to help students with difficult concepts, CourseSmart can make life a little easier. See how when you visit **www.coursesmart.com/instructors**.

CourseSmart for Students (978-0-13-218125-9)

CourseSmart goes beyond traditional expectations–providing instant, online access to the textbooks and course materials you need at an average savings of 60 percent. With instant access from any computer and the ability to search your text, you'll find the content you need quickly, no matter where you are. And with online tools like highlighting and note-taking, you can save time and study efficiently. See all the benefits at **www.coursesmart.com/students**.

Technology Specialists

Pearson's technology specialists work with faculty and campus course designers to ensure that Pearson technology products, assessment tools, and online course materials are tailored to meet your specific needs. This highly qualified team is dedicated to helping schools take full advantage of a wide range of educational resources, by assisting in the integration of a variety of instructional materials and media formats. Your local Pearson sales representative can provide you with more details on this service program.

MySearchLab

MySearchLab offers extensive help to students with their writing and research project and provides round-the-clock access to credible and reliable source material.

Research

Content on MySearchLab includes immediate access to thousands of full-text articles from leading Canadian and international academic journals, and daily news feeds from The Associated Press. Articles contain the full downloadable text—including abstract and citation information—and can be cut, pasted, emailed, or saved for later use.

Writing

MySearchLab also includes a step-by-step tutorial on writing a research paper. Included are sections on planning a research assignment, finding a topic, creating effective notes, and finding source material. Our exclusive online handbook provides grammar and usage support. Pearson SourceCheck™ offers an easy way to detect accidental plagiarism issues, and our exclusive tutorials teach how to avoid them in the future. And MySearchLab also contains AutoCite, which helps to correctly cite sources using MLA, APA, CMS, and CBE documentation styles for both endnotes and bibliographies.

To order this book with MySearchLab access at no extra charge, use ISBN 978-0-13-282385-2.

Take a tour at **www.mysearchlab.com**.

Pearson Custom Library

For enrollments of at least 25 students, you can create your own textbook by choosing the chapters that best suit your own course needs. To begin building your custom text, visit www.pearsoncustomlibrary.com. You may also work with a dedicated Pearson custom editor to create your ideal text—publishing your own original content or mixing and matching Pearson content. Contact your local Pearson representative to get started.

CHAPTER 1

Colonialism and Aboriginal Peoples

LEARNING OBJECTIVES

After reading this chapter you should be able to:

1. Explain the seven stages of the colonization process.
2. Compare and contrast French-Aboriginal and English-Aboriginal relations prior to Confederation.
3. Understand how Aboriginal and non-Aboriginal relations have changed since Confederation.
4. Identify two key ways of establishing identity and how they differ.
5. Explain the Aboriginals' economic loss and the non-Aboriginals' gain.
6. Describe the structural racism perspective.

INTRODUCTION

How does a people become marginalized in society? The history of Aboriginal–non-Aboriginal relations in Canada reveals both an active interference and a benign neglect on the part of the federal and provincial governments as they dealt with Aboriginal people over time. The marginalization that Aboriginal people experience today is not a recent event but rather is rooted in historical circumstances. In this book we will take what is called a political-economy approach, which utilizes economic and political factors in the development of relations between governments and Aboriginal people. Such structural impacts began to affect Aboriginal people at the time of contact with Europeans and became increasingly influential as the settler population grew. As the Canadian domestic economy became integrated with the world political economy, these structural effects relegated Aboriginal peoples in Canada to a peripheral position in society. In short, what we find today in Canada bears similarities to the plight of Aboriginal people around the world who have been marginalized within their own societies.

What are these processes? How have they affected Aboriginal people? We wish to approach the problem from a perspective that involves social structural factors—e.g., the organization of the society, the alignment of social institutions, the change in demographic factors. While we will not deny that Aboriginal people are exposed to a great deal of prejudice and discrimination, their greatest obstacle is the very structure of society itself, which prevents them from effectively participating in its social, economic, and political institutions. Furthermore, we feel there is a link between structural effects (the institutional arrangements of our society) and the behaviour of groups and individuals.

Using a macro perspective allows us to present the Aboriginal community as an internal colony that is exploited by the dominant group in Canada. In this model, Canadians are seen as the colonizing people, while Aboriginal persons are viewed as colonized. By conceptualizing the Aboriginal community as an internal colony of a larger nation, it is possible to see beyond the individual factors involved in inter-group behaviour and focus on the structural arrangements.

Why were Aboriginal people so overwhelmed by European settlers? Europeans settling Canada argue that their own superiority in technology and the inferiority of Aboriginal society (e.g., they were primitive, too few in number, superstitious) contributed to their colonization. In addition to being self-serving, these arguments fail to provide an adequate explanation.

Our explanation focuses more on the structural impact of colonization in New Canada. During the 16th and 17th centuries, England and France were intent on participating in the worldwide competition for faith and fortune and turned their attention to the new lands of America. In competition with the Dutch and Spanish, they explored the new continent, established trading missions, extracted primary resources, and dispatched missionaries. The impact of their activities was devastating.

As Wright (2003) notes, " . . . the great death raged for more than a century . . . perhaps more than 90 million died . . . It was the greatest mortality in history" (Doybns, 1983: 395). Bodley (1999) estimates that from the time of first contact, 80 percent of Indigenous people have been annihilated. He estimates that 60 million Indigenous people were annihilated in the 20th century alone. European diseases such as typhus, yellow fever, influenza, and smallpox often wiped out tribes by as much as 90 percent. It has been estimated that during the first century of colonization, an average of 1.5 percent of Aboriginal people died each year from chronic and epidemic diseases (Thornton, 1987). Regardless of the original number, we know that after nearly 20 new diseases were introduced to North America over the span of five generations, less than a tenth of the original population remained. In this catastrophic loss of people, leaders, intellectuals, and military strategists, as well as spiritual and political leaders, died.

Many will object to the numbers presented above, and while they are certainly controversial, much of the opposition to these statistics is related to the myth of the **"empty land"** that was created by the white settlers—and the development of the doctrine of *terra nullius* that was incorporated into our law. Put another way, Canada developed a legal system based on the concept of discovering an uninhabited land! Canadians object to large estimates of the number of Aboriginal people killed because doing so allows them to evade the issue of genocide, which resulted from the practices of the settlers and the government.

These obvious points have eluded Canadians for the past 500 years, yet we have built stories upon these myths that support the current view that Europeans discovered Canada and built what we have today through the efforts of hardworking settlers and dedicated colonial leaders. As Wright (2003) notes, these myths become maps by which succeeding generations navigate and make sense of their world. Once the stories are told and re-told, they take on a sense of legitimacy and their veracity is rarely questioned. Canadians are loath to accept that perhaps the past is not as they think.

THE COLONIZATION MODEL

Our model suggests that historical colonialism shaped the organization of our society and set in motion a number of factors that propelled Aboriginal people to its margins. First of all, Aboriginal participation in the Canadian economy has become economically redundant over time because of changes in the structure and technology of the national economy. After the buffalo hunts ended and the fur trade all but ceased, Aboriginal people were restricted from participating in the newly emerging economy. As Canadian society moved first to an agricultural and then to an urban industrial base, Aboriginal peoples did not possess, and were not in a position to acquire, new technologies or skills. The result is that Aboriginal people found themselves operating a subsistence economy parallel to that of the more modern economy. Today their lack of education, technical expertise, and access to technology continues to keep them out of the new knowledge economy. This new knowledge economy focuses on the development of information rather than the production of goods. In other words, there are two economies in our society. The industrial, technological, and knowledge-based modern sector is dynamic: Change promotes further change. The traditional, subsistence sector, however, resists change: It clings to the old ways and is unable to adopt new technology (Wien, 1986). This suggests that, as our economy becomes increasingly knowledge-based, barriers continue to be created that hinder or prevent the entrance of Aboriginal people into the knowledge era. Certain technical and social skills are now prerequisites for entering the labour force. People without these skills will be kept from participating as full-time members in the modern national—and international—labour markets. Already, researchers have noted the "digital divide" between Aboriginal and non-Aboriginal communities.

As individuals are prevented from entering the modern economy, a cultural ethos emerges that is quite different from the one expressed in the dominant sector. When the goals of higher status are denied to people, other forms of adaptation are created—for example, withdrawal and rebellion (often self-destructive)—in order to deal with the despair and hopelessness that are central to the **culture of poverty**. This encourages individuals to develop a different perspective on life and on how to deal with everyday occurrences.

Once an individual is placed outside the primary labour market, it is almost impossible for him or her to enter it. As stated above, the lack of certain technical and social skills keeps Aboriginal persons from entering the modern labour market. And as that market becomes increasingly segmented into primary and secondary markets, there is greater difficulty in moving from the secondary to the primary market. As a result, Aboriginal persons are increasingly shut out of the primary market.

COLONIALIZING CANADA'S ABORIGINAL PEOPLE

The Historical Context

Colonization first needs to be put in its historical context before we discuss the process. It emerged out of the belief that papal claims of authority provided explorers with the right to discover new lands and claim them for the "mother" country. However, by the 15th and

16th centuries, kings and queens (French and English) were signing letters of patent giving people like John Cabot and Jacques Cartier authority to explore and claim lands from heathens and infidels. By 1670, Charles II issued the Hudson's Bay Company charter, which restated their disregard for any Aboriginal claims to much of present-day Canada. Maybury-Lewis et al. (2009) note that within a short time after the Hudson's Bay Company charter was signed, the French met with Aboriginal groups and asserted French national claims to all of Canada. At the time, there was no thought about the possibility that Aboriginal people might actually own the land or its resources. By the time the English had defeated the French and won the Indian wars, ousting the French and their military, the pattern for dealing with Aboriginal people was set. The *Royal Proclamation* (1763) then became the standard policy by which the British began to base their relations with Aboriginal people. This document outlined in principle the manner in which lands would be transferred from Aboriginal peoples. However, in practical terms, the Proclamation was duly ignored by colonists and settlers in Canada.

When European settlers came to Canada, they had no interest in any aspect of Aboriginal culture. Colonists viewed the Aboriginal people as impediments to the cultivation of the land and to civilization in general. They were, in many respects, viewed in the same light as mountains or rivers: implacable obstacles that had to be dealt with. Unless the Aboriginal people vanished, which was highly unlikely, the settlers typically tried to pacify and resettle them away from the land required by the newcomers. The settlement of Canada by Europeans, with their machines and microbes, was an attempt to control the new land and its inhabitants and to turn them into a profit. It was planned that the land itself could be made profitable through the introduction of Western technology (e.g., agriculture) and a capitalist economy. However, the inhabitants of the land posed a problem in bringing this policy to fruition. Their culture was strange and diverse and did not fit into the new European way of life. It was clear that if the colonizers wanted the new land to yield a profit, they would have to harness, or at least neutralize, the activities of the Aboriginal population (Axtell, 1981).

The Colonization Process

The **colonization process** can be considered to have seven different dimensions (Kennedy, 1945; Blauner, 1969). The first concerns the incursion of the colonizing group into a geographical area. This usually takes the form of forced-voluntary entry; acting in its own interests, the colonizing group forces its way into an area. In Canada, both French and English settlement followed this pattern. Lands and resources were taken from Aboriginal people and reallocated to settlers. At present, many Aboriginal people argue that forced-voluntary colonization is still occurring in the North.

The second attribute of colonization is its destructive effect on the social and cultural structures of the Indigenous group. In Canada's case, European colonizers destroyed the Native peoples' political, economic, kinship, and, in most cases, religious systems. The values and norms of Aboriginal people were either ignored or violated. For example, after the War of 1812, when a large number of European settlers arrived, the colonial government decided that Aboriginal persons should be forced to surrender their traditional lifestyles. Official programs were developed, and, between 1830 and 1875, legislation was enacted to carry out this destructive policy (Surtees, 1969). Over time, rules and regulations were imposed on Aboriginal people in order to stop them from engaging in traditional ceremonies (e.g., potlatches, sundances) and force them to take on more settler-like behaviour.

As Titley (1986) points out, the federal government's policies were in harmony with the demands of non-Aboriginal people. The creation of "trust authority" over Indian lands and assets demonstrates the government's commitment to dictating what resources would be exploited, in what quantities, and by whom. However, in principle, the government implemented a relationship that was more of a "guardianship" than a trust. As Cohen (1960) points out, guardianship is a relation that limits the personal and group rights of the Aboriginal, while a trusteeship is a relation that limits the property rights of a trustee and makes the trustee the servant of the trust beneficiary. As the government implemented the guardianship role with Aboriginal people, it allowed the determination of Aboriginal behaviour for what purpose and at what cost. There was a conflation of guardianship and trusteeship that allowed the government to reinterpret treaties and other agreements they had made with Aboriginal people such that government officials could carry out actions that were in their best interest. In the end, the land base of Aboriginal people was diminished and their culture undermined.

As Wright (2003) argues, it was important that the reserves be made to look "self-governing" so that they would be exempt from normal business practices and thus subject only to the unique rules established by Indian Affairs. The protests of Aboriginal people were futile, and when they took action to support their claims in the late 1860s, harsh repression followed, including the bombardment of British Columbia coastal villages by British warships (Tobias, 1976). By the late 1890s, the federal government had amended the *Indian Act* (of 1876) so that "surplus" or "idle" Aboriginal land could be made available for the use of non-Indians. In 1911, amendments to the *Indian Act* gave even greater coercive powers to the federal government. For example, Section 46 allowed portions of reserves to be taken by municipalities or companies for roads or similar public purposes with the consent of the governor-in-council (today called the cabinet) but without a surrender (Carter, 1990; Imai and Hawley, 1995).

While it was agreed that Aboriginal people were redeemable, it was also recognized that they were still in a state of "savagery," which meant they were some distance from Christianity. And, in order to redeem them, Aboriginal people needed to be first "civilized" and then educated in the Christian way of life. The major problem with Aboriginals, as seen by the colonists, was their unpredictability and their savagery—both of which emerged from their cultural deficiencies. Aboriginal peoples had to be rendered predictable if the new land was to be settled and developed. Initially, the missionaries took on this task of "Christianizing" the Aboriginal population and making them more like the settlers in ways of thought and behaviour. In short, the conversion of Aboriginal people not only focused on religion but sought to replace their culture with a European one and to change their behaviour by substituting predictable European modes of thinking and feeling for unpredictable Aboriginal modes. By aiming to control the Aboriginal way of life, missionaries lent, unwittingly or not, powerful support to the European assault upon Aboriginal people by carrying out their own subversive invasion within (Axtell, 1981).

During this time, a symbiotic relationship emerged between various churches and the state. For example, a review of all the colonial charters of the French and English during the 16th and 17th centuries explicitly reveals the wish to extend the Christian church and to save the "savage" souls as a principal motive for colonization. Even the Recollect priests coming to Canada in the early 17th century noted that Indians were to be regulated by French laws and modes of living in order to render them capable of understanding Christianity (Le Clercq, 1834). As Christianity was enforced, names and clothing were changed, hair had to be cut, and many other cultural attributes of Aboriginal life altered. In addition, there were structural changes implemented in order to bring the Aboriginals into a state of "civilization." However, over time, the English, with their sense of cultural superiority—infused with racism—realized that Aboriginal people would remain Aboriginal no matter how "civilized" or Christianized they became. Moreover, church officials felt that because certain components of Aboriginal culture were incompatible with Christianity, they should be eradicated. They therefore convinced the state to pass legislation outlawing a variety of ceremonies that were an integral component of Aboriginal culture—for example, the potlatch.

The third and fourth aspects of colonization are the interrelated processes of external political control and Aboriginal economic dependence. In the standard practice of colonization, the mother country sends out representatives through which it indirectly rules the newly conquered land. In our model, the representative ruler is the Department of Aboriginal Affairs and Northern Development (known as AAND). Until 1940, what was then Indian Affairs created a "pass system" which determined who could leave reserve lands, when, and for what purpose. Aboriginal **self-government** was effectively prevented through the introduction of new techniques of selecting chief and council. Moreover, any decision taken by chief and council had to have the approval of the local Superintendent of Indian Affairs. Until the latter part of the 20th century, band funds could not be used by Aboriginal people to develop social and political organizations of their own (Whiteside, 1972).

In 2006, the federal court ruled on a case involving Indian monies that allowed a First Nations community in Alberta to control funds obtained from the development of natural resources on the reserve. After 10 years of litigation and a cost of over $50 million, the First Nations won, only to have the government appeal the decision to the Federal Court of Appeal, which overturned the initial ruling. A further appeal to the Supreme Court upheld the Federal Court of Appeal decision. This control over Aboriginal people continues today, as exhibited by Canada's refusal to initially sign the Declaration on the Rights of Indigenous Peoples, which was endorsed in 2007 by 143 countries around the world. What is particularly problematic is that the Conservatives under Prime Minister Harper have not provided an intelligible explanation as to why they would not sign the Declaration.

The minister of Aboriginal Affairs and Northern Development can suspend almost any right set forth in the *Indian Act*. Acting through cabinet, Aboriginal Affairs can also veto any decisions of band councils. For example, Section 82 of the *Indian Act* allows a band to enact money bylaws. However, cabinet must first find that the band has reached a "high state of development" before allowing the band to pass such a bylaw. Section 68 of the Act allows a band to "control, manage, and expand in whole or in part its revenue moneys." No band was actually permitted to do so until 1959, and to date, fewer than 20 percent have received permission. Section 60 allows a band "the right to exercise such control and management over lands in the reserve occupied by that band as the Cabinet considers desirable." To date, cabinet has found this desirable for less than 15 percent of reserves. Section 35 of the Act explicitly states that reserve land can be expropriated by the federal government at any time. Unfortunately, this provision has been implemented many times over the past half-century.

As Alfred (2009) points out, political and social institutions as well as service agencies that influence and govern Aboriginal life today are shaped and organized to serve the interests of the state, not those of Aboriginal people. He argues that the structures and responsibilities of these agencies conform to the interests of governments as their source of legitimacy is found in Canadian law, not in Aboriginal interests or laws.

During early days of trade between Aboriginal people and European settlers, a pattern of dependency began to emerge. For example, while many trade goods were simple substitutions for traditional items used by Aboriginal people (e.g., cloth for animal skins, metal for stone or wooden tools), it meant that once the substitution took place, the dependency began. However, there were some items that radically transformed Aboriginal culture. Specifically, the introduction of guns and alcohol brought about large and long-lasting changes to the traditional Aboriginal way of life.

Aboriginal people remain economically dependent on the larger society because their reserves are treated as geographical and social hinterlands for Euro-Canadian exploitation. Initially, Euro-Canadian settlers claimed sovereignty over the land. They then extended this to the land's people, and today continue the process by claiming sovereignty over resources found on the land—all inanimate materials. Euro-Canadians control businesses; exploit non-renewable primary resources such as oil, minerals, water, and forest products; and ship these resources to urban industrial centres for processing. This practice has two important consequences for Aboriginal people on reserves: the development of Aboriginal-owned industries is pre-empted, and Aboriginal occupational activities remain at a primary level. As the treaties and the *Indian Act* show, federal policy has always tried to orient Aboriginal occupations toward agriculture and primary industries (Carter, 1990). Today this orientation continues with the federal government's cap on financial support for young Aboriginal people who want to attend post-secondary educational institutions.

In the colonization process, a two-level system develops in which the colonizers own, direct, and profit from industries that depend upon exploitation of colonized peoples, who provide an unskilled, seasonal work force. For example, on the reserves, the long-term result has been an Aboriginal population that lives at subsistence level, working at unskilled, seasonal jobs in primary industries and practising subsistence agriculture to survive. Although the profits from raw material production are based on reserve resources and cheap Aboriginal labour, they disappear from the reserve into the pockets of non-Aboriginal entrepreneurs. One must remember that First Nations do not own their lands. The federal government has total legal jurisdiction on these lands and manages them for the use and benefit of First Nations people.

The federal government has effectively discouraged the economic development of reserves, as the *Income Tax Act* and the *Indian Act* show. If Aboriginal people create a limited corporation to engage in business on reserves, they lose the benefit of exemption from taxation as individuals or as a band. As a result, income earned by a corporation wholly owned by Aboriginal people is subject to the same taxation as any corporation, even if the income is derived solely from activities on a reserve. While some provisions of the *Income Tax Act* have changed, the overall thrust remains the same today. The structural complexities involved in the payment of property taxes on reserve lands also prevent Aboriginal people from profitably leasing their lands. In other cases, non-Aboriginal business interests have not developed large-scale commercial and industrial projects on First Nations reserves because of "regulatory gaps." These gaps refer to differences between provincial and federal laws with regard to economic activities taking place on the reserves. It would take more than 100 years for the federal government to finally enact the *First Nations Commercial and Industrial Development Act* in 2009 in order to rectify this situation. While this change still requires government permission for First Nations communities that wish to take advantage of the Act, they now may request permission to operate under the Act. The federal government's explanation of this gap was that they never thought that First Nations communities would want to engage in economic development projects.

A fifth attribute of colonization is the provision of low-quality social services for colonized Aboriginal individuals in such areas as health and education. This aspect of colonization has been operating for many centuries.

A survey by the former Department of Indian and Northern Affairs confirms a desperate need for adequate health and social services (Canada, 2001). As illustrated elsewhere in this book, the survey's findings show a lower life expectancy than in the general population, a higher level of support from social assistance organizations, and an unhealthy lifestyle imposed by poverty. Although some housing conditions have improved, social problems, new diseases (e.g., diabetes, AIDS), alcohol abuse, welfare dependency, and water pollution have increased. The provision of health care is normally considered a provincial responsibility, although there is considerable debate between the provinces and the federal government as to who provides social services for Aboriginal people. Kirmayer and Valaskakis (2009) further argue that it is likely that Aboriginal experiences with collective trauma, disorientation, and government policies are the major determinants of health problems experienced by many Aboriginal communities across Canada.

The sixth and seventh aspects of colonization relate to social interactions between Aboriginal and non-Aboriginal people and refer to racism and the establishment of a colour-line. Traditional racism is a belief in the genetic or cultural superiority of the colonizers and the inferiority of the colonized people. At the time of contact, there was widespread agreement among the colonizers that Aboriginal people lacked several basic qualities essential to being "men"—order, industry, and manners. As a result, both missionaries and colonial governments used a variety of strategies to elevate the Aboriginal's status beyond the level of "savage." There were three obstacles to overcome. First, Aboriginal people did not recognize forms of government beyond "chiefdoms." The Europeans were accustomed to kings and queens, standing armies, and bureaucratic structures (e.g., parliaments) to deal with everyday life and so "chiefs" were viewed with distain. Second, Aboriginal people were migratory and eschewed the concept of permanent settlements. Even those engaged in more sedentary activities generally moved in a seasonal fashion. Finally, colonial powers found Aboriginal people deficient in industry or what we would call "work." This didn't mean Aboriginal people didn't work in order to produce food and housing. However, for the colonial powers, it meant they did not work "laboriously" in the sense of severe, compulsory work. Colonists found "idleness" endemic to the Aboriginal way of life, which, defined in religious terms, meant "the devil's hand." As a result, colonial action attempted to bring the Aboriginal way of life "in line" with that of the settlers.

With a colour-line, indicators such as skin pigmentation and body structure form the basis for determining superiority and inferiority. For example, a recent Environics (2010) survey found that over 60 percent of adult non-Aboriginal Canadians believe that Aboriginal people are subject to prejudice and discrimination. Interaction is found to take place only among members of the same group: Non-Aboriginals interact with non-Aboriginals and Aboriginal people with Aboriginal people. In Canada, for example, Native people have the highest rate of marriage within their own ethnic group—almost 90 percent.

In short, settlers brought with them an ethnocentric ethos and viewed Aboriginal life through that lens. What they perceived to be "disorder" and "idleness" were thought to be weaknesses that characterized Aboriginal culture as well as the individual (Axtell, 1981). However, over time this pure form of racism has transformed into what is called "structural" or "systemic" racism. The prevailing fundamental belief was that no person in his/her right mind (a civilized person) would choose to be an Indian.

Structural Racism

Today it would be difficult to find a Canadian who would publicly state that some groups of people are racially inferior to others. This is because, over time, overt biological racism has given way to a new form of racism. This new form of racism is covert, structural, and best described as the emergence of whiteness. All people other than whites are "raced." This embodies the assumption that white people are not racially seen or named, and, as such, they function as the "human norm"—i.e., white people are just people. It also conveys the message that others are something else. This perspective was necessary for conquest, colonization, and enslavement to take place. As a result, an institutional set of structures and relations was established which still determines how Canadians think about non-white people. Those who were white were able to dominate powerful positions in our organizations and institutions. Once a particular perspective (a white one) is built into the laws, norms, and mores of a society, it becomes part of the "way things are" and remains an uncontested definition of normality. Most Canadians, rather than actively refusing to comply with the law, go along with the norm, particularly if they think the law doesn't affect them personally. In short, whiteness functions as a large ensemble of practices and rules that give white people all sorts of advantages and privileges in life that they have trouble giving up. White privilege is the ability to make decisions that affect everyone without taking others into account. It is a standpoint, a location from which to see others, a product of history, and a relational category. Whites have created the dominant images of the world, and they don't see that they have constructed the world in their own image.

White culture and identity have no content (e.g., no definable attributes or "ethnic markers"); consequently, white people can't see that they have anything that accounts for their position of privilege and power. Much of this ingrained privilege is not exhibited deliberately and maliciously, but the impact is the same—it stratifies society into whites and non-whites. Today the structural arrangements are seen as "normal" even though they disadvantage non-whites. Moreover, it is not always the intent of a white person to make use of the unearned benefits received on the basis of skin colour. In fact, many go through their day-to-day activities unaware that they are white or that it even matters. Nevertheless, throughout Canadian history, white power holders have made decisions that have affected white people as a group differently than groups of non-whites. White privilege allows white people *not* to see race in themselves and to be angry with others who do. In the end, whites live in the centre, Aboriginals live on the margins.

Whites do not recognize their unearned privileges because whiteness operates by invisibility—so ubiquitous and entrenched as to appear natural and normative. Thus, whiteness operates as the unmarked norm against which other identities are marked and realized. On the other hand, while whiteness is invisible to whites, it is hyper-visible to Aboriginals. Whites never have to "speak for their race," nor are they viewed as the "white" teacher or lawyer. At the same time, Aboriginals seldom see themselves broadly represented in the media and educational curricula, and when they do, it is usually not in a positive light. Aboriginal people have to grapple with these issues, which impose an important social and psychological cost. The advantage of being white is not to have to absorb this cost, or even to have to be aware of the benefits being received.

Today, for a variety of reasons, questions concerning the rights of Aboriginal people in Canada have taken a curious prominence in Canadian politics. The federal government has, for the past half-century, conveyed a message to Canadians that it has, or is just about to, resolve the issues that Aboriginal people are bringing forth (Churchill, 1999). Thus it is not surprising that most Canadians find it difficult to understand the demands being made by Aboriginal people. Moreover, Canadians find they are not prepared or able to link historical actions with contemporary events. In other words, it is difficult to see how historical events are causal agents of today's actions. Most people tend to see historical events as discrete events that have little or no bearing on today. One goal of this book is to show the reader how historical events, even though they may have happened 100 years ago, have an impact on today's conditions.

Consequences of Colonization

The ultimate consequence of colonization is a reduction in the resistance of Aboriginal people to a point at which they can be controlled and will disappear as a people through assimilation or elimination. Whether the motives for colonization are religious, economic, or political, the rewards are clearly economic. White Canada has gained far more than it has lost in colonizing its Aboriginal peoples. Aboriginal people have struggled to address what they see as historic wrongs and injustices. Such battles have long histories, but with long-term profits to the state and private enterprise at stake, these institutions are not about to give up easily.

In the initial stages of colonization, Aboriginal people generally accept their fate. Only later do they reject their powerless position. Aboriginal leaders on reserves today tend to be considerably more militant than those who initially signed treaties. But even if Aboriginal peoples no longer accept their subordinate status, there is little they can do to change it. Actions taken against government and the private sector must be channelled through a legal system that was created and is maintained for the existing political and economic elite. Although, as Boldt (1980a) showed, many Aboriginal leaders view extra-legal activity as a viable method of pressing their claims, others have surrendered to the current legal system and display a general apathy and dispiritedness—the long-term impact of colonization. The process of acculturation and the demise of indigenous Aboriginal tribal associations have eroded Aboriginal self-identification. Communal bonds have broken down among individual Aboriginals and among bands, contributing to the continued failure of Aboriginal organizations. Leadership responsibilities on reserves have become further divided and are poorly defined, exacerbating this disorganization. In the political arena, Aboriginal people have been ineffectual for several reasons. Most importantly, historically they have been prevented from voting or running for office. Aboriginal persons did not receive the right to vote in provincial elections until after World War II and did not receive the federal franchise until 1960. Needless to say, this exclusion severely restricted their interest in political affairs and their ability to make political demands. Those with no voice in the political structure that governs their lives have few means of influencing or sanctioning the policies that affect them. Even after receiving the vote, Aboriginal people have continued to be skeptical of their rights, although this attitude is changing.

Aboriginal people who continued to live as Indigenous peoples after colonization were met with ridicule. Aboriginals have long been devalued by the dominant group, which has resulted in damage to their individual and collective identities. First Nations people have suffered a collective distortion in their relation to self and have internalized this negative self-image; this has prevented them from developing a healthy cultural identity of their own. This self-hate has been turned inward. Aboriginals have had to understand and deal with the source of their own disempowerment without being able to do anything about it. Alfred (2009) argues that men express the colonized mindset by channelling their rage externally (e.g., with violence), while women express it through self-destruction or suicide. Thus it has been difficult to maintain a cohesive Aboriginal community as colonialism has continued to exert its forces.

Cultural Domination

When Aboriginal people and Europeans first encountered each other, two different cultures came into contact. Aboriginal people were hunters and gatherers (although there were some agricultural tribes) who lived in harmony with their physical environment. Their limited technological developments made few demands on the ecology, and the small numbers of people meant that population pressures were light (Miller, 2000). Europeans, on the other hand, were continually developing their technology to achieve control over nature. They were ethnocentric in outlook and had a mission to Christianize the world. During the early British period of the early 19th century, officials gave little consideration to what role Aboriginal peoples would play in the development of Canadian society (Nichols, 2009).

Settlers demanded access to lands and resources that lay unused and ripe for exploitation. They saw Aboriginal people as "owning" lands yet not utilizing them to extract their potential economic benefit. As such, politicians gave way to this increasing "anti-Indian" sentiment. Lands ceded to Aboriginal people were taken back or reduced for settler and corporate exploitation. Moreover, settlers became "monitors" of Aboriginal activity in that they reported to authorities the actions of Aboriginal people if they moved away from their communities, even for short periods of time. The clash of these two cultures was resounding, and while there is no doubt that Native people have taken the brunt of this collision, they have, surprisingly, retained considerable elements of their culture. They have, whenever possible, taken a "controlled acculturation" perspective, adopting certain behaviours and ideas from the Euro-American culture while retaining other valued mental constructs from their own. Perhaps the creation of reserves and its resulting high level of isolation for many Aboriginal people allowed this selective retention to occur (Brown, 1980; Brown and Vibert, 2003).

The reader might claim that people are far more enlightened today. To be sure, most people today would not argue that one group of people are biologically inferior to another. However, this biological racism has been supplanted by a new form of social/cultural racism that focuses on the inferiority of a group's way of life, their ethos, and their assumptions about the world. In taking the latter view, people may escape being accused of "biological racism"; they are prepared to accept the biological similarities of different groups of people. However, they are not prepared to accept cultural equality or the impact of historical structured inequality. As such, individual racism has given way to structural (systemic) racism. Examining **structural racism** allows one to focus on the way discrimination is built into systems of power and institutions in Canada (Nichols, 1998).

Some readers will be angered by these statements and indignant that Canada should be labelled racist. After all, they will claim, they do not engage in individual racist activities. They will point out that other history books do not make such claims. But history is humanity's way of recording past behaviour; historians are extremely susceptible to the political and social forces that prevail while they are writing. What Aboriginal people have been encouraged to write histories? And when Aboriginal histories have been written, why have they been dismissed as fabrications?

The history of hostility and conflict established between Aboriginal people and political and legal enforcement bodies has contributed to the contemporary relationships between them, which are based on suspicion, disrespect, and mistrust on both sides. Through enactments legislated through colonial parliaments, the institutions in this country have been used to segregate Aboriginal peoples from the dominant culture and to legitimize paternalistic control over all aspects of their lives. However, while being granted rights (in their own country) may have helped Aboriginal people alleviate some of the consequences that emanated from the horrific colonial era, no attempts have been made in political or judicial quarters to address the discriminatory and biased legal provisions that were used to deny them parity and equality with their dominant counterparts. The historical situation provided the initial conditions, and, by apathy and indifference rather than intentional exploitation, those conditions have continued to exist. While the introduction of the *Charter of Rights and Freedoms* in 1982 was assessed as a significant step toward enacting a degree of reform in this area, the Aboriginal population found little comfort in it because of the inadequacies that were attached to its legislative jurisdictional powers.

The old ways by which non-Aboriginal people look at and relate to Aboriginal people have been reflected in the way government has treated them. Moreover, they have become a forgotten people. However, some of these old views are now coming under scrutiny and being challenged. Weaver (1981) points out that the **Penner Report** on Aboriginal self-government (Penner, 1983) and the *Coolican Report* on comprehensive land claims (DIAND, 1986) broke new ground in conceptualizing issues involving Aboriginal people. The **Royal Commission on Aboriginal Peoples** brought into focus what Aboriginal people were thinking and reflects their current view of how they should fit into Canadian society.

What is this new conceptualization? First, a new idea about the relationship between Aboriginal and non-Aboriginal people is presented. Whereas non-Aboriginal people previously tended to view the linkages as eventually resulting in the "termination" of Aboriginal persons and/or their full integration into non-Aboriginal society (i.e., assimilation), these reports view the relationship as parallel over time, with the two cultures adjusting to each other as time and context change. In other words, they see the relationship as equal, flexible, and evolving.

Second, the courts have recently brought about a new relationship between governments and Aboriginal people. This new relationship focuses on the notion of sanctioned rights, which is defined as those rights recognized by the state as justified claims against its actions toward a particular group. At the public level, there is a new commitment to being direct, honest, and honourable in government dealings with Aboriginal people. This new ethic has been brought to the forefront not by government but as a result of a number of court decisions that have gone against the government. From these decisions, governments have been forced to rethink their relationship with Aboriginal peoples. In many cases the courts have found that the old rules don't apply and new methods of relating to Aboriginal peoples have to be forged. However, in many cases, the results of these limited judicial decisions have been negated when their application is implemented in real life (e.g., the duty to consult) because existing structural arrangements continue to neutralize the impact of courts' decisions.

The Royal Commission on Aboriginal Peoples noted that if the social position of Aboriginal people is to change, then the relationship must be restructured. These new ideas have begun to challenge the old views, but before they can become dominant in government thinking, old conceptualizations will have to be dropped. As the government reflects on possible changes, their agent, the Department of Aboriginal Affairs and Northern Development, has undergone turbulent times in recent decades as proponents of each perspective try to make their position the basis for action. This is one reason why the government seemingly takes contradictory stands in dealing with Aboriginal people. For example, Sanders (1990) points out that even the Supreme Court has not been consistent in its rulings with regard to Aboriginal people. In some cases the inconsistencies reflect the evolution of doctrine, while others defy explanation. Yet the changes do seem to reflect the emergence of a new perspective and a new place for Aboriginal persons in Canadian society. However, whether or not this new view of First Nations people will become the dominant one remains to be seen.

Confrontations and Conflict

Press reports on confrontations between Aboriginal and non-Aboriginal people tend to focus on specific complaints, overlook broader issues, and reflect an old definition of Aboriginal people and their role in Canadian society. Hence, in many cases where conflict emerges, Aboriginal persons are labelled as malcontents, troublemakers, and opportunists—labels that can only be defended through a distorted and abbreviated view of history (Lambertus, 2004). For example, the Oka confrontation in 1990 was defined by the media as a "law and order" problem that, once interpreted in this manner, required and justified the harsh and extraordinary measures that the federal government took. A similar definition has been applied to the more recent Caledonia conflict in Ontario. This conflict involves a dispute between a housing developer and Aboriginals who claim that the land upon which houses are being built was illegally taken from First Nations people many years ago.

As at Oka, the stage for clashes between Aboriginal and Euro-Canadian people has generally been set by historical facts and existing structural relations, though few people are interested in examining these. For example, the Lubicons in Alberta, who have block-aded roads and shut down oil pumps, have generally been depicted as irresponsible trou-blemakers. Yet surely the reasons for their protests were linked to the fact that the band has been fighting for land to be set aside for a reserve promised 50 years ago, and for compensation for energy and forestry development that has taken well over $5 billion in natural resources from the area. More broadly, they are protesting on behalf of the Aboriginal children who die before their first birthday, the Aboriginal people who are unable to get jobs, and the large number of Native people who are unable to secure ade-quate housing. Nevertheless, when confrontations erupt, the implication is that the fault (and the cause) lies largely with Aboriginal people. This assumption reveals a biased and short-term perspective. Such an assumption ignores the subtle violence that has been perpetrated against Aboriginal people since the arrival of the European explorers. It also serves those who want to remain in power and maintain a status quo that excludes Aboriginal people from a share in their country's bounty and that allows them to remain hungry, uneducated, and inadequately housed in the midst of plenty.

WRITING A HISTORY

An author's explanation of social events depends on an individual point of view. Because overt social behaviour can be interpreted in many different ways and one can't always ask the individual why she/he did something, the historian must always infer the actors' motives, whether discussing individuals or groups.

Until recently, our historians have largely been Euro-Canadian; as a result, they have largely based their inferences on the same primary assumptions and have therefore pre-sented similar views of social reality (Trudel and Jain, 1970). Canadian histories written before the 1980s barely mention Aboriginal people when discussing the history of Canada after the 18th century. Those authors who did write about Aboriginal peoples were colonial elites who had an interest in representing Aboriginal peoples' social and cultural life as "barbaric." As the 20th century began, a lack of technological skills rele-gated Aboriginal people to second-class citizens. While many history books acknowledge the interaction of Aboriginal people and Europeans, they tend to characterize Aboriginal persons as passive, always responding to actions taken by Europeans. In short, descrip-tions of the interaction between the two parties usually portray Europeans as the proac-tive agents, asserting their vision of Canada regardless of Aboriginal people. There are some exceptions to this general pattern (Miller, 2000), but the history of Aboriginal–Euro-Canadian relations in Canada has generally been told from the perspective of non-Aboriginal people. As Dickason (2002) points out, problems of interpretation become problematic when considering Europeans' accounts of their exploits in the new America.

She notes, for example, that there can be differences in the connotations of words as used in the 16th or 17th centuries versus today. She also points out that in the case of published historical accounts, what appears in print may not be what the author wrote. Historically, publishers were more interested in the economic value of material than in its veracity.

Throughout recorded time, empowered groups have been able to define history and provide an explanation of the present. In the 18th and 19th centuries, Canadians were focused on finding the best route to the Pacific coast in an attempt to tie Ontario to the West and the Asian market. However, during this period, little thought was given to Aboriginal people and their way of life. It would not be until after the American Civil War and the purchase of Alaska by the Americans that Canadian politicians realized they would have to engage in some defensive expansionism to block the American seizure of all of North America. It should be noted that no notice was given to tribal groups or their claims to the land. Government policies relating to Aboriginal people were, as Prime Minister Alexander Mackenzie (1877) noted, cheap, humane, just, and Christian. As such, Indian affairs were kept far from the centre of political debate. The only attention Aboriginal groups received during the early years was when they were needed as economic partners or were involved in land cessions. For example, in the 1783 *Treaty of Paris,* the Mohawks and the Iroquois (who had been allies with the British Americans in the Revolutionary War) discovered that their contributions and the promises made to them were to be ignored. As such, these Aboriginal groups moved into present-day Ontario partly through the urging of Canadian officials. During this time, Canadian officials encouraged Aboriginal peoples to resist American demands and welcomed them into Canada. They encouraged Aboriginal people who moved to Canada to maintain their American ties as a strategy to weaken and disrupt American control over the West.

In the history books, when Aboriginal people attacked a non-Aboriginal village or fort and won, the result was called a massacre. If Europeans attacked an Aboriginal village and won, it was described as a victory. Because the colonist is able to make these interpretations and definitions, it is also able to keep others from initiating alternative explanations or definitions. History gives credence and legitimacy to a society's normative structure; to legitimize its power, the dominant group must reconstruct social history whenever necessary. The early reconstructions of Canadian history were effective: Today, most Canadians continue to associate "savage" and "heinous" behaviour with Canadian Aboriginal people. As Churchill (1999) points out, the standard European/Canadian depiction of Aboriginals has been one of a small number of people who wandered about in scattered bands, grubbing out an existence through hunting and gathering, never developing writing or serious appreciation of art, science, or mathematics. It has been believed that, aside from utilizing furs and hides for clothing and housing, there were few attributes that distinguished Aboriginal people from other higher orders of mammalian life.

In another example, Euro-Canadian history reveals that scalping was a notorious activity carried out by Aboriginal people. Few Canadians know that scalping was not practiced by Aboriginal people prior to colonization. It began in 1694 when the General Court of Massachusetts passed an act that offered bounties for every hostile "Indian" adult or child that they could kill or bring to the authorities as a prisoner. However, the question remained as to how you could tell whether a hostile Indian had been killed. Since 50 pounds (later increased to 100—an incredible amount of money at the time) was provided for each "kill," authorities had to be sure that a hostile Indian had indeed been killed. The issue was resolved by demanding that the scalp of the Indian be provided to authorities to authenticate the kill (Washburn, 1957). Hence scalping was one that was introduced and sanctioned by settlers and the colonial powers.

As Patterson (1972) points out, alien history is pulled down and discredited, and national history replaces it. Continuity of tradition for any group is truncated when the communication channels are taken over by others who wish to transmit different information. How often have we known something to be true only to find out many years later that the government, or some other group, distorted information that might have led us to believe something quite different? Brown (1971) and Andrist (1964) have vividly portrayed American-Indian history from an alternative point of view. Their information concerning Aboriginal–non-Aboriginal relations is quite dissimilar to that provided by "established" historians. Recent histories by such authors as Miller (2000), Churchill (1999), Warry (2006), and Nichols (1998) portray a more balanced perspective of events and reveal the Aboriginal side of Canadian history.

Readers have reacted quite differently to books by Cardinal (1969), Pelletier (1970), and Waubageshig (1970) than to books by Morton (1963), McInnis (1959), and Lower (1957). The layperson typically rejects the conclusions of the first three authors as the product of bias. But the same person tends to accept the explanations provided by the second group of "established academic" authors. We are not suggesting that the first are right or the second wrong, but both groups deserve to be read and judged fairly. As a new generation of Aboriginal authors emerge (Waters, 2004; Cajete, 2000; Bastien, 2004), new data and views of history are being presented to readers. While some resistance to the new history still exists, many readers have responded with "I didn't know that," reflecting a grudging acceptance.

Walker (1971) characterized Canadian historians in their analysis of Aboriginal people in Canada as ignorant, prejudiced, and, in some cases, dishonest. But we do not have to attribute motives of deliberate falsification. In any reconstruction of the past, the author shapes an interpretation of events according to individual perceptions, memories, analytical preferences, and social background. Whether deliberately or unconsciously, a reshaping of the past occurs. No historian is free of bias; no history is capable of presenting only the facts.

A Western perspective asserts that the history of North America began with the arrival of the settlers. In short, there was no "history" before they arrived. Many authors argue that there is no written history prior to the settlers' arrival and thus a history cannot be presented. Others will note that, while we have few written materials regarding many ancient civilizations, we are still able to use artifacts to reconstruct the history of a people. Nevertheless, in Canada, history traditionally begins with the arrival of European settlers. While there is certainly a history of Aboriginals presented as they came into contact with settlers, there is a built-in assumption that as Aboriginals were assimilated, their history would disappear. As Dockstator (2005) points out, a Western historical perspective involves three factors regarding Aboriginal people: (1) they are a vanishing race; (2) they are a single homogenous group; and (3) Aboriginals are a mixture of what he calls simultaneous contrasts—e.g., noble yet savage, robust yet dying, existing but not really existing. For example, settlers had little interest in Aboriginal perspectives, and from the duality of their perspective, Aboriginal people were nations when it came to signing treaties but not nations once they were signed. In the end, from a Western perspective, Aboriginals are always placed at the margins of mainstream activity. There has been, and continues to be, a belief that Aboriginals will, through various legal acts (e.g., treaties, Indian acts, federal bills) disappear and the end of their history will be written.

When contact occurred, Aboriginals recognized Western culture as legitimate yet found it perplexing that the settlers and colonial powers did not recognize their own culture with the same respect. And, while Aboriginals regarded the newcomers as their equals, settlers always viewed themselves as superior. Aboriginals interpreted the negotiation of treaties as reflecting a principle of equality. As Dockstator (2005) concludes, Aboriginals believed in the equality of the two nations, although they certainly understood that the indicators of equality would change over time. Aboriginals never viewed themselves as a vanishing race nor as a single homogeneous group. They were keenly aware of the cultural and linguistic differences among their various groups. Over the past four centuries, Indigenous peoples have consistently maintained that their concept of nationhood originated long before the settlers came, and it remains intact. They also argue that even after contact with the settlers, a balanced relationship between themselves and the settlers reflected two nations of equal status.

Canadians are mostly unaware of the "underside" of history and our relationship with Aboriginal peoples. This is one more attribute of a colonial society in that only the settlers' side of the story is told and perpetuated through myths and stories. As Alfred (2005) notes, government and law manifest in fictive legal constructs that legitimize non-Aboriginal people's usurpation. This is turn becomes a feigned legitimacy in order to normalize the structure of racism. Over time, it is integrated into the literature and art that further demonstrates the "facts" required to justify colonial privilege.

RELATIONS BETWEEN PEOPLES

The balance of this chapter will provide an overview of the history of the relations between the two dominant Canadian groups and Aboriginal peoples. Before discussing Aboriginal–non-Aboriginal relations, we should point out that Aboriginal–Aboriginal relations are also an important component in the way Canada developed. Europeans were able to establish themselves in Canada partially due to the fact that a large number of Aboriginal people allowed them to and supported them in doing so (Trigger, 1985; Dickason, 2002). Since in the beginning Aboriginal people controlled the fur trade and were militarily superior to the newcomers, European entry onto the land could not have been accomplished without their cooperation (Coates, 1991).

A major shift in government–Aboriginal relations in Canada emerged after the British solidified their position in Canada. After the American Revolution, more than 100 000 American refugees were invited to come to Canada and they settled near Aboriginal populations in Ontario. In order to provide land for these refugees, government officials began to expropriate land from Aboriginal groups. At first, small parcels of land were provided to the refugees, but over time, through force or fraud, more and better portions of the land were taken. Moreover, most of these Americans (United Empire Loyalists) had strong anti-Aboriginal prejudices, which perpetuated more myths and spread violence to other areas of Canada. As Maybury-Lewis et al. (2009) point out, Canadian dealings with Aboriginal people can be characterized as the government doing as little as possible until circumstances dictated that they take some action. By the 1800s, Aboriginal people in Ontario discovered—too late—that earlier agreements with Canadian officials were no longer being honoured and more and more land was being expropriated for the use of settlers.

Once Britain (and earlier, France) took over control of what is now Canada, they took the stance that their earlier recognition of Aboriginal nationhood and sovereignty were no longer relevant political positions. While they certainly endorsed such political statements in their earlier relations with Aboriginal people when they needed them as allies against other European competitors, once control over what is now Canada was secured, such positions were dropped. As Alfred (2009) points out, the British ignored the earlier recognition of Aboriginal nationhood and sovereignty as well as the legal guarantees to land ownership established by the treaties. Moreover, by this time, the Aboriginal population had been decimated by disease and hardship, so they were no longer a formidable military force nor a potential political opponent. As such, the British could act freely and without opposition to consolidate their control over Canada. They were now able to pursue a political course that focused on the elimination of First Nations as legal and political entities, on the implementation of a reserve system to control them, and on a movement to gradually civilize the Aboriginal population (Rotman, 1996). The end result of such activities produced a long-lasting "dependency" of Aboriginal peoples on mainstream society.

Colonialism produced a new Aboriginal existence as the new capitalist economy was introduced. As Alfred (2009) points out, every aspect of their lives was affected by the implementation of capitalism. Wotherspoon and Satzewich (1993) note that Aboriginal peoples' lives were destroyed as they were not given any opportunity to participate in this new economy. Exclusion and limitations upon Aboriginal participation in the larger economy still echo today. The continued and cumulative impact of natural resource extraction on and near First Nations lands continues to disrupt traditional patterns of existence through pollution, disruption of flora and fauna, and the rejection of any meaningful Aboriginal involvement. In other cases, government action stymied Aboriginal involvement in the fisheries through federal and provincial regulations. Newell (1993) shows how regulatory laws were passed under the guise of environmental regulation (conservation), although their impact was designed to ensure cheap Aboriginal labour for the canneries and to prevent Aboriginal people from becoming competitors with non-Aboriginal economic interests. Her work reveals both the covert and overt actions taken by government to keep Aboriginal people from participating in the fisheries industry.

French–Aboriginal Relations

With the establishment of Quebec in 1608, the French created a centre for the growing fur trade. Their policy was to treat Aboriginal people with consideration, avoid violence with them, and transform them into Frenchmen (Dickason and Newbigging, 2010). With early settlements short of French women, intermarriage, or "wintering in," between French trappers and Indian women soon became common practice and was encouraged by French authorities who wanted to strengthen Aboriginal relations so that the fur trade would continue. These marriages between French men and Indian women were not meant to be exploitative; the relationships were stable, and the man was considered legally responsible for his wife and offspring (Brown, 1980). However, the reader should understand that intermarriage was not a policy that originated in Canada. The French had used this technique when they colonized Brazil a century earlier. Moreover, intermarriage was eased for the French by the belief that Aboriginals were really white, turning brown because they ate certain foods and were out in the sun. If one looks at formal records of intermarriage, the incidence would indicate a small number. However, other documents suggest that the rate was quite high and was supported by the missionaries as a form of concubinage. Thus both economic and religious institutions supported intermarriage between Aboriginal women and French men. Nevertheless, by the mid-18th century, the practice was no longer supported by the structures that had earlier facilitated its process.

In general, the French tried to expand their territories in North America by peaceful means (Francis, 1983). Usually they succeeded, because their agricultural style of existence only minimally disrupted Aboriginal life. Because they used the seigneurial system of agriculture, the French always remained near major waterways and did not intrude into the interior of New France. After they had settled a territory, the French asked the Indians to join in a treaty to acknowledge submission to the king of France. In this way, the French usually won territory without actually expropriating it. In 1611, Champlain sealed a pact of friendship with Chief Anadabijou, which allowed the French to establish themselves on Montagnais territory. In entering this alliance, the French were following a practice that they had developed a century earlier in Brazil and that was successful in establishing trade relations (Wright, 2003). The French had long come to realize that diplomatic protocol and negotiations (by means of gift distributions) were the process by which alliances could be built with Aboriginal people. However, the process was not always peaceful, and the French were certainly prepared to use force when they found it expedient to do so. When the Marquis de Tracy was placed in charge of Canada in 1663, his commissions included a provision for the use of arms to subjugate the Aboriginal peoples if necessary.

The two strongest ideological influences in 17th-century New France were Roman Catholicism and **mercantilism**. The latter was the economic theory that had prevailed in Europe during the 18th century and had two basic tenets: The mother country was entitled to accumulate wealth in any form, and the mother country was entitled to exploit its colonies as a source for raw materials and a market for finished products, thereby maintaining a favourable balance of trade. As well, the French utilized the missionary zeal of the Catholic clergy to convert Aboriginal people.

Thus, with the full support of the French monarchy and its colonial officials, Catholic missionaries began the process of "civilizing" the Aboriginals and converting them to Christianity. Both Jesuit and Recollet missionaries dealt with Aboriginal groups from the Gulf of St. Lawrence to Georgian Bay, encouraging them to take on a sedentary life and to adopt the beliefs and values of Catholicism (Furniss, 2000). French policy, rather than treating Aboriginal people as distinct and inferior, tried to make them into French citizens, at least in Canada. Two additional factors contributed to the relatively peaceful relations between the French and the Indians: the military alliance of the Huron, the Algonkian, and the French; and the fact that the French settled in an area occupied by the Algonkian, who were migratory hunters (Jenness, 1937) with no real tribal organization and were themselves recent arrivals in the area (Cumming, 1969). This ideology of "**Frenchification**" is illustrated in various exchanges of letters between religious and state leaders of the day.

When war broke out with England in the 18th century, the demand for fur decreased and the French mercantilistic philosophy came to an end. War also brought a change in the French policy toward Aboriginal peoples (Jaenen, 1986). Aboriginal land rights began to be systematically ignored (Harper, 1947: 131). Letters signed by Louis XV at this time gave companies headed for New France full ownership of the land, coasts, ports, and havens of New France, and full right to dispose of these properties in any way they desired (French, 1851). Similar provisions can be found in the privileges, power, and requirements given to the Company of One Hundred Associates by Cardinal Richelieu nearly a century earlier.

The king of France understood that, if he was to colonize Canada, he would have to spend time, money, and energy in maintaining alliances with the Aboriginal peoples. He also realized that they were important allies in times of war, and they would support the French if treated properly. Others have noted that the French used their Indian allies as "outposts" in the new world and thus reaped the benefits of low costs and accurate information. In the end, as Dickason (2002) points out, the French dealt with Aboriginal groups on a practical basis. It was a blend of give-and-take: giving when alliances were necessary, taking when the profits of the fur trade allowed. However, French domination in New France came to an end when the *Treaty of Paris* (1763) was signed and the French handed over their vast territory to the British. Moreover, Aboriginal people found that they now occupied a new niche in New France, devoid of any bargaining between the French and English. This niche was characterized by a loss of protection of their land and a halt to the recognition of Aboriginal leaders and the provision of gifts to them.

British–Aboriginal Relations

As the English cemented their control over North America, Aboriginal people found themselves in a very different world. Their experience with the English was considerably more negative than that with the French. This was partly due to the operation of different structural variables—e.g., a new religious ideology, new racist philosophies, a different economy, and the intrusion of thousands of new settlers on the land. Mercantilism as an economic theory had been discarded and the importance of the fur trade was dwindling; colonization in its true sense was now important. In addition, the religious ideology of the British had a very different basis than that of the French. As other religious denominations entered Canada, they continued the expansion of Christianity. Finally, the British based their actions on the ideology that no natural community exists on its own through natural processes. They believed that group life was an artificial creation and that the individual's needs and interests would always come into conflict with the desire to create a homogenous society. In creating a society, the state has to use systematic violence (supported by the rule of law). Out of this philosophy, British colonists insisted that the creation of political order required that laws had to be capable of coercive enforcement. As such, as they settled in what is now Canada, their intent was to create a centralized state and reject any other social organization exhibited by the Indigenous people. As the British continued their colonization of the new country, their political and social systems moved further away from the ideas of justice and equality toward the increasing use of force. As such, the underpinning of their empire was increasingly based upon a philosophy of violence toward Aboriginal people. Henderson (2008) argues that the British built their Canadian empire out of cruelty and the destruction of the Indigenous population. Specifically, he notes:

Eurocentrism established its primary elements of individual and subjective interests in the construction of an artificial political and social order regulated by violence and punishment. (pg. 15)

Thus it seemed reasonable to deal with Indigenous peoples, who were seen inferior, from a perspective that legitimized the use of violence (Catellani, 1901).

As Thomas (1972) points out, Aboriginal people were not even mentioned in discussions when land was given to companies or settlers as they took over control of what is now Canada. Until 1755, the English followed a policy of expediency they had developed and refined in dealing with Aboriginal people in the Thirteen Colonies (now the eastern United States). At first, they chose to ignore the Aboriginal population. When allies were required, Aboriginals were courted and provided with resources. Later, when this was no longer necessary or feasible due to westward expansion, the English chose to isolate Aboriginal people through the reserve system or to annihilate them, as with the Beothuk of Newfoundland. As far back as 1755, Indian agents, today called superintendents, were appointed, formally establishing Canada's policy of treating Aboriginal peoples as wards of the state. Significantly, the Indian agents initially placed in control of the reserves were always military men.

By 1830, the government questioned the value of the Aboriginal person in developing Canada's future. Although it remained a concern for some, invasion from the south by the United States was no longer an immediate and direct threat. Because there were no other potential attackers, Aboriginal people were not likely to be needed for support in military efforts. Without their status as military allies, Aboriginals had no value for a "white Canada." Thus, in 1830, Indian affairs were removed from military control and became a branch of the public service (Surtees, 1969). This change of jurisdiction allowed the British to adopt a more humanitarian attitude toward Aboriginal people (Doerr, 1974). The new image of Aboriginals reflected a more general humanitarian ideology that had arisen through various social reform movements in Britain and the United States (Furniss, 2000). It also gained widespread popularity through the writings of individuals such as James Fenimore Cooper and George Grant as well as by the paintings of artists of the day.

By the mid-1880s, most areas in Canada had been claimed by some religious denomination. Manifest Destiny and the Hamlite rationalization pervaded the British secular way of life, exemplified in the Protestant ethic that hard work and no play would bring salvation. The philosophy of Manifest Destiny, though usually associated with American expansion, was more broadly a belief that Europeans should control the world, or at least large parts of it. A related belief, the Hamlite rationalization, was a belief taken from the Bible that Ham was cursed by God and turned into a non-white person so that "he and his descendants should remain cursed and be subservient to Whites from then on." To the British, the Indians were clearly descendants of Ham.

During this time the interests of the various settler groups—e.g., fur traders, missionaries, settlers, and government officials—were sometimes in agreement, while at other times they conflicted. For example, missionaries and fur traders supported each other, although traders were more pragmatic in their dealings with Aboriginals. Traders also saw disruptions to Aboriginal communities as against their interest—i.e., they would hinder their ability to gather furs for trade.

POST-CONFEDERATION ABORIGINAL– NON-ABORIGINAL RELATIONS

The French chose to exploit resources by encouraging settlers to remain permanently on the land while the British exploited resources through the fur trade (Satzewich and Liodakis, 2010). Nevertheless, the colonizers, under the watchwords of law, order, and peace, justified their violence against Aboriginal people. This justification continues to provide the legal underpinnings of a British philosophy that is now accepted by most Canadians. Moreover, this philosophy of life and action is not viewed as a "privileged norm" but rather is argued to be a universal and general philosophy that all other societies must embrace. Under the terms of the *British North America Act*, the federal government took on legal responsibility for "Indians and Indian lands." The first *Indian Act* after Canadian Confederation was passed in 1876, bringing together a number of disparate pieces of legislation relating to Aboriginals. The intent of the Act was to control and manage the operation of reserves. It was first revised in 1880 (and placed under the Department of Indian Affairs), and received minor alterations in 1884 and 1885. For the next 65 years, the Act underwent annual minor changes. However, in 1951, a major revision was undertaken and, although there have been subsequent alterations, only one or two major changes have been made since that time. Interestingly enough, the 1880 version of the Act and the present one are remarkably similar, indicating that the Indian Affairs Department has not yet undergone any major ideological shifts in the past hundred years of dealing with the Aboriginal population.

Diffusionism

Since Confederation, Canadian officials have borrowed the earlier British philosophy and built upon it when it comes to dealing with Aboriginal people. Specifically, they created what has been called by Henderson (2008) "epistemological **diffusionism**." This philosophy is based on a basic tenet that most human societies are uninventive, although there are some that are highly innovative and thus become permanent centres of cultural change. Thus, it was no stretch to argue that British (and European) society was the single inventive, progressive culture while Aboriginal people were historical, stagnant, and unchanging. Only British people were intellectually able to create, imagine, or innovate. Blaut (1993) argues that this belief became the normal and natural way of viewing Indigenous peoples and informed relations with them as the settlers continued to take over the land.

Table 1.1 outlines the basic attributes of diffusionism. Colonialism brings civilization, which in turn brings innovation and change. Only if the Aboriginal people would accept the colonial way of life would they escape their stagnant and unimaginative one. This belief is still with us today in that the Department of Justice refuses to acknowledge the existence of "Aboriginal knowledge." Their response is that there is "traditional Aboriginal knowledge" but it is just that—traditional, and it cannot ever be modern.

TABLE 1.1	British World View of its Own Culture and that of the Aboriginal 1700–1900
British Culture	**Aboriginal Culture**
• Civilized	• Savage
• Progressive	• Stagnant
• Scientific	• Spiritual
• Uses Abstract Reasoning	• Practical
• Rational	• Emotional
• Disciplined	• Spontaneous
• Adult	• Child-like

We find that the policy governing Aboriginal–non-Aboriginal relations was administered differently throughout Canada over time. First of all, until 1830, Aboriginal peoples were viewed as military objects and were treated as such. If their presence would support the military campaign, they were given consideration. On the other hand, if their presence gave no military advantage, Aboriginals were ignored. By 1850 they would be defined as dangerous and dealt with accordingly. In Ontario and Quebec until 1860, the imperial government handled all the affairs and expenses of Aboriginal people. As the British began to settle Canada, they devised a strategy by which land would be taken away from the Aboriginals and opened for settlement. As a result, treaties and pieces of legislation of all kinds were passed to legitimize the takeover of land once occupied and settled on by Aboriginals. At that time, a Crown Lands Department was established and a commissioner appointed to assume the role of Chief Superintendent of Indian Affairs. In other areas of Canada, the Indian Affairs office was administered directly by the various provincial or colonial governments (Hawley, 1990).

Included in the *British North America Act* of 1867 was a special provision allowing for the administration of Indian Affairs to come under the control of the government of Canada. Initially, Indian Affairs was the responsibility of the Department of the Secretary of State, but in 1873 it was transferred to the Department of the Interior. In 1880, a separate Department of Indian Affairs was formed and by 1936 it was shifted to the jurisdiction of the Department of Mines and Resources. In 1950, it was shifted again to the Department of Citizenship and Immigration, and from 1953 to 1966, Indian Affairs was handled by the Northern Affairs and National Resources Department. In 1966 it was renamed the Department of Indian Affairs and Northern Development. This was followed by a change to Indian and Northern Affairs Canada (INAC). More recently, the name has been changed to Aboriginal Affairs and Northern Development (AAND). Hence, the administration of Indian affairs has been shunted from one department to another and has never been allowed to develop consistent, long-range policies.

Summary

- History determines the structure of contemporary Canadian society.
- Colonialism characterizes the history of Canadian society; the Four *D*s—Disease, Disorientation, Disempowerment, Discord.
- The marginal position occupied by Aboriginal people is a concern for all Canadians (e.g., land claims).
- Power relations between Aboriginal people and the government have changed over time.

Key Terms

Charter of Rights and Freedoms p. 12
colonization process p. 4
culture of poverty p. 3
"empty land" p. 2

diffusionism p. 22
"Frenchification" p. 19
mercantilism p. 19
Penner Report p. 12

Royal Commission on Aboriginal Peoples p. 13
self-government p. 6
structural racism p. 12

Questions for Further Discussion

1. What impacts did each stage of the colonization process produce?
2. How did French-Aboriginal relations differ from English-Aboriginal relations prior to Confederation?
3. When did the federal government pass the first *Indian Act* and how did this effect Aboriginal and non-Aboriginal relations?
4. Do you think "white Canada" has gained more than it has lost? Explain your answer.
5. Why was the structural racism perspective necessary for white Canadians in order for colonization and enslavement to take place?

CHAPTER 2

Aboriginal Identity and Belonging

LEARNING OBJECTIVES

After reading this chapter you should be able to:

1. State the result of the first statutory definition in 1850 of who was an Indian.

2. Know the differences between treaty/non-treaty and reserve/non-reserve Indians.

3. Explain the term "enfranchisement."

4. Explain the benefits and downfalls of *Bill C-31*.

5. Know the importance of Sections 6(1) and 6(2) of the *Indian Act*.

6. Identify the four types of membership rules for several First Nation groups.

7. Understand the social impact of legal definitions of Aboriginal people.

8. Explain the significance of the Lavell and Bedard cases.

LABELLING AND IDENTITY

Every society uses a variety of labels to identify people located within different socio-political economic and demographic situations. These labels are used to identify specific groups and to attach both subjective and objective social attributes to each group. In the end, labelling allows members of society to interact with each of the differently identified groups. Aboriginal people have long argued that Aboriginal identity has been essential-ized, making the implementation of the governments' policy toward Aboriginal people easier. They have maintained that colonizers have developed a system of thought and representation to mask their oppressive behaviour. Colonizers use an ideology to legitimate and entrench the unequal power relations set up by the entire process of colo-nization. This ideology in turn creates a language that celebrates colonial identities while constructing the colonized as the antithesis of human decency and development (LaRocque, 2010). Such constructions dehumanize Aboriginal people and allow them to be labelled as savages, in contrast to civilized European people.

In other cases, various tribal affiliations are ignored, and all individuals who share the same label are treated the same way. The effect of such labelling is to obscure the varia-tions among Aboriginal peoples. Moreover, the lack of a homogeneous worldview by Aboriginal people complicates the application of a single description of "Aboriginality." For example, those Aboriginal people who remain in rural areas have different cultural values than those who have moved into urban centres; the Cree have a different cosmos than the Mohawk. Social identity is also influenced by other factors, such as religion. For example, some Aboriginal people have accepted Christianity while others have resisted.

Thus, there are Christian Aboriginal people and traditionalists who did not succumb to the efforts of Christian missionaries, each with a very different Aboriginal identity.

From an Aboriginal perspective, it is important to note that Aboriginal people spring from many nations and traditions, and there is a need to acknowledge these differences. At a legal level, we recognize Indians, Inuit, and Métis as being "Aboriginal," once again noting that one label encompasses three distinct groups. However, within these broad categories there are many sub-groups—e.g., Red River Métis, Western Métis; Inuvialuit, Nunavut; Cree, Ojibwa, and the list goes on. Nevertheless, in many cases, Canadians ignore these differences and simply ascribe the single identity of Aboriginal to those people.

CREATING AN IDENTITY

Our identity reflects the image we believe others have of us. People are sufficiently sensitive to other people's definitions of them to incorporate that image into their identity. Identity is intimately connected to the reactions imputed to other people. Thus, identity is a social product, socially created and maintained. However, identity is a fragile concept—temporal, situational, and constrained, and defined by those we encounter on a day-to-day basis. What is key is that identity is actively shaped and reshaped. It is not something solely acquired at birth, remaining fixed and static. It is rooted in other people, different situations, and varying contexts. Identity is never gained or maintained once and for all; it is constantly lost and regained. Moreover, both self-identity and group identity are constructed. They are made and remade, altered and refined, disrupted and negotiated through an interaction process. Through our social interactions, identities are forged and validated but always with the threat of change or reconstruction.

Over the life history of an individual, he/she moves through the structure of society. At various stages of life, individuals experience changing status and identity (e.g., graduation, marriage, divorce) as they progress through a series of statuses, roles, and positions—all of which have an impact on their identities. Moreover, as our society becomes more differentiated, "official agents" and institutions of the state often impose identity. When these labels are made public, they create a "credential" that defines who we are and what we are meant to be.

As such, an individual's identity is not constructed in isolation from others but is closely connected to their approval. Moreover, there is a multiplicity and flexibility of identities. An individual's identity can also be fragmented, meaning it can remain uncertain. The constitution of identity is accomplished amid a puzzling diversity of options and possibilities. Individuals must create coherence yet continuously revise incoming data to form a cohesive identity. We no longer conceptualize identity as an entity but rather understand the construction of the self as an orientational process. Central to this idea is the examination of self-processes as reflectional and involving engagement in, and with, the physical and social environments. Society plays a constitutive role in the identity of an individual by providing certain basic orientations that structure the social and behavioural environments.

The reality of identity is that it is dynamic not static, multiple not monolithic or homogeneous, and a social construction not at all naturally inherited. Identity is not a property of individuals but of social relationships. Critical to this notion is the extent to which identity validation is the basis upon which consensual roles are enacted. Identities are established when identity announcements (information given by an individual to others) corresponds to identity placements (categories that others place the person in). The degree of correspondence between these two can range from no fit (leading to identity invalidation and role enactment confusion) to complete fit, resulting in consensus. Thus, identities are variable, ranging from stable and enduring to unstable and transient, and, because they are information-dependent, they are always constructed and potentially negotiable.

Interfering with Identity Construction

The impact of colonialization has created extensive cultural discontinuity over time for Aboriginal people. This has produced structural problems in subsequent generation identity. In addition, Aboriginal people have to contend with a dominant society that exerts its power position over all aspects of Aboriginal life (e.g., the *Indian Act*) as well as other forms of legislation. LaRocque (2010) points out that non-Aboriginal people have supported their "eminent merits" by constructing the Aboriginal demerits. In the end, the framework worked out by white Canadians creates an ideology that allows for the systematic construction of Aboriginal people as savages who inevitably had to yield to the superior power of Euro-Canadians (LaRocque, 2010). The historical impact of colonialism is very present and the vestiges of such a structure still remain part of Canadian society. Aboriginal people find it virtually impossible to develop an integrated collective identity. The result is that many individual Aboriginals have no clearly established schema for their identity, nor do they have a schema for understanding the dominant collective identity. However, today as the "devolution" process unfolds, Aboriginal people are attempting to re-capture their Aboriginality (Berry, 1999).

Identity for Aboriginal people is at a crossroads. When groups of individuals have problems establishing their collective identity or are unclear as to what their collective identity is, they lack purpose, direction, and commitment. They have no goal objective and the behaviour of the group is devoid of meaning. Being Aboriginal in Canada means having to confront the dominant society and its integrating culture, while at the same time having to retain or manage a "heritage" collective identity (Taylor, 1997). Aboriginal people must cope with the fact that "racial" identity is what perpetuates the homogeneity myths that the dominant society imposes while failing to reflect cultural variations among Aboriginal groups.

Personal identity and its value are contingent upon whether the individual is a member of an Aboriginal group that has established a clear collective identity and placed a positive value on that collective identity. Unless an individual can clearly demarcate the standards of the collective identity, he/she is unable to establish personal identity. And until the collective positively values its culture, an individual cannot develop a strong and vital Aboriginality. Collective identity is most important for any Aboriginal group so that individual members can establish their personal identities. Moreover, the collective has to place a positive value on that identity if the individual is to have positive self-esteem.

However, when an Aboriginal group is able to provide its members with clear referential standards upon which to build a strong collective identity, members of the group will be able to establish a defined collective identity (Nagy, 2002; Myers, 2006). Until this happens, young people are confronted with a multiplicity of alternative standards that serve to confuse and hinder efforts to develop a collective identity. In the case of Aboriginal people, colonialism first destroyed group standards and then forced Aboriginals to assimilate so quickly that young people have become unable to develop an Aboriginal collective identity, becoming what Taylor (1997) calls "collectively demotivated." This, in turn, has had devastating consequences for Aboriginal people in general and younger generations in particular. The growth of Aboriginal gangs in cities like Regina and Winnipeg attest to the outcome for young people who are collectively demotivated. Becoming members of gangs and engaging in activities that would not be defined as acceptable by their families or communities fulfill their aspirations and sense of identity.

Aboriginal people, banned from the economic and political structures of Canadian society, have been relegated to a marginal position. They have been forced "inward" as families and communities. Substantial cultural resources have been developed among these communities to develop the elements of autonomy and opposition needed to survive. Omi and Winant (2006) refer to this as a *"war of maneuver."* This strategy was developed by Aboriginal people in an attempt to preserve and extend a definite social boundary, to combat violent assaults imposed upon them, and to develop an internal society as an alternative to the repressive social system they encounter on a daily basis. Recently, this strategy has been replaced by a *"war of positions,"* by which Aboriginal people use political strategies to achieve their goals. Aboriginal people, since obtaining the vote in the 1960s, have followed sustained strategies into the mainstream political process (e.g., Meech Lake, the use of the courts, overt conflicts—Oka, Caledonia, Gustafson Lake) to resolve differences.

Awareness of their stigmatized status leads people to become vigilant and use this status as a "lens" through which they act and judge the actions of other people. It creates a mindset that causes them to be constantly "on-guard" for actions by other people that might be interpreted as "racist" or exhibiting prejudice. This state of vigilance and awareness begins to temper an individual's activity and leads them to scrutinize the actions of others. As such, these individuals are always looking to see if they are operating in a threatening environment where they might be stigmatized or devalued through racist or discriminatory actions on the part of others. In many cases, these strategies will lead to disengagement and dis-identification (Butera and Levine, 2009). Coping strategies allow an individual to disassociate their self-esteem from threatening contexts. Young Aboriginal men are able to do this as they enter high school when they do not link their self-esteem with academic achievement. Their self-esteem comes from peers and family and, in some cases, they cope with their marginalized status by defining themselves in opposition to the prevailing white culture.

PREVAILING IDEOLOGY

As Berry (2001) points out, the maintenance of ethnic identity is an important factor in the creation of positive self-esteem and the establishment of positive relationships with other ethno-cultural groups. At the same time, there is considerable pressure from politicians and others to force minority ethno-cultural groups to "give up" their ethnicity and take on the attributes of the majority. Their argument is that it is important to create a common "superordinate" identity as a means of reducing the incidence of ethnic conflict. The thesis of this ideology is that aggressively pursued assimilation policy will generate social inclusion and integration and produce a society with high social cohesion.

Aboriginal people have four choices in terms of how they wish to relate to mainstream society. They can attempt to integrate (maintain their ethnicity *and* develop new relationships with mainstream society), assimilate (give up ethnic identity and take on the identity and culture of mainstream society), separate (maintain ethnic identity and not develop ties with mainstream society), or marginalize (give up their ethnic identity without developing a new identity) (Hornsey and Hogg, 2000). Current research in the area of ethnic conflict reveals that the assimilationist approach, long advocated by Canadians, is not the best strategy (Portes and Hao, 2002) for developing a cohesive, integrated society. First, Aboriginal people realize that even if they do give up their ethnicity and take on the attributes of the majority, they will not be fully accepted by the majority until several generations have passed. For many Aboriginal people, their acceptance (no matter how much they change their language, dress, and deportment) by the majority may never come about. As such, there is considerable resistance to giving up one's Aboriginal identity and assimilating into the larger social system.

Nevertheless, government officials have steadfastly argued that Aboriginal people should adopt the "assimilationist" position in order to reduce conflict and allow Aboriginal people to better function within society. The logic is that as the similarity between Aboriginal people and mainstream society increases, there will be less conflict in the relations between the two and greater social inclusion of all groups. Since most Aboriginal peoples have "dual" identities, they identify both with their native ethnic identity as well as with the dominant society (Tran, Kaddatz, and Allard, 2005). When Aboriginal people are pressured to assimilate by the dominant society, they experience an identity threat. Aboriginal people, who consider their ethnicity highly salient and important, react in a negative fashion to assimilation and have been resistant to such pressures for generations. Assimilationist pressures that are seen as identity threatening (e.g., giving up language, dress, values, religion), creating resistance by which Aboriginal people strategically emphasize their ethnic identity (or their dual identities).

Assimilative pressures also produce a threat to the distinctiveness component of Aboriginal identity because assimilation not only undermines the distinctiveness of the group but also devalues its identity. Huo and Molina (2006) argue that pressures to assimilate can reduce feelings of respect for Aboriginal people as well as Aboriginal peoples' self-definition because the definition is imposed rather than preferred by the group. This constant pressure to "assimilate" is viewed as an assault on Aboriginality, which is, after all, the basis of First Nations identity (Nesdalel and Mak, 2003). The continued positioning of Aboriginal people in a category that they are not prepared to accept has resulted in their rejection of the imposed identity and the concurrent affirmation of the neglected identity (Barreto and Ellemers, 2009).

Aboriginal people have continually undermined the usefulness of such unwanted categorization processes, neither following nor accepting norms of imposed social categorization by the majority. They have been resentful and resistant and have engaged in differing forms of conflict with the majority group in an attempt to maintain their distinctive ethnic identities. These pressures, in turn, have resulted in second and third generations of Aboriginals feeling threatened.

Pursuing an assimilation policy has led to conflict (at various levels) between Aboriginal people and mainstream society, and thus actually weakens the ties between the two groups. In addition, since Aboriginal people feel coerced into taking on new values and behaviours, assimilation has a negative impact on their lifeways. Nevertheless, "passing" is a strategy attempted by some Aboriginal peoples who have internalized the assimilation policy. However, individuals who "pass" as a member of the dominant society risk "exposure" of the fact that they are not really a member of the majority. Research has shown that despite the benefits that people think passing will bring, the strategy has major costs (Paxton, 2002).

Verkuyten (2005) notes that assimilationist ideology justifies the superiority of the dominant culture, and thus ethnic minority group members are evaluated on how close they come to the dominant template. Aboriginal people find that they must give up attributes that make them deviants (in relation to the prototype of the dominant society) and also to endorse attributes that enhance the likelihood that the majority will perceive a closer "match' to that template. In summary, in a society that forces the assimilationist ideology, minority ethnic group members are put in a disadvantaged state since they have to give up their identities, devalue what they have learned up until this point, and agree that the identity of the majority is superior.

At the same time, Aboriginal people find themselves the focus of discrimination that reinforces the differences between themselves and the dominant society. Aboriginal people are frequently targets of discrimination in which they receive unfair or derogatory treatment based upon their social membership. This can include overt behaviour, covert acts of prejudice, and other more subtle forms of discrimination (e.g., poor service at a restaurant, being the focus of jokes). Aboriginal people experience racism and prejudice on a daily basis—at work, at school, and in their neighbourhoods (Environics, 2010). However, over time, legislation and changing social norms have reduced the extent of overt discrimination. In its stead, social exclusion is used to marginalize Aboriginal individuals and groups. Such treatment produces marginalization, and those affected are likely to perceive (accurately or not), that they do not belong to the same social structure as others. Aboriginal people feel they do not matter and that they are unable to contribute or effect change within society; they believe that, for all intents and purposes, they are "invisible" to the larger society.

When assimilation is pursued by the majority, it produces a distinctive threat through the attempt to do away with the social boundaries established by Aboriginal people. This is important in that all groups seek some sort of distinctiveness because it clarifies the norms and boundaries of belonging and acceptable and unacceptable behaviour. This is what Barreto and Ellemers (2009) refer to as "optimal distinctiveness," which states that groups of people try to differentiate themselves only to the extent that it does not threaten inclusion in a higher order category.

Moreover, we find that the extent to which ethnic minorities feel that the majority have some respect for their way of life and institutions influences their feelings of threat. There is also some suggestion that the perception of respect is a precondition to the acceptance of the superordinate culture (Huo, 2003). Huo and Molina (2006) also find that ethnic group members who feel that the majority society has respect for their "culture" are also more positive in evaluating the cultures of other minority groups in society.

The nature of the relationship between Aboriginal people and the dominant group depends upon the nature of the state policies with regard to how minority groups fit into society and the approach accepted by Aboriginal people. If there is not an alignment of perspectives, conflict will emerge. That is, if the dominant group insists on assimilation while Aboriginal people prefer integration, a misalignment will emerge and the result will be conflict. In summary, if Aboriginal people are viewed in a respectful manner and are supported for their contribution to the dominant society, the level of stress and tension in society will decrease, social cohesion will increase, and the level of integration of Aboriginal people will proceed more smoothly.

ABORIGINAL–WHITE CONTACT

At the time that Europeans made first contact with the peoples of what is now Canada, they met Aboriginal peoples from a variety of cultural backgrounds (e.g., the Beothuk of Newfoundland and the Mi'kmaq of Nova Scotia, as well as a large number of Indigenous peoples from the eastern regions of Quebec). There was a kaleidoscope of **Indigenous** groups, each one unique in its economic organization as well as in its language, religion, and values. Incoming Europeans found this diversity hard to deal with and quickly found a way to resolve the dilemma. Europeans simply labelled all Indigenous people as Indians. There would be some recognition of the different tribes, usually because of linguistic differences, but there was no real attempt to view Aboriginals as distinct cultural entities or to understand the cultural differences. When differences were acknowledged, they were considered minor attributes and were subsumed under the master trait of "Indian," which was a more meaningful and universal term from the Europeans' point of view (Hedican, 1995).

Over the years, Indigenous people in Canada have had different labels, some by their own choice, mostly others imposed upon them. For example, northern Indigenous peoples were called **Eskimos** (a term still used by Americans) but are now called **Inuit** or Inuvialuit. While we refer to Métis today, yesterday they were referred to as "half-breeds." Similar name changes have taken place for those Indigenous people called "Indians." Terms such as "Native" were once used to refer to "Indians," and "Native" is still used by the lay public. Nevertheless, over the years, the term "Indian" has become demeaning, offensive, and loaded with negative stereotypes such that Indigenous people created a new name to identify themselves—First Nations. The term chosen has no legal standing (as does the term "Indian") but has become more commonly used by Indigenous people themselves, government officials, and the lay public. At the same time, generational differences exist in the use of terms such as "Indian," "Native," and the new label "First Nations." Older people sometimes still use the term "Indian" to refer to themselves while younger and more politically active Indigenous people use the term "First Nations people."

The term "First Nations" is a Canadian term that came about as a result of historical and political events. The National Indian Brotherhood first used the term in the 1970s to address the Canadian rhetoric about the "two founding nations." In creating this term, they differentiated themselves from other Aboriginal groups—e.g., Inuit, Métis (and from being considered one of the many ethnic groups living in Canada)—and found that the new title was a powerful symbol that not only provided a positive identity for but also had cachet in dealing with political issues as well as with identity. The term generally refers to those individuals who self-identify as descendents of the Indigenous peoples who settled in North America long before European settlers came. In reality, it turns out that the concept is most commonly used to refer to "status (or legal) Indians." Overall, there is some vagueness in the use of the term but it does tend to focus on people who have a confirmed legal status by the government of Canada.

SOCIAL EXCLUSION

The experience of social exclusion is distressing as well as painful and unlikely to be moderated by situational forces. As one scholar noted, it is like the shock of a cattle prod (Williams and Carter-Sowell, 2009). Social exclusion threatens four basic needs: belonging, control, meaningful existence, and self-esteem. As Cherubini (2008) points out, Aboriginal peoples have repeatedly argued for the redirection of these entitlements from mainstream political control, yet policy makers and political authorities have been non-responsive in their recognition of these requests. Once individuals see themselves as socially excluded, they will attempt to deal with their threatened needs through a variety of affective and behavioural responses. In short, they will cope with the exclusion by attempting to find ways to enhance their sense of belonging, self esteem, control, and meaningful existence.

Yet the question remains: Why do people maintain loyalty to a group that is devalued by others if they have a chance to leave the group? Why don't Aboriginal people leave their communities and become part of the larger society? Put another way, what does membership in an Aboriginal community provide? Devalued groups such as Aboriginal people place an emphasis on intergroup differentiation. Since it is clear that Aboriginal people will never be able to fully "assimilate" into the larger society, other steps need to be taken to maintain their identity and positive self-esteem. First Nations groups emphasize "us" versus "them," which can serve to raise awareness of their devaluation. This in turn produces a heightened salience of the in-group's identity and the treatment it receives from other groups, and facilitates the development of a sense of common fate among group members. The group develops a "politicized identity" that allows it to respond to its devalued status as a group rather than individually (Simon and Klandermans, 2001).

IDENTITY MAINTENANCE

Given the desire to control the terms used to refer to themselves as a people, Aboriginals jealously guard those they have come to adopt. In addition, they are concerned about how the terms are used. For example, they feel that the concepts of "Aboriginal," "Métis," "Inuit," and "First Nations" should be capitalized, as they refer to a human group with respect to nation and nationality. If you talk about "Canadians," you would capitalize the term just as you would "Quebecers". Also, given that there are many First Nations people who have nation-to-nation relationship with the Crown, the independence of those relationships needs to be expressed. An appropriate wording would be "First Nations in Canada" or "First Nations citizens." This terminology reflects a meaning that, for First Nations people, Canada is theirs, rather than that Canada "owns" First Nations. The term "Indian" has all but been removed from discourse today with the exception of making specific legal statements. This chapter will define the various terms used to identify the growing number of Aboriginal peoples in our society (see Figure 2.1). The reader will find that many Aboriginal groups have discarded the names given to them by the settlers and have re-taken on traditional names they used before they were colonized—e.g., Sarcee now call themselves Tsuu T'ina Nation, and Blackfeet now call themselves the Siksika Nation. In short, Aboriginal people have rejected the labels imposed upon them for the past three centuries and have tried to create their own.

Aboriginal people are in an identity crisis situation. After two centuries of oppressive colonization, they are now beginning to have a clear vision of their own "heritage" culture as distinguished from "mainstream" society. Over the past half-century, Aboriginal people have started developing a new collective identity. As Taylor (1983) points out, collective identity arises when a culture is able to provide to its members a clear compliance ideology (a society's collective orientation through which all members make decisions and resolve dilemmas) upon which to build a strong unified ethos. One strand that links Aboriginal people is the general sense of betrayal and injustice they believe has been meted out over the past century. In other cases, political and economic issues have brought together various Aboriginal groups. Finally, a commonality in culture (e.g., spirituality, kinship, cultural ethos) has linked previously uncoupled groups together.

CRYPTOMNESIA

Aboriginal people have long attempted to influence how government and other non-Aboriginal people treat them. We can see that over the years, their influence involved five stages in terms of bringing about social change. The first stage is revelation, during which Aboriginal people demonstrate opposition to the actions of the non-Aboriginal population. In this phase, they register their opposition and try to bring public attention to the issue (e.g., treaties, rights). The initial reaction by government to such action by Aboriginal people is to reject and show distain for the idea. The second stage of social change is called the incubation period, where Aboriginal resistance is persistent and support for Aboriginal claims from external sources (e.g., religious groups, foreign governments) forces the majority to consider the claims of Aboriginal people, which many times reveal legitimate concerns. The 1950 and 1985 changes to the *Indian Act* are good examples. Once the government has to take the concerns expressed by Aboriginal people seriously, the third phase of social change occurs—the conversion stage. This is the phase where the government finally accepts the Aboriginal complaints, internalizes the arguments, and moves toward the Aboriginal position at the covert level. Then, once the government is convinced that other Canadians have agreed with the position raised by Aboriginal people, they reveal their new opinion publicly—the innovation stage. Finally, the government moves into the fifth stage, where it engages in **social cryptomnesia**. Here, the government now takes ownership of the idea and ignores the fact that the idea originated with Aboriginal people. Aboriginal people are not perceived as the authors of their own ideas; instead, government and non-Aboriginal people claim ownership and moral leadership in creating and implementing changes long ago requested by First Nations people (Butera et al., 2009).

There are many examples of cryptomnesia in the history of Aboriginal–non-Aboriginal relations, but *Bill C-31* is one of the best examples. Aboriginal women have, for over 100 years, argued that the *Indian Act* is discriminatory. When changes were made to the Act in 1985, the government claimed these changes were part of their program of removing discriminatory actions against First Nations women. When subsequent claims were made that *Bill C-31* was still discriminatory, government officials rejected the claim. Only when the BC Supreme Court found that indeed *Bill C-31* was discriminatory did the government once again move to change it.

In a recent document (INAC, 2010), the government stated that "On June 2, 2009 it was announced that Canada would not seek leave to appeal the decision to the Supreme Court of Canada and would begin the process of implementing changes to the *Indian Act*" (p. 1). In August 2009 the federal government announced that it would develop legislative amendments to respond to the McIvor decision. It is clear that the voice of Aboriginal people has been lost and the focus is instead on the government's moral and legal responsibilities toward Aboriginal people. Other examples abound and involve complaints about treaties and Aboriginal rights, where Aboriginal people have long held that the existing laws and regulations are illegal, inappropriate, or morally unjust. Only after many years has the government made changes but, in doing so, has given themselves credit for authoring the change. This has important ramifications for the identity of Aboriginal people and their sense of positive perspective.

Aboriginal people also realize that the continued failure of government to deal with Aboriginal issues or to consult with them has contributed to their sense of isolation in Canada, but has also led to their resolve to create a better life. The inability of government to act in a prudent manner to protect Aboriginal peoples continues to reinforce the belief that the achievement of any goals will have to come from within Aboriginal communities, and that if they act in a collective manner they will have a greater impact on bringing about the changes necessary. Nevertheless, there remains an overall lack of Aboriginal identity, which has resulted in an inability to generate consensus on policy issues, in chaos (with various segmented groups constantly vying for popular legitimacy), and in an impotence felt by many members living in First Nations communities (Wilkins, 1999; Sawchuck, 1998).

ABORIGINAL DIVERSITY IN CULTURE AND LANGUAGE

Figure 2.1 identifies the cultural and linguistic divisions among Aboriginal people in Canada. The figure reveals that there are numerous cultural divisions—divisions that have continued into the present. Having noted the diversity among Aboriginal peoples, it must be pointed out that in a number of other ways there is some commonality. For example, Aboriginal people interpret life from a certain common perspective at variance with that of Europeans. Europeans in the 16th and 17th centuries viewed science and religion as closely linked. They envisioned a rigid vertical hierarchical order of life with God on top; below God was a complex order of angels; below the angels, all other forms of life were ordered according to their descending levels of importance. These "natural" inequalities were fixed and ordained by God. Thus, poor people were not equal to rich people, and ethical considerations appropriate for rich people did not need to be applied to the poor. Aboriginal peoples' view of their reality was and continues to be quite different. They view all things (living and non-living) as having souls with a spiritual essence. Humans are no different than the trees, the lakes, or the bears. For Aboriginal people, humans do not have any predestined significance in the world; while humans are different from other elements on earth, they are basically the same—they have a spirit that gives them life.

FIGURE 2.1 | Aboriginal Language and Cultural Divisions

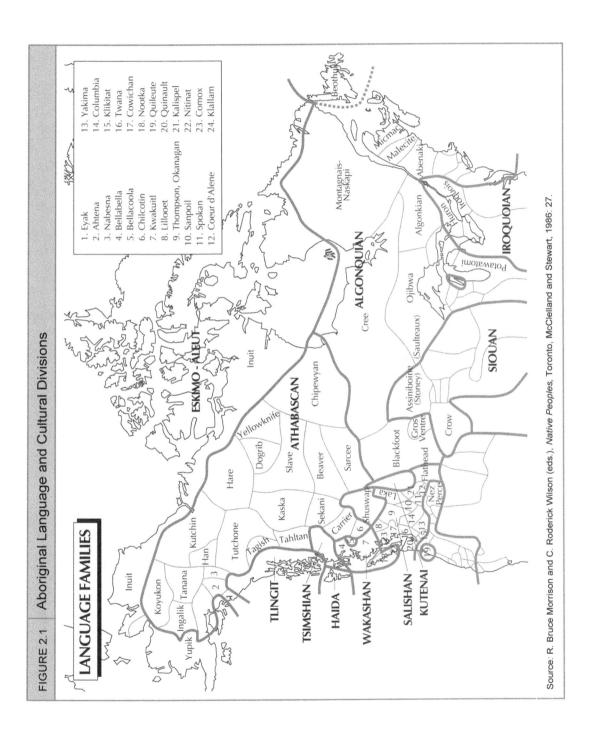

LANGUAGE FAMILIES

1. Eyak	13. Yakima
2. Ahtena	14. Columbia
3. Nabesna	15. Klikitat
4. Bellabella	16. Twana
5. Bellacoola	17. Cowichan
6. Chilcotin	18. Nootka
7. Kwakuitl	19. Quileute
8. Lillooet	20. Quinault
9. Thompson, Okanagan	21. Kalispel
10. Sanpoil	22. Nitinat
11. Spokan	23. Comox
12. Coeur d'Alene	24. Klallam

Source: R. Bruce Morrison and C. Roderick Wilson (eds.), *Native Peoples*, Toronto, McClelland and Stewart, 1986: 27.

MAJOR GROUPS OF ABORIGINAL CANADIANS

Since the late 19th century, there have been four major Aboriginal subgroups—legal or status Indians, non-status Indians, Inuit, and Métis. However, even though these four groups are officially recognized in the Canadian Constitution, they are not recognized in all parts of Canada. The legal status of each of these categories varies across the country—e.g., in Quebec Métis are not recognized by the provincial government, while in Alberta there are formal Métis settlements with official rolls denoting the membership. Nevertheless, there has been a social and now legal recognition of the four groups. The category of **non-status Indians** (who sometimes call themselves people of "Aboriginal ancestry") became diffuse during the 20th century, although these people have long lobbied for some official recognition and legal rights. More and more attention was given to the legal category of "Indian" during the last century because of its financial and resource implications. The label "Métis" began to decline in importance with regard to the federal and provincial governments (Moore, 1978), although with the inclusion of "Métis" in the *Constitution of Canada,* 1982, as a legal subcategory of Aboriginal, their prominence has been reasserted.

In censuses taken before 1941, ethnic origin was traced through the mother. Since eastern Indian tribes were matrilineal and matrilocal, this seemed a satisfactory means of distinguishing Indians from other ethnic groups. Before 1941, children whose mother was Indian were also defined as Indian. However, this was only true for those people who had been previously defined as Indian under the ***British North America Act***. Statistics Canada also made a distinction between Indian and "mixed origin." In 1941 the definition was changed so that, for off-reserve Indians, the father's ethnic status determined that of his children. For those who lived on a reserve, both the mother's and father's lineages were used (Romaniuc and Piche, 1972). It was at this time that the federal government removed any ability of an individual to identify him/herself as Métis. The right to identify as Métis was not reinstituted until the 1991 census.

In 1951, a more complex legal definition of Indian was introduced, stating that only those individuals who fell under the *Indian Act* would be classified as Indians. Today, the federal (and some provincial) government(s) recognizes a legal and fiduciary obligation to legal (registered) Indians, Métis and Inuit. However, non-status Indians and those of Aboriginal ancestry, while given recognition in the census and other official government documents, are not considered a responsibility of Aboriginal Affairs.

Today's definition of an Aboriginal is purely a legal one. For example, even if someone exhibits all the racial and cultural attributes traditionally associated with "Indianness," if the individual does not come under the terms of the *Indian Act,* that person is not an Indian in the eyes of the federal and provincial governments. The following sections explain the categories in the government typology (Levine, 1970).

DEFINING AN INDIAN: FIRST ATTEMPTS

For the first 300 years after sustained contact was made with Aboriginal people, there was little difficulty in determining who was or was not an Aboriginal person. Nor was there any real need to establish a legal definition. Residents living in a small community were aware of who was Aboriginal. Ancestry, physiology, and way of life were the determining factors. This is not to say the question never arose, but rather, when it did arise, the answer was clear from the local residents' perspective. And it should be noted that there was not always consensus on the answer. But for the most part, local community residents understood who was, and who was not, Aboriginal.

However, as the population of Canada grew, as settlement became the goal of the Europeans, and as mobility became a fact of life, tension between Aboriginal people and the settlers intensified. From the settlers' point of view, it became necessary that a clearer demarcation as to who was an Aboriginal person had to be established if social and legal relations were to be determined. Yet it was not until 1850 that the first statutory definition of who was an Indian was enacted. At this time the concept of Indian was a mixture of biology and culture. People of mixed ancestry were assigned either to Indian or Euro-Canadian society and did not constitute a separate category; only Indians and non-Indians existed (Hedican, 1991).

However, once the criteria were established to identify a legal/formal definition of an "Indian," individuals could then, when in question, revert to these attributes to categorize people. As the utility of such a categorization scheme became evident, this definitional strategy was employed by the dominant group without consideration of Aboriginal people. Nevertheless, changes to the definition of who is an Indian have been made over time. For government, one of the first changes in defining an Indian was to drop the blood quantum factor—that is, having a certain proportion of Indian blood. However, in the past decade, some bands have re-introduced "blood quantum" to determine who is a band member (which is different than answering the question of who is an "Indian").

REDEFINING WHO IS AN INDIAN

For some time after contact, phenotypical, cultural, and linguistic attributes became the master traits associated with "Indianness" and "whiteness." Thus, if a person evidenced a certain way of life, he or she was designated Indian or non-Indian, although in everyday life having evidence of visible biological traits (e.g., dark skin colour, straight black hair) made it difficult to pass oneself off as a non-Indian. Nevertheless, if the individual gave ample evidence of being "white," he or she would be treated almost as white—but never totally. For example, if individuals lived in a house rather than a tipi, wore cotton or wool clothes rather than clothes made out of animal hides, held a permanent job and had short hair, they may have been treated as non-Aboriginal in most social contexts (i.e., because the individuals followed a white or European lifestyle). The result of this was that the early ethnic system was divided into two categories—Indians and non-Indians, Inuit and non-Inuit (Bartlett, 1980).

As negotiations with Aboriginal people began over land issues, it became increasingly clear that more refined definitions would have to be determined. With the establishment of the *Indian Act* (1876) and the subsequent creation of an **Indian roll**, it became possible for the government to track and identify who was or was not Indian. By 1880, the federal government excluded Métis from falling under the provisions of the *Indian Act,* although at the present time, the constitutional status of the Métis is undecided. Parliament claims that the Métis are not "Indians" while the provincial legislatures claim that they are. As new legislation was passed, the Indian status of each person listed on the roll could be evaluated according to any criteria that was in place. Those who met the criteria remained on the roll and retained their Indian status (Chartrand, 2004). However, those who did not measure up to the criteria were dropped from the roll and by definition were no longer Indian. Whether their offspring retained their listing on the roll also varied according to the existing legislation at the time. Nevertheless, it is important to remember that those struck from the roll were not necessarily considered Métis, although a large number who were denied Indian status began to define themselves by that term. If people struck from the roll were not Métis, how were they defined? Legally, they were classified as non-status Indians, which meant they were neither Indian nor Métis. At the social level it was clear they were not "white" (Laing, 1967). Changes in definitions were continual, and the movement of large numbers of people in and out of categories is evident. Moreover, federal ministries in charge of keeping records were sloppy in documenting who was or was not Indian. Even when discrepancies were identified, federal ministries were more interested in reducing or limiting the number of people who would be labelled Indian and were slow to change their records, if they ever did. This process continues today and, under *Bill C-31*, thousands of individuals who applied to be defined as Indian were denied their "Indian status."

Registered Indians

The terms "legal," "registered," and "status" are generally used interchangeably to identify an Aboriginal person who is of federal concern. **Registered Indians** are defined in a legal manner and are different from other types of Aboriginal persons who do not have the same legal status. In short, "Indian" refers to a person who, pursuant to the *Indian Act,* is registered as an Indian or is entitled to be registered as an Indian. Put another way, the minister of Aboriginal Affairs and Northern Development has the unilateral right to determine who is and who is not an Indian. First Nations communities can decide who will be part of the band and who can live on the reserve but they cannot determine whether an individual is an Indian. Criteria for determining who is or is not an Indian are part of the *Indian Act* and remain firmly entrenched in the ministers' portfolio, implemented through the content of the Act.

Today it is estimated that nearly 800 000 Canadians are defined as registered Indians. Being registered means that, with some exceptions, an individual is attached to a band and is on the "roll" in Ottawa. As noted earlier, over the years, the federal government has used a number of different criteria to decide who is and who isn't an Indian. For example, between 1868 and today the following groups of people have at times been defined as Indians and at other times as non-Indians:

1. Indian women married to non-Indian men.

2. Children of a non-Indian mother whose father also had a non-Indian mother.

3. Indians residing outside Canada for over five years.

4. Indians with a university degree.

5. Half-breed persons outside Manitoba who accepted scrip.

As identified in Figure 2.2, there are several subtypes of legal Indians. First, legal Indians can be categorized according to whether they have "taken treaty"—that is, whether they or their ancestors signed a treaty with the federal government. As Figure 2.3

FIGURE 2.2 Social–Legal Categories of Aboriginals Residing in Canada

Indians

Registered					Non-Registered
Band Membership				No Band Membership	Band Membership
Treaty		Non-Treaty			
Reserve	Non-Reserve	Reserve	Non-Reserve		
385 000	240 000	140 000	40 000	80 000	11 000

Métis

Off-settlement	On-settlement
190 000	23 000

Inuit

Without disc number	With disc number
41 000	15 000

Indian Ancestry

over 1 000 000

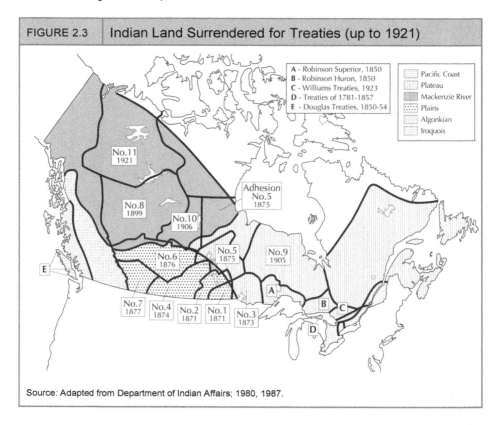

FIGURE 2.3 | Indian Land Surrendered for Treaties (up to 1921)

A - Robinson Superior, 1850
B - Robinson Huron, 1850
C - Williams Treaties, 1923
D - Treaties of 1781-1857
E - Douglas Treaties, 1850-54

Pacific Coast
Plateau
Mackenzie River
Plains
Algonkian
Iroquois

No.11 1921
Adhesion No.5 1875
No.8 1899
No.10 1906
No.6 1876
No.5 1875
No.9 1905
E
No.7 1877
No.4 1874
No.2 1871
No.1 1871
No.3 1873
A
B
C
D

Source: Adapted from Department of Indian Affairs; 1980, 1987.

shows, Indians in British Columbia (with the exception of Vancouver Island), Yukon, Quebec, and the Atlantic provinces did not sign any treaties involving land transfers. Other groups, like the Iroquois of Brantford and Tyendingaga, who emigrated from the United States, are considered non-treaty registered Indians.

Regardless of whether their ancestors signed a treaty, Indians are further subdivided into reserve and non-reserve, according to whether their ancestors were provided with reserve lands. For example, although a treaty (No. 11) was signed by Indians in the Northwest Territories, virtually no reserves exist in this area. And although British Columbian Indians have not taken treaty, many of them live on reserves.

In summary, the classification of a group of people as Indian arises from an historical and legal definition. However, one must remember that the concept of "Indian" today does not solely reflect social, cultural, or racial attributes. The distinction between an Indian and a non-Indian is strictly a legal one.

Non-Status Indians

Although people in this group—i.e., people described as having some social or biological linkage to Indians—may exhibit all the social, cultural, and racial attributes of "Indianness," they are not defined as Indians in the legal sense. Members of this group are not considered registered Indians because they have not been defined as Indian by the Crown. Included in this category are those Indians who have undergone "**enfranchisement**"—that is, they have lost their Indian status through changes in the definition of an Indian, are the product of an Indian–non-Indian marriage, or have been dropped from the Indian roll by the Indian Register.

Enfranchisement (loss of Indian status) occurred in several ways, although coercive enfranchisement by the government was stopped in 1986. For example, until 1960, Indians had to give up their legal status in order to vote in a federal election. Until 1980, an Indian could choose to give up his or her Indian status by applying formally to Ottawa. In so doing, that person also surrendered status for all heirs. For years, one of the most common ways of losing Indian status was through intermarriage. Under the old *Indian Act,* any legal Indian female who married a non-legal Indian male lost Indian status for herself and for her children. However, if a legal Indian male married a non-Indian female, the female became legally Indian as did any offspring that may have resulted. One of the major concerns that the then Department of Indian Affairs and Northern Development (DIAND) had with regard to the changes in the *Indian Act* was the financial cost. In a once-secret DIAND document entitled "Amendments to Remove Discriminatory Sections of the *Indian Act,*" estimates ran from $312 to $557 million (*Indian News,* 1981: 7). Other ways of losing Indian status included obtaining the right of title (fee simple) of land.

In general, a move from Indian to non-Indian status is made on the basis of legal criteria that are set forth by Parliament through the *Indian Act.* However, informal changes to the Act also affect movement between categories—e.g., the then minister of Indian Affairs, at the request of band councils, declared the government would suspend certain sections of the *Indian Act* that discriminated against Indian women who married non-Indians, as well as against their children. The government of Canada has empowered the Department of Aboriginal Affairs to declare that any portion of the Act may not apply to any Indian individuals, groups, or bands. These powers under Section 4(2) were recently invoked for members of certain bands in Quebec. Finally, as noted earlier, until the mid-20th century, Indian Affairs was notoriously lax in keeping accurate, up-to-date records about who was an Indian—using its own criteria. As Giokas and Chartrand (2002) point out, before the 1951 revision to the *Indian Act*, there was no well-organized or well-maintained manner of compiling a list of Indians who were to be on the Indian roll. The result was that many people who should have been on the list were omitted. When people's names were provided by the band for inclusion, Indian Affairs did not add them to the list. Even after 1951, Indian Affairs did not exhibit "due diligence" in trying to establish an up-to-date and accurate list. Giokas and Chartrand (2002) suggest that there were several reasons: the very broad definition of "Indian" in existence, the loose supervision of officials in the field, the pressures of trying to put a list together in a short time, and an indifference to placing names on the roll. They also argue that irregular band members and non-treaty Indians were not considered by the registrar for inclusion on the roll at that time. The end result was the removal of many persons and their children and children's children who would have legitimately been defined as Indian.

Today the minister for Aboriginal Affairs and Northern Development also serves as the federal interlocutor for Métis and non-status Indians. In playing that role, the minister maintains links with the Aboriginal organizations that represent Métis and non-status Indians (e.g., Congress of Aboriginal Peoples, Métis National Council). In addition, the federal interlocutor implements the urban Aboriginal strategy that deals with Aboriginal people living in major urban centres.

Inuit

The category of "Inuit" has also undergone a number of redefinitions. Until Confederation, there was no legal definition of Inuit, nor any real need to make such a distinction. And, since the issue was limited to local concerns, the government did not see fit to enter the debate. However, in 1938, a major dispute between Quebec and the federal government emerged over who had responsibility for the Inuit. The province felt that the federal government had responsibility while the federal government argued that it fell under the province's jurisdiction. In 1939 the Supreme Court of Canada ruled that for administrative purposes, Inuit were Indians and thus fell under the auspices of the *Indian Act.* Since that time, Aboriginal Affairs and Northern Development (AAND) has created Indian and Inuit Affairs, which emerged from the *Indian Act*. In 2005, the Inuit Relations Secretariat was established to liaise with national and regional Inuit organizations as well as to serve as a focal point for Inuit issues and to develop policy and programs unique to Inuit.

When Canada began to think of developing the North in the early 20th century, the government decided that a census was needed to establish the actual number of Inuit. As a result, a "disc" number was allotted to each Inuk; for a time, only those with numbers were officially defined as Inuit. However, other definitions have developed since and continue to be changed. A more detailed profile and discussion on Inuit will be provided in Chapter 9.

Métis

As the treaties were being established in the 1800s, mixed ancestry people (Métis) were often forced to "**take treaty**" and became Indians under the *Indian Act.* However, some were declared non-Indian and were treated accordingly. Both before and after Confederation, it was possible to treat people of mixed ancestry, either individually or in groups, as Indians or non-Indians. However, over time, even individuals initially defined as Indians were arbitrarily removed from the roll and made "non-Indians." The rationale for this action was that the fewer individuals considered Indian at the time of signing of a treaty meant that the total cost of the treaty would be lessened (Chartrand, 2004). At the time of treaty signing, negotiators made it clear that Métis could become Indians, and thus participate in the benefits granted to Indians under the treaty, or live as non-Indians on the reserve—if the Indians agreed. However, they would not be acknowledged as a separate legal entity. This distinction was important because when land was to be given to Indians, government officials had to know who the appropriate recipients were. Social mores also demanded that an individual's ancestry be public so that the community could respond accordingly (Dunning, 1972; Kaye, 1981). As such, Métis, for many years, were forced by the government to fall into one of these two categories. In some cases they were forcibly placed on the roll, while at other times they were unilaterally defined as non-Aboriginal.

The original legislation for deciding who was a Métis used a **blood-quantum** (the percentage of different blood ancestry) definition—if at least one quarter of one's blood was non-Aboriginal, then a person was not considered an Indian (Naumann, 2008). For a more detailed discussion of Métis, consult Chapter 8. Today there are two very different definitions of who is Métis. For the Congress of Aboriginal Peoples, Métis identity is simply defined as those individuals who emphasize their Aboriginal ancestry and heritage. The Métis National Council, while accepting a "self-definition," requires that this identity be mediated by the history of political relations between the ancestors of the Western Métis and the political action (Chartrand, 2002). In other words, the Métis National Council wants to present itself as representing a "nation" of people and not just a group of people who "feel" they are Métis. As such, the Métis National Council requires that for a person to be Métis, he or she must have some connection to the historic Métis and be a descendant of the original Métis people who lived in northern Ontario and the Prairie provinces. In either case, Chartrand (2002) notes that in most nations, "mixed-blood" peoples are usually part of the Indigenous population or part of the new colonial society. Seldom is a new ethnic category created to define social communities created by the colonization process. Nevertheless, the current federal approach to defining Métis is arbitrary, self-serving, and focuses on individual identities, not collective identities.

TOWARD A NEW CONCEPTUALIZATION

Early Attempts at Change: The Lavell and Bedard Cases

Two legal cases from the early 1970s involving the sex-discriminatory status regulations in the *Indian Act* clearly illustrate the issue of definitions, the process of developing social divisions among Aboriginal groups, and the complexity of the Aboriginal women's sexual equality problem. The *Lavell* **and** *Bedard* cases also had a profound effect on the establishment of the Native Women's Association and on the way that organization manifested vis-à-vis national male-dominated Aboriginal organizations (King, 1972).

Jeanette Corbiere Lavell, a status Ojibwa from the Wikwemikong reserve in Ontario who was to marry a non-Aboriginal man in December 1970, had already declared before the date of her marriage that she intended to contest Sections 12(1)b and 14 of the *Indian Act* in court.

A precedent had been set in 1967 by a court case involving a liquor infraction in the Northwest Territories. An Indian man named Drybones was convicted under Section 94(b) of the *Indian Act* for being intoxicated off-reserve. Drybones successfully challenged his conviction before the Supreme Court in 1969 on the basis that this particular section of the *Indian Act* contravened Section 1(b) of the Diefenbaker *Canadian Bill of Rights* (1960) that prohibited racial discrimination. The *Drybones* case proved that it was possible for the *Indian Act* to be overruled by the *Bill* (Cardinal, 1979; Jamieson, 1978). The *Drybones* case and the report of the Royal Commission on the Status of Women, together with the withdrawal of the 1969 *White Paper* on Indian policy, resulted in renewed pride in Indian identity (Krosenbrink-Gelissen, 1983) and an incentive to challenge the *Indian Act*.

In June 1971, an Ontario County Court dismissed Lavell's case on the grounds that, despite the loss of her Indian status, she had equal rights with all other married Canadian women. As such, it was found that she was not deprived of any human rights or freedoms contemplated in the *Bill of Rights*. The court did not find her inequality within her own class of people contrary to the *Bill* and thus overlooked the fact that the *Indian Act* reinforced an inferior position of Indian women in relation to other Canadian women (Chapman, 1972; INAC, 1983; Jamieson, 1978; Krosenbrink-Gelissen, 1984b).

In October 1971, Lavell made an appeal to the Federal Court of Appeals and won. The three judges concluded that the *Indian Act* resulted in different rights for Indian women than those of Indian men when women married non-status males or Indians from different bands. The court decided that Sections 11(1)f, 12(1)b, and 14 of the *Indian Act* contravened the *Bill of Rights* and should therefore be repealed in due course. Right after the decision from the Federal Court of Appeals, the federal government declared that it would bring the *Lavell* case before the Supreme Court of Canada (House of Commons, 1982). There it would be considered together with a second case—that of Yvonne Bedard, a non-status Iroquois woman from the Brantford reserve in Ontario.

Ms. Bedard had separated from her non-Aboriginal husband and returned to her reserve to live in the house that was willed to her by her parents. A year later, Bedard was evicted from the reserve by the band council, although DIAND had informed the council that on the basis of local control several other bands had decided not to implement that particular section of the *Indian Act*. Bedard successfully presented her case before the Supreme Court of Ontario on the same grounds that Lavell had used (Cheda, 1977; Jamieson, 1978; Weaver, 1978).

In February 1973 the *Lavell* and *Bedard* cases appeared before the Supreme Court of Canada. The Attorney General had made the appeal in response to suggestions from government officials who were afraid of the far-reaching implications if the lower court decisions in the *Lavell* and *Bedard* cases should be upheld. Most important, the appeal was also made in response to pressure from the National Indian Brotherhood. The federal government did not want a revision of the *Indian Act,* in view of the previous negative reactions by Indians when change was suggested, and because the abolition of sex discrimination in the Act would bring about substantial financial liabilities (Murphy, 2001). The number of status Indians would increase dramatically if non-status Indian persons were to regain status and corresponding government services.

The Supreme Court decided, in a five-to-four vote, against Lavell and Bedard. The *Canadian Bill of Rights* could not overrule the *Indian Act,* and the fact that Indian women were treated differently upon marriage to a non-status man or an Indian from another band was not considered relevant (Eberts, 1985; Jamieson, 1978; Kerr, 1975). Both the federal government and the National Indian Brotherhood saw the decision as a victory. The National Indian Brotherhood saw it as a victory for Indian rights. The fact that Indian women were denied Indian rights was ignored, since it was thought not relevant to their political mandate.

Nevertheless, the *Lavell* and *Bedard* cases awakened both the Canadian public and the Indian people. The cases presented a moral dilemma over which the women's movement and the Indian movement collided; the Indian ideology of special status was perceived as irreconcilable with the equal rights ideology of the women's movement. However, to Indian women the issue had never been as described above. They had never asked for equal rights with other Canadians, but for equal rights with other Indians: "We can't begin discussing universal women's rights because at this time we can't even get Indian rights for Indian women" (*Indian Rights for Indian Women*, n.d.: 15). Misinterpretations of Indian women's political goals on the part of both the Indian movement and the women's movement were due to a lack of understanding of the true character of the Indian or Aboriginal women's movement, as the Native Women's Association of Canada was to argue in the 1980s.

Bill C-31: More Changes to Who is an Indian

As noted, until the late 20th century, the government focused on deleting Indians from the roll and minimizing their legal and financial liability. However, in 1985, the Government of Canada, after considerable lobbying by Aboriginal peoples, international pressure, and the fact that the government had implemented the *Charter of Rights and Freedoms*, introduced *Bill C-31* (*An Act to Amend the Indian Act*), which once again redefined who is, and is not, Indian. Three key provisions are part of this amendment to the Act:

1. Reinstatement as Indians for those who lost their registration under earlier versions of the Act and the registration of their children.

2. New rules with regard to who could register as an Indian.

3. The ability of First Nations to determine their own rules for determining First Nations membership.

This amendment, for the first time, began to add people to the roll in a most peculiar fashion. *Bill C-31* was passed so that sexual discrimination would be eliminated, bringing the *Indian Act* into line with the *Canadian Charter of Rights and Freedoms*. It also abolished the concept of enfranchisement and provided for the partial reinstatement of people who had lost their Indian status. Moreover, the bill defined eligibility for various benefits that the federal government provided for registered Indians. While the government argued that the overall effect of *Bill C-31* was to ensure that no one would gain or lose status through marriage, it did not have that effect.

The new Act identified four different types of Indians in addition to the differentiation between treaty and non-treaty: (1) status with band membership; (2) status with no band membership; (3) non-status, but with band membership; and (4) non-status, non-band. As a result, one may hold legal status and be on the roll but not be a member of a band. Previously, no such distinction was made. While people who lost their Indian status through marriage or enfranchisement may now reapply for status as a legal Indian, and also apply for band membership, those individuals whose ancestors (more than one generation removed) lost their status are not eligible. Those individuals applying to regain their Indian status are reviewed by Aboriginal Affairs and Northern Development (AAND) and a decision is made as to whether the individual has a legal right to claim it. Well over 250 000 applications have been received by Aboriginal Affairs, and thus far only about 120 000 have been accepted.

Others who were reinstated had to wait for two years to come under Sections 6(1) and 6(2) of the new *Indian Act*. Because acceptance into a band means that resources such as housing have to be shared, many band councils are reluctant to accept reinstated Indians onto their band membership lists. If a band failed to establish a membership code by the deadline, then all individuals who had been reinstated as Indians and had some historical basis for claiming membership to a particular band were automatically given band status. If, however, they did not meet the band criteria, they were counted as part of a new category of Indians (legal Indians with no band status).

The *Bill* also addressed the issue of transmitting one's status (Section 6 of the new *Indian Act*):

6(1) Subject to Section 7, a person is entitled to be registered if

    (a) that person was registered or entitled to be registered immediately prior to April 17, 1985.

    (b) that person is a member of a body of persons that has been declared by the Governor in Council on or after April 17, 1985, to be a band for the purposes of this Act.

    (c) the name of that person was omitted or deleted from the Indian Register, or from a band list prior to September 4, 1951, under subparagraph 12(2)(a)(iv), paragraph 12(2)(b) or subsection 22(2) or under subparagraph 22(2)(a)(iii) pursuant to an order made under subsection 109(2), as each provision read immediately prior to April 17, 1985, or under any former provision of this Act relating to the same subject-matter as any of those provisions.

    (d) the name of that person was omitted or deleted from the Indian Register, or from a band list prior to September 4, 1951, under subparagraph 12(1)(a)(888) pursuant to an order made under subsection 109(1), as each provision read immediately prior to April 17, 1985, or under any former provision of this Act relating to the same subject-matter as any of those provisions.

    (e) the name of that person was omitted or deleted from the Indian Register, or from a band list prior to September 4, 1951.

        (i) under section 13, as it read immediately prior to September 4, 1951, or under any former provision of this Act relating to the same subject-matter as that section or

        (ii) under section 111, as it read immediately prior to July 1, 1920, or under any former provision of this Act relating to the same subject-matter as that section: or

    (f) that person is a person both of whose parents are or, if no longer living, were at the time of death entitled to be registered under this section.

6(2) Subject to Section 7, a person is entitled to be registered if that person is a person one of whose parents is or, if no longer living, was at the time of death entitled to be registered under subsection (1).

Applying for Birthright

Sections 6(1) and 6(2) serve to define who will be a status Indian in the future. Moreover, Section 6(1) identifies those who lost or were denied status as a result of the *Indian Act* prior to 1985. This includes such events as having married a non-Indian man, having been the child of a non-Indian man and a woman who was a status Indian at the time of birth, and enfranchisement. While at first reading it might seem as though the discriminatory aspects of the *Indian Act* had been removed, closer inspection will reveal that sex discrimination still remained, although the government would deny it for the next 25 years. As Giokas and Groves (2002) and Loh and George (2003) point out, Section 6(1)(f) registers all those persons whose parents (living or dead) were registered or entitled to be registered under either Section 6(1) or 6(2). Section 6(2) registers only the child of one parent who was, or was entitled to be, registered under only Section 6(1).

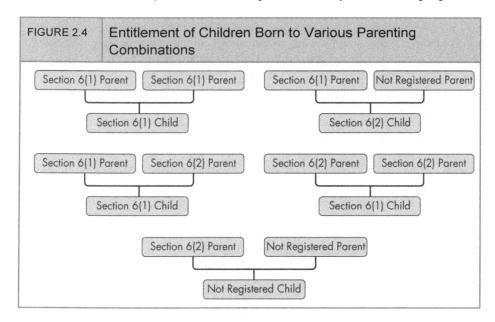

FIGURE 2.4   Entitlement of Children Born to Various Parenting Combinations

As such, the children of a 6(2) parent are immediately penalized if that parent marries a non-Indian. At the same time, the penalty for a 6(1) person to marry a non-Indian does not have the same impact on the children of such a union. In summary, the changes to the *Indian Act* revealed that for 6(1) Indians, after two consecutive generations of marrying a non-Indian, Indian status will be lost. For 6(2) Indians, only one generation of marrying out will result in the children losing their Indian status. Similar issues arise when dealing with "illegitimate" Aboriginal children. Figure 2.4 shows the outcome of different types of marriages with regard to the status of their children.

The above scenarios show that individuals who have obtained status through Section 6(2) and then marry a non-Indian will have children who are non-Indian. However, if they marry an Indian, any children will be Indian. If those individuals who are registered under the conditions of Section 6(1) marry Indians, their children will be Indian. However, if they marry a non-Indian, the children will become Indian under Section 6(2) and will be unable to pass Indian status to their children if they marry a non-Indian. One final possibility would be to have two Indians under Section 6(2) marry. In this case, the children would be Indian under the provisions of Section 6(1). All children born "out of wedlock" will automatically be registered as Indians under Section 6(2) unless the mother can prove that the father was a status Indian, in which case they would be registered under Section 6(1).

The consequence of this new system is that the probability of an Indian marrying a non-Indian is much greater than marrying another Indian. For example, if 100 male Indians and 100 female Indians live in a community, and if they wish to marry a member of their "in-group," there can only be 100 marriages. However, if they marry someone who is non-Indian, there could be 200 marriages. As a result, as the out-marriage rate increases, the number of Indians will decrease. It has been suggested that within five generations, there will be far fewer Indians than today. And by 10 generations, there will be virtually no Indians in Canada.

An example provided by Giokas and Groves (2002) illustrates the point. Assume that a status Indian brother and his status Indian sister both marry non-Indians. The children of the sister who married out prior to the 1985 amendments will be "new status," since they all fall into the 6(2) category at the outset because they will only have one parent who was registered under *Bill C-31*. The children of the brother who married out prior to the 1985 amendments will be "old status" because both their parents already had status. They will therefore be 6(1) and will start off with an advantage over their similarly situated 6(2) cousins in terms of status transmission. This has nothing to do with the actual **Indian ancestry**, since the brother and sister have exactly the same degree of Indian ancestry. In the end, the new *Bill* may sow the seeds of discontent between factions of a community and bring further tension and conflict within the reserve.

Table 2.1 reveals the impact on the Indian population registered under *Bill C-31*. From 1985 until 1997, the addition of *Bill-C-31*-registered Indians was significant. We also see that as of 2001, the number of Indians registered through *Bill C-31* has been minimal, and projections show that the trend will continue. However, the important issue is that even though *Bill C-31* has lost its impact in terms of adding "disenfranchised" Indians, other parts of the new Act will have major effects upon the Indian population. Today, the pool

TABLE 2.1	Registered Indians and Indians Registered Under *Bill C-31*, Average Annual Growth Rates, Canada 1981–2004				
	Registered Indians			Average Annual Growth (%)	
Year	Excluding *Bill C-31*	*Bill C-31* Population	Total	Excluding *Bill C-31*	Including *Bill C-31*
1981	323 782	0	323 782	2.59	0.00
1982	332 178	0	332 178	2.95	0.00
1983	341 968	0	341 968	2.00	0.00
1984	348 809	0	348 809	2.82	3.28
1985[a]	358 636	1 605	360 241	3.16	7.66
1986	369 972	17 857	387 829	2.40	7.24
1987	378 842	37 056	415 898	2.71	6.73
1988	389 110	54 774	443 884	2.65	5.06
1989[b]	399 433	66 904	466 337	4.20	5.11
1991	429 178	92 282	521 460	3.55	4.23
1996	506 005	104 869	610 874	2.83	3.01
2001	517 226	105 675	622 901	2.16	1.93
2004	527 570	106 456	637 227	2.00	2.03

a. In 1985, the *Indian Act* was amended to allow, through *Bill C-31*, the restoration of Indian status to those who had lost it due to discriminatory clauses in the *Indian Act*.

b. The high annual growth rate between 1989 and 1991 is due in part to the upward adjustments of the Indian Register for the purposes of the projections and to the Department's estimate of 86 000 *Bill C-31* registrants in 1990-91 plus the growth due to natural increase.

Sources: *Adapted from Basic Departmental Data*-1990, pp. 7, Indian and Northern Affairs Canada; Clatworthy, 2004; DIAND, 2004; Ram, 2004; Romaniuc, 2003.

of potential applicants is exhausted, and it is likely that *Bill C-31* will no longer have a substantial impact on the number of legal Indians. Nevertheless, it does show that the growth rate for Aboriginals is about twice that of the overall Canadian population.

The data show that the average annual growth rate for Aboriginals between 1985 and 1991 was three to seven times higher than the overall Canadian growth rate. The addition of *"Bill C-31"* people to the Indian roll created substantial social and political problems for reserve Indians as well as financial problems for the federal government. A serious rift now exists between Indians who have spent their lives on the reserve versus those who were enfranchised or otherwise forced to live off the reserve and now find themselves with Indian status. The return of urban Indians to the reserves has brought about bitterness, jealousy, and factions within the reserve community. In many areas, such as in educational institutions, a great deal of animosity exists between "traditional" Indians and *"Bill C-31"* Indians.

Because enfranchisement meant that Indians had to leave the reserve, most migrated to urban areas. Thus, many *Bill C-31* Indians have lived and raised their children in urban areas, and, over a generation of absence from the reserve, have been assimilated, taking on the attributes of non-Aboriginal culture. Under the new legislation, some of these Aboriginals are allowed to be reinstated, to claim their Indian identity (or what they have retained of it), and to benefit from the social and economic programs that are available to Indians. In some cases, this means access to a reserve and possible resettlement. Land allocation can be applied for and a share of band profits will have to be allocated to these new Indians. In other cases, it means access to financial support to go to school or to receive health care benefits. In still other cases, it provides an individual with his or her birthright as an Indian. In the latter, the financial benefit is not at issue but rather the right to identify oneself with the group—Indians.

There are a number of complex problems involved in the implementation of *Bill C-31*. First, at a family level, it means that brothers and sisters may have different legal status. A second problem concerns band membership. Although some children (dependants—6[2]) have a right to reside on a reserve, it is not certain that independent 6(2) children and their non-Indian fathers are allowed to reside on the reserve. A further problem of *Bill C-31* centres on band membership for reinstated women and their children. Bands have been given control over their membership, and some of these bands have adopted the old *Indian Act* band membership system and thus are able to exclude reinstated Indians.

White, Maxim, and Beavon (2003) and Clatworthy (2004) have carried out a review of the membership rules of various First Nations and found four different types, as depicted in Table 2.2. Individuals reinstated through *Bill C-31* technically have the right to reside on a reserve. In the past, nearly all registered Indians were members of a band. However, because this new legislation allows for each Indian band to adopt its own rules governing membership, there are major differences between the number of people who are registered and the number who are members of bands. This difference may seem unimportant, but upon closer inspection several issues emerge. For example, if you are a band member, you are eligible to vote and to stand for band council membership. In addition, being a band member makes you eligible for a number of programs that are offered by the community—e.g., housing, social assistance, health. Moreover, if you are a band member you may be exempt from paying certain taxes. These are important considerations for any community, and they have not been taken lightly by First Nations people.

TABLE 2.2	Different Band Membership Rules by Number of First Nations and Population	
Type of Membership Rule	% of First Nations Community	% of Population
Indian Act Rule	71.4	70.8
Unlimited One-Parent[a]	13.8	12.5
Two-Parent rule[b]	10.5	6.9
25–50% Blood Quantum	4.3	13.8
Total Population Covered	609	725,700

[a]Unlimited one-parent rules, where eligibility requires that at least one parent be a member;
[b]Two-parent rules, where eligibility requires that both parents be members of the band.

The introduction of *Bill C-31* has also affected the demography of the Aboriginal population. White, Maxim, and Beavon (2003) show that substantial age differences exist between *Bill C-31* and pre-*Bill C-31* populations. For on-reserve populations, the average age of the *Bill C-31* population registered under 6(1) was 43.5 years, or about 15 years older than its pre-*Bill C-31* population. For those registered under 6(2), the difference was 24 years older on average. They note that age differences for Indians off-reserve were even greater. While the immediate impact of *Bill C-31* was to increase the Indian population, its long-term effects are also of great interest. Clatworthy (2010) has developed a projection methodology that explores the future impact of *Bill C-31* on the population entitled "Estimates of Demographic Implications from Indian Registration Amendment—*McIvor v. Canada*". The total population of survivors and descendants is projected to increase to slightly more than 2 million within four generations. However, the population entitled to be registered as "Indian" would grow for two generations to a peak of just over 1 million, and then an accelerating decline would take place over the next two generations. By the end of the fourth generation, only 750 000 would be registered as Indian, a number similar to today's population. After that, he projects a decrease in numbers such that, by the end of the sixth generation, there would be less than 100 000 individuals classified as "Indian" (White, Maxim, and Beavon, 2003).

When *Bill C-31* was passed, the federal government argued that it had addressed the issue of sex discrimination. However, as Giokas and Groves (2002) point out, injustices remain. First, they observe that not all persons of Indian ancestry were included in the new registry. Second, they note that sex discrimination has not been eliminated because the effects of the earlier sex discrimination fall harder on Indian women and their descendants than on Indian men. Third, band membership codes do not deal with every person who has Indian status. Fourth, even where bands have been unable to exclude the new band members that the bill added, other ways are found to exclude them from the benefits of band membership—e.g., in one case, per-capita disbursements under the *Indian Act* were stopped and the funds moved to a band-controlled account from which new members were not provided with per-capita disbursements. Finally, there are problems in how children are defined.

McIvor v. Canada

Bill C-31 was challenged in the courts by Ms. McIvor, an Indian woman. She argued that despite amendments made by *Bill C-31*, there is still sex discrimination. It would take several years for the courts to respond to her challenge, but in 2007, the Supreme Court of British Columbia found that indeed, Section 6 of the *Indian Act* infringed on Section 15 of the *Canadian Charter*. After two years of assessing the decision, the federal government did not seek leave to appeal the decision to the Supreme Court of Canada. The court gave the government one year to make the necessary changes so that the Act no longer infringed upon the *Canadian Charter*. The federal government hastily amended the *Indian Act* and attempted to meet with various Aboriginal organizations to seek approval of their suggested amendments. While the amendments are specific and pertain to the issue considered by the Supreme Court, they do not deal with larger issues surrounding Indian registration, band membership, and First Nations citizenship.

Nevertheless, the amendments were implemented in the fall of 2010. These amendments accomplished the goal of providing Indian registration under Section 6(2) of the *Indian Act* to the grandchild of a woman:

> who lost status due to marrying a non-Indian; and whose child born of that marriage parented the grandchild with a non-Indian after September 4, 1951 as well as any sibling of that grandchild born before September 4, 1951. (INAC, 2010)

SOCIAL DIVISIONS AMONG ABORIGINAL PEOPLE

The definitions of "Indian," "non-status," "Métis," and "Inuit" are far from settled. Many of the decisions will rest with the courts. Indeed, it is clear that no single definition of Aboriginal peoples has been agreed upon. However, as Mallea (1994) argues, whatever the definition of "Indians," the legislation in place led the government to a strategy of "divide and conquer" as well as assimilation. She contends that it allowed the government to create an apartheid system by placing Aboriginal peoples on reserves. Moreover, the changing definition of who is an Indian has an impact on who is defined as Métis and/or Inuit. Why have these legal distinctions been inflicted upon Canadian Aboriginal people? Those in power have surely been aware that such nominal distinctions have a "divide and conquer" effect. Aboriginal people became easier to control as they began to fight among themselves. The distinctions between non-treaty and the treaty Indians are particularly divisive; the two groups receive different privileges, different amounts of money from different sources, and different rights.

Summary

- Aboriginal identity has become complex and fragmented.
- Aboriginal identity transcends political borders (e.g., pan Canadian).
- Aboriginal people have been faced with changing definitions and identities.
- A collective consciousness is beginning to connect diverse Aboriginal groups.

Key Terms

British North America Act
   p. 36
blood-quantum p. 42
enfranchisement p. 41
Eskimos p. 31
Indian Act p. 27

Indian ancestry p. 48
Indian roll p. 37
Indigenous p. 31
Inuit p. 31
Lavell and *Bedard* cases
   p. 43

non-status Indians p. 36
registered Indians p. 38
social cryptomnesia p. 33
"take treaty" p. 42

Questions for Further Discussion

1. Explain why there was no statutory definition of who was an Indian before 1850.
2. Explain how the classification of a group of people such as treaty/non-treaty is strictly for legal reasons.
3. Why was enfranchisement abolished and what did this mean for an Indian whose rights had been lost?
4. What was the overall effect of *Bill C-31*?
5. Describe the important aspects of Sections 6(1) and 6(2) of the *Indian Act*.
6. Why have legal distinctions been inflicted upon Canadian Aboriginal people?
7. How do the legal cases *Lavell* and *Bedard* illustrate the issue of definitions?

CHAPTER 3

Demographic Profile of Aboriginal Peoples

LEARNING OBJECTIVES

After reading this chapter you should be able to:

1. Appreciate the significance of reserves in Canada.
2. Understand the distribution of registered Indian populations on and off reserves.
3. Recognize the importance of population size and growth rate for First Nations.
4. Understand health issues for First Nations.
5. Understand the impact of social and economic problems on Aboriginal health.
6. Recognize the quality of life experienced by Aboriginal people.
7. Analyze the challenges experienced by Aboriginal people living on reserves.

INTRODUCTION

The role of Aboriginal people in Canadian society today can be summed up by a song Bob Dylan wrote nearly 50 years ago when he sang that things change over time. For nearly three centuries after the coming of the Europeans there was a depopulation of Aboriginal people. It was only after the turn of the 20th century that a stabilization and slow recovery began (Romaniuc, 2003). Since that time, Aboriginal people have increased their population nearly five times. How did this happen? What is the future for this group?

To answer these and other questions, we need to examine demography. Demography is the study of populations and their size, distribution, and change. It provides an understanding of how societies and groups change over time and examines how changes in a population act upon and change culture and society. It is also useful for helping us understand enduring conflicts and competing interests within and among societies. Finally, demographic information provides the context in which governments make policy and program decisions regarding Aboriginal people.

To ensure up-to-date information, every 10 years a census is undertaken that collects data from every Canadian. This systematic collection of data allows governments (federal, provincial, and municipal) to assess their policies as well as project into the future what programs will be required in order to address the problems facing people. The Department of Aboriginal Affairs and Northern Development (**AAND**) also collects information on Aboriginal people. Unfortunately, the census data differ widely from the AAND data, partly due to differences in the groups' definition of an Aboriginal and their methods of enumeration. Box 3.1 provides a general definition of terms that will be used in this book.

Box 3.1	Terminology

Aboriginal Affairs and Northern Development (AAND): In May 2011, the Harper Conservative government changed the name of Indian and Northern Affairs Canada (INAC). The change reflects the increasing involvement of the federal government in Inuit, Métis, and non-status Indian peoples. Thus the new title reflects a broadening of the federal government's mandate to deal with all Aboriginal people and not just First Nations people.

Aboriginal peoples: The descendants of the original inhabitants of North America. The Canadian Constitution recognizes three groups of Aboriginal people—Indians, Métis, and Inuit. These are three separate peoples with unique heritages, languages, cultural practices, and spiritual beliefs.

Aboriginal rights: Rights that some Aboriginal peoples of Canada hold as a result of their ancestors' long-standing use and occupancy of the land. The rights of certain Aboriginal peoples to hunt, trap, and fish on ancestral lands are examples of Aboriginal rights. Aboriginal rights vary from group to group depending on the customs, practices, and traditions that have formed part of their distinctive cultures.

Aboriginal self-government: Governments designed, established, and administered by Aboriginal peoples under the Canadian Constitution through a process of negotiation with Canada and, where applicable, provincial governments.

Aboriginal title: A legal term that recognizes an Aboriginal interest in the land. It is based on the long-standing use and occupancy of the land by today's Aboriginal peoples as the descendants of the original inhabitants of Canada.

band: A body of Indians for whose collective use and benefit lands have been set apart or money is held by the Crown, or declared to be a band for the purposes of the *Indian Act.* Each band has its own governing band council, usually consisting of one chief and several councillors. Community members choose the chief and councillors by election, or sometimes through custom. The members of a band generally share common values, traditions, and practices rooted in their ancestral heritage. Today, many bands prefer to be known as First Nations.

Bill C-31: The pre-legislation name of the 1985 *Act to Amend the Indian Act*. This *Bill* eliminated certain discriminatory provisions of the *Indian Act*, including the section that resulted in Indian women losing their Indian status when they married non-status men. *Bill C-31* enabled people affected by the discriminatory provisions of the old *Indian Act* to apply to have their Indian status and membership restored.

custom: A traditional Aboriginal practice. For example, First Nations peoples sometimes marry or adopt children according to custom, rather than under Canadian family law. Band councils chosen "by custom" are elected or selected by traditional means, rather than by the election rules contained in the *Indian Act.*

First Nation: A term that came into common usage in the 1970s to replace the word "Indian," which some people found offensive. Although the term First Nation is widely used, no legal definition of it exists. Among its uses, the term "First Nations peoples" refers to the Indian peoples in Canada, both status and non-status. Some Indian peoples have also adopted the term "First Nation" to replace the word "band" in the name of their community.

Indian: Indian people are one of three cultural groups, along with Inuit and Métis, recognized as Aboriginal people under Section 35 of the *Constitution Act.* There are legal reasons for the continued use of the term "Indian." Such terminology is recognized in the *Indian Act* and is used by the Government of Canada when making reference to this particular group of Aboriginal people.

To change the name of Indian and Northern Affairs Canada, a rigorous process would have to be undertaken, involving changing the legal term used in the *Indian Act* and *Constitution Act* to describe First Nations people in Canada. As long as the term "Indian" remains in these two acts, it will continue to be used when referring to Indian people in a legal context. However, Indian and Northern Affairs Canada uses the term First Nations in most instances.

status Indian: A person who is registered as an Indian under the *Indian Act.* The Act sets out the requirements for determining who is an Indian for the purposes of the *Indian Act.*

non-status Indian: An Indian person who is not registered as an Indian under the *Indian Act.*

treaty Indian: A status Indian who belongs to a First Nation that signed a treaty with the Crown.

Indian Act: Canadian federal legislation, first passed in 1876 and amended several times since. It sets out certain federal government obligations and regulates the management of Indian reserve lands, Indian moneys, and other resources. Among its many provisions, the *Indian Act* currently requires the minister of Indian Affairs and Northern Development to manage certain monies and lands belonging to First Nations and to approve or disallow First Nations bylaws. In 2001, the national initiative Communities First: First Nations Governance was launched to consult with First Nations peoples and leadership on the issues of governance under the *Indian Act.* The process will likely take two to three years before any new law is put in place.

Indian status: An individual's legal status as an Indian, as defined by the *Indian Act.*

Innu: Naskapi and Montagnais First Nations (Indian) peoples who live in Northern Quebec and Labrador.

(Continued)

Inuvialuit: Inuit who live in the Western Arctic.

Inuit: An Aboriginal people in Northern Canada, who live in Nunavut, Northwest Territories, Northern Quebec, and Northern Labrador. The word means "people" in the Inuit language—Inuktitut. The singular of Inuit is Inuk.

land claims: In 1973, the federal government recognized two broad classes of claims—comprehensive and specific. Comprehensive claims are based on the assessment that there may be continuing Aboriginal rights to lands and natural resources. These kinds of claims come up in those parts of Canada where Aboriginal title has not previously been dealt with by treaty and other legal means. The claims are called "comprehensive" because of their wide scope. They include such things as land title, fishing and trapping rights, and financial compensation. Specific claims deal with specific grievances that First Nations may have regarding the fulfillment of treaties. Specific claims also cover grievances relating to the administration of First Nations lands and assets under the *Indian Act*.

Métis: People of mixed First Nation and European ancestry who identify themselves as Métis, as distinct from First Nations people, Inuit, or non-Aboriginal people. The Métis have a unique culture that draws on their diverse ancestral origins, such as Scottish, French, Ojibway, and Cree.

the North: Land in Canada located north of the 60th parallel. AAND's responsibilities for land and resources in the Canadian North relate only to Nunavut, Northwest Territories, and Yukon.

Nunavut: The territory created in the Canadian North on April 1, 1999 when the former Northwest Territories was divided in two. Nunavut means "our land" in Inuktitut. Inuit, whose ancestors inhabited these lands for thousands of years, make up 85 percent of the population of Nunavut. The territory has its own public government.

off-reserve: A term used to describe people, services, or objects that are not part of a reserve, but relate to First Nations.

oral history: Evidence taken from the spoken words of people who have knowledge of past events and traditions. This oral history is often recorded on tape and then put in writing. It is used in history books and to document claims.

reserve: Tract of land, the legal title to which is held by the Crown, set apart for the use and benefit of an Indian band.

surrender: A formal agreement by which a band consents to give up part or all of its rights and interests in a reserve. Reserve lands can be surrendered for sale or for lease, on certain conditions.

tribal council: A regional group of First Nations members that delivers common services to a group of First Nations.

Source: **INAC**. Retrieved from www.ainc-inac.gc.ca/ap/tln-eng.asp.

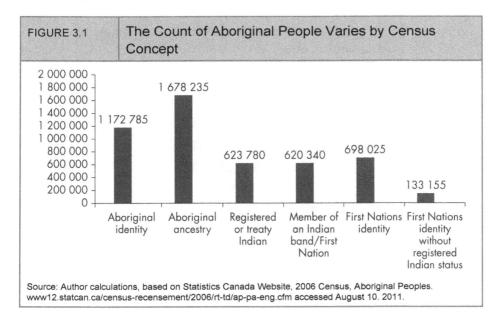

FIGURE 3.1 — The Count of Aboriginal People Varies by Census Concept

Source: Author calculations, based on Statistics Canada Website, 2006 Census, Aboriginal Peoples. www12.statcan.ca/census-recensement/2006/rt-td/ap-pa-eng.cfm accessed August 10. 2011.

Nevertheless, statistics coming from one agency are not strictly comparable with statistics from the other and the lack of standardized data confuses the layperson and poses problems for short-term trend analyses, while at the same time making future projections difficult. Moreover, because the definition of an Aboriginal has changed over time, statistics reported by the same agency can show wide discrepancies. Figure 3.1 reveals the discrepancies among the various categories of Indigenous peoples in Canada.

It is crucial for policy and program analysts to have information regarding the size of the Aboriginal population with which they are dealing. Improper interpretation of demographic data can have a detrimental impact on understanding population trends as well as on the implementation of policies related to those trends. In order to properly interpret these factors, analysts must also be clear about the base population size and the growth rate (Guimond and Robitaille, 2009). The growth rate is dependent upon three factors: fertility, mortality, and immigration. Other factors, such as policy and legislation, also have an impact on the size and growth of a people. To begin with, we will briefly look at Aboriginal residential patterns and growth rates and how policy and legislation have affected both the size and growth of Aboriginal people in Canada.

RESIDENTIAL PATTERNS

Where do Aboriginal people live? They reside in all parts of Canada, although they are not evenly distributed. Figure 3.2 reveals the broad geographical dispersion of Aboriginal peoples across Canada. It shows that eight out of ten Aboriginal people live in Ontario and in the Western provinces. However, it should be noted that just because those who live in Ontario and the West make up a large proportion of the Aboriginal population, they do not represent a large portion of the population within these provinces. Even though nearly a quarter of a million Aboriginal people reside in Ontario, they make up only about 2 percent of the Ontario population.

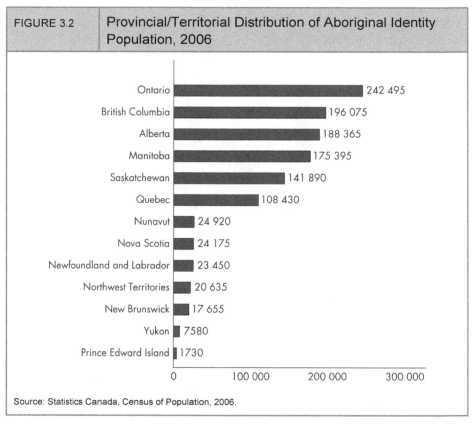

FIGURE 3.2	Provincial/Territorial Distribution of Aboriginal Identity Population, 2006

Ontario 242 495
British Columbia 196 075
Alberta 188 365
Manitoba 175 395
Saskatchewan 141 890
Quebec 108 430
Nunavut 24 920
Nova Scotia 24 175
Newfoundland and Labrador 23 450
Northwest Territories 20 635
New Brunswick 17 655
Yukon 7580
Prince Edward Island 1730

Source: Statistics Canada, Census of Population, 2006.

Looking at the distribution of Aboriginal people from a different perspective, we find that nearly half the Aboriginal population live in urban centres across the country (see Figure 3.3). The data show that just over one-quarter of Aboriginal people live on reserves, with nearly equal amounts (21 percent) living in non–Census Metropolitan Areas (CMAs) and rural areas. Nearly one-third live in CMAs. However, if we compare these figures with the non-Aboriginal population we see striking differences. First, two-thirds of the non-Aboriginal population live in CMAs while the remainder are equally split between non-CMA and rural areas. Making this more complex, if we look at the different categories of Aboriginal people, we see major differences among them. All of this suggests that policies dealing with Canadians cannot take a "one size fits all" approach, as there are different demographic profiles for the various sub-groups. Projections suggest that growth for all different types of Aboriginal people will continue over the next decade.

Approximately one-fourth of the Aboriginal population of Canada lives in Ontario, and another 16 percent in each of Saskatchewan and British Columbia. Other Western provinces show similar numbers, while much smaller populations reside in Quebec and Atlantic Canada. Population projections suggest average population growth by province/territory over the next 15 years and show Nunavut with the greatest (70 percent), followed by Alberta (64 percent) and Saskatchewan (64 percent), and then Manitoba (53 percent). In summary, the Prairie regions will experience the highest growth rates in the country, far exceeding the national average (47 percent) for Aboriginal people.

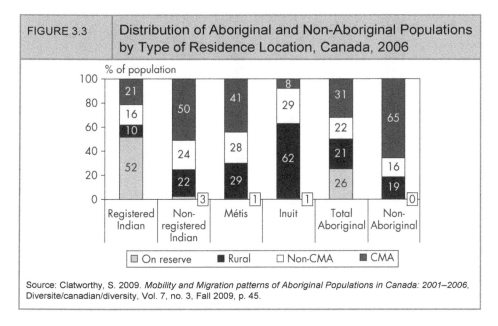

FIGURE 3.3   Distribution of Aboriginal and Non-Aboriginal Populations by Type of Residence Location, Canada, 2006

Source: Clatworthy, S. 2009. *Mobility and Migration patterns of Aboriginal Populations in Canada: 2001–2006*, Diversite/canadian/diversity, Vol. 7, no. 3, Fall 2009, p. 45.

When we focus on the off-reserve population, we see that all regions have experienced increases (Table 3.1). However, the largest increases in off-reserve Aboriginal populations from 1966 to 2006 were in Saskatchewan and Alberta, with Quebec having the lowest. Thinking about the future, the data suggest that Alberta and Manitoba will continue to have substantial increases in off-reserve Indians. If we look at the geographical distribution of Métis and non-status Indians in 2005, we find that about 29 percent of enumerated Métis live in Alberta while an additional 42 percent live in the other two Prairie provinces. Focusing on non-status Indians, we find that 40 percent live in Ontario while an additional 30 percent are in British Columbia. We now turn to a more detailed look at the demography of "registered Indians."

Registered Indians (Commonly Called First Nations) on Reserves

Canada has some 2720 **reserves**, though this number, like the number of bands (615), varies over time according to the policy of the federal government. Reserves also vary in size. Although there is no minimum area, 71.5 hectares per person is the maximum (the Blood reserve—900 square kilometres—in Alberta is the largest in the country), while some reserves in British Columbia cover only a few hectares. In Eastern Canada each band is generally limited to one reserve, while in the West one band may encompass several reserves. British Columbia has over 1600 reserves but fewer than 200 bands (Allan, 1943; Siggner and Locatelli, 1980). Figure 3.4 reveals the population size of First Nations communities across Canada. The data show that most of the reserves have fewer than 500 people, and that less than 10 percent have more than 2000 members. These data demonstrate that most First Nations communities are small and that their viability is at stake as new policies and legislation come into existence.

TABLE 3.1	Registered Indian Population by Region, 1966–2006										
	1966		1976		1986		1996		2001		2006	
Region	No.	%	No.	%	No.	%	No.	%	No.	%	No.	%
Atlantic	8 494	3.8	10 891	3.8	16 460	4.1	21 835	3.8	23 398	3.8	41 800	5.3
Quebec	23 186	10.3	29 580	10.2	40 200	10.0	53 280	9.3	56 125	9.0	76 500	9.7
Ontario	52 408	23.4	64 690	22.4	91 250	22.6	126 755	22.1	134 372	21.6	175 600	22.3
Manitoba	31 000	13.8	42 311	14.6	59 064	14.7	84 684	14.8	93 020	14.9	112 200	14.2
Saskatchewan	31 362	14.0	43 404	15.0	62 232	15.5	93 250	16.3	105 830	17.0	107 100	13.6
Alberta	25 432	11.3	34 130	11.8	44 653	12.3	75 954	13.2	84 684	13.6	105 400	13.4
B.C.	46 543	20.8	53 342	18.5	69 822	17.3	96 472	16.8	102 552	16.5	146 500	18.6
Yukon	7 300	1.0	3 181	1.1	4 626	1.1	7 133	1.2	7 602	1.2	5 739	2.6
N.W.T.			7 409	2.6	9 735	2.4	13 906	2.4	15 318	2.5	13 700	1.9
Canada	224 164	100	288 938	100	403 042	100	573 269	100	622 901	100	786 400	100

Sources: Adapted from 1966–1989: *Indian Register*, DIAND; 1996–2001: *Population Projections of Registered Indians, 1986–2011*, DIAND, 1990; *Projections of the Aboriginal Populations, Canadian Provinces and Territories, 2001–2017*, Statistics Canada, 2005.

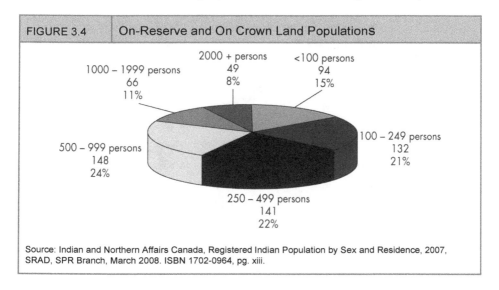

| FIGURE 3.4 | On-Reserve and On Crown Land Populations |

Source: Indian and Northern Affairs Canada, Registered Indian Population by Sex and Residence, 2007, SRAD, SPR Branch, March 2008. ISBN 1702-0964, pg. xiii.

The reserve/settlement system provides security and roots for many Aboriginal people. These rural-based communities are where the majority of Aboriginals have grown up, among family and friends. Even for those who leave, reserves continue to provide a haven from the pressures of Euro-Canadian urban society. These factors, combined with the prejudicial attitudes of the non-Aboriginal culture, create a strong internal pull and external push toward remaining on, or returning to, the reserve. Even if an increasing number of Aboriginal people leave the reserve, the absolute population of those who remain will still show a sizeable increase. Table 3.2 reveals the massive changes in numbers of registered Indians on and off reserve over a 50-year time period. It illustrates a dramatic increase in off-reserve residence over this time, as well as major changes taking place at the territorial/provincial level.

These changes could pose a number of issues for Canada. Reserves are potential hotbeds of political and social discontent. If First Nations on reserves become economically developed, they could pose a competitive threat to some Canadian corporate structures. Already, in Western Canada, First Nations have angered local business people by building housing developments and strip malls, and by proposing casinos on reserve lands close to major cities. The population growth rate for First Nations people may be affected by these demographic and residential changes. All of these issues will have a major impact on federal and provincial policies developed in relation to First Nations people.

Reserves are situated in a variety of geographical contexts that have significant implications for development potential, population mobility, and transportation routes. Aboriginal Affairs and Northern Development has characterized First Nations' communities in four ways: urban, rural, remote, and **special access**. Reserves/settlements within 50 kilometres of a service centre are considered urban. Rural is a zone where the reserve/settlement is located between 50 and 350 kilometres from a service centre.

| TABLE 3.2 | Registered Indian Population On/Off-Reserve by Region, 1966 and 2005 |

| | On Reserve | | | | Off Reserve | | | |
| | 1966 | | 2005 | | 1966 | | 2005 | |
Region	No.	%	No	%	No	%	No	%
Atlantic	6 444	75.9	18 810	60.7	2 050	24.1	12 141	39.2
Quebec	18 720	80.7	46 709	67.9	4 466	19.3	20 503	29.8
Ontario	36 508	69.7	79 979	48.1	15 900	30.3	84 581	50.9
Manitoba	26 752	86.3	75 075	61.8	4 248	13.7	44 598	36.7
Saskatchewan	26 920	85.8	58 419	48.7	4 442	14.2	59 730	49.7
Alberta	22 573	88.8	59 788	61.8	2 859	11.2	34 033	35.6
B.C.	37 019	79.5	58 415	48.7	9 524	20.5	61 263	51.0
Yukon	2 620	82.4	5 482	95.5	561	17.6	–	–
N.W.T.	7 143	96.4	–	–	266	3.6	–	–
Canada	180 418	80.5	397 980	53.2	43 746	19.5	326 188	43.6

Sources: 1966–1989: *Indian Register*, DIAND; 1996–2001: *Population Projections of Registered Indians*, 1986–2011, DIAND, 1990; Statistics Canada, 2005.

A remote reserve/settlement is located beyond the 350-kilometre limit but is accessible by a year-round road. The special access designation is for any First Nations community that has no year-round road connecting it to a service centre (Siggner, 1980).

Table 3.3 shows the distribution and proportion of Aboriginal people in each of the designated zones. While a majority of people live in urban and rural zones, considerable numbers live in remote and special access reserves. The data show that over one-third of the First Nations people in Manitoba and over one-quarter in Ontario live on reserves that have no road access to a service centre. A substantial number in Quebec and British Columbia reside in special access areas. Conversely, fewer than 20 percent of Aboriginal persons in Alberta and Saskatchewan live in either remote or special access areas. Data gathered by Indian Affairs reveals that the pattern of residence has not changed substantially over the past two decades. When we look at just Inuit, we find that 90 percent live in remote areas and only 10 percent are considered urban, although many live in small villages and towns.

Changes over time that are discernable show an increasing number of First Nations people living in urban areas (35 to 37 percent) as well as rural ones (40 to 44 percent). Concurrently, there has been a decrease in the number of Indians living in remote and special access areas (5 to 2 percent and 21 to 18 percent, respectively). These reserve lands make up a little less than 3 million hectares of land. The total area of reserve lands per capita has decreased over the past 20 years, although in the past five years, through major comprehensive land claims settlements, there has been an increase in the actual land base. For example, in the first five years of the 21st century, approximately 25 land

TABLE 3.3	On-Reserve Registered Indians by Region and DIAND Geographic Zone, 2007			
	Geographic zone			
Region	Urban & Rural %	Remote %	Special Access %	Total Number
Atlantic	100%	0.0	0.0	32 219
Quebec	71.2	17.9	10.9	70 946
Ontario	73.2	0.0	26.8	171 953
Manitoba	70.2	0.0	29.8	127 159
Saskatchewan	92.9	1.7	5.5	125 666
Alberta	93.0	0.0	7.0	101 161
B.C.	78.4	6.4	15.2	123 927
Yukon	60.4	32.5	7.0	8 221
N.W.T.	54.5	8.5	37.0	16 798
Canada	79.4	3.7	16.9	778 050

On-reserve includes Crown lands and settlements. Excludes Cree and Naskapi bands in Quebec.

Sources: Adapted from *Basic Departmental Data*, 2002, Indian and Northern Affairs Canada, Indian and Northern Affairs Canada, *Aboriginal Demography*, 2010, Registered Indian Population by Sex and Residence, 2007 INAC, 2008.

claims were settled, and additional lands added to the existing inventory. However, because of high population growth, per capita allocations are less today than they were previously. In 1959, across Canada, there were 13 hectares per capita; by 2001, that number had decreased to 12.6 hectares (see Table 3.4). The exceptions to this are in the North and in recent comprehensive treaty settlements, where Aboriginals have signed agreements with the federal government that give them control over vast areas of land.

First Nations Bands

Nearly all registered (status) Indians are affiliated with one of the Canada's 615 bands. A band is a group of Aboriginal people who share a common interest in land and money and whose historical connection is defined by the federal government. It is important to point out that the term "band" is also a political term; it is arbitrarily imposed on registered Indians, regardless of cultural differences, for the government's administrative purposes. The Department of Aboriginal Affairs can create and do away with band designations, so the number of bands often varies from year to year.

When the federal government first divided various Indian tribes into bands, it showed very little concern for the impact of these divisions on Aboriginal culture. For example, some tribes were matrilineal, tracing descent through the mother's side, while others were patrilineal. Yet when the band system was established, tribes were arbitrarily thrown together, and all were treated as patrilineal. This produced serious social disorganization and a wide-ranging disruption of tribal culture.

TABLE 3.4 | Registered Indian Population and Indian Lands, by Region, 2007

	Atlantic Provinces	Quebec	Ontario	Manitoba	Sask.	Alberta	B.C.	N.W.T.	Yukon	Canada
Total Indian population	32 219	70 946	171 953	127 159	125 666	101 161	123 927	8 221	16 798	778 050
% of total Indian population	4.0	10.0	22.3	14.8	15.6	12.6	17.2	2.3	1.1	100.0
% of total provincial/territorial population	0.6	0.5	0.9	4.9	5.4	1.9	2.2	17.2	16.5	1.4
% living off-reserve	28.8	20.3	36.1	28.3	36.0	28.1	38.6	7.7	42.0	31.9
Number of Indian bands	33	39	126	62	70	44	198	16	26	614
% of Indian bands	5.2	6.6	21.3	10.1	11.5	6.9	33.1	2.4	2.9	100.0
Number of reserves and settlements	67	33	185	103	142	90	1610	29	25	2284
% of reserves and settlements	2.9	1.4	8.1	4.5	6.2	3.9	70.5	1.3	1.1	100.0
Approximate area of reserves (hectares)	31 800	85 450	736 210	235 120	645 010	725 010	372 300	–	–	2 830 900

Source: Adapted from *Registered Indian Population by Sex and Residence 2002*, Ottawa, 2003 (Ct. No. R31-3/2002E.); *Registered Indian Population by Sex and Residence, 2007*, INAC, 2008.

At present, nearly 400 000 First Nations people live on reserves. The largest is the Six Nations band, near Brantford, Ontario, with a population of 8200. Each band is adminis-tered by one of 87 agencies across Canada. The Caughnawaga agency handles only one band, while the New Westminster agency handles 32. The average size of **Indian bands** in Canada has increased from 200 in 1950 to approximately 500 people today. If we look at the size of communities of First Nations and Inuit south of the 60th parallel, we find that 43 percent live in communities of less than 400, 34 percent in communities between 401 and 1000, 21 percent in communities between 1001 and 3000 people, and only 2 percent in communities larger than 3000.

Table 3.5 reveals the 20 largest bands in Canada and shows that while the size of the land base has increased slightly, the population base is increasing at a much faster rate. These fig-ures demonstrate that managing bands has become a major activity for First Nations as their size increases and the complexity of operating them is beginning to equal that of small towns.

TABLE 3.5	The 20 Largest Bands in Canada, December 31, 2007	
Band	**Region**	**Indian Register Population**
Six Nations of the Grand River[1]	Ontario	22 969
Mohawks of Akwesasne	Ontario	10 607
Blood	Alberta	10 253
Kahnawake	Québec	9 570
Saddle Lake	Alberta	8 770
Lac La Ronge	Saskatchewan	8 462
Peguis	Manitoba	8 281
Mohawks of the Bay of Quinte	Ontario	7 706
Peter Ballantyne Cree Nation	Saskatchewan	8 334
Wikwemikong	Ontario	7 104
Fort Alexander	Manitoba	6 719
Cross Lake First Nation	Manitoba	6 768
Bigstone Cree Nation	Alberta	6 954
Samson	Alberta	6 826
Norway House Cree Nation	Manitoba	6 493
Siksika Nation	Alberta	6 289
Oneida Nation of the Thames	Ontario	5 261
Sandy Bay	Manitoba	5 408
Nisichawayasihk Cree Nation	Manitoba	5 027
Montagnais du Lac St-Jean	Québec	4 886

[1] Six Nations of the Grand River consists of the following 13 Registry Groups: Bay of Quinte Mohawk, Bearfoot Onondaga, Delaware, Konadaha Seneca, Lower Cayuga, Lower Mohawk, Niharondasa Seneca, Oneida, Onondaga Clear Sky, Tuscarora, Upper Cayuga, Upper Mohawk, Walker Mohawk.

Source: *Registered Indian Population by Sex and Residence, 2007*, pp. xi, Indian and Northern Affairs Canada, 2008. SRAD, SPR Branch.

POPULATION GROWTH

In studying the population dynamics of a people, it is important to understand how and why population changes over time. From a biological perspective there are two factors that impinge upon the size and structure of any population: fertility and mortality. In addition, migration may have an impact on the number of people in a specific geographical location. For example, if many individuals either leave a group or become members of a group, this may decrease or increase the numbers accordingly. In the case of Aboriginal people, however, migration is a minor issue with little effect on the total number of Aboriginal people, since few actually leave Canada. Figure 3.5 illustrates the slow but steady growth of the Aboriginal population during the first part of the 20th century, which increased rapidly after 1980.

For Aboriginal people, there are legislative and political decisions that have an impact on the population and its profile. These are decisions taken by government and Aboriginal people themselves that are related to defining who is an Aboriginal. Hence, a change in the law may mean that some people are no longer considered "Indian," Métis, or Inuit. Or, alternatively, a change in law may add people who previously were not included to these three categories.

The case of *Bill C-31,* passed in 1985, had exactly that impact on one group of Aboriginal people—registered Indians—whom we have records on. It redefined who was or was not an "Indian." It should be noted that the changing view of Aboriginal people and possible benefits to them affected other groups, such as the Métis. Both fertility and mortality as well as other external factors can have an impact on a population's size and profile. To better understand the demography of Aboriginal people, we will look at three factors.

To begin with, we should determine whether the Aboriginal population has changed over time. Table 3.6 reveals the population growth of First Nations people over the past century. It shows that a small but steady growth has taken place since the latter part of the 19th century. Figure 3.6 illustrates a more detailed analysis of change in the registered

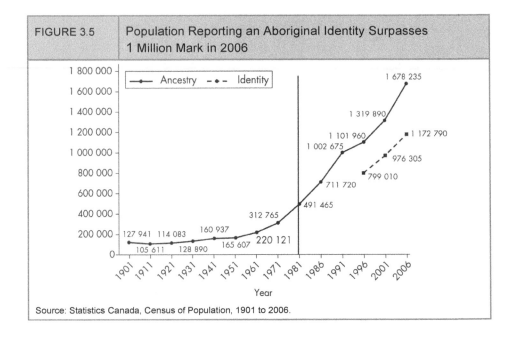

| FIGURE 3.5 | Population Reporting an Aboriginal Identity Surpasses 1 Million Mark in 2006 |

Source: Statistics Canada, Census of Population, 1901 to 2006.

TABLE 3.6	Population of Registered Indians in Canada, 1881–2007
Year	**Registered Indian Population**
1881	108 547
1901	127 941
1929	108 012
1939	118 378
1949	136 407
1954	151 558
1961	191 709
1971	257 619
1981	323 782
1986	403 042
1991	521 461
1992	531 981
1996	573 269
2001	622 901
2006 (estimated)	713,100
2007	778 050

Sources: Information Canada, *Perspective Canada I* (Ottawa: Queen's Printer, 1974), 240; *Perspective Canada II* (Ottawa: Queen's Printer, 1977), 282; Siggner (1986), 3; *Native Agenda News*, March, 1992; T. Courchene and L. Powell, *A First Nations Province*, Queens University, Institute of Intergovernmental Relations, Kingston, Ontario, 1995, 20; *Registered Indian Population by Sex and Residence*, 2007, Ottawa, 2008, Strategic Research and Analysis Directorate, Strategic Policy and Research Branch.

FIGURE 3.6	Percentage Change in Registered Indian Population, Canada, 1981 to 2003

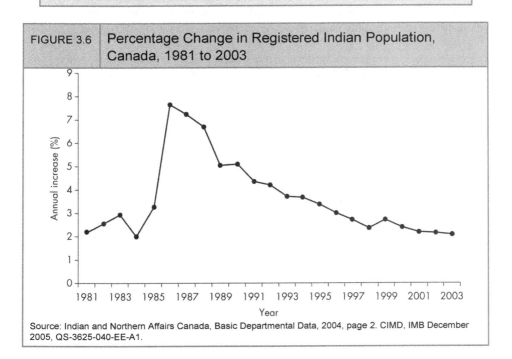

Source: Indian and Northern Affairs Canada, Basic Departmental Data, 2004, page 2. CIMD, IMB December 2005, QS-3625-040-EE-A1.

Indian population for the period 1981–2003, showing a remarkable increase over the past three decades. Much of the increase has been the result of the number of individuals who, prior to 1985, were not Indians, but became Indians under *Bill C-31*. As a result, nearly 130 000 people have been added to the Indian Register and, depending upon marriage patterns, the children of these individuals may also be included." The figure shows population increases that defy the natural growth limit of 5.5 percent per year. From 1986 to 1988, population increases were above 7 percent. Then, from 1989 to 1992, the annual growth rate was well above 4 percent, unheard of in modern times. Although since this time the annual increase in the number of registered Indians has fallen, these numbers reveal that the increases are far above the Canadian average of .7 percent per year. In addition, the B.C. Supreme Court's decision to add more individuals to the Indian Register when it recognized the McIvor (2010) appeal (discussed later in the chapter) means that approximately 40 000 more people will be included, changing the demography of this people in the process.

Over the first three-quarters of the 20th century, the growth in the Aboriginal population averaged about 3 percent per year. The increase in population was mediated by high mortality rates. In addition, for First Nations people, exogamous marriages that resulted in women and their children being removed from the Indian roll had an impact on the growth and size of the population. However with the advent of *Bill C-31*, all of this changed.

After the introduction of *Bill C-31* in 1985, the registered Indian growth rate increased to over 7 percent and averaged well in excess of 6 percent until the 1990s, when it decreased to about 2 percent. These rates must be compared to the general Canadian growth rate of about 1 percent over the past decade. The overall Aboriginal population (Indian, Métis, and Inuit) is growing very fast; it is estimated that by 2027 it will be in excess of 1.5 million (see Figure 3.7). Figure 3.8 shows the age distribution of registered Indians in 2005 with an average growth rate. The proportion of males and females under the age of 18 is similar for both on- and off-reserve populations, but when we look at the 18–64 age group, there are significantly more registered women than men living off reserve.

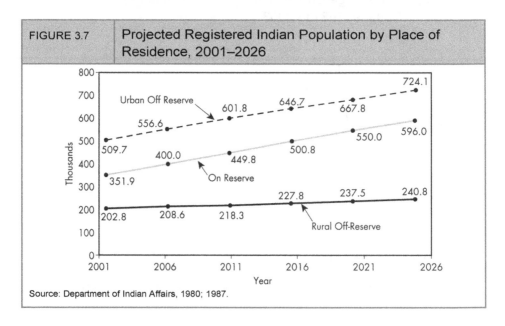

| FIGURE 3.7 | Projected Registered Indian Population by Place of Residence, 2001–2026 |

Source: Department of Indian Affairs, 1980; 1987.

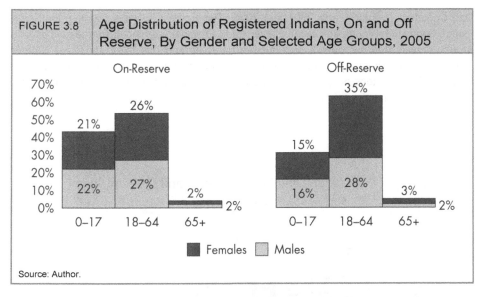

| FIGURE 3.8 | Age Distribution of Registered Indians, On and Off Reserve, By Gender and Selected Age Groups, 2005 |

Source: Author.

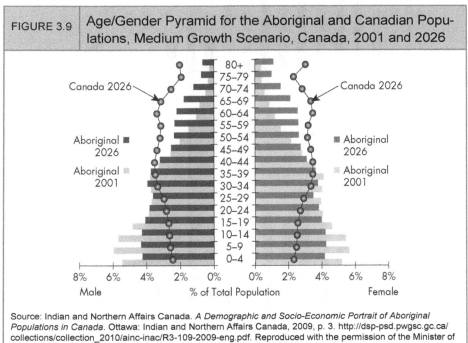

| FIGURE 3.9 | Age/Gender Pyramid for the Aboriginal and Canadian Populations, Medium Growth Scenario, Canada, 2001 and 2026 |

Source: Indian and Northern Affairs Canada. *A Demographic and Socio-Economic Portrait of Aboriginal Populations in Canada*. Ottawa: Indian and Northern Affairs Canada, 2009, p. 3. http://dsp-psd.pwgsc.gc.ca/collections/collection_2010/ainc-inac/R3-109-2009-eng.pdf. Reproduced with the permission of the Minister of Public Works and Government Services Canada, 2011.

Age/Sex Distribution

Before we discuss the future population of Aboriginal peoples, we need to look at age/sex distribution. This demographic component is important in understanding future size as well as future policy. Figure 3.9 shows the age/sex distribution for the Aboriginal and Canadian populations in 2001 and 2026. The figure illustrates that the Aboriginal population is very young and exhibits every sign of remaining young for the next decade. It also reveals that the Canadian population is aging and that there are fewer children being born for this group. Figure 3.10 looks as the existing age/sex distribution specifically for First Nations people. Again, the pattern reveals a very young population, with nearly half less than 25 years of age.

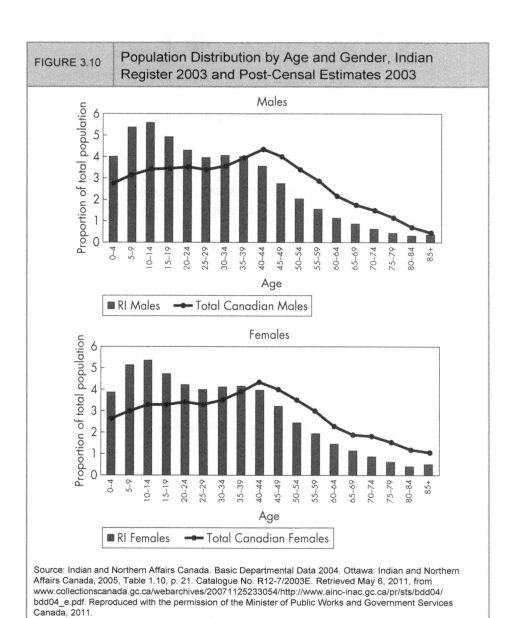

| FIGURE 3.10 | Population Distribution by Age and Gender, Indian Register 2003 and Post-Censal Estimates 2003 |

Source: Indian and Northern Affairs Canada. Basic Departmental Data 2004. Ottawa: Indian and Northern Affairs Canada, 2005, Table 1.10, p. 21. Catalogue No. R12-7/2003E. Retrieved May 6, 2011, from www.collectionscanada.gc.ca/webarchives/20071125233054/http://www.ainc-inac.gc.ca/pr/sts/bdd04/bdd04_e.pdf. Reproduced with the permission of the Minister of Public Works and Government Services Canada, 2011.

COMPONENTS OF POPULATION GROWTH

We now turn our attention to the three factors that make up the population size and growth of a people—fertility, mortality, and other factors. Let's begin with fertility.

Fertility

Fertility describes the number of children born to a woman over her lifetime. In the early 20th century, the average fertility rate for Aboriginal people was nearly six children per woman within child-bearing age (15–40). This seems high by today's standards, but it should be noted that for non-Aboriginal people, the rate was just less than five children. Thus, it can be seen that the fertility rate for Aboriginal women was reasonably high. As a result of infant mortality, disease, and a number of other factors, however, many people did not live to adulthood. High fertility rates continued until the mid 20th century. At that time, Canada was still a "child-centred" society in which families considered children to be important. Families catered to children in an attempt to ensure they would have a better life than their parents. At the same time, birth control activities were not condoned.

The pattern began to change over the next half-century. In 1921, the crude birth rate for Aboriginal people was over 5.0 per 1000 population. By the 1970s, this rate had decreased to 2.85, and by 2017 it is expected to further decline to 2.35, although still remain at nearly double the national average. Romaniuc (2003) has noted that the decline in the birth rate can be deduced from looking at the child/population ratio. The ratio of children under five years of age to the total Indian population fell from 19 percent in 1961 to 12 percent in 2001. Further evidence of fertility decline can be inferred from the average number of children born to never-married women 20–24 years of age. The latter was 2.3 in 1961 but fell to less than 1.5 in 2001. The number of childless never-married women in the age category 20–24 went up from 11 percent in 1961 to 29 percent in 2001. When we compare fertility rates for on-reserve Indians and the general Canadian population for women aged 15–49, we find substantial differences. In 1986, on-reserve women had 3.2 children, while in the general Canadian population the number was 1.67. By 2004 the number for Aboriginal women had decreased to 2.7 children while the overall Canadian number had dropped to 1.57.

The birth rate is also significantly influenced by the average age of marriage. Although, overall, the proportion of married Indians is lower than the national average, the proportion of married Indians in the highest-fertility age group of 20 to 24 exceeds that of non-Indians. Moreover, the fertility of Indians between ages of 20–24 appears to be twice the Canadian average.

The average number of children by age group also reflects changes that have taken place in Aboriginal communities. In 2008, Aboriginal women had an average of 3.23 children, compared to 1.57 for non-Aboriginal women. When controlling for age, we find that older Aboriginal women (65 and over) had 6.2 children during their child-bearing years (3.0 for non-Aboriginal women), and Aboriginal women 45–64 years of age had 6.0 (3.2 for non-Aboriginal women). It is projected that in 2021, the fertility rate will decrease to 2.71 for on-reserve women (still twice as high as non-Aboriginal women) and 1.63 for off-reserve women (nearly equal to that for non-Aboriginal women). There are, however, considerable regional variations in Aboriginal birth rates. Aboriginal women living in Eastern Canada have similar fertility rates to those of non-Aboriginal women, while Aboriginal women in the Prairies have much higher ones.

In Canada as a whole, as we entered the 1960s, the outlook toward children began to change. Canadians began to move to the cities, giving up the country as a place to live and work. Children were now being seen as a liability rather than an asset and families started to become adult-centred with a reduced number of children. In addition, birth control was no longer considered deviant and techniques for carrying out birth control (e.g., birth control pills, abortions) were made easily available, and thus women began to control their reproductive rates as part of their right. As such, the number of children produced began to decrease over time. By the start of the 21st century, Canadians had a total fertility rate of just under 1.5. This means that every woman of child-bearing age who makes the decision to give birth has, on average, 1.5 children. This rate is unsustainable; a rate of at least 2.1 children is necessary in order to reproduce the population. Anything less means the society will decline in population.

Aboriginal people did not flock to the cities, however, and their ethos of "child-centred" families remains a cherished value. In addition, birth control techniques are less likely to be used by Aboriginal women. As a result, while their fertility rate has decreased over the past century, it still remains about 2.35—well above the replacement value. Moreover, young women in Aboriginal communities have children at a much younger age than their non-Aboriginal counterparts. For example, Aboriginal women between the ages of 15–19 have a fertility rate 11 times higher than the general Canadian population. The result of this high fertility rate is that the Aboriginal population is very "young," with nearly 50 percent under the age of 25.

Mortality

As noted earlier, mortality (death) rates also determine the size and nature of a population. The mortality rate for Aboriginal youth (15–30) per 1000 in 1981 was 75, dropping to 39 by 2006. Comparable figures for Aboriginal women were 34 and 21, respectively. To place these rates in perspective, the overall Canadian rate for men in 2006 was 7 while for women it was 4. Thus, while it is true that the mortality rates for Aboriginal people have decreased substantially over the past three decades, they lag well behind their non-Aboriginal counterparts.

One good overall indicator of mortality is life expectancy. Between 1926 and 2005, the life expectancy of males increased by 20 years, while females gained an additional 23 years. These increases are due to improved health care facilities, better nutrition, and lifestyle changes. As such, for Canadians, there has been an increase in life expectancy. In 1978, men could expect to live to 71 and women to 78 years. By 2008 this had increased to 77 for men and 82 for women.

However, if we focus solely on the Aboriginal population, we find that while mortality rates have certainly been reduced over the past 30 years (in 1978 the age of death was 60 for males and 67 for females, compared to a rate in 2008 of 70 for males and 75 for females), the gap remains. In short, today Aboriginal people have achieved the same life expectancy that non-Aboriginal people had achieved 30 years ago.

Figure 3.11 shows the life expectancies at birth for status Indians and all Canadians by sex. It illustrates that the general trend of increasing life expectancy continues. Nevertheless,

FIGURE 3.11	Life Expectancy at Birth, Status Indians and All Canadians, 1981, 1991, 2001, 2020

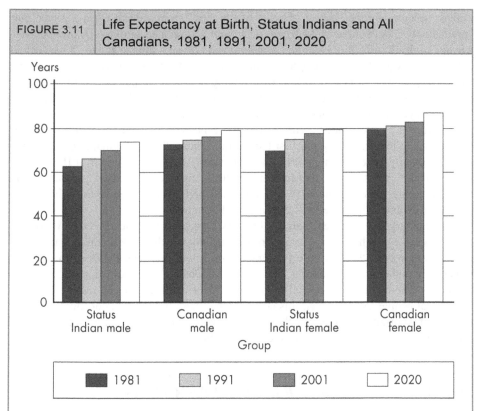

- In 1981, the life expectancy at birth for status Indians was approximately 10 years less than that of the national population, the same as it had been 20 years earlier. However, life expectancy at birth for status Indians is increasing. Between 1981 and 2020, the life expectancy at birth for status Indians is projected to increase by five years for both sexes, but will still be five years less than that for other Canadians.

Sources: Indian and Northern Affairs Canada, 2010. Highlights of Aboriginal Conditions, 1981–2001, Part II, Social Conditions, p. 5, Statistics Canada, 2005; Health Policy Research Bulletin, Health Canada, 2003.

non-Indians still live longer than status Indians, but this gap is narrowing; by the start of the 21st century life expectancy for Indian men in comparison to non-Aboriginal men was 70 versus 76, and for Indian women in comparison to non-Aboriginal women it was 77 versus 83. Overall standardized death rates in 1981 show 9.2 per 1000 for Indians compared to just 6 among the total Canadian population. In 2008, the Aboriginal mortality rates were almost 1.5 times higher than the national rates.

Infant mortality (deaths of babies before the age of one) is perhaps an even more important factor in determining the growth rate of a population. The number of First Nations deaths per 1000 live births was nearly 80 in 1960. Although this number decreased to 11.6 in 2003, the Canadian rate was 6.5.

As we entered the 21st century, studies by Indian Affairs showed that the potential years of life lost for First Nations and Canadians differed significantly. This statistic accounts for the number of years of life "lost" from a death when a person dies "prematurely." In the case of Aboriginals, it would be defined as dying before the average age of death of 75. For example, a person who commits suicide at age 25 has lost 50 potential years of life. For Aboriginals, suicide and unintentional injuries are the leading causes of potential years of life lost, contributing to nearly 40 percent of all deaths for youth. Suicide accounts for approximately 108 potential years of life lost per 1000 population each year (three times the 2001 Canadian rate) (Trovato, 2001).

Aboriginal people, since the turn of the 20th century, have gone through three stages of birth–death trends. During the first half of the century the Aboriginal population was characterized by extremely high birth and death rates. Then, after World War II, the death rate decreased substantially (because of medical advances, increased sanitation, and better housing), although the birth rate remained high. Today we see the third phase, which is a decline in both the fertility and mortality rates.

In summary, we can see that fertility has decreased significantly for Aboriginal people over the past half-century, and projections indicate that it will continue to slowly decrease. However, there is little to suggest that it will meet the levels of the general Canadian population. The mortality rate has also dramatically decreased, particularly for newborns. The reduction in mortality is also evident in the increasing number of older Aboriginal people. At one level, this suggests that there will be a major increase in the number of Aboriginal people over the next half-century. However, before we accept this projection, we need to enter "other factors" into the equation—those having to do with legislation.

Legislative Changes: *Bill C-31* and AAND Policy

The Aboriginal population profile has been confounded by the introduction of *Bill C-31*, which changed the definition of an "Indian." As discussed earlier, migration is not an important factor in population levels in the Aboriginal community, since few leave the country. However, in/out migration is another matter. In/out migration does not refer to Aboriginals leaving or entering the country. Rather, it reflects the different definitions and self-identities of who is and is not an Aboriginal. Legislation has played a key role in this regard.

The federal *Bill C-31* restored Indian status and membership rights to individuals and their children who had lost them as a result of discriminatory clauses—e.g., 12(1)(b)—in the previous *Indian Act.* After the Constitution was patriated in 1982 and *Bill C-31* was proclaimed in 1985, thousands of individuals who had not previously been considered "Aboriginal" were, overnight, now proclaimed as such—Indian, Métis, or Inuit. Only individuals who are considered Indians by the government are eligible for specific social services such as health benefits, educational support, and possible tax relief. As such, it is important for AAND to know just how many Indians there are in Canada. After *Bill C-31* came into effect, it was projected that about 150 000 individuals would be added to the Indian Register. While that may seem like a great number, the real impact on the numbers comes from the children of those individuals currently considered Indians as a result of *Bill C-31* and/or those individuals who had been considered Indians before *Bill C-31.*

When *Bill C-31* came into effect, the government decreed that there would be two different types of Indians: Section 6(1) and Section 6(2). Individuals who were considered Indians prior to *Bill C-31* would be considered 6(1) Indians. Those who were added to the register might either be 6(1) or 6(2), depending upon their genealogy and the marriage patterns of their parents and grandparents. Reconsider Figure 2.4, which illustrates the process of continuing Indian status through future marriage patterns and the status outcome of the children.

What this means is that if a 6(2) Indian marries a non-Indian, the children will not have any status and will not be included in the registry. Thus their children will have 6(2) status. If these children marry non-Indians, their children will not be considered Indians. At present it is estimated that about one-third of all Indian parents are married to non-Indians. In addition, AAND implemented a policy (in 1985) stating that if a mother attempts to register her child with AAND, the father must be identified in such a way that AAND can determine what status the father has—6(1), 6(2), or non-Indian. If the father's name is not provided, AAND assumes the father is a non-Indian and the child takes on the appropriate status. At present, about 15 percent of all children have unknown fathers and thus these children may not be afforded Indian status (see Figure 2.4). As such, about one-half of the children born to Indian women will have "less" status than their mothers.

As noted above, these changes in law and policy will substantially revise projections about the future registered Indian population. Added to this mix is a court challenge by Sharon McIvor, which was ruled on by the Supreme Court in 2009. She argued successfully that *Bill C-31* remained discriminatory toward women. The Court ordered the government to revise the *Bill* to redress this injustice. As a result of McIvor's successful challenge, an additional 45 000 people will be added to the Indian Register. In addition, many of these individuals' parents may be able to switch from 6(2) to 6(1) Indians. However, neither the exact number of individuals who will apply for a status change nor the number who will be able to claim Indian status are known at this time.

We have now discussed the three factors that determine the size and growth of a population. While some of the factors are well-known—for example, decreasing fertility and an increased life expectancy—the rate of change is an unknown quantity because of the legislative changes that continue to be implemented by the federal government with regard to defining who is and is not an "Indian." Moreover, the legislative and policy changes identified above will also vary over time; they too, will have a substantial impact on the Aboriginal population.

Band Membership

The issue of whether an individual is an "Indian" is quite separate from the issue of having "band membership." It turns out that you can be a legal registered Indian but not a member of a band. Or alternatively, you can be a band member and not be a legal Indian. How did this come about? When *Bill C-31* was passed, there was a provision for each band to establish their membership criteria. It is important to recognize that all bands do not have the same membership criteria. Being a band member is important because there are specific rights, such as access to housing, that go along with membership.

POPULATION PROJECTIONS

Over the past decade, the non-Aboriginal population has increased 8 percent while the total Aboriginal population has increased 45 percent. When we look at the three categories of Aboriginal people, we find large differences. The populations of First Nations people have increased 29 percent, Métis 91 percent, and Inuit 26 percent. We also find that projections for the number of Aboriginal people in Canada will increase substantially in the next decade, although for Inuit the increase will be larger. The Inuit population has nearly doubled since 1981 and similar increases are expected over the next decade. Figures 3.12 and 3.13 identify the projected Aboriginal population by place of residence

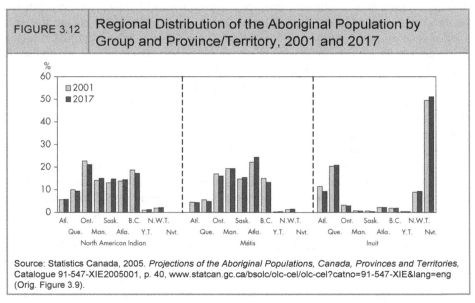

| FIGURE 3.12 | Regional Distribution of the Aboriginal Population by Group and Province/Territory, 2001 and 2017 |

Source: Statistics Canada, 2005. *Projections of the Aboriginal Populations, Canada, Provinces and Territories,* Catalogue 91-547-XIE2005001, p. 40, www.statcan.gc.ca/bsolc/olc-cel/olc-cel?catno=91-547-XIE&lang=eng (Orig. Figure 3.9).

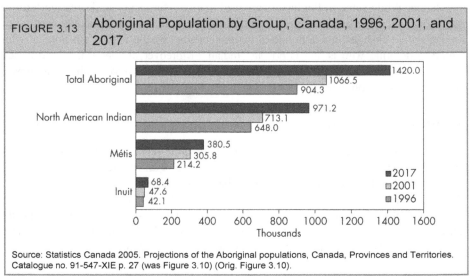

| FIGURE 3.13 | Aboriginal Population by Group, Canada, 1996, 2001, and 2017 |

Source: Statistics Canada 2005. Projections of the Aboriginal populations, Canada, Provinces and Territories. Catalogue no. 91-547-XIE p. 27 (was Figure 3.10) (Orig. Figure 3.10).

and various Aboriginal groups for 2017. They clearly illustrate the differing projections by group and allow a comparison with the base Canadian population. Projections for the next quarter-century show that there will be continued increases in the Aboriginal population, with an expected 47 percent increase by 2026. Within the overall groupings, there will be nearly an 80 percent increase in the number of non-status Indians, a 62 percent increase for Inuit, and lower increases for registered Indians (45 percent) and Métis (37 percent). However, these increases will be moderated in the long term by *Bill C-31*.

In summary, demographers predict that status Indian and Inuit populations will continue to experience higher growth rates than the Canadian population for the next three decades. Other data confirm that the growth rates are extremely high. The Aboriginal population more than doubled since 1966, and as we entered the 21st century, the estimated registered Indian population was nearly 800 000. These data also show that in 1966, 80 percent of the Indians lived on a reserve; by 2010, this number had decreased to 50 percent (Piche and George, 1973; Basic Departmental Data, 2007).

Nevertheless, while fertility and mortality certainly have an impact on the population profile, legislation and policy changes implemented by government have an even larger impact. Moreover, the question as to how many Indian people will "out-marry" still remains unanswered. We have some hints, however. Nearly 80 percent of the people registered as Indians as a result of *Bill C-31* lived off reserve because most of these people were women who had married non-Indian men, and before *Bill C-31*, they were automatically removed from the register. We also know that these women have a lower fertility rate than women who remained on the reserve. In addition, mixed marriage literature shows that when people live in large urban centres, the likelihood of out-marriage is increased substantially. Should out-marriage (20 percent on the reserve, 40 percent off the reserve) occur in more than two generations, the children produced will not be registered Indians. Unknown paternity is characteristic of 13 percent of all births today. Clatworthy (2001) predicts that given the above assumptions,, the number of registered Indians will increase until about 2060, then there will be a dramatic decrease such that by the end of the 21st century, there will be fewer Indians than today. He also notes that in smaller reserves, by the third generation there will be no more "Indians" living on those land bases.

There are a number of ways to project the future population sizes of the various Aboriginal groups. AAND has been undertaking such projections for the past 50 years in an attempt to introduce policy and develop financial plans. Inuit, the smallest population of all Aboriginal groups, are projected to grow to about 75 000 in 2026 (assuming an annual growth rate of 2.1 percent). This projection is based on a fertility rate of 3.4 and a decrease in Inuit mortality rates. And, like other Aboriginal populations, the Inuit population is very young, with a median age of just over 20. Nearly 60 percent of Inuit are less than 25 years of age.

For Métis, it was estimated that the 2010 population was about 316 000. This number is expected to increase by about 37 percent over the next two decades to nearly 400 000. Métis populations in urban areas are expected to increase by 1.4 percent over the next two decades, with a fertility rate of 2.1 children per woman. The Métis also have a young population, with just under half under the age of 25. While fertility explains some of the growth in population, much is a result of changes in "self-reporting" of ethnic identity. This process, sometimes called "ethnic mobility," refers to the increasing number of individuals who report "Métis" as their primary ethic identity on the Census.

The non-registered, non-status Indian population was estimated to be about 140 000 in 2010. It is expected that by 2026, this population will grow to just under 200 000— representing an increase of 77 percent from 2000. This population is overwhelmingly urban, with only a few individuals living in settlements (in Alberta). In addition, because of the changes introduced in 1985, many individuals who previously considered themselves "non-status non-Indian" were redefined as Indians—thereby decreasing the number of people who self-identified as Métis. Projections show that this population will increase dramatically by 2030. While there will be a decrease in fertility rates as well as increased urbanization, these factors will be offset by the number of people who out-marry and whose children will not be eligible for Indian registration. In addition, the number of children with unknown paternity will increase substantially, leading to increased numbers of people who will no longer be considered Indian.

A HISTORICAL NOTE

The number of registered Indians, as discussed earlier, is affected by external legislation that goes well beyond fertility and mortality. People have been removed from and placed on the Indian roll over the past century at the will of the Crown. It is estimated that in the first half of the 20th century approximately 50 000 status Indians directly lost their status through government action such as the "enfranchisement" policy. Given the fertility rate at that time, we can assume an additional 250 000 descendants also lost their status as legal Indians. Others lost their Indian status through sloppy bookkeeping, concern about costs, and failure to register births. When confronted with these issues, Indian Affairs ignored or rejected the claims without any serious investigation. Then, between 1955 and 1982 (when the general policy of enfranchisement was phased out), an additional 13 502 adults and children (as well as their descendants) were formally enfranchised (removed from the Indian roll and no longer defined as Indians under the *Indian Act*). In all, it is estimated that since the early 20th century, well over 500 000 individuals have been denied their Indian status.

Both the enfranchisement rules and the "double mother" rule in the *Indian Act* have now been changed. As early as 1980, Indian and Inuit Affairs allowed bands that wanted to opt out of the conditions of 12(1)(b) and 12(1)(a)(iv) to do so. By 1984, 103 bands had opted out of the former section, while 309 had acted on the latter. When *Bill C-31* was passed in 1985, new rules prevailed. However, under this new change, only the first generation of those listed above are eligible for registration. If these children are themselves parents at the time of registration, their children cannot be registered. If the individual is eligible to be registered, their children have the capacity to transmit status to any children they have thereafter. In summary, projections suggest that the overall registered Indian population will increase until 2041, at which time it will level off at around 1 million. After that, it is expected to decrease, and the number of registered Indians will once again change as a result of a definition established nearly 50 years earlier.

HEALTH

The prevalence of disease in any group of people also affects its size and growth over time. While disease and genocide were important forces during the 17th, 18th, and early 19th centuries, they have played a different role in 20th century population dynamics of Canadian Aboriginal people. The federal government believes that, with certain exceptions, it does not have any legal or fiduciary obligations with regard to health care for Aboriginal people except in certain exceptional circumstances such as Treaty 6, which explicitly refers to the provision of a "medicine chest." Aboriginals disagree and claim the right to special treatment. Provincial governments agree with Aboriginal people and have pressed the federal government to cover the cost of various health issues. As a result, hospital, pharmaceutical, and dentistry costs for registered Indians and Inuit are generally covered by the federal government. However, for Métis, these same costs are the responsibility of the province/territory.

Disputes between the First Nations and the federal government regarding the provision of health care revolve around three issues. First is the conflict in definitions of health. Second is how health policy is implemented for Aboriginal people. Third is the funding of First Nations health services, including the statutory, constitutional, or fiduciary obligations of the federal government regarding the provision of health services (Speck, 1989). The federal government has accepted some responsibility for Aboriginal health. Under Health Canada, six major health programs are supported: Community Health Services, Environmental Health and Surveillance, Non-Insured Health Benefits, the National Native Alcohol and Drug Abuse Program, Hospital Services, and Capital Construction. While there is no direct federal government legislation for the provision of these services, custom and historical commitment provides the basis and rationale for covering their cost. Over time, however, new issues emerge that result in changing boundaries about health.

Federal Health Policy

Until 1945, the Department of Indian Affairs was the sole provider of health care services to Indians on the reserve. In that year, the Department of Health and Welfare was created and took over providing services to First Nations and Inuit. In 1962, the Indian Health Services Unit (a division in Health and Welfare) was merged with six other federal health programs to form a specific branch: Medical Services. In 1964, treaty Indians were defined as insured persons under provincial medicare. By 1970, the present structure of Indian Health Services was in place, although the 1974 *Lalonde Report* for the federal government first set the stage for the transfer of health care away from the federal government. This policy document reiterated that no statutory or treaty obligations exist to provide health services to Indians, but the federal government wanted to ensure that services would be provided to Indians and Inuit when normal provincial services were not available. In 1979, a new Indian Health Policy was enacted to ensure that the needed community development would take place. It was at this time that the Medical Services Branch started to work toward transferring management of health services to First Nations.

See Box 3.2 for a discussion of the Aboriginal Healing Foundation.

Box 3.2	The Aboriginal Healing Foundation

As part of the settlement of the residential school abuses, the federal government established the Aboriginal Healing Foundation in 1998 with a budget of $400M. Once the funds have been spent, there will be no additional funds provided by the federal government. Participants in the program include Métis, Inuit, and First Nations people. Over the past decade, the Foundation has developed and supported programs to help Aboriginal people build and reinforce sustainable healing processes. These programs have taken different approaches (e.g., Aboriginal, Western) to "heal" individuals who experienced abuse in the school system. Four volumes have now been published identifying the results of the work of the Foundation.

The Aboriginal Healing Foundation (www.ahf.ca) is a not-for-profit, Aboriginal-managed national funding agency that encourages and supports community-based healing efforts addressing the intergenerational legacy of physical and sexual abuse in Canada's Indian Residential School System. Over the years, nearly 250 community projects have been funded across Canada.

The Aboriginal Healing Foundation's goal is to:

— Deliver funding to support community-based healing services and activities that address the intergenerational legacy of physical and sexual abuse in Canada's Indian Residential School system;

— Be an effective funding delivery mechanism;

— Foster a supportive public environment for healing; and

— Promote reconciliation between Aboriginal and non-Aboriginal people.

In March 2010, the Aboriginal Healing Foundation (AHF) Board of Directors acknowledged Canada's decision not to provide funds to the Foundation in the 2010 Federal Budget. This decision by the federal government means that a nationwide network of community-based healing initiatives will no longer have AHF support after March 31, 2010, when current funds run out.

Aboriginal Healing Foundation president Georges (Erasmus noted that this budget cast "a dark shadow however over the good and effective work being done in Aboriginal communities, by Aboriginal people, to address the destructive residential school legacy and to create healthier, stronger communities" Erasmus, 2010).

Concerning the future, he added, "Without additional funds, community services will disappear at the end of this month, and the Aboriginal Healing Foundation will have no recourse but to wind down its operations."

By 1981, a proposal to transfer responsibility for health care services to Indian communities was approved, and in 1982 Indian health services standards were developed as a way of measuring the extent to which Aboriginal health needs were being met. The

Nielsen Report was leaked in 1985, which, in addition to exposing the duplication of services, focused on the federal government's insistence that it had no statutory or treaty obligations in this area.

In 1986, Health and Welfare (Medical Services Branch) announced a new policy initiative: the Indian Health Transfer Policy. This new policy, which centred on the concept of self-determination, was to facilitate a developmental approach to transferring health care and services to Aboriginal communities. It was hoped that it would lead to First Nations autonomy and to community control of health care services (Speck, 1989). The transfer policy was a continuation of the "**devolution policy**" developed by Indian and Northern Affairs Canada a decade earlier, in that it proposed that a larger share of the responsibility once allocated to the federal government be taken on by First Nations. This policy began to transfer 27 programs over to Aboriginal communities. However, the policy stated that 14 programs—for example, tobacco control, HIV/AIDS, dental—would never be transferred to Aboriginal communities. From 1990 to 2004, a further seven programs were transferred, but in 2005 the federal government decided to stop the transfer process. That decision remains in place today. In 2000, the Medical Services Branch was renamed the First Nations and Inuit Health Branch. Its mandate is to ensure the availability of and access to health services for Aboriginal people. It has also pledged to help First Nations address local health issues and to build strong relationships between Health Canada and First Nations communities. As of 2002, about 70 percent of eligible First Nations and Inuit communities have taken on some degree of administering their own community health programs. Today, more than 80 percent of the funds for federal community health programs are channelled through agreements with First Nations and Inuit organizations.

There is considerable conflict between the two parties with regard to how and under what conditions the transfer of management will take place and what the nature of the relationship will be.

Today, in all but two of the provinces, insurance premiums are paid by provincial governments through tax revenues. A variety of arrangements exist in these provinces for the payment of premiums by registered Indians, ranging from bulk payments to general means tests. The specific features that differentiate Aboriginal from non-Aboriginal health services are the payment of medical and hospital insurance premiums by the federal government for three provinces, the provision of public health services by the federal rather than the provincial government, and the federal funding of additional non-insured services for registered Indians. Regardless of the source of funding, a full range of medical services is provided to First Nations, although the specifics of this care vary from one province to another.

Medical Services Delivery

While the *Indian Act* says little about the specifics of medical services delivery (see Section 73[1]) and its main focus is on the prevention of the spread of infectious diseases, there remains a strong financial commitment to Aboriginal health care through a variety of programs (Woodward, 1989). The mandate at the First Nations and Inuit Health Branch is to assist Aboriginal people in achieving levels of health comparable to that of other Canadians, to ensure their access to sustainable health services, and to build capacity in the health field for all First Nations and Inuit communities. To ensure the achievement of these goals, the branch works with the Assembly of First Nations and the Inuit Tapiriit Kanatami, who have representatives sitting on the branch executive committee. In addition, each regional branch office has established joint committees with the regional First Nations and Inuit groups.

Health and Welfare Canada operates a number of programs that provide health care to Aboriginal people throughout Canada. The first major program is Community Health Services, which focuses on communicable disease control, health education, mental health, nursing, and the provision of medical advice and assistance. The second is the non-insured health benefits program. Through this program, Aboriginal people are provided general health care through access to provincial medicare systems and supplemental programs. In addition, the program includes the transportation of patients, dental services, and other medical appliances and services. The third major program is one in which funding is provided to train and employ local health care workers under the aegis of Community Health Services.

The provision of services for Aboriginal people is carried out through all three levels of government. Those services provided by provincial and municipal agencies are generally fully reimbursed by the federal government. At the federal level, the First Nations and Inuit Health Branch supplies doctors and nurses. Over 500 community health workers are also contracted by the First Nations and Inuit Health Branch to provide health care for Aboriginal people. At the beginning of this century, there were almost 2000 Aboriginal health workers. Approximately 800 were Aboriginal nurses and over 80 were Aboriginal physicians. On a per capita basis, the First Nations and Inuit Health Branch spends about $800 per year per Aboriginal person, approximately the same spent on non-Aboriginal people in Canada. Overall, Health Canada spent about $2.2 billion on health services to First Nations in 2007, compared to just over $1 billion in 1995. Just under half of these funds were allocated for non-insured health benefits. The remainder was spent on transfer agreements, management and support, and community health programs and community-based health services.

Health services are also provided through contributions and contract arrangements with Aboriginal organizations, bands, and post-secondary education institutions. Community Health Services carry out this program through four main activities: health care and treatment services, public health services, involvement of Indians in the health care system, and the provision of physical facilities. One of the changes that has been implemented is the limitation of non-insured health benefits. All registered Indians were previously eligible to receive prescription medication, medical supplies, dental services, medical transportation, optometry services, and mental health services. The cost of this program exceeds $600 million per year and has become the target of fiscal restraint. Specifically, off-reserve Indians have been cut off from such benefits (Adelson, 2005) and are now under the provision of provincial/territorial governments.

The overall structure for providing medical and health services to Aboriginal people is complex. At the national level, several government agencies interact to set policies, determine programs, and establish funding levels—e.g., Deputy Minister of Health and Welfare; director general, Policy and Evaluation, Treasury Board; and the directors of Indian/Inuit Policy, Planning, and Evaluation. At the provincial level, the regional director oversees implementation of the programs for each health zone, which involves doctors, nurses, and environmental health officers. At the local level, for those bands

involved in health care delivery, band councils make decisions regarding training programs and who will be admitted to various health programs.

In 2004–05, Health Canada directly awarded $1 billion to the First Nations and Inuit
Health. In addition, nearly an additional $1 billion was indirectly given to cover First
Nations and Inuit health issues. The bulk of the direct payment was for integrated Indian
and Inuit community-based health care services ($360 million), while administration
costs for First Nations to provide health care added an additional $240 million. Contribu-
tions to Aboriginal associations and groups made up $110 million and various prevention
projects added $55 million. The remaining funds went to universities and renovations
($10 million each), head start programs ($35 million), Capital contributions for nurse
residences ($25 million) and other—e.g., health information dissemination, provision of
health care facilities ($56 million).

Aboriginal Health

Research over the past 25 years has brought to light that abuse of alcohol and other sub-
stances is a major problem in First Nations communities. In the recent Aboriginal Peoples
Survey, nearly three-quarters of respondents said that alcohol and drug abuse was a problem in their community. In this same survey, one in five Aboriginal youth reported having used solvents—and one in three solvent users is under the age of 15. One of the most
widely-known health services provided by Health Canada is in the area of substance
abuse. In addition, research has shown that diabetes, HIV/AIDS, and respiratory problems are now a major concern for Aboriginal health. Many of the statistics about disease
and illness among Aboriginal people have been published and are well-known. Illnesses
resulting from poverty, overcrowding, and poor housing have led to chronic and acute
respiratory diseases, which take a heavy toll on Aboriginal people. In addition, when we
compare the health of Aboriginal people with non-Aboriginal people we find that most
major health issues for non-Aboriginal people occur during the last 13 years of their life.
Up until that time, they live largely healthy lives. However, Aboriginal people are beset
with health issues from birth that continue.

Laurie (2008) notes that over one-third of First Nations households live in poverty.
More importantly, she shows the link between poverty and poor health. Her data demonstrate a strong relationship between income and indicators of health status, ranging from life
expectancy, infant mortality, and mental health to chronic health conditions. In all cases,
people with low incomes do worse than people with higher incomes, regardless of the
health indicator used. Phipps (2004) also concludes that there is little doubt that poverty
leads to ill health. She points out that inadequate nutrition, obesity, overly-cramped living
quarters, high levels of stress, and poor access to health care contribute to ill health. Laurie's
work shows that Aboriginal people experience chronic diseases such as arthritis, diabetes,
cancer, and hypertension at nearly twice the rate of the general Canadian population. If
poverty levels were reduced by 20 percent, the savings from such a reduction would result
in a decrease of $7.6 billion per year in health care expenditures (Laurie, 2008).

In terms of crude mortality rates for First Nations, there were 354.2 deaths per 100 000
in 2005. However, while the standardized death rate for the Aboriginal population was
more than double that of the general Canadian population—15.9 versus 6.6 deaths per 1000
during the 1980s (Nuttall, 1982; INAC, 1988)—it is now similar to the general Canadian

population. The overall death rate among Aboriginal people has decreased by nearly one-half since 1978 to a rate similar to the national average (662 versus 661 per 100 000 population). However, there is a gap between Aboriginals and the general Canadian population, particularly for ages 15 to 44: Aboriginals in this age group are more than twice as likely to die than the average Canadian. Moreover, the cause of death by age group varies. Figure 3.14 shows the leading causes of death in First Nations by age group.

Infant mortality has a tremendous impact upon the population of all societies, since infants will (if they live) contribute to the growth of the population when they reach child-bearing age. Over the years, there has been a substantial decrease in infant mortality rates. Today the infant mortality rate among Indian people is now less than one-sixth of what it was in 1960. However, it should be noted that, as late as 1990, it was double that of the general Canadian population: 7.9 versus 17.5 per 1000. After 1988 a disturbing trend emerged, showing that while the infant mortality rate for all Canadians decreased, it increased for registered Indians. Fortunately this trend reversed in the late 1990s and the gap has closed, though it was still 20 percent higher than the Canadian rate in 2005. A closer look at the infant mortality rate shows that Aboriginal rates of perinatal death (stillbirths and under one week of age) are twice as high as in the general population. Neonatal (birth to one month) death rates for the two groups are very similar. Post-neonatal (one month to one year) death rates are more than three times higher for First Nations. These rates reflect the unavailability of good health care facilities, poor housing, and other environmental conditions (all indicators of poverty) that Aboriginal children are born into (Canada, 1980).

The effectiveness of the Native health care system is related as much to the environmental conditions in which Aboriginal Canadians live as to the treatment and facilities provided. Health care provided is sometimes countered by social and economic problems such as overcrowding, poor nutrition, chronic unemployment, and community and family violence. For example, Figure 3.15 shows the relationship between overcrowding and the incidence of tuberculosis. An Aboriginal person, after receiving effective medical treatment, finds himself or herself returning to the social conditions that created the problem in the first place. In short, the causes of poor mental and physical health are not being dealt with (Health Canada, 2003).

What are the specific causes of death? Over one-third of all registered Indian deaths (compared to 8 percent in the general population) are due to accidents and violence. Aboriginal people are up to 6.5 times more likely than the total Canadian population to die of injuries and poisonings. For all age groups up to 63, Aboriginal people are four times as likely as other Canadians to die from these causes. The most frequent are motor vehicle accidents, drowning, and fire. Although these rates are still extremely high, they have decreased by over 40 percent since 1980.

What is most striking in Figure 3.14 is the cause of death for different age groups. It shows that 38 percent of deaths for children aged 10—19 are due to suicide and self-inflicted injuries. A similarly high rate of suicide is noted for the 20–44 age group. The other major causes of death (in order) are diseases of the circulatory system, diseases of the respiratory system, cancer, suicide, and chronic conditions (e.g., tuberculosis and diabetes). Heart diseases, hypertension, and AIDS are "new" diseases for Aboriginal people, although for each of the diseases listed, the incidence is much greater for Aboriginal people than for the general Canadian population.

FIGURE 3.14	Leading Causes of Death[1], by Age Group, Registered First Nations[2], Western Canada, 2001-2002 (average)	
Age group (N = # of deaths)	Cause of death	Percentage of deaths
1 to 9 (N=71)	External causes of morbidity and mortality[a]	46.5
	Neoplasms	8.5
	Diseases of the nervous system	8.5
	Congenital malformations, deformations and chromosomal abnormalities	7.0
	Other causes	29.6
10 to 19 (N=162)	External causes of morbidity and mortality	72.2
	Other causes	27.8
20 to 44 (N=852)	External causes of morbidity and mortality	59.0
	Diseases of the digestive system	6.5
	Neoplasms	5.5
	Other causes	29.0
45 to 64 (N=987)	Neoplasms	20.4
	Diseases of the circulatory system	20.0
	External causes of morbidity and mortality	15.3
	Diseases of the digestive system	9.9
	Endocrine, nutritional and metabolic diseases	6.2
	Diseases of the respiratory system	5.2
	Other causes	23.1
≥65 (N=1,379)	Diseases of the circulatory system	31.4
	Neoplasms	18.8
	Diseases of the respiratory system	11.1
	Endocrine, nutritional and metabolic diseases	7.7
	Diseases of the digestive system	5.6
	Other causes	25.5

[1] Refer to **Appendix 1** for a description of the ICD-10 chapters; only 19 of the 21 ICD-10 chapters were used in the analysis.
[2] Includes on-reserve populations for Manitoba and Saskatchewan, and on- and off-reserve populations for Alberta and British Columbia.

Note:

a. Refers to accidents and suicides

Source: A *Statistical Profile on The Health of First Nations in Canada: Vital Statistics for Atlantic and Western Canada, 2001/2002*, p. 29. Health Canada, 2011. Reproduced with the permission of the Minister of Health, 2011.

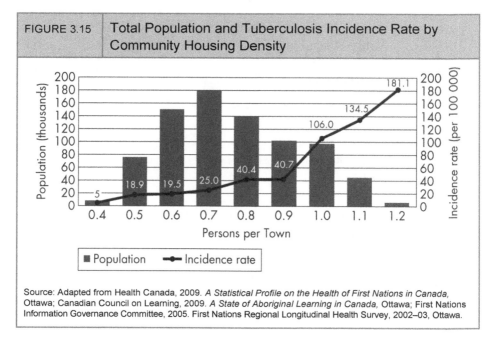

FIGURE 3.15   Total Population and Tuberculosis Incidence Rate by Community Housing Density

Source: Adapted from Health Canada, 2009. *A Statistical Profile on the Health of First Nations in Canada,* Ottawa; Canadian Council on Learning, 2009. *A State of Aboriginal Learning in Canada,* Ottawa; First Nations Information Governance Committee, 2005. First Nations Regional Longitudinal Health Survey, 2002–03, Ottawa.

Health Canada (2009) assessed the level of health conditions facing First Nations on-reserve, comparing it to the general Canadian population. Figure 3.16 illustrates the prevalence of selected health conditions. High blood pressure, diabetes, and asthma

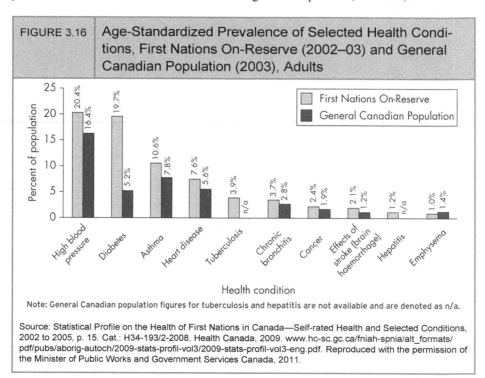

FIGURE 3.16   Age-Standardized Prevalence of Selected Health Conditions, First Nations On-Reserve (2002–03) and General Canadian Population (2003), Adults

Note: General Canadian population figures for tuberculosis and hepatitis are not available and are denoted as n/a.

Source: Statistical Profile on the Health of First Nations in Canada—Self-rated Health and Selected Conditions, 2002 to 2005, p. 15. Cat.: H34-193/2-2008. Health Canada, 2009. www.hc-sc.gc.ca/fniah-spnia/alt_formats/pdf/pubs/aborig-autoch/2009-stats-profil-vol3/2009-stats-profil-vol3-eng.pdf. Reproduced with the permission of the Minister of Public Works and Government Services Canada, 2011.

account for the highest reported incidences of disease. And the incidence for First Nations people is much higher than for the general population. When comparing other health conditions, while First Nations have a higher incidence, the difference is much smaller. However, it points to the fact that First Nations people have poorer quality of life than the general population. If we look at selected mortality rates for specific diseases, we find that in the case of lung, colorectal, and breast cancer, First Nations people have a lower rate than Canadians. On the other hand, for prostate cancer, acute myocardial infarction, and stroke, Aboriginal people have much higher rates.

However, when chronic conditions (health conditions lasting at least six months) were considered, over 60 percent of the off-reserve population reported at least one chronic condition, while less than half of the non-Aboriginal population reported this. Arthritis/ rheumatism had the highest prevalence in the Aboriginal population (26 percent), followed by high blood pressure (15 percent) and diabetes (9 percent). When compared to the general Canadian population, these rates were much higher. For example, the diabetes rate was twice as high as that of the general population (Tjepkema, 2002). When long-term activity restrictions were assessed, over 16 percent of the off-reserve Aboriginal population reported such restriction, which was 1.6 times higher than in the non-Aboriginal population. When compared to Aboriginals living on-reserve, non-Aboriginal people reported similar levels of activity restriction. Surprisingly, middle-income off-reserve Aboriginals were more likely to report activity restrictions than other middle-income Canadians, while Aboriginals from high income groups reported lower levels of restriction compared to high-income non-Aboriginal Canadians. The survey found that over 13 percent of off-reserve Aboriginals had experienced a major depressive episode in the past year—nearly twice the level reported by the non-Aboriginal population (Tjepkema, 2002).

New Diseases in the Aboriginal Community

Tuberculosis   Since the 1940s when antibiotic treatment was introduced, the incidence of TB declined throughout Canada. After treating tuberculosis (TB) in the Aboriginal community for nearly 50 years, by the end of the 1950s Canada had finally won the war. However, low income, elderly, and Aboriginal populations have not been fortunate. TB began to return to First Nations communities in the mid-1980s, achieving near epidemic proportions. After a major TB elimination program was implemented in 1992, the number of new and relapsed cases decreased until 1999, when they once again began to increase to 1990 levels. In 1992, the incidence per 100 000 people was 67.8, decreasing to 54.6 throughout much of the 1990s until 1999, when the rate went back up to nearly 62. Today we find the age-standardized rate of TB for First Nations is 34—six times greater than the Canadian rate and 31 times greater than the rate of Canadian-born non-Aboriginals. These figures reveal a TB rate that is 10 times that of the entire Canadian population. It is important to realize that the incidence of TB is not uniformly distributed across Canada. Seventeen percent of TB cases reported in 2004 were Aboriginal people. Within this category, three-quarters were registered Indians, 15 percent Inuit, 7 percent non-registered Indians, and 3 percent Métis.

Figure 3.15 shows the TB incidence rate in relation to housing density, which is once again reflective of poverty. Saskatchewan had the highest incidence (ranging from 104.3 to 155.7 per 100 000) over the past decade, but Alberta and Manitoba tend to experience higher rates than the national average. Mortality from TB is low due to aggressive case findings and effective treatment. While fewer than 50 individuals died from TB in 2005, its infection takes an individual out of the labour force, requires family support, and enhances the chances of acquiring other respiratory diseases.

Diabetes   Diabetes was virtually non-existent in the Aboriginal population before the 1940s. Today its incidence among Aboriginal people is estimated to be two to five times higher than in the non-Aboriginal population, and to be increasing rapidly (Wells, 1995; Health Canada, 2009). Its importance is heightened by the fact that it is increasingly showing early onset, greater severity at diagnosis, high rates of complications, lack of accessible services, increasing incidence, and increasing prevalence of risk factors for a population already at risk (Young et al., 1998). Health care officials in British Columbia reported increases of 85 percent between 1992 and 2002. A comparison of life tables (length of life) between the Aboriginal and non-Aboriginal populations over the past 20 years shows that there has been little improvement in diabetes rates for Aboriginal people, and even a deterioration in the past decade (Nuttall, 1982; Young, 1984; Bobet 1997; Health Canada, 2009).

Based upon Statistics Canada data, it is estimated that between 80 000 and 120 000 Aboriginal people 15 years of age and over have diabetes (generally type 2). The latest First Nations and Inuit regional health survey conducted by the National Steering Committee estimates that the above figures are underestimated by 20 percent. Recent figures show that, among all First Nations people, the incidence of diabetes is 6.4 percent. For those living on reserves, the rate is 8.5 percent. Métis have reported a prevalence of 5.5 percent while Inuit report a 1.9 percent incidence. Figure 3.17 shows the prevalence of all types of diabetes for both First Nations people and the general Canadian population and reveals that the age-standardized prevalence of diabetes for First Nations people is three to five times that of the general population. This is true for all age categories.

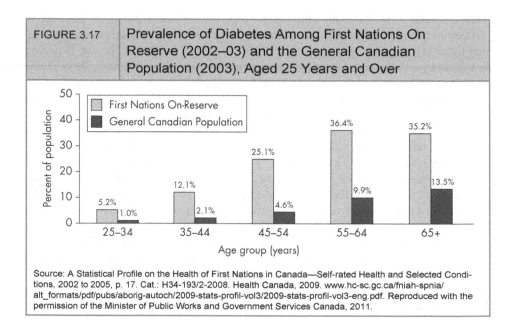

| FIGURE 3.17 | Prevalence of Diabetes Among First Nations On Reserve (2002–03) and the General Canadian Population (2003), Aged 25 Years and Over |

Source: A Statistical Profile on the Health of First Nations in Canada—Self-rated Health and Selected Conditions, 2002 to 2005, p. 17. Cat.: H34-193/2-2008. Health Canada, 2009. www.hc-sc.gc.ca/fniah-spnia/alt_formats/pdf/pubs/aborig-autoch/2009-stats-profil-vol3/2009-stats-profil-vol3-eng.pdf. Reproduced with the permission of the Minister of Public Works and Government Services Canada, 2011.

According to a regional health survey, 53 percent of the First Nations people with diabetes are 40 years old or younger and 65 percent are less than 45 years old. The average age of onset of diabetes for Aboriginal people is 30 to 35. This is in contrast to the general population, where type 2 diabetes typically begins at age 40 and is highest for those 65 and older. Bobet (1997) found that approximately two-thirds of the First Nations people diagnosed with diabetes are women—a pattern that is not reflected in the general Canadian population. Aboriginal women have over five times the rate of diabetes compared to women in the general population, and Aboriginal men have over three times the corresponding rate for men in the general population. In a survey of First Nations adults, Health Canada (2006) asked whether they had been informed by a health care professional that they had one or more types of diabetes. Fifteen percent of respondents claimed to have been informed. Most of these individuals said they had type 2 (80 percent) diabetes.

With the high rates of diabetes for Aboriginal people, it should not be surprising that health complications emerge. Secondary illnesses such as strokes, macrovascular disease, heart attacks, lower limb amputations, and high blood pressure are just some of the related health care issues. While national projections are not available, in Manitoba is has been estimated that the number of First Nations diabetes cases will increase three times over the next 20 years (Green et al., 1997). The impact of diabetes over the next decade will be significant, and the disease will impose a high cost in resources if this problem is not addressed today. For example, the annual costs for diabetic drugs through the non-insured health benefits program are now in excess of $16 million per year (Health Canada, 2000).

Related to diabetes is cardiovascular disease. While Canadians are experiencing a decline in rates of cardiovascular disease, Aboriginal people have experienced a dramatic increase (Anand et al., 2001). The prevalence in First Nations communities is three times greater than for other Canadians. It is estimated that just over 40 percent of the First Nation population have metabolic syndrome, a primary cause of cardiovascular disease. Moreover, nearly three-quarters of the Aboriginal population are overweight, which is a determinant of both diabetes and cardiovascular disease (First Nations Centre National Aboriginal Health Organization, 2004; Harris et al., 2002).

HIV/AIDS Unlike in the general population, where the number of AIDS cases has levelled off, the number of AIDS cases among Aboriginals has dramatically increased over the past two decades (see Figure 3.18). From 1998 to 2001, over one-fourth of all reports of HIV-positive tests were from Aboriginal people. In cases where the ethnicity of the individual who has AIDS is known, the proportion of Aboriginal cases has increased from 1.5 percent to 5.6 percent. Smylie (2001) found more than 10 percent of those with AIDS are Aboriginal. The proportion of AIDS cases among Aboriginal persons climbed from 1 percent of all cases in Canada before 1990 to over 12 percent in 2002 (Health Canada, 2005). A dramatic increase of HIV and its primary and secondary (related to TB) conditions in First Nations communities has emerged in recent years. A study in B.C. identified one-third of HIV/TB patients as Aboriginal. Mobility between cities and rural communities has been identified as an important factor in the introduction and spread of HIV.

Injection of drugs continues to be the most prevalent manner (38 percent) in which AIDS is spread among the Aboriginal population. However, homosexual encounters accounted for 35 percent and heterosexual relationships made up 16 percent. The remaining cases have a variety of other causes, such as blood transfusions. These figures can be compared to the

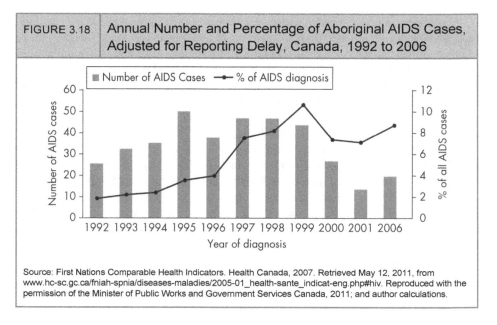

FIGURE 3.18 | **Annual Number and Percentage of Aboriginal AIDS Cases, Adjusted for Reporting Delay, Canada, 1992 to 2006**

Source: First Nations Comparable Health Indicators. Health Canada, 2007. Retrieved May 12, 2011, from www.hc-sc.gc.ca/fniah-spnia/diseases-maladies/2005-01_health-sante_indicat-eng.php#hiv. Reproduced with the permission of the Minister of Public Works and Government Services Canada, 2011; and author calculations.

non-Aboriginal population, with 6 percent transmission through injecting drug users, 71 percent through homosexual encounters, and 14 percent through heterosexual relationships.

Evidence indicates that the HIV epidemic in the Aboriginal community shows few signs of stabilizing. Aboriginal peoples make up a growing percentage of positive HIV tests and reported AIDS cases. Moreover, Aboriginal women now make up a large part of the HIV epidemic, and Aboriginal peoples are being infected at a younger age than non-Aboriginals (Public Health Agency of Canada, 2004).

Suicide Suicide accounts for up to one-quarter of all injury deaths among First Nations people. The majority of suicides occur in individuals aged 15 to 24, although in recent times there has been a doubling of suicides in the 1–14 age group. In 2001, suicide accounted for nearly 40 percent of all deaths in Aboriginal youth (ages 10–19) and nearly one-quarter of all deaths in ages 20–44. Overall, the First Nations suicide rate in 2001 was 27.4 deaths per million, which suggests that a sustained decrease has not occurred over the past 25 years. Data show that suicides occur in "clusters" of specific areas and time periods, and in some areas the rates of suicide are extremely high. While the overall rate for young people is high, in areas such as Sioux Lookout, it is 50 times higher than the general Canadian average for the 10–19 age group. Overall, between ages 15–24, the suicide rate in First Nations women is almost eight times that of the same age group for all of Canada, while for men it is five times higher. While completed suicides are typically much higher among males, in general, females attempt suicide far more often—a pattern also seen in the general Canadian population (Whitehead et al., 1996).

In conclusion, rates of suicide and self-inflicted injuries are three times higher (six times higher for the 15–24 age group), homicide rates are twice as high, congenital anomalies are 1.5 times higher, and pneumonia more than three times higher than the national average. Aboriginal people have five times the rate of child welfare; four times the death rate; three times the violent death, juvenile delinquency, and suicide rates; and twice the rate of hospital admissions compared to the average Canadian population. Aboriginal people also have three times the rate of heart problems and hypertension.

Chandler and Lalonde (2006) have shown that bands in British Columbia that have preserved their cultures and have met with success in recovering community control over their lives have suffered very few or no youth suicides over the past 15 years. In communities where this has not occurred, the youth suicide rate is more than 150 times the national average.

Self-Reported Aboriginal Health

O'Donnell and Tait (2004) conclude that a majority of non-reserve Aboriginal people report excellent or very good health, and this is particularly true for young Aboriginals. Overall, the off-reserve Aboriginal population reported better health than their non-Aboriginal counterparts and, as incomes increased, the proportion of people reporting fair or poor health decreased. However, on-reserve self-reported health was worse than that of the general Canadian population. In fact, the gap between the health status of older Aboriginals and Canadians widened over the past decade. The proportion of Aboriginal people with fair or poor health is about double that of the Canadian population (O'Donnell and Tait, 2004).

Health Canada (2006) found that compared to Canadians in general, 40 percent of First Nations adults felt they had the same level of access to health services. One-quarter felt they had better access while 36 percent claimed to have less access. First Nations adults were also asked about barriers to receiving health care, and one-third claimed the waiting period was too long. Thirty-seven percent stated that services required were not covered by Indian Affairs or were actually denied to them and thus they could not afford to access them. A similar percentage felt that health practitioners were not available in their area. About 17 percent felt that the actual health care received was inadequate.

| FIGURE 3.19 | Distribution of Community Well-Being Index for First Nations and Other Communities in Canada, 2006 |

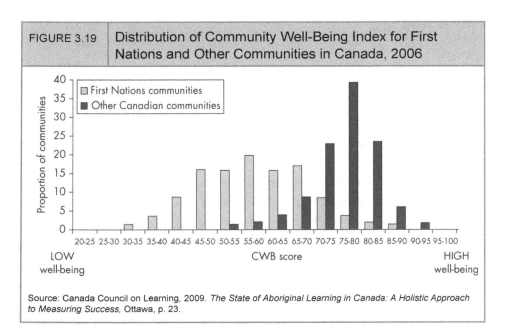

Source: Canada Council on Learning, 2009. *The State of Aboriginal Learning in Canada: A Holistic Approach to Measuring Success*, Ottawa, p. 23.

In terms of seeking health care services, over three-quarters of the off-reserve population had visited a general medical practitioner at least once in the previous year, and this was similar to the non-Aboriginal population. Contact with medical specialists was also similar between the two groups. When contact with dentists was assessed, Aboriginals were much less likely to have seen them than their non-Aboriginal counterparts.

In a novel assessment of Aboriginal health, Health Canada (2006) asked First Nations adults how often they felt that they were in balance in the four aspects of their life—physical, emotional, mental, and spiritual. Seventy-one percent claimed to be in balance in their physical and emotional aspects of life. Seventy-five percent claimed to have achieved balance in the mental aspect, and just over two-thirds felt they had achieved spiritual balance. Figure 3.19 compares the distribution of well-being for First Nations and other communities in Canada and reveals substantial differences.

Summary

- The demographic profile of Aboriginal people is unique.
- The demographic profile of Aboriginal people has changed substantially over the past century.
- Policy and legislation have moderated the demography of Aboriginal people across Canada.
- Population projections suggest increases in the Aboriginal population followed by dramatic decreases before the end of the 21st century.
- Fertility, mortality, and immigration within the Aboriginal population have changed over the past century

Key Terms

AAND p. 53   devolution policy p. 81   reserves p. 59
Bill C-31 p. 54   Indian bands p. 65   special access p. 61

Questions for Further Discussion

1. How could reserves create a potential economic threat to some Canadian corporate structures?
2. How much has the registered Indian population increased over the past century?
3. Explain current health policy for First Nations and what they are denied.
4. What would happen if Health Canada discontinued a number of programs that provide health care to Aboriginal people? How would this affect their lives?
5. To what do we attribute the many diseases and illnesses among Aboriginal people?
6. Give examples of challenges experienced by Aboriginals on reserves.

CHAPTER 4

Social Profile of Aboriginal Peoples

After reading this chapter you should be able to:

1. Understand the implications of aging for the Aboriginal and Canadian populations.
2. Appreciate the impact of Christianity upon Aboriginal people.
3. Discuss the factors that influence an individual's quality of life.
4. Distinguish between paternalistic ideology and democratic ideology.
5. Explain how the *Indian Act* affected the Aboriginal education process.
6. Discuss Aboriginal living conditions.
7. Understand variations in religion among Aboriginals.
8. Explain current marital status among Aboriginal people.
9. Discuss the history and quality of Aboriginal education.

INTRODUCTION

When you think about how a population grows and changes, it allows you to form a mental picture of that population and a means to imagine the future. Most children born today will, like their parents, mature and bear children of their own. The question is, what will the social components of the population look like? For students of international relations, the concern for a population's changing size and shape is vitally important. At a domestic level, controlling how the Canadian population reproduces itself is an alternative approach to policing our nation's borders (Connelly, 2008). For example, just a few decades ago the average life expectancy for Aboriginals was less than 50 years, and many babies did not live to see their first birthdays. Most lived on the land and pursued agricultural pursuits. Their housing was rudimentary and infrastructure services such as roads and sewage were minimal. Today this has all changed. Will there be more changes? In order to answer this question, we should start by looking at a more general social profile of the Aboriginal population. Such statistics provide a base line regarding the social attributes of the Aboriginal population and, when possible, comparisons with the Canadian population. This will allow us to place the Aboriginal population in context within Canadian society. The profile will also allow policy analysts to better see the differences between Aboriginal and non-Aboriginal peoples and to understand the kinds of programs needed to deal with the problems facing Aboriginal people. We will begin with a basic age/sex profile.

AGE AND DEPENDENCY

Table 4.1 shows the age distribution of First Nations, illustrating a very **young population.** Well over one-third of the Aboriginal population is younger than 15 years of age and half is younger than 25. Of the total Canadian population, only about one-fifth is under 15 and about one-third is under 25. Over 70 percent of the Aboriginal population is under 40 years of age, evenly divided between males and females. Thirty-seven percent of on-reserve Indians and Inuit are under age 15, while nearly two-thirds of them are under 25.

As noted in the previous chapter, the proportion of young people in the overall Aboriginal population is growing. However, this growth is slowing as the Aboriginal population ages. For example, in 1981 the median age for Aboriginal people was 19, while for the overall population it was 32. Today the Aboriginal median age is 27, while the overall population has only increased to 38.

The **dependency ratio** is one way of assessing the burden of care placed on the working age population. The dependency ratios are outlined in Table 4.2. They show that, again, while the Aboriginal young dependency ratio is falling, it is substantially larger than that of non-Aboriginal people. At the same time, the age dependency ratios have remained the same over the past decade. The overall dependency ratio for the Canadian population has remained stable over the past decade and will continue at this level well into the 21st century. The overall dependency ratio for Aboriginal people, however, declined from 1981 to 2005. In the specific case of Inuit, it declined from 84 percent to 61 percent in 2001. We also know that with the decreasing birth rate for Canadians, the shape of the age pyramid is changing quickly. Figure 4.1 maps the past, present, and future with regard to population age distribution. As shown, the Canadian population is becoming a diamond-shaped population with few old people and few young people and most of the population in their middle productive years. However, 50 years from now, the middle-aged population will have grown old with continued low reproduction rates, producing few children. Contrast that picture with the population distribution of Aboriginal people. This raises basic questions such as: Who will pay the pensions of this large number of old people since the work force will be much smaller than today? What will the major policy issues for Canada be? Will they be focused on an aging population? And what relevance would this focus have for a young Aboriginal population?

An increasing Aboriginal population growth rate means a continued modest **fertility rate** as well as a decreasing death rate. Unless birth rates also decrease, more and more Aboriginal people will be entering the prime employment category of 15–40, and the demand for jobs will increase. As Table 4.2 shows, the dependency ratios are already over twice as high for Aboriginal people as for the general population; this means that the working-age population must support a large number of non-productive people. Unemployment is already rampant among Aboriginal Canadians, and, as more Aboriginals move into the prime employment category, greater competition for jobs is likely to take place. Data from Census Canada show that the number of people in the labour force age range (15–64) increased from 46 percent in 1966 to nearly 65 percent by 2001, but has since declined and is projected to continue that decline. How will immigration policies address this issue? In 2010, the Government of Canada allowed nearly 300 000 new immigrants to enter the country in an attempt to address the labour shortage. How long it can sustain such levels remains an open question. Moreover, the impact of such large numbers on the social cohesion of Canadian society and how immigrants will be received also remains to be seen.

TABLE 4.1   Registered Indian Population by Type of Residence, Age Group, and Sex, December 31, 2005

Age	On Reserve				Off Reserve				Total			
	Male		Female		Male		Female		Male		Female	
	#	%	#	%	#	%	#	%	#	%	#	%
0–4	18 941	4.5	17 890	4.2	9 958	3.1	9 696	3.0	28 899	3.9	27 586	3.7
5–9	23 890	5.7	22 594	5.4	13 683	4.2	13 460	4.1	37 573	5.0	36 054	4.8
10–14	25 502	6.0	24 309	5.8	15 251	4.7	14 534	4.5	40 753	5.4	38 843	5.2
15–19	23 246	5.5	21 882	5.2	14 386	4.4	14 202	4.4	37 632	5.0	36 084	4.8
20–24	19 422	4.6	18 460	4.4	13 220	4.1	13 156	4.0	32 642	4.4	31 616	4.2
25–29	16 457	3.9	15 329	3.6	12 389	3.8	13 260	4.1	28 846	3.9	28 589	3.8
30–34	15 290	3.6	14 662	3.5	13 174	4.0	14 052	4.3	28 464	3.8	28 714	3.8
35–39	15 262	3.6	14 308	3.4	13 466	4.1	14 848	4.6	28 728	3.8	29 156	3.9
40–44	14 392	3.4	13 808	3.3	12 817	3.9	15 516	4.8	27 209	3.6	29 324	3.9
45–49	11 949	2.8	11 751	2.8	10 105	3.1	13 367	4.1	22 054	2.9	25 118	3.4
50–54	9 032	2.1	8 740	2.1	7 059	2.2	10 538	3.2	16 091	2.2	19 278	2.6
55–59	6 822	1.6	6 732	1.6	5 241	1.6	8 236	2.5	12 063	1.6	14 968	2.0
60–64	5 090	1.2	5 012	1.2	3 668	1.1	5 948	1.8	8 758	1.2	10 960	1.5
65+	9 862	2.3	11 549	2.7	7 522	2.3	13 436	4.1	17 384	2.3	24 985	3.3
Unstated	0	0	0	0	0	0	0	0	0	0	0	0
Total	215 157	51.0	207 026	49.0	151 939	46.6	174 249	53.4	367 096	49.1	381 275	50.9
Total – both sexes	422 183	56%			326 188	44%			748 371	100%		

Note: On reserve includes on Crown land.

Source: Adapted from Statistics Canada, 2005. *Projection of the Aboriginal Population, Canada, Provinces and Territories, 2001–2017*, Catalogue No. 91-547-XIE; Statistics Canada, 2010, *Population Projection for Canada, Provinces and Territories, 2009–2036*.cat. No. 91-520-X; Statistics Canada, 2008, Canadian Demography at a Glance, Ottawa, 91-003-XIE; INAC, 2008. *Registered Indian Population by Sex and Residence*, 2007, Ottawa, ISSN 1702–0964.

TABLE 4.2   Age Distribution and Dependency Ratio of Aboriginal and Non-Aboriginal Population

| | Age Group | | | | Population | Dependency Ratio[a] | | | |
| | 0-14 years (%) | 15-64 years (%) | 65 years and over (%) | No age given (%) | | Young | | Aged | |
						Indian	Non-Indian[b]	Indian	Non-Indian[b]
1924	32.2	51.2	5.9	10.7	104 894	62.9	56.5	11.5	7.9
1934	34.7	55.4	6.2	3.7	112 510	62.7	50.3	11.1	8.8
1944	37.5	55.9	6.6	–	125 686	67.0	42.4	11.8	10.2
1954	41.7	53.2	5.1	–	151 558	78.5	49.0	9.6	12.5
1964	46.7	49.1	4.2	–	211 389	95.0	58.1	8.6	13.1
1974	43.2	52.4	4.2	0.2	276 436	82.4	47.5	8.1	13.0
1981	39.0	57.0	4.0	–	323 000	68.4	48.8	7.0	12.8
1991	35.0	60.0	4.0	–	521 500	65.2	46.3	7.0	13.6
1999	29.5	65.3	5.2	–	604 400	59.5	29.4	6.3	17.9
2002	29.2	66.1	4.7	–	611 300	58.4	31.2	5.7	18.2
2005	28.0	66.3	5.7	–	748 371	43.2	29.5	8.5	18.4

a. The dependency ratios reflect the relationship between the groups least likely to be involved in the workforce (i.e., the young and the elderly), and the working-age population.
b. Data were not available for the corresponding year; the years represented are: 1921, 1931, 1941, 1951, 1961, 1971.

Sources: Information Canada, *Perspective Canada II*, (Ottawa: Queen's Printer, 1977), 287; *Census of Canada*, 1981; Indian and Northern Affairs Canada, *Quantitative Analysis and Socio-Demographic Research*, 1992; *Registered Indian Population by Sex and Residence*, 2002, INAC, Ottawa, 2003, Cat. No. R31-3/2002E; Health Canada, A Statistical Profile on *The Health of First Nations in Canada*, Ottawa, 2002.

FIGURE 4.1	Population Distributions, 1950–2060, Aboriginal and Canada

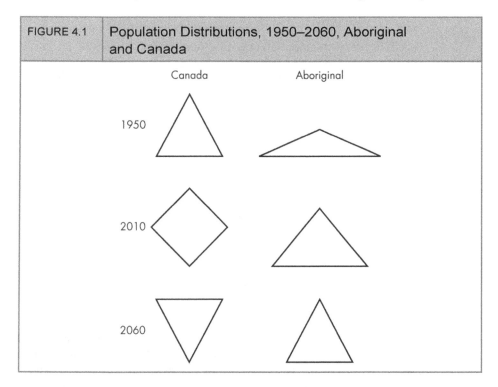

LANGUAGE USE AND RETENTION

Language is often recognized as the essence of a culture. Canada has a rich diversity of Aboriginal languages that reflect the various histories and cultures of First Nations, Inuit, and Métis (Galley, 2009). The **language** of any group is the repository of concepts, images, and history that allows individuals to organize their social environment. As Little Bear (2000) points out, language embodies the way a society thinks. And, through learning and speaking a language, an individual absorbs the collective thought processes of a people. Moreover, he notes that most Aboriginal languages are oriented toward process and action rather than objects (as are Western languages) and are free of dichotomies (e.g., black/white, either/or, animate/inanimate). It is important to know the extent to which Aboriginal people use and retain their languages. Price (1981) and Norris (1998) have investigated the potential for the survival of Aboriginal languages in Canada. Norris (2009) provides information on the regional diversity, endangerment, and vitality of languages, which have important policy implications for language planning and programs (see Table 4.3 for the prevalence of Aboriginal languages). The Inuit Tapiriit Kanatami found that 64 percent of Inuit overall claimed Inuktitut as their mother tongue, 50 percent used it as their home language, and 69 percent claimed to have the ability to converse in that language (Inuit Tapiriit Kanatami, 2008).

There are approximately 50 languages being used by Canada's Indigenous peoples, belonging to 11 major **language families** (Norris, 1998). Norris found that some language families are large and strong, while others are small and endangered. Overall, she (2009)

TABLE 4.3	Percentage of First Nations and Métis who have Knowledge of an Aboriginal Language by Age Group, 2006.			
Age Group	First Nations		Métis	Inuit[a]
	On	Off		
0–14	39	8	2	51
15–24	43	9	2	51
25–44	56	13	3	52
45–64	67	21	6	58
65–74	79	26	9	60
75+	83	24	12	63
Total	51	12	4	53

[a] Inuit figures are for retention of mother tongue.

Source: Statistics Canada, Aboriginal Peoples in Canadian 2006: Inuit, Métis and First Nations, 2006 Census, Inuit Tapiriit Kanatami, 2007.

contends that only about a third of the Aboriginal languages now being used have a good chance of survival and only half will still be in use by 2060. However, the three largest families, consisting of Algonquian (147 000), Inuktitut (28 000), and Athapaskan (20 000), have high vitality and high probabilities of persisting for some time in the future. Estimates are that long-term future viability has been secured for at least 18 Aboriginal languages (the three largest are Inuktitut, Cree, and Ojibwa) for which there are more than 1000 speakers. An additional 16 languages are spoken by an estimated 100 to 1000 Aboriginal people and could be considered "endangered." The remaining 16 languages have less than 100 speakers and are considered "near extinction," meaning that they are beyond the possibility of revival.

While Aboriginal people have maintained a relatively high degree of adherence to their mother tongues (language first learned and still spoken), it has diminished over time. In 1941, fewer than 10 percent of Aboriginal people claimed English as their mother tongue. The figure reached 15 percent in 1951 and over 25 percent in 1961; another 2 percent claimed French. By 2010, 78 percent claimed English as their mother tongue and fewer than 5 percent were bilingual (i.e., spoke an Aboriginal language as well as either English or French). Of those who claimed Aboriginal dialects as their mother tongues, more than 40 percent were "somewhat" bilingual. Among non-reserve adults, only one-third said they could speak or understand an Aboriginal language, although less than 15 percent said they were able to speak it. Of the three groups, Métis were the least likely to know an Aboriginal language, but Inuktitut is spoken and understood by 90 percent of Inuit adults. Today about one-third of First Nations people can speak an Aboriginal language well enough to carry on a conversation. For on-reserve people, 51 percent could carry on a conversation whereas only 12 percent of off-reserve people could do so.

Notwithstanding widespread signs of language erosion, most Aboriginal people consider speaking an Aboriginal language to be an important issue (Norris, 2007; Statistics Canada, 2003). There is considerable evidence of Aboriginal language revitalization through the efforts of parents as teachers (O'Donnell and Tait, 2004). Specifically, Aboriginal communities are creating language and teaching environments that allow young people to pick up their Indigenous language as a "second language." Community programs are now offered to youth and middle-aged individuals who have not learned their mother tongues. In addition, band schools (as well as provincial schools) have implemented local Aboriginal language classes for students at all levels. The overall dwindling of Aboriginal-language use is somewhat mediated by primary and secondary schools through language instruction programs. Almost 34 000 students (or 42 percent of Aboriginal enrolments) received some Aboriginal language instruction in school during 2009 In addition, the number of students taking courses in which an Aboriginal language was the medium of instruction more than half the time increased by more than 40 percent during the 2000–2010 period. However, like other ethnic minorities, Aboriginal people have learned that, to integrate into the larger society, they must also learn to speak English or French. To a certain extent, the decreasing number of Aboriginal-language speakers reflects an increasing move away from the reserves and increasing contact with non-Aboriginal persons. Second language learning is a good indicator of the revitalization of endangered Aboriginal languages. Home language use, another measurement of language vitality, reveals an equally skewed distribution, with almost 80 percent claiming English as the home language. The data also indicate that 80 percent of Aboriginal people claim to have a working knowledge of one official language.

Overall, 22 percent of the nearly 1.5 million Aboriginals in Canada speak an Aboriginal language at home. Of those who listed an Aboriginal language as their first language, 43 percent speak Cree, 14 percent speak Inuktitut, 13 percent speak Ojibwa, 3 percent speak Athapaskan, and 1 percent speak Sioux. The average age of Aboriginals who claim to speak an Indigenous language is well in excess of 40. This suggests the older segment of the population retains the language and not the younger generation. Norris (1998) found that the index of continuity was at 76 percent in 1981, but 15 years later it had decreased to just below 65 percent. This means that for every 100 people with an Aboriginal mother tongue, the number who used an Indigenous language most often at home declined from 76 to just under 65. However, by the time of the 2006 Census, the decline had stabilized and Indigenous language use even marginally increased, suggesting that secondary language programs and community involvement have had an impact on language loss.

Nearly all Aboriginal people who change language shift to English (96.8 percent). Inuit and other Aboriginal people living in the north of Canada are the most reluctant to change languages, while Métis are most likely to do so. The young (under 14) and the old (65+) are least likely to take on English as their operating language. Younger children will, as they grow older, be more fully exposed to the larger society and will begin the process of linguistic shift. The fact that some young people retain their Aboriginal tongue is no indication that they will be fluent in that language as they enter the labour force (Jarvis and Heaton, 1989; Bougie, 2010). The 2006 Census found that 80 percent of on-reserve First Nations seniors spoke an Aboriginal language, compared to 24 percent of those living off reserve.

Even though the number of persons reporting an Aboriginal mother tongue has increased by 25 percent over the past 15 years, proportionately fewer of these individuals use this Indigenous language at home. However, as Norris (2009) points out, Aboriginal language vitality is stabilizing and revitalization efforts by Aboriginal communities are moderating the decline. The link between perceptions regarding children's grasp of Native culture and language is clear: Turcotte and Zhao (2004) show that nearly two-thirds of Aboriginal parents believe it is important for their children to speak and understand an Aboriginal language. Aboriginal peoples have realized that a key component in the creation of a healthy community requires the revitalization of traditional languages. It is not only a means of communication but a link that connects people with their past and grounds their social, emotional, and spiritual needs (Statistics Canada, 2003). Parents are key language teachers for their children, but the question remains as to whether they will be able to teach, since many have lost their ability to speak their Indigenous tongue.

RELIGION

Many followers of Native American spirituality do not regard their spiritual beliefs and practices as a "religion" in the way that many Canadians do. Their beliefs and practices form an integral and seamless part of their very being.

Box 4.1	Amerindian Religions

Europeans discovered a rich and complex spirituality among the Aboriginal peoples, who believed in the existence of a supreme being. The Iroquois called this being 'the one to whom all things belong'; the Outaouais referred to 'the master spirit of life.' Nearly all Aboriginal peoples shared a belief in the flood, a worldwide deluge in which all mankind died [except] one elder from each nation [who] was saved with his family and a few animals because he had the presence of mind to have a great canoe built. As soon as a boy could use a bow and arrow, he underwent an initiation rite meant to put him in contact with the *manitou* [spirit] that would guide and protect him all his life. Fasting played an important role in ritual practices—it induced dreams in which the spirit appeared in animal form.

The religious belief of the Inuit is grounded in the idea that *anua* (souls) exist in all people and animals. Individuals, families, and the tribe must follow a complex system of taboos to assure that animals will continue to make themselves available to the hunters. Many rituals and ceremonies are performed before and after hunting expeditions to assure hunting success.

An underwater goddess, Sedna or Takanaluk, is in charge of sea mammals. She is part human and part fish. She observes how closely the tribe obeys the taboos and releases her animals to the hunters accordingly. There is a corresponding array of deities who release land mammals. They are called Keepers or Masters, and there is one for each species.

Other spiritual elements found in many Aboriginal communities are:

(1) a Creator who is responsible for the creation of the world and is recognized in ritual, song, and prayers;

(2) a Hero or Trickster—a mythical individual who teaches culture and proper behaviour and provides sustenance to the tribe.

This dual divinity encapsulates the belief that there are also spirits who control the weather, spirits who interact with humans, and others who inhabit the underworld, although the Master of humans is the Creator.

In general, Native groups have no precise belief about life after death. Some believe in reincarnation, with a person being reborn as either a human or animal after death. Others believe that humans return as ghosts, or that people go to another world. Still others believe that nothing can definitively be known about one's fate after this life. Combinations of belief are common.

The sundance of the Plains Natives is perceived as a replay of the original creation. Its name is a mistranslation of the Lakota *sun gazing dance*. Other tribes use different names. The Sun Dance fulfilled many religious purposes: to give thanks to the Creator, to pray for the renewal of people and earth, to promote health, and more. It also provided an opportunity for people to socialize and renew friendships with other groups. Sweat lodges purify the participants and ready them for lengthy fasting and dancing. Although the Sun Dance was successfully suppressed by the government in the early 20th century, it survived and is now increasingly celebrated.

According to present statistics, 44 percent of Aboriginals in Canada are Catholic. This reflects the early Jesuit and Oblate missionary work among the Aboriginal people. Protestants make up an additional 29 percent, while "no religion" adds another 17 percent and "other" religions make up 9 percent (Statistics Canada, 2001). These figures show some changes over the past decade. For example, the percentage of Catholics has increased by 5 percent, and that of Protestants has decreased by 8 percent, while "other" and "none" have increased from 23 to 30 percent. The second largest Aboriginal religious denomination is Anglican, with 18 percent. Another 10 percent of Aboriginal peoples belong to the United Church, and the remaining 8 percent are evenly distributed among the other Christian churches in Canada. No information has been gathered regarding the extent to which Aboriginal people adhere to pre-Christian religious traditions, but apparently a significant percentage have retained their Indigenous spiritual beliefs. Christianity has had a definite impact on Aboriginal culture during the past three centuries and its ideology of acceptance and obedience has contributed significantly to a widespread conservatism and fatalism among Aboriginal peoples.

MARITAL STATUS AND FAMILY

In many respects, history has influenced and helped to shape the structure, roles, and meaning of family for Aboriginals today. Aboriginal people define family as fictive and non-fictive kin (blood-related and non–blood-related), extended family, and tribal community (Nabokov, 1999). In this regard, a First Nations person is never alone without family or a kinship network. This is summed up in the often heard "all my relations." Some Aboriginal groups are patriarchal and patrilocal in structure; others are matriarchal and matrilocal.

Today, some believe that the core of Aboriginal culture is maintained through Aboriginal women. This is a progressive and feminist view that does not apply across all Aboriginal communities in Canada. Others view the role of women as based on an ethic of care in which women are principally concerned with the responsibility and activity involved in the care of others and their development (Miller, 1986). In essence, Aboriginal women see themselves as providing an integral role centred around the connection between relationship and responsibility. Women's activity—in relation to others—is more aptly depicted in language such as "being able to encompass the experiences and well-being of the other." Aboriginal women are best described as having an "active participation in the development of others" (Miller, 1986: x). The role of contemporary Aboriginal women is very much rooted in historical tradition, but in a modernized way.

Active participation occurs daily. As women interact with adults and children, they engage in a relational connection. By looking at the conventional ways women have been socialized to carry out the expressive activities and functions of the so-called female role—that is, wife, mother, and nurturer, responsible for child rearing and the private sphere of home—it is clear that these activities are focused on serving others' needs (Red Horse et al., 1978). For Aboriginal women, then, ties to others represent affiliations based on an ethic of care—the connection between relationship and responsibility (Silvey 1997).

In their role, Aboriginal women are viewed as the carriers of culture, or, put another way, keepers of the culture. As such, the women are not suppressed, although the same is not true for Aboriginal men. The cultural context of the larger society has negatively affected the role and status of Aboriginal men compared to Aboriginal women. From an historical perspective, the role and status of Aboriginal women and men has been one of cultural adaptation and evolution as opposed to tradition.

Many Aboriginal men play prominent roles within their communities as band councillors, administrators, and casino operators. However, it is still far easier for Aboriginal women to find jobs that enable them to provide for their families and establish a career than it is for Aboriginal men.

The structure of the Aboriginal family is often misunderstood by non-Aboriginal people. The expansive nature of the family structure, inclusive of extended family systems, is confusing because of the number of non–blood-related members inherent in it. Not all members may be of the same tribal affiliation. Moreover, a non-blood or fictive member may be an elder who is referred to by members as an uncle. Adding to this confusion is the number of people who reside together; it is not always possible to tell by looking at members who is fictive or non-fictive (Red Horse, 1980;

Silvey, 1997). At the same time, Aboriginal children reside in twice the number of "lone-mother" families as other Canadians. Overall, 35 percent of Aboriginal children live with a lone parent compared to 17 percent for all of Canada. It is projected that by 2029, there will be 81 000 lone-parent families on the reserve and 51 000 off reserve (INAC, 2006).

Nevertheless, the goal of family and parental support, within the context of the Aboriginal family of origin, is to foster interdependence as well as independence. The family serves as a facilitator in the development of its members and does so according to family or cultural roles, not necessarily according to age (Red Horse, 1980). Family and parental support encompasses cultural and spiritual maintenance, satisfaction of physical and emotional needs, and the themes of providing care, being cared for, and preparing to care for, throughout the lifespan. In this regard, the family is strengthened, and lifelong interdependence among members is fostered. This approach contrasts with European-Canadian family support systems in that the goal of the latter is independence of members rather than interdependence among members.

Statistics suggest that Aboriginal family patterns depart from non-Aboriginal norms. About 60 percent of Aboriginal people living together are officially married, as compared to 67 percent of the overall Canadian population (Statistics Canada, 2006). Figures on the marital status of Aboriginal people do not support the stereotype of the broken Aboriginal family. Data shown in Table 4.4 reveal the marital status of the female Aboriginal population aged 15 and older in 2001. It shows that there were differences among the various Aboriginal groups and the non-Aboriginal population. For example, the proportion of married varies from 47 percent for off-reserve Aboriginals to nearly 60 percent for non-Aboriginals. Less than one-quarter of non-Aboriginals have never married, while on-reserve residents have the highest marriage rate at 36.

Related to marital status is the number and growth rate of Aboriginal families. In 2006 there were 163 000 families, a major increase from 1986. Projections to 2029 suggest that there will be 420 000 First Nations families, an increase of 71 percent. For on-reserve Aboriginals, this means an increase of 106 percent, and for those off reserve, an increase of 41 percent.

TABLE 4.4	Marital Status of Female Aboriginal Population Aged 15 and Older versus Canada, 2001					
Registered	Total Abor.	On Reserve	Off Reserve	Métis	Inuit	Non-Aborig.
Married	49.3	50.6	46.6	50.1	55.7	58.4
Separated	4.4	3.1	5.3	4.9	2.0	2.8
Divorced	6.0	3.1	7.0	7.3	1.7	6.3
Widowed	5.2	6.6	4.9	4.7	4.9	8.9
Never Married	35.1	36.5	36.2	33.0	35.7	23.6

Source: Adapted from Hull, J. 2006. *Aboriginal Women – A Profile from the 2001 Census*, p. 31. Catalogue: R2-162/2001E-PDF. Accessed May 25, 2011 at http://dsp-psd.pwgsc.gc.ca/Collection/R2-162-2001E.pdf

SOCIO-ECONOMIC STATUS

Canada is an internally stratified, unequal society. It can be divided into unequal or hier-archical categories that persist over time. Inequalities between categories thus become crystallized into social classes such that some groups perennially have more resources than others, translating into a better quality of life. Those who rank high are able to enjoy the benefits of modern industrial society with its enhanced educational, medical, and lei-sure activities. Those who place low in our hierarchical system will not be able to benefit from the increased technological innovations to enhance their quality of life. Four factors influence one's ability to participate in modern industrial society: income, labour force participation, occupational status, and education.

Income

In 1966 the *Hawthorn Report*—a national study commissioned by the federal government of the Aboriginal person's position in Canadian society—established that the per capita income per year for Aboriginal persons was about $300, and for other Canadians, about $1400. Census data from 2006 shows that the median income for Aboriginal people was $18 962, more than $8000 less than that of the general Canadian population—and

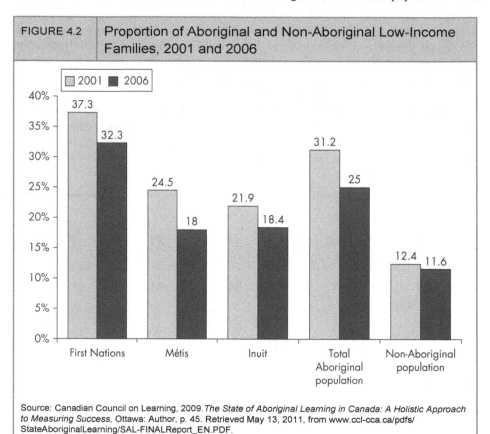

FIGURE 4.2 | **Proportion of Aboriginal and Non-Aboriginal Low-Income Families, 2001 and 2006**

Source: Canadian Council on Learning, 2009. *The State of Aboriginal Learning in Canada: A Holistic Approach to Measuring Success*, Ottawa: Author, p. 45. Retrieved May 13, 2011, from www.ccl-cca.ca/pdfs/ StateAboriginalLearning/SAL-FINALReport_EN.PDF.

TABLE 4.5	Income by Sex and Aboriginal Group, 2005					
Registered	Total	On Res.	Off-Res.	Métis	Inuit	Non-Aborig.
Women	$16 519	13 968	16 654	18 144	16 863	25 955
Male	$21 268	14 907	23 221	26 634	21 103	37 365

decreasing. At this rate, it would take 63 years for income equity to be attained. Figure 4.2 illustrates the proportion of Aboriginals living in low-income families. It shows that although this proportion is decreasing, more than twice as many Aboriginal families live in low-income situations compared to non-Aboriginal families. The average household income for non-Aboriginals in 2006 was $36 000, $12 000 higher than the average income for Aboriginal families.

When we review the average individual income by different Aboriginal groups, we find substantial differences. The data in Table 4.5 show dramatic differences in income among Aboriginal groups as well as between Aboriginals and non-Aboriginals. Aboriginal people make less regardless of sex, location, or education level. Moreover, despite the increased educational attainment of Aboriginal people, the disparity in relation to the non-Aboriginal population is growing (Wilson and Macdonald, 2010).

Before discussing income further, it is important to fully appreciate that income can be generated from a number of sources. The most general categories used in this review are those of wage (earned) and non-wage (unearned or transfer). Data from Statistics Canada show that earned income is the major source of income for all groups and employment income makes up at least 60 percent. For on-reserve Aboriginals, 20 percent comes from government transfer payments, in comparison to 10 percent for non-Aboriginals. Only non-Aboriginals have a substantial proportion of "other" income— e.g., interest, bonds, and stocks. Another way of illustrating the income of groups is to look at family income. When we compare the total family income (regardless of source) for Canadians compared to Aboriginal families, 40 percent of Aboriginal families make less than $20 000 per year, compared to only 10 percent of non-Aboriginals. At the other end of the continuum, 36 percent of non-Aboriginal people make more than $70 000 per year, while only 7 percent of Aboriginal families have that high an income.

We now turn to the issue of Aboriginal versus non-Aboriginal income. At least 75 percent of the total Canadian population (over the age of 15) has some income. However, nearly one-fourth of the Aboriginal population reported no income in 2006, while only 10 percent of the Canadian population reported no income (Wilson and Macdonald, 2010).

In summary, the disparity of income between Aboriginal and non-Aboriginal Canadians, as noted by Hawthorn in the 1960s, still exists. In addition, the data suggest that the gap between the two groups is getting larger. This startling fact emerges despite the large and complex structure we have put in place to help Aboriginal people find a niche in Canadian society and integrate into the economic structure (Pendakur and Pendakur, 2008). However, as Sharpe et al. (2007) point out, it will provide a significant benefit to the Canadian labour force in the future if Canada focuses on enhancing the employment of Aboriginal people.

Income Polarity While the data presented above demonstrate that, as a group, Aboriginal people are economically disadvantaged (consistent with the data presented by George et al. (2001) and Brunnen (2003)), the question arises as to whether these disparities are increasing or decreasing. Walters, White, and Maxim (2004) noted that the Canadian population experienced a greater increase in family income during the 1990s than ever before. Maxim and White (2003) observe that, on average, Canadian incomes increased 1.7 percent per annum during the past decade. Have the incomes of Aboriginal people followed that trend? Data from Maxim and White show that, while the overall increase was just under 2 percent per year, the top quintile (upper 20 percent) of Canadian families experienced a 6.6 percent increase each year, while the lowest quintile experienced a 5.2 percent decrease. Given that we know that most Aboriginals have incomes in the lowest quintile, we can infer that they have experienced a decrease in income over the past decade, thus exacerbating the **income polarity** that existed a decade ago. Even when transfer payments—e.g., old age pension, disability, interest, dividends—are added to the total income of individuals, there is no decrease but in fact an increase in disparity. This suggests that wealthy people are making more in government transfers than poor people are.

Labour Force Participation

Participation in the labour force affects the income of an individual or family and provides an indicator of the degree of social integration in society. Labour force participation is highly differentiated between Canadians and Aboriginal Canadians. In Table 4.7, data from Indian and Northern Affairs Canada show a gap in Aboriginal labour force activity, illustrating that Aboriginal involvement is much less than that of non-Aboriginal people.

Aboriginal and Canadian labour force participation increased between 1980 and 2005. In 1981, only 42 percent of Aboriginal people were employed, and by 2006, 75 percent were employed. Comparable figures for non-Aboriginals were 51 percent and 80 percent. While an increasing number of Aboriginal people entered the labour force over the past three decades, their percentage of unemployment doubled; for Canadians as a whole, the increase was minor. In 2006 the unemployment rate on reserves was triple the official national rate of 7 percent. This disparity was larger on an age-specific basis. The gap between First Nations and Canadian participation in the labour force was widest among the 15–24 age group, with a difference of 30 percent. For all age groups and sexes, the First Nations unemployment rates were at least twice as high, and the highest unemployment rate was in the 15–24 age group (Health Canada, 2003; see Table 4.6). These figures illustrate the degree of exclusion of Aboriginal people from the Canadian economy. To achieve parity with all Canadians, nearly 100 000 more Aboriginal people would have to be employed.

Participation in the labour force may involve full-time or part-time/seasonal work. Data show that, in 2000, over 40 percent of Aboriginal women and 32 percent of Aboriginal men did not work during the year. This is compared to 36 percent and 25 percent for non-Aboriginal women and men. Looking at the other end of the continuum, 36 percent of Aboriginal women and 40 percent of Aboriginal men worked more than 40 weeks (full-time) during the year. This is in contrast to 47 percent and 59 percent of non-Aboriginal women and men, respectively, for the same year. Even if the level of education is controlled for, there is no increase in the **labour force participation** rate. However, the labour force participation rate for Aboriginal people does not match that of the non-Aboriginal population. This reveals that education does not "pay off" for Aboriginal people.

TABLE 4.6	Labour Force Activity of Aboriginals Aged 15+ (percentage), Canada, 2001					
Total	Registered Abor.	On	Off	Métis	Inuit	Non-Aborig.
Women						
Part. Rate	57	47	55	65	60	61
Unempl. Rate	17	22	19	12	19	7
Employ. Rate	47	37	45	57	48	56
Men						
Part. Rate	67	56	68	75	65	73
Unemp. Rate	21	33	21	15	25	7
Empl. Rate	53	38	53	64	49	68

Source: Adapted from Hull, J. 2006. *Aboriginal Women – A profile from the 2001 Census*, pp. 54–55. Catalogue: R2-162/2001E-PDF. Accessed May 25, 2011, at http://dsp-psd.pwgsc.gc.ca/Collection/R2-162-2001E.pdf.

Table 4.7 reveals the occupations of Aboriginals by group and sex. The data show that over half of the jobs held by Aboriginal men in 2001 were made up of skilled, semi-skilled, and other manual occupations. In fact, one-fourth of the jobs held by Aboriginal males were in manual labour. Just over 10 percent of the Canadian population held level

TABLE 4.7	Occupations of Experienced Labour Force by Sex and Aboriginal Identity, 2001 (percentage)					
	Total Aboriginal	Registered		Métis	Inuit	Non-Aboriginal
		On	Off			
Men						
Level A	12.9	13.3	12.5	12.7	14.5	26.2
Level B	33.2	30.8	33.5	35.3	29.2	33.0
Level C	30.4	27.6	30.8	31.5	29.9	27.6
Level D	23.5	28.2	23.1	20.6	26.4	13.3
Women						
Level A	17.9	20.0	18.0	16.5	22.2	24.8
Level B	25.2	27.6	26.4	24.9	24.9	25.9
Level C	36.5	32.4	36.5	39.7	27.2	36.1
Level D	20.4	20.0	21.1	18.9	25.8	13.1

Level A consists of senior and middle managers as well as professions. Level B are semi-professionals, supervisors, senior clerical and skilled sales, service crafts and trades. Level C are clerical personnel, intermediate sales and service and semi-skilled manual. Level D are other sales and service and other manual.

Source: Adapted from Hull, J. 2006. *Aboriginal Women – A profile from the 2001 census*, pp. 69–70. Catalogue: R2-162/2001E-PDF. Accessed May 25, 2011, at http://dsp-psd.pwgsc.gc.ca/Collection/R2-162-2001E.pdf.

D (manual labour) occupations. When we look at the upper scale of the occupational list (upper- and middle-level managers and professionals), we find over 25 percent of the total Canadian population employed there, but less than half that percentage of Aboriginal people. Overall, compared to the total population, there are fewer Aboriginal persons in upper-status occupations and more in lower-status occupations.

When we look at females in the labour force, we find a different distribution than that evidenced by the male population. At the upper ends of the occupational scale, similarities exist between Aboriginal women and Canadian women, even though Aboriginal women are slightly underrepresented. The major differences between Aboriginal women and all females are in two occupational categories—clerical and services. Nearly 30 percent of all female Canadians in the labour force hold jobs as clerks. For Aboriginal women, it is less than 23 percent. One-fifth of the Aboriginal females are in service occupations, compared to just over 10 percent of the total female population in the labour force.

EDUCATION

Canadian culture places a great emphasis on the value of education and is generally seen as essential to success; young people who do not show academic potential are usually regarded as early failures. Certainly, education has a great impact on lifestyle and life chances. Yet for a variety of reasons, not all Canadians are able to use the educational system as effectively as possible. Aboriginal people in particular are excluded from the benefits of Euro-Canadian education by several factors.

Federal expenditures for Aboriginal education were $13.5 million in 1956; by 1980, they had reached well over $270 million, or 39 percent of the total Indian–Inuit Affairs budget. Today AAND spends about $1.2 billion for operations and an additional $200 million for building capital and maintenance to support the 130 000 First Nations students. About 75 000 attend the 350 band schools on reserves. The remaining students attend schools off the reserves (INAC, 2008). AAND covers the cost of any registered Indian who is attending primary or secondary school, either on or off reserve. The actual amount and means by which schools are paid are determined by each province, and there are a number of different types of agreements. AAND also spends about $200 million annually to support school infrastructure projects in First Nations communities across the country. However, First Nations are considered the owners and operators of infrastructure on reserves and are thus responsible for the operation, maintenance, and minor renovations of their schools.

Today education represents less than 20 percent of AAND's total budget. Expenditures per student have increased, representing an average annual growth rate of 7.1 percent. By 2007, the per capita average had increased to nearly $11 000 per year (AAND, 2008). In comparison, over the past five years the federal government contributed over $7 billion to the education of non-Aboriginals, for activities that are outside the mandate of the government. Over the past decade, the federal government has kept Aboriginal education funding at a ceiling of 2 percent per year, although an analysis of enrolment increases in First Nations schools demonstrates that it should have risen to over 3 percent. This means that funding for education has decreased in terms of real, inflation-adjusted, per-student dollars (Mendelson, 2006). Over a decade ago the Auditor General (2000) noted that AAND's funding showed a provision of between $5500 and $7500 per student. However, at the same time, the Auditor General also found that the student per-capita expenditures were between $6800 and $8400 for non-Aboriginal students. When the high cost for factors such as isolated location, special needs students, and high levels of socio-economic need are taken into consideration, these figures reveal a major gap in funding.

What is troubling with the above picture is that, as the Auditor General pointed out in her 2004 report, "The Department of Indian Affairs does not know whether funding to First Nations is sufficient to meet the education standards it has set" (Section 5.1). An evaluation study of Aboriginal education in British Columbia (Postl, 2005) and Saskatchewan (QED, 2004) revealed that federal funding was not at the level of provincial funding and that federal funding did not cover special needs students or administrative support for teachers.

For the past three decades, only 30 percent of on-reserve, First Nations students have graduated from Grade 12 as they finished their third year in high school. There are a number of individuals who graduated in their fourth and fifth year (or even later), but the fact remains that while 80 percent of non-Aboriginal students graduate from Grade 12, the gap between the two groups is startling. As information from the 2006 Census emerged, there was considerable optimism that the graduation rate for Aboriginal students would dramatically increase—particularly for those in the 20–24 age cohort. However, when the data was analyzed, the rate had not changed and the gap between reserve students and non-Aboriginal students had actually increased.

There was considerable hope that when the federal government made a major concession to First Nations communities regarding control of their education in 1973, 40 years later this would have translated into major changes in the number of students in primary and secondary schools, the graduation rate, and the number of students attending post-secondary educational institutions (Mendelson, 2008).

AAND has been under scrutiny by the federal Auditor General for some time, and in 2004 the Department established a dedicated education branch. There was hope that the branch would work within the community to establish an Indian education act, but after two years of meetings, the branch seems to have disappeared. The Auditor General (2004) was critical of AAND's handling of elementary and secondary education for First Nations people. As of 2011, little has been put in place by the Department to show its roles and responsibilities toward Aboriginal education. Moreover, Mendelson (2008) claims that there is no policy statement or funding envelope through which the Department committed itself to fund First Nations schools at a level comparable with provincial funding and support. The only comparable component between the two school systems is that they both must have provincially certified teachers. However, in terms of outcome, no measure has been established.

History of Aboriginal Education

In 1830, legislation was passed that transferred the responsibility of education to the provincial or local governments (Special Senate Hearing on Poverty, 1970: 14, 59), thus beginning the state's role in the provision of education for Aboriginal people. In general, European settlers were indifferent to Aboriginal education: A public fund was not established for this purpose until 1848. In some cases, European settlers encouraged the school enrolment of Aboriginal children in order to pressure the province to establish more schools. As the density of the non-Aboriginal population grew, however, Aboriginal education was increasingly ignored. The federal government was reluctant to operate schools for Aboriginals and passed the responsibility to other, mainly religious, agencies. With the passage of the *British North America Act, 1867,* Canada's parliament was given the power to administer Aboriginal affairs, including education, and nine years later the *Indian Act* provided the legal basis for federal administration of Aboriginal education. In addition, most treaties signed after 1871 contained an educational commitment to maintain schools on the reserve and provide educational services when required.

Federal and provincial government policy on Aboriginal education can be considered in two phases. The first, from 1867 to 1945, has been labelled the "paternalistic ideology" phase. Until 1945, Aboriginal schooling was "education in isolation." During this period, schools and hostels for Aboriginal children were established, but scant attention was paid to developing a curriculum geared to either their language difficulties or their sociological needs. A few Indian bands established schools for their children on the reserves, but the majority had neither the financial resources nor the leadership to build and operate their own schools. Provincial governments were too preoccupied with their own priorities to become involved in Aboriginal education. Missionaries provided a modicum of services, but their "noble savage" philosophy effectively insulated the Indians from the mainstream of society (Special Senate Hearing on Poverty, 1970: 14, 59). However, four churches— Roman Catholic, Anglican, Methodist, and Presbyterian—began to educate Aboriginal children in denominational or **residential schools**. Of these, the Catholics and Anglicans have had the greatest impact on Aboriginal people in Canada, and continue to do so.

Education was traditionally viewed by government and religious organizations as the best way to assimilate Aboriginal people. The missionaries, who until the 1960s controlled Aboriginal education, were far more concerned with converting the students than with teaching useful, practical knowledge and skills. Because they felt that Aboriginal people would always live in isolation, the missionaries made no attempt to prepare them for successful careers in modern Canadian society. Instead, they concentrated on eradicating all traces of Aboriginal languages, traditions, and beliefs (Fuchs, 1970) and on converting them to their religious beliefs. Because religious ideologies are fundamentally conservative, they discouraged protest and revolt on the part of the Aboriginal people. For example, Roman Catholicism holds that poverty is not a social evil but is God's will. Instead of struggling against God's will, Catholics are encouraged to humbly accept their fates in order to ensure a place in heaven. Roman Catholicism discourages social change, particularly that which involves force: In heaven "the first shall be last and the last shall be first" (Matt: 19:30).

Churches that operated schools were given land, per capita grants, and other material rewards for their efforts. Often these grants resulted in the material exploitation of the Aboriginal peoples as churches pursued property and profits (McCullum and McCullum, 1975; Grant, 1996). To accommodate the education of young Aboriginal students and facilitate their assimilation, residential schools were established throughout the country. Residential schools were almost all built in rural locations, far from non-Aboriginal settlements. These schools limited the contact between Aboriginal children and their parents to facilitate the transformation of the students from "heathens" to Christians. The schools were highly regimented and insisted on strict conformity. There were few adults, and most of these were non-Aboriginal persons. As a result, normal adult–child relations could not develop. Few of the teachers were academically well qualified; they neither stimulated the children nor acted as positive role models. The average annual staff turnover was never less than 21 percent and often higher, particularly after 1955.

The second period, from 1945 to the present, has been called the "democratic ideology" phase (Hawthorn, 1967). This second phase simply refers to the "open-door policy" that enabled Aboriginal students to attend school off the reserve. It was a radical departure from the earlier policy of isolation, and residential schools began to decline in enrolment. After the early 1960s, the number of Aboriginal children attending residential schools drastically declined. The unpopularity of these schools should come as a surprise to no one.

Once the new policy came into effect, Aboriginal students could attend either federal schools (generally church-operated) or integrated (provincially/federally funded) joint-schools. There were four types of federal schools, some still in existence today: day schools. denominational (also called residential or religious) schools, boarding and hospital schools, and band schools. Day schools were the largest group under federal control. They were located on the reserve and provided education only for those who lived there, including the non-Aboriginal children of teachers. The last residential school in Canada closed its doors in 1996.

Hospital schools provide classes for Aboriginal students in government hospitals, from the pre-school level through to adult education. Boarding schools are for Aboriginal orphans or children from broken homes, and may or may not be on the reserve. All federal-residential (religious) schools have been closed. In turn, "integrated" schools and "band" schools were established.

Provincial integrated joint-schools were established to encourage Aboriginal students to leave the reserve and enrol in provincial schools. Provincial governments had overbuilt their schools, particularly in rural areas, and empty spaces needed to be filled. If they could make arrangements with the federal government, these schools were willing to take new students. Essentially, these are provincial schools that allow Aboriginal students to attend and in turn are paid a fee by Indian and Inuit Affairs for each student. The structure and curricula of these schools are established by the provincial government. Although education is a provincial responsibility, the provincial governments argue that Aboriginal children are a federal responsibility and thus, if they attend a provincial school, the province must be compensated.

The creation of **band schools** emerged out of the political lobbying that Aboriginal people participated in during the late 1960s and early 1970s. While they are technically federal schools, they have taken on an air of independence and largely manage themselves even though they receive federal dollars to operate. In 1973, the National Indian Brotherhood produced a document, *Indian Control of Indian Education,* which was later accepted by the federal government and adopted as official educational policy for Aboriginals. This policy explicitly incorporated the principles of parental responsibility and local control. It was, for Aboriginal people, a time when they believed that they would become active participants in affecting their own educational experiences. Indian Affairs established guidelines and procedures for school transfers to bands and introduced a national formula-funding system for the allocation of resources for band-operated schools.

By 1980, well over 100 band-operated schools were in existence. By 1990 the number had increased to 300 and today there are 500. Band-operated schools make up an increasing portion of the total Aboriginal student enrolment. Today over 60 percent of the primary and secondary school Aboriginal population attends First Nations (band) schools, with just over one-third attending provincial joint-integrated schools and others attending federal or private schools. Over the years, secondary schools on the reserves have been closed, and while most primary Aboriginal students attend band schools, the number of secondary students attending provincial schools continues to increase.

Data from the Indian–Inuit Affairs Program show that, from 1964 to 1981, over 800 agreements were made between local school boards and the Department of Indian Affairs in order to secure positions for Aboriginal children in provincial schools. The data provided in Table 4.8 demonstrate the historical increase in Indian enrolment from 1961 to 2007. The decrease from 1991 to 2001 is a result of the higher number of registered Indians resulting from *Bill C-31*. These young Aboriginals do not attend a federal, band, or provincial integrated school, but rather a regular provincial urban school, not as an Aboriginal student but as a provincial citizen. Thus, while the rate looks low, if these additional students are counted, the school participation rate is about 89 percent. Subsequent to this, there have been dramatic decreases in the percent of Aboriginal students attending school. These figures represent the high drop-out rate, a change in the definition of a First

TABLE 4.8	Enrolment in Kindergarten, Elementary, and Secondary Schools On Reserve, Canada, 1960/61-2007-08				
Year	Enrolment[a]	Population 4–18 years	Enrolment Rate	On-Reserve	Off-Reserve
1960/61[b]	41 671	57 550	72.4%	87%	13%
1965/66[b]	54 670	73 632	74.2%		
1970/71	68 449	81 531	84.0%		
1975/76	71 817	88 660	81.0%		
1980/81	82 801	88 581	93.5%		
1985/86	80 623	92 080	87.6%		
1986/87	82 271	94 169	87.4%		
1987/88	84 271	95 336	88.4%		
1988/89	85 582	96 606	88.6%		
1989/90	88 158	97 751	90.2%		
1990/91[c]	96 501	102 605	92.2%		
2000/01[d]	119 574	179 967	66.4%	61	39
2003/04[d]	120 421	178 223	67.6%	61	39
2007/08	130 996	221 563	59.1%	61	39

Note: On reserve includes Crown lands and settlements.

a. Total enrolment includes registered and non-registered Indians and Inuit in kindergarten to Grade 13.

b. A breakdown of on/off-reserve Indian population was not available in 1960/61 and 1965/66. Based on 1975 Indian Register data, off-reserve was estimated to be 26 percent of the total population. Data also were not available for the 4-18 age population for 1960-61, estimated to be 42 percent of the total Indian population.

c. Data are based on population age 5-14, single response.

d. Data are based upon ages 6-16.

Sources: In *Basic Departmental Data* 1990, p. 35; *Basic Departmental Data* 2001-02, p. 36; *Basic Departmental Data* 2002-03, 37; *Basic Departmental Data* 2003-04, Indian and Northern Affairs Canada, p. 45; Basic Departmental Data 2004; Mendelson, 2009.

Nations person, and a change in the manner in which statistics are kept by provincial and federal agencies. While the official figures reveal dramatic decreases, the reality is that there are some decreases, but not in the magnitude demonstrated in Table 4.10.

School Attendance: Primary and Secondary

Most Indian children attend federal schools until Grade Six, then switch to provincial schools for their middle and secondary education.

The switch from one school system to another has a serious disruptive influence (both socially and academically). Initially, Aboriginal children enter federal schools as a distinct cultural group with minimal knowledge of English or French. Because they share a similar social status, no one is at a disadvantage. However, when these students transfer, the cohort is usually broken up and the individuals are sent to different provincial schools, where they become minority outsiders among Euro-Canadian students for whom English or French is the mother tongue.

Aboriginal students at provincial schools face considerable discrimination. On the reserve these students have already met indirect, institutionalized racism; Aboriginal students in integrated provincial schools, however, are exposed daily to direct discrimination from teachers and other students. In the long term, racism results in a serious and permanent distortion of the Aboriginal child's self-image. In addition, the Aboriginal cohort in these schools becomes the reference group by which Aboriginal students measure their success. Not surprisingly, social disruptions eventually result in low grades and a high drop-out rate.

The rate of Aboriginal students attending school has generally increased over the past two decades. This is particularly true for the younger ages. For example, in the late 1950s only about 43 percent of Aboriginal children aged four to five went to kindergarten. By the late 20th century, this figure had increased to 80 percent. Overall, about 39 percent of First Nations students aged 15 to 24 are attending school full-time, while over 44 percent of the general population in that age group is doing so. Looking at the issue from another perspective, the differences are clearer: 16 percent of Canadians aged 20 to 24 did not complete high school in 2001, compared to Aboriginal young adults at 43 percent. As Mendelson (2006) points out, in 2001, an astonishing 58 percent of young adults (age 20–24) living in a First Nations community did not complete high school. In the cities, more than one-third of young Aboriginals failed to complete high school in 2001—more than double the rate of the total population.

Aboriginal education outcomes differ from those of non-Aboriginal groups. We know that high school completion rates for Aboriginal people are much less than for non-Aboriginal youth. However, we also know that proportionately, more Aboriginal youth than non-Aboriginal youth are returning to school and completing high school after age 24 (Richards, 2008). Richards et al. (2008) found that by Grade Four, a sizeable gap exists between Aboriginal and non-Aboriginal student performance. By Grade Seven, there are major gaps in reading, writing, and numeracy levels. However, there are some schools that stand out in revealing high academic performance for Aboriginal students. The success of these schools demonstrates that when schools emphasize Aboriginal education success as a long-term priority, involve Aboriginal leaders and the community, and follow through on policy implementation, Aboriginal students excel in their academic studies.

TABLE 4.9	Percentage of High School Graduates Who Were Enrolled in Grade 12 or 13, On-Reserve Population, Canada, 1994-95 to 2003-04		
School Year	Enrolment	Graduates	Graduate Rate
1994-95	5743	1662	28.9
1995-96	5909	2001	33.9
1996-97	5618	1785	31.8
1997-98	5948	1975	33.2
1998-99	6036	1939	32.1
1999-00	6463	2072	32.1
2000-01	7063	2168	30.7
2003-04	7287	2203	30.2

Sources: Adapted from *In Basic Departmental Data*, 2002, p. 38. Indian and Northern Affairs Canada; Mendelson, 2006; 2008; Richards et al., 2008; Postl, 2005; QED Information Systems, 2004.

Until the 1970s, the educational curriculum was dominated by an assimilationist ideology. Even today, the curriculum used in Aboriginal schools is regulated by the provincial government and is the same as that designed for white middle-class students in all other public schools. Under the current *Indian Act*, First Nations manage their own schools, although each band can enter into agreements with the Crown in terms of what that management agreement contains. Today there are only a handful of agreements that allow a First Nations "Education Authority" to function in the way of a provincial school board, providing teacher and school certification and setting standards for curricula and examinations for participating First Nations (Mendelson, 2006).

The reasons for the high drop-out rate among Aboriginal students are complex yet straightforward. Researchers have noted that the distorted image of Aboriginals presented in curricula is not the chief source of the alienation most Indian children experience in the white school system. Far more significant and detrimental is the fact that the verbal symbols and theoretical constructions the Indian child is being asked to manipulate bear little or no relation to the social environment with which he or she is most familiar. Students must acquire and accept a new form of consciousness, an orientation that not only displaces but often devalues the world views they bring with them (Castellano, 1970; Hampton, 1993; Barnhardt, 2001). Finally, as noted earlier, discrimination (individual and systemic) results in high drop-out rates and low grades.

In addition to systemic and individual racism, Aboriginal students must contend with the poor image of themselves projected by the mass media, including films and books used in schools. It has been argued that a lack of parental support is an additional factor in the drop-out rate. There are many structural reasons for it, however. Not surprisingly, because Aboriginal parents have little to no control over curricula, textbooks, or staff, until recently they have come to regard the educational system as an "outside" racist institution, to be tolerated but not supported. Parents who have had no education or endured negative experiences with the educational system as children are reluctant to endorse such a system. Active adult community support for education will only develop when Aboriginal people who live on the reserve are allowed to control the curricula, hold teaching and administrative positions, and determine the teaching techniques. To blame parental neglect for the high drop-out rate is naive; when all the structural variables are considered, the reaction of Aboriginal parents to the educational system is not apathetic but actively and understandably hostile (Battiste and Barman, 1995).

Quality of Aboriginal Education

The quality of Aboriginal education is determined by a variety of factors, including operation and maintenance costs, pupil–teacher ratios, teacher qualifications, proportion of Aboriginal teachers, community involvement, educational expenditures, and overall per-student education costs. In addition, reserve schools do not have the professional backup resources—for example, curriculum development specialists and language consultants—that are present in most provincial schools. Finally, there is no teachers association that federal teachers can join to improve their teaching and educational skills. In addition, since the creation of the band schools, teachers and curricula have been increasingly subjected to political battles that take place in the community. While the proportion of Aboriginal administrators and teachers in federal schools more than tripled between 1966 and 2001 to over 36 percent, there is considerable turnover. Finally, it should be noted that when standardized testing takes place, Aboriginal students achieve scores that are equal to non-Aboriginal students two years below their level (Mendelson, 2006).

Recently, AAND commissioned a national working group on education to look at ways to improve education for First Nations children and youth. The resulting report, *Our Children—Keepers of the Sacred Knowledge,* made several major recommendations, and AAND has set aside funds for their implementation. The question remains as to whether the funds set aside will be allocated to the recommendations or whether other priorities will take precedence.

Educational Attainment

In 1981 (when systematic data was first collected), there was evidence of a major gap between Aboriginals and non-Aboriginals in every level of educational attainment. For example, 17 percent more non-Aboriginals graduated from elementary school than Aboriginals. Ten years later, this gap had been reduced to 10 percent. However, since that time, the gap has remained unchanged. An even larger gap existed between Aboriginal and non-Aboriginal people for high school graduation. In 1981 the gap was 23 percent, and by 2001 it was reduced to just under 20 percent. Gaps between the two groups for successful completion of post-secondary education also remain, although not as large as those above. In 2001, 23 percent of registered Indians attained a post-secondary certificate, diploma, or degree. For non-Aboriginals, the rate was 38 percent. These data show the changes (or lack thereof) that are taking place within both the Aboriginal community and all of Canada. Unfortunately, current data reveal a gap that is as wide as that evidenced 20 years earlier (see Table 4.10).

TABLE 4.10	Level of Education by Aboriginal Group and Non-Aboriginal, 2004					
Females						
Education Level	Total Aboriginal	On Reserve	Off Reserve	Métis	Inuit	Non-Aboriginal
‹ Grade 9	16.2	26.6	13.5	10.0	32.7	11.2
Grade 9–13	39.5	36.7	40.9	40.4	31.2	34.8
Non-Univ.	30.3	25.3	30.0	34.6	29.5	29.1
University	14.0	11.4	15.7	15.0	6.6	29.9
All Post-Sec.	44.3	36.7	45.6	49.7	36.0	54.0
Males						
‹ Grade 9	17.6	27.5	12.8	12.2	31.2	10.3
Grade 9–13	41.8	39.2	44.0	42.6	31.5	33.0
Non-Univ.	30.6	26.8	30.6	33.3	33.3	30.7
University	10.1	6.5	12.6	11.9	4.0	26.0
All Post-Sec.	40.6	33.3	43.1	42	37.3	56.7

Post-Secondary School Attendance

In 1960, 200 status Indians enrolled at a college or university. By 2001, this number had increased to almost 30 000, but it has levelled off over the past decade. Several factors explain this profile. First Nations' increasing control over their own education and the provision of funds by Indian and Inuit Affairs account for some of the dramatic increase. In addition, more Aboriginal students are completing Grade 12 and are ready to enrol in a post-secondary educational institute. However, the decision by Indian and Inuit Affairs to limit the increase of funds to support Aboriginal people to only 2 percent each year since 2001 has resulted in a slowdown in post-secondary enrolment. And, finally, the quality of on-reserve secondary schools seems to be in question with regards to preparing graduates for a successful transition to post-secondary school.

The data on Aboriginal participation in post-secondary education is discouraging. The rate of Aboriginal students obtaining a university degree fell when comparing the period 1996–2006. Also disappointing is the educational achievements for Aboriginal students in non-university post-secondary certification programs. There has been a slight increase over the past decade (14 to 17 percent) but because there is a large proportion of Aboriginal people in the 20–24 age group, the proportion of Aboriginal people who have a non-university post-secondary certificate actually decreased over this time period.

Because of the increased number of high school graduates (see Table 4.9), more and more Aboriginal students wish to attend post-secondary educational institutions. By 2004 this number had reached approximately 30 000 students. This reflects an increase from less than 1 percent to about 6 percent over the past two decades for Aboriginals in the 17–34 age group. Nevertheless, this is still considerably lower than the overall national rate of over 12 percent. From a modest $2.5 million budget in 1981, the post-secondary budget increased to over $315 million in 2005—representing a per capita expenditure of $10 500. However, since these funds are distributed to bands, the latter make decisions as to whom and how much is provided to successful applicants. If a student comes from a band with few applicants, his or her chances of being successful (as well as receiving a sizeable stipend to go to school) are high. If there are many applicants from the band, chances of success and the monies available will be low. While the number of Aboriginal students receiving assistance has more than quadrupled since 1981, because the Indian Studies Support Program has been capped, many individuals eligible to attend university will not be able to do so. In 2003, the government created a $12 million endowment for scholarships for Aboriginals who want to go on to post-secondary schools. Nevertheless, the funding is insufficient and the focus is not toward enhancing the secondary system so that high school graduates can successfully compete in a university system.

While there has been a dramatic increase since the early 1960s in the number of Aboriginal students attending college and/or university, most of these students are in college programs, working toward certificates or diploma. It is estimated that about 80 percent are college registrants and 20 percent are enrolled in a university degree program. Within universities, Aboriginal students generally make up less than 2 percent of the student population, while at colleges, they make up in excess of 10 percent. To address the lack of Aboriginal enrolment, a number of universities have tailored special programs to meet the interests and needs of Aboriginal students, while others have provided remedial services to assist Aboriginal persons who are entering university. However, despite a rapid increase in Aboriginal enrolment, the Aboriginal participation rate is still less than half the national level. Today less than 10 percent of the Aboriginal population between the ages of 18 and 24 is enrolled in university, while 31.2 percent of the non-Aboriginal youth population is enrolled. Even more dismal than the enrolment figures are the statistics that reflect the rate of graduation from post-secondary institutions. It is estimated that about 28 percent of Aboriginal students enrolled in university programs graduate (Mendelson, 2010). These figures have remained constant for the past decade and there is no evidence that they will change in the near future.

To remedy the lack of success in post-secondary educational institutions, Aboriginal organizations have recently entered the arena. Several major agreements have been signed in Western provinces. For example, the Nisga'a have contributed $250 000 to the University of Northern British Columbia to offer courses in the Nass Valley, the traditional home of the Nisga'a. To implement the program, the Wilxo'oskwhl Nisga'a Post-Secondary Institute was created. The University of Manitoba began offering social work classes to isolated First Nations communities. The University of Calgary's Virtual Circles Program is a similar arrangement that has been established for distance education in Alberta. The creation of the First Nations Adult Higher Education Consortium, made up of several First Nations community colleges in Western Canada, is another strategy being employed. These community colleges are working out partnership agreements with nearby public educational institutions so that students completing their programs in Aboriginal colleges will be able to seamlessly enter the university system.

Aboriginal Studies programs were created in the late 1980s at various Canadian universities, which allowed Aboriginals to gain entrance to the schools under conditions different from those of non-Aboriginal students. In addition, support services have been added to help

Aboriginal students. These programs started small but have grown in size over the years, and in some schools, graduate programs in Aboriginal Studies have been implemented. Nevertheless, as universities continue to experience budget cuts, Aboriginal Studies programs are currently under review as "untraditional programs" and are vulnerable to budget cuts.

Even if the *Indian Act* were changed, it is unlikely that Aboriginal people could take control of the education process unless other structures and processes in place are changed. First, the federal government has more trust in provincial school authorities (with regard to finances) than in Aboriginal people. Second, because the federal government does not operate an educational system, it relies on provincial curricula and standards. Thus it is not interested in developing new approaches to education that would be appropriate or relevant to the diversity of Aboriginal communities (Longboat, 1987). Finally, AAND's education policy is developed and carried out by department officials; it is not a cooperative effort between Aboriginal people and the government. For example, even though the government adopted a stance acknowledging Indians' right to control education in the early 1970s, it added an important condition: Any agreement that had already been signed with provincial officials will be honoured until its term expired. In other words, local control of education will not be discussed until the terms of any federal–provincial agreement has concluded. Because most of the capital agreements (agreements to pay a percentage of the school board's capital and building costs) are 20- to 25-year contracts, Aboriginal communities will have to wait an entire generation before they can begin to discuss local control of their schools (Longboat, 1987).

Overall, the educational attainment of Aboriginal people has increased over the past 50 years. These increases are a result of several factors. They are due in part to the increased number of band-operated schools. Almost all of the schools on reserves are administered by First Nations themselves, and many are secondary schools. There has also been an increase in federal funding for post-secondary education, and a major expansion of Aboriginal Studies programs in Canadian universities. Finally, universities are starting to implement policies that will render the institutions more welcoming to Aboriginal students.

JUSTICE AND THE LAW

The concept of law and justice in Canada was brought by settlers reflecting a European world view. Aboriginal peoples were never consulted, and over time the settler view of justice was enshrined into Canadian law. How different these two conceptions are is revealed in Table 4.11

Since the settlers were able to enshrine their laws, Aboriginal people have been forced to accept this authority, although they do not condone it.

Given these discrepancies, how has the implementation of these laws affected Aboriginal people? Table 4.12 shows the federal statute as applied to incidents reported to police on First Nations communities for 2004. It reveals very different profiles between Aboriginals and non-Aboriginals with regard to being charged with a crime. Fifty percent of the cases against Aboriginal people were considered violent crimes (e.g., assault, sexual assault), while only 39 percent of non-Aboriginals were charged with such a crime. On the other hand, 37 percent of incidents in which non-Aboriginals were charged with a federal statute offence involved a property crime (e.g., break and enter, mischief), while just over one-fifth of the Aboriginal population faced such a charge.

TABLE 4.11	Canadian versus Traditional Native Conceptualizations of Justice

Anglo-Canadian Justice	Traditional Indian Justice
• laws formulated by elected representatives	• laws formulated by the community through tradition and consensus
• laws tied to man-made economy	• laws tied to the natural environment, only a few universally condemned actions
• Protestant ethic and Christianity the moral foundation of the law	• traditional Native religions the foundation of Native codes of behaviour
• personal offences seen as transgressions against the state as represented by the monarch	• personal offences seen as transgressions against the victim and his/her family; community involved only when the public peace threatened
• law administered by representatives of the state in the form of officially recognized or operated social institutions	• law usually administered by the offended party, e.g., the family, the clan
• force and punishment used as methods of social control	• arbitration and ostracism usual peacekeeping methods
• individualistic basis for society and the use of the law to protect private property	• communal basis for society, no legal protection for private property. Land held in trust by an individual and protected by the group

TABLE 4.12	Characteristics of All Persons Involved in Adult Correction Services, 1999–00 to 2003–04, Saskatchewan

	Aboriginal	Non-Aboriginal
Violent Offences	50.6	38.5
Serious Violent Offences	18.0	9.0
Sexual Offences	4.4	5.2
Robbery	3.3	2.5
Common Assault	19.6	21.4
Other Violent Offences	5.2	10.4
Property Offences	19.8	37.2
Break and Enter	7.0	11.8
Theft	8.0	19.3
Fraud	2.7	18.8
Other Property Offences	2.0	7.1
Offences Against Administration of Justice	7.9	14.4
Other Criminal Code (No Traffic)	4.6	13.5
Criminal Code (Traffic)	10.7	37.0
Drug Offences	3.4	20.7
Other	3.0	11.5

TABLE 4.13	Aboriginal Inmates in Correctional Institutions by Region		
Region	Aboriginal Inmates in Provincial Institutions (% of all inmates)	Aboriginal Inmates in Federal Institutions (% of all inmates)	Off-Reserve Registered Indians (% of all Registered Indians)
Atlantic Provinces	3	3	33
Quebec	2	1	22
Ontario	8	4	46
Manitoba	49	39	34
Saskatchewan	68	52	46
Alberta	34	31	34
British Columbia	18	14	47
N.W.T.	91	37	21
Yukon	63	94	54

Sources: Adapted from Boe (2000); Johnson (2005); Wood and Griffiths (2000); and Beattie (2006).

Table 4.13 reveals the percentage of Aboriginal intake for both provincial and federal prisons in 2000. These numbers are to be compared to the overall population of Aboriginal people, which now stands at less than 4 percent.

These data show that Aboriginal people are more likely to come into contact with the Canadian judicial system than non-Aboriginals. In addition, once they become involved with the legal system, they are more likely to be sentenced and spend greater time in jail, and less likely to be released on parole. While most Canadians hold the court system in high regard, Aboriginal people tend to see the courts as a tool of oppression. Aboriginal people do not experience the courts as being accountable to their communities, nor do they see them as resolving disputes between parties. For Aboriginal people, justice can only be obtained through the establishment of alternative dispute resolution processes such as day courts and justices of the peace. These courts would be staffed by Aboriginal people and would provide a suitable compromise, allowing justice to be more equitably distributed. This arrangement would allow Aboriginal people to become more involved in the system, and the participation of elders and laypersons would lend greater legitimacy to the process. And, in the end, their involvement would be more effective in resolving problems in the community (Royal Commission on Aboriginal Peoples, 1996a).

QUALITY OF LIFE

The term "**quality of life**" refers to specific objective factors that affect an Aboriginal person's ability to maintain a lifestyle commensurate with that of other Canadians. This includes such considerations as the availability and quality of housing and the provision of community services such as health care and welfare. We begin with a comparison of income or social assistance for the general Canadian and on-reserve populations.

Social Assistance

Aboriginal people rely upon social assistance more than any other ethno-cultural group in Canada. Participation in social assistance programs is just one more indicator of poverty. The funds provided through social assistance enable Aboriginal people to maintain basic levels of health, safety, and family unity. They provide recipients with food, clothing, and shelter, as well as counselling to enable them to achieve independence and self-sufficiency. In addition to the social assistance program, Aboriginal Affairs also offers welfare services to ensure that Aboriginals who need protection from neglect or who need help with personal problems have access to a variety of services (Canada, 1979b).

The data examined show that this reliance is increasing, even though a variety of economic development projects have been implemented. The extent of social assistance provides a negative indicator for both the quality of life of Aboriginal people and how well the economic programs are working. Table 4.14 shows the number of people (First Nations and the general population) on income or social assistance for 1997 and 2003. In terms of dollars spent, in 1973, about $53 million was spent on social assistance. By 2003, this number had increased to $625 million. The 1997 expenditures for First Nations people were about $400 million. Table 4.14 shows that in 1997, 7 to 10 percent of the general population was receiving social or income assistance. By 2003 this had decreased to between 4 and 7 percent. When we look at the First Nation part of the equation, in 1997 between 31 and 81 percent of the population was receiving assistance. By 2003 these numbers had also decreased but still ranged from 23 to 44 percent. The average annual number of First Nations recipients per month has increased by nearly 30 percent over the past 10 years, and nearly 40 percent of the First Nations people living on reserve are receiving social assistance. This expenditure represents a 30-percent increase over the 1990 level and stands at about 3 percent of the overall total Canadian social assistance budget. In addition, $600 million is allocated for social support services and an additional $225 million is earmarked for Aboriginal welfare services. Child and family services (78 percent) and adult care (22 percent) make up the rest of this program's budget.

In addition to the expenditures for social assistance, in 2003–04, over 700 adult registered Indians were in institutional care, with a cost of over $23 million per year. This represents a ratio of 3.2 per 1000, which has decreased only slightly from 1971, when the ratio was 3.7 per 1000.

The number of Indian children in care in 1966 was 3.4 percent of the total child population (aged 16 and under). Subsequently, there was an increase in the late 1970s, when in-care services peaked at 6.5 percent. Just under 6 percent of Aboriginal children are currently under state care. This represents about 9000 children in care facilities with a cost of well over $100 million—a sevenfold increase since 1970. Even with this increase, provincial agencies provide 22 percent more funding per child than First Nations agencies receive from the federal government. It should also be noted that today, there are more than 27 000 First Nations children in state care (including both federal and provincial). This means that one out of every ten First Nations children is in care, compared to 1 in 200 non–First Nations children.

In summary, social assistance is a far more serious problem for Aboriginal people than for other social groups in our society. Overall, over half of the total Aboriginal

TABLE 4.14	Comparison of Income or Social Assistance Coverage Rates – On-Reserve Population and General Population, 1997 and 2003					
Province/Territory and Canada	1997			2003		
	Total Population at March, 1997	Number of People on IA or SA at March, 1997	Percentage	Total Population at March, 2003	Number of People on IA or SA at March, 2003	Percentage
General Population (excluding on-reserve population)						
Canada	29 819 070	277 900	9.3%	31 543 355	1 745 600	5.5%
British Columbia	3 931 016	321 300	8.1%	4 135 769	180 700	4.3%
Manitoba	1 135 851	79 100	6.9 %	1 159 917	59 900	5.1%
Atlantic	2 373 558	247 300	10.4%	2 342 835	165 800	7.0%
Ontario	11 180 472	1 149 600	10.2%	12 193 256	673 900	5.5%
On-reserve Population						
Canada	369 163	152 746	41.4%	423 631	147 300	34.8%
British Columbia	72 448	22 749	31.4%	80 103	18 009	22.5%
Manitoba	62 554	29 853	47.7%	74 038	32 483	43.9%
Atlantic	15 645	12 634	80.8%	18 420	11 818	64.2%
Ontario	73 109	18 004	24.6%	82 774	18 615	22.5%

Source: National Council of Welfare, 2007. *First Nations, Métis, and Inuit Children and Youth: Time to Act*, Vol. 127, p. 28. Retrieved May 13, 2011, from www.ncw.gc.ca/l.3bd.2t.1ils@-eng.jsp?lid=88.

population received social assistance or welfare payments in 2000. An even more astounding fact is that nearly 90 percent of Indians, at one time in their lives, have received social assistance/social support. These figures compare with 14 percent for non-Aboriginal people. Structural factors have produced the problems that have forced Aboriginal people to become dependent on social assistance, yet most Canadians engage in a form of personal attack, implying or asserting that Aboriginal people themselves are the cause of their need for social assistance. Maintaining that Aboriginal people, as a group, have brought on their own problems draws our attention away from dealing with the structural issues preventing them from fully participating in Canadian society. Neglect remains the form of maltreatment most closely associated with poverty (Assembly of First Nations, 2007).

Environmental Hazards

Aboriginal people are also exposed to severe environmental hazards. Industrial and resource development have polluted water and disrupted fish and game stock for many reserve communities, seriously affecting quality of life. For example, residents of the White Dog and Grassy Narrows reserves in Ontario were found to have 40 to 150 times more mercury in their blood than the average Canadian (Bolaria, 1979). Various environmental disturbances have upset other Aboriginal communities, such as Cluff Lake (uranium pollution), Serpent River (acid discharge), and St. Regis (fluoride pollution). Obviously, Aboriginal lifestyles vary considerably from those of non-Aboriginal people (Ram and Romaniuc, 1984), as they are more likely to harvest and consume local game and plants. In the second diagnostic study of the health of First Nations and Inuit people, researchers found that 60 percent of Inuit children under the age of 15 and 40 percent of Inuit women of childbearing age on Broughton Island, Nunavut, have polychlorinated biphenyl (PCB) levels well above government definition of "tolerable." A similar study in Quebec found that concentrations of PCB in newborn children in Quebec Inuit and the Montagnais were four times higher than the concentrations in Southern Quebec infants. The concentrations of mercury in Quebec and Northwest Territories Inuit were 6 to 14 times higher than the levels in the Southern Quebec newborn population. Another study in the James Bay area showed that although mercury levels exceeding government levels had decreased over the past two decades, they were still higher than government standards in 2002. Today the Tar Sands is under scrutiny for its potential pollution to the land and water in surrounding environs. To date, there has been little systematic data collection to ascertain the health impacts or the cost of such pollution. Nevertheless, many Aboriginal communities across the country have argued, to no avail, that modern technology has negatively affected their quality of life.

Housing

The federal government argues that it has no legal or treaty obligation to provide housing units or to repair existing ones for Aboriginal people. However, it does have a historical commitment to provide housing for Indians, which, so far, it has chosen to continue. With a birth rate double the national average, there is an ever-increasing demand for housing.

To support this activity, the Department of Aboriginal Affairs provides support to First Nations communities through the Capital Facilities and Maintenance Program.

Housing needs for any population are generally measured in terms of affordability, adequacy (condition), and suitability (overcrowding). However, it is to be remembered that most of the housing stock on reserves is owned by the First Nation or by a corporate entity owned or controlled by the First Nation and allocated by the First Nation directly rather than through some pricing or market mechanism. Thus we will only look at the condition and overcrowding indicators.

Overall, just over one-quarter of housing stock on reserves was reported to have no housing deficiencies in 2006 and only required regular maintenance. An additional quarter of the households reported that their dwelling required minor repairs but met other occupancy standards. As such, just over half of the Aboriginal households in First Nations communities are considered acceptable. However, this means that the remaining half is not acceptable in terms of condition (36 percent), overcrowding (22 percent), or both (10 percent) (see Figure 4.3). Moreover, Clatworthy (2007) found that "family doubling" was a common occurrence for on-reserve families. Nearly 12 percent of all Aboriginal family households living on reserve contained more than one family in

FIGURE 4.3	Proportion of Aboriginal and Non-Aboriginal People Living in Overcrowded Housing or in Housing in Need of Major Repairs, 2006

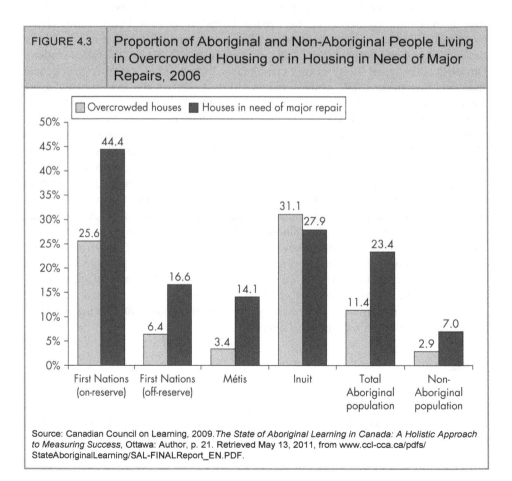

Source: Canadian Council on Learning, 2009. *The State of Aboriginal Learning in Canada: A Holistic Approach to Measuring Success*, Ottawa: Author, p. 21. Retrieved May 13, 2011, from www.ccl-cca.ca/pdfs/ StateAboriginalLearning/SAL-FINALReport_EN.PDF.

2006—particularly in Quebec and the Prairies. The number of Aboriginal homes with more than one person per room is 200 to 300 times that of the overall Canadian population. The average number of Aboriginal persons per dwelling is 3.5, while for all of Canada it is less than 2. The average Canadian dwelling has 7.2 rooms, while the Aboriginal dwelling has 5.8. This overcrowding decreases the lifespan of a house and worsens social and health problems in communities.

Today, about 46 000 (out of a total of 91 600) housing units have been built on reserves under the Indian and Inuit Housing Program, at a cost of well over $250 million in 1999–2000. In addition to this, rural and Aboriginal housing programs have provided $123 million to subsidize housing for Inuit, Métis, and non-status Indians. Data relevant to the growth rate in the number of dwellings in relation to the growth rate of the population shows that between 1983–84 and 1989–90, an average of 3263 new dwelling units per year were built on reserves. In 1991 the number was slightly above 4000. However, since this time the number of new housing units each year has decreased, and by 2001 the number had decreased to fewer than 2000.

During the 2001–2006 period, Canada Mortgage and Housing Corporation built 3544 new housing on reserves, and 4098 renovations were completed during that time. However, Clatworthy (2007) found that an additional 11 000 new units needed to be built just to address the "doubling" issue. Another 5000 needed to be built to replace those housing units no longer habitable. He also found that an additional 25 000 bedrooms needed to be added to the existing stock of housing to address the issue of overcrowding. Finally, he noted that another 25 000 housing units would need to be renovated to acceptable standards. The total cost for addressing these housing issues is estimated at about $3 billion. If the current policy and fiscal commitment is to continue, the above scenario reveals that the housing crisis will not be resolved and in fact will worsen over the next decade. In terms of needed renovations, 28 percent of housing in First Nations communities required major repairs. This is in contrast to 15 percent for Aboriginal people living off reserve and 7 percent for the general Canadian population.

The above figures must also be interpreted in the context of public housing standards. Aboriginal housing units, because of the standards employed by AAND, have a lifespan of 15 to 20 years—less than half the national average lifespan. Thus, even though there has been an increased number of housing units built on reserves, the poor quality of the houses and the increase in the number of people living on the reserves intensifies the competition for good housing. Much of the housing on reserves is provided by the federal government, and because individual title is severely limited, most homes are not owned by individuals but by the band. The band councils "rent" the houses at a break-even point to keep the costs down. As a result, the absence of individual ownership and the lack of validation of home ownership reduce the chances that the occupant will maintain the unit in good repair. Houses on the reserves are built almost exclusively as traditional single-family units, rendering the housing stock less suitable for single people and multigenerational families.

The federal government has not seriously dealt with the problem of housing until recently. A latent function of its policy of reducing the number of available housing units was to force more and more First Nations people to move off the reserve and into the cities. By 2000, the total number of houses on reserves was nearly 80 000 and, of these, only about half were considered "adequate." But in 1996 the government introduced a new housing policy. This new approach gives Aboriginals control of their housing design, construction, and placement. Under this First Nations Innovative Housing Initiative, new housing designs and types of construction—e.g., log houses—are being built in Aboriginal communities. In addition to the $138 million provided annually to support First Nations housing on reserve, Aboriginal Affairs has committed another $220 million to support the 1996 policy. Between 1996 and 2002, the total number of houses on reserve increased by more than 17 percent. During the same period, the number of houses considered to be in adequate condition increased by nearly 25 percent. In addition, the Innovative Housing Fund introduced in 1998 provides $2 million in annual funding for new building technology, alternative house designs, and alternative energy sources. Finally, Aboriginal Affairs provides ministerial loan guarantees and has increased the department's guarantee authority for these housing loans from $1.2 to $1.7 billion. Off the reserve, less than 40 percent of Aboriginals own a home, compared to nearly three-quarters of the non-Aboriginal population. A study of homelessness in 19 urban areas across Canada revealed that over one-quarter of the homeless population was Aboriginal. In the end, core housing needs (i.e., containing at least one dedicated room for each basic need such as cooking, bathing, and sleeping) for Aboriginals is about 25 percent, while for non-Aboriginals it is less than 10 percent.

Infrastructure Services

The number and extent of government services available to Aboriginal people have a considerable impact on their quality of life. A major factor in the provision of services is accessibility by road or rail; without good transportation access, services are difficult and costly to provide. Yet only about one-third of the reserves have year-round road access. Nearly half of all reserves and settlements are accessible only by water. And only 18 percent are accessible by both rail and road.

Over 90 percent of all homes in First Nations communities have electricity. While this may seem high, it still means that 1 out of every 10 homes does not have electricity. However, less than three-quarters of Aboriginal homes have central heating, in contrast to over 90 percent of non-Aboriginal homes. Figure 4.4 presents the quality of the infrastructure services that communities expect to have. It shows that nearly all communities have some form of water accessibility. On the other hand, over 20 percent have inadequate water services, according to Health Canada standards. In addition, over 50 communities have "boil water" conditions. With regard to sewage, 5 percent have none, while an additional 14 percent have inadequate infrastructure. Finally, nearly one third of First Nations communities have no fire protection and an additional 17 percent have inadequate fire protection.

Over the past decade a number of First Nations communities were confronted with water quality issues. In four cases, members were physically removed from the community and placed in a nearby town while the quality of the water was dealt with. A survey by INAC in 2006 revealed that 17 percent of all First Nations communities had water quality issues that required immediate attention. One year later, only two of the communities had been provided with new infrastructure to enhance the water quality. In Nunavut, over one-third of the people claimed that there were times of the year when their water was contaminated.

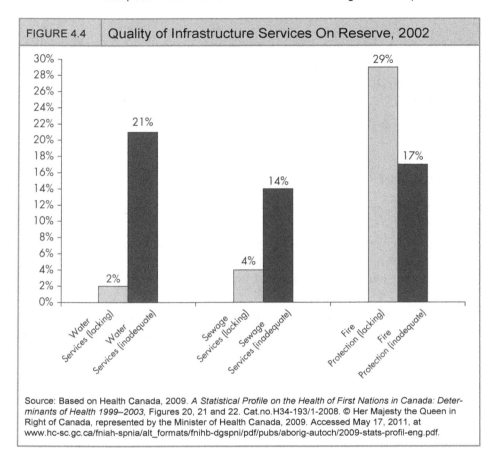

FIGURE 4.4 | Quality of Infrastructure Services On Reserve, 2002

Source: Based on Health Canada, 2009. *A Statistical Profile on the Health of First Nations in Canada: Determinants of Health 1999–2003,* Figures 20, 21 and 22. Cat.no.H34-193/1-2008. © Her Majesty the Queen in Right of Canada, represented by the Minister of Health Canada, 2009. Accessed May 17, 2011, at www.hc-sc.gc.ca/fniah-spnia/alt_formats/fnihb-dgspni/pdf/pubs/aborig-autoch/2009-stats-profil-eng.pdf.

While the infrastructure on reserves is better than it was in the past, when we compare these figures with the overall picture of Canadian infrastructure, we find that Aboriginal dwellings are still far behind when it comes to having basic necessities that most Canadians take for granted.

Summary

- Aboriginal people are marginalized and remain socially and economically at the periphery of Canadian society.
- Historical subjugation and economic displacement of Aboriginal people are a result of government policy and legislation.
- Individual and institutional racism still permeate Canadian society.
- Human rights are enshrined in Canadian legislation but programs to implement policies in relation to Aboriginal people are not evident.
- The social and economic gap between Aboriginal people and the general Canadian population remains wide, and projections suggest that this disparity will increase.

Key Terms

band schools p. 111

dependency ratio p. 94

fertility rate p. 94

Hawthorn Report p. 104

income polarity p. 106

labour force participation
  p. 106

language families p. 97

language p. 97

quality of life p. 120

residential schools p. 110

young population p. 94

Questions for Further Discussion

1. What are the implications for the economy of aging Aboriginal and Canadian populations?

2. What positive impacts has Christianity had on Aboriginal people? Do you think it has had a negative impact? Why or why not?

3. What factors lead to a poorer quality of life for Aboriginal people than for other Canadians?

4. Define and then compare and contrast paternalistic ideology and democratic ideology.

5. If there had been no legal basis for the federal administration of Aboriginal education, which direction do you think the Aboriginal education process would have taken? Explain your answer.

6. What effect has religion had on Aboriginal culture?

7. Why do you think Aboriginal communities have a marriage rate so much higher than the rest of Canada?

CHAPTER 5

Great Strides and New Challenges: City Life and Gender Issues

INTRODUCTION

The title of this chapter may seem an odd pairing of subjects. What is the connection between urbanization and gender issues? There are three answers to that question. First, until 1985, women (and any children they had) who were previously deemed "Indians" were subsequently denied their Indian status if they married a non-Indian male. So, if they were not "Indians," they had no right to live on the reserve nor to obtain services provided to Indians by federal/provincial authorities. Amid such a context, most women moved to cities and began the urbanization process. Second, Aboriginal women are much more educated than Aboriginal men. Yet life on the reserve is patriarchal—it's a "man's world" in terms of power and authority. It is true that there are some women who occupy positions of authority on the reserve, but the number is small. As such, many Aboriginal women find that if they are to use their educational/technical skills, they have to look to the urban centres for work. Third, many Aboriginal women have left the reserve due to housing and family-related reasons. Many are single parents moving with their children because they cannot obtain adequate lodging. Others have left because of violence and abuse. While a small number of Aboriginal women depart for cities each year, the numbers are cumulative. Over the past 50 years, the total number of Aboriginal women who have settled in cities is substantial. The long-term consequence of this trend is that in 2010, more Aboriginal women than men resided in urban areas.

Although *Bill C-31* reversed the legal refutation of "Indian" status for women who "married out," the die was cast. Even though these women and their children were once again considered "Indians" and so were eligible to live on the reserve, most of the reserves now began to revise their band list requirements, making many of these women and their children no longer eligible for band membership. At the same time, many women did not want to return even though they were now redefined as "Indians" since they had good jobs, had developed social networks in their communities, and were able to maintain social networks with their Aboriginal community while living in town. Finally, because housing on the reserve continues to be scarce, living on the reserve is difficult—and this continues to be an issue for women who would like to return. But the decision on the part of Aboriginal people to live in cities does not constitute a rejection of Aboriginal culture. Moreover, what are now large cities in Canada were once historical gathering places for Aboriginal people. As more and more settlers began to take over these gathering places, Aboriginal people were pushed into the margins and later onto reserves that were some distance from these urban centres. As such, it should be understood that many urban centres today are considered part of the traditional "territory" of Aboriginal people (Browne et al., 2009). So the connection between urbanization and gender is complex. While there is a linkage between the two, there are also differences. This chapter will explore the intersection and divergence of the two issues. We begin with a discussion on urbanization and then turn to gender issues.

URBANIZATION

At the beginning of the 20th century, fewer than 5 percent of Aboriginal people lived in urban areas. Nearly 50 years later, in the 1951 Census, just short of 7 percent of the Aboriginal population had taken up residence in cities. However, by 2008, nearly two-thirds of Aboriginal people were living off the reserve or in settlements across Canada. This influx of Aboriginal peoples to the cities is a result of both structural and individual factors. The urban setting, as a permanent residence, is particularly attractive to those who are qualified to actively participate in it. Moreover, there are expectations of prosperity and an enhanced quality of life in the city. However, migration away from the reserve/rural environment is as much a result of "push factors," such as a lack of housing, jobs, and educational opportunities, as it is "pull factors." Aboriginal people decide to leave the reserve or rural way of life when they are forced to by an absence of housing and employment opportunities or by other factors such as domestic violence. A combination of structural and individual factors, then, reflecting various social and cultural conditions, is instrumental in pushing/pulling Aboriginal people off the reserve or rural environment and into the urban context. The decision to return to the reserve is also influenced by these factors (Ablon, 1965; Peters, 2000).

While some First Nations people do succeed in the city, many experience racism, poverty, marginalization, and exclusion (Peters, 2004) and decide to return to the reserve. Others settle into urban life with the intention of returning to the reserve or rural community later. However, evidence suggests that once they settle into the city, few Aboriginals return to their rural roots. Successful immigration to the city requires the ability to find a job and adequate housing, develop successful social networks, and obtain access to cultural activities. Although small numbers have remained in the cities each year, over time the urban population has grown considerably.

As the number of Aboriginal people living in cities has grown, they have fundamentally changed the character of urban areas. With Aboriginals becoming increasingly visible in city life, new relationships between Aboriginals and non-Aboriginals are emerging. While this visibility has been evident for some time in some Western cities, it is now increasingly apparent across the country. Greater visibility is not just due to increasing numbers, but is also a result of the emergence of Aboriginal communities, businesses, institutions, networks, and, in some cases, urban reserves in urban centres. Moreover, members of different Aboriginal groups who meet in cities serve as a communications link for their respective Aboriginal communities in rural areas (Levesque, 2003). As a result, new ties are being forged among different Aboriginal groups as well as between urban and rural Aboriginal communities. The Aboriginal presence in Western urban centres is particularly important, and it is estimated that by the end of the next decade, one-sixth of the labour force population in places such as Winnipeg, Saskatoon, and Regina will be Aboriginal (Mendelson and Battle, 1999).

Despite concerns about the Aboriginal quality of life expressed by various levels of government, there is a paucity of any concrete measures to improve their plight. Since urban Aboriginals are hypermobile and tend to blend into the general population of the urban poor, statistics are particularly difficult to obtain; politicians, as well as academics, tend to concentrate their efforts elsewhere. For example, Norris et al. (2002) observed, in an examination of **mobility** over a span of a decade, that 70 percent of urban Aboriginal residents moved, compared to just under 50 percent of the non-Aboriginal urban population.

As Canada shifted from a rural, agricultural economic system to an urban, industrialized one after WWII, rapid urban growth occurred. As a result, Aboriginal people found themselves migrating to urban centres in larger numbers than before, looking for employment or better services, or simply an escape from the reserve. For example, in Manitoba the urban Aboriginal population jumped over 300 percent between 1966 and 1986. Table 5.1 shows the current picture of **urbanization**.

Overall, between 1996 and 2006, the proportion of the Aboriginal population living on reserves and in rural areas declined from 53 to 47 percent, while there was a commensurate increase of people living in urban areas. Table 5.1 shows that Métis people are the most highly urbanized, with just over two-thirds living in cities—still less than the overall Canadian rate of 80 percent. Inuit are the least urbanized and continue to live in rural areas.

Nearly 80 percent of off-reserve Aboriginal people live in large metropolitan centres. Table 5.2 shows the population size as well as the rate of growth in the Aboriginal population for selected cities between 1951 and 2006. Clearly, the Aboriginal urban population

TABLE 5.1	Urbanization Patterns for Aboriginal People, 2006			
	First Nations	Métis	Inuit	Registered Indian
Total Population	698 025	389 780	50 480	623 780
On Reserve	43.1%	1.1%	0.9%	48.1%
Rural/Non Reserve	12.2%	29.5%	61.5%	11.3%
Urban	44.7%	69.4%	37.6%	40.6%

TABLE 5.2	Growth of Aboriginal and Métis Population in Selected Urban Centres, 1951-2006						
	1951	1971*	1996	2001	2006	Change 2001-06	% of total pop.
Calgary	62	2 265	23 450	21 915	40 310	+46%	2.5
Edmonton	616	4 260	44 150	45 930	52 100	+12	5.1
Halifax	–	–	7 795	8 100	10 210	+21	1.4
Hamilton	493	1 470	11 020	12 200	13 900	+21	1.5
London	133	1 015	8 200	8 200	9 350	+12	1.3
Montreal	296	3 215	6 775	11 275	17 865	+37	0.5
Ottawa-Hull	–	–	6 915	13 915	20 590	+32	1.8
Regina	160	2 860	14 570	15 760	17 105	+8	8.9
Saskatoon	48	1 070	18 160	20 275	21 535	+6	9.3
Toronto	805	2 990	14 205	20 595	26 575	+23	0.5
Vancouver	239	3 000	26 030	37 265	40 310	+8	1.9
Winnipeg	210	4 940	35 150	55 970	68 385	+18	10

* Does not include Inuit.

Source: Adapted from, Government of Canada, *Perspective Canada I* (Ottawa: Queens Printer, 1974), 244; Canadian Metropolitan Areas, *Dimensions*, Statistics Canada, Table 9, 1986; Newhouse and Peters, 2003; INAC, *Registered Indian Population Projections*, 1998-2008, 2000; Siggner & Costa, 2005; Browne, et al., 2009; University of Saskatchewan, 2010.

has experienced rapid growth. The table reveals that in all cases, there has been an increase in Aboriginal people entering cities. It also shows the percentage of the Aboriginal population in each city, ranging from 5 percent in large cities such as Toronto and Montreal to nearly 10 percent in smaller western cities.

URBAN ABORIGINAL PROFILE

The urban Aboriginal population is composed of three major groups—First Nations, Métis, Inuit—with considerable diversity within each. For example, within the category of First Nations, a number of different of groups will be resident in a single city (e.g., Cree, Ojibway, Mohawk, Dene, Blackfoot). As discussed earlier, most urban Aboriginal people are first or second generation and have come to the cities seeking education, work opportunities, and the various amenities and services not available on the reserve. However, for Aboriginal women, an additional reason for moving to cities pertains to housing and family issues. And while very few urban Aboriginals ever move back to their home communities once they leave, nearly all continue to maintain contact and establish a social network with their home community.

The history of Aboriginal urbanization varies by city. Some cities, such as Winnipeg, have had a sizeable Aboriginal population for many years, while other towns like Calgary, Ottawa, and London have only recently had an influx of Aboriginal peoples. As such, the institutional infrastructure in cities varies depending on the size of the Aboriginal population and the length of time it has lived there. Our analysis finds that early Aboriginal migrants to the city were hesitant in establishing permanent residences. In turn they demonstrated considerable circular mobility—moving from the reserve to the city and back again. These mobility cycles were characteristic of pioneers who made the transition from rural to urban centres. However, today there is a core of permanent Aboriginal residents who have acted as the vanguard for new and future immigrants. They provide newcomers with necessary information, access to social networks, and linkages with the home community. Therefore, more recent immigrants to the city are more likely to remain even though they have strong personal linkages or linkages through their parents and grandparents (second generation) on the reserve.

In a major study carried out by the Environics Institute (2010), it was found that most urban Aboriginal people who reside permanently in the city like their city and are satisfied with their current quality of life. This level of satisfaction is constant among Métis, First Nations people, and Inuit and is invariant across social class. At the same time, these individuals have a strong sense of their Aboriginal heritage and exhibit considerable attachment to their Aboriginal group. Overall, they maintain a great reverence for their heritage and express strong Indigenous identity. Long-term residents have become "**bi-cultural**" in that they are able to adapt to the mainstream culture while holding a strong Aboriginal identity. Most urban Aboriginal peoples express a strong sense of pride in their identity and few say that they ever downplay or hide their heritage. Most Aboriginal peoples agree that there is considerable availability of Aboriginal cultural activities—e.g., language, customs, traditions—within the city and, if desired, the option to participate in the cultural activities in their "home" community. However, actual participation in cultural activities is linked to age. Older Aboriginal residents are frequent participants in Aboriginal cultural activities while younger Aboriginal people are less likely to participate. This generational difference has important implications for First Nations communities in urban centres.

The choice of neighbourhood in a city is generally dictated by economic conditions. In other words, people live where they can afford the housing. In addition, establishing a permanent residence is influenced by "chain" migration, where individuals migrating to the city from a particular community will chose their destination in the city based on the location others from the same community have chosen at an earlier time. The end result is the creation of a "community of likeness" within the urban centre. However, economics is a powerful determinant at the outset, and once permanent residence is undertaken, small Aboriginal enclaves form. Maintaining a community of likeness is a result of social networks that emerge. While "family and friends" are the most important factor, a sense of community in the neighbourhood and with those of similar ethnic backgrounds are powerful determinants of connection and belonging. Smaller Aboriginal communities in an urban centre generally reveal that there are extensive and personal networks across the groups and subgroups. Everyone knows everyone, and there are locally recognized leaders within the community. However, as the community increases in size, this sense of intimacy decreases, and diverse and smaller social networks develop within the neighbourhood (e.g., people from Treaty 6 will form enclaves, Dene will know other Dene, and Cree will create social networks with other Cree). Nevertheless, for a variety of activities such as pow wows, rodeos, social events, or political issues, these diverse communities will coalesce and cooperate. The end result is that the networks expand in interlocking grids and, as the individual continues her/his stay in the urban centre, their network of influence and recognition expands. These new linkages are no longer "personal" but functional and important in the economic and political sense. Not surprisingly, most urban Aboriginal people tend to see their city of residence as "home."

We now turn to a more detailed profile of urban Aboriginal people, which will provide insight as to their social and economic integration.

Age/Sex Distribution

The age and sex distribution of urban Aboriginals and non-Aboriginals is quite different, as depicted in Figure 5.1. First, the Aboriginal population in urban areas is young: Half the Aboriginal population now living in urban areas is below the age of 24, considerably more than the 31 percent in this age group for the rest of Canada. This means that in another decade, there will be more than 1 million Aboriginal young people entering the labour market in these urban areas, particularly in Western Canada. Second, the non-Aboriginal urban population is increasingly aging, and a considerable number of older people migrate to urban centres. These different population pyramids reveal potential conflict in policy development and program implementation between the two populations in an urban setting.

As noted above, today nearly 40 percent of the urban Aboriginal population is below the age of 24. The numbers shown in Figure 5.1 support the observation that urban migration is stabilizing and the resident population is aging. When age groups of Aboriginal

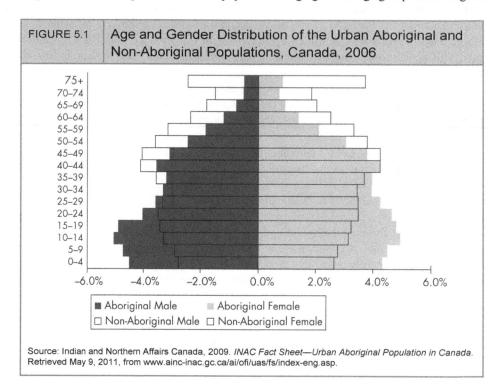

| FIGURE 5.1 | Age and Gender Distribution of the Urban Aboriginal and Non-Aboriginal Populations, Canada, 2006 |

Source: Indian and Northern Affairs Canada, 2009. *INAC Fact Sheet—Urban Aboriginal Population in Canada.* Retrieved May 9, 2011, from www.ainc-inac.gc.ca/ai/ofi/uas/fs/index-eng.asp.

migrants are compared, however, no substantial difference emerges in migration patterns. This suggests that members of all age groups migrate in almost equal numbers to urban centres, although somewhat fewer Aboriginals over age 50 migrate. The high proportion of migrating children under the age of 14 years old shows that many Aboriginal people bring their children with them as they enter the city. At the national level, one-third of all children in the age group 0–14 live in urban centres. An additional 17 percent are aged 15–24. Forty percent of Aboriginals between the ages of 25 to 54 also live in urban centres, while less than 7 percent of those over the age of 55 live in cities (Siggner and Costa, 2005). In comparison, for the non-Aboriginal population, 33 percent of urban inhabitants are under age 25. What is of particular importance is that in most metropolitan areas, Aboriginal children (0–14) account for nearly 40 percent of the Aboriginal population in Western cities.

Health

Assessing the health of urban Aboriginal people requires consideration many factors. For example, life expectancy is a general indicator of health. Frohlich et al. (2006) noted that life expectancy (as of 2001) at birth for men was 67.1 years on reserve and 72.1 years for urban Aboriginals, compared to 76 years for non-Aboriginal men. For women, the figures were: 73.1, 77.7, and 81.5, respectively. Research focusing on Aboriginal women from birth to death shows that they do not have levels of health comparable to other urban Canadian women. The life expectancy for urban Aboriginal women is about five years less than that of non-Aboriginal women living in the city. Other indicators of health show that urban Aboriginal women have a suicide rate eight times that of non-Aboriginal women. Compared to non-Aboriginal women, urban Aboriginal women have higher incidences of diseases such as diabetes, tobacco addiction, and HIV/AIDS. In 1990, Aboriginal women accounted for less than 1 percent of AIDS cases in Canada. Today that number has increased to nearly 10 percent of all cases. And the rate of infection for tuberculosis is 10 times higher for Aboriginal women than for women in the general population in Canada.

Table 5.3 reveals that considerably more urban Aboriginal people are receiving government transfer payments than non-Aboriginal urban people. The percentage of low-income Aboriginals in urban areas is almost twice that of urban non-Aboriginals. The data also show that the percentage of young children living in low-income families is more than twice as high for urban Aboriginal people as for urban non-Aboriginal people.

With regard to the use of traditional healers and medicines, there is little difference between rural and urban Aboriginals. However, urban Aboriginal people have more access to social support, and there is some reason to suspect that they enjoy better mental health than those living on reserves. On the other hand, the levels of homelessness, substance abuse, lack of affordable housing, and deinstitutionalization of patients with mental illness all contribute to the high rates of mental illness among urban Aboriginal peoples (Browne et al., 2009). The Native Women's Association of Canada (2007a) notes that Aboriginal women's health is significantly worse in comparison to that of Aboriginal men.

The number of children in care and the infant mortality rate are additional indicators of health. While Aboriginal children make up about 5 percent of the total child population in Canada, nearly 40 percent of children under government care are Aboriginal. In Vancouver, nearly 70 percent of children under provincial care are First Nations.

TABLE 5.3	Selected Demographic Indicators for Urban Aboriginals and Non-Aboriginals, 2006			
	Urban Area			
	<100 000		>100 000	
Indicator	Aboriginal Identity	non-Aboriginal Identity	Aboriginal Identity	non-Aboriginal Identity
% of pop. Age 15-19 < high school	19%	14%	18%	16%
% of pop Age 25-44 with university degree	7	16	13	33
Unemployment rate	12.7	6.6	10.6	6.1
Average total income (all sources)	26 134	32 331	27 029	37 594
Average employ-ment (full time) Income	41 406	46 204	41 861	54 267
% receiving government transfer payments	16.5	14.3	15.0	9.6
Incidence of low income before tax among "economic families"	25.5	9.2	31.2	13.8
Incidence of low income before tax among unattached individuals	50.1	34.6	58.4	38.7
% of children under age 15 In low-income families	36.2	15.3	44.8	20.5
Lone parent families as a % of all census families	23.0	16.0	24.0	17.0

Source: Adapted from Indian and Northern Affairs Canada, 2009. *INAC Fact Sheet – Urban Aboriginal Population in Canada.* Retrieved May 9, 2011, from www.ainc-inac.gc.ca/ai/ofi/uas/fs/index-eng.asp

Education Levels

While levels of education for off-reserve Aboriginal people are lower than the national average (Hanselmann, 2001), when these figures are compared to those of 1981, school attendance among urban Aboriginal youth has increased substantially. However, non-Aboriginal urban youth are staying in secondary school at higher rates, so the difference between the two groups is becoming wider. When comparing the education levels of on- and off-reserve Aboriginal people, the difference is not significant. In other words, there is no "brain drain" operating in the rural communities. Nevertheless, Table 5.3 illustrates major differences in educational achievement between urban Aboriginals and urban non-Aboriginals. Urban Aboriginals have a greater percentage of young people without a high school education and, conversely, a smaller percentage who hold a university degree.

Involvement in the Labour Force

A number of surveys over the past two decades have been undertaken to assess the labour-force involvement of urban Aboriginals (Stanbury and Fields, 1975; Norris, 2000; Norris et al., 2002; Wotherspoon, 2003; Norris and Jantzen, 2003). All the data show that the unemployment rate for off-reserve Aboriginals is five to six times higher than for non-Aboriginal people living in urban areas. Table 5.3 shows that in 2006, the unemployment rate for urban Aboriginal adults was almost twice as high as that of urban non-Aboriginal adults—11.6 versus 6.4. Not only were unemployment rates higher, but the length of time that Aboriginals have held jobs is also much shorter than that for non-Aboriginal people. Only about one-fifth of the urban Aboriginal population has held jobs for more than a month (Hanselmann, 2001). Unemployment rates for Aboriginals are two to three times that of non-Aboriginals.

Unemployment among off-reserve Aboriginal people is generally the result of a lack of training and a need to attend to family responsibilities. However, Siggner (2001) found that discrimination in employment is also a significant barrier. Because of the low labour-force participation rate, high unemployment, and low educational attainment, the income levels of urban Aboriginal people are very low. Well over half of the Aboriginal people in urban centres had incomes well below the poverty level in 2001, compared with less than one-fourth for the non-Aboriginal population. Hanselmann (2001) reviewed the population aged 15 years and older and found between 40 to 51 percent of urban Aboriginals made less than $10 000 per year, while for non-Aboriginals in the same cities only about 25 percent made less than $10 000. As seen in Table 5.3, on average, Aboriginal people living in small urban areas have an average total income significantly lower than that for urban non-Aboriginals. Table 5.4 reveals that the median employment income for urban Aboriginals is between 60 and 70 percent of the income of non-Aboriginal people.

Because of their difficulty in obtaining employment and their low incomes, many Aboriginal people in urban centres have a lower standard of living than their non-Aboriginal counterparts. Siggner and Costa (2005) show that, while the number of Aboriginal people with employment incomes of $40 000 or more increased by nearly 300 percent between 1980 and 2005, the number of Aboriginals making less than $14 000 grew faster. As a result, their lives require extensive social assistance—e.g., for housing,

TABLE 5.4	Median Employment Income in Constant 2005 Dollars for Aboriginal and Non-Aboriginal Populations in Selected Cities	
	Aboriginal	Non-Aboriginal
Montreal	20 033	25 216
Ottawa-Hull	26 080	30 802
Toronto	26 040	29 990
Sudbury	20 043	25 068
Thunder Bay	18 449	27 598
Winnipeg	16 918	24 796
Regina	16 932	25 556
Saskatoon	15 000	22 953
Calgary	20 061	28 026
Edmonton	17 925	26 026
Vancouver	20 038	27 834

Source: Environics Institute, *2010 Urban Aboriginal People Study*, Toronto; Statistics Canada, 2006. *Aboriginal Peoples in Canada in 2006 – Inuit, Metis and First Nations*; Richards, J and M. Scott, 2006. *Aboriginal Education, Strengthening the Foundations*, Ottawa, Canadian Policy Research Network.

child care, and food. Their lower standard of living also leads to an increased risk of family and social problems and an increased risk of homelessness. Aboriginal people who live in urban centres attempt to utilize more services than those living on reserves. However, because of legal disputes between the federal and provincial governments and the establishment of specific **service organizations**, Aboriginals are not able to gain access to this multitude of services. Their lack of access is also a result of their poor understanding of their rights as Canadians and their unwillingness to press for the services they might need. Consequently, many urban Aboriginal people continue to live in poverty, as they did on the reserve. Jantzen (2003) has carried out an analysis of Métis residing in urban areas, and her work confirms this finding. She concludes that urban Métis—especially those reporting a single Métis origin—are not faring as well as the non-Aboriginal population.

The Justice System

It is well known that Aboriginal people are overrepresented in the criminal justice system, both as victims and offenders. While Aboriginal people make up just over 3 percent of the total Canadian population, they account for nearly one-quarter of the individuals sentenced to custody in the provincial and federal correctional system (Statistics Canada, 2009). This disparity is particularly evident in the Western provinces. For example, while Aboriginal people make up about 10 percent of the population, they account for between 70 to 80 percent of the jail population. Brzozowski et al. (2006) show that Aboriginal people are three times more likely than non-Aboriginal people to be victims of sexual assault, robbery, or physical assault.

In its survey of urban Aboriginals, the Environics Institute (2010) discovered that nearly two-thirds of urban Aboriginal people have had some serious contact with the criminal justice system in their lifetime—e.g., they have been arrested or charged with a crime or have been a witness to a crime. Moreover, their involvement is often from the viewpoint of both victim and witness. Contact with the justice system is directly related to both income and education. Individuals with low incomes (less than $10 000) and low education levels (less than high school graduation) are three times as likely to come into contact with the justice system than those with higher incomes and educational attainments.

More than half of the urban Aboriginals interviewed in the Environics study had little or no confidence in the criminal justice system. A similar study by the Department of Justice in 2010 found that 75 percent of non-Aboriginal Canadians had strong confidence in the criminal justice system. Overall, urban Aboriginal peoples appear to be more than twice as likely as Canadians generally to have low confidence in the criminal justice system. Urban Aboriginal peoples felt that an alternative Aboriginal justice system should be established to deal with Aboriginal people encompassing concepts such as sentencing circles.

In summary, our analysis of urban Aboriginals reveals a profile that is different from non-Aboriginals living in major urban centres. The data confirm that urban Aboriginal people (1) are more likely to have low levels of education, (2) have low labour force participation rates, (3) have higher unemployment rates, (4) have low income levels, (5) have high rates of homelessness and greater housing needs, (6) are overrepresented in the criminal justice system (both as victims and offenders), (7) have poor health status (particularly in areas such as diabetes, HIV and AIDS, suicide, and substance abuse), and (8) are over twice as likely to have lone-parent families and to experience domestic violence. These results portray a sub-population in the urban context that needs special attention as it tries to integrate into the larger social and economic structure of the industrial economy.

URBAN ABORIGINAL STRATEGY

Until the 1980s, governments at all levels did not see urbanization as an issue that required any specific legislation or programs. During the 1990s, the Royal Commission on Aboriginal Peoples had an opportunity to address the plight of urban Aboriginal people, but did not forcefully address the issue (Anderson and Denis, 2003). The Assembly of First Nations has not had an interest in urban issues until recently, and it only represents "registered Indians." Nevertheless, the issue of Aboriginal urbanization has recently been brought to the attention of municipal, provincial, and federal governments by such indirectly related issues as social services, unemployment, and urban crime (Hanselmann and Gibbins, 2002). In short, Aboriginal urbanization has been defined as a "social problem" that needs to be dealt with.

In 1998, the federal government (involving a number of departments, including Human Resources Development Canada, Western Economic Diversification Canada, Health Canada, and Justice Canada) developed a policy to build partnerships in order to address urban Aboriginal needs. They began in 2003 by investing $25 million (later adding an additional $25 million) for a three-year term. Starting with eight partner cities, over the years the project has expanded to include 13 cities, and is slated to end in 2011. This

Urban Aboriginal Strategy Pilot Projects Initiative was formed to develop innovative techniques to integrate Aboriginal people into urban centres. The objectives of the program were to address the needs of Aboriginal people in urban centres, to align federal programs with provincial and municipal programs directed toward Aboriginal people, and to improve the socio-economic conditions of urban Aboriginal people. The actual programs implemented varied by city and ranged from health and employment to the provision of safe water and educational programs (Canada, 2010).

In addition, Canada's Economic Action program has been implemented to promote greater participation by Aboriginal people in the Canadian economy. As part of a pilot project in 2009–2011, the federal government invested $1.4 billion to meet the specific needs of Aboriginal people living in urban and rural areas. A review of the first two years reveals that while considerable funds have been allocated, there is little to show in terms of concrete changes in quality of life for Aboriginal people. While the brief period of time that has elapsed may be one reason for the lack of evident change, it may be that the funds have been directed to "crisis" needs of urban Aboriginal people and have only upheld the status quo without bringing about meaningful change. For example, funding a project on adequate housing simply means that Aboriginal people will find some level of safe housing—a condition that most Canadians take for granted.

For many years there has not been any policy developed to support the urbanization of Aboriginal people. In addition, conflict between federal, provincial, and territorial governments has exacerbated the problem. The jurisdictional tug of war between the different levels of government has resulted in a justification for not developing policy. There has been, and continues to be, a jurisdictional dispute as to which level of government has legislative authority and responsibility for urban Aboriginal people. The federal government is quick to agree that it is responsible for all registered First Nations people who live on reserve or on Crown land. However, the authority and responsibility for other Aboriginal people is subject to disagreement, and the federal government argues that the provinces have a primary (but not exclusive) responsibility for all non-reserve Aboriginal people. The provinces, in turn, have argued that all Aboriginal people are the primary responsibility of the federal government, and that provincial responsibility is limited to serving Aboriginal people as part of the larger provincial population for services controlled by the provinces. The provincial governments have therefore not developed an inclusive policy with regard to urban First Nations people (Hanselmann, 2001). The consequence is a "policy vacuum" that has resulted in urban Aboriginals being ignored (Canada, 1996d: 538).

As Hanselmann (2001) points out, a policy reflects an overarching public written statement that sets out a government's approach to an issue. Unfortunately, there are few government-wide policies with regard to urban Aboriginals. While policies are generally implemented through programs, they may be unique and "one off" in design. Just because there is no policy does not mean there are no programs, however. In fact, this has been one of the problems faced by urban Aboriginals. Various levels of government have funded programs but have no policy to link them to. As a result, within short periods of time, these programs are stopped and other "ad hoc pilot" programs are funded. Hanselmann's work reveals a paucity of provincial and municipal policy with regard to urban Aboriginal integration. He shows that issues regarding Aboriginal urbanization are not systematically being addressed. Rather, as he points out, the responses to the challenges facing urban Aboriginal people are taking place in a "differentiated policy environment" (Hanselmann, 2001: 17). The existing policy environment (disagreement between the federal and provincial governments as to who has primary responsibility for urban Indians) continues to thwart any comprehensive system of policy development with regard to urban Aboriginals. Moreover, his analysis shows that there are major gaps in the policy fields. For example, there are no policies in the areas of childcare and family violence, and only partial coverage for issues such as income support, housing, and human rights. The policies that exist are not well linked to the everyday experiences of urban Aboriginals. For example, housing is a major concern for urban Aboriginals, and yet only half of the cities in Canada have a policy with regard to urban Aboriginals.

Social Organizations and Aboriginal Urbanization

Over the years, various levels of government have established agencies to provide support to Aboriginals entering urban centres in an attempt to encourage Aboriginal people to abandon their reserves and treaty rights, therefore mobilizing them as Canadian citizens but not as "citizens plus" (Canada, 1969; Weaver, 1981). "Citizens plus" refers to the view that, since Aboriginal people were the first inhabitants of Canada, they should be afforded special status and rights. By curtailing services on the reserves, most noticeably in the areas of housing and economic development, the government has tried to push Aboriginal people into the cities. In addition, by transferring the provision of services from the federal to the provincial government and more recently to the Aboriginal communities themselves, the federal government has attempted to reduce its obligations and expenditures.

However, the federal government does not have jurisdiction over many of the social services, particularly education and social welfare, that have been used to expand citizens' rights and to urbanize members of the lower classes. In Canada, these services are generally provided by provincial agencies. While the provincial educational system has made some effort to increase Aboriginal levels of literacy and formal certification, the welfare system has not been expanded to incorporate Aboriginal people into urban society. Although the number of Aboriginal persons on welfare has increased in cities, Aboriginal people generally receive only short-term services relieving temporary problems of urban subsistence (Bol, 2003).

The Transition

Early Aboriginal migrants to cities found few programs and services to help them out. As a result, a series of cyclical movements occurred as these pioneers moved in and out of urban areas. However, once an Aboriginal enclave was established, it led to increased out-migration from the rural regions. Social networks were in place and supported the integration of newcomers. In addition, a variety of service agencies were introduced to temporarily deal with Aboriginal migrants. Nevertheless, Aboriginal people entering the city have usually found the process difficult and problematic. Many find that they must utilize the services of a variety of organizations within in order to remain. Even disregarding social and cultural factors, many Aboriginal people entering urban areas do not have the qualifications necessary to get work, obtain social services, or succeed in school. Most cannot even qualify for employment insurance. Their poverty, combined with their unconventional lifestyles, exposes them to much higher-than-average levels of detention and arrest by the police. In the end, many Aboriginal people take considerable time to successfully adapt to city life. In some cases, they give up and return to their original home.

Because of their unique position, urban Aboriginal people are similar to other foreign-born immigrants in coming into direct contact with service organizations that regulate and monitor social behaviour. Aboriginal people, like some immigrant groups, have consistently posed problems for those organizations in their attempts to establish public order and provide various services. Organizations that attempt to deal with Aboriginal urban problems can be broken down into four categories: public service, acculturating service, accommodating service, and member organizations. Table 5.5 outlines the attributes of each type.

As a citizen, each individual has the right to a basic education, a basic standard of living, and equal treatment before the law. **Public service organizations**, especially education and justice systems, also are important mechanisms for encouraging the participation of individuals in society. For example, educational achievement draws individuals out of their immediate locales and moves them into a socio-economic framework through entry into the labour force. Similarly, the basic requirements of public health and order encourage normative social behaviour. Public service organizations provide a single, specific service, such as justice, education, or welfare, to the general public and are designed to provide certain minimum levels of service. They work within the prevailing

TABLE 5.5	Types of Service Organizations: Values, Composition and Structure
Public Service	These organizations recruit from the general population and provide single services to their clients. They are highly effective in providing their service and have a high probability of placing their clients. Their values as well as their staff represent middle-class white Canada.
Acculturating Service	These organizations are very selective in their recruitment and generally operate on a "sponsorship" basis. Their services offered are "multiple integrated". Acculturative organizations are highly effective and show a high probability of placing their clients. Both their values and staff represent middle-class white Canada.
Accommodating Service	These organizations draw their clients from the general population and provide a single service for their clients. Their organizational effectiveness is low and their ability to place clients is also considered low. Their values reflect an Aboriginal perspective. The ethnic composition of the staff of such an organization is mixed, with some Aboriginal sand some middle class whites.
Member	These organizations provide a single service and are moderately effective in doing so. They draw their clients from the Aboriginal community but have a low probability of successfully placing them. Their values reflect Aboriginal culture and most of their staff is Aboriginal.

Source: Based on W. Reeves, and J. Frideres, (1981). "Government Policy and Indian Urbanization: The Alberta Case," *Canadian Public Policy*, vol. 2:(4)(autumn), 584-595. Table 2, p. 589. http://economics.ca/cgi/jab?journal= cpp&view=v07n4/CPPv07n4p584.pdf.

Canadian system of values and beliefs and are typically staffed by middle-class executives, clerical workers, and members of service-oriented occupations. In Canada, public services have failed to integrate Aboriginal people into urban society. Aboriginal persons who have come into contact with these organizations have tended to become virtually permanent clients, as evidenced by recurrent patterns of detention and arrest, high rates of hospitalization and premature death, and the inability of most Aboriginal people to leave the welfare rolls. In the educational system, where permanent subsistence is not permitted, Aboriginal students tend to drop out before achieving the minimum standards of attainment for success in the labour force. In short, public service organizations do not assist most Aboriginal people to live in the city as competent citizens. Indeed, as currently constituted, these organizations more often present a barrier that denies Aboriginal citizens entry into mainstream urban Canadian life.

A second type of service organization is the **acculturating organization**. Like the public service, acculturating service organizations draw their staff from the middle class and act to promote or maintain the assimilation of Aboriginal people into Euro-Canadian culture. Acculturating service organizations include post-secondary institutions such as colleges and universities, provincial apprenticeship branches, and the Canada Mortgage and Housing Corporation. They usually obtain many, if not most, of their clients through a system of referrals from public service organizations. Whenever possible, they exercise discretion when accepting prospective clients, taking only those who have a good chance of succeeding in their programs. Once accepted, their clients typically do succeed: Formal and informal counselling services, along with other sources of support, minimize drop-out rates. Nevertheless, acculturating service agencies have few Aboriginal clients, as most simply do not have the minimal qualifications necessary to be referred to or accepted into such programs. Furthermore, Aboriginal people have found it difficult to obtain services from these organizations because they have difficulty understanding and coping with non-Aboriginal rules and procedures.

A third type of service organization, the **accommodating organization**, attempts to compensate for the lack of preparedness of Aboriginals in their contact with Euro-Canadian society. These agencies are often funded by public service organizations to deal with problematic clients. For example, the Special Constables Program of the RCMP, the Courtworkers' Program, and the race relations units of municipal police forces all attempt to handle the problems that have arisen among Aboriginal citizens, the public, and the courts. These agencies try to protect the rights of Aboriginal people and, at the same time, render the legal system more efficient. Also, several acculturating service organizations support the work of accommodating service organizations; examples include the Aboriginal counselling and Aboriginal studies programs of various universities.

The ability of an accommodating service organization to actually alter the fate of its clients is extremely limited. These agencies support the work of public and acculturating service organizations and generally operate within a white, middle-class value system. They have managed to attract Aboriginal clients by hiring a greater proportion of Aboriginal staff members and by modifying some operating procedures to reflect their clients' cultural background. However, because funding is short-term and often depends on enrolment figures, this "accommodation" of Aboriginal interests is not entirely altruistic. Programs offered by these organizations usually lack scope and continuity. Accommodating agencies are generally expected to simply direct their clients to existing services provided elsewhere. Indeed, accommodating service organizations are often limited simply to registering, screening, and referring their clients to other organizations. Moreover, they are unable to offer any real assistance to Aboriginal people in their dealings with those other organizations.

Unlike the other three types of service organizations, **member organizations** tend to work against the assimilation of Aboriginal people into mainstream Canadian society. Member organizations represent the interests of Aboriginal people as members of a distinct people. They provide some employment for Aboriginal persons, promote the revitalization of Aboriginal culture, and attempt to provide the broad range of social support necessary to allow people to lead an Aboriginal lifestyle. Some organizations, like provincial Aboriginal associations, advocate Aboriginal economic and political rights. Others, like the Aboriginal friendship centres, promote an Indigenous lifestyle in the cities. These organizations also function to encourage the emergence of an Aboriginal elite that has not been co-opted into the staff of various other types of public service organizations.

Although member organizations successfully provide services to urban Aboriginal people, their effectiveness is weakened by a virtual absence of employment suited to Aboriginal people as Aboriginal people. Member organizations have tried to promote the institutional completeness needed for in-group cohesiveness and solidarity. However, it cannot be achieved without the creation of jobs for their members. To remedy this problem, Aboriginal people need to establish and run their own businesses and organizations. At present, an inability to do this stymies the success of Aboriginal member organizations. Like those who rely on public service organizations, Aboriginal persons who belong to member organizations continue to be excluded and stigmatized by non-Aboriginal, urban society. Unlike the clients of public service organizations, however, Aboriginal people in member organizations are less likely to regard themselves and their fellows as failures (McCaskill, 1981).

How has mainstream society reacted to the inability of public service organizations to help Aboriginal people adapt to urban life? As more and more Aboriginal people moved to the city in the late 1960s, public and acculturating service organizations came under increasing pressure. In coping with this influx, public service organizations experienced a disproportionate decrease in effectiveness and a disproportionate increase in costs. Although schools experienced some problems in assimilating Aboriginal children, the brunt of this problem was felt by the police and courts. Moreover, young Aboriginal people who migrated to the cities lacked the prerequisite skills for employment and were unable to cope in a conventional fashion with the demands of urban society. Frustration and unemployment combined with divergent values produced a style of life that frequently deviated from the social norms and laws in the cities. While greater expenditures on law enforcement increased the number of Aboriginal persons being processed (and reprocessed) in the system, they did not reduce the threat to public order. This simultaneous decrease of effectiveness and increase in costs was underscored by social scientists, who pointed out that nearly half the inmates in provincial jails in the 1960s were Aboriginal.

Managers of acculturative service programs were also faced with escalating costs accompanied by decreased effectiveness. Their programs were sporadic, unevenly implemented, and made little attempt to find standardized solutions to Aboriginal problems. In addition, they were under pressure to "debureaucratize" existing legitimate programs. Acculturating service organizations were also criticized on a different ground. Because Aboriginal people as a group were systematically undercertified, exceedingly few of them enrolled in university, entered unionized occupations, or qualified for credit assistance in purchasing a home or establishing a business. With greater urbanization, Aboriginal people became a more visible minority, demonstrably denied access to many of the avenues to success in Canadian society. Aboriginal member organizations publicly questioned the legitimacy of training programs and assistance agencies that failed to recruit proportionate numbers of Aboriginal people into their publicly funded programs.

Like the public service organizations, then, the acculturative service agencies were faced with a credibility problem: Those Aboriginal people most in need of their services were clearly not receiving them. Both in public and acculturative service organizations, middle-level managers, who were responsible for day-to-day internal administration, funding, personnel, and clientele, felt that some action was necessary. Although the issue of legitimacy did not actually threaten their budgets, it did increase public scrutiny of funding and internal administration, reducing managerial discretion and hindering the management of day-to-day operations.

In order to reach a greater number of Aboriginal people, middle-level management in public and acculturating service organizations began to fund new projects proposed by accommodating service organizations. In some cases, existing Aboriginal member organizations were co-opted to run these programs, including Native counselling services, Native employment transitional services, and Native alcoholism services. In other cases, funding was provided for the formation of new Aboriginal-oriented service organizations.

Whatever their origins, accommodating service organizations tend to enhance the legitimacy of existing service organizations. Accommodating service programs essentially deal with the problem clients of public service organizations, and leave other operations intact. For example, Aboriginal students unable to complete their secondary education in public high schools are referred to "alternative" public schools run by Aboriginal personnel.

By registering, screening, and referring problematic clients, accommodating organizations can forecast or even regulate the number of clients they deal with, and accommodating agencies can tailor specific projects to particular problematic groups. These special programs justify their high costs and provide a rationale by which public service organizations can offer special treatment to—and acculturating service organizations can relax entry and performance standards for—certain preferred groups, such as Aboriginal people. Over the years, as Newhouse (2003) points out, a number of member institutions have been established by urban Aboriginals. However, over time, many of these institutions have ceased to function due to a lack of funding, or they have evolved into accommodating service organizations and are not distinguishable from other, non-Aboriginal accommodating service organizations.

Ironically, accommodating organizations inherit the same problems of legitimacy that plague public and acculturating service organizations. Accommodating organizations are generally small, independent, voluntary associations that undergo major program and staff transformations every few years. Their instability is partly due to the nature of their financial support. They face serious problems establishing a permanent source of funding and, therefore, a clearly defined mandate. Usually their budgets are mostly made up of grants from public service organizations. These grants are generally earmarked for specific projects designed to last for a limited period of time, often one to three years. In addition, they are aimed at protecting the rights of individual clients and do not attempt to address the general problems of Aboriginal people in urban settings. As a result, accommodating service agencies generally offer services for Aboriginals that are far too restricted in focus to adequately address the low quality of life experienced by Aboriginals in the city.

To obtain funding, accommodating organizations orient their programs toward Aboriginal culture in hopes of attracting Aboriginal clients. However, the placement of these clients then becomes problematic. Because non-Aboriginal businesses generally refuse to hire them, Aboriginal people become perpetual clients of these agencies and are locked into a limbo between the reserve and the city. As a result, a large number of them enter accommodating organizations, but few graduate. Also, because the organizations to some extent encourage Aboriginal values and lifestyles, they do not prepare Aboriginal people for white, middle-class society; at best, they produce marginal Aboriginals.

Because the federal and provincial governments desire to provide social services on an equal basis to individual members of the general public, they have been unwilling to address the problems of particular groups or communities. The current political climate exacerbates this problem. At the constitutional level, the provincial government has refused to accept sole legal responsibility for the social support of status Indians off the reserve. To avoid giving even *de facto* recognition to the collective rights of Aboriginal people, these governments have restricted their support of organizations for Aboriginal persons to narrow-range, small-scale, temporary projects. As a result, the precarious status of accommodating agencies undermines their effectiveness. Overly specific short-term programs discourage the regular, full-time participation of Aboriginal people. Moreover, remedial programs are often too narrow to ensure continued Aboriginal participation without a broad range of additional social support to counteract the effects of poverty and unemployment. To obtain this support, accommodating organizations must refer their clients to the system of social services offered by public and acculturating organizations, despite the fact that their own projects often run counter to, and are not integrated with, these social services. Clearly, whatever the efficiency of accommodating organizations under ideal conditions, the absence of wider social support sabotages their effectiveness and undermines what few gains they manage to achieve.

URBAN RESERVES

With increasing numbers of First Nations people living in urban areas, and projections that there will be more to come, there is a push for the creation of **urban reserves**. For these individuals, city life is now an integral attribute of "urban" Indians (Environics, 2010). Moreover, this urban migration was brought about because of an aggressive federal policy started over half a century ago. Prior to the Royal Commission on Aboriginal Peoples, it was agreed by the male-dominated national Aboriginal organizations to downplay issues relating to urban Aboriginal people. This tacit agreement came about for several reasons. First, "urbanization" is generally equated with "assimilation," and it was agreed that this would not add clarity to the issue of land-based issues in non-urban centres. Second, there was an acknowledgement that if there were constitutional amendments concerning Aboriginal people on rural reserves, they would also apply to urban Aboriginals. As a result, urban Aboriginal peoples were not represented at the First Ministers' Conferences on Aboriginal constitutional matters. The long-term impact of these decisions, appropriate as they might have been at the time, has resulted in a dearth of policy with regard to the issue of urban First Nation reserves. Nevertheless, today the *First Nations Commercial and Industrial Development Act* (and subsequent amendments), along with treaty settlements, has allowed First Nations communities to purchase land in urban centres and create urban reserves on which they can establish large-scale commercial and industrial projects.

Aboriginal people now make up a part of the urban landscape and will remain there for a long time. However, rather than assimilating into the larger society, these residents maintain close ties to their communities of origin and desire a quality of life that maintains a distinctive culture as well as one that allows the exercise of self-governance (Environics, 2010). Newhouse and Peters (2003) point out that, for Aboriginal people in the city, maintaining their identity is an essential and self-validating pursuit. Contemporary urban Aboriginal people see their communities in urban centres as real and no different than the rural communities they came from. These residents have a growing interest in self-determination and self-government in cities, and there are attempts to coordinate all levels of government to support their urban communities. This new view sees urban Aboriginals as part of their communities, with goals and needs that they want to attain within an urban landscape (Peters 2001).

Nevertheless, some First Nations people object to the creation of urban reserves on the basis that government will begin to define some existing reserves as "non-viable" and thus move First Nations people to urban peripheries (Quesnel, 2010) under the guise of "urban reserves." Other non-Aboriginal organizations, such as the Canadian Taxpayers Federation, have been vocal opponents of urban reserves. Opponents have charged that urban reserves would create an "uneven playing field" between urban reserve businesses and non-Aboriginal businesses in the area. Aboriginal people argue that such arrangements will in fact provide a "level playing field" that has, up until now, been tipped in favour of the non-Aboriginal businesses. In some cases, municipalities were resistant to the idea because they felt that the intrusion would usurp the city's planning authority, lessen the potential tax base, and create social problems. However, in most cases the strong opposition was mediated by compromise between First Nations communities and the municipality. For example, since reserves do not pay taxes, some First Nations agreed to provide the municipality with an "annual grant" to compensate their lack of tax revenue. In other cities such as Saskatoon and Yorkton, this was not an issue, and city council was very supportive of the creation of urban reserves, arguing that the increased economic activity in the municipality would add to economic development and attract additional investment for the cities.

Wilmont (2003) points out that today there are more than 50 urban reserves in Western Canada, the vast majority in B.C. and Saskatchewan. The context for these reserves is in unsettled treaty agreements from years past. For example, in Manitoba, a Treaty Land Entitlement signed in 1997 provided 20 First Nations communities with nearly 450 000 hectares of land to fulfill the 1871 and 1910 treaties. While much of the land taken thus far has been in northern Manitoba, one First Nations community purchased a 40-hectare area in Winnipeg with the intent of developing it for commercial outlets. Similarly, in Regina, property in the city's north-central area has been purchased by a First Nations group. In both cases, servicing agreements between the First Nation and the city have been agreed upon, but in neither case is the band be required to pay property taxes. With urban reserve status, which has to be approved by Ottawa, band members would be able to buy products on the new property without paying provincial or federal sales tax.

As diverse urban Aboriginal people become an "urban community of interest," they may develop a social organization that "creates" itself so that it spawns specific organizations to each deal with a single policy sector, or they may create a single city-wide body that exercises self-government in a range of policy sectors through a number of different organizations. However, given the diversity of Aboriginal groups in any city, fragmentation of the population may emerge as the various groups compete for limited resources. As such, before such organizations can be created, the diverse groups residing within the cities will need to resolve their differences and engage in collaborative activities. In some cities, such as Winnipeg, there is an impressive array of urban Aboriginal service organizations that are now in the process of developing an integrative structure.

We now turn to a discussion of gender issues in the Aboriginal context. The role of women in Aboriginal society has been pivotal, and in the urban context even more important. They were the pioneers of urbanization and the creators of social networks to help new Aboriginal migrants survive. Through their organizational efforts, they have also promoted **gender equity** and social justice. For example, the Native Women's Association and the Indian Rights for Indian Women organization worked for years to remove section 12(1)(b) from the *Indian Act*. Their efforts were resisted by Aboriginal men who wanted to keep their power and resources via the systematic exclusion of women through their removal from the Indian Registry.

GENDER ISSUES IN ABORIGINAL LIFE

In most Aboriginal societies, women are not only highly regarded and protected, but occupy positions of authority in both secular and religious affairs. Every member of a tribe belongs either through birth or adoption to a clan. Historically, many Aboriginal societies were matrilineal (tracing descent through the female line), characterized by the man moving to the woman's family location after marriage. Other Indigenous communities were matriarchal—societies in which women were actively involved in tribal governance (Abbott, 2003). For example, Leigh (2009) and Allen (1992) point out that prior to European settlement, Aboriginal families were organized communally, non-hierarchically, and without coercive authority. Aboriginal women held unique and influential positions in their societies, held leadership and governing positions, and had the responsibility for adjudicating disputes that arose. Emberley (2001) goes on to note that Aboriginal women were the centre of the circle of life and held spiritual roles as well as decision-making power over the allocation of food and crops. In some Aboriginal societies, women rather than men owned property (e.g., Chippewa, Iroquois). Mohawk female elders held special positions of power, and grandmothers were the only ones who had "almost walked a full circle" (Monture-Angus, 1995: 87). As such, they were the holders of wisdom and power and solely responsible for the discipline of all community members. Lineal descent, inheritance of property, and the hereditary right to public office and trust developed through the female line. In no cases where the clan system had been established were women without property rights (Terrell and Terrell, 1976). Thus, prior to European settlement, Aboriginal women held power, land, and property and were influential in the organization and functions of their communities.

In addition, D'Anglure (2005) points out that gender roles were not linked to biological sex, and men and women could move between perceived gender-specific tasks based on individual preference or ability. In short, sex in pre-colonial Aboriginal society typified "different-but-equal" relations and high status for women in their communities. In societies of hunting and gathering, the distinction between work and home was less evident. As D'Anglure (2005) points out, it was only through industrialization that the production of goods became linked to economics, making the male "breadwinner" the more powerful role. Pre-colonization, concern over "blood lines," adoption, casual sex, and homosexuality were not the basis of stigmatization, as each was incorporated into the social norms and mores of Aboriginal society. "Two spirited" individuals, for example, played special roles in various religious ceremonies. They were accepted as falling within the range of legitimate gender roles and were considered integral to tribal communities. In short, there was a kind of gender fluidity in pre-colonized Aboriginal society that allowed individuals to move between genders.

As colonization took place in Canada, the organization and role of Aboriginal family and gender changed dramatically. As settlers began to migrate, the Aboriginal family was forced to change in both organization and function—aligning it with the conceptualization of settler families. First, families were moved from matrilocal to patrilocal societies, in which "maleness" had higher status and more importance and was embedded with more authority and power. This realignment silenced the voices of Aboriginal women—a condition that many Aboriginal men did not object to, even though in 1906 both Aboriginal men and women were "non-persons" under law (Blair, 2005). The subsequent implementation of the *Indian Act* was the beginning of the formalization of this process and it has held sway until this day. For example, in the early *Indian Act,* Indian women were defined through their relationship to Indian men. As Leigh (2009: 75) points out, in this way, Aboriginal men were recognized as "subjects" in exchange for dispossessing Aboriginal women of their power. The creation of "chief and council" in the *Indian Act* removed women's powers, since only men could stand for election as chief. At the same time, Christianity was being imposed upon Aboriginal society, which meant that sexual practices, homosexuality, and other cultural activities were redefined in such a way that women were again subjugated to a patriarchal system. Other practices, such as the census, also imposed a redefinition of gender in society. The end result was a rooted "maleness" within Aboriginal society that remains in place today and has precipitated what some have called the "gender wars" of the 21st century.

Over time white settler society has controlled the image of the Aboriginal woman, portraying her as the "squaw"—a faceless, immoral, unfeeling, lustful, and dirty person. Aboriginal women have become, in the process, dehumanized. While this stereotype of Aboriginal women has evolved, it persists in the media. And Aboriginal men have come to accept the stereotype and have acted upon it accordingly.

Some researchers note the difficulty Aboriginal men have faced in attempting to deal with the forces of colonization. For example, the attributes of silence and observation are important and useful in hunting and gathering societies, but are not of particular significance in a business setting. Aboriginal women, whose communication and organizational skills are more relevant to non-Aboriginal society, are able to enter the workplace and complete secondary and post-secondary educational pursuits more easily.

Bill C-31 and the McIvor Case

Bill C-31 continues to accelerate what some regard as the extermination policies of Canadian government with regard to Indigeneity. Daniels (1998) notes that from an Aboriginal perspective, the *Bill* is the "Abocide Bill," intended to do away with "legal" Indians and their rights and responsibilities. Moreover, it does not ensure equal treatment of First Nations people, but rather creates a new "caste" system. The *Bill* gives bands the right to define who is on their "band list," with the result that a number of bands have chosen to exclude all individuals (mostly women) who were given "Indian status" as a result of being redefined as "Indian." Unfortunately, the federal government has not challenged these discriminatory requirements. It is estimated that in less than five generations, the number of "legal Indians" will be far less than today, and by the beginning of the next century, few "legal Indians" will remain.

As we saw in Chapter Two, in a civil lawsuit against the federal government, Ms. McIvor argued that *Bill C-31* and the *Indian Act* discriminate between men and women with respect to who is defined as an Indian. As such, it violates the *Charter of Rights*. In 2009 the Court of Appeal for British Columbia found that indeed the registration provisions of the *Indian Act* were unconstitutional and violated the *Charter of Rights*. The Court gave the Government of Canada one year to resolve the issue. In early 2010, the federal government introduced *Bill C-3* (the *Gender Equity in Indian Registration Act*) in order to deal with the findings of the B.C. Court of Appeal.

Specifically, the federal government suggested the following amendment:

> . . . the government proposes to amend the *Indian Act* to accomplish the goal of providing Indian registration under s. 6(2) of the *Indian Act* to the grandchild of a woman: a) who lost status due to marrying a non-Indian, and b) whose child born of that marriage parented the grandchild with a non-Indian after September 4, 1951 (when the "double mother" rule was first included in the Indian Act, as well as any sibling of that grandchild born before September 4, 1951). To accomplish this goal, a new paragraph 6(1)(c1) will be added to the *Indian Act* granting entitlement to registration to any individual: 1) whose mother lost Indian status upon marrying a non-Indian man, 2) whose father is a non-Indian, 3) who was born after the mother lost Indian status but before April 17, 1985, unless the individual's parents married each other prior to that date, 4) and who had a child with a non-Indian on or after September 4, 1951. (INAC, 2010: 2-3)

Thus, the government proposed a solution to First Nations people. The negative response it received was due to several factors. First, Aboriginals argued that there had been no meaningful "consultation" with First Nation peoples with regard to these changes, pointing to the Supreme Court ruling that the Government of Canada has a "duty to consult" any time there are changes that may have an impact on First Nations rights. Instead, the government simply presented the proposed changes and, while noting the objections of the First Nations, clearly did not take them into account. At the end of the day, the above amendment was passed! This case is a good example of meaningful consultation failing to take place.

Second, First Nations women were concerned about the lack of recognition of the historical **discrimination** perpetuated against them. They noted that discrimination against Aboriginal women had been formalized in the *Indian Act* since 1876. The amendment under *Bill C-31* is restricted to grandchildren of women who lost status due to marrying a non-Indian born after September 4, 1951. This assumes that it is only after this date that Aboriginal women began to experience discrimination through the *Indian Act,* failing to take into account the thousands of women (and their descendants) who were denied their Indian status from 1876–1951. Third, the amendment will only apply to grandchildren and not to other matrilineal descendants. Yet descendants of male Indians face no such restrictions! The amendment focuses exclusively on the grandchildren of women who lost status due to marrying a non-Indian born after September 4, 1951. Consequently, it does not remedy the ongoing and past sexual discrimination toward Indian women or matrilineal descendants (Quebec Native Women, 2010).

Aboriginal Women's Organizations

Aboriginal women's associations (member organizations) have existed throughout Aboriginal history. Today they, like other Aboriginal organizations, obtain funding from the government, existing pan-Canadian Aboriginal organizations, and the private sector in order to achieve their mandates. Organizations such as the Native Women's Association and the Congress of Aboriginal People are focused on domestic issues such as domestic violence, governance, and gender equality. The Congress of Aboriginal Peoples is one of the only organizations active on the national or provincial level with respect to urban issues relating to Aboriginal women. For the most part, Aboriginal organizations such as the Friendship Centres have advocated for urban Aboriginal women on a local basis.

Other women's organizations, such as Indigenous Women of the Americas (founded in 1993), have attempted to build links among the Indigenous women of Latin and North America. Their central focus is to ensure that Aboriginal women's contributions are included in the shaping of Canadian society. Other organizations, such as the Métis National Council of Women (organized in 1995) and the Pauktuutit Association (established in 1984), advocate for equity and social improvements for their constituencies. While ostensibly non-political, these organizations have entered the political arena at various times in an attempt to achieve their mandate of equity and social justice for women. In addition to the major national organizations, there are hundreds of regional and local Aboriginal urban organizations. Many are single-focused and provide a specific service—e.g., services for the homeless, businesses, or leadership.

The Economy

The situation of Aboriginal women shows that even though they have higher educational attainments than Aboriginal men, they are less likely to participate in the labour market. And, if they do enter the labour market, they earn less than Aboriginal men and non-Aboriginal women. Low wage rates, part-time work, lack of affordable daycare, and the failure of the legal system to ensure that men pay an appropriate share of family support have contributed to an increasing number of Aboriginal women living in poverty. Aboriginal women are just one group that makes up the increasing feminization of poverty. The growing number of Aboriginal women, specifically lone-parents, migrating to the city has led to a state of social and economic impoverishment (Williams, 1997). The combination of low educational achievement and high unemployment has resulted in great difficulty in coping with city life. Moreover, as women and minority group members, they are exposed to double jeopardy. For example, their average annual income is nearly $10 000 less per year than non-Aboriginal women, who in turn make considerably less than their non-Aboriginal male counterparts. While the proportion of urban Aboriginal children in low-income families decreased from 2001–2006, this number is still twice of that of the general Canadian population (see Table 5.3).

Violence/Abuse

Violence and abuse against Aboriginal women have reached epidemic proportions, and Browne et al. (2009) contend that it will continue at an alarming rate. In 2004, the rate of spousal assault against Aboriginal women by a current or ex-spouse was more than three times higher than that of spousal assault reported by non-Aboriginal women (AFN, 2007). The unequal status of Aboriginal women in Canadian society has resulted in their increased vulnerability to exploitation and violence (Mann, 2005). The forms range from physical to psychological violence and are evident on both regular and episodic bases. Traditionally, anyone who abused their family members would have to account for their behaviour to the community and generally the "abuser" was shunned by the community until he/she apologized and stopped the behaviour. Today, the process has been reversed in that the victims of abuse are now asked to account for their behaviour. As a result, even though three-quarters of Aboriginal women claim to have been physically abused by the time they are 25, few report the abuse and/or seek help.

Aboriginal women report spousal assault at a rate (21 percent) that is three times higher than that for non-Aboriginal women. Research shows that women are, on average, abused 35 times before they leave the relationship and seek help. Aboriginal women only report the most severe and potentially life-threatening forms of violence—e.g., assault, choking, having a gun or knife used against them, or being sexually assaulted—and this rate (54 percent) has been consistent for the past decade; yet for non-Aboriginal women, the rate of severe violence has decreased to nearly 35 percent. Overall homicide rates for Aboriginal women are about eight times the rate for non-Aboriginal women. Non-spousal violence is much higher on the reserve than off (AFN, 2007).

These startling statistics are a result of Aboriginal women's economic and social marginalization; a history of colonial government policies, including residential schools; and a legal system that dispossessed Indian women who married outside their community (Mann, 2005). Poverty and the use of alcohol and drugs have also contributed to spousal and non-spousal violence against Aboriginal women.

Family

Fertility rates are much higher for Aboriginal women (2.6 percent) than for non-Aboriginal women (1.5 percent). In addition, Aboriginal women are twice as likely as non-Aboriginal women to be lone parents (19 versus 8 percent). Nearly one-quarter of registered Indian children live in single-mother families, compared to 14 percent of non-Aboriginal children. Aboriginal women aged 15–24 are more than three times as likely to be single mothers than the general population in that age group. There are more women among the Aboriginal homeless population than are found in the non-Aboriginal population. And well over one-third of the Aboriginal homeless population is female, compared to just over one-quarter of the non-Aboriginal homeless population. While there are a number of personal factors that cause Aboriginal women to become homeless, including violence, abuse, and out-marriage, there also are structural factors such as shortage of housing in First Nations communities, lack of affordable housing in urban centres, and deinstitutionalization of women without adequate supports. Finally, it should be noted that Aboriginal women with children have high rates of "relative" homelessness—i.e., they pay a large proportion of their income for housing and/or live in substandard or unsafe housing.

Urban Aboriginal women have high rates of mobility and high rates of housing instability. In addition, they are disproportionately found in the inner city cores; accounting for nearly one-third of this population. Given their marginal status in the city, they are particularly vulnerable to related problems and risks such as sexual exploitation and violence. Overall, there is an increasing proportion of First Nations children being born in urban as compared to rural areas. A greater percentage of Aboriginal mothers are living in urban areas in the lowest quintile of neighbourhoods, as compared to non-Aboriginal mothers (40 versus 23 percent). And 57 percent of urban Aboriginal mothers are unmarried, compared to 64 percent of rural Aboriginal mothers. However, there are no significant differences between rural and urban neonatal and post-neonatal death rates. Overall, urban Aboriginal women and their children live in poverty and are exposed to high risks of violence in urban areas although the death rates for young children are the same as for those living on a reserve.

Complexity surrounding Aboriginal families arises because of additional rules and regulations implemented by the government. Prior to 1985, children with unreported fathers were allowed to register as Indian provided that their registration was not successfully protested within 12 months of birth. In practice, however, Indian and Northern Affairs Canada consistently challenged any attempt by the mother to register these children and thus they were never registered. This speaks volumes about the relationship between theory and practice. After the passage of *Bill C-31*, a child's entitlement to registration became based on the registration characteristics of the child's parents (Clatworthy, 2003). The sexism of this policy is clear in terms of how "**indigeneity**" is transmitted. When a child's father is not reported, the child's registration entitlement can only be based on the mother's entitlement. If the father is unreported and the mother is registered as a section 6(1) Indian, the child is allowed to be registered as a 6(2). In the case where the mother is registered as a 6(2) Indian and the father is unreported, the child cannot be registered.

In order for a child to be registered as a "status" Indian, a birth certificate must be signed by both the mother and the father. In short, the federal government requires that they be able to assess the "Indian" status of both parents. If the father has not signed the birth certificate, the assumption is that the father is not Indian and thus the child will then take on the status of 6(2) or not be allowed to register. This cost-saving measure has resulted in over nearly 40 000 people being denied their "Indian" status between 1985 and 2000. The impact will be compounded further over the next generation.

Why would an Aboriginal woman not report the father of her child? Although as some would argue it is no business of the federal government, women might not want to acknowledge paternity for many reasons. They might be concerned with personal safety, they might want to maintain privacy in a small community, or they might wish to avoid custody claims. It is also possible that a mother may have had to leave her community to give birth and thus the father was unable to sign the birth certificate. If the father wished to sign the birth certificate later on, it would involve a lengthy bureaucratic process and a fee would be charged. In other cases, the mother might voluntarily choose not to state the paternity of her child or the father might refuse to sign the certificate (Mann, 2005a). In some First Nations communities, children are not named at birth; names are given by the grandparents at some later ceremony. Thus, for purposes of birth registration, a child is initially registered as "unnamed" and remains that on the official birth registry unless an amendment is subsequently filed. As such, the father is, for legal purposes, unnamed, which means the father's birth registration has to be amended in order to have his identity included on the birth registration.

The incidence of unknown paternity cases is very high in some regions of the country. In Manitoba, Saskatchewan, and the Northwest Territories, more than one in every four children born to women registered under section 6(1) have unstated fathers. Overall, it is estimated that nearly 28 percent of all Aboriginal births have an unstated father (Clatworthy, 2003). From the point of view of Aboriginal Affairs, the fewer the number of individuals identified as "Indian," the less liability. As such, the department has not tried to resolve the problem, although the McIvor case has recently forced them to address it.

Justice

Current data reveal that Aboriginal women experience discrimination within the justice system, as seen by their disproportionate rate of being charged, prosecuted, and convicted of crimes and by their overrepresentation in prison. Some researchers note that the number of missing Aboriginal women and the lack of concern shown by police reflects the low value placed on the lives of Aboriginal women. For example, in the *Voice of Our Sisters in Spirit*, it was found that over 500 cases of missing and/or murdered Aboriginal women and girls in Canada had taken place since 1970. Data from the past four decades show that the trend is not on the decline.

Aboriginal women are overrepresented in jails (more so than Aboriginal men), particularly in maximum-security prisons. Currently, they make up nearly half of all maximum-security federally-sentenced women, a third of the medium-security population, and a quarter of the minimum-security prison population. Overall, Aboriginal women make up 2 percent of the women in Canada, but nearly one-third of women in federal prisons. There also is a higher proportion of Aboriginal women serving federal sentences in prison (as opposed to being released on bail or placed under supervision in the community) than there is for non-Aboriginal women. From 1996–2002, there was an increase of nearly 40 percent of Aboriginal women sentenced to federal institutions, while the increase for the same time period for Aboriginal men was 5 percent. Moreover, the lack of appropriate facilities has additional effects on Aboriginal women in jail. First, the facilities are not near Aboriginal communities, meaning that the women are deprived of links with their family and/or community. Second, many Aboriginal women are housed in men's federal prisons and psychiatric wards. Third, funding for women's jails is less than for men's jails. Finally, the Native Women's Association of Canada (2007) points out that once Aboriginal women are placed in jail, they experience discrimination within the correctional facilities from other inmates and staff.

Overall, the overrepresentation of Aboriginal women in the criminal justice system is linked to their victimization, which in turn is rooted in colonization and perpetuated by current legal practices. For example, Aboriginal women may be charged for reacting to abuse or when they are contending with the poor social and economic conditions brought about by double discrimination. First Nations women face both racism and sexism not just as Aboriginals and not just as women, but as Aboriginal women, commonly objectified and dehumanized in racial and sexual stereotypes that create a high risk of physical, emotional, and sexual violence. In 2004, the Canadian Human Rights Commission noted that systemic human rights problems remain, particularly with regards to Aboriginal women. This systemic discrimination may in part contribute to the growing numbers of federally incarcerated Aboriginal women.

Matrimonial Property

Canadians have little knowledge of the laws and conditions that affect Aboriginal women. For example, Aboriginal women have fewer rights regarding their **matrimonial property** when a marriage ends than do people living off-reserve. This has not gone unnoticed by Aboriginal women's groups or other groups such as the National Action Committee on the Status of Women. What are the differences? First, there is bias in favour of men receiving certificates of possession for the matrimonial home. That means that 9 out of 10 certificates of possession are issued to men. It is not because women are not allowed to hold such certificates; rather, it is because when they are told they cannot, they do not know they are legally entitled to do so. In this respect, their position mirrors that of many Canadians who are not aware of their legal rights. Once the certificate is issued, a court cannot change who holds it. In practical terms, this means that when a marriage ends in divorce, the man holds on to the matrimonial property and the wife or partner has to leave. Given the shortage of housing on reserves for the past 50 years, in practical terms this means the wife must find housing off the reserve. Even when the certificate of possession is jointly held by both partners, there are no enforceable rules about who gets to stay in the matrimonial home. The result is "force makes right," and the partner that can garner the most support and force will take over the house. If the certificate is held by an abusive partner, then the rest of the family has to leave and he/she can remain in the matrimonial home. There is no legal remedy available to the abused spouse for obtaining possession of the matrimonial home for her/himself. In fact, the Supreme Court of Canada supported this in a 1986 decision that said that as a result of the *Indian Act*, a woman cannot possess or apply for a one-half interest in on-reserve property for which her husband holds a certificate of possession. In other words, there is no way this dispute can be dealt with by provincial law. This dynamic has been taking place since the advent of the *Indian Act*. Why has this situation not been remedied? The answer is self-evident. People in power do not want to give it up.

Rights of Aboriginal Women

When English common law was introduced in Canada, it excluded all women from property ownership and from holding positions of power. Moreover, women were defined as property, owned first by their fathers and then by their husbands. While these laws have since been repealed for non-Aboriginal women, exemplified by the famous 1930 "Persons" case, the same is not true for some Aboriginal women today.

Prior to the implementation of *Bill C-31*, a number of Aboriginal women attempted to force the Canadian government to rethink its position on the *Indian Act* and its discriminatory provisions. Four Aboriginal women were at the forefront of actively challenging the federal government. All had married a non-Indian male and, some time later, their husbands had died or divorced them. All wanted to return to their Aboriginal communities but were denied because under the *Indian Act* they had lost, irrevocably, their Indian status through "out-marriage." Ms. Lavell's and Bedard's challenges (as discussed in Chapter 2) were implemented in the early 1970s and were rejected, and the Ontario

County Court found that Ms. Lavell's status had actually improved such that throughout marriage, she was elevated from "Indian" to "white" and thus was not discriminated against by the *Indian Act*. These two cases eventually went to the Supreme Court of Canada, which found that since "registration" was a prerequisite to Indian status, there was no inequality of treatment between Indian men and women. Thus their claims were denied and Section 12(1)(b) was ruled not discriminatory.

Mrs. Two Axe Early also married a non-Indian, and when he died, she wanted to return to her Aboriginal community. She was able to move back to the reserve only because her daughter was an "Indian" and she could live with her. Nevertheless, Mrs. Two Axe Early was a pioneer in challenging the *Indian Act*'s provision that removed Indian status.

Perhaps the most famous case is that of Sandra Lovelace, in which she challenged the provisions of the *Indian Act* regarding marriage rules. In 1977, Ms. Lovelace started a legal challenge to Section 12 of the *Indian Act*, just as others had done. However, unlike the others, she chose to ignore the domestic Canadian courts and approached the United Nations for help. The Canadian government responded by arguing that the *Indian Act* was designed to protect the "Indian minority" (which was allowed under Section 27 of the *International Covenant*) and that a definition of "Indian" was needed because of their special rights. Moreover, they argued that traditionally Aboriginal communities were patrilineal (which is not true) and family relationships were taken into account for determining legal claims. They asserted that in the farming communities of the 19th century, reserve land was felt to be more threatened by non-Indian men than non-Indian women. If non-Indian men marrying Indian women would become Indians, in short order the reserve lands would be taken over by whites who had been given Indian status. The federal government argued this rationale was still valid in 1977.

Three years later, the United Nations found that given the fact that Ms. Lovelace, after her failed marriage, had no right to live in the community where she grew up, Canada had violated Article 27, which states that ". . . in states which ethnic, religious or linguistic minorities exist, persons belonging to such minorities shall not be denied the right, in community with other members of their group to enjoy their own culture, to profess and practice their own religion or to use their own language." Since Ms. Lovelace was a member of a minority (the government didn't argue against this point), her rights were interfered with because of Section 12 of the *Indian Act*. The Canadian Constitution was amended in 1982 and the *Charter of Rights and Freedoms* became part of Canadian constitutional law. The Charter prohibits discrimination on the basis of race, national or ethnic origin, colour, religion, age, sex, or mental or physical disability. However, it would not be until 1985 that *Bill C-31* was implemented and that Section 12 of the *Indian Act* was repealed (Wong, 2002).

Adding to the complexity of Aboriginal women's rights, Section 67 of the *Canadian Human Rights Act* shields actions of the Minister of Aboriginal Affairs and Northern Development from court scrutiny, even if such actions are in violation of human rights laws. While many have argued that the temporary measure (Section 67) should be removed from the *Human Rights Act*, thus far it remains. In summary, the application of the *Canadian Human Rights Act* is based on whether the *Indian Act* explicitly provides authority to the band council or AAND to undertake the action complained of. If the answer is yes, then Section 67 exempts any further review by the tribunal. If the answer is no, then the tribunal may begin investigation and make a judgment after reviewing all of the facts (Blair, 2005).

Prior to 1951, Indian women were eligible for election to chief and band council. However, under Section 75 of the *Charter of Rights and Freedoms*, this right was removed. Section 75 noted that only band members could be elected councillors; as such, non-status Indian women could not stand for election. In an important case (*Goodswimmer*) the courts were asked to rule on a situation where the elected chief was married to a band member and lived on the reserve but was not a status Indian or a band member. She had been elected to the position of chief. Was she entitled to that position? The courts ruled that if she ran for councillor, she had to be a band member, but if she ran for chief, she did not have to be Indian or belong to the band—and thus her election as chief was upheld.

Summary

- Aboriginal people are becoming more urbanized over time.
- Increased urbanization brings changes in values, norms, and ideology.
- The organizational structures of service-providing organizations maintain marginal status for Aboriginal peoples in the city.
- Aboriginal women find themselves in a "war of the sexes."
- Aboriginal women have adapted to life in urban centres better than Aboriginal men.

Key Terms

accommodating organization p. 143

acculturating organization p. 143

bi-cultural p. 133

discrimination p. 150

gender equity p. 148

indigeneity p. 153

matrimonial property p. 155

member organizations p. 144

public service organizations p. 142

mobility p. 131

service organizations p. 138

urbanization p. 131

urban reserves p. 146

Questions for Further Discussion

1. Compare Aboriginal challenges and non-Aboriginal challenges when faced with living in a major urban centre.
2. What structural, social, and cultural factors affect Aboriginal urbanization?
3. What are the positive and negative consequences of urbanization for Aboriginal people?
4. Why has Aboriginal institutional completeness failed to develop in the urban centres?
5. What is meant by the "gender wars" in Aboriginal communities?
6. Why are urban reserves so contentious?
7. What is the demographic significance of *Bill C-31* and the McIvor case?
8. How are the rights of Aboriginal women different than those for Aboriginal men?

CHAPTER 6

David and Goliath: Aboriginal Organizations and the AAND

LEARNING OBJECTIVES

After reading this chapter you should be able to:

1. Explain the details of the Indian and Inuit Affairs Program.

2. Understand the organizational structure of the Department of Aboriginal Affairs and Northern Development.

3. Outline the goal of devolution.

4. Discuss some of the recommendations made by the Royal Commission that involved political action.

5. Describe Aboriginal reaction to the Royal Commission Report.

6. Assess the history of Aboriginal organizations.

7. Identify the four broad categories of Aboriginal organizations.

INTRODUCTION

Confronting the bureaucratic behemoth that is the Department of Aboriginal Affairs and Northern Development (AAND) is no small challenge for Aboriginal communities. Overseeing most aspects of the daily lives of Aboriginal people, the federal government looms large in the affairs of Native communities, although the provincial governments also play a role. As we will discuss, AAND is one of the largest and most complex federal agencies in this country. Over time, it has grown in size and complexity as new mandates and issues have developed. Traditionally, AAND dealt with Aboriginal peoples on the reserves and their lands. However, with the introduction of *Bill C-31*, the outcomes of several court cases, and the changing demography of Aboriginal people, AAND has increasingly dealt with urban, education, and housing issues well outside the confines of rural communities or reserves. At the same time, Aboriginal people have come to realize that they need to take action to challenge AAND's policies, as well as its tendency to implement change unilaterally Their task is to develop appropriate strategies to convince the federal government to instead pursue policies advocated by Aboriginal people. However, given that the Aboriginal population is spread widely across Canada and constitutes less than 4 percent of the total population, it has become a Herculean task. Compounding this difficulty is the fact that Aboriginal organizations are highly dependent upon the federal government since much of their funding comes from this source.

We will begin by outlining the mandate of AAND, along with its structure and activities over the past 30 years. Then we will provide a brief history of the emergence of Aboriginal organizations in Canadian society. Finally, we will examine the major pan-Canadian organization—the Assembly of First Nations (AFN).

One of the most important challenges to government is to ensure stability and to manage change successfully. The administration of Aboriginal affairs is no exception. The British Indian Department, the first department set up by the Crown in America, was established in 1755 to handle Aboriginal issues. However, 1830 is considered the true beginning of an ordered system of civilian Aboriginal administration in Canada. Thirty years later, responsibility for Aboriginal affairs was transferred by the British government to the government of the province of Canada. At the time of Confederation, the *British North American Act*, now called the *Constitution Act, 1867*, gave the new Canadian federal government legislative authority over "Indians and lands reserved for Indians." In 1939, a Supreme Court decision allowed this bureau to also deal with Inuit affairs, even though the Inuit were not considered Indians as defined by the *Indian Act*. Over the years, Aboriginal affairs have been under the control of many different government departments —even Agriculture and Citizenship, at one time. It was snot until the 1960s that the current structure was put into place.

Aboriginal organizations have emerged to restrain, react, and modify the actions of AAND. These organizations have had the unenviable task of trying to deal with this large and complex federal government unit. Nevertheless, Aboriginal organizations have, on occasion, been able to bring about change in the policies and programs enunciated by AAND; for example, the retraction of the federal government's *White Paper* in 1969. The tension between the two has sometimes spilled over to the courts. Surprisingly, as discussed in earlier chapters, the courts have sometimes sided with the position of the Aboriginal peoples. However, the ratio of court decisions in favour of Aboriginal positions compared to those in favour of the government stands at about 1:20. Moreover, the many Aboriginal organizations that exist today lack sufficient funding, possess inadequate organizational resources and political clout, and have different goals and objectives with the result that presenting a unified response on a specific issue is sometimes a challenge. For example, on the issue of women's rights, there is a significant split between Aboriginal women's organizations and the Assembly of First Nations.

ABORIGINAL AFFAIRS AND NORTHERN DEVELOPMENT

The Department of Aboriginal Affairs and Northern Development (or **AAND**)— sometimes referred to by its previous names, the Department of Indian and Northern Affairs Canada (INAC) or the earlier Department of Indian Affairs and Northern Development (DIAND)—comprises a complex number of programs, sectors, branches, directorates, and secretariats. The Department is responsible for two mandates, Indian and Inuit Affairs and Northern Development, which together support Canada's Aboriginal and northern peoples in the pursuit of healthy and sustainable communities and broader economic and social development. The Inuit Relations Secretariat was established in 2005 to serve as a focal point for Inuit issues and to advocate for the inclusion of Inuit-specific concerns in federal program and policy development. This Secretariat reports to the Deputy Minister and is the principal liaison with national and regional Inuit organizations.

This makes AAND the lead federal department for two-fifths of Canada's land mass, with a direct role in the political and economic development of the territories and significant responsibilities for resource, land, and environmental management. In the North, the territorial governments generally provide the majority of programs and services to all northerners, including Aboriginal people.

Both mandates also include an international dimension: AAND is actively engaged in international Indigenous and circumpolar activities involving Aboriginal and northern organizations, states, and international organizations.

Under Indian and Inuit Affairs, AAND negotiates comprehensive and specific land claims and self-government agreements on behalf of the Government of Canada; oversees implementation of claim settlements; delivers provincial-type services such as education, housing, community infrastructure, and social support to Status Indians on reserves; manages land; and executes other regulatory duties under the *Indian Act*.

In recent years, the Department's responsibilities for the planning and coordination of government-wide activities relating to Aboriginal and northern priorities have been expanded, including, in particular, AAND's new role in Aboriginal economic development activities, and in the development of the government's Northern Strategy. Over the planning period, there will be a further expansion of AAND's government-wide policy development activities relating to Aboriginal and northern priorities.

Within the Department, the **Indian and Inuit Affairs Program** architecture has five sectors that have been created to deal specifically with Aboriginal people—government, people, land, economy, and the North. All of these units are identified in Figure 6.1 to illustrate the size and complexity of the program. And it should be noted at the outset that the size and complexity of the organization's structure have certain implications for how it operates.

Furthermore, these branches, directorates, and secretariats are not the only federal agencies that deal with Aboriginal people. For example, Citizenship and Immigration Canada, the Department of Justice, Industry Canada, and Health Canada all have units within their departments that have Aboriginal people as part of their mandate. In addition, there are many other areas in both the federal and provincial governments—e.g., revenue, corporate affairs—that deal with Aboriginal people. Hence, the scope and complexity of the structure of government involved with Aboriginal issues should be clear to the reader. The attendant problems of coordination and delivery are great indeed. It should come as no surprise, then, that there is a great deal of overlap, confusion, and tension among and between the many organizations that deal with Aboriginal people. Likewise, it should be clear that Aboriginal people find this complex web of uncoordinated organizations difficult to contend with. Finally, the lack of answerability of such a structure should also be clear. It is almost impossible to attribute blame to a specific individual or unit, and unsuccessful initiatives cannot be clearly traced to any single unit. In short, accountability is not possible under such a structure—a point that the Auditor General's office has made for many years.

AAND is responsible for all federal policies and programs concerning Canadian registered Indians and Inuit; it also administers the Northwest Territories, Nunavut, and Yukon. Moreover, it includes the **Office of the Federal Interlocutor** for Métis and non-status Indians. The Office of the Federal Interlocutor is derived from an Executive order

FIGURE 6.1	Indian and Northern Affairs Canada—Program Activity Architecture

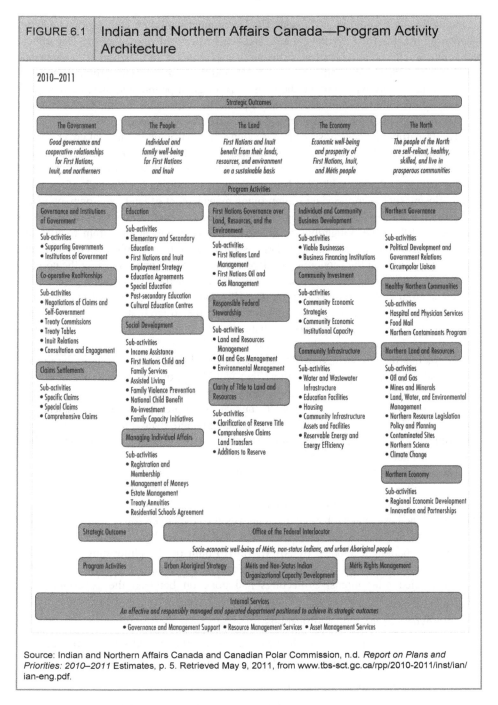

Source: Indian and Northern Affairs Canada and Canadian Polar Commission, n.d. *Report on Plans and Priorities: 2010–2011* Estimates, p. 5. Retrieved May 9, 2011, from www.tbs-sct.gc.ca/rpp/2010-2011/inst/ian/ian-eng.pdf.

giving the minister the power to strengthen the government's relationship with various Aboriginal organizations—specifically those Aboriginal people who do not live on reserves and are not registered Indians. Overall, AAND administers over 50 separate acts, encompassing every region in Canada. The Department's mission is to facilitate a better quality of life for First Nations, Inuit, and northerners. In doing so, the Department collaborates with other federal departments and provincial and territorial governments, identifies both short-term and long-term goals, and then puts in place programs and services that ostensibly will improve the lives of Aboriginal people and increase their self-sufficiency. In summary, this department is primarily responsible for the Government of Canada meeting the legal commitments it makes to Aboriginal people.

The Department's current strategic directions were based on the federal government's philosophy and action plan outlined in the 1998 document *Gathering Strength—Canada's Aboriginal Action Plan*. The actions to be taken by the Department were based on transforming relations with First Nations through supporting healthy and safe communities; closing socio-economic gaps; improving management of land, environment, water, and natural resources; and honouring responsibilities and commitments. Specific actions included fulfilling the obligations of the federal government arising from treaties, the *Indian Act*, and other legislation; negotiating settlements in respect of claims to Aboriginal rights; and supporting the economic development of the North and protecting the northern environment, including Arctic seas. Its mandate also includes coordinating settlement implementation and continuing to promote self-reliance, establishing and implementing new funding arrangements with Aboriginal communities to facilitate their education, and assessing existing program delivery mechanisms and related organizational structures to establish Aboriginal control and community self-sufficiency.

Over a quarter-century ago the Department decided to play a new role in the lives of Aboriginal people through "**devolution**" that would support Aboriginals in developing healthy, sustainable communities and in achieving their economic and social aspirations. This change to the role of an "enabler" and an advocate for initiatives launched by Aboriginal people has been difficult to implement and even more difficult for the Department to accept. This new identity stands in stark contrast to the previously held role of controller and regulator of Aboriginal issues.

The then Department of Indian and Northern Affairs argued that its mandate was derived from the Canadian Constitution as well as from the many pieces of federal legislation and regulations assigning responsibility for Aboriginal issues to its department. Yet there was a tacit acceptance that the mandate would change over time as the courts continued to resolve issues between Aboriginal people and the federal government.

The new paradigm adopted by AAND (2010) built on the philosophy and assumptions evident in the document *Gathering Strength* and is designed to achieve goals that were identified after intensive meetings had gone on between the government and Aboriginal people. Specifically, the Department now sees its "raison d'être" as:

improving educational qualifications;

supporting new strategies to achieve effective governance and self-governance;

empowering Aboriginal people and protecting those most vulnerable;

resolving outstanding land claims; and

supporting sustainable economic development for Aboriginal peoples.

In an attempt to achieve these goals, the Department shifted more decision making to Aboriginal communities (specifically First Nations communities), attempted to remove barriers to economic growth, and tried to develop better housing, education, and social services in order to respond to local needs. Finally, it hopes to achieve better management of First Nations lands and monies and to protect the special relationship that exists between the federal government and Aboriginal peoples. In short, the Department is trying to strengthen Aboriginal governance, reduce the socio-economic gap, and encourage healthy communities.

As discussed earlier, AAND is not the only organization that funds activities related to Aboriginal people. Nevertheless, the Department has certain outputs that directly impinge upon Aboriginal people, and this "operational circle" represents activities over which the Department has direct control—e.g., funding, monitoring, policy. However, the Department is equally cognizant that because many other agencies (e.g., Health Canada) also include Aboriginals in their mandates, it needs to develop partnerships with these organizations and engage in collaborative actions. These partnerships may be with other government departments or agencies, with First Nations, or with the private sector. Unfortunately this collaboration has not generally been successful, although there are some "best practices" that typify this type of thinking (e.g., the Mushuau Innu Relocation Agreement and the Labrador Innu Comprehensive Healing Strategy). Finally, AAND has taken an even broader perspective in adopting a "global circle" of influence. This describes both the existing conditions that affect strategic outcomes as well as desired changes. Although these conditions are beyond the Department's direct influence, they are still an important focus, as they affect First Nations people in the long term.

Structure and Activities of AAND

AAND traditionally has been highly centralized, with its headquarters in Ottawa. It is responsible for policy development, resource allocation, and planning for First Nations and Inuit through a variety of methods—for example, direct service delivery, grants, and loans. However, since the late 1970s, when a policy of devolution was introduced, the 10 regional offices—one in each territory, one for the Atlantic provinces, and one in each of the remaining provinces—have begun to develop their own programs. These programs have emerged from the structures serving specific districts within each region (except in Manitoba). Thus, the districts have become influential, except in Alberta, where control is retained in the regional office, and of course in Manitoba. The complexity of the operations should be apparent.

At the same time, AAND also supports Aboriginals in their quest to preserve and develop their culture. Support is channelled through three streams. First, financial assistance is given to bands, councils, or non-profit corporations that support Aboriginal heritage. Second, a cultural development program supports Aboriginal artists. Third, community social services provide advice and guidance to band councils, their staff, and community service organizations.

AAND policies, objectives, priorities, and programs are established by senior executives and then passed down and back up the bureaucratic ladder. Budgets must be developed for each program and approved by Parliament. Most of the budget of AAND (74 percent) is nondiscretionary; that is, it is set aside for specific items and is non-transferable to other activities. However, as the year proceeds, AAND usually requests additional funds to cover the costs of unanticipated events, such as floods, fires, and destruction of infrastructure.

Today about 17 percent of the total number of employees of AAND are of Aboriginal ancestry. However, Aboriginal workers in the Department have not yet gained access to policy-setting positions; only 4 percent of the Aboriginals employed AAND are at the senior- and middle-management levels. The largest proportion—30 percent—is at the operational level, primarily involved in teaching. Less than 12 percent of AAND employees have been with the Department for more than 15 years and it is this group ("the old guard") that has almost total control over policy development and implementation.

The Cost of AAND

The government of Canada operates more than 100 programs directed in whole or part toward Aboriginal people. The cost of these programs is well in excess of $12 billion (see Table 6.1) and is directed toward a number of different activities. The beneficiaries of these programs—Indians, Inuit, Métis, and non-status Indians—add up to about a million people. However, as indicated in Table 6.1, AAND is not the only federal agency that provides services for Aboriginals.

Table 6.2 identifies federal expenditures for Aboriginals as just under $8 billion dollars in 2009-2010. Over two thirds of the total budget directed toward Aboriginal people is covered by AAND, with Health Canada being the second largest contributor.

TABLE 6.1	Approximate Federal Expenditures for Aboriginal Peoples[1]							
	Expenditures by Department[2] ($ Millions)				Federal Departments			
Year	INAC	NHW	EIC	CMHC	ISTC	SS	Other	Total
1975-76	587	74	-	3	26	13	-	703
1980-81	1134	155	57	58	44	23	4	1475
1985-86	1990	341	159	156	15	53	22	2736
1990-91	3081	578	152	199	85	45	22	4162
1991-92	3412	639	200	240	79	62	42	4674
1992-93	3647	706	200	272	76	51	89	5041
2003-04	5471	1682	337	307	40	69	1905	9811
2004-05	5832	1705	417[3]	370	39	-	2406	10769
2008-09	6268	2010	478	392	45	-	2896	12089

Note:
1. Federal departments and agencies with Aboriginal programs include Indian and Northern Affairs Canada (now AAND); Health and Welfare Canada; Employment and Immigration Canada; Canada Mortgage and Housing Corporation; Industry, Science and Technology Canada; Secretary of State; Solicitor General; Fisheries and Oceans; Public Service Commission; Justice; and National Defence. Data are from annual reports of the respective departments.
2. 1991-92 and 1992-93 figures are from Main Estimates. Figures include spending on Aboriginal employment equity programs, but do not include spending on programs available to all Canadians, such as Old Age Security and Unemployment Insurance. Data are from annual reports of respective departments.
3. This represents a combination of Health and Welfare as well as Human Resources and Skill Development.

TABLE 6.2	Budgets for Federal Programs Directed to Aboriginal Peoples (Millions)				
	1993-94	2003-04	2009-10	% of INAC(09-10)	% of Total (03-04)
Indian and Northern Affairs Canada (INAC)					
Self-government	18.3	137	641	8	2
Claims	70.9	673	829	11	8
Economic Development	98	152	218	3	2
Lands, Revenues, and Trusts	140.3	119	112	2	1
Education	903.3	1431	1705	22	16
Social Development	816.3	1194	1458	19	13
Capital Facilities	665.1	1027	1327	17	12
Band Management	269.4	377	30	1	4
Northern Affairs	572.4	133	324	4	2
Office of the Federal Interlocutor	–	–	40	1	
Other (includes internal service)	92.9	902	1030	13	10
Subtotal (amount/percentage)	3647	6145	7714	101	70

In 1975, federal expenditures on Aboriginal programs represented 2.1 percent of overall federal expenditures (excluding expenditures on public debt). By 2008, this had increased to 4.8 percent of the federal budget. Overall, federal spending during this time grew 7 percent, while spending on Aboriginals increased at a rate of about 10.4 percent annually. Spending for AAND from 2009 onward reveals some projected reductions in expenditures. These decreased amounts reflect the government's cap on increases for AAND as well as reductions on treaty and claims payments that were established years previously and are now coming to an end.

Nearly all federal expenditures flow through four main routes. **Quasi-statutory programs** receive 40 percent of the total budget. These programs are directed toward First Nations people living on reserves, and they reflect the legal obligations of Canada through the *Indian Act, Constitution Act, 1982*, and other legal directives implemented over the past two centuries. Basic services (36 percent) include expenditures on schools, community infrastructure, health, housing, and local government. The third category of expenditures is land claims. While this program only made up 3 percent of the total budget a decade ago, it has increased substantially as the backlog of claims has been settled (15 percent). The fourth avenue is through **"discretionary" funds** that are allocated during the year on an "as needed" basis through supplementary estimates (e.g., relocation, safe drinking water, housing, residential schools settlements). Table 6.3 compares funding allocated for Aboriginal peoples by federal agency over a 10-year period. Table 6.4 illustrates the expenditures on voted and statutory expenditures for AAND from 2008–2010. Nearly one-quarter of the AAND budget is set, and Parliament has no vote on these items. However, the remainder of the budget is annually voted on. This reveals the extent of control that government has over AAND expenditures and the allocation of those monies to various activities.

TABLE 6.3	Funding Allocated for Aboriginal Peoples by Federal Agency, 1993–2004 (in Millions of Dollars)		
Other Government Departments/Agencies	1993-94	2003-04	% of total (03-04)
Health Canada	706.4	1682	19
Canada Mortgage & Housing	271.8	307	3
Fisheries & Oceans	8.0	164	2
Solicitor General	44.7	84	1
Justice	9.7	13	–
National Defence	4.3	8	–
Secretary of State (Heritage)	51.3	69	1
Human Resources	200	337	4
Industry	76	40	–
Correctional Services	–	28	–
Indian Residential Schools and Resolution Canada	–	58	1
Natural Resources	–	17	–
Privy Council Office	–	15	–
Subtotal	1372.2	2822	31

On a per capita basis, the data show a steady increase over the past quarter century. In 1981, the per capita cost of operating the then INAC was $5678. By 1993 it was well in excess of $12 000—a 54 percent increase, although it subsequently decreased to just over $9300 in 2004, partially a result of the increase in the number of Aboriginal people. As noted earlier, AAND covers two-thirds of all Aboriginal expenditures. See Figure 6.2 for the allocation of its budget. The actual programs and services delivered to Aboriginal people vary by group and location. Some are provided directly by the Indian and Inuit Affairs Program, while others come from territorial governments that are, in turn, reimbursed for their costs. Aboriginals living on reserves deal directly with the federal government. On the other hand, off-reserve Aboriginals face a complicated pattern of eligibility for government services. The federal government takes the position that off-reserve Aboriginals should avail themselves of provincial services, while the provinces argue that registered Indians, no matter where they live, are a federal responsibility. Sometimes proof of residence is required (e.g., proof of having lived 12 months off the reserve) before provinces consider registered Indians eligible for provincial services.

FEDERAL EXPENDITURES: A COMPARISON

Courchene and Powell (1992) attempted to estimate the dollar value of federal spending on registered Indians living on the reserve. Overall, they found that on-reserve Indians received about $9300 per capita per year. If administrative costs were added to this figure, the value increased to $10 100. If we compare this value with the contemporary

TABLE 6.4	Voted and Statutory Items Displayed in the Main Estimates		
		\$ millions	
Vote # or Statutory Item (S)	Truncated Vote or Statutory Wording	2008–09 Main Estimates	2009–10 Main Estimates
Indian and Northern Affairs Canada			
1	Operating expenditures	665.4	937.7
5	Capital expenditures	22.7	44.4
10	Grants and contributions	5314.9	5657.9
15	Payments to Canada Post Corporation	27.6	27.6
20	Office of the Federal Interlocutor for Métis and Non-Status Indians – Operating expenditures	5.3	9.0
25	Office of the Federal Interlocutor for Métis and Non-Status Indians – Contributions	21.4	29.9
(S)	Contributions to employee benefit plans	52.4	61.1
(S)	Minister of Indian Affairs and Northern Development – Salary and car allowance	0.1	0.1
(S)	Grants to Aboriginal organizations designated to receive claim settlement payments pursuant to Comprehensive Land Claim Settlement Acts	74.3	65.5
(S)	Grant to the Nunatsiavut Government for the implementation of the Labrador Inuit Land Claims Agreement pursuant to the *Labrador Inuit Land Claims Agreement Act*	18.0	18.0
(S)	Liabilities in respect of loan guarantees made to Indians for Housing and Economic Development	2.0	2.0
(S)	Payments to comprehensive claim beneficiaries in compensation for resource royalties	1.5	1.5
(S)	Indian Annuities Treaty payments	1.4	1.4
(S)	Grassy Narrows and Islington Bands Mercury Disability Board	–	–
	Total budgetary	6207.0	6856.1
L30	Loans to Native claimants	25.9	47.4
L35	Loans to First Nations in British Columbia for the purpose of supporting their participation in the British Columbia Treaty Commission Process	34.6	30.4
	Total non-budgetary	60.5	77.8
	Total	6267.5	6933.9
Canadian Polar Commission			
40	Program expenditures	0.9	0.9
(S)	Contributions to employee benefit plans	0.1	0.1
	Total	1.0	1.0

Due to rounding, figures may not add to totals shown.

Source: "Voted and Statutory Items Displayed in the Main Estimates." In Report on Plans and Priorities: Indian and Northern Affairs Canada and Canadian Polar Commission, 2009-2010. Ottawa: Indian and Northern Affairs Canada, 2010, p. 14. www.tbs-sct.gc.ca/rpp/2009-2010/inst/ian/ian00-eng.asp. Reproduced with the permission of the Minister of Public Works and Government Services Canada, 2011.

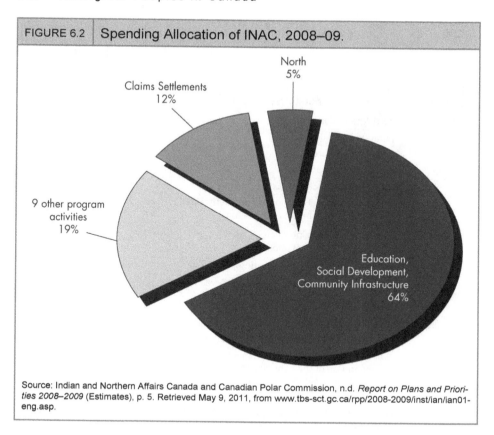

FIGURE 6.2 | Spending Allocation of INAC, 2008–09.

North
5%

Claims Settlements
12%

9 other program
activities
19%

Education,
Social Development,
Community Infrastructure
64%

Source: Indian and Northern Affairs Canada and Canadian Polar Commission, n.d. *Report on Plans and Priorities 2008–2009* (Estimates), p. 5. Retrieved May 9, 2011, from www.tbs-sct.gc.ca/rpp/2008-2009/inst/ian/ian01-eng.asp.

total provincial expenditures per capita, the overall expenditure for all Canadians was $10 500, although this value varied by province, with a low of $9700 in Newfoundland and Labrador and a high of $11 700 in Nova Scotia. This suggests that on a per capita basis, Indians are receiving expenditures similar to other Canadians. While the numbers have changed in the past decade, a similar pattern exists today.

However, Aboriginals argue that, because of their inferior position in Canadian society, the government needs to increase its expenditures to "catch up" for past inequities. For confirmation of this view, the **Royal Commission on Aboriginal Peoples** recommended that additional expenditures be allocated to Aboriginal people in order for them to shed their low socio-economic status.

It should be noted that services provided to Aboriginals far exceed the federal government's constitutional and legislative responsibility. Many programs and services, such as housing, have been implemented as a strategy to lessen Aboriginal poverty and distress. While some programs have produced positive results, many have been dismal failures—both in the short and the long term.

In the early 1980s nearly 60 percent of Indian Affairs's expenditures were made through contribution arrangements to Indian bands or various Aboriginal organizations. In turn, these groups provided specific services as outlined in the contract or agreement. As the new "devolution" policy was implemented, more and more of the budget was managed by First Nation communities. In addition to the allocation of funds, there have been major changes in the distribution of those funds. In the early 1960s over half of the budget was used to meet operating expenses, while the rest was evenly split between the other two categories—capital and grants and contributions. By 2010, however, operating expenditures accounted for only 14 percent of the budget, while capital expenditures on additions and betterments had decreased to 4 percent. At the same time, expenditures on grants and contributions had increased substantially and made up nearly 83 percent of the total budget (see Table 6.4). This reallocation continues and suggests a wide-scale transfer of the administrative costs of AAND programs to provincial governments.

The actual spending patterns of the Indian and Inuit Affairs Program also have substantially changed in recent years. In the early 1960s approximately 45 percent of the budget was spent on education, but by 1990 that number had decreased to 33 percent. Today it represents 26 percent. Other activities funded by the Indian and Inuit Affairs Program also show changes in fiscal priorities. Community affairs accounted for about 43.1 percent of the budget in 1970 but decreased to 24 percent in 2000. Economic development, previously a low priority ranging from between 6 and 9 percent of the total budget, has recently been identified as a high priority for Indian Affairs. However, the data show that in the 2003–04 planning estimates, it only accounted for less than 3 percent of the budget. Indian Affairs argues that funding in other areas such as capital facilities and social development will lead to an increase in economic development. Moreover, they note that, with the introduction of new Aboriginal economic programs, private–public partnerships will result, with greater leveraging abilities and thus greater economic impact.

In 1967 the Indian and Inuit Affairs Program accounted for 1.06 percent of the government's total budget. This figure peaked at 1.74 percent in 1972–73 before it was reduced to 1.7 percent in 1980, and in 1987 it stood at about 1.6 percent. It has slowly increased since this time, so that by 2003 the federal expenditures on Aboriginal programs represented 4.1 percent of the federal budget. In 1965, the Indian and Inuit Affairs Program was allocated about one-half of the total Indian and Northern Affairs Canada budget. This proportion increased to nearly 75 percent in 1969 and today constitutes 83 percent of the total AAND budget.

OPERATIONS OF AAND

The program architecture of AAND is outlined in Figure 6.3, with approximately 75 percent of its employees delivering more than 500 distinct services in 10 regions across the country. There are 10 major sectors in the Department: Economic Development and Special Initiatives, Policy and Strategic Direction, Lands and Trust Services, Claims and Indian Government, Northern Affairs, Corporate Services, Socio-Economic Policy and Programming, Legal Services Support, Federal Interlocutor, and Office of the Corporate Secretariat. This structure shows that each sector of AAND communicates directly to the deputy minister, while no formal linkages exist among the units. However, informal communication goes on between the various units on a routine basis in an attempt to keep each sector informed of other activities being carried out in the Department.

The Department administers the statutory requirements defined in the *Indian Act*, including the registration of Indian people, the deployment of reserve lands and other resources, and the regulation of band elections. It also attempts to ensure that the federal

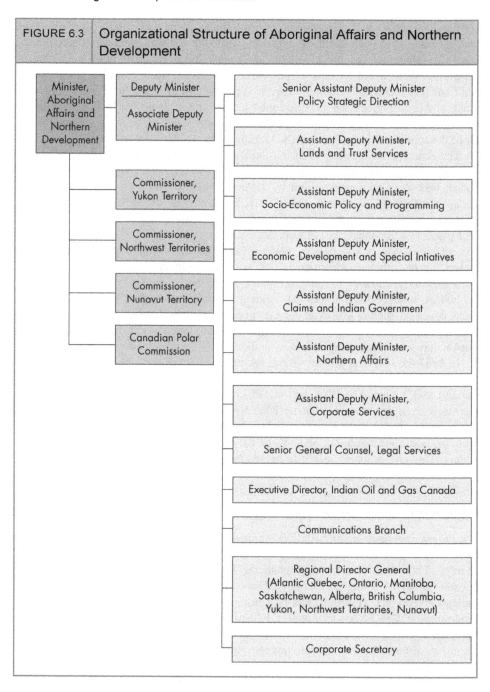

FIGURE 6.3 | Organizational Structure of Aboriginal Affairs and Northern Development

government's lawful obligations to registered Indians and Inuit under the *Indian Act* and the treaties are fulfilled. Overall, the Department provides a wide range of services of a federal, provincial, and municipal nature to Aboriginal people. In meeting its responsibilities, the Indian and Inuit Affairs Program works closely with other federal departments and agencies such as Health Canada and Justice Canada. In keeping with the principle of self-development, the Department attempts to assist and support Aboriginals in achieving their cultural, educational, and social aspirations. In addition, the agency tries to promote the economic and community development needs of Aboriginals and to ensure that Canada's constitutional and statutory obligations and responsibilities to Aboriginals are fulfilled.

We now present a brief overview of each of the functions carried out by AAND as well as the goals and objectives of each unit.

Economic Development

In 2008, the federal government established a new framework for Aboriginal economic development. This new program was aligned with the overall economic policy published in the government's *Advantage Canada: Building a Strong Economy for Canadians.* In 2009, Canada's Economic Action Plan introduced $1.4 billion over the following two years to meet specific needs of Aboriginal people and communities in a number of areas such as education, health care, housing, skill development, clean water, and employment. However, at the end of 2011, this funding was scheduled to end. As usual, new pilot programs are to be initiated. This lack of continuity and interconnectedness means that new projects do not build upon completed ones nor do they integrate into future programs. Each of the programs is a "stand alone" project that does not leverage other funding or fit into a larger vision.

Policy and Strategic Direction

This unit oversees all of the other branches in the department to ensure that policies from within Indian Affairs as well as from other departments in the federal government that are developed for Aboriginal people are consistent and aligned. It also develops long-range goals and objectives for its own department. It carries out both internal and external environmental scans, such population projections, to assess the political, legal, social, and technological changes that are taking place within Canada and globally.

Lands and Trust Services

This sector is supposed to administer the *Indian Act* and the Crown regulatory mechanisms that have been established over the years. It has recently been reshaped as a facilitator of change necessary for First Nations so they can take on greater responsibility and control over their lives. At the same time, it is a delivery agent of programs, services, and policies. From an operations perspective, it is divided into three interdependent branches that manage 21 business lines: the Registration, Revenues, and Band Governance Branch; the Lands and Environment Branch; and the Policy, Partnership and Coordination Branch.

The Registration, Revenues, and Band Governance Branch is responsible for elections, maintenance of Indian registration and lists, bylaws, Indian monies, estates, and transfer of control of membership, to mention just a few of their activities. The Indian registry administers about 3 million hectares of land and processes some 100 000 transactions per year, including birth and death certificates. The trust fund managed over $3.4 billion in

2005, with revenues of $1.9 billion and disbursements of well over $1 billion. Recently this unit has come under scrutiny by the federal Auditor General, who points out that First Nations are not getting the land to which they are entitled. She notes, for example, that since 1994 only 12 percent of the land allocated to First Nations in Manitoba and Saskatchewan by the courts or through negotiation has actually been handed over to them.

The Lands and Environment Branch is responsible for First Nations land management initiatives, natural resources (forestry and minerals), land management, surveys, and land registration, as well as all forms of environmental protection and remediation activities. Over the past 10 years, this directorate has added 220 000 hectares of land to the total existing reserve land base in Canada (now at 2 846 000 hectares), an area roughly half the size of Nova Scotia. This branch also provides bands and Indian organizations with advisory, technical, and other support to deal with environmental problems.

Finally, the Policy, Partnership and Coordination Branch acts as a facilitator of change necessary for First Nations to assume greater responsibility and control over their lands and governance systems. It also acts as a catalyst for legislative reform and an agent for change and devolution.

It should be noted that these three branches maintain linkages with other federal and arm's-length organizations. In addition to the implementation of the **Canadian Aboriginal Economic Development Strategy**, Lands and Trust Services also works in the area of Aboriginal taxation and in the administration of the *Indian Oil and Gas Act*. Indian Oil and Gas Canada's mandate is to identify, administer, and tender for permit or lease Indian petroleum and natural gas rights on behalf of Indian bands. The Indian Taxation Advisory Board was created in the Economic Development Sector (as a result of *Bill C-115*, the 1988 amendment to the *Indian Act*) to consider new taxation bylaws. For example, the board granted bands broad powers to tax interests in Indian lands. The Indian Taxation Advisory Board, which used to be part of Indian Affairs, is now an arm's-length agency that deals with taxation-based issues in First Nations and maintains extensive linkages with Lands and Trust Services. It also links with Indian Oil and Gas Canada to facilitate the development of fossil-fuel–based resource harvesting.

The Department has been admonished for its role in administrating Indian funds and land. Recently the courts have awarded individuals and bands damages or other redress because AAND has not carried out proper administrative procedures. For example, the Musquean band of British Columbia (*Guerin v. the Queen*, 1984) brought a breach of trust suit against the Crown. The federal government had not carried out the terms of a lease requested by the Indians and did not inform them of this breach. Almost a decade after the suit was launched, the Supreme Court ruled that a breach of trust had indeed occurred and found in favour of the First Nations community. This ruling overturned a federal Court of Appeal decision that had overturned the original judges' decision. The importance of the ruling lies in the judges' statement that the band had a pre-existing right to its traditional lands and that the Crown had breached a fiduciary obligation to the band. This decision forced the government to clarify its role when negotiating with third parties over Indian land, as well as to obtain informed consent from the band on whose behalf it is acting.

For nearly a decade, lawyer J. O'Reilly represented the Samson Cree in an attempt to take "Indian monies" out of *Indian Act* control and give them to an independent trust for the use of First Nations. In 2005, the court ruled in favour of the transfer of all the Samson money (which had been held by the federal government since 1892) to an independent trust, known as the Kisoniyaminaw Heritage Trust. While the government initially agreed with the decision, it appealed in 2006. By 2009 the case had been accepted by the Supreme Court of Canada, which disagreed with the lower court decision. In the end, the Supreme Court ruled that AAND (then INAC) had the right to control Indian monies and had not breached a fiduciary obligation to the band, and the Aboriginal communities had to accept the policies outlined and practiced by AAND.

Claims and Indian Government

This sector manages the negotiations, settlement, and implementation of land claims agreements, as well as special claims settlements and self-government arrangements. Within this sector, four branches have been created: Comprehensive Claims, Specific Claims, Implementation, and Self-Government.

The Comprehensive Claims Branch represents Canada in all negotiations of comprehensive land claims with Aboriginal groups. This branch (also known as the modern-day treaties branch) has the responsibility to negotiate the settlement of land claims and to ensure that Aboriginal people are protected. Its primary goal is to provide a clear and long-lasting definition of rights to lands and resources for Aboriginals and other Canadians. It is also responsible for ensuring that settlements provide economic opportunity for Aboriginal groups, that settlements respect the fundamental rights and freedoms of Canadians, and that the interests of the general public are respected.

Through the Specific Claims Branch, the Claims and Indian Government Sector undertakes the assessment of specific claims submitted by Indian bands and conducts negotiations on behalf of the government. The assessment process entails determining whether the federal government has breached legal obligations to a band and compensating the band if so.

The Indian Specific Claims Commission was created in 1985 to conduct an impartial inquiry when a First Nations claim is rejected by the minister of AAND. It provides for mediation and facilitation services, if appropriate, in an attempt to resolve the dispute. In 2004, the commission worked on more than 60 inquiries and mediation efforts with a total budget of $6.3 million. However, the government is not mandated to abide by the commission's ruling. In 2003 a new claims resolution centre was established, although it has yet to come into force. As the centre takes on the role of resolving Aboriginal claims, the Indian Specific Claims Commission will be phased out of existence.

The Implementation Branch monitors and manages the implementation of comprehensive land claims and self-government agreements. This branch also provides policy support and expertise where specific claims agreements are being settled. It ensures that what the parties agree to is in fact carried out. There are two steps to this process. The first is the development of an implementation plan, while the second phase is the monitoring and management of actual implementation activities. Today, parties to a land claim and/or self-government agreement must negotiate a plan, which becomes an integral part of the overall agreement. This plan identifies what must be done to put the agreement into effect, who will be responsible for which implementation activity, and how and when these activities will be undertaken.

The fourth branch of the sector is Self-Government. Self-Government agreements identify arrangements for Aboriginal groups to govern their internal affairs and assume greater responsibility and control over the decision-making that affects their communities. Because Aboriginal groups have different needs, the federal government has recognized that there is no single model of self-government for all negotiations. As such, self-government arrangements take many forms based on the diverse historical, cultural, political, and economic circumstances of the Aboriginal groups, regions, and communities involved.

Northern Affairs

The Northern Affairs sector assists the social, cultural, political, and economic development of Yukon, Nunavut, and the Northwest Territories, and, while not specifically directed toward Aboriginal people, it does place particular emphasis on the needs of northern Aboriginal peoples. The program operates directly and indirectly through the governments of the three territories. It also is responsible for the Polar Commission.

The Northern Affairs sector's activities, as they relate to Aboriginals, focus on the settlement of land claims, establishing cooperative mechanisms to support economic development, and the enhancement of Arctic sovereignty and circumpolar cooperation. The Constitutional Development and Strategic Planning Branch, the Natural Resources and Economic Development Branch, and the Comprehensive Claims Branch make up the focus of this program. The first branch's goal is to establish transfer programs resembling provincial programs for territorial governments, thus encouraging the development of northern political institutions and diversification of the economy as well as reinforcing Canadians' sovereignty. The Natural Resources and Economic Development branch has myriad functions, ranging from the Biological Division—which focuses on the management of wildlife—to carrying out the responsibilities of the North American Air Defence Modernization Project.

Corporate Services and Legal Services

This unit within AAND focuses on ensuring that operations within Indian and Northern Affairs are carried out effectively, efficiently, and legally. In addition, Legal Services oversees the various claims and grievances that are presented, as well as ensuring that all contracts between Indians and the government of Canada are appropriate.

GOVERNMENT POLICY

Policies are developed by AAND bureaucrats at its headquarters in Ottawa and amended by bureaucrats from other government units that are likely to be affected by the suggested policies. As Weaver (1980) points out in her analysis of the 1969 *White Paper*, the Privy Council Office, the Prime Minister's Office, the Treasury Board, and the cabinet wield the most direct influence on federal policy concerning Aboriginal peoples. In the 1969s the Privy Council Office and the Prime Minister's Office were restructured to assert the primacy of the prime minister and cabinet in setting policy and monitoring programs. This restructuring allowed these offices and the cabinet to maintain much closer control of Indian and Inuit Affairs Program activities and to evaluate those activities in the context of other government departments.

The changes removed policy development and implementation from the total control of particular departments and ensured that policies would be evaluated in the context of other departments. Policy advisory councils were created to report to the cabinet; in effect, these councils are one step above the cabinet in power. Information from each department is now filtered through the Privy Council Office and Prime Minister's Office instead of passing directly from senior bureaucrats to cabinet ministers (Cairns, 2004; 2005; Ponting and Gibbins, 1980).

The federal government acknowledges a special relationship between itself and Aboriginal Canadians. It agrees that registered Indians and Inuit possess special rights, privileges, and entitlements, whether they live on or off the reserves. But, although the federal government acknowledges its responsibility to on- and off-reserve Aboriginals, it claims that they also should look to other levels of government for certain services. In addition, the federal government regards its responsibility for off-reserve services in a different light than that for on-reserve services. More specifically, under Section 91(24) of the *BNA Act* the federal government has accepted responsibility for on-reserve services in more program areas than for off-reserve services.

The federal government, then, maintains that each level of government has its respective responsibilities based on separate, distinct bonds with Aboriginal peoples. Aboriginals who live off reserves are residents of provinces and often contribute to provincial tax revenues. In addition, the federal government often provides indirectly many other resources to the provinces, which are included in the calculation of transfer and block payments. The provinces, on the other hand, take the position that registered Indians are a federal concern and are not under the jurisdiction of provincial governments. If provincial governments become involved in providing services for Aboriginal peoples, they argue they must be compensated.

In early 1991 Ottawa decided to limit spending on social services for registered Indians, and it has continued to enforce this limit. For example, it decided that it would no longer pay social assistance to registered Indians for the first year after they leave a reserve. Provinces have reiterated their stance that it is the federal government's responsibility to provide for the welfare of Indians regardless of whether they reside on or off the reserve. Registered Indians likewise agree with the provinces' stand, and argue that the social services question is a federal responsibility and should not be transferred. Today this issue remains unresolved, but the effect is that registered Indians do not have access to social services from the federal government during the first year after leaving the reserve.

DEVOLUTION

Indian and Inuit Affairs has been in the process of decentralization/devolution (decolonization) since 1964. In 1969, the then Department of Indian Affairs and Northern Development simply stated in the *White Paper* that First Nations peoples were to become a provincial responsibility and the legal status of "Indians" would be terminated. This policy was rejected by Aboriginal organizations, provincial governments, and a host of other social organizations. The government withdrew the *White Paper* as proposed policy, and in the mid-1970s a new policy emerged that involved the transfer of federal responsibility to First Nations communities rather than to the provinces. At the same time, administrative responsibilities were being shifted from Ottawa to the regional and district offices of the Department of Indian Affairs and Northern Development. As a result, First Nations gained greater involvement in the policy formation of the Indian and Northern Affairs Program (Ponting and Gibbins, 1980).

In 1976 a new mega-policy was introduced by the minister of the then Department of Indian and Northern Development to promote Indian identity within Canadian society. The definition and evolution of Aboriginal identity were to be treated as flexible and dynamic. In general, the policy continues to recognize Aboriginal status, treaty rights, and special privileges resulting from land claims settlements. Within Aboriginal band and reserve communities, local self-determination and control of Aboriginal affairs are encouraged. In addition, the policy noted, for the first time, that different needs, aspirations, and attitudes among Aboriginals in all parts of Canada rule out a single uniform strategy. As a result, the policy emphasizes joint participation in program development with organized Aboriginal leadership at all levels. Under the new policy, the federal government takes the initiative in defining the aims and general shape of strategies applied to Aboriginal issues. If the government chooses, this process can involve Aboriginal representatives at various levels. The major goal of the new policy is to transfer the administration of programs and resources to band governments. The rate of transfer is determined by the desire and ability of each to assume control of its own affairs, including the implementation of programs.

The devolution of responsibility for the delivery and management of services and programs from Indian and Northern Affairs to the direct control of First Nations began in earnest in the late 1970s. This process occurs through a range of mechanisms—funding contributions, alternative funding arrangements, grants, and flexible transfer payments. For example, in 1993 there were 110 signed alternative funding arrangements with 198 bands, totalling nearly $400 million. Today this figure has nearly tripled. These alternative funding arrangements provide bands with the maximum level of authority available under existing legislation and policy—the *Indian Act*. They also allow First Nations communities to have some power in redesigning programs and re-allocating funds that meet community priorities.

From 1983 to 1993, the number of people working in the Indian and Inuit Program decreased by 42 percent. As a result, phase I of the Devolution Plan—which involved the transfer of community services such as social development and education to First Nations communities—is complete.

The shift of responsibility to First Nations communities is continuing. First, funds for program management are being transferred from the Indian and Inuit Program to the direct control of bands. This transfer began in 1968; by 1971, bands were managing about 14 percent of a $160-million budget and, by 1978–79, about 35 percent of a $659-million budget. Today they manage over 70 percent of a budget exceeding $4 billion. Second, **core funding** grants are provided for the basic administrative costs of chiefs, councils, and band managers. In 1978–79, these grants represented 4 percent of the total DIAND budget; today this has nearly doubled to 7.5 percent. Third, band training and support services are supplied to encourage management skills and to provide technical support.

At present, the bands administer about 60 percent of the total capital and 80 percent of the school budgets. Approximately 90 percent of bands are involved in the core funding program, but these figures show considerable regional disparity—for example, Manitoba bands control a great deal of their operational expenditures, while Yukon bands control very little. Overall, more than 80 percent of Indian and Inuit Affairs Program expenditures flow through Aboriginal governance structures. We also know that the number of full-time federal employees in the program has decreased by 51 percent, from nearly 4000 in 1987 to less than half that number today.

This policy of devolution was designed to promote the autonomy of Aboriginal communities and to support self-government. It marks a shift in federal policy from programs that promoted assimilation to those that encourage First Nations community government and cultural self-sufficiency. Band councils are increasingly responsible for financial allocations. However, although the Indian and Inuit Affairs Program is relinquishing specific management over expenditures, it still retains control of the overall allocation of funds and demands an accounting of funds spent. In effect, this policy has shifted critical attention away from the Indian and Inuit Affairs Program to the local chief, council, and manager.

Again, this attempt to provide a forum for Aboriginal participation reflects a shift in federal policy from a desire to assimilate Aboriginals toward an increasing emphasis on tribal responsibility and Aboriginal governance. The tripartite (i.e., federal/provincial/Aboriginal) discussion partly arose from a belief by Indian Affairs personnel that Aboriginals had developed enough political leadership skills to articulate their needs. In addition, the provinces are willing to discuss priority issues set forth by Aboriginals, largely to avoid being excluded from any far-reaching negotiations that might take place elsewhere in Canada. However, despite promises to the contrary, Aboriginal peoples are still effectively excluded from much of the negotiation process. Currently, much of the discussion between federal and provincial officials circumvents Aboriginal involvement through the use of personal communications, confidential documents, and so on.

In today's environment, the government has stated it will support strong, sustainable communities through such means as establishing government-to-government relations as well as enhancing First Nations communities' ability to establish proper governance structures. As an immediate activity, the Department has tried to empower First Nations constituents to hold their governments to account by providing them with the tools to implement modern, effective governance regimes and practices. This has been supported by a number of legislative governance packages that have been introduced over the past decade (e.g., the *First Nations Governance Act*, the *Specific Claims Resolution Act*, the *First Nations Fiscal and Statistical Management Act*, and the *First Nations Land Management Act*). It is hoped that these pieces of legislation will allow First Nations communities to engage in activities such as leadership selection, administration, financial management, land resource management, citizen redress, and organization support. At the same time, the federal government will then be able to decrease its involvement in the day-to-day operations of First Nations communities. Therefore, the capacity of First Nations to achieve self-sufficiency and to develop their own public services will be enhanced.

THE LATENT FUNCTIONS OF THE INDIAN AND INUIT AFFAIRS PROGRAM

Like many other organizations, AAND is a highly structured, rational system that espouses specific policies and pursues specific goals. It has defined Aboriginal welfare as its sole concern; overtly, all its activities are geared to improving that welfare. Also like other organizations, however, AAND pursues certain latent goals that are quite independent of its stated formal goals. As Perrow (1961) and several others have observed, organizations often exist not only to serve their stated goals but to serve other interests as well. In fact, some would even argue that the stated policy and goals of an organization largely function only to legitimize its existence. An organization makes its stated goals explicit through its formal policy statements. Its latent goal structure becomes apparent only through an examination of the services that it provides for interest groups other than those it manifestly serves.

The organizations dealing with Aboriginal people all possess a number of latent functions. For the past half-century, the Indian and Inuit Affairs Program and its forerunners have stated that their primary manifest goal is the maximum participation by Aboriginals as equals in Canadian society. The latent goals of these organizations include such self-referential aims as cost-efficiency and freedom from conflict within their own structures. Another latent function is to provide resources for other organizations. Many institutions make extensive use of the nearly $700 million and 2000 employees provided to the Indian and Inuit Affairs Program at public expense; examples range from Aboriginal organizations and educational institutions to businesses.

Although other latent functions could be documented here, none is as extensive as the latent attempt by federal administrators to control the lives of Aboriginals. Throughout its history, the major latent function of the various Aboriginal programs has been the regulation of Aboriginal behaviour. Aboriginal people have been lured to cities, where their dependent status forces them to conform, or they have been segregated on reserves, concealed from the view of middle-class Canadians. They have been arbitrarily dispersed throughout cities or forcibly bused out of town, back to the reserve. Often the control of Aboriginals has been achieved through the behavioural requirements attached to various social services. For example, the off-reserve housing program requires applicants to have steady full-time jobs before they are eligible for loans. The insistence of the federal government of control over its Aboriginal wards has characterized federal government–Aboriginal relations since Confederation. As Whiteside (1980) points out,

> Perhaps we should recall the various measures the bureaucrats introduced during this period to ensure "orderly administration": (1) the development of a single piece of legislation in 1876, to govern all the Indian Nations, regardless of varying traditions and history; (2) the systematic destruction of tribal governments and replacement of them with band councils which were really an extension of the Department's [Indian Affairs'] structure; (3) the systematic attempt to destroy Indian culture and the outlawing of Indian religious ceremonies; (4) the introduction of compulsory enfranchisement provisions to control bad Indians; (5) the systematic attempts to harness and discredit Indian leaders who attempt to develop or strengthen Indian political organization. (p. 6)

On the reserve, the various federal programs are a "total" institution in that they have a monopoly on the delivery of services to a captive clientele (Breton, 1964). AAND is characterized by specialization, hierarchy, and regimentation, while its clients are relatively uneducated, unspecialized, and varied. By limiting the choices available to its Aboriginal clients, the Indian and Inuit Affairs Program shapes and standardizes Aboriginal behaviour at minimal cost and risk to itself.

The success of the Indian and Inuit Affairs Program is not assessed on the basis of the assistance it provides to Aboriginals but rather on the basis of how effectively it has kept

Aboriginal behaviour under control. The brighter officials at the Indian and Inuit Affairs Program know perfectly well that they will not be fired, transferred, or demoted for failing to help Aboriginals receive decent education, find jobs, mend broken homes, and settle into life in the city. Rather, the officials' assessment will be based on the number of Aboriginals they handled, and at what cost per person. Programs that fail to meet their announced goals do not result in fired personnel or radical organizational changes. The upper management of the Indian and Inuit Affairs Program can simply blame failures on a need for organizational restructuring, a lack of adequately trained fieldworkers, a poorly allocated budget, and so on.

Internal forces acting upon the Indian and Inuit Affairs Program cause it to downplay its stated goal of improving the quality of Aboriginal life. First, government officials tend to become disproportionately concerned with the number of their employees, the size of their budgets, and the quantity, rather than the quality, of their programs. Because it is difficult, time-consuming, and speculative to assess the effectiveness of an organization, readily quantifiable criteria become the indicators of a successful program. Because these indicators measure cost efficiency rather than program effectiveness, they are simple to tabulate, highly visible, and extremely responsive to changes.

A second internal factor is the emphasis on stability within the Indian and Inuit Affairs Program. There is an implicit rule that conflict should not be evident in any federal department. If conflict does exist, it must remain an internal affair. The preoccupation of the Indian and Inuit Affairs Program with remaining conflict-free results, once again, in a downplaying of stated goals and objectives.

In all of the organizations that deal with Aboriginal issues, officials accept and promote the existing expectations, norms, and mores of a free-enterprise, class-based system. This places severe limitations on the programs offered to Aboriginal people. For example, not one organization has suggested that most of the Indian and Inuit Affairs Program's budget should be given directly to Aboriginal people or used to organize Aboriginals into an effective political force. Quite the contrary. One of the better-known attempts to organize Aboriginals politically in a Western urban centre resulted in the dissolution of one district office and substantial reassignment of personnel. A similar response ended the ill-fated Community Development Program, which was phased out within a few years of its inception.

Today's Aboriginal policy reflects the recent decisions of the courts. Courts have become more intrusive in government–Aboriginal relations and have clearly identified the rights and responsibilities of each party. In addition, the Royal Commission identified key issues that needed to be addressed immediately if the mission of AAND is to be achieved. We now turn to a brief analysis of the Royal Commission.

THE ROYAL COMMISSION ON ABORIGINAL PEOPLES

The Royal Commission evolved out of the Oka crisis in 1990 and subsequent overt conflict that was erupting throughout the country as Aboriginals attempted to deal with legal and economic issues confronting them. The Commission started in 1991, but it would take five years before it tabled a six-volume, 5000-page document on the status of Aboriginal people in Canada. After five years and nearly $60 million, it laid out a 20-year plan to deal with First Nations peoples. A one-line summary of the report is that Canada can no longer allow Aboriginal peoples to remain in a state of dependency.

The report begins by noting that Canada systematically denied First Nations their nation status, violated most agreements made with First Nations, and suppressed their culture and institutions. In short, the report claims that Canadians built a great liberal democracy in part through the dispossession of Aboriginal people. As a result, Aboriginals exist in conditions of poverty and social upheaval. A key recommendation of the Commission was not to allocate more money but to address the fractured historical relationship between Aboriginals and Canada. The roots of injustice lie in history, and it is there that the key to regeneration of Aboriginal society and a new and better relationship with the rest of Canada can be found.

Report Recommendations

The Commission was specific in its recommendations, and its major point was to encourage the federal government to move immediately to make major changes. The Commission recognized that the relationship between First Nations and Canadian society needed to be restructured before positive outcomes could be achieved in the social, economic, and health dimensions of Aboriginal life. The chief elements of the proposed restructuring included:

- **New Royal Proclamation** Reiteration of Canada's affirmation of Aboriginal and treaty rights
- **Recognition of First Nations** Implementation of First Nation governments by the federal government, and recognition of these governments by the federal and all provincial governments
- **Administration** Elimination of the current government structure, to be replaced by a minister of Aboriginal Relations and a minister of Indian and Inuit Services
- **Treaty Commission** Establishment of a tribunal to deal with specific claims and all treaties
- **Fiduciary Responsibility** Clear financial responsibility and policies to support it
- **Land and Resource Distribution** Development of a procedure by which First Nations would be ensured their fair share of the wealth of Canada
- **Healing Centres** Develop an integrated service delivery structure for First Nations

The report recommended that, over the next 20 years, the federal government spend an additional $38 billion on Aboriginals. The report reveals that $2.5 billion per year is spent to offset Aboriginal poverty ($50 billion over 20 years). It also states that about $1 billion is spent annually on social assistance on reserves, where unemployment hovers around 80 percent and Aboriginal communities endure Third-World living conditions. But it notes that lost productivity, lost income, and lost potential taxes bring the total economic cost of the unhealthy relationship with Aboriginals to over $7 billion, equivalent to 1 percent of Canada's gross domestic product ($140 billion over the 20-year period). The report states that, since over half of the Aboriginal population is under 25 years of age, if nothing is done the estimated cost for dealing with Aboriginals by the year 2016 would increase to $11 billion. The Commission forecasted that if monies are now invested, the result would be a huge saving by 2016.

The report proposed that the federal government increase its spending for Aboriginals to $1.5 billion for the next seven years and to $2 billion for the following 13 years. The logic of such a recommendation was that within 10 years there will be a fall in the remedial costs and a rise in government revenues as Aboriginal people become more productive and begin to make a net contribution to the economic development of Canada. For example, the expensive "front end" cost of addressing the housing crisis on reserves would cost nearly $3 billion. However, in 10 to 15 years the savings would be in excess of twice that value. The extra money would go toward building new health centres, stimulating the Aboriginal economy, upgrading the infrastructure on reserves, and dealing with crisis conditions now found in Aboriginal communities. Then a long-term program of training Aboriginals would be put in place. Later, monies would be used to settle land claims and to implement self-government.

Most of the cost of forgone earned income ($5.8 billion in 1996) is borne by Aboriginal people in the form of lost income. The rest is borne by governments in the form of taxes forgone and various forms of assistance paid out. These costs to governments are not included in the amount given for "cost to Aboriginal people." Table 6.5 outlines the projected results of the Royal Commission's strategy.

Aboriginal Reaction

Aboriginal leaders were supportive of the Commission's report and felt that for the first time in many years they had something to look forward to. However, they also noted that if this report were not taken seriously, Canadians should be prepared to face some significant social and economic consequences. In summary, most Aboriginal peoples responded favourably to the report and felt that positive outcomes would result.

The Assembly of First Nations (AFN), in its 10-year retrospective, noted than *none* of the above recommendations have been implemented. While there have been some increases in funding, it has been specific to targeted areas—e.g., water management, diabetes, and sewage infrastructure. In these cases, caps of 2 percent on increases have been evident for the past 10 years. First Nations communities today continue to live in poverty, and increasing gaps in health, mortality, and economic indicators are widely evident.

The AFN noted that, in their assessment of government action over the past decade, there has been no sustained investment in meeting the basic needs of First Nations communities. There have been no structural changes in the relationship between First Nations and the Canadian government, and the First Nations action plan proposed in accordance with the *Gathering Strength* policy (the government's formal policy response to the report of the Royal Commission) has never been pursued after changes in political leadership. The later Kelowna Summit agreement in 2005 was rejected when a new federal government took over. Of the 66 recommendations issued by the Royal Commission, the AFN's report card (2006) showed that only one recommendation received an "A" grade, three received a "B" grade, and 12 were assigned a "C." The remaining 50 recommendations received "D" or "F" grades, reflecting a clear lack of action on the key foundational recommendations of the Royal Commission and a resultant lack of progress on key socio-economic indicators.

While some funds have been allocated to issues identified under the *Gathering Strength* policy, they have been inadequate. Moreover, while other government agencies have been allocated an annual 6 percent increase, the government has placed a 2 percent increase for Aboriginal funding. This means that lost funds to First Nations communities from 1996–2006 totalled over $10 billion. In comparing the social development of communities, First Nations rank 76th out of 174 nations, while non-Aboriginal communities rank 8th in the world.

TABLE 6.5	Projected Results of the Royal Commission's Strategy		
		Additional allocation in the year	
		2001	2016
		($ millions)	($ millions)
Structural Measures			
Tribunal and treaty commissions		50	50
Nation rebuilding		50	0
Nation governments		50	425
Land claims settlements		0	1000
Total for Structural Measures		**150**	**1475**
Social and Economic Measures			
Healing, education, youth, and culture		300	150
Health care		100	(450)
Social services		100	(425)
Justice		25	(325)
Economic Opportunities and Living Conditions			
Economic development		350	225
Income transfers		0	(250)
Housing and infrastructure		400	350
Human resource development		150	425
Total for Social and Economic Measures		**1425**	**(300)**
Government Revenue Gains		-	(1550)
Overall Total		**1575**	**(375)**

Notes:
  Positive entries (figures without parentheses) show the increase in spending by all governments needed to implement the strategy.
  Reductions are shown by numbers in parentheses in the second column. These relate to amounts saved as a result of the strategy (that is, amounts that would be spent if the status quo were to continue) and to additional revenues collected by governments.

  Figures are rounded to the nearest $25 million.

Source: Adapted from Report of the Royal Commission on Aboriginal Peoples, 1996. Table 3.2: Changes in Government Finances Under the Strategy: Long Term Gains ($Millions). Reproduced with the permission of the Minister of Public Works and Government Services, 2011, and Courtesy of the Privy Council Office.

In 2004, the AFN published a document titled *Federal Government Funding to First Nations: The Facts, the Myths, and the Way Forward.* In this document, the Assembly challenged the existing funding arrangements, the amount of funds allocated to First Nations, and the myths that are being perpetuated about funds allocated to First Nations. They point out that even though AAND has a budget of over $10 billion per year, only two-thirds are allocated to AAND while the remaining one-third is allocated to other agencies to support Inuit, Métis, and "non-status Indians" as well as for administration and bureaucracy at the federal or other levels of government and private sector organizations. The government of Canada provides about $7200 per First Nations person, while it spends about $6000 on each of Canada's non-Aboriginal persons. However, for non-Aboriginals, an additional $2900 is provided by provincial and municipal governments. Figure 6.4 shows that both the core program and the total spending of AAND over the past five years have decreased 13 percent and 3.5 percent, respectively. These figures show that, while AAND claims to have increased its budget, the facts show a decrease as expenditures for the general Canadian population has remained stable over this time.

There are some areas of expenditure for First Nations that exceed the per-capita non-Aboriginal person. For example, housing costs per Aboriginal person is $5.1, while only $1 is spent for non-Aboriginals. Other areas of core programming such as education, health care, and social services also show a greater expenditure for First Nations than for non-Aboriginal people. These increased expenditures reflect the fact that most First Nations are in remote or northern areas where the cost of providing materials and service is much higher. Second, because of the demographic distribution of First Nations (e.g., higher number of youth), education costs are higher. Finally, the history of neglect, displacement, and disenfranchisement has driven social costs higher for many First Nations.

Nearly all of the funds provided to First Nations are related to the provision of basic services such as health, education, roads, and potable water. The provision of these services by the federal government is intended to be comparable to what non-Aboriginal Canadians already receive from the three levels of government. The figures discussed

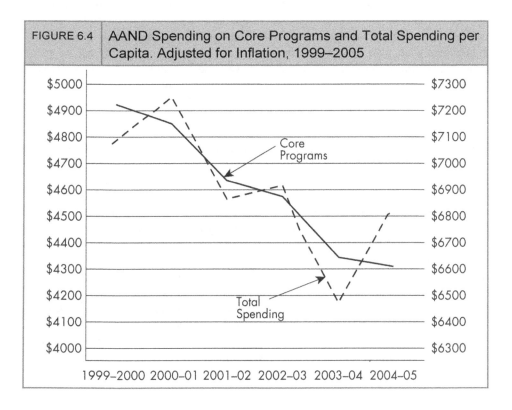

FIGURE 6.4 **AAND Spending on Core Programs and Total Spending per Capita. Adjusted for Inflation, 1999–2005**

show that First Nations people are not receiving comparable services (as outlined in the *Constitution Act, 1982*).

Additional funds are allocated to First Nations because of lawful obligations of the Crown in the form of claims, treaties, and litigation. With regard to resolving lawful obligations, the federal government has consistently taken a strategy (e.g., stall and delay resolution of claims, lengthy court battles) that costs First Nations and the Canadian public large sums of money and provides no benefits to either group. In fact, the 1998 *Report of the Joint First Nations–Canada Task Force on Specific Claims Policy Reform* recommended that other strategies be undertaken to reduce the time and cost for resolving these lawful obligations.

Government Reaction

The initial response by the government to the Royal Commission was one of indifference and hostility. For some time, the federal government did not respond to the Commission's report. The minister of Indian Affairs noted that the report, because it was two years late in being submitted, had already been eclipsed by changes in the then Department of Indian and Northern Affairs, and claimed that these changes had already addressed many of the issues raised in the report.

The federal government's formal reaction to the report came on January 7, 1998, with the publication of the document *Gathering Strength—Canada's Aboriginal Action Plan*. This document, in tandem with another government document, *Sustainable Development Strategy*, outlines the goals of helping develop strong, healthy First Nations communities and setting up new relationships founded on mutual respect, with responsible, transparent, accountable, sustainable governance structures and institutions. It was an integrated, government-wide plan to address the major challenges facing Aboriginal people—structural reform of the federal government's Aboriginal programming to promote self-sufficiency and economic development and the enhancement and strengthening of the capacity of Aboriginal governments and organizations to run accountable, responsive government systems. Some initial investments were made for "healing" and reconciliation, but these "one time" funds have since been exhausted and there has been no attempt to measure their impact. However, the federal policy failed to endorse the national action plan recommended by the Royal Commission (Chartrand, 2002). Instead, the federal government opted for its traditional strategy of trying for slow, incremental policy shifts. As Chartrand (2002) points out, the federal policy response seemed to reflect the government's philosophy that incremental change is more politically manageable than the kind of fundamental change that was recommended by the Royal Commission.

In 2005, the last of a series of meetings between Aboriginal people and first ministers came to a close in Kelowna, B.C. In that last meeting, the first ministers and First Nations leaders agreed, through a document called "First Ministers and National Aboriginal Leaders Strengthening Relationships and Closing the Gap," to embark on a 10-year effort to close the gap in the quality of life that now exists between Aboriginal peoples and other Canadians. There was agreement that additional funds ($5.1 billion) for clean drinking water, health, education, and housing programs, as well as for economic development, would be made available over the next decade. However, in spring 2006, the newly elected Conservative government refused to honour the negotiations and rejected the agreement.

Each year, AAND outlines its goals and objectives and provides a listing of the strategies it has taken (and plans to take for the next year) to achieve these goals. In its annual reports, the Department identifies targets and outcomes for each of the strategies and goals identified. For example, it was very clear in 1999 that it would be trying to enhance Aboriginal governance capacity. Other goals outlined by the federal government in 2000 have not been achieved at this time—e.g., to have 50 to 60 specific claims settled and to conclude up to 18 comprehensive claim settlement agreements-in-principle and up to 17 final agreements by 2003. Nevertheless, the accountability framework adopted by INAC, and subsequently used by AAND, allows tracking of its progress in achieving goals (or lack thereof) over time. It also allows the matching of resource investment with goals to assess if the allocation is appropriate and sufficient.

We now turn to an analysis of Aboriginal organizations that have been created to deal with issues they regard as a priority. These organizations have been formed to respond to actions taken or proposed by the federal government or AAND. To fully appreciate the actions of Aboriginal organizations, we will need to begin with a brief historical account of these organizations and how they have culminated in the creation of major pan-Canadian organizations.

ABORIGINAL ORGANIZATIONS IN CANADA

Daugherty (1982) has suggested that the first Aboriginal association in North America was established in about 1540 when the League of Iroquois was formed (Seneca, Mohawk, Onondaga, Oneida, and Cayuga). However, it would not be until 1870 that the first Canadian Aboriginal political organization was created—the Grand General Indian Council of Ontario and Quebec. For the next 70 years, Aboriginal political and social organizations focused on local or regional issues; it would not be until the 1940s that Aboriginals from across the country formed a national organization—the Canadian Indian Brotherhood (later renamed the **North American Indian Brotherhood**). Later, in 1954, the National Indian Council was formed, and, in 1961, it became the official organization for both status and non-status First Nations people. By the end of the 1960s, it had split into two organizations: the National Indian Brotherhood for status First Nations and the Canadian Métis Society for non-status Aboriginals and Métis. In 1970 the Métis Society became the **Native Council of Canada** and later renamed itself the Congress of Aboriginal Peoples. While the Métis National Council represents only members of the Métis Nation, the Congress represents anyone who claims either Métis or non-Indian status. Inuit have also created organizations to deal with their specific concerns. The national organization, the Inuit Tapiriit Kanatami, was created in 1970 but since then several other organizations have emerged, focusing on their specific regional and cultural interests. As a result, the Tungavik Federation of Nunavut, an umbrella organization, was created to represent the Inuit organizations east of the Mackenzie Delta. Overall, early Aboriginal organizations were generally tied to specific concerns, such as particular land claims and unfulfilled treaty promises. These organizations had a single focus, were relatively simple in structure, and were limited to a particular area or group of Aboriginal people. Only since the mid-1950s have Aboriginal organizations become multifaceted, complex in structure, and representative of Aboriginal people from across Canada (Patterson, 1972).

Many Aboriginal organizations have emerged over the past century, but some have faded into oblivion and their records have been lost to history. Their emergence was precipitated by the introduction of the government's *White Paper*, which proposed doing away with the legal status of Indians. However, a second issue also fed the creation of Aboriginal organizations—the federal government's willingness to fund Aboriginal organizations. At the same time, the demise of many of the early organizations was generally the result of suppression by the federal government (e.g., the *Indian Act, 1927* prohibited the political organization of Aboriginal people beyond local levels of government) and of internal discord among Aboriginals themselves. These problems continue to plague many Aboriginal groups (Warry, 2007) in the 21st century. The short-lived and ineffectual structure of many Aboriginal organizations has been the result of outside interference, mistakes made by Aboriginal leadership, and the inappropriateness of certain social structures within a larger social system. For example, the burgeoning number of Aboriginal organizations representing a myriad of goals and objectives has prevented Aboriginal people from pursuing a cohesive and integrated set of objectives. Different tribal and linguistic groups have slowed the emergence of cohesive strategies, thereby limiting the extent to which they are able to develop their social capital.

The Need for Aboriginal Organizations

The creation and sustainability of organizations involves the development of social capital and speaks to the importance of social networks, communication, and the sharing of resources (Kay and Johnston, 2007). Social capital can also be seen as a cultural mechanism to establish and solidify boundaries of groups. However, social capital is less tangible than physical capital in that it exists in the relations among individual human beings. It consists of the sharing of resources through networks of social relations along with the norms that are attached. It represents the willingness of individuals to work together and to engage in cooperative activities. In short, the concept has come to mean the willingness of individuals to create and sustain relationships through voluntary associations (Portes and Landolt, 1996).

As such, organizations are one of the keys to ethnic survival. Voluntary organizations produce a sense of community, solidarity, and mutual obligation in order to support collective activities. In addition, they allow Aboriginal communities to develop economically, to enter the world of politics, to become advocates for their goals, and to develop social cohesion, solidarity, and social integration among themselves. In dealing with the dominant society, Aboriginal organizations play an important role in ensuring that their voices are heard, their needs understood, and the achievement of their goals attained. Nevertheless, while broad social capital is easy to build in homogeneous communities, it is more difficult to develop and maintain in diverse settings. Individuals are more likely to trust others like themselves and less likely to trust those they perceive to be different (Uslaner, 2002). As we have pointed out in earlier chapters, there is a great deal of diversity among Aboriginal groups across the country as well as in urban centres, which has posed a major barrier to the development of the shared trust and common objectives required to sustain multi-Aboriginal voluntary associations.

Nevertheless, the Aboriginal "movement" has had both a political and a social impact on Canadian society. Aboriginal organizations have instigated and supported legal challenges that have resolved conflicts, provided new opportunities for Aboriginal people, and outlined new perspectives for non-Aboriginal people. Many times they have been the centre of controversy in the legal or the political field. The nature of the goals set by the various organizations has been problematic for Aboriginal people. Some groups have tried to pursue local objectives, while others have focused more on regional or national matters. Their goals have been political, social, religious, or economic, and this diffusion of focus has led to divisions among those pursuing them.

Voices and Partners

Aboriginal people argue that in order for Canada to have legitimate political authority, it must not be the product of an unjust usurpation of a previously existing legitimate authority (Moore, 2010). Moreover, Aboriginal people argue that they have been treated unjustly by the imposed, coercive federal government. They maintain that the government of Canada has assumed, since its creation, that the Aboriginal peoples are culturally backward and that they need to be assimilated into mainstream society. First Nations leaders have argued that the governments' assumptions of superiority are embedded in the process of treaty making and in the content of the treaties. In their view, the signing of a treaty is itself an act of recognition and signifies mutual respect and consent. However, this was not evident in the treatment of Aboriginal people by Canadian officials. The treaties offered to Aboriginal people were generally unfair, and if tribes were unwilling to sign a treaty as offered, they were coerced into it by Euro-Canadians taking advantage of illness, starvation, or some other calamity. As such, treaties were not entered into in good faith and do not serve as a just basis for inter-communal relations (Moore, 2010).

Furthermore, once the treaties were put in place, they were systematically ignored or violated and the governments' sense of superiority provided the justification for abrogating them. As such, the relationship between Aboriginal people and the government has a long history of "broken promises." Aboriginal organizations have taken the stance that the concept of "justice" embodies the idea of fair treatment that has not characterized Aboriginal–non-Aboriginal relations in Canada. Moreover, Aboriginal organizations have argued that the assumptions of Aboriginal cultural inferiority and the merits of assimilation affected state policies with respect to First Nations. The result of such state policies has meant that Aboriginal people have few cultural, land, or financial resources available to them today. First Nations organizations also argue that these policies are not just the result of one government but rather are part of a long progression of abuses and injustices enacted by governments since the 18th century. Thus the "problem" is not simply due to the actions of various governments or the specific administrative structure related to Aboriginal peoples, but rather is the result of something that is endemic in the state order. It is their goal to address these issues and to push the government to make substantive changes that will address the systemic inequalities and injustices embedded in the Canadian social, legal, and political structure. Aboriginal organizations argue that, in some respects, the current state is not legitimate and until it makes substantive changes to address the systemic unjust policies and legislation, self-government continues to be a viable alternative.

Aboriginal organizations are also faced with the issue of how to deal with the human rights abuses that Aboriginal people have experienced over the past two centuries. In some instances, Aboriginal groups have argued for the creation of a "restorative justice" system to be implemented, though the government is strongly resistant of such a move. In other cases, they have argued that liberal constitutionalism needs to be implemented. Moore (2010) argues that this involves a "pre-commitment" to resisting certain undesirable propensities of the state. This would require the government to design various legislation and policies that would prevent mainstream institutions from engaging in discriminative and unjust activities. For example, we have built in safeguards for free speech because we understand that sometimes the dominant group is inclined to attack minority views. In this respect, many Aboriginal organizations have tried to convince the government to think about extending the constitutional tradition to include Aboriginal rights given their long history of being victims at the hand of the state. In short, their goal is to build structural and legal protections for Aboriginal people to keep them from being subjected to future injustices.

Contemporary Aboriginal organizational structure has largely resulted from the above ideology as well as from increased urbanization, the need to develop formal organizations to achieve goals, and the changing role of advocacy groups in Canada. Although many Aboriginal organizations operate within an urban context, their members are generally rural in orientation and are concerned with rural issues such as land claims and treaties. Today's organizations are imbued with a sense of cultural nationalism, or what Smith (1981) calls "ethnic revival." The genesis of this outlook lies partially in the emergence of Aboriginal intellectuals graduating from non-Aboriginal schools. These individuals are equipped to research and piece together an account of the past several centuries as seen from an Aboriginal perspective. And they are able to promote the historical legacy they discovered. This was reinforced when the National Indian Brotherhood reorganized itself under the rubric of the Assembly of First Nations. In addition, in their efforts to achieve their goals, Aboriginal organizations are beginning to use new tactics, such as confrontation, protest, and lobbying. Aboriginal people are being taken seriously because they are (1) viewed as a threat to national security, and (2) now able to hire experts, including lawyers, who have an expertise in Canadian law as it pertains to Aboriginal rights. Finally, the new tactics being employed have generated a great deal of publicity— Aboriginal issues now receive media attention and have entered everyday discourse. The result has been some additional pressure brought to bear on government officials to make changes to legal and social policies (Fleras and Maaka, 2000).

ABORIGINAL ORGANIZATIONAL STRUCTURE: A TYPOLOGY

There are four broad categories of Aboriginal organizations: band, local, urban, and pan-Aboriginal. Band organizations, which deal with the federal government, are based on historical precedents and have their authority vested in the *Indian Act*. Relations between Aboriginal people and government at this level are formal and regulated by the terms and conditions outlined in federal statutes. Local, urban, and pan-Aboriginal organizations, in contrast, have no statutory basis for their dealings with the government. Nevertheless, these organizations have had extensive dealings with both government and non-government agencies over the years.

Local organizations in First Nations communities have emerged through specific efforts of individuals or groups living in a specific community, focusing on a specific issue. They are usually singular in focus, short-lived, and ineffective. Overall, these individual organizations pursue goals widely ranging from particular services to treaty rights to changes in federal Indian policy. In the 1960s two events occurred simultaneously that had a tremendous effect on these two types of Aboriginal organizations. First, new programs were introduced into the reserves, which brought substantial funds to an otherwise poor constituency. Second, the urbanization of Aboriginals meant that for the first time a large number of Aboriginal people would not be effectively served by a band or local organization. This meant that urban Aboriginal people had to develop their own organizations. The original Aboriginal urban organizations focused on economic and social welfare goals. The central goal of these organizations was to change Aboriginal–non-Aboriginal relations to accommodate urban Aboriginal communities and their interests (Cornell, 1988; Cornell, 2000). The increase in the number of Aboriginal persons entering urban areas resulted in a proliferation of organizations, reflecting the varied goals and objectives of each group. After a time of working at cross-purposes, some of the organizations began to carry out cooperative efforts. After several successful ventures, new pan-Aboriginal organizations began to emerge. More recently, **pan-Aboriginal organizations** have attempted to reduce federal control and increase their own control over band and tribal affairs (Aggamaway-Pierre, 1983; Cairns, 2005).

Cornell (1988) has developed a typology of Aboriginal organizations that is based upon their goals; it illustrates and provides an understanding of their actions (see Figure 6.5). The first distinction he makes is between reformative and transformative goals. A "reformative" organization focuses its efforts on changing the role of Aboriginal people without changing the structure of Aboriginal/non-Aboriginal relations. This approach is based on a belief that there must be a redistribution of social power and/or rewards to allow Aboriginal people their share, and that this can take place within the existing system. For example, they feel that more Aboriginal people should be hired by Indian Affairs, that more Aboriginal people should be in senior management positions, and that social services on the reserves need to be expanded. In summary, these organizations accept and endorse the existing structure of Canadian society and feel that only some changes are needed to make the existing system work better.

"Transformative" organizations agree that a redistribution of rewards and power needs to be undertaken, but not within the existing social structure. They feel that a fundamental change is required—for example, phasing out Indian Affairs, allowing Aboriginal people to establish their own legal system, and reopening treaties. In summary, their goal is to change the existing structures that impinge upon Aboriginal people (Grand Council of the Crees, 1998).

The second distinction Cornell makes among Aboriginal organizations is the degree to which each is integrative or segregative. This distinction reflects the degree of acceptance or rejection of dominant institutions. Organizations with an integrative perspective accept the appropriateness of the dominant culture and thus promote the dominant institutions as the way of maximizing Aboriginal interests. As a result of their general acceptance of the dominant institutions, they also believe that Aboriginal communities should be built on this model.

FIGURE 6.5	Types of Aboriginal Organizations		
		Aboriginal-White Relations	
		Reform	Transform
Orientation to institutions of dominant society	Integrate	1	2
	Segregate	3	4

Source: Adapted from S. Cornell, *The Return of the Native*. New York: Oxford, 1988: 154.

On the other hand, Aboriginal organizations with a segregative ideology argue against accepting the dominant institutional structure as a role model. These organizations promote goals and objectives that are fundamentally anti-assimilationist. The relationship between these two variables is portrayed in Figure 6.5; they result in four basic types of Aboriginal organizations.

We now turn to look at one national Aboriginal organization that represents one group of Aboriginals—registered Indians (First Nations). The Assembly of First Nations has been an important Aboriginal organization and has taken leadership on a number of issues regarding Aboriginal peoples across the country. While it does not speak for all Aboriginal peoples, its leaders have been visionary in their mission and have provided leadership for other Aboriginal groups in dealing with the federal government.

ASSEMBLY OF FIRST NATIONS

In 1982, the Assembly of First Nations (AFN) emerged as the primary national Aboriginal organization, replacing the defunct National Indian Brotherhood. It represents First Nations peoples and has recently concentrated its efforts on constitutional issues and self-government. Notwithstanding opposition from many provincial premiers, the AFN takes the position that First Nations have the right to self-government, and that this prerogative exists as an inherent Aboriginal right that has never been surrendered, relinquished, or diminished by any formal treaty or agreement, nor by the Constitution, legislation, or policies of non-Indian governments in Canada. This right, although it exists, has yet to be exercised by the First Nations. Consequently, no contemporary national institutions exist as a derivative government for First Nations.

At the third Annual Assembly of First Nations held in Penticton, B.C., in 1982, a new structure for the AFN was formally adopted by the chiefs of provincial and territorial or regional associations. This new organization was deliberately established outside the corporate structure defined by Canadian law and was the culmination of two years' work by the Interim Council of Chiefs. The Confederacy of Nations was mandated to formulate policy and oversee the direction of the executive and secretariat between sessions of the Assembly. There is no direct comparison between the AFN and any body within government or, likely, within traditional First Nations structures. The intention of the AFN is to represent the needs and wishes of First Nations people across Canada.

The AFN was established by chiefs to respect the sovereignty of each individual First Nation. It can be described as an organization involved in a process of transition from the statutory origins of the National Indian Brotherhood toward a national political institution that derives its existence and direction exclusively and entirely from the First Nations. In some respects, it remains an organization that has not completely divorced itself from its statutory foundations (Final Report to Assembly of First Nations, February 18, 1985, mimeo).

In 2003, the Assembly of First Nations Renewal Commission was formed to examine the purpose and structure of the AFN. At that time, the chiefs felt that it had been 20 years since the creation of the Assembly and it needed to change structure and organization in order to better deal with new issues emerging (e.g., the need for consultation on *Bill C-31*). Moreover, with recent court decisions and land claims literally changing the landscape of Canada's First Nations, a huge contingent of First Nations peoples living in urban centres, and an increasingly young population, the AFN needed to assess whether its structure and processes required change. After nearly two years, the commission tabled its report and, in 2006, it was ratified by the AFN (Assembly of First Nations, 2005).

Figure 6.6 identifies the new structure of the AFN. Three groups inform the Assembly, in addition to the regional chiefs. A circle of elders, a women's council, and a youth council now support the general and special assemblies. However, while the three groups have representation on the National Council, they do not have any voting rights. Only the national and regional chiefs are voting members of the council.

The circle of elders develops the rules and procedures of the AFN for ratification by the entire Assembly. They are a resource for the AFN and its constituents. The elders are viewed as the custodians of the Assembly's rules and procedures, as they are for other traditional and customary laws. They have responsibility for the development, implementation, and maintenance of a redress system that provides mechanisms for impeachment, discipline, and loss of membership. The circle of elders also investigates and arbitrates any disputes within the Assembly. In addition, the elders select and present the speaker of the Assembly to the chiefs. They guide the speaker in the exercise of his/her duties and in seeking consensus of the Assembly. The women's council was created to give women a strong voice and allow them to participate in the Council activities. Finally, the creation of a youth council came about AFN officials recognized that new members of the community needed to have a voice in decisions made by the Council.

At the present time, the ongoing political work of the AFN is carried out by the Office of the National Chief. He represents the only body or person within the Assembly who can truly be held accountable by the chiefs. Between assemblies, the Confederacy of Nations tries to function as an executive committee and gives its own political mandates and direction to the Office of the National Chief. Ten regional chiefs have portfolios as needed. They also provide a means of communication between the national chief, the Council, and their regions. But in almost all cases, this function is secondary to their provincially or regionally held positions, such as president of a provincial First Nations association. Finally, the new structure incorporates four national advisors (all without a vote) to provide the necessary expertise required when making decisions.

The national office has historically avoided running programs or providing services. At the same time, there is a desire to have the national office valued and respected within

First Nations communities. Therefore, a role must be identified for the national office—
one that goes beyond support for the national executive on major political issues (which
have already been fairly well defined).

FIGURE 6.6	Organizational Structure of the Assembly of First Nations

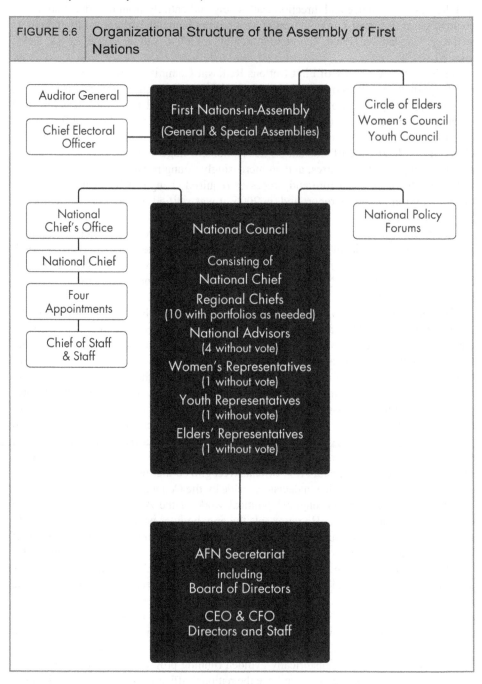

Since its creation, the AFN has established several committees, commissions, and portfolios to address the many issues confronting First Nations people. As such, the Assembly deals with a issues ranging from health and education to land rights, and has portfolios for regional chiefs to ensure these issues are dealt with. Resolutions are brought forward at both the general assembly and at special assemblies to ensure that all members of the Assembly are informed and have the opportunity to discuss resolutions.

Since the AFN is the national organization that represents all First Nations people in Canada, the chiefs meet annually to set national policy and direction through resolution. In addition, the members meet three to four times a year in a forum called the Confederacy of Nations, which gives members a guide for future actions. The AFN is active in the politics of Canada and met with provincial premiers four times during the 1985–87 period to convince them that Aboriginal people had an inherent right to self-government. In the last meeting, most of the premiers were adamant that they did not, and only Ontario, Manitoba, and New Brunswick were prepared to support the AFN position. The AFN was involved in the Meech Lake Accord of 1987, the Charlottetown Accord of 1992, the Free Trade Agreement with the United States, and other legislative business. It works closely with other Aboriginal organizations and lobby groups.

The AFN argues that any national institution established to represent or advance the interests of First Nations must reflect the sovereign jurisdiction of First Nations as the source of all that it does on behalf of the citizens of First Nations and, for that matter, on behalf of the governments of First Nations. Therefore, all powers, mandates, or responsibilities exercised on behalf of a First Nation are merely delegated, and the passage of time does not alter the delegated nature and quality of the power, mandate, or responsibility.

In conclusion, the AFN is an organization composed of members from varying backgrounds, cultures, histories, and philosophies. Out of respect for diversity and for the maintenance of solidarity, the AFN attempts to develop some basic principles of organization that are acceptable to all First Nations.

LIMITS OF ABORIGINAL ORGANIZATIONS

A review of Aboriginal political organizations reveals a substantial impact on the social and legal landscape of Canada over the years. These organizations have granted Aboriginal people input into the federal and provincial policies that affect them, thus providing instruments needed to bring about social change. The government has found that dealing with such organizations has many benefits. Because the bureaucracies within Aboriginal organizations are similar to those in government, both can interact in an orderly, legitimate fashion. Government funding of most Aboriginal political organizations makes them more vulnerable to government control. As a consequence, Aboriginal leaders find themselves in the position of having to play by the government's rules in order to achieve their own goals—goals that may be at variance with those of the government. On the other hand, the government's power over Aboriginal organizations should not be overestimated. Governments also face a dilemma: Without sufficient funds, Aboriginal organizations will not be able to negotiate; with sufficient funds, Aboriginal organizations will become too powerful (Krosenbrink-Gelissen, 1991).

As noted earlier, the overall aim of many Aboriginal organizations is to gain input into the government decisions that affect them. They have learned to focus on the bureaucratic organizations that affect them most directly, whether at the federal, provincial, or municipal level. Aboriginal organizations can also influence government in other ways, such as through annual submissions to cabinet on aspects of federal policy. Local and provincial Aboriginal organizations may deal directly with the government at any level, or may channel their appeal through whatever nationwide organizations they possess (Tanner, 1983).

The impact of an Aboriginal organization varies in direct proportion to its resources. By resources, we mean group assets such as solidarity, well-structured organizations, and money, which can be directed toward social action that enhances the capacity of the group to achieve its goals. During the first half of the 20th century, Aboriginal resources were extremely limited; however, since the 1960s they have markedly increased. The nature and extent of these resources have varied over time. Depending on the action taken by Aboriginal people, those resources utilized are built up and remain part of the total supply available to them in future. The relative importance of different types of resources may vary from time to time and from situation to situation. For example, economic resources are important, but they may be subordinate to political or legal resources under certain conditions. Furthermore, some resources (primarily economic) are portable, or transferable, while others have limited application (e.g., legal).

Cornell (1988) argues that a useful way to classify resources is by function. He identifies two types of resources: direct and mobilizational. Direct resources are those that directly influence the socio-political structure. Mobilization resources are those used in the process of bringing direct resources to bear on the issues under consideration. One of the most common direct resources that organizations can use is their number of members and/or supporters. However, because Aboriginal people are both dispersed and factionalized, they have been unable to convert this resource into a major force. Commodities that are held by an organization may also be a direct resource. However, the commodity must be one desired by others. In the case of Aboriginal people, such commodities usually take the form of land, resources, or some other special right. Land and natural resources commanded by various Aboriginal organizations have been and continue to be valued bargaining resources, although government has tried to implement legal steps that mediate their value. A third type of direct resource is the extent to which an organization has allied itself with other organizations, particularly those with power. Aboriginal organizations' success in the past has been the result of linkages with other non-Aboriginal organizations—e.g., religious organizations, human rights groups, and conservation groups. Some of these organizations have the aid of Aboriginal people as a primary purpose; others have related political agendas and find the alliance with Aboriginal people useful for obtaining their own goals and objectives (e.g., the Sierra Club).

As noted above, direct resources may not be useful if they are not mobilized. Having alliances, money, and land is of little use if one cannot mobilize them at the time one need to exert power. An example of an organization with good mobilization is the Native Women's Association of Canada. There are some 400 local chapters spread over the country with no fewer than 100 000 members. These informal groups foster networks, facilitate communications, and provide Aboriginal women with an opportunity to develop organizational skills. These local groups are linked to provincial and national offices; this affords quick communication and the ability to spread information quickly (NWAC, 1981).

TABLE 6.6	The Organizational Structure of Interest Groups
Institutional	**Issue-oriented**
Possess organizational continuity and cohesion.	Have limited organization and cohesion.
Are knowledgeable about government sectors that affect them.	Possess poor information about government.
Have a stable membership.	Have a fluid membership.
Have concrete and immediate operational objectives.	Show an inability to formulate long-term goals.
See credibility of the organization as important.	See goal achievement as important.

Sources: Adapted from P. Pross, ed., *Pressure Group Behaviour in Canadian Politics.* (Toronto, McGraw-Hill, 1975); P. Pross, "Pressure Groups: Talking Chameleons," in M. Whittington and G. Williams, eds., *Canadian Politics in the 1980s.* Toronto: Methuen, 1981.

What are the resources that allow organizations to mobilize and direct their activities? First, if an organization is to engage in sustained, focused activities, it must maintain a structure and retain relationships with other organizations. A major explanation for a group's failure or success seems to lie in its basic organizational structure. In Table 6.6, Pross (1975) delineates differences between two types of interest groups. Institutional interest groups can be placed at one end of a structural spectrum, and issue-oriented groups at the other.

Because of their lack of organizational structure, issue-oriented groups are generally less effective in pursuing and achieving their goals. Moreover, their goals are restricted to a narrow focus and can only be pursued one at a time. The highly structured institutional groups, however, are free to pursue a number of broadly defined issues simultaneously. Issue-oriented groups have a small membership and a minimal, usually volunteer, staff to handle communications. Institutional groups, meanwhile, can bring extensive financial and human resources to bear on a variety of issues. Clearly, the Aboriginal organizations that are more institutional in nature have a greater chance of achieving their goals. Institutional organizations can choose from a variety of persuasive techniques, such as advertising, and can cultivate long-term formal and informal relations with government officials and senior civil servants (Wuttunee, 1972).

An organization with a strong network forms a basis for recruiting. And a sharing of recruits among organizations leads in turn to a sharing of some of the same ideas. Hence, the ability of a group of Aboriginal people to achieve their goals is also a function of the social cohesiveness of the organization to which they belong. Thus, the linkages of the network are continually strengthened. An institutional type of organization is in a position to distribute many more ideas than can an issue-oriented one. Organizations within a network also find that decision making is facilitated and that coordinated action is more possible.

Certain factors associated with issue-oriented groups can reduce their effectiveness. For example, the emergence of divergent (or different) goals of various sub-interest groups leads to a decrease in ability to achieve goals as well as an increase in the amount of intergroup conflict. In addition, as the organization increases in scope and area, new sub-interest groups emerge—e.g., band affiliation, province, legal status, linguistics, and religion—that contribute to the multiple cleavages permeating Aboriginal organizations.

The internal leadership structure of an Aboriginal organization is also an important determinant of that organization's effectiveness in achieving its goals. Particularly important is the ability of Aboriginal leaders to exert strategic control over the goals and objectives of the organization. Organizational leaders must be adept at spanning boundaries at all times. They must monitor and control such factors as their clients' needs, funding opportunities, and reserve politics as they attempt to achieve their organization's goals. This requires leaders to be constantly vigilant in promoting their clients' interests, while at the same time maintaining their legitimacy in the eyes of external power groups (Howard, 1951).

As Pfeiffer and Salanchik (1978) point out, an organization survives when it is able to quickly adjust to external conditions and also cope with the environment in which it operates. For example, Aboriginal organizational leaders invest considerable time and effort in dealing with and attempting to influence such external agencies as AAND, the Department of Industry, and various economic boards while also attending to the needs of their own constituents (Nielsen, 1991). The Native Women's Association of Canada was able to utilize the court rulings of the *Lavell* and *Bedard* cases as the basis for further lobbying efforts. They were able to identify "sex-equality" as the central issue of their organization and focus on that single goal (Cantryn, n.d.).

The organizational processes that have to be undertaken by Aboriginal organizations to survive are continuously in flux. Organizations with stable leadership and members are more likely to embark upon strategies that allow the organization to continue its existence. Oliver (1990) identifies several factors that push organizations into a "balancing" mode. Let us take each in turn.

Necessity comes into play when the organization must take an action in order to meet some legal or regulatory requirement. Non-compliance with this requirement will lead to negative sanctions against the organization (e.g., loss of funding). Thus, when government officials require Aboriginal organizations to comply with certain legal standards, the organizations must put themselves into a balancing mode. Reciprocity motivates an organization when it attempts to collaborate or coordinate its activities with those of another in the hope that there will be a mutually beneficial outcome. There is anticipation that the benefits of establishing a partnership will outweigh the disadvantages. A third factor that makes it necessary for an organization's leadership to strive for balance is efficiency. All modern organizations are assessed in terms of their ratio of inputs to outputs. The cost–benefit ratios of Aboriginal organizations are continually being monitored. The establishment of a stable organization (resource flow and exchanges) is important if the Aboriginal organization is to remain in existence over time. Finally, the issue of legitimacy is significant to organization leaders. The image or reputation of the organization is important if it is to remain credible in the eyes of both its constituents and the broader society.

As noted, resources are not useful if they cannot be mobilized and brought to bear when needed. Aboriginal people have, in the past, mobilized some resources in the form of sporadic, incidental, collective action. However, if this mobilization is not sustained, within a short time the organization will fall into disarray. Historically Aboriginal people have lacked the structural organization necessary to carry out political action. However, new organizational structures, such as the AFN, form a basis for recruiting new members, linking existing members, and providing them with a vehicle to develop shared ideas and mutual respect (Cornell, 1988). Thus it helps develop a collective consciousness. Organizations also disseminate ideas that can be used to facilitate decisions and carry out concerted action.

Aboriginal people have always had organizational structures. However, these structures were local (tribal) and focused around kinship. It has only been in recent years that pan-Indian and national Aboriginal organizations have emerged. Through this process, various Aboriginal groups have become linked in their political action. However, while the organizational structures have emerged from the rural-based Aboriginal people, organizations are usually located in urban centres, and this disconnect has placed one more obstacle in their effective functioning.

Why haven't Aboriginal people become more involved in changing their lives? Why haven't they taken action in the past to provide themselves with the opportunities available to others? First, the answer is that they have. However, through the process of cryptoamnesia, Canadians have long forgotten the role of Aboriginal organizations and their quest for social change. A second answer is that the degree of impact has been lessened because of their inability to amass the correct resources for the goals they want to achieve. As a rule, the greater the number and variety of resources held by a group, the greater their power. However, it is important to note that the importance of any resource is related to the issue being considered. As Cornell (1988) points out, not all resources are equally valuable, and their relative value depends on a variety of factors. For example, the size of a minority population is an important resource in a democracy because it will have more political influence than in a dictatorship. Legal skills are important if decisions are made by a judiciary but are not as important if they are made through a political process. Resources can also be assessed in terms of their convertibility, reusability, and applicability. For example, education is convertible into jobs, income, and power. It also can be used over and over and has a wide applicability to a number of situations. On the other hand, legal skills have a limited applicability but can be used over and over.

Summary

- The Department of Aboriginal Affairs and Northern Development is an all encompassing institution—from birth to death, from the bedroom to the boardroom.
- AAND conveys a lack of vision and operational means to bring about meaningful change to the lives of Aboriginal people.
- AAND is only one of 34 different agencies that deal with Aboriginal people.
- Aboriginal people have developed a myriad of organizations to resist the unilateral decision making of AAND.

- Most Aboriginal organizations have been ineffectual in bringing about social change.

Key Terms

AAND p. 159

Canadian Aboriginal Economic Development Strategy p. 172

core funding p. 176

devolution p. 162

discretionary funds p. 165

Indian and Inuit Affairs Program p. 160

Native Council of Canada p. 185

North American Indian Brotherhood p. 185

Office of the Federal Interlocutor p. 160

pan-Aboriginal organizations p. 189

quasi-statutory programs p. 65

Royal Commission on Aboriginal Peoples p. 168

Questions for Further Discussion

1. How does the Indian and Inuit Affairs Program support Aboriginal people in their quest to preserve and develop their culture?

2. How has the federal government been shifting responsibility since the mid 1970s?

3. Federal expenditures flow mainly through what four main routes?

4. What new role has been created in the Office of the Federal Interlocutor? What does this mean for non-status Indians?

5. Why has the process of decentralization taken so long?

6. How can the Royal Commission Report help rebuild Aboriginal and non-Aboriginal relationships?

7. When was the first Aboriginal political organization in Canada formed? What was it and who formed it?

8. Compare and contrast reformative and transformative perspectives.

9. What are two types of resources?

CHAPTER 7

First Nations: Contesting Title and Ownership

LEARNING OBJECTIVES

After reading this chapter you should be able to:

1. Explain what pre-Confederation treaties attempted to accomplish.

2. Understand the importance of the Jay Treaty of 1796.

3. Discuss the significance of the *Royal Proclamation* of 1763.

4. Define "treaty entitlement."

5. Discuss land claims.

6. Identify the three types of claims.

7. Understand the significance of the *White Paper* of 1969.

INTRODUCTION

When William Robinson was sent to deal with Indian complaints about the intrusion of whites looking for minerals on land along the eastern and northern shores of Lake Superior, a new era in Indian–white relations emerged. Robinson met with the Ojibwa leaders and the first land-based treaties were established (the Robinson–Superior and Robinson–Huron treaties of 1850). These treaties provided a template that would be used by Robinson's successors and would forever change the social landscape of Canada. Later treaties were intended to give recognition to Indian interests in the land, to provide compensation, and to establish an orderly transition of land ownership from one group to another. The treaties also established the rules of the relationship between Indians and the federal government once land was transferred (Daniel, 1980).

There did develop in British North America a consistent body of precedent and tradition that was utilized on new frontiers where fairly rapid settlement or resource exploitation took place. This involved negotiations by which Aboriginal peoples surrendered most of their territorial rights and in return gained various forms of compensation. Although numerous land surrender treaties had already been made in the Thirteen Colonies, it was not until after the American Revolution that surrender/compensation was first systematically used in Canada (Ray, 1974).

Nevertheless, many Canadians feel that treaties are no more than outdated contracts between a group of Indians and the federal government. There is also a belief that, since treaties are old, the agreements within them can be breached. However, in a Supreme Court decision concerning hunting rights (*Simon* v. *The Queen*, 1985), the court held that treaties are neither contracts nor international instruments. They are to be regarded as agreements *sui generis*; that is, they exist in force and are legally binding.

Aboriginal treaty and land claims today involve much more than legal questions about the collective title and property rights of Aboriginal peoples. In addition, they are not simply concerned with determining an appropriate amount of financial compensation (Moss and Niemczak, 1991). Land claims are a balance between negotiation and litigation, and between government action and inaction, and are subject to passive and active resistance by both Aboriginal people and governments (Hodgins, Heard, and Milloy, 1992). They are perhaps the most sensitive and socially volatile issues now confronting Aboriginal peoples and successive Canadian federal governments (Mallea, 1994).

In the 19th century, Aboriginal land fuelled Canadian and American economic growth. However, dispossession had an opposite effect on the Indian nations. It contributed to their underdevelopment to the extent that Aboriginal peoples were unable to sustain themselves. Within a century, this process had destroyed the Aboriginal economic base, wherever their societies were. In addition, the land base was unequally distributed. The most fertile land was taken for European settlers, control over water went to the government, and the environment was altered to the disadvantage of Aboriginal people. As Cornell (1988) points out, they struggled to adapt, but their economies were falling apart and they had no way of entering the new emerging capitalist structure. The result was a spiral toward economic marginalization and dependency. Today many Aboriginals remain among the most marginalized and poorest communities, discriminated against and often exposed to grave abuses of their fundamental rights.

While the Canadian government has publicly stated that it wants to make Indigenous rights a reality (despite its actions and, just as frequently, its inactions) the results have not changed First Nations' status in over a century. This lack of commitment is most clearly demonstrated in the way government has been dragging its feet with regard to land claims. Large-scale projects for the construction of infrastructure or the extraction of natural resources on Indigenous lands have been, until the late 20th century, pursued without consultation or thought as to how they will affect the lives and health of Aboriginal people.

The reactive stance that Aboriginal people have typically adopted can be seen in a variety of institutional settings—religious, economic, and educational. Often, the inability to coordinate their actions, the lack of funding, and the lack of understanding of the political process have led to this failure to control the agenda when dealing with federal and provincial governments. The emergence of various factions within the Aboriginal community has also hindered their planning and political strategies. Attempts to establish any sense of community and/or compromise among Aboriginal groups have been lacking—a situation ostensibly at odds with the traditional Aboriginal "consensus" model of decision-making.

The lack of consensus has been exploited by agencies and organizations dealing with Aboriginal people. It has allowed them to act in any way they wanted to, justifying their actions through the inability of Aboriginal people to agree. However, conditions have changed over the past several decades and Aboriginal people are beginning to act in a concerted and proactive manner. They have come to realize that, if they do not, decisions will be enacted that will seal the fate of Aboriginals as peoples relegated to a marginal position in the political economy of Canada (Lutz, 2007).

Aboriginal people have begun to think in proactive terms, not constrained by existing bureaucratic rules in their dealings with provincial and federal governments. But over a century of control and marginalization has had its impact, and dependence has been created. It is this sense of limited capacity to act, or lack of agency, that must be overcome. Aboriginal people are also prioritizing the goals they are prepared to pursue. Boundaries are being established in order to determine when and how they will take action. Agendas are being clearly spelled out, and strategies planned. Community divisiveness is being addressed and ranks are being closed to ensure a unified response to government. Finally, fiscal issues are being considered as only one component in a highly complex matrix of decision-making. If decisions are always based on financial considerations, then the process of consultation and negotiation is reduced to economic choices, a substantial handicap for any group trying to advance its agenda (Sanders, 1983a; 1983b).

One issue about which Aboriginal people have become more proactive is their concern over land. They have, after many years, realized that they can successfully pursue land claims even though results are not easily achieved. The early and disappointing outcomes of their land claims slowed their initiatives. However, as they have become more skilled at legal confrontation, their successes have increased. They have also come to more fully appreciate the connection between land and their culture. As Altman and Nieuwenhuysen (1979) point out, the special relationship that Aboriginal people have with the land seems best described by the word "spiritual." Having fully reclaimed this perspective, Aboriginal people have now taken on the challenge of reclaiming land that they feel rightly belongs to them. As Mallea (1994) and Isaac (1995) have pointed out, the law on this subject has developed rapidly, and concepts and precedents have even been applied across international borders.

ORIGIN OF THE TREATIES: COLONIAL STRUGGLES AND THE MAKING OF CANADA

Some of the earliest agreements between Indians and the government have been called **Peace and Friendship treaties**, and were carried out primarily in the Maritime area. These **pre-Confederation treaties** generally dealt with military and political relations and did not involve specific land transfers, annuities, trading rights, or compensation for rights limited or taken away (Sanders, 1983a). Yet by no means are these early treaties unimportant, even today. Good examples of "Peace and Friendship" treaties are those signed between the Mi'kmaq and the governor of Nova Scotia in 1760–61. It was these treaties, and specifically the right within them to catch and sell fish for profit (including lobster), that were at the centre of the controversial and highly publicized **Marshall case**, argued in the Supreme Court of Canada (*R. v. Marshall,* 1999; Coates, 2000). Pre-Confederation agreements continue to be reinterpreted and to generate new court rulings over access to different resources.

With the fall of the French fortress at Louisbourg, Cape Breton, and by the Treaty of Paris in 1763, which ended hostilities, France ceded all its North American possessions to Great Britain, with the exception of Saint Pierre and Miquelon Islands (which it still retains) and Louisiana (which it later ceded to Spain). In the spring of that year, the crystallization of Indian misgivings gained expression through the activities of Chief Pontiac (fighting against the English and the intrusions of the missionaries), although particular provisions in the *Royal Proclamation* concerning the protection of Indian-occupied lands were designed to allay such fears. The ***Royal Proclamation of 1763*** did indeed define lands that were to remain, at the sovereign's pleasure, with the Indians as their hunting grounds, but Rupert's Land and the old colony of Quebec were specifically exempted. In what was to become Canada, the hunting grounds in the east comprised a relatively narrow strip between the northern bounds of Quebec and Rupert's Land, along with all of what was to become Upper Canada; in the Northwest, they comprised an amorphous area bounded by Rupert's Land, the Beaufort Sea, and the Russian and Spanish claims to the west and south.

With the Revolutionary War of 1775 to 1783, the emphasis in the colonies of Nova Scotia and Quebec changed irrevocably to settlement, development, lumbering, fishing, and trade; the dissolution of the 200-year-old partnership between Indian and fur trader was well on the way. The most immediate effect was a 50-percent increase in population in the two colonies occasioned by the influx of United Empire Loyalists, who were primarily interested in farming, homesteading, and business. These were followed, particularly in Upper Canada after 1791, by a steady stream of settlers from the south with like interests. They brought with them the desire for peace, law, good order. and the other concomitants of settled living.

The Treaty of Paris signed between Great Britain and the United States in 1783, established the boundary from the Atlantic to the Lake of the Woods. In one stroke, Canada lost the entire southwestern half of the vast inland domain that French and British adventurers had discovered, explored, and exploited with the help of the Aboriginals. Along with it went that portion of the Indians' hunting grounds, established in 1763, that was bounded by the Great Lakes and the Ohio and Mississippi rivers. A natural point of departure for the future boundary at the 49th parallel of latitude was also ensured. The inevitable dissension with the Indian people that followed, however, was reaped by the United States rather than Great Britain.

By the *Constitutional* (or *Canada*) *Act* of 1791, the British Parliament divided Quebec into the provinces of Upper Canada and Lower Canada, abolished the conciliar form of government that had existed in Quebec for two centuries, and established representative government in both provinces. Land was to be granted in freehold tenure in Upper Canada and could be so granted in Lower Canada, if desired.

In 1796, by the terms of the *Jay Treaty*, the fur-trading posts of Niagara, Detroit, Michilimackinac, and Grand Portage—which were still in British hands—were handed over to the United States in accordance with the boundary provisions agreed to in 1783. In order to facilitate what remained of the fur trade, an article in the *Jay Treaty* provided for the free passage of Indian trappers back and forth across the boundary with "their ordinary goods and peltries"; it is on the basis of this provision that the present-day Iroquois claim duty-free passage across the international boundary (Innis, 1970).

On the Pacific coast, the leading protagonists changed over the course of time from Russia, Britain, and Spain to Russia, Britain, and the United States, but it was not from the sea that this contest was to be settled. Although Captain Cook had made his landfall at Nootka Sound in 1778, the traders who followed him lost their vessels and furs to the Spanish, who were engaged in a last endeavour to enforce their claims to the northwest coast. In 1791, Captain George Vancouver arrived to officially acknowledge the restoration of British rights after the Nootka Convention with the Spanish; the Russians were concurrently pushing down from the North, following the seal and sea otter.

The only firm and lasting links with the Pacific coast, however, would have to be established by land, and these were established by Alexander Mackenzie in 1793, by way of the Peace River canyon to Dean Channel; Simon Fraser in 1808, by the tumultuous river that bears his name; and David Thompson in 1811, down the Columbia to its mouth. These Canadian Scots were all members of the North West Company and were rivals not only of the Spanish, Russians, and Americans, but also of the Hudson's Bay Company. With their exploits, the chain of discovery and exploration, whose initial links had been forged in the quest for furs along the Atlantic coast over the preceding two centuries, was complete from ocean to ocean—all in the name of the fur trade. In each instance, the ubiquitous Scot was accompanied, guided, and sustained by Aboriginal companions (Wildsmith, 1985).

The outbreak of war in 1812 saw 500 000 British Americans (of whom fewer than 5000 were regular troops) confronted by a population of 8 million in the United States. Great Britain was not only at war with the United States but had its strength committed to the struggle against Napoleon. Through a combination of dogged determination on the part of the British Americans (aided by several hundred Indians under Shawnee Chief Tecumseh) in throwing back invasion forces and ineffective planning on the part of the enemy, Canada managed to hold out until the defeat of Napoleon in 1814, allowing Britain to bring all its forces to bear in America.

The United States considered the Jay Treaty of 1796 to be abrogated by the War of 1812–14, but the Convention of 1818 settled the outstanding boundary matters by confirming the border to the Lake of the Woods and extending it along the 49th parallel to the Rocky Mountains. The Treaty of Ghent in 1814 reinstated the provisions of the Jay Treaty affecting Indian people, but, as the conditions of the former were not considered to be self-executing, it became the individual responsibility of each of the governments concerned to give effect to the relevant provisions by appropriate legislation (Leslie and Maguire, 1978).

In terminating the international boundary at the Rocky Mountains, the Convention of 1818 left one major area subject to contention with the growing neighbour to the south—the so-called Oregon Territory, jointly occupied by Britain and the United States. The first large-scale movement of American settlers into Oregon in 1842 naturally created a clamour for annexation to the United States. Fortunately, the contention was resolved through the Treaty of Washington in 1846, by which the boundary was continued to the sea along the 49th parallel and Vancouver Island was confirmed as a British possession. For all intents and purposes Canada's external boundaries now were fixed and its attention could be concentrated on consolidation.

Pre-Confederation treaties were often little more than territorial cessions in return for one-time grants, usually in goods. However, there is evidence that some of the Indians involved felt that the government was assuming broader trusteeship responsibilities as part of the bargain. Annuities, or annual payments for the ceded land rights, first appeared in a treaty in 1818 and thereafter became routine. At this stage, the provision of land for Indian reserves only occasionally formed part of the surrender terms. Similarly, the right to continue hunting and fishing over ceded territories was very rarely mentioned in the written terms of surrender. Not until 1850, when cessions of land rights were obtained by William Robinson along the northern shores of Lakes Huron and Superior, were treaties made that granted to the Indians all four items: one-time expenditures, annuities, reserves, and guarantees concerning hunting and fishing. It was for this reason that Alexander Morris, the most widely known of the government's negotiators, noted in the early 1870s that the Robinson Treaties were templates to be used for all future treaties made by the recently created Dominion.

Most cessions made in Ontario after 1830, for example, were concluded in trust. The government assumed responsibility for disposing of the ceded lands on the Indians' behalf, with the proceeds of sales usually going to the particular Indians involved. As with land cessions made earlier, which were at times outright surrenders with the government as purchaser, there are strong arguments that inadequate compensation was given. Surrenders concluded prior to 1818 provided for a lump-sum payment along with a nominal yearly rent; in one 1816 surrender of Thurlow Township, for instance, the yearly rent was fixed at one peppercorn. In an 1836 surrender, it was considered sufficient to promise the Chippewa claimants agricultural and educational aid in exchange for their surrender of 1.5 million acres south of Owen Sound. The Robinson–Huron and Robinson–Superior Treaties also supplied only minimal payments to the Indians, although they contained provisions for a limited augmentation of annuities in the future. (One oversight in the Huron Treaty possibly left Aboriginal rights intact at Temagami.)

TREATIES AND TREATY MAKING AFTER 1867

As discussed, pre-Confederation treaties were made with the Crown through representatives of the British government. Later, after Confederation, treaties would be made through the Canadian government. All the terms of the pre-Confederation treaties were turned over to the Canadian government at the time of Confederation. When the *Royal Proclamation* of 1763 was issued, Indian rights were specifically referred to for the first time in Canadian history. The *Royal Proclamation* confirmed that **Aboriginal rights** existed. However, the question remains as to how much of what is now Canada is covered by the proclamation. Driben (1983) pointed out that it is difficult today to determine the boundaries of what the *Royal Proclamation* referred to as "Indian territory."

When the Hudson's Bay Company (HBC) surrendered Rupert's Land in 1869, Canada inherited the responsibility for negotiating with the resident Aboriginal tribes. Prior to the transfer, the *Royal Proclamation* had established the "equitable principles" governing the purchase and surrender of Aboriginal lands. The Imperial order-in-council that transferred this responsibility is stipulated in Article 14:

> Any claim of Indians to compensation for lands required for the purposes of settlement shall be disposed of by the Canadian government in communications with the Imperial government; and the Company shall be relieved of all responsibility in respect of them.

The administrators who were subsequently appointed to negotiate federal treaties with the Indians were inexperienced and unfamiliar with Aboriginal customs. Lacking firsthand knowledge, these administrators fell back on the legacy of the Hudson's Bay Company's treatment of Aboriginal people, as well as on some sketchy reports of the negotiations behind the Robinson Treaties of 1850 and 1862 and the Manitoulin Island Treaty, also of 1862.

Preliminary negotiations between the Indians in Manitoba and representatives of the government began in 1870. By 1871, Treaties Nos. 1 and 2 were signed, and in 1873 the lands between Manitoba and Lake Superior were ceded in Treaty No. 3. Northern Manitoba and the remainder of the southern Prairies were surrendered by Aboriginal peoples between 1874 and 1877 in Treaties Nos. 4, 5, 6, and 7.

The land taken by the Canadian government under Treaties Nos. 1 through 7 provided sufficient land for the mass settlement of immigrants entering Canada for the time being. However, by 1899 the pressures of settlement and mineral development again caused the government to negotiate for new lands from the Aboriginal peoples. Although these later treaties, Nos. 8 through 11, differed in many respects from the earlier ones, they were clearly modelled upon earlier treaties. Subsequent modern agreements may, in turn, be modelled upon and indeed even replace these numbered treaties, as is the case with Treaty 11 (noted later in this chapter and for some details on the 2003 Tlicho [Dene/Dogrib] Agreement).

The federal government decided to negotiate with the Aboriginal peoples largely because its own agents foresaw violence against European settlers if treaties were not established. However, this perception was not based on particular threats or claims on the part of the Aboriginal peoples, who simply wished to carry out direct negotiations with the government for compensation for the lands they'd occupied prior to European settlement. After the first treaty was signed, neither the government nor the Aboriginal people attempted to find alternative means to deal with "Indian claims." Government officials based future treaties on prior ones, and Aboriginal groups insisted on treatment similar to that received by those who had signed earlier treaties.

Despite specific differences, the contents of all the treaties are remarkably similar. Treaties Nos. 1 and 2 set the stage. They created reserve lands granting 160 acres per family. Annuities of $3 per person, a gratuity of $3 per person, and a school on each reserve were agreed upon. Other promises were also made orally during the negotiations; some of these were later given formal recognition by an order-in-council. Treaty No. 3 contained the same provisions as Treaties Nos. 1 and 2, except that its reserve allotment was increased to 640 acres per family of five.

The federal government desired treaties that were brief, simple, and uniform in content. Nonetheless, although constrained by these government-imposed limitations, negotiators were often forced to make minor additions to a treaty. Sometimes these took the form of verbal promises, presumably to avoid deviations from the standard written form. For example, the government negotiators for Treaty No. 6 were forced to add several benefits, such as medicine chests and provisions for relief in times of famine.

In general, however, the government negotiators had by far the best of the bargaining. Most treaties were written by the government and simply presented to the Indians for signing. The terms of Treaty No. 9, for example, were determined by the Ontario and Canadian governments well in advance of discussions with Aboriginal people. Moreover, there is evidence that, in many cases, hard-won oral promises have never been recognized nor acted upon by the government.

In their negotiations with the Aboriginal people, treaty commissioners always avoided discussing the nature or extent of Aboriginal land rights. Although the commissioners obscured the issue, the Aboriginal people clearly surrendered rights to land by signing the treaties. In many cases, the commissioners argued that the Indians had no land rights at all. If the Aboriginal negotiators objected to this argument, the commissioners would enlist support from missionaries or traders whom the Aboriginal people trusted. In the end, however, no Indian treaty was ever brought before Parliament. Instead, the treaties were presented to cabinet and ratified by an order-in-council. This suggests that they were accepted by the Government of Canada both as recognition of Aboriginal land claims and as a means of their negotiation and resolution.

British Columbia: A Special Case

British Columbia was a special case in its handling of treaties. Between 1849 and 1854, James Douglas, the governor of the colony, negotiated a series of treaties with the Indians on Vancouver Island. After 1854 this policy was discontinued. Although the Colonial Office in England supported the treaties, it would not provide Douglas with monies to continue them. British Columbia settlers refused responsibility for negotiations with the Indians and would not release public funds to settle land claims.

As Berger (1981: 222–23) points out, British Columbia's House of Assembly had initially recognized Aboriginal land titles. However, when told by London that it would have to provide the funds to settle those titles, the House of Assembly withdrew recognition of Indian land claims. This meant that, technically, the Aboriginal peoples were not entitled to any compensation by the province.

No further treaties were made in British Columbia until the late 20th century. The only exception was the northeastern part of the province, which was to be covered by Treaty No. 8. With the entry of British Columbia into Confederation in 1871, the administration of Indians and Indian lands in the province fell under the jurisdiction of the federal government. However, the federal government's interpretation of this jurisdiction has remained controversial up to the present (Duff, 1997).

When British Columbia entered Confederation in 1871 as Canada's sixth province, the actual terms concerning the treatment of Aboriginal people were unclear. The terms of union clearly stated that all public lands were to be the property of the provincial government; this meant that the federal government owned no land outright in the province to give to the Aboriginal people. Some provision was made, however, for Aboriginal lands. The province agreed to relinquish to the federal government "tracts of land of such extent as it had hitherto been the practice of the British Columbian government to appropriate for that purpose" (Berger, 1981: 224).

Unfortunately, the practice of the British Columbian government was to supply considerably less land than did the federal government. When allotting land, non-Aboriginal settlers received 320 acres of land per homestead from the province; Aboriginal people were granted considerably less. In 1887 the federal government asked the province to determine the size of the reserves by relinquishing 80 acres per Indian family. The province set aside only 20 acres per family, a much lower acreage than that set aside for other Aboriginal peoples by the Canadian government. Understandably, Indians in British Columbia objected strongly and insisted on their Aboriginal rights.

British Columbian Aboriginals continued to oppose the establishment of reserves and to argue title to their own lands. The federal government dissolved its commission in 1910 after the provincial government refused to sanction any more reserves. In the early 1900s, Indians sent delegations to Victoria and to England in an attempt to argue their claims for Aboriginal rights. The federal government partly supported these claims and tried unsuccessfully for a hearing before the Supreme Court of Canada. The province refused to participate in the legal proceedings and thus thwarted the efforts of the federal government.

In 1913 a Royal Commission was established by the federal government, partly to adjust the acreage of the reserves in British Columbia. In 1916 the Commission produced a report detailing lands to be added to and removed from existing reserves. The added land was to be twice the size of the land taken away; however, the land to be taken away was, at that time, worth twice as much money.

As the federal government tried to implement this report, it met increased opposition from the provincial government and from Aboriginal peoples. The province finally confirmed an amended version of the report in 1923, but the Aboriginal peoples never accepted it. The Allied Indian Tribes of British Columbia emerged to become a powerful political force uniting Aboriginal opposition to the decision. In 1923 the Allied Indian Tribes of British Columbia presented a list of far-reaching demands to the federal government and agreed to relinquish their Aboriginal title claim only if the demands were met. These demands were remarkably similar to those met by previous treaties in other provinces—namely, 160 acres per capita, hunting rights, and the establishment of reserves.

The Allied Indian Tribes of British Columbia demanded that either a treaty be negotiated or that their Aboriginal title claim be submitted to the judicial committee of the Privy Council. In essence, they argued that, contrary to the beliefs of the federal and provincial governments, there had been no final settlement of their claims. As a result of the Indians' petition, a special joint committee of the House and Senate was convened to hear evidence and make a decision. This committee decided that the Indians had not established any claims to land based on Aboriginal title; however, it did recommend that an annual sum of $100 000 be spent for the good of Indians in British Columbia.

In order to prevent an appeal of this decision, the federal government passed an amendment to the *Indian Act* that prohibited the collection of funds by Aboriginal people for the advancement of a land claim. This amendment remained law until the middle of the 20th century. As a result, Aboriginal groups became powerless to press their claims, and were successfully ignored by the federal government throughout the Depression and World War II. Of necessity, local issues replaced larger concerns during this time. The Native Brotherhood of British Columbia was established in 1931 and, in 1942, became prominent in its fight against income tax for Aboriginal fishermen. But Aboriginal claims in British Columbia (McGhee, 1996) did not emerge again as an issue until the 1960s, when they played an important role in, among other things, the creation of the Indian Land Commission.

Chapter 10 will outline recent developments in British Columbia, from the 2002 Referendum on Aboriginal Treaties to the Lheidli T'enneh Final Agreement signed in 2006, turned down by First Nations members in 2007 but expected to come into effect in April 2011 (Price, 2009: 160–161; Indian and Northern Affairs website, accessed November 7, 2010). The Tsawwassen First Nation Final Agreement, signed in 2009, is the first treaty negotiated under the British Columbia treaty process initiated between 1990 and 1993 (Indian and Northern Affairs, February 2010).

The Historical, or Numbered, Treaties

Treaties Nos. 1 to 7 were made during the 1870s in the territory between the watershed west of Lake Superior and the Rocky Mountains, in what was then Canada's newly acquired Northwest. These treaties utilized many features of the earlier transactions, but were far more comprehensive in their provisions and more uniform and consistent with one another. Their characteristics and relative similarities were not due to a broad policy worked out in advance by the federal government. Immediately before the first of these treaties was made, the government had little information about the Indians of its new territory, let alone a policy. It proceeded to deal with the Aboriginal occupants in an ad hoc fashion as necessity dictated. Almost inevitably the patterns of earlier Canadian experience were adapted to a new time and place. The seven treaties that emerged were partly shaped by the Indians themselves and were indirectly influenced by United States policy and practice.

The government's purpose in negotiating treaties in the Northwest was to free land for settlement and development. A corollary of this was the urgent desire to satisfy the Indians sufficiently so that they would remain peaceful. The nature and extent of Indian rights to the territory were not discussed at the negotiations, nor were they defined in the treaties themselves. It is evident from the texts, nevertheless, that the government intended that whatever title the Indians might possess should be extinguished, since the opening clauses of all seven agreements deal with land surrender. This emphasis was not reflected in the preliminary treaty negotiations. There, the stress was on what the Indians would receive rather than on what they were giving up. The commissioners gave them assurances that the Queen understood their problems and was anxious to help them (Henderson, Benson, and Findlay, 2000).

The loss of control over land use and the diminishing game supply threatened the traditional Aboriginal way of life. While the Indians attempted to retain as much control as possible over their own territory and future, a secondary desire was the attempt to gain sufficient compensation and support to ensure their survival amid rapidly changing conditions. As a result of hard bargaining, Indians did manage to have some additional provisions included in the treaties beyond those the government had originally intended. These included agricultural aid and certain liberties to hunt and fish (Rotman, 1996). Aboriginal people today make several points in relation to these treaties. The major one is that the treaty texts do not reflect the verbal promises made during the negotiations and accepted by a people accustomed to an oral tradition. They state that their ancestors understood the treaties to be specifically designed to protect them and help them adapt to the new realities by developing an alternative agricultural base to complement their traditional livelihood of hunting and fishing. An excellent example and discussion of the Aboriginal view of treaties and their intent, expectations, and interpretation is presented in a study by Treaty 7 Elders and Tribal Council (1996).

Aboriginal associations strongly deny that the treaties obligate the government only to fulfil their terms as they appear in the essential treaty texts. They uniformly insist that the written versions must be taken together with the words spoken by the government's agents during the negotiations. In a submission to the commissioner on Indian claims, the Federation of Saskatchewan Indians states that:

In his various addresses to Chiefs and Headmen at treaty meetings, Commissioner Morris had a single message for the Indians: The Queen was not approaching the Indians to barter for their lands, but to help them, to alleviate their distress and assist them in obtaining security for the future. "We are not here as traders, I do not come as to buy or sell horses or goods, I come to you, children of the Queen, to try to help you. The Queen knows that you are poor: the Queen knows that it is hard to find food for yourselves and children: she knows that the winters are cold, and you(r) children are often hungry: she has always cared for her Red children as much as for her White. Out of her generous heart and liberal hand she wants to do something for you. . . . "

These verbal assurances and statement of Crown intent, and the many others like them given by Morris in his address to Chiefs and Headmen, cannot be separated from treaty documents because they were accepted as truth by the assembled Indians. (Saskatchewan Indian Federation, Saskatchewan Indian, 1982: 30)

The nature and extent of the implementation of treaty provisions are another source of grievance in this area. The government's open policy of detribalization, which held as its goal the assimilation of Indian people into the dominant society, motivated a number of specific policies that were destructive of Indian efforts to develop within the context of their own cultures. The field of education is one of the most conspicuous examples of this process, since it is easy to appreciate the effects of isolating children in residential schools, where they were taught that their parents' language and culture were inferior, and where a set of alien customs and values were instilled in them (Pennekeok, 1976).

In the Aboriginal peoples' view, during the late 19th and early 20th centuries, the government failed to provide the expected agricultural assistance and unduly restricted Indian agricultural development. It encouraged the surrender of some of the best agricultural land from the reserves when its efforts failed to turn the Indians into farmers.

All of the Prairie Aboriginal organizations, along with the Grand Council of Treaty No. 3 in northern Ontario, think the treaties should be reworded in terms that will embody their original spirit and intent. As in the area of Aboriginal title, the results of such settlements could, they say, provide the basis for revolutionizing the future development of Aboriginal peoples and reserves on Aboriginal terms. The treaty Indians' organizations have outlined some specific objectives and proposals for an approach to development. A primary characteristic of these is their rejection of the concept of assimilation or detribalization, and, stemming from this, the conviction that Aboriginal people must initiate and control the development effort themselves.

Only at the turn of the 20th century, when mineral exploitation provided the impetus, were treaties made to the north of the areas surrendered during the 1870s. Treaty No. 8 was concluded in the Athabasca District, Treaty No. 9 in northern Ontario, and Treaty No. 10 in northern Saskatchewan. In addition, adhesions to Treaty No. 5 were taken in northern Manitoba to extend the limit of ceded territory to the northern boundary of the province. Finally, in 1921, following the discovery of oil at Norman Wells, Treaty No. 11 was made in the Northwest Territories.

The numbered, or historical, treaties between the Indians and the Dominion thus began in the mid-1800s (in southern Ontario) and moved westward, eventually encompassing all of Manitoba, Saskatchewan, and Alberta. The treaty period ended in 1921 with the signing of Treaty No. 11, which encompasses almost all of the Mackenzie

Valley of the Northwest Territories. Today, only British Columbia, the Yukon, parts of Quebec, and Newfoundland have not "treatied" with the Indians. It should be emphasized that, where treaties have not been made, **Aboriginal title** is said to still exist, thus providing the basis for subsequent land claims and the modern-day treaty-making process (McGhee, 1996).

TYPES OF CLAIMS

There are essentially three categories of claims: **Aboriginal rights** (which include "title" and self-government), treaty and scrip settlement grievances, and land claims. Chapter 8 will detail scrip issues, Aboriginal treaty rights (called *specific claims*), **band claims**, and land claims (called comprehensive claims). Chapter 10 will deal with the broader issues and claims relating to self-determination and self-government.

The notion of Aboriginal rights is the prime rationale underlying all Aboriginal claims in Canada. Aboriginal people assert that their rights to land derive from their original occupancy and point out that Aboriginal title has been recognized by the dominant society through numerous judicial decrees and actions of the government going back to the *Royal Proclamation* of 1763. It is important to note that no treaties were made for about half the territory in Canada where Aboriginal people surrendered their lands. On this basis alone, both status and non-status Indians, as well as Inuit, are now developing or negotiating treaty terms.

Treaty Indians have a number of claims that relate to the agreement for the cession of their lands. Some of these rest on an insistence that specific treaty terms have not been fulfilled, or that the broader spirit of the treaties has not been acknowledged by the government. As discussed, a frequent claim is that verbal promises made at the time of the negotiations were not included in the written texts. In some areas, Indian people also emphasize in their treaty claims that these transactions constituted inadequate settlements, even if all their terms were fulfilled (for example, treaty land and/or reserve entitlement claims). These claims involve assertions about the way in which treaties were negotiated, the disparities between the two contracting parties, and the alleged unfairness of the terms.

Most status (or registered) Indians have rights to reserve lands held in common for their band. Most bands, whether in treaty or non-treaty areas, usually have specific claims to make. The most numerous and widespread are those stemming from reserve land losses. Reserve land was sometimes lost through squatting by non-Aboriginal people, or through error, or by being re-surveyed. Most typically it was lost as a result of formal surrenders to, and expropriations by, the federal or provincial governments. Claims may be based on the dubious legality of these occurrences or on the propriety of certain methods of land alienation. Claims based on such land (reserve) losses are sometimes called "surrender claims," involving either a technical breach (of the *Indian Act*) or a fiduciary breach in the case of a surrender that was not in the First Nation's best interests (Indian Claims Commission, 2005).

Management of band funds, reserve resources, and the administration of band affairs, particularly with regard to economic development, are the bases of some band claims discussed later in this chapter.

Land is an extremely important element in Aboriginal claims in general. As mentioned, Aboriginal peoples are becoming more articulate about their unique relationship to the land, both past and present, and about the meaning it has for them. They are also aware that the material standard of living that has been achieved generally in Canada derives ultimately from the land and its resources. As a consequence, they seek not only a role in determining the way in which the land and other resources are used, but also an equitable portion of the substantial benefits derived from their exploitation. This theme is basic in Aboriginal rights claims, but it also appears in treaty claims, where the original land agreements may be in question, and in band claims concerning lost reserve land or other natural resources.

For Aboriginal people, trusteeship, a fundamental element in their claims, involves both protection and assistance. When the federal government assumed political control over Aboriginal people, it undertook responsibilities for reserve land and band finances and imposed special limitations on Indians as a feature of Indian status. It adopted a protective role over Indians and their affairs analogous to that of the duty of a guardian or trustee toward a ward or beneficiary (Rotman, 1996). From this fiduciary relationship (or duty) flows grievances and claims that pertain to the government's management of Indian resources (DIAND, 1982a; 1985).

CLAIMS REGARDING TREATIES

Treaties have been the focal point for specific claims that have been pursued by Indians. These claims focus on several aspects. First, Indians argue that the treaty texts do not include the verbal promises made by the government during the negotiation period prior to the actual signing. Hence, they argue that the treaties oblige the government to keep promises made in both verbal and written contexts—e.g., Treaties Nos. 8 and 11 (Melville, 1981). Second, inequality among the various treaties' land provisions has provoked specific claims—for example, Treaty No. 5 provides for 71 hectares per family while other treaties provide 285 hectares.

Treaties have three possible interpretations. In one sense they can be viewed as agreements between two or more nations. Most Aboriginal people claim this interpretation when they refer to the various treaties with the federal government. On the other hand, it is clear that the Canadian government (as evidenced through certain legislation and court decisions) does not interpret the treaties in the same manner (Weaver, 1983).

Treaties have at times been interpreted as contracts. While there is some legal support for this interpretation, the nature of the jurisprudence dealing with this issue is so specific that one must be cautious in interpreting treaties from this perspective. Nevertheless, former prime minister Pierre Trudeau publicly stated that treaties are analogous to contracts.

Finally, treaties can be viewed as pieces of legislation. This interpretation is plausible, since many Indian treaties were made before such legislation as the *Indian Act.* Hence, any legal means that attempts to establish an orderly relationship between people could be viewed as analogous to legislation (Marule, 1977).

Even today, it is unclear which interpretation prevails (for a meticulous historical overview, see Miller, 2009). Nevertheless, the courts have viewed treaties as enforceable obligations, which has required the federal government in large part to live up to those obligations. Section 25 of the *Canadian Charter of Rights and Freedoms* and Section 35, or Part 2, of the Canadian Constitution (1982) have enshrined "existing" treaty rights.

Treaties are therefore legal arrangements between Aboriginal peoples and the Government of Canada. Moreover, treaties confer benefits upon successors even though at times it is difficult to identify who those successors are. The Supreme Court of Canada has identified a number of conditions that determine if a document is a treaty:

- continuous exercise of a right in the past and at present;
- the reasons that the Crown made a commitment;
- the situation prevailing at the time the document was signed;
- evidence of relations of mutual respect and esteem between the negotiators; and
- the subsequent conduct of the parties.

If, after reviewing the above, ambiguity still remains, the court decided that one could look at extrinsic evidence, such as the historical context, information about what went on at the time the document was signed, and the subsequent conduct of the parties. In all instances regarding the interpretation of treaties, the Supreme Court encourages and supports interpretations in favour of, and for the benefit of, Indian people as part of fiduciary doctrine. The reasoning of the court and federal government extends even to the "Peace and Friendship" treaties of the 18th century, as shown by the Marshall decision in September 1999. Subsequent treaty claims in the Maritimes involving the Mi'kmaq (treaties signed in 1726, 1752, 1759, and 1761 for example) revolved around the right to practice traditional trading activities in modern ways and modern contexts.

Land Claims Before 1969

The modern specific claims process traces its roots to 1947, when the federal government struck a special joint committee of the House and Senate to investigate matters relating to Indian Affairs. This committee operated for one year and heard presentations from Aboriginals across the country. The committee recommended the creation of an independent administrative tribunal to adjudicate claims, but this did not come to pass. Ten years later another joint committee was created. It made the same recommendation as the previous committee but, as before, nothing came of the recommendation (Prentice and Bellegarde, 2001). Similar recommendations were made for the next 20 years, but a lack of political will was demonstrated in that no such tribunal was ever established. As such, prior to the establishment of the Indian lands commissioner (1969) and the Office of Aboriginal Claims (1974), Indian claims were handled on an individual basis. The processing of a claim was dealt with either by the then Department of Indian Affairs and Northern Development or by the Department of Justice. There was a dual filing system utilized by DIAND through which all claims were sorted. One was labelled "petitions and complaints," the other "claims and disputes." The former label was interpreted by government officials as representing grievances and as such did not require any legal action on their part. However, the claims in the latter file were interpreted as legitimate and thus required the department to respond (Daniel, 1980; Wright, 1995).

By 1969, the federal government decided to take a different course and offered its infamous *White Paper* to deal with such thorny issues as land claims, Aboriginal rights, and other disputes between Aboriginal and non-Aboriginal peoples. The recommendations in the *White Paper* would have solved the issue of Indian claims in that Indians would not, in a legal sense have a basis upon which to bring claims forward (McNab, 1999).

As Daniel (1980) points out, the 1969 *White Paper* on Indian policies was vigorously repudiated by Indian leaders. They were joined in their opposition by a number of non-Indian social and political organizations, and the policy soon became the *bête noire* of government–Indian relations. However, one recommendation of the *White Paper* was for the appointment of an Indian claims commissioner. In late 1969 Dr. Lloyd Barber was appointed Canada's first and only Indian claims commissioner, a position he would hold until 1977 when the office was terminated. The commissioner's mandate was to receive and study grievances and to recommend measures to adjudicate any claims. He himself did not have powers of adjudication since his role was only advisory. Nevertheless, he played an important role in educating government officials and the public at large (Morse, 1991). The Indian Claims Commission and the Indian claims commissioner's office had divergent aims, and this was partially a result of the government's insistence that Indians had no legal basis on which to make claims. The creation of the commissioner's office was an interim structure developed by the government that was meant to be phased out once a new policy could be drafted (Sanders, 1983c; 1985a).

TREATIES TODAY

Are treaties signed years ago still valid, even those signed before Canada became a country in 1867? Canadians woke up on September 17, 1999, to find that they are indeed. On that day a Supreme Court decision (the Marshall decision) upheld a 240-year-old treaty between the King of England and the **Mi'kmaq Indians**. The Supreme Court ruled that the treaty gave Mi'kmaq the right to fish for daily needs and/or to obtain a moderate livelihood, including food, clothing, and housing, supplemented by a few amenities. This decision has forced the federal government to reassess its position on the over 800 outstanding treaty cases considered by the Department of Aboriginal Affairs (as of November 2010). The impact of this decision is far reaching, and Aboriginal people on the West coast have argued that they also have fishing and hunting rights under the 150-year-old Douglas Treaty. Russell Barsh has noted that the high court's ruling includes a "way of life" provision that will have a dramatic effect on provincial hunting and fishing regulations in Canada. For example, he noted that members of Treaty 7 could hunt legally in national parks and on unoccupied Crown land.

As a result of the treaties, the government of Canada received millions of acres of land from the surrender of First Nations while, in return, 0.32 percent of Canada's land mass was set aside for reserves. Many irregularities emerged in the allocation of this land, and in many cases treaty land entitlements could be claimed. While these entitlements are complex and complicated, they are legal obligations recognized in the Constitution that must be dealt with by the Government of Canada. The term *treaty land entitlement* is used to document land claims that flow from Treaty Nos. 1 through 11. There are two forms. The first is called initial or "late" entitlement, which reflects the fact that the First Nations did not receive the land promised under a treaty. The second is a shortfall, which refers to the situation in which a calculation for the amount of land to be set aside did not include all the eligible population. To resolve these specific claims requires considerable time and money to ensure that all factors are taken into consideration during evalutation.

One of the major recommendations presented by the Royal Commission on Aboriginal Peoples (Canada, 1996d) was that the federal government develop a trilateral relationship with regard to establishing new treaties. These new treaties would establish integrated processes on a regional level to deal with governance and jurisdictional issues. This recommendation has been accepted and is now in force in several provinces. With a new federal policy emphasizing a renewed partnership with Aboriginal peoples and an agreement that land claims need to be settled, it comes as no surprise that considerable activity has focused on land and land compensation.

British Columbia is by far the most active in establishing new treaties and, by 2003, 51 Aboriginal groups, representing over 70 percent of B.C.'s First Nations, were active in treaty negotiation through the tripartite lands commission. Setting the stage, the province established a **Treaty Negotiation Advisory Committee** in 1996 to provide input and advice to the government with regard to establishing treaties in the province and settling outstanding claims by Aboriginal peoples. Progress is equally dramatic in other jurisdictions, as shown by the example of the Tlicho final agreement (August 25, 2003), which effectively replaces the 82-year-old Treaty No. 11 from the Northwest Territories (see Box. 7.1).

Box 7.1	Tlicho Land Claims and Self Government

In 2005 the Tlicho, the government of the Northwest Territories, and the federal government signed the **Tlicho Land Claims and Self-Government** Agreement, which is the first combined land and self-government agreement in the Northwest Territories and the second in Canada. This land claims treaty gives the Tlicho ownership of a single area measuring 39 000 square kilometres surrounding the four Tlicho communities of Behcho ko, Wha ti, Gameti, and Wekweeti, as well as the subsurface resources. The Tlicho government is to receive $152 million over a 14-year period as well as a share (not yet determined) of resource royalties annually from resource developments in the Mackenzie Valley. Equally important, *Bill C-14* made major amendments to other acts, primarily the *Mackenzie Valley Resource Management Act.*

In its provision for self-government, the agreement created a regional Tlicho government with law-making authority over all Tlicho citizens who live in their communities and on their lands. This authority includes areas of education, adoption, family services, income support, social housing, and language and culture. Moreover, the agreement created the Tlicho community services agency, encompassing those services previously supplied by the government of the Northwest Territories as well as certain services provided by the federal government.

The Tlicho Nation's new government replaced the Indian Act Bands and Northwest Territories's municipal corporations, which previously had governing authority. The agreement also created a Tlicho constitution that sets out the structure of the Tlicho government and describes the main roles and responsibilities of officials. Moreover, under the agreement, the chief and half of the community councillors must be Tlicho citizens. From each of the four community governments, the chief and two councillors are appointed to the Tlicho government. The Tlicho community governments represent and serve all residents of the Tlicho communities and are responsible for municipal services. Through agreements with principal investors in the North and through impact benefit agreements, the Tlicho people will directly benefit from these agreements and will now have the power to manage their destiny in a way that is congruent with the norms and values of their society.

By far one of the most important settlements is the 2000 **Nisga'a Treaty**. This treaty is the first in British Columbia since 1899 and is the 14th modern-day treaty in Canada. The settlement was approved amid considerable political controversy, and over 500 public events and consultations took place in the negotiations between the Nisga'a and the provincial Treaty Negotiation Advisory Committee, composed of 31 individuals representing various third-party interests. The Nisga'a Final Agreement was accepted by the Nisga'a council, ratified in the House of Commons, in the B.C. legislature, and by the Nisga'a people.

The Nisga'a treaty took well over 100 years to be settled and represents a milestone in treaty settlements in British Columbia. It gives the Nisga'a a central government with the authority to make laws concerning social services (including child and family issues) and adoption and health services, as well as tribal jurisdiction over education. While laws can be established by the Nisga'a, they must be in agreement with the existing provincial and federal statutes. Laws established by the Nisga'a will have standing in any court dispute. In addition, the Nisga'a will administer and deliver federal and provincial social services.

How this will take place will be agreed to by both the provincial and federal governments. Under the treaty, the Nisga'a will continue to provide the services they have been and will then have full jurisdiction over them. These services will be funded through a federal transfer of funds. However, as soon as the Nisga'a begin to generate their own income, perhaps through taxation, the transfer funds will be reduced commensurately. On the face of it, the treaty seems to give the Nisga'a municipal status. However, the fact that they will be in control of their social services, health, and education makes their system different from a mere municipal structure. For example, the treaty notes (Section 27) that, in the event of an inconsistency between Nisga'a laws and federal and provincial laws of general application, Nisga'a law will prevail. Finally, the treaty stipulates that voting rights on Native territory will be restricted to people of Nisga'a descent.

Several criticisms of the treaty have been identified. First, critics claim that the treaty is "race based" and thus gives the Nisga'a rights that other "races" do not have. A closer look at the treaty characterizes the Nisga'a as a linguistically and culturally identified group, not a race. Others claim that the treaty is an example of modern-day apartheid. As

Foster (1998–99) points out, there is something hypocritical about stripping a people of their resources in one generation and then describing a complex and careful attempt by the next generation to restore some of those resources as "apartheid" or as a violation of equality before the law. A second criticism is that the government "gave it all away." In truth, the Nisga'a will only be getting about 10 percent of the land they are able to demonstrate as belonging to their traditional territories.

In British Columbia, Indian reserves make up about 0.35 percent of the province, and the treaty adds little to this figure. Surely this cannot be viewed as an exorbitant land settlement. Some critics claim that the treaty amends the Constitution because it requires a referendum by both the provincial legislature and the federal House of Commons. On the contrary, the treaty does not amend the Constitution but rather ensures that both levels of government confirm the treaty and take it seriously (Section 25 of the *Charter of Rights and Freedoms* and Section 35 of the Canadian Constitution). Finally, it is argued that it is not prudent for Canada and British Columbia to sign a final agreement with the Nisga'a when it is still not clear whether the 1997 *Delgamuukw* decision has given the Nisga'a more or fewer rights than the Nisga'a will get in the agreement. According to federal and provincial authorities, they, along with the Nisga'a, reviewed the decision before deciding to carry on negotiations and have agreed that the treaty is a final settlement of Nisga'a land claims. Behind these criticisms, it is easy to think that the real reason for objecting to the Nisga'a treaty is that it sets a benchmark for all others now being negotiated. No Aboriginal negotiator will take less than the Nisga'a, and that might be a real problem—or one that simply leads to unrealistic expectations. Whichever the case, the treaty has definite implications for future negotiations (Gibson, 1998–99).

In addition to non-Aboriginal criticism of the treaty, questions have been raised by other Aboriginal groups (Sterritt, 1998–99). They argue that the Nisga'a do not have a claim to the entire Nass watershed (based upon the critics' own evidence) and thus the treaty violates the rights of other nearby Aboriginal groups. They point out that the failure of the provincial and federal governments' response to the claims made by the Gitksan and Gitanyow submissions has serious consequences for their "overlapping" claims (Rotman, 1997). There has emerged a splinter group among the Nisga'a themselves, which has spoken out against alleged discrimination, financial irresponsibility, unaccountability, and "dictatorship" on the part of the Nisga'a Government (*The Province*, October 11, 2007).

GOVERNMENT LAND NEGOTIATIONS

Canadian jurisprudence has taken the position that Canada was acquired by discovery or settlement (Bartlett, 1984) and, although the concept of existing Aboriginal rights (from which Aboriginal title flows) is now entrenched in the Canadian Constitution (Sections 25 and 35), it is unclear what the words "existing Aboriginal rights" actually mean (W. Henderson, 1983; Sanders, 1985b; 1990).

One of the first legal rulings on the issue of Aboriginal title was handed down in 1885 (*St. Catharines Milling and Lumber Company* v. *The Queen*). This ruling characterized Aboriginal title as a possessory right, a right to use and occupancy similar to a **usufructuary right**—that is, a right based on *traditional* use and occupancy (R. Thompson, 1982). The Privy Council in 1888 changed this interpretation slightly when it characterized

Aboriginal title as a personal usufructuary right, dependent upon the goodwill of the sovereign. It would not be until nearly a century later, when in 1973 the *Calder et al.* v. *Attorney General of British Columbia* case came before the Supreme Court of Canada, that the basis of this right was re-examined. Even though the Nisga'a Indians did not win this case, three of the seven Supreme Court justices ruled that Aboriginal title did exist in common law irrespective of any formal recognition—that is, independent of the *Royal Proclamation* of 1763. These justices argued that once Aboriginal title has been established it is presumed to continue until the contrary is proven (making it an inherent right), and that the onus is upon the government to prove that it intended to extinguish Indian title through various legislation ordinances. Since no specific legislation was enacted that provided for Indian title to be extinguished, these judges concluded that the Indians may indeed still be in possession of Aboriginal title.

Prior to the Calder case, the federal government held that Aboriginal land rights were so general and undefined that it was not realistic to view them as claims capable of remedy through law. However, after the Calder case, the government announced a change in its policy with regard to legal obligations to legitimate claims being pursued by Indians. The government indicated that it was willing to negotiate settlements with Native groups where Native rights based upon usufruct had not been explicitly extinguished by treaty or otherwise superseded by law (Bankes, 1983; Asch, 1993).

Other writers, such as Driben (1983), Cumming and Mickenberg (1972), T. Clark (1994), and Asch (1993, 1997), have gone beyond the Supreme Court's ruling and have suggested that Aboriginal interest rests on a solid legal foundation. They point to the *Royal Proclamation* of 1763, which pledged, in a legal context, that Aboriginal title would be respected. The surrender or extinguishment of title could only take place if Indians approved of the action at a public meeting with public officials. When the surrender took place, it could only be to the Crown. Today, according to the courts, Aboriginal rights are vested in Native people by virtue of both the *Royal Proclamation* of 1763 and by the fact that they were the sovereign inhabitants in Canada before the land was considered French or English property (Indian Claims Commission, 1975).

All told, the Canadian government has shown somewhat of a reluctance to negotiate with Aboriginal people over land issues since Confederation. Each time the federal government developed a land claims policy, Aboriginal people denounced the content. As Mallea (1994) points out, on the whole, Aboriginal people have found negotiating with the government to be a frustrating exercise. In most cases the government has been viewed as an obstruction to achieving justice.

In approaching land claims, Aboriginal groups have been required by the courts to meet four conditions to establish proof of Aboriginal title. This is referred to as the "Baker Lake Test" (***Baker Lake*** v. ***Minister of Indian Affairs and Northern Development***, 1980). The requirements are:

1. that they and their ancestors were members of an organized society;

2. that the organized society occupied the specific territory over which they assert the Aboriginal title;

3. that the occupation was to the exclusion of other organized societies; and

4. that the occupation was an established fact at the time sovereignty was asserted by England.

In 1990 the Supreme Court of Canada, in a landmark decision, set specific guidelines for determining Aboriginal rights in general. This decision (*R. v. Sparrow* [1990]—see below) held that an Aboriginal right could be claimed even though it was not otherwise supported by a treaty. The court also ruled that existing Aboriginal rights should not be subject to Section 33 of the Charter (the "notwithstanding" clause) and that any proposed legislation negatively affecting Aboriginal people may only be enacted if it meets a strict legal test that justifies such an interference.

Sparrow and *Delgamuukw* : Turning Points

Aboriginal land rights were given a serious blow in the ***Delgamuukw* v. *British Columbia*** (1991) case when B.C. Supreme Court judge Alan McEachern ruled that 8000 Gitksan and Wet'suwet'en British Columbian Indians do not hold Aboriginal rights to the land. He stated that the *Royal Proclamation* of 1763 has never applied to the province of British Columbia, and that Aboriginal interest in the land did not include ownership of, or jurisdiction over, the territory. He also ruled that pre-Confederation colonial laws, construed in their historical setting, show a clear intention to extinguish Aboriginal interests in order to give unburdened titles to the settlers, and that the Crown extinguished all Aboriginal rights implicitly (because no specific extinguishment act was passed) even before the province entered Confederation in 1871. Therefore, he argued, since Confederation the province has had title to the soil of the province and the right to dispose of Crown lands unburdened by Aboriginal title. However, the judge did acknowledge that the Indians could use vacant Crown land, but that this is not an exclusive right—their use of Crown land is subject to the general laws of the province.

The trial took more than four years, during which communities and forestry and mining companies fought the Aboriginal land claims. Their $1-billion investments were deemed at risk until the judgment was made. Uncharacteristically, the judgment ended with a stern lecture from the judge. He insisted that only political negotiations could solve the land issue, and questioned the focus on legal and constitutional matters such as ownership, sovereignty, and rights. He also noted that the issues now facing Aboriginal people could not be solved by continuing the reserve system, which, he argued, had created "fishing footholds and ethnic enclaves" (*Delgamuukw* v. *The Queen*, 1991). He concluded his judgment by arguing that enlarging the reserves is not in the best interest of anyone, and suggested that Indians must leave the reserve and enter the urban centres of Canada so that they can participate in the economic activities found there. The Gitksan-Wet'suwet'en Nation appealed the decision and the case eventually went to the B.C. Court of Appeal.

Before discussing the appeal, it might prove instructive to discuss the Supreme Court's decision. First, the judge (McEachern) assessed Aboriginal society using a very ethnocentric perspective—e.g., since Aboriginal people did not use the wheel, have a written language, or use domesticated animals for food production, he claimed that they did not have an organized, integrated society. In fact, he argued that early Aboriginal life was "nasty, brutish and short." He concluded that "many of the badges of civilization, as we of European culture understand them, were indeed absent" (p. 31). In short, the judge introduced highly ethnocentric and biased perspectives about what constitutes "civilization" and/or "development" and concluded that, since Aboriginal people did not have many of the cultural artifacts of Europeans, they could only be considered "primitive."

The findings of McEachern were puzzling and without precedent. He rejected testimony from certain experts out of hand and without adequate justification, while allowing testimony from others. For example, he rejected testimony from anthropologists but accepted it from historians and linguists. Furthermore, there are well-accepted principles that the judge did not follow. For example, all testimony must be understood by the judge (since he/she must make a ruling); otherwise, the judge must simply accept the conclusions of the experts unless those are successfully challenged by information from other experts. Nevertheless, the transcripts of the trial show that the judge openly acknowledged that he did not understand the logic or the argument of certain witnesses, yet he accepted their conclusions unquestioningly, even when the illogical and unintelligible arguments were questioned by others. The judge's insistence on seeing himself as a social scientist was without precedent. Much of the data presented to him by anthropologists were rejected with no good explanation. He then proceeded to develop his own biased and ethnocentric explanation about Aboriginal people, totally devoid of evidence or logic (Elliott, 1991).

The *Delgamuukw* Appeal

In 1993 an appeal of the *Delgamuukw* decision was heard by the British Columbia Court of Appeal. A majority of the judges agreed with the trial judge that certain Aboriginal rights were in force when British sovereignty was established. Moreover, the Appeal Court agreed that these rights were *not* ownership rights. However, it disagreed with McEachern in finding that the Aboriginal rights had not been extinguished and based its decision on a test much less stringent than that adopted by the *Sparrow* court (see below).

This B.C. Court of Appeal decision modified the meaning of the *Sparrow* decision in that it redefined what it thought the Supreme Court meant when it delivered that judgment. There have been few comparable cases since the *Delgamuukw* appeal, so it is difficult to interpret its impact. Subsequent well-known cases that have variously expanded upon *Sparrow,* mostly in favour of Aboriginal people, and that have served as important precedents for the final 1997 *Delgamuukw* Supreme Court of Canada decision (1997) include *R.* v. *VanDerPeet* (1996), *R.* v. *NTC Smokehouse* (1996), *R.* v. *Gladstone* (1996), and *R.* v. *Côté* (1996), among others.

In the *Guerin* v. *Regina* (1984) and *Sparrow* (1990) cases, the Supreme Court acknowledged and reinforced the **fiduciary relationship** between the Crown and Aboriginal people. These precedent-setting judgments forcefully noted that the government has a responsibility to act in a fiduciary capacity with respect to Aboriginal people. The Court pointed out that the relationship between the government and Aboriginal people is trust-like rather than adversarial, and contemporary recognition and affirmation of Aboriginal rights, as reflected in the (1997) *Delgamuukw* decision, must continue to be defined in light of this historic relationship.

Beyond its fiduciary obligation toward Aboriginal people, the federal government is also required to guarantee the rights and freedoms found in the Charter. Actions by government toward Aboriginal people reveal that there are numerous violations of Aboriginal civil liberties. For example, the presentation by the Indigenous Bar Association to the Standing Committee on Aboriginal Affairs regarding the events of Kanesatake and Kahnawake during the summer of 1990 noted that the most serious violation of Aboriginal civil liberties was when the then minister of Indian Affairs signed an agreement on preconditions to negotiations with Aboriginal peoples! This meant that the federal government would only agree to negotiate if First Nations people agreed to certain conditions—conditions that were contrary to the claims being pursued by the Kanesatake and Kahnawake (e.g., the amount of land to be considered in the negotiations, the value of the compensation). One precondition, that the Mohawk disperse from their roadblocks, was tantamount to denying the Mohawk freedom of assembly.

The pivotal *Sparrow* (1990) case in B.C. attracted the attention of all individuals interested in Aboriginal–non-Aboriginal affairs. The case involved an Indian who was fishing at the mouth of the Fraser River. In 1987, in what amounted to a sting operation, agents working on behalf of the Fisheries Department acted as individual Canadians who wanted to buy fish illegally from band members. While the "sting" resulted in 25 Indians being charged, none were convicted of illegally fishing. It was at this time that the Fisheries Department implemented another procedure to reduce the number of fish caught by Aboriginal people—it reduced the net depth from 38 to 25 fathoms so that the Indians would not catch as many fish.

After the new regulations were in place, Sparrow, an Indian fisherman, was caught fishing with a net over 25 fathoms and was subsequently charged under the new regulations. Even though historical data showed that Indians had fished this area since time immemorial, the provincial court found Sparrow guilty. The court ruled that Aboriginal rights had been extinguished at the beginning of the century. This was appealed to the county court, then to the Court of Appeal of British Columbia and eventually to the Supreme Court of Canada. The Supreme Court ruled that, while the provincial regulations were legal and forced Indians out of their fishing activities, the province could not extinguish Aboriginal rights through the application of provincial or federal regulations. The regulations would have to specifically (explicitly) state that Aboriginal rights were to be extinguished. Moreover, the Supreme Court ruling also stated that, in cases where regulations are ambiguous or vague, the interpretation would favour Aboriginal people. This reasoning was upheld specifically in such cases as *Gladstone* (1996) and *NTC Smokehouse* (1996).

Comprehensive Claims

As mentioned earlier, there are two major categories of claims now being pursued by Aboriginal peoples in Canada. The first is referred to as comprehensive claims or Aboriginal title claims, while the second is called **specific claims** and will be discussed later. Progress in some jurisdictions has been significant, as examples in this chapter have shown. In British Columbia, for example, these claims make up nearly 75 percent of the province.

These claims take two different forms that are, to some extent, regionally based. In the North, the claims focus on a demand for formal legal recognition of Aboriginal land title and all the rights that are derived from it. In the South, comprehensive claims place more emphasis on cooperation between Aboriginal peoples and the government for the extinguishment of Aboriginal title and the restitution of specific rights—e.g., hunting and fishing rights (Canada, n.d.).

The map in Figure 7.1 identifies the major areas in Canada that are under comprehensive claims processing at the present time. Almost the entire Canadian North is claimed by Aboriginal groups, and various Aboriginal associations are actively pursuing their cases. Areas in the Arctic are being pursued by the Inuit, while the Métis and Indians in the Mackenzie Valley area of the Northwest Territories and in the Yukon have filed several claims.

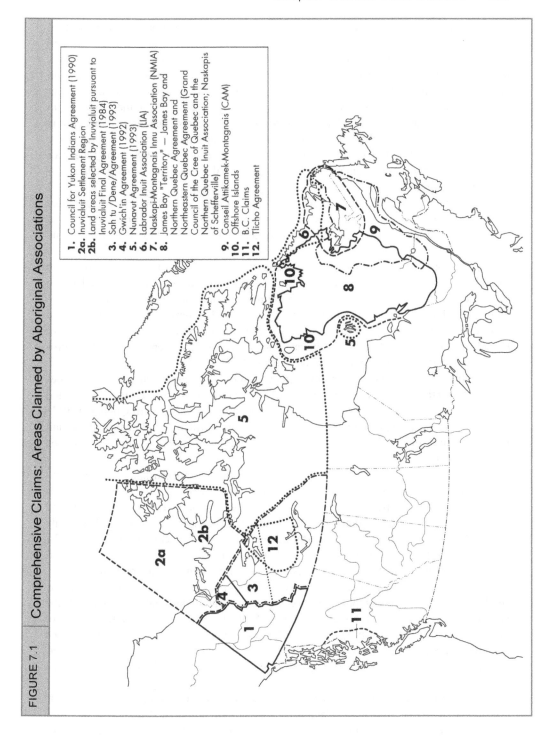

FIGURE 7.1   Comprehensive Claims: Areas Claimed by Aboriginal Associations

1. Council for Yukon Indians Agreement (1990)
2a. Inuvialuit Settlement Region
2b. Land areas selected by Inuvialuit pursuant to Inuvialuit Final Agreement (1984)
3. Sah tu /Dene/Agreement (1993)
4. Gwich'in Agreement (1992)
5. Nunavut Agreement (1993)
6. Labrador Inuit Association (LIA)
7. Naskapi-Montagnais Innu Association (NMIA)
8. James Bay "Territory" — James Bay and Northern Quebec Agreement and Northeastern Quebec Agreement (Grand Council of the Cree of Quebec and the Northern Quebec Inuit Association; Naskapis of Schefferville)
9. Conseil Attikamek-Montagnais (CAM)
10. Offshore Islands
11. B.C. Claims
12. Tlicho Agreement

Comprehensive claims are not negotiations about grievances related to the interpretation and the shortcomings of previous treaties. Rather, they are land claims that deal with areas of the country where various Aboriginal people continue to live and where treaties were never entered into (and where presumably Aboriginal title still exists and has not been extinguished or surrendered). An exception to this is the Dene/Métis claim in the Northwest Territories, where Treaty 8 encompasses some of the land but no reserves were ever established. The policy of establishing **comprehensive land claims** began in 1973, and has subsequently been revised and updated several times. As Harry Swain, then Deputy Minister of Indian Affairs, pointed out in 1988, comprehensive claims are a unique arrangement in which Aboriginal people can finally settle outstanding land issues.

The process is one through which Aboriginal groups agree to exchange their Aboriginal title over all or most of the land covered in return for land, money, certain rights, and other conditions designed to protect and enhance their social, cultural, and economic well-being.

The comprehensive land claims agreements that emerge from these negotiations are formal, legal, and binding documents. Also known as modern-day treaties, they have to be ratified by the Aboriginal groups and communities concerned and by the federal government, and are then enacted into law by Parliament. They now constitute a substantial body of law and have helped to redefine the relationship between the Government of Canada and many of its Aboriginal citizens. Since 1982, these agreements have been protected constitutionally; future agreements will also be protected.

The first of these landmark comprehensive land claims agreements was the **James Bay and Northern Quebec Agreement**, which was reached between the federal and provincial governments and the Cree and Inuit communities of Northern Quebec in 1975 (Niezen, 1998). This was followed by the Northeastern Quebec Agreement in 1978, and later by an agreement with the Inuvialuit of the Mackenzie Delta and the Beaufort Sea region in 1984.

By March 2002, 53 First Nations were participating in modern land claim negotiations. There were also 18 other comprehensive land claims taking place throughout Canada involving 78 communities. Since the inception of the program in 1973, 15 final land claim agreements had been completed (Indian and Northern Affairs Canada website, July 17, 2003); by 2006 several more important agreements had been completed (see Box 7.2 for an example). Refer to the AAND website (www.ainc-inac.gc.ca) for current provincial and regional information on the status and number of claims in the "pipeline."

Each of these land claims is distinctive and has taken into consideration the unique conditions of history, geography, culture, and economic circumstances that exist in the particular region and communities concerned. Still, there is a similar pattern to all of these claims—a pattern set initially in 1973 and reinforced in the government's revised comprehensive land claims policy of 1986. As a result, while there are individual differences, considerable precedent has been established in the terms and conditions provided in these settlements.

When faced with the decision to cede, or surrender, in whole or in part, their Aboriginal title to certain areas, Aboriginal Canadians are naturally concerned that in return they receive benefits that will enable them to prosper and survive as distinct and definable

Box 7.2	Maa-Nulth First Nations Sign Historic B.C. Land Treaty

After years of little progress and costly negotiations, five Vancouver Island First Nations signed a treaty Saturday worth almost $500 million, a treaty that includes more than 24 000 hectares of land.

The Maa-nulth First Nations live on the West coast of Vancouver sland with some of the land bordering the scenic Pacific Rim Park near Tofino. Five Maa-nulth chiefs, B.C. Premier Gordon Campbell, and federal Indian Affairs Minister Jim Prentice gathered Saturday for a ceremony in Victoria. . . .

The deal must still be ratified by the 2000 Maa-nulth people and the federal and B.C. governments. Once ratified and enacted as legislation, Prentice said the treaty

benefits both the province and First Nations. . . .

The Maa-nulth are part of Vancouver Island's 14-member Nuu-chah-nulth Tribal Council, but the five bands decided to negotiate a treaty as a separate group. . . . The financial component of the Maa-nulth treaty includes cash in lump sum and timed payments. The First Nations will receive $90 million in cash, up to $45 million over 25 years for potential revenue sharing projects, and $150 million over eight years for program financing. Estimates for the value of the treaty lands range between $100 million and $200 million.

groups. The most basic concern is for land. All the agreements are, at heart, land settlements. All designate specific lands that the claimant group will own outright, as well as land-related rights in areas where they have certain interests in perpetuity. But Aboriginal concerns go beyond mere ownership of land. Essentially they seek terms and conditions that will allow them to:

- continue to maintain to the greatest degree possible their traditional lifestyle and culture;
- participate in the decision-making process regarding land and resource management within their claim area; and
- receive a fair share of the economic opportunities and economic benefits that may exist in the claim area.

As a result, comprehensive claims agreements cover a range of issues besides land and basic compensation. Issues include surface and sub-surface resource provisions, guaranteed rights for wildlife harvesting and fishing, resource revenue sharing, participation in renewable resource management, and environmental protection measures. An excellent example of a modern-day treaty, or comprehensive claim, wherein these issues are paramount is the 2000 Nisga'a Treaty. Six major issues are present in comprehensive claims. They include:

- *Land:* All agreements confer on the beneficiaries' primary interest over extensive areas of land.
- *Cash:* In consideration for certainty of title over their settlement regions, all signed agreements provide significant financial compensation packages. These are considered payments in exchange for rights.
- *Wildlife:* Wildlife management and Aboriginal control over wildlife harvesting are usually negotiated. These are an important part of traditional Aboriginal lifestyles. The agreements in principle or sub-agreements also provide for harvesting rights, priorities, and privileges. Various rights and privileges under these agreements include permit or tax exemptions; the right to sell, barter, exchange, and give freely the harvested wildlife; the right of first refusal for new hunting, fishing, and tourism lodges over settlement regions; and the right of first refusal for the marketing of wildlife and wildlife parts and products.
- *Environmental protection:* All agreements have provisions for the protection of the environment and of the Aboriginal societies in the settlement areas; these provisions spell out the terms and conditions of any future development, and subject all developers to specific duties and responsibilities.
- *Economic participation:* The agreements recognize the necessity to preserve Aboriginal cultural identity and values, in part through enabling Aboriginal people to become more equal participants in Canada's economy. The comprehensive claims policy provides for resource royalty sharing.

All agreements in principle and sub-agreements contain various similar provisions to support the beneficiaries and businesses under their control. These cover such items as access to information relating to business ventures and opportunities, tax exemptions, incentive measures, contract splitting, and financial and technical support measures.

- *Interim protection:* The present policy permits the negotiation of interim measures to protect Aboriginal interests while the claim is being negotiated. They are identified in the initial negotiating mandate. These measures operate over the claimed territory and remain in effect until a final agreement has been signed. They can impose general or specific obligations on the parties that relate to land and its future development; the protection of traditional hunting, fishing, and trapping activities; and the other rights that are generally negotiated in a comprehensive claim.

The measures enable negotiations to proceed in good faith, thus lessening the need for court intervention that could have the effect of freezing any type of development in a claimed area. It must be said, however, that an agreement on interim measures does not affect the rights of any party to seek judicial recourse should they consider their interests to be endangered.

- *Other provisions:* There is a whole range of other provisions in the agreements, covering in substantial detail areas such as access to Aboriginal lands, establishment of protected areas, fisheries, social protection, and the incorporation and management of local governments. These are positive measures intended to provide a genuine opportunity for Aboriginal economic and cultural progress.

The terms and conditions of the agreements are established in Canadian law and, under the Constitution, cannot be unilaterally changed. They are not subject to override by other existing laws, nor by any future legislation that may be enacted. The comprehensive claims process has resulted in long-term agreements between Canadian governments and Aboriginal peoples, agreements that have in fact redefined in a truly unique way the relationship between Aboriginal people, the Canadian government, and other Canadians.

By 1990 the government had come under attack because of its handling of comprehensive claims. Aboriginal people accused the government of pursuing a goal of extinguishing the "burden" of Aboriginal rights and minimizing its legal obligation. A working group composed of Indian leaders representing Aboriginal interests across Canada was established to identify problem areas and recommend change. Later in the year, the policy of restricting the number of comprehensive claims being investigated to six was removed. Amendments to the comprehensive claims policy removed the idea of "blanket extinguishment" of all Aboriginal rights, including title, and allowed for the retention of Aboriginal land rights, provided these rights do not conflict with the negotiated settlement agreement.

The Assembly of First Nations (1990a) has claimed that the existing comprehensive claims policy excludes self-government provisions. The federal government has argued that this claim is untrue. Yet when the *Delgamuukw* case was appealed to the Supreme Court of Canada after 1993, Chief Justice Lamer rejected "the respondents' submission with respect to the substitution of Aboriginal title and self-government for the original claim of ownership and jurisdiction." Aboriginal negotiators have consistently sought to settle their land claims and to establish the right of self-determination through the process of self-government. The government has been prepared to give "advanced" bands some legal powers similar to those of a municipality, but not additional powers.

Specific Claims

A specific claim deals with treaties and scrip (scrip is discussed in Chapter 8) and band claims. It is, as the term implies, specific to a particular concern; for example, a clause in a treaty, or land withdrawn from a reserve. Since 1970, hundreds of claims have been presented to the Office of Native Claims for adjudication, though very few have been resolved (see Box 7.3).

Box 7.3	Comprehensive and Specific Claims: Liability for the Future

Over the past four decades, 26 comprehensive claims, such as the James Bay and Northern Quebec Agreement, the Kluane First Nation Final Agreement, and the Teslin Tlingit Council Final Agreement, have been resolved. Nearly 20 more are in the negotiating stage and have yet to be signed or ratified by the federal government. These claims are complex and require considerable review and investigation by both the litigant and the federal government before they can be resolved. On average, these claims require about 20 years before they move into the implementation phase.

Specific claims dealing with Canada's obligations under treaties or the way it has managed First Nations funds or assets are much less complex. In 2010, over 40 specific claims were resolved across the country. Some of these were settled through negotiation, while others were not accepted for negotiation on the basis that they did not involve any lawful obligation by the federal, provincial, or territorial government. Today, about one-fifth of the claims are from Ontario, 10 percent from Quebec, 20 percent from the Prairies, and 44 percent from British Columbia, with the remainder coming from the Atlantic provinces and the North. During that same year, 27 new specific claims from across Canada were accepted for negotiation.

Between 2007 and 2010, 313 specific claims were addressed. As of 2007, 800 outstanding specific claims were being processed and attempts were being made to resolve the claims. In contrast, in 1993 there were less than 400 claims being processed. The rate has steadily increased over the past two decades. Despite these gains, it is clear that the process is not working. The Indian Specific Claims Commission (ICC) was created to conduct independent reviews of the government's decision process in resolving specific claims. The commission does not have the power to make binding decisions, although it can recommend to First Nations people that they pursue their claims through the courts. It is estimated that it will take until 2100 before most of the specific claims being brought forward will be resolved.

Clearly, of the number of specific claims submitted and accepted, many are at different stages of resolution (for example, in litigation, under review, before the Indian Claims Commission, or rejected). As is evident from the low number of claims that have been settled, the Office of Native Claims and subsequent agencies have not substantiated all of the Native claims. This is obviously unacceptable and has sparked protest, often violent, across the country.

From the late 1980s until the turn of the millennium, the government spent less than $5 million per year on the Indian Claims Commission (ICC) for mediation services, public education, and ongoing inquiries with regard to Aboriginal land claims. Since then, there has been a slight increase to nearly $6 million per year. During the decade that the ICC existed, it facilitated the process by which First Nations would enter negotiations with the federal government. For example, in 2002–03 the ICC handled nearly 60 cases. It recommended that the government accept 42 of these for negotiation. The government accepted most of the recommendations. The commission also recommended that seven cases not be sent to negotiation. The remainder of the cases considered by the commission were dealt with in different ways. Some were sent back to the First Nations community for additional work, others were actually settled, and still others remained under review by the commission.

The history of Aboriginal claims shows that that there has been sustained pressure on the Government of Canada to reform the specific claims process and establish an independent claims body. Yet this did not happen until 2003. It takes the government five to eight years to complete its validation process in assessing any particular First Nations claim. Then it takes another five to seven years to negotiate the resolution of a claim. On average, since 1973, the government has resolved only 7.5 claims per year. This means it will take 50 years to settle existing claims without adding new ones. From 1991 to 1999, Canada settled 23 specific claims, totalling nearly $33 million and involving the return of nearly 15 000 acres of land back to Aboriginal people.

In 2003, the Government of Canada passed the *Specific Claims Resolution Act*, creating the Canadian Centre for the Independent Resolution of First Nations Specific Claims, which replaced the ICC. The new centre has two separate components: a commission and a tribunal. In addition, the centre facilitates negotiated settlements using mediation, negotiation, and other means of dispute resolution. It provides these services for all claims, regardless of the potential amount of a claim, although there is a $10-million ceiling on settlements. The tribunal is a quasi-judicial body able to make final decisions on the validity of claims that were not reached through a negotiated settlement.

Band Claims

A type of specific claim encompassing the multifarious, scattered, but not insubstantial claims of individual Indian bands is called a band claim. Several categories of these can be identified at present, including claims relating to the loss of land and other natural resources from established reserves, as well as issues pertaining to the government's stewardship of various bands' financial assets over the years. Underlying all these claims is the difficult question of **trusteeship**.

The full story of the government's management of reserve resources and band funds across Canada is only gradually being pieced together from the files of AAND, from the accounts of missionaries and other Euro-Canadian sources, and from the oral testimony of Indian people themselves. Reserve resources include not only land but also minerals, timber, and water. Band funds in most cases derive from land and other resource sales. Where land was surrendered or sold off from reserves, the capital went into band funds to be administered in trust by the federal government.

Land losses from established Indian reserves account for by far the majority of band claims (or surrender claims) brought forward to date. Groups of them are probably sufficiently similar to be classified on a regional and historical basis. Grievances arising in New France have certain elements in common, as do Indian claims in the Maritimes, in Ontario, in the southern Prairies, and in British Columbia. The problem of pressure for reserve-land acquisition by speculators and settlers is central to all.

The French, who were the first European power to control the northern half of North America, were the first to establish any sort of Canadian Indian policy. There are conflicting interpretations of whether Indian territorial rights were affirmed or extinguished under the French regime; treaties were never concluded for territory either in New France or in Acadia. Land was given to Indians through imperial grace, just as it was to European colonists. However, the Crown, instead of granting such tracts directly to the Aboriginal people, handed them in trust to the religious orders, the most efficient civilizing and Christianizing agencies then known. Six Indian reserves were formed in this manner.

At the time of the British takeover in 1760, France's Indian allies had been given land for their exclusive use. By 1851, 230 000 acres (92 000 hectares) were set aside as Indian reserves and a further 330 000 acres (132 000 hectares) were similarly appropriated by the Quebec *Lands and Forests Act* of 1922.

As far as the Indian people were concerned, the arrival of the British in New France did not favourably alter their condition. The same could be said for the Indians in the Maritimes. As British settlement and power increased, large tracts were set apart for Indian use and occupation. Although these lands were called Indian reserves, they were not guaranteed to the Indians through treaties and were subsequently reduced as more land was required for settlement. With Confederation, the existing reserves were transferred to the jurisdiction of the federal government, though for a long time the underlying title lay with the respective provinces.

Claims have been presented to the federal government for past reserve-land losses. Within this category, several main types of claims have emerged. A large number contest the legal status of surrenders and expropriations of reserve lands. These include submissions on surrenders processed without proper Indian consent, uncompleted sales of surrendered land, sales of lands prior to their being surrendered, lack of letters of patent for completed sales, expropriations for highway rights-of-way, public utility easements, and even forged Indian signatures or identifying marks on surrenders.

Indian people have claimed that unjust cessions and legally questionable government expropriations of reserve lands were common right across the board. Government initiatives, along with pressure from non-Aboriginal speculators and settlers, were, as usual, dominant factors. The Six Nations' Grand River surrender in 1841, the Mohawks' cession of Tyendinaga Township in 1843, the Moore Township surrender made by the Chippewa later that year, and the 1847 cession by the St. Regis Iroquois of Glengarry County are prime examples of cases where surrenders were attained under pressure. All these lands were ceded in trust, although there is evidence that the trust provisions were not always upheld. Similar grievances pertain to the government's acquisition of unceded islands. Equally familiar was the variety of expropriation that allowed the sale of individual lots from Indian reserves for clergy and state purposes. Disputes over the status of territory were also prevalent. These were generally related to squatter infiltration and occasionally extended into inter-tribal conflicts for reserve lands and, accordingly, for annuities.

The social and economic factors underlying the loss of Indian reserve lands in central and eastern Canada found expression on the Prairies. In the years following the making of the treaties and the setting aside of the reserves, the southern Prairies were gradually settled. Towns and cities sometimes grew on the very edges of reserves or even around them, and railways ran through them or along their boundaries. As in Ontario, Prairie reserves located on good farming land were coveted by settlers. For all these reasons, political pressure frequently developed for the surrender of all or a portion of a reserve. In many cases Indian Affairs responded by obtaining a surrender of the reserve land in question; proceeds from the sales of such land were credited to the particular band's fund and administered under the terms of the *Indian Act* (Hall, 1991).

At the heart of many Indian grievances in the Prairies is the issue of unfulfilled treaty entitlements to land. Complex in themselves, such claims have been further complicated by the need for provincial assent to any proposed transfer of lands to Indian reserve status. Under the 1930 Natural Resources Transfer agreements, the three Prairie provinces obliged themselves to transfer to the federal government, out of the unoccupied Crown lands, sufficient area to meet unfulfilled treaty obligations. Aboriginal people have felt that there has been provincial reluctance to comply with this, and disputes have arisen over the exact nature of the commitments. The Island Lake bands in Manitoba, for instance, have raised the matter of what population base should be utilized in the granting of unfulfilled treaty entitlements. A substantial proportion of the bands' allotments under Treaty No. 5 were made in 1924, but the land assigned was approximately 1200 hectares short, if based on the populations at the date and on the terms of the treaty. The bands maintain that their total entitlement should be computed using a more up-to-date population total, with the 1924 allotment simply subtracted from the new allocation.

In British Columbia the history of Indian reserves is different from those in the other provinces. During the 1850s, when Vancouver Island was still provisionally governed by the Hudson's Bay Company, certain minor surrenders were concluded by the company's chief factor, James Douglas, for several parcels of land there. But these, along with the territory in the northeastern corner of the mainland part of the province included in Treaty No. 8, are the only areas covered by treaty. The dual governorship of the two colonies of Vancouver Island and British Columbia under Douglas in 1858 was soon accompanied by the establishment of comparatively liberal reserves both within and outside the treaty areas. But then expanding European settlement motivated Douglas's successors to reverse his policy of allowing the tribes as much land as the Indians themselves judged necessary. Accordingly, they set out to reduce the reserves wherever possible. Only with great reluctance did the colonial government allot new reserves in areas opening to settlement (Flanagan, 1983a).

By 1871, when the colony entered Confederation, Indian complaints concerning the failure to allot adequate reserves and reserve land reductions were already numerous. The Terms of Union that year did nothing to allay these grievances. Fundamentally, the terms provided for the transfer of responsibility for reserves to the Dominion, and for the conveyance of land for new reserves from the province to the Dominion. Since no amounts were agreed upon, a dispute immediately arose between the two governments over the appropriate acreage to be allotted per family. The province declared 10 acres sufficient; the federal government proposed 80. An agreement establishing an Indian reserve commission was concluded in 1875 to review the matter, but there continued to be provincial resistance against attempts to liberalize reserve allotments.

This is just one more source of Indian claims in British Columbia. A report by the Union of British Columbia Indian Chiefs, entitled *The Lands We Lost* (1974), details others. They include the by-now familiar pattern of encroachment by non-Indian people, together with questions about various government surveys and commissions, federal orders-in-council, and reserve land surrenders. The primary cause of such losses and the major grievance expressed in this regard were the work of the federal–provincial McKenna–McBride Commission, set up in 1912 to resolve the outstanding differences between the two governments respecting Indian land in British Columbia. The commissioners were appointed to determine the land needs of the Indians and to recommend appropriate alterations to the boundaries of Indian reserves. All reductions were to require the consent of the bands involved, but in practice this stipulation was not followed. The recommendations were subsequently ratified by both governments under legislation that authorized these reductions irrespective of the provisions of the *Indian Act* controlling the surrender of reserve lands.

In summary, most of the band claims now being dealt with by the federal government have come primarily from the Maritime provinces and the Prairies, with a lesser number from Quebec, Ontario, and British Columbia. A recent one from Ontario, however, has been called the largest specific claim offer to a First Nation in the history of Canada by the band involved. The Mississaugas of the New Credit voted unanimously to accept a $145 million land claims settlement that resolves unfairly compensated *urban* land acquired in 1797 and 1805 (pre-Confederation!) in what are now the cities of Burlington and Toronto, respectively (CTV News/Bell Canada, June 8, 2010). A total of 253 450 acres of urban land was in dispute.

CLAIMS POLICY TODAY

After the 1973 Supreme Court decision with regard to the Nisga'a Indians in British Columbia, the federal government developed new land claims policy. The new policies on comprehensive and specific claims identified the procedures and limitations of negotiating. The policies also provided the philosophical assumptions (on the part of the government) underlying them. These new policies divided land claims into the two types mentioned before—comprehensive and specific. Furthermore, it suggested that comprehensive claims from British Columbia, northern Quebec, the Yukon, and parts of the Northwest Territories would receive more favourable treatment than comprehensive claims from southern Quebec and the Atlantic provinces. However, the policy also specified that Aboriginal claims would be dealt with through direct negotiations between Indian and Northern Affairs and the Aboriginal claimants. The government felt that, in southern Quebec and the Atlantic provinces, historical negotiations had taken place between the government and the Indians, however imperfect those negotiations had been. There was some evidence that the government had taken treaty with these Indians. But in British Columbia, northern Quebec, the Yukon, and areas of the Northwest Territories, it was clear that no negotiations had ever taken place.

The comprehensive claims policy was adopted in 1981 with the publication of the document *In All Fairness: A Native Claims Policy, Comprehensive Claims* (Canada, 1981). The policy stated that the federal government was willing "to exchange undefined Aboriginal land rights for concrete rights and benefits" (1981: 19). Some of these benefits would entail land, wildlife, sub-surface rights, and monetary compensation. With regard to land rights, the document stated that lands to be selected by Aboriginal peoples would be limited to traditional lands that they currently use and occupy. It also stated that "third parties" would be fairly dealt with on the issue of sub-surface rights and that the government was prepared to grant some sub-surface rights in certain areas. Finally, the compensation (in whatever form) was to be "specific and final." However, the policy paper adopted the use of the term Aboriginal "interests" rather than "rights" (Iverson, 1990; Swain, 1988).

The process for resolving these comprehensive claims is to follow a negotiating procedure culminating in a compromise settlement. In summary, Aboriginal people are limited in (1) the scope of what they can negotiate, (2) their standing in relation to other "interests," and (3) the extent of their involvement in trying to settle their claim (Hatt, 1982). The actors involved in the process usually consist of the federal government, the Aboriginal group, and a provincial or territorial government. Because of the scope of such undertakings, the federal government earlier had limited to six the number of separate negotiations that may proceed at any time. For example, in the 1990s it negotiated with the Council for Yukon Indians, the Dene/Métis of the Northwest Territories, the Tungavik Federation of Nunavut, the Conseil Attikamek–Montagnais, and the Labrador Inuit Association.

In 1982 the government published its policy with regard to specific claims in a document titled *Outstanding Business* (DIAND, 1982a). This policy reaffirmed the government's commitment to resolving specific claims and in some respects expanded on the previous role it had played in settling claims. As noted previously, specific claims relate to the administration of land or other Indian assets under the *Indian Act* and to the fulfilment of treaties or other agreements. Box 7.4 is an excellent example of a specific claim/band claim grievance other than a land dispute.

Box 7.4	**First Nations File Claims for Bullets and Twine Never Received from Ottawa**

About 14 First Nations in Canada are waiting to settle claims for compensation with the federal government that they filed because they allege they did not receive bullets and fishing twine from Ottawa a century ago. Sixteen First Nations originally filed ammunition and twine claims, but two were settled in the 1970s, and the rest are still waiting for the claims to be resolved. Many of the claims are under review.

Bradford Morse, a law professor at the University of Ottawa, said he thinks the federal government is reluctant to resolve these claims because, even though they involve some relatively inexpensive items, the cost to settle them now is high due to inflation. "You start thinking this is just a little bit of string, a couple of bullets. The small item of thinking in terms of 10 dollars [sic].

Now you're talking tens of millions of dollars."

The First Nations, which include the Driftpile First Nation in Alberta, say Ottawa failed to give them the ammunition and twine they needed when hunting for food as a key to their survival in Canada.

Christopher Devlin, a Victoria, B.C., lawyer representing the Driftpile First Nation, said its members did not get ammunition and twine from 1899 to 1952. It's not a question of Canada showing up with a tractor trailer of bullets and spools of twine, and saying, "OK, sorry for not giving it to you earlier, but here it is now." Devlin says it was a treaty violation and the people deserve compensation.

Under the terms of the policy for specific claims, the process of handling the claims is a combination of adjudication and negotiation. Claims are first submitted to the minister of AAND, acting on behalf of the Government of Canada. After the claim is submitted, the Office of Native Claims (ONC) reviews the case and analyzes the material. The claim and supporting materials (both *for* or *against*) are referred to the Department of Justice for advice. On the basis of the Department of Justice's advice, the ONC (1) negotiates a settlement with the claimant, (2) rejects the claim, or (3) returns the claim for additional documentation. If the claim is accepted, the ONC and the claimant negotiate the terms of settlement; for example, land, cash, or other benefits. Once the claim has been settled it represents final redress, and a form release is obtained from the claimant so that it cannot be reopened at some later time.

Because Aboriginal peoples do not have their own financial resources to carry out research in order to document their claims, the federal government has made substantial contributions to various Aboriginal organizations that are engaged in this research process. Since 1973 the federal government has spent in excess of $100 million on negotiations, but has produced only three agreements. For example, between 1972 and 1982, more than $22 million in contributions were made for research into Aboriginal rights, treaties, and claims, plus an additional $94 million in loans between 1974 and 1982. Since the creation of the ONC in 1974, more than $26 million has been spent on the operation and management of the claim process (both specific and comprehensive). If the claim being submitted by the Indians is substantiated and compensation paid, part of the "contribution" portion given to the Indians is repaid. Thus far about $15 million has been repaid by Aboriginal groups who have signed final agreements. On the other hand, if the claim is dismissed, no repayment is necessary. This infusion of money into Aboriginal organizations has enabled them to pursue vigorously many claims that, without the funds, would never have been researched and brought forward.

Research contributions and loans are provided to Aboriginal people for both specific and comprehensive claims. Funding for specific and comprehensive claims in the late 1970s was about $8 million. In the early 1980s, this was increased to about $14 million, where it remained until 1989. As we entered the 1990s, major expenditures were provided to settle a growing backlog of comprehensive and specific claims.

In 1985 a task force that had been struck to review comprehensive claims policy reported to the minister of the then Indian and Northern Affairs. The report noted that the negotiating process used up until then to resolve Aboriginal claims had tried to incorporate two principles: (1) to encourage the cultural development of Aboriginal people, and (2) to provide a climate for the overall economic growth of Canada. The government, in dealing with Aboriginal peoples, had argued that Aboriginal goals could be best pursued by settling claims through an extinguishment of all Aboriginal claims once and for all. Unsurprisingly, Aboriginal peoples have not accepted this philosophy. As a result, negotiations stalled and settlements of various First Nations claims were few. The task force recommended that a blanket extinguishment of all Aboriginal rights was unacceptable. Some of the noteworthy recommendations were:

1. Agreements should recognize and affirm Aboriginal rights.

2. The policy should allow for the negotiation of Aboriginal self-government.

3. The process should be open to all Aboriginal peoples who continue to use and to occupy traditional lands and whose Aboriginal title to such lands has not been dealt with either by a land-cession treaty or by explicit legislation.

4. Parity among agreements should not necessarily require that their contents be identical.

5. Given the comprehensive nature of agreements and the division of powers between governments under the Canadian Constitution, the provincial and territorial governments should be encouraged to participate in negotiations. The participation of the provinces will be necessary in the negotiation of matters directly affecting the exercise of their jurisdiction.

6. Agreements should enable Aboriginal peoples and the government to share both the responsibility for the management of land and resources and the benefits from their use. (DIAND, 1985: 31–32)

Previous claims were settled through one of two options: (1) by the signing of a final agreement extinguishing all Aboriginal rights, or (2) by doing nothing and maintaining the status quo. Contemporary policy does not see a settlement as a final agreement but rather as an agreement that will settle immediate issues and define the context for issues that emerge later on. It argues that there is no need to insist on extinguishment of Aboriginal rights, including title, when a voluntary surrender of rights has been obtained from the Aboriginal peoples. This procedure has been made more acceptable by all parties because of the difficulties that emerged after the signing of the James Bay Agreement, when DIAND found that there were problems of implementation, unresolved disputes, and, in some cases, a failure to fully implement the agreement in its spirit and intent (DIAND, 1982a; Mendes and Bendin, n.d.).

The task force suggested several alternatives to the claims process. One alternative is to return to the legal technicalities used in pre-Confederation treaties. Specific rights such as land and wildlife harvesting would be subjected to extinguishment or retention. However, the loss or retention of one right would not affect other rights; each would have to be subjected to a court of law (Dyck, 1990).

A second option is to separate land rights from all other rights. Thus, land rights could be dealt with by negotiations or through the courts but would be separate from other Aboriginal rights such as culture and religion.

Finally, a third option would be to set aside the issue of Aboriginal rights altogether when discussing land rights. Although this would not provide an answer with regard to the existence of Aboriginal rights, it would allow Aboriginal groups and other parties to continue to carry out economic activities. An example of this approach in another area is that of the federal and Nova Scotia governments' approach to the ownership of offshore rights: The issue of ownership of offshore oil has been set aside for now so that development of natural resources can proceed.

Regardless of the option(s) pursued, there must be some flexibility in their application, since Aboriginal groups come from different regions, have different interests, and operate in different political contexts. The task force recommended that negotiations continue to be the major mode of settling claims. The force's members felt that litigation fosters an adversarial approach that is not conducive to settling claims and to developing a true social contract between Aboriginal and non-Aboriginal people. The task force's report goes on to suggest that, prior to negotiations, the process of "scoping" be undertaken. This process, in which important issues and alternatives are dealt with by both parties prior to actual negotiations, is now used in social impact assessments. The task force also felt that negotiations must deal more expeditiously with Aboriginal claims and that Aboriginal interests should be protected during the negotiations.

In summary, the task force felt that new approaches to settling Aboriginal claims must be undertaken. Contemporary policies have not really been effective, either in social or economic terms. If Canada is to continue to develop as a nation these issues must be resolved. At the same time, if Aboriginal people are to retain their identity and self-worth by developing communities that will actively participate in Canadian society, settlements must be negotiated. As the members of the task force so eloquently stated in their report:

> Much is at stake in working towards consensual settlements with those Aboriginal peoples who have never entered into agreements concerning the destiny of their traditional lands within Canada. In the deepest sense, what is at stake is our identity as a nation that resolves its internal differences not through coercion or domination by the majority, but through agreements based on mutual consent. (Canada, 1985a: 101)

The government has since "streamlined" procedures to deal with land claims under a half-million dollars. In addition, the then DIAND was given complete authority to approve settlements of up to $7 million without the Treasury Board having to review and accept the proposal. There was a belief that more than 250 outstanding claims could be settled within the first few years of the new millennium. However, at the end of the first decade of the 2000s, fewer than 30 land claims had been settled, and thus the backlog continues to grow.

THE *WHITE PAPER* AND THE INDIAN CLAIMS COMMISSIONER: A SHORT HISTORY LESSON

The first of a series of contemporary responses to Indian claims started with the 1969 *White Paper* on Indian policy. This event marked the beginning of a new era of unprecedented claims activity. The government proposed an approach that it said would lead to equality of opportunity for Aboriginal peoples. This was described as " . . . an equality which preserves and enriches Indian identity and distinction; an equality which stresses Indian participation in its creation and which manifests itself in all aspects of Indian life" (Canada, 1969: 6). To this end, the *British North America Act* would be amended to terminate the legal distinction between Indians and other Canadians, the *Indian Act* would be repealed, and Indians would gradually take control of their lands. The operations of the Indian Affairs branch would be discontinued, and services that had previously been provided on a special basis would be taken over by the federal or provincial agencies that serve other Canadians. Economic development funds would be provided as an interim measure. In short, Indians would come to be treated like all other Canadians: Special status would cease.

In laying out these proposals, the government continued to recognize the existence of Indian claims, and proposed the establishment of an Indian claims commission, but solely as an advisory body. It was made clear that the government was no longer prepared to accept Aboriginal rights claims: "These," the paper said, "are so general and undefined that it is not realistic to think of them as specific claims capable of remedy except through a policy and program that will end injustice to Indians as members of the Canadian community. This is the policy that the government is proposing for discussion" (Canada, 1969: 20). Treaty claims, while acknowledged, were also placed in a dubious light.

Rather than proceeding with the kind of commission discussed in the 1960s, it was decided that further study and research were required by both the Indians and the federal government. Accordingly, the contemporary form of commission was established under the *Public Inquiries Act* to consult with the Indian people and to inquire into claims arising out of treaties, formal agreements, and legislation. The commissioner would then indicate to the government what classes of claims were judged worthy of special treatment and would recommend means for their resolution.

Given the nature of Indian views on their rights and claims as we understand them, it is not surprising that their reaction to the 1969 *White Paper* was strongly negative. The National Indian Brotherhood (NIB) immediately issued a statement declaring that:

> the policy proposals put forward by the Minister of Indian Affairs are not acceptable to the Indian people of Canada. . . . We view this as a policy designed to divest us of our Aboriginal, residual and statutory rights. If we accept this policy, and in the process lose our rights and our lands, we become willing partners in cultural genocide. This we cannot do. (NIB, June 3, 1970)

In the following months Aboriginal groups across the country forcefully and repeatedly echoed this response. When the commissioner, Dr. Lloyd Barber, was appointed in December 1969, the National Brotherhood rejected his office as an outgrowth of the unacceptable *White Paper*, viewing it as an attempt to force the policy on Aboriginal people. Indians saw the *White Paper* as the new articulation of a long-resisted policy of assimilation. The proposal was denounced as a powerful, threatening extension of traditional Indian policy in Canada. In rallying to oppose this apparent challenge to their rights, the Aboriginal peoples in turn produced extensive statements of their own positions.

In August 1973, the government signalled a substantial change in its position on Aboriginal rights by announcing that it was prepared to negotiate settlements in many areas where they had not been dealt with. Then, in April 1975, on the basis of proposals developed through consultations between Indian leaders and the commissioner, the government accepted an approach to the resolution of Indian claims based upon negotiation.

This new policy would take the issue of land claims out of the legal arena and provide an alternative forum to solve problems. This also meant that there could be greater flexibility in introducing and using certain documents—for example, historical and anthropological ones—in the negotiating process. In addition, the government felt that this process would provide a forum that would take into account the interests of non-claimant groups who reside (or have an interest) in an area that could be affected by a settlement. Finally, and perhaps most importantly, it was believed that the process would allow for transforming the Aboriginal-rights concept into concrete and lasting benefits. In addition, the process would be final and not subject to reassessment at some later time.

THE OKA CRISIS OF 1990: A SLIGHTLY LONGER HISTORY LESSON

No other situation in the recent history of Aboriginal–Euro-Canadian relations has brought the complexity of comprehensive and specific claims into sharper relief than the **Oka crisis** of the summer of 1990. For 78 days the Oka standoff kept Canadians wondering how this armed conflict would be resolved. The events of Oka have remained fresh in our minds as we remember the barricades, tanks, low-flying aircraft, and nightly interviews with municipal, provincial, and federal officials recounting the events of the day. After watching these events, Canadians were convinced that this conflict would produce substantive changes in our treatment of Aboriginal people.

There are six Mohawk communities in Canada—Kanesatake, Kahnawake, Akwesasne, Tyendinaga, Wahta, and Six Nations at Ohsweken—totalling about 40 000 persons. We will focus on Kanesatake, since it was central to the events at Oka. Other groups in the Six Nations were involved in the resolution of the Oka dispute, but they played a more supportive role.

In the 17th century, the Mohawks were located in the northern part of New York State (from the Adirondacks in the east to the five Finger Lakes in the west). In the middle of that century, following the arrival of the Europeans, a number of Mohawks converted to Catholicism and joined settlements of New France. The origin of land disputes between Aboriginal and non-Aboriginal people in the region of Kanesatake and Oka can be traced to the 1717 land grant by the king of France to the ecclesiastics of the Seminary of St. Sulpice of Montreal. Around 1721, the Sulpicians established a settlement of religious converts, composed of Iroquois (Mohawk), Nipissing, and Algonquin people, within the 1717 seigneurial grant at Lac-des-Deux-Montagnes. The original grant was subsequently enlarged by the king of France in 1735. It is generally acknowledged that these tracts of land were granted to the Sulpicians for the purpose of protecting and instructing the Indigenous people (a policy reflecting the ethnocentrism and paternalism of that time). However, the precise nature of the obligations of the Sulpicians to the Aboriginal people has remained a point of controversy ever since. (Later, seigneuries were granted to the Jesuits and the Sulpicians for the benefit of the Indians living in the Montreal area, at Kahnawake and Oka, respectively. By the mid-18th century, a portion of the Mohawks of Kahnawake settled in St. Regis, where the Akwesasne reserve was later created.)

Although the *Royal Proclamation* of 1763 recognized that Indian lands had to be purchased by the Crown before settlement could occur, it was not applied in the St. Lawrence Valley or the Atlantic colonies. Thus the Sulpicians' claim at Kanesatake was accepted, even though the claim made by the Mohawks in neighbouring Kahnawake against the Jesuits of Sault St. Louis had been recognized. After 1787, the Mohawks publicly protested the Sulpicians' claim several times, but to no avail. They continued their protest well after the mid-19th century.

Conflicts between the Aboriginal people and the Sulpicians over the land were frequent, particularly over the issue of sale of the land to third parties. In response to petitions from the Indians of Oka during the 1800s for title to the land granted to the seminary, the legislature of Lower Canada enacted a statute confirming the full proprietary title of the seminary to the disputed land while retaining the somewhat vaguely defined obligations to the Aboriginal population. *An Act Respecting the Seminary of St. Sulpice* incorporated the members of the seminary, and provided that the corporation "shall have, hold, and possess" the "fief and seigneury" of Lac-des-Deux-Montagnes as proprietors in the same manner and to the same extent as the seminary did under the original land grant. Local Mohawks continued to dispute the right of the seminary to sell the land and complained about the manner in which the land was managed.

In the early part of the 20th century, the federal government attempted to resolve this issue by initiating a court action on behalf of the Indigenous people at Lac-des-Deux-Montagnes to determine the respective legal rights and obligations of the seminary and the Aboriginal population. In determining the nature of the land rights of the seminary, its ability to sell the land unencumbered to third parties would also be clarified. This legal action culminated in the 1912 decision of the Judicial Committee of the Privy Council (then the final court of appeal for Canada). The court stated that the effect of the 1841 legislation "was to place beyond question the title of the respondents [the seminary] to the Seigneury; and to make it impossible for the appellants to establish an independent title to possession or control in the administration." The Privy Council also said that the Mohawks could not assert title over the land because they had not been in the area from time immemorial. Furthermore, it was accepted that the French had extinguished whatever title the Indians might have had. The Indians had not taken treaty, nor had the land been set aside for them in trust. The Privy Council went on to suggest that there might be the possibility of a charitable trust, but that the issue was not argued in this case. In essence, the court held that the Mohawk people had a right to occupy and use the land until the Sulpicians exercised their unfettered right to sell it.

The conflict between the seminary, which continued to sell off parts of the original grant, and the Aboriginal people continued. In the 1960s the Mohawks pursued legal action. However, resistance at the departmental level prevented the claim from being acted upon. One of the obstacles to creating a reserve base under the *Indian Act,* or any future legislation, was that Sulpician land purchased earlier in 1945 consisted of a series of blocks interspersed with privately held non-Aboriginal lands within the municipality of Oka. Both the community of Kanesatake and the municipality of Oka were faced with the dual problems of making decisions regarding land use and management that might affect each other, and of dealing with the effects of decisions made by one or the other community. Not surprisingly, the question of coordinating land-use policies had been a source of considerable friction between the two communities for some time.

In 1975 the Mohawks of Kanesatake presented a joint claim under the federal comprehensive land claims policy with the Mohawk people of Kahnawake and Akwesasne, asserting Aboriginal title to lands along the St. Lawrence and Ottawa rivers in southern Quebec. Comprehensive claims, as we have seen, involve claims to an existing Aboriginal title, and presume the need to negotiate a range of matters such as land to be held under Aboriginal control, lands to be ceded, compensation, and future legislative regimes to be applied to the territory in question (see Figure 7.2). The Mohawk comprehensive claim includes the southwestern part of the province of Quebec, encompassing the area along and adjacent to the St. Lawrence and Ottawa rivers stretching south and east to the U.S. border and north to a point near the Saguenay River, and including areas to the north and west of the St. Lawrence and Ottawa rivers.

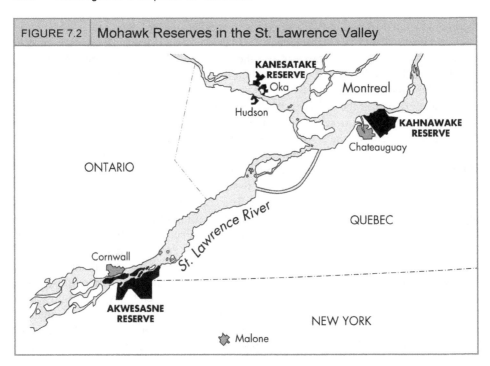

FIGURE 7.2 **Mohawk Reserves in the St. Lawrence Valley**

The federal government rejected the Mohawk 1975 comprehensive claim and the then Department of Indian Affairs restated its view that the fundamental weakness of the Mohawk land claim in the area of Oka is that the historical record, as the department viewed it, failed to demonstrate exclusive Mohawk use of the territory since time imme-morial—relative to other Aboriginal peoples and non-Aboriginal people such as the Sulpicians. From the Mohawk perspective, the claims of Canadian governments and non-Aboriginal settlers are at least equally flawed.

The Mohawk claim was also been expressed another way. Since the department had described the Mohawks at Oka as descendants of the Iroquois, Algonquins, and Nipissings, then the Indigenous people of Kanesatake could demonstrate traditional use and occu-pancy of the land not just as Mohawks but also as descendants of all Aboriginal peoples who used that territory prior to and since the arrival of Europeans.

As an alternative argument to the comprehensive claim, Mohawks said that the Sulpician land grant was intended for the benefit of the Indigenous people. Accordingly, the Sulpician Order was not free to sell any of this land without the consent of the Aboriginal people concerned. If this argument was used, then this ought to be regarded as a specific claims issue, since specific claims arise from allegations of government mismanagement of particular Indian lands. With respect to any specific claim in this region, the federal government took the position that the 1912 Privy Council decision (*Corinthe* v. *Seminary of St. Sulpice*) fully answered the question of any outstanding legal obligation of the federal government. The answer was *none.*

The Mohawks then submitted a specific claim in June 1977, which was ultimately rejected in October 1986. The Department of Justice advised that a lawful obligation on the part of the federal government did not exist. However, in a letter to the band informing them that no outstanding lawful obligation on the part of Canada existed, then minister of Indian Affairs Bill McKnight expressed the federal government's willingness to consider proposals for alternative means of redress of the Kanesatake band's grievance.

In summary, Mohawk claims to land have been advanced on a number of grounds, each representing a separate legal argument but also related to one another:

1. territorial sovereignty flowing from status as a sovereign nation;

2. treaty rights;

3. the *Royal Proclamation* of 1763;

4. unextinguished Aboriginal title under common law; and

5. land rights flowing from the obligations imposed on the Sulpician Order in the 18th-century land grants to the order by the king of France.

The Mohawk people today argue that, independent of the arrival of Mohawk religious converts in 1721 at the Sulpician mission at Lac-des-Deux-Montagnes, the Mohawk nation used and occupied that territory and exercised sovereignty over it long before the land grants by the king of France. The Mohawk people make reference to a number of treaties with European powers (Holland, France, and England), which they say acknowledge the sovereign status of the Mohawk people throughout their territory in Canada and the United States. They also question the legality, under international law, of the land grants. For example, if these lands were unoccupied by non-Aboriginal people before 1717 but were occupied and used by Indigenous people (whether Mohawk, Nipissing, or Algonquin), by what international legal principle could a European power assert sovereignty over the territory in the absence of conquest or cession?

Contrary to this position, the municipality of Oka, the federal and provincial governments, and persons claiming a clear title through the seminary argued that the Aboriginal people have no proprietary rights outside the federally purchased lands, and that this issue had been conclusively settled by legislation and litigation. In 1936 the Sulpician Order sold nearly all of the land to a Belgian real estate company. The company began to sell the land in parcels for agricultural development. In 1945 the Department of Indian Affairs purchased the seminary's unsold lands plus some additional surrounding land. The seminary retained a small parcel, which is used for religious purposes. The land question continued to be important to the Mohawks, but the government felt that the issue had been resolved. Lacking funds and legal expertise, the Mohawks were unable to further pursue their claims. It would not be until the 1990s, in the face of the Oka affair, that the federal government would act on the claim.

The conflict was over 39 hectares of land. The municipality wanted to use this land to expand an existing nine-hole golf course. This land included an Aboriginal cemetery and parts of a pine forest that the Mohawks consider theirs. Ottawa has since purchased the land for $5.2 million and turned it over to the Mohawks.

In 1992 the grand chief of the Mohawk Council of Kahnawake and the minister of state for the then Department of Indian Affairs and Northern Development signed a framework agreement to start negotiations on a new relationship between the government and Kahnawake. In the long term, the Mohawks proposed to revive the structures, institutions, and principles of the Great Law of the Iroquois of Six Nations. In the meantime, they intended to change their existing relationship with the federal government in order to obtain recognition of their jurisdiction in a variety of areas—e.g., policing. Negotiations include the nature and scope of Mohawk government, justice, land management, land control, environment, social services, health, education, and cultural matters. But just as one crisis is settled, others loom on the horizon. The early new millennium has seen its share of standoffs and confrontations, such as the Caledonia land claims dispute that erupted in 2006. Seemingly the more things change, the more they stay the same.

LATE 20TH- AND EARLY 21ST-CENTURY CLAIMS

Since the establishment of a federal policy for the settlement of Aboriginal land claims in 1973, a significant number of major comprehensive claims agreements have come into effect in Canada. An American claim in Alaska (1971) became the model for subsequent Canadian settlements—e.g., in James Bay (1975) and the Western Arctic (1984). These include the Northeastern Quebec agreement (1978), the Inuvialuit final agreement (1984), the Nunavut land claims agreement (1993), the Sahtu Dene and Métis agreement (1993), the Selkirk First Nation (1997), the Nisga'a Treaty (2000), the Tli Cho Agreement (2003), and others since. These settlements involve three major components: land cession to the Aboriginal groups, financial payment for cession, and the creation of corporate structures to deal with land, money, or environmental issues. Aboriginal corporate and political structures were also established. A more detailed description of a selection of these settlements can be seen in the "Prime Examples" section below.

In British Columbia, direct action by Aboriginal people in the 1970s and 1980s prompted the federal government to re-evaluate its policy and programs. Although the provincial government continued to deny the existence of Aboriginal title, by the late 1980s it had become more responsive to Aboriginal concerns. The Ministry of Native Affairs and the Premier's Council on Native Affairs were created to meet with Aboriginal groups regarding a range of Aboriginal issues. In 1990 the British Columbia government agreed to establish a process by which Aboriginal land claims could be received and placed on the negotiating table. The province agreed to join Aboriginal groups and the federal government in negotiating land claims settlements. This meeting resulted in the creation of a tripartite task force to develop a process for negotiations.

It is estimated that British Columbia land claims (both specific and comprehensive) will cost in excess of $10 billion when they are all settled. Under provincial–federal agreements, land claims are equally shared by both parties. The federal government will contribute most of its share in cash while the province will pay most of its share in land. As discussed earlier in the chapter, British Columbia is a special case in that Aboriginal title in most of the province still exists except in the northeast (where title was extinguished by virtue of Treaty No. 8) and the small reserves established on Vancouver Island. There has thus been pressure on the provincial government to accelerate the treaty process and settle claims quickly. In 2002 the British Columbia government proposed a province-wide referendum to determine both support for and direction of treaty negotiations, perhaps in the hopes of ending the process entirely. Ultimately, the referendum and its results were rejected on the basis that the process itself constituted an attack on the agreements between the Crown and Aboriginal people, and on decisions of the courts that have established Aboriginal rights. In addition, there was a significant lack of voter support. The First Nations and their supporters (including the Canadian Jewish Congress, the

B.C. Federation of Labour, and the David Suzuki Foundation) considered the referendum a shameful act for the B.C. government to have carried out and argued that the rights of a minority should not be determined by a vote of the majority. Voters were asked to consider and vote "yes" or "no" to some eight principles, including the following:

1. Private property should not be expropriated for treaty settlements.

2. Parks and protected areas should be maintained for the use and benefit of all British Columbians.

3. The existing tax exemptions for Aboriginal people should be phased out.

Notwithstanding the fact that these were "loaded" statements in the first place, it was the potential precedent of specifically targeting minority group rights that angered First Nations and most citizens. The 2002 B.C. referendum provides a clear example of how strong feelings are in relation to treaties and claims, and how far some governments are willing to go to deal with them (Ponting, 2006).

An argument for Canada to reopen the historical (numbered) treaties might be made. The *White Paper* in 1969 brought to the collective attention of Canadians the problems of Aboriginal groups and their claims. This was buttressed by a Supreme Court decision in 1973 (*Calder* case) and the Berger Commission (1974), which both gave some credence to Aboriginal claims. However, by the late 20th century public interest and support had waned somewhat (Ponting, 1987). The issue of land claims is still being overshadowed by other domestic and international concerns such as economic recession, the environment, health care, energy policies, and Quebec secession.

COMPREHENSIVE LAND CLAIMS: PRIME EXAMPLES

James Bay

This agreement ushered in a new relationship between Aboriginal people and government and set the stage for future comprehensive land claims. The James Bay and Northern Quebec Agreement (1975) and the Northeastern Quebec Agreement (1978) required the federal and Quebec governments to enact special legislation in respect to local government and land administration for Aboriginal people in the area. Between 1976 and 1979 a number of bills were passed to enact the agreements. Thirty-one boards, committees, commissions, and councils were established in order to deal with the organizational structure that resulted from the agreements—for example, the Cree School Board, the Income Security Board, and the Cree Trappers Association (see Figure 7.3). The agreements also required that the traditional financial arrangements between Aboriginal groups in the area and the federal government be changed as bands began to take on more political control and accountability. The new agreements (confirmed in the *Cree/Naskapi Act, 1984*) provided for:

1. funding for local government, safeguarding of community infrastructure, and delivery of essential services;

2. the determination of funding needs;

3. the principle of local autonomy and the elimination of unnecessary central administration;

FIGURE 7.3 | The James Bay Hydroelectric Project

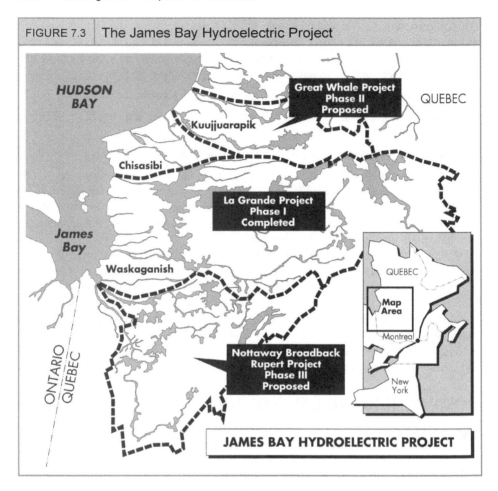

4. unconditional grant funding; and

5. grants that will be submitted to Parliament annually based on five-year agreements. (Indian and Aboriginal Program, 1985; 261–262)

In return for the Cree allowing phase I to proceed, they received $136 million from the Quebec and federal governments. This money was invested in the Cree Regional Economic Enterprises (CREECO) and the Cree Regional Authority Board of Compensation. CREECO dominates the Aboriginal economy by means of its $36 million in revenues and through its control of the airways and housing projects. Both companies have expanded and created hundreds of jobs. However, profit was slow to come, and CREECO registered a $5.2 million deficit in 1989. In addition to the above revenues, CREECO obtained over $30 million in Hydro-Quebec contracts in 1989 and over $50 million in 1990. This created permanent jobs for the Cree and changed their lifestyle considerably. With assets of over $140 million, the Cree have invested in Quebec government bonds, debentures, and blue chip stocks (which were required under the terms of the agreement), thus generating over $11 million revenue. Other monies received were used by communities to build infrastructure and develop creative investments; for example, Waskaganish Enterprises Development Corporation entered into a joint venture with Yamaha Motors Canada to build fibreglass freighter canoes.

Proponents of Hydro-Quebec's James Bay development, which diverts and stores the waters that flow into James Bay and Hudson Bay, feel that the production of 26 000 megawatts of power is reason enough for its existence. The original project altered the flow of several rivers in the region. When the water from the Caniapiscau River was first diverted to a reservoir, the volume (19 billion cubic metres) was so great that a minor tremor was felt.

The battle over this $50-billion-plus project once again came to the foreground as the first phase reached completion (in 1984) and the provincial government moved into the second and third stages. For over two decades, the Cree (10 000 of them) fought against development, but eventually agreed to allow the project to proceed after the provincial and federal governments agreed to compensation (Raunet, 1984).

As phase II continued, the Cree asked the court to declare the original settlement null and void because the agreement was based upon the assumption that hydroelectric power development was compatible with the Cree way of life, and this, the Cree argued, is not true. In phase I Hydro-Quebec erected 215 dams and dikes, and more than 10 000 square kilometres of new lake were created. Some consequences were not anticipated; for example, flooding released mercury from the bedrock and thus contaminated certain fish. But the more dramatic and significant consequences are the social impacts. The sudden modernization and urbanization of a previously nomadic society will continue to have immediate and long-term effects (Wertman, 1983), and has prompted both a re-examination of the original treaty and additional lawsuits (see Box 7.5).

After the completion of phase I, the Province of Quebec and Hydro-Quebec began planning the Great Whale phase to enlarge the hydro generating capacity of the region. After 10 years of legal wrangling, the province dropped the project. However, after 1990,

---

Box 7.5	Quebec's Innu Launch $11 B Lawsuit

The Pessmit Innu are relaunching an $11-billion lawsuit against Quebec, the federal government, and Hydro-Quebec, saying 13 dams were built on their ancestral land 50 years ago without their consent. Innu Chief Raphael Picard says the three parties violated his people's rights by building the hydroelectric dams. He figures $11 billion is about the amount that Quebec society has made from the development of the land.

The suit was first launched in 1998 for $500 million, but Picard suspended it when he became chief four years ago. Now he says that was a mistake, and that negotiations with the government are going nowhere. "The first goal for my community: that the two governments respect our title and native rights on the territory because 50 years ago, the Quebec government (did) not respect our rights and title," Picard said Tuesday.

Source: © Canadian Broadcasting Corporation, June 27, 2006. Reprinted with permission.

Hydro-Quebec and the provincial government developed plans for a new hydro dam project in the region and, in 2002, secured the support of the Cree. That project is now moving forward. The agreement with the Cree will see them receive $70 million a year for the next 50 years as well as timber rights in a large area of northern Quebec.

Almost 50 percent of the people in northern Quebec, including the Cree, are unemployed. The tradition of community food is no longer part of their customs. Alcoholism, substance abuse, and spouse abuse are rampant, as are suicide attempts. On the other hand, the villages established now have water, sewage, electricity, and schools. Children no longer have to be sent to southern schools to be educated in English.

The Nisga'a Treaty

The most recent comprehensive claim to be settled was with the Nisga'a and reveals how claims settlement has changed since the James Bay Agreement over 35 years ago. Canadian history was made on August 4, 1998, at the initialling of the Nisga'a Final Treaty Agreement. Ratified first by the Nisga'a and the province of British Columbia and then by Parliament in Ottawa, the final agreement came into effect on May 11, 2000. It was British Columbia's first treaty since 1899—some 112 years after the Nisga'a first went to Victoria to attempt to settle the land issue. By this agreement, the Nisga'a Aboriginal rights under Sections 25 and 35 of the Constitution are modified into both treaty rights and a land claims agreement. To the extent that any Aboriginal rights or title that the Nisga'a have, or may ever have, differ from those set out in the treaty, those rights are released by the Nisga'a. The treaty also reaffirms the Nisga'a Nation as an Aboriginal people of Canada, while acknowledging that the Canadian *Charter of Rights and Freedoms*, the Canadian Criminal Code, and other federal and provincial laws of general application apply to Nisga'a government.

The Final Agreement sets aside approximately 2000 square kilometres of the Nass River Valley as Nisga'a lands (of the original land claim of 24 000 square kilometres) and establishes a Nisga'a central government with jurisdiction and powers similar to those of other local municipal-style governments, including law making, policing, corrections services, and establishment of a Nisga'a court. The 56 Indian reserves cease to be reserves and become instead Nisga'a communal and fee simple property. Under the terms of the treaty, the Nisga'a will own surface and sub-surface resources on Nisga'a lands and have a share in the Nass River salmon stocks and Nass area wildlife harvests.

The treaty also provides for a financial transfer of $190 million (with a formula for how the cost will be shared between British Columbia and Canada) payable over 15 years, as well as $21.5 million in other benefits. These payments will support economic growth in the region and should help to break the cycle of dependency. In addition, the Final Agreement specifies that personal tax exemptions for Nisga'a citizens will be phased out. Other provisions in the treaty specify that, after a transition period of 12 years, the Nisga'a will cease to be administered under the *Indian Act*, will become subject to all provincial and federal taxes, and will become responsible for an increasing share of the cost of public services as the Nisga'a develop their own sources of revenue.

Despite continued opposition and criticism from some federal and provincial political parties, some resource companies, and some non-Aboriginal people, the Nisga'a treaty set a new precedent for settling the approximately 100 outstanding Aboriginal land and rights claims in British Columbia. The treaty is considered a milestone, particularly considering that between 1890 and the 1960s Nisga'a negotiators were banned from the legislature in Victoria and prohibited from publicly raising their claims.

The Prince George Treaty

The third example is the **Prince George Treaty**, which is likely to become the first agreement reached under a government and Aboriginal negotiation process since the late 1990s. Should it be successfully concluded, the treaty will represent a final agreement between the 315-member Lheidli T'enneh Band and the federal and B.C. governments.

The major components of the treaty, as so far negotiated among the three parties, will include a sockeye salmon fishing agreement, rights to 43.3 square kilometres of land in and near the central B.C. city of Prince George, and more than $13 million in cash. The fish component of the treaty would provide the Lheidli T'enneh with a one-time grant of $3 million to monitor and assess salmon stocks in the Upper Fraser River area. A significant amount of the land parcels in the treaty are within Prince George city limits. The treaty will include an agreement among the band, the city, and Prince George regional district that would harmonize property taxes, land-use plans, and municipal services. In exchange for the salmon, land, and cash, the Lheidli T'enneh Band would agree to give up their income-tax–free status, just as the Nisga'a did.

On March 30, 2007, the band rejected the claim settlement in a 53 percent vote. This means that the treaty is still in the process of negotiation, and illustrates the difficulties, frustrations, and challenges facing all parties.

Summary

- Indian treaties began with "Peace and Friendship" agreements during colonization.
- The *Royal Proclamation* of 1763 still remains an important agreement between the Crown and Aboriginal peoples.
- Land transfer treaties began in 1850 and led to the 11 numbered treaties between 1871 and 1921.
- Treaties have not been established in British Columbia, the Northwest Territories, and other areas of Canada.
- Treaties opened vast areas of Canada for settlers.
- Aboriginal people and governments vary considerably in terms of how the treaties are interpreted.
- New modern treaties have been signed and reflect changing relationships between Aboriginal people and governments.

Key Terms

Aboriginal rights p. 204

Aboriginal title p. 210

Baker Lake v. *Minister of Indian Affairs and Northern Development* p. 217

band claims p. 210

comprehensive land claims p. 222

Delgamuukw v. *British Columbia* p. 218

fiduciary relationship (or duty) p. 219

James Bay and Northern Quebec Agreement p. 222

Marshall case p. 201

Mi'kmaq Indians p. 213

Nisga'a treaty p. 215

Oka crisis p. 236

Peace and Friendship treaties p. 201

pre-Confederation treaties p. 201

Prince George Treaty p. 245

Royal Proclamation of 1763 p. 202

specific claims p. 220

Tlicho Land Claims and Self-Government Agreement p. 214

Treaty Negotiation Advisory Committee p. 214

trusteeship p. 227

usufructory rights p. 216

Questions for Further Discussion

1. Why are pre-Confederation "Peace and Friendship" treaties still important today?

2. Who is Alexander Morris and why was he important in the early 1870s?

3. In the *Royal Proclamation* of 1763, what was specifically referred to for the first time in Canadian history?

4. What two forms are used to document land claims?

5. Who dealt with the processing of land claims?

6. Why was the *White Paper* introduced?

7. Briefly explain the Oka standoff.

CHAPTER 8

The Métis: The "Original" Canadians

LEARNING OBJECTIVES

After reading this chapter you should be able to:

1. Explain the historical origins of the term "Métis."

2. Discuss the ways in which Métis culture is separate and distinct from its Indian origins and roots.

3. Understand the 18th and 19th century origins of the Métis Nation, especially in relation to the creation of Manitoba as a province.

4. Explain the details of Métis scrip, and scrip as a source of contemporary rights claims.

5. Explain why some Métis chose to become Indian and why some Indians chose to become Métis in relation to both *the Indian Act* and the *Constitution Act* of 1867, and how this illustrates the complexity and personal nature of identity.

6. Discuss the importance of the Powley case and its bearing on the Métis as a rights-bearing community with historic and modern claims for land and resources.

7. Understand the differences between Indian and Métis rights claims and how the courts have approached each Aboriginal group differently.

INTRODUCTION

The question of who is a Métis has long gone unanswered. Although it has always been important, with constitutional recognition and affirmation of the Métis as an Aboriginal people with rights, the question has taken on heightened importance. We must therefore provide a definition that has clearly articulated criteria. To begin to generate such a definition, we need first to provide a brief historical overview as well as some background regarding the often confusing legal status of persons of mixed Aboriginal and non-Aboriginal ancestry. It has been difficult for many Euro-Canadians and First Nations to accept that a new Aboriginal people with Euro-Canadian ancestry evolved in Canada. The idea seems to defy deeply held notions about loyalty to one's ethnic ancestry and the entitlements of the "first peoples." Canadians have never been comfortable with the possibility of individuals or a collective having multiple identification opportunities, a concept that suggests an unfair advantage or preferential rights. Mixed race individuals have traditionally elicited discomfort in others. This negativity can be explained by the fact that mixed race people challenge established racial hierarchies or boundaries. There is also a theory that mixed race peoples such as the Métis do not have a permanent identity. This theory envisions the Métis as a people who bridge the so-called "primitive" and "modern worlds."

Before the Canadian Constitution was repatriated in 1982, there were different legal terms for most of the Aboriginal peoples of Canada. Today, it is common to use the terms First Nations, Inuit, and Métis. Previously these same people were known in law as Indians, Eskimos, and Half-breeds. None of these terms accurately reflect the cultural societies embodied in them. For example, "Indians" includes over 50 nations of people stretching from coast to coast. Since 1982, Indians have generally adopted the term "First Nations." The people we now know as the Inuit were previously known as "Eskimos," and although they are not culturally "Indians," they were included within the meaning of "Indians" for the purposes of federal jurisdiction under Section 91(24) of the *Constitution Act, 1867*. This was accomplished by means of a reference case to the Supreme Court of Canada in 1939. The constitutional use of the term "Métis" in 1982 officially replaced the term "Half-breeds" in English legal language.

The Métis, as a collective, are a people of many names. Many of these names come from the attempts of outsiders to label the Métis either in their own language or according to their own understandings. These labels often say more about the person employing the label than about those to whom the label is attached. Because the Métis travelled widely over a vast area, they had relationships with many different peoples who spoke many different languages. Each of these groups had their own names for the Métis. The names reflect a variety of emotions and opinions—from the pejorative to claims of kinship. French language names include the terms *michif, métis, gens libre, hommes libre, bois brûlé,* and *chicot*. English language names include freemen, Half-breed, country-born, and mixed blood. Most of the different terms reflect one or the other of three concepts: (1) that the Métis belong to one of the existing hegemonies—Amerindian or Euro-Canadian; (2) reference to their skin colour; and/or (3) reference to their "mixed ancestry." The Métis themselves prefer the term "Métis" or "**Michif**" (Bakker 1997) and rejected the term "Half-breed" as early as the days of Louis Riel.

The Métis have as paternal ancestors the former employees of the Hudson's Bay and North-West companies and as maternal ancestors Indian women belonging to various tribes. The French word Métis is derived from the Latin participle mixtus, which means "mixed"; it expresses well the idea it represents. Quite appropriate also was the corresponding English term "Half-Breed" in the first generation of blood mixing, but now that European blood and Indian blood are mingled to varying degrees, it is no longer generally applicable. The French word "Métis" expresses the idea of this mixture in a more satisfactory way.

The unfortunate reality is that the Métis identity is confusing to everyone. There are several reasons for the confusion. First, the term "Métis" is often used to describe two distinct groups. Until the 1960s, references to the Métis were generally references to the historic Métis of the Northwest—the people in the northwest central part of Canada usually associated with Louis Riel. However, in the 1960s the common usage of the term expanded significantly to include all persons of mixed Aboriginal and non-Aboriginal ancestry.

Another source of the confusion with respect to Métis identity arises from the close geographic and kinship relationship between Indians and Métis. Intermarriage between Indians and Métis has been a constant fact of history. Because of this intermarriage some individuals may be Métis (from one ancestor) and Indian (status or non-status from another ancestor). Such an individual might, if he or she chooses, identify as Aboriginal, or self-identify as Métis or Indian. While Métis individuals such as Louis Riel have been well recognized in Canadian history, the Métis collective, community, or society has been, since the 1885 hanging of Louis Riel, largely invisible. The collective features of the Métis of the Northwest have either not been recognized or have been misunderstood by outsiders. Instead of seeing the collective features of the Northwest Métis as indicia of a society, observed cultural markers have been seen as factors that undermine a sense of collectivity.

Since 1885, the Métis collective has remained largely invisible to the rest of Canadian society. Their invisibility is the result of several factors: One, the fact that historically there were only two identity options in Canada—white or Indian—because no one wanted to recognize the existence of a mixed-race people; two, the erasure of historic Aboriginal geographic boundaries; three, the fact that the Métis are not phenotypically distinct; and four, a general disinclination to publicly identify following the events of 1870 (the *Manitoba Act*) and especially 1885 (the execution of Riel).

THE HISTORICAL BACKGROUND ON THE ORIGINS OF THE MÉTIS

The Northwest Métis developed from two very distinct cultures—Euro-Canadian and Amerindian. They are the children of the fur trade—the result of marriages between Amerindian women and the French voyageurs and, subsequently, English Hudson's Bay Company (HBC) employees. History shows that Métis communities were evolving throughout the Northwest during the 1700s and that Métis often acted together with Indians to protect their lands and resources. The earliest incidence of Métis participating in such political activities with Indians was in the Great Lakes, when the Pontiac Uprisings began in the summer of 1763. In 1763, at the end of the Seven Years War, New France was ceded to the British Crown in the Treaty of Paris. With the formal capitulation by France, Britain caused further discontent among the Aboriginal peoples of the Great Lakes. The British had recently discontinued the French practice of reaffirming peaceful relations with Aboriginal peoples by means of the symbolic giving of presents. This lack of recognition gave evidence to Aboriginals that the new settlers did not recognize the legitimacy of First Nations culture or governance. Moreover, there were an increasing number of transgressions regarding land being taken over by settlers.

In particular, the British discontinued giving guns and ammunition. The withdrawal of weapons fed suspicions among the Aboriginal peoples that the British were about to implement a military takeover, and they would lose their lands. This resulted in uprisings, which were led by an inspirational Ottawa chief named Pontiac. The British were particularly concerned about the Métis in the Great Lakes area because of their French background and because they were formerly the allies of the French. General Amherst, the British military commander in North America, believed that the Métis, in seeking to protect their lands and resource access, were inspiring the uprising.

While the Pontiac Uprisings ended rather peacefully, they contributed to the development of British policies respecting Aboriginal people and representatives of the British Crown. In order to quell the discontent, the British called a meeting at the Crooked Place (Niagara) in the summer of 1764, which was intended to secure peace, friendship, and trust with the Aboriginal people and in particular with France's former allies, including the Métis. The intention was to assure Aboriginal people that the British would respect First Nations territories and resources. The meeting was also intended to impress the

Aboriginal people with an unprecedented show of wealth. The Crown distributed over £20 000 worth of presents. Over 2000 Aboriginal people, many from thousands of miles away, attended the meeting that summer. Most of the Indigenous people from the Great Lakes attended the meeting. It was at this meeting that the British "proclaimed" policy with respect to Aboriginal people in the *Royal Proclamation.*

The policy recognized Aboriginal peoples as autonomous political units capable of entering into negotiations and agreements with the Crown. It also recognized that Aboriginal peoples were entitled to continue in possession of their territories, including their hunting and fishing grounds, unless or until they ceded them to the Crown. The *Royal Proclamation* and the Royal Instructions that followed set out the equitable principles under which Aboriginal territories could be ceded. These equitable principles subsequently guided Canadian policy, law, and treaty-making with respect to First Nations. Even in 1763, the equitable principles in the *Royal Proclamation* were not new. They were the consolidation of previous British and French practices. However, the meeting at Niagara was the occasion for the official announcement of the policy to the Aboriginal peoples. The practice of giving presents, begun by the French and re-established by the British at Niagara in 1764, then became an important annual event. This ceremony reaffirmed the Crown's commitment to the principles of the *Royal Proclamation* and to the protection of Aboriginal peoples. Presents were distributed annually to all Aboriginal peoples who attended, including the Métis.

The Northwest Metis also were active in Red River from 1812–1816. It is here that the Métis first began to self-identify as the Métis Nation and it was at this time that the first Métis Nation flag was flown. The cause that spurred this self-identification was the need to assert themselves to protect their livelihood. The newly arrived Selkirk settlers were seen as a threat because they were farmers, and their activities would severely affect the Métis, who were dependent on the fur trade and the buffalo. The interests of the Métis coincided with the aims of the North West Company and together they sought to actively discourage settlement. Later, Métis leader Cuthbert Grant disassociated his loyalties from those of the North West Company and pursued the ideal of a new Métis Nation.

In 1815, the HBC signed a treaty with the Métis that appeared at first to resolve the issues. The settlers left, and the Métis returned to the buffalo hunt. However, in the fall a new governor arrived and matters deteriorated rapidly. The Selkirk settlers returned and began to rebuild the colony. Tensions increased between the Métis and the settlers. In June 1816, Grant and a contingent of Métis met Governor Semple and a group of settlers. Within 15 minutes virtually all of the settlers, including the new governor, were killed. The colony was dissolved again and all colonists left. This was known as the Battle of Seven Oaks. Several unsuccessful attempts were made to arrest Grant for the murder of Semple. Finally, Grant voluntarily surrendered and was taken to Lower Canada for trial. There, a Grand Jury found no cause to try him for murder, and he was released and returned to Red River. Later, Grant was tried again by proxy in the Courts of Upper Canada. Once again he was cleared of any charges.

By 1830, there are records of the Métis meeting in council at Sault Ste Marie to protest attempts by the Crown to cut them out of the distribution of presents. To promote their cause, they joined forces with the Ojibway. Thus, the government remained deeply concerned about the Métis. In general, the Métis in the Great Lakes were seen to be too Indian, too French, and too Catholic. The government sought to remove the Métis from their lands and by the mid 1840s it was aided by mining and timber speculators who wanted exclusive control over the land and its resources around Sault Ste Marie. The area was surveyed in 1848, and by 1849, initial discussions were started to investigate the willingness of the Aboriginal people to enter into treaty negotiations.

While the government maintained its optimism that a treaty could be achieved, the general air of optimism masked a serious rupture in relations. On November 9, 1849, an armed party of Métis and Ojibway from Sault Ste Marie took over a mining camp at Mica Bay on Lake Superior. The mine was taken without bloodshed, and the miners were evacuated safely within a week. Soldiers were sent to Sault Ste Marie but the ringleaders voluntarily turned themselves in. They were arrested and sent to Toronto to stand trial. The charges were dismissed on procedural grounds. But while events were unfolding in Toronto, the situation at Sault Ste Marie remained tense and rumors abounded that 2000 **Red River Métis** were coming to act as allies. Instructions were soon issued to William Robinson to negotiate a treaty. The Métis in Sault Ste Marie asked to participate as a separate group, and when this request was denied they asked to have their lands protected in a separate clause in the treaty. Robinson denied that he had any authority to deal with the Métis, and they were not included in the treaty as a separate people. The land speculation that followed the 1850 Robinson Treaties, combined with the westward movement of the main fur trade, contributed to the dispersal of many Métis from the Upper Great Lakes to points farther west, particularly Manitoba and the Prairies (see Figure 8.1).

The Métis of Red River asserted their economic rights during the *Sayer* trial of 1849 (Weinstein 2007: 4). The Métis also fought with the Sioux over control of grazing lands and the buffalo. In 1851, after generations of fighting, a crucial battle took place at the Grand Couteau. The Métis were victorious and became known as the undisputed "masters of the plains." Perhaps the best-known events associated with the Métis of the Northwest surround the activities of Louis Riel. In 1869, a provisional government was formed to negotiate the terms of Manitoba's entry into Canada. The events at Red River led to the inclusion of the Métis in the *Manitoba Act* and the *Dominion Lands Act*. This event, which should have heralded a new relationship with the Métis, in fact led to a tragically flawed system of land grants and a scrip process (discussed below) that intended to extinguish the Aboriginal land rights claimed by the Métis. The formal political rights of the Métis were overwhelmed by brute power and the numbers of eastern financial interests. New settlers from Ontario were anti-Catholic, anti-French, and racist. The execution of Thomas Scott by the provisional government had whipped up hatred of the Métis, and many of the new settlers were bent on revenge. Riel, a symbol of Métis national sentiment, was forced into exile by the Canadian government. Physical and psychological abuse of the French Métis went unpunished in Red River. Many Métis were driven from their land by settlers from Ontario while provincial troops stood by and did nothing to prevent the illegal seizures. The government deliberately delayed the distribution of the 1.4 million acres promised to the Métis. The land speculation that followed led to the forced dislocation of many Métis to points even farther west and north. Some went to the United States, some to Fort Edmonton, and some to settlements in St. Laurent, Batoche, and Duck Lake on the South Saskatchewan River. Meanwhile, perhaps in response to the events at Red River, in 1875 the government agreed to let the Métis of Rainy Lake and Rainy River adhere to Treaty 3. This unique example of Métis adhesion to a treaty guaranteed the Métis important lands and hunting, fishing, and gathering (harvesting) rights.

FIGURE 8.1	The Distribution of Métis Populations in the Prairie Provinces, 2007

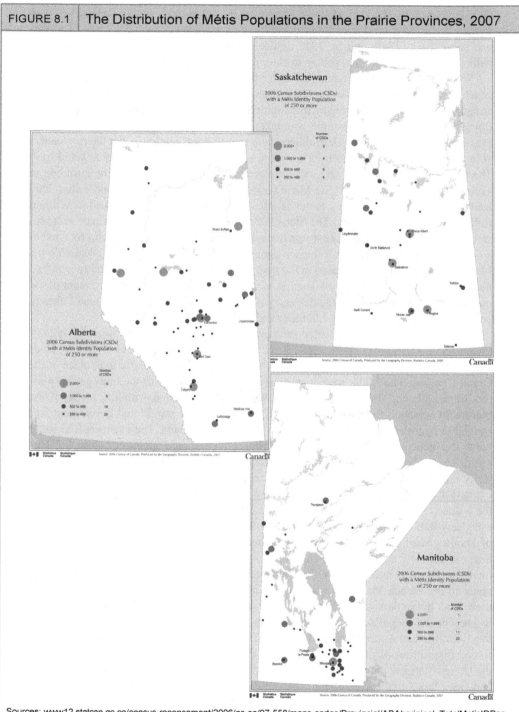

Sources: www12.statcan.gc.ca/census-recensement/2006/as-sa/97-558/maps-cartes/Provincial/ABAboriginal_TotalMetisIDPop_ec.pdf; www12.statcan.gc.ca/census-recensement/2006/as-sa/97-558/maps-cartes/Provincial/MBAboriginal_TotalMetisIDPop_ec.pdf; www12.statcan.gc.ca/census-recensement/2006/as-sa/97-558/maps-cartes/Provincial/SKAboriginal_TotalMetisIDPop_ec.pdf.

MÉTIS SCRIP: A SOURCE OF CONTEMPORARY RIGHTS ISSUES

The conditions for the transfer of land to the Métis were outlined in the *Manitoba Act* and *Dominion Lands Act*, as mentioned above. In the case of the Métis, the allocation of land (or money) was through the process of scrip. Scrip is a certificate giving the holder the right to receive payment later in the form of cash, goods, or land (Sawchuk, Sawchuk, and Ferguson, 1981). This process differed from Indian treaties in that it involved grants to individuals; it did not purport to set up the Métis as a continuing corporate entity or community. For over 30 years (1885–1923), there was a series of scrip allotments to Métis. Each time a new part of the Prairie provinces or the Mackenzie Valley was ceded by Indians, persons of mixed blood who did not participate were allocated scrip redeemable in land (Flanagan, 1983a).

Prior to 1870, the Métis had not been dealt with as a separate group. However, expediency, or perhaps humanitarian reasons, led to a change; under Section 31 of the *Manitoba Act, 1870,* a proportion of 623 000 hectares originally calculated as unoccupied land was set aside for the children of Métis families in Manitoba. This land was reserved for "the benefits [sic] of the families of the half-breed residents." It was to be divided "among the children of the half-breed heads of families" residing in the province at the time of its transfer to Canada. Initially, the amount of land set aside was thought to provide each child with 290 acres (116 hectares). However, due to miscalculations, the government also had to issue money scrip in lieu of land. In 1874 the heads of Métis families were also provided with scrip (71 hectares or $160). Under the *Dominion Lands Act* in 1885, all Métis resident in the Northwest Territories outside the limits of Manitoba in 1870 were granted 107 hectares. By this time, the government had allotted 579 264 hectares of land and $509 760 to Métis in Manitoba. Four years later this would be extended to Métis residents in the area ceded by the adhesion to Treaty No. 6 (Taylor, 1983). In 1899 Métis in the Athabasca and Peace River areas were given scrip, and in 1906 all Métis permanently residing in the territory ceded at the time of making Treaty No. 10 were provided with 107 hectares. Finally, in 1921 each Métis of the Mackenzie River district received $240 to extinguish their Aboriginal rights (Sealey and Lussier, 1975). In all, the government handled more than 24 000 Métis claims (14 000 in the Northwest Territories, Saskatchewan, and Alberta, and 10 000 in Manitoba). These claims involved over a million hectares of land and in excess of $3.6 million.

Scrip came in two forms and looked as follows.

A typical land scrip certificate read:

Dominion of Canada

Department of the Interior

This Scrip note is receivable as payment in full for ONE HUNDRED and SIXTY ACRES of Dominion Lands, open for ordinary Homestead only if presented by _____ at the office of Dominion Lands of the District within which such lands are situated in conformity with Scrip Certificate form _____ granted by the North West Half Breed Commission this _____ day of _____, 18 _____.

A typical money scrip certificate read:

Dominion of Canada

Department of the Interior

In conformity with Certificate form No. _____ granted by the North West Half Breed Commission, it is Hereby Certified that under the authority of an order of the Honorable Privy Council dated _____ day of _____, 18 _____ as amended by the order of _____ of _____, 18 _____, and in accordance with the provisions of subsec. (e), Sec. 81, 46 Vic. Cap. 17 _____, a Half-Breed is entitled to TWO HUNDRED AND FORTY DOLLARS IN SCRIP. The coupons attached to this will be accepted in payment of Dominion Lands on presentation at the office of Dominion Lands of the District within which such lands are situated.

Issued at the Department of the Interior, Ottawa, this _____ day of _____, 18 _____.

After passage of the *Manitoba Act* of 1870, which set aside lands for Métis, the government began a systematic process of amending the Act so that land set aside would not actually be allotted. From 1873 to 1884, 11 amendments were passed, referred to as Manitoba Supplementary Provisions. Nearly half of these amendments altered substantive portions of the original law. The effect of all of the amendments was the dispersal of the original Métis people in Manitoba. Only about 20 percent of the claimants received and made use of their land allotments. A similar percentage of river-lot occupants obtained patents and remained on the land they occupied in 1870. Over half the potential recipients were denied their land through a number of government manoeuvres (Sawchuk, 1978; 1998).

Perhaps the single most important factor that prevented Métis from reaping the potential benefits of land claim settlements was the 1874 amendment to the 1870 Act, which restricted eligibility for the initial allotment. It should be noted that even in the original allotment many children were omitted from participating in the benefits of the Act. The 1874 amendment, which declared that heads of families were entitled to the same benefits as children, excluded the heads from receiving any part of the original 1.4 million acres set aside. Instead they were awarded $160 in scrip that could be used to purchase Crown land (Dickason, 1992). As Dickason points out, "Fortunes were made at the expense of the Métis—half-breed scrip millionaires" were created (p. 317). Scrip was sold to land speculators (bankers and wealthy individuals) for as little as half its face value. In some cases, accepting scrip left Métis poorer than before.

Children who received an allotment were not adequately protected. For example, their allotments were subject to payment of local taxes from the moment the allotment was drawn. Thus, even if they were minors and had no way of paying the tax, they were expected to do so. Failure of tax payment meant loss of the property. Finally, Métis river-lot claimants were not compensated by the government for railway or other public expropriation. However, homesteaders were. The federal government acted in many other ways that placed the Métis in a disadvantageous position (Peterson and Brown, 1985).

Some writers, such as Flanagan (1983a), claim that Métis only wanted money scrip and thus were not interested in obtaining land scrip. He also notes that some Métis insisted on receiving their entitlements in as liquid a form as possible. He points to the

Métis of Lesser Slave Lake, who refused to accept scrip until it was rewritten "payable to the bearer." He also argues that Métis were good negotiators and that they operated in a "willing buyer–willing seller" market. We would acknowledge that some Métis preferred money scrip and we would concur that some were skilful negotiators. However, the structural conditions under which Métis operated did not allow for the exercise of choice, nor did they fully understand the implications of not having land deeded to them. For example, nearly 60 percent of the Métis were illiterate, a definite liability when dealing with banks and lawyers. The Métis Association of Alberta also pointed out in its study *Métis Land Rights in Alberta: A Political History* (1981) that the use of **land scrip** came about because Métis opposed money scrip and wanted land grants. Métis of the Qu'Appelle Lakes refused to accept **money scrip**. Thus, land scrip was considered a compromise. There is also no doubt that most of the land scrip issued to Métis was eventually owned by banks and financial agents.

Evidence today is clear that when fraud was committed in obtaining these certificates, the government did little or nothing about it. For example, in 1900 two federal commissioners found that many powers of attorney were signed without the forms being completed. In other cases, Métis who anticipated receiving scrip were asked to sign power of attorney to brokers hoping to make money out of scrip settlements (Purich, 1988). Other evidence shows that land owned by minors was not safeguarded and was lost to non-Aboriginal land speculators for much less than it was worth. It is clear that large-scale land transfer from Métis to land agents and banks took place. More problematic has been how the government has resolved these fraudulent transfers and what their consequences have been (E. Pelletier, 1974; 1975).

LATE 19TH- AND EARLY 20TH-CENTURY EVENTS AND CIRCUMSTANCES

By 1885, increased immigration, encroachments on lands and resources, and the loss of the buffalo led to serious unrest for the Indians and Métis, particularly in western Canada. Once again the two peoples joined together in an attempt to protect their livelihood. It was an economic struggle for land carried out by an alliance of Métis workers and plains hunters. A strong element of national liberation also motivated the Métis. Batoche, Duck Lake, and Fish Creek are names that evoke the battles in Saskatchewan in 1885. Métis and Indians who participated in the battles were found guilty of treason and sentenced to terms of imprisonment. Seventy-one men were charged with treason for partaking in the uprising in 1885, including Big Bear, Wandering Spirit, and Poundmaker. In the end, nine Indians were hung and 50 were sentenced to penitentiary terms for participating in the uprising. Eleven Métis councilors were sentenced to prison for seven years. Three others were sentenced to three years in prison, four got one-year sentences and seven prisoners were discharged conditionally. The cases of some of the Métis participants were not litigated. Gabriel Dumont escaped to the United States, but Riel himself was captured, tried, and convicted of high treason. He was hanged in Regina on November 16, 1885.

By the 1890s, the government had begun to implement its new policy of "civilizing" Indians. It began to promote individual enfranchisement and assimilation as well as to introduce and enforce the "out-marriage" provision in the *Indian Act*. The Half-breed/Métis who had "taken treaty" with the Indians were approached and requested to "take scrip," thereby removing them and their descendants from the Indian roll and saving the government money. Giokas and Chartrand (2002) point out that the 1885 Street Commission reported that one-third of the scrip claims allowed were issued to persons withdrawing from treaty. One year later, another Half-breed commission noted that nearly 90 percent of the individuals taking scrip were Half-breeds leaving treaty. They also assert that in the case of the treaty adhesion in the Lesser Slave Lake region, nearly 600 Indians were removed from the band list on the sole basis that they were of mixed ancestry. Although an inquiry was held and the presiding judge found that only about 200 people should have been removed from the roll, the department only reinstated about one-third of those recommended to be put back on. Métis do not necessarily have to be part of the historic Red River or Rupert's Land Métis nations. Nor is there any real distinction between Métis and Indians or non-status Indians other than the fact that the two groups seem to have chosen different ways of addressing their land claims: Indians took treaty and lived on a reserve, while the Métis took scrip. Giokas and Chartrand (2002) conclude that if judicial rulings continue the way they have in the recent past, scrip-takers may have an actionable claim to the restoration of Indian and band status as well as to treaty and reserve land rights (p. 94). In the early 1950s, several bands asked the Department of Indian Affairs to expel "mixed ancestry" residents from the reserve. Changes to the *Indian Act* in 1958 effectively ended this attempt to expel members from the reserve. However, it created two different types of scrip-takers—those who were band members and status Indians prior to that date (1958), and those who were not.

As is evident from Métis history, as early as 1763 the Métis were beginning to take action to defend their livelihood. This activity culminated sadly in the events of 1885 and from that time until the mid-20th century the Métis lived on the margins of society between First Nations and Canadian cultures. From being the "masters of the plains" and the "diplomats and culture brokers" of emerging Canadian society, the Métis who lived in the southern and central parts of the Prairie provinces became marginalized, poverty-stricken, and known as the "road allowance people." During the late 1800s and early 1900s, some Métis attempted to challenge the land grant system that disentitled them from their lands. While a couple of these cases document individual Métis attempting to reclaim their lost scrip, most are about non-Métis purchasers trying to capitalize and gain on the scrip they acquired from Half-breeds.

THE 20TH CENTURY: MIXED RESULTS FOR THE MÉTIS

Beginning in 1902, the federal government began to establish some Métis townships in Saskatchewan at Green Lake. The creation of these townships and farms continued over the next four decades. In the 1930s, the Alberta government set aside lands that became the Métis settlements (see Box 8.1 and Figure 8.2). The Saskatchewan Métis settlements are largely lost today, and the Green Lake townships are now the subject of litigation. The Alberta settlements have continued, although there are less of them than there used to be. With the new **1990 *Métis Settlements Act***, the future of the currently established and recognized settlements is hopefully more secure. From the 1930s to the 1960s, organizational work was carried out in the Prairie communities by many Métis leaders.

In the 1930s, the Ewing (Half-breed) Commission (1935) asserted the existence of Métis claims. By 1969, the Indian claims commissioner also argued for the Aboriginal rights of Métis, stating that they were well established in Canadian law. According to the commissioner, various actions of the federal government, such as scrip allocation in Western Canada and the Adhesions to Treaty No. 3, granted special status to the Métis both morally and legally. However, even while recognizing Métis claims, the federal and provincial governments have continually tried to wish them away. The rights of the Métis in the Northwest Territories were ignored until rebellion was threatened in 1885. In the 1940s the federal government deleted "Métis" from the census as a separate ethnic category. In 1944, Indian Affairs removed the names of nearly 1000 Indians from the roll, arguing that they were really Métis. Although a subsequent judicial inquiry forced the department to replace most of the names, clearly the government was hoping that the Métis would simply assimilate into Euro-Canadian society and disappear, along with their claims (Barkwell et al., 1989).

In their attempts to retain their ethnic status and to receive compensation for Aboriginal rights, the Métis, like the Indians and Inuit, have created complex and highly political organizations. The Native Council of Canada (NCC) was established in 1970 and became the political arm of the Métis. The NCC became known as the **Congress of Aboriginal Peoples** (CAP) in 1994. By the mid-1970s, there were 10 Métis organizations representing Métis in all regions of Canada. The overall mandate of the congress and its many provincial affiliates for these groups is to seek improved social conditions and a land base, and to deal with historical grievances (Purich, 1988; Sawchuck, 1998). The Métis argue that those whose ancestors did not take treaty or receive scrip or land still have Aboriginal rights. By the 1960s and 1970s, provincial and national Métis organizations had been established to pursue these rights. The political work of the Métis organizations reached a high point in 1982 with the inclusion of Métis in the *Constitution Act, 1982*. Since then, the Métis, in a series of cases, have sought to establish their land and resource rights in the courts. *MacPherson, Manitoba Métis Federation* v. *AG Canada, Morin and Daigneault, Powley,* and *Blais* are just some of the cases that are significant for Métis rights claims across Canada.

At present, the relationship between the Métis and the federal and provincial governments varies from province to province. In the Yukon, Métis demands have gone relatively unnoticed, or at least have been treated with less legitimacy than Inuit or Dene demands (Coates and Morrison, 1986). On the other hand, in the Northwest Territories, the Métis are working alongside status Indians and Inuit to negotiate an agreement with the federal government. Until the 1990s, the British Columbia government refused to recognize the special rights of certain Aboriginal peoples in the province, including the Métis (Hatt, 1972).

Saskatchewan excludes Métis from any land claim registration now taking place with status Indians. In Saskatchewan, "farms" have been established for Métis, with land bases of less than four square kilometres each. Although Manitoba has historically recognized the Métis, it has recently refused to acknowledge their existence officially. The few monies that the Métis Association had been receiving from the provincial government for special education and cultural activities were cut off in 1982.

In Ontario, the Métis are recognized and are eligible to receive funds from a Native Community Branch. Although Quebec claims to define Métis and non-status Indians as Indians, it refuses to fund or implement programs for these special groups. In order to be officially recognized by the Quebec government, the Métis would have to reject the *Indian Act* and accept new terms outlined by the provincial government. Provincial policy with regard to Métis has been (with the exception of Alberta, which has accepted partial responsibility for Métis) one that claims that Métis fall under Section 94(21) of the Constitution and that they are thus a federal responsibility. In the Atlantic provinces, most governments simply refuse to acknowledge the existence of the Métis. Although Prince Edward Island recognizes them, it has no special policy because there are so few of them.

Today there is no legislation in Canada that formally recognizes a group referred to as Métis prior to the acquisition of the HBC in Rupert's Land in 1870. Nevertheless, Métis have been recognized as a people through the *Manitoba Act* and other acts of legislation. However, there has not been a consistent or coherent national policy on Métis (Groves and Morse, 2004). Early in the history of Canada there was a belief that the Métis (however defined) would eventually integrate either into the Indian or non-Indian population and would thus no longer be a people. As such, the country would not need a long-term policy with regard to this group. It is now evident that the Métis have been part of the political, social, and legal fabric of Canada since at least 1763. The recognition of the Métis and their inclusion in the *Constitution Act, 1982* is therefore not a new recognition. It is part of a long history of government recognition of the Métis. In 1992, both the House of Commons and the Senate passed unanimous resolutions that promised to act to further recognize the Métis.

At the federal level, the Métis have only in recent years received formal, legal, and constitutional recognition beyond that established in the *Manitoba Act* of 1870. The Métis argue that, under this Act, they were recognized as a separate people with certain rights. Furthermore, because the Act cannot be changed without Britain's consent, Métis and non-status Indians continue to have separate legal status. The federal government has established a cabinet committee on Métis and non-status Indians to investigate more fully the claims and issues put forward by them. Currently there is considerable debate about the legal status of Métis and their rights.

In early 1981 the federal government recognized and affirmed the Aboriginal and treaty rights of Indians, Inuit, and Métis. These rights have been affirmed in the Constitution (1982, Sec. 35(1)), with the proviso that only "existing and treaty rights" are to be recognized. The Métis argue that their rights are a special case of Aboriginal rights, that they stem from the self-perception of the Métis people as an Indigenous national minority (Daniels, 1981), and that they are derived from their Aboriginal ancestry and title—both of which constitute the national identity of the Métis.

In 1983, members of the Métis Nation created the Métis National Council, whose goal was to achieve a clear definition and defence of Métis rights. By the time the First Ministers' Conference on Aboriginal Affairs convened that same year, a separate invitation had been issued to the Métis National Council, thereby severing the formal relationship with the Native Council of Canada, which had previously represented the Métis.

The Métis National Council has published material that identifies its criteria for determining whether a person is Métis:

The Métis are:

- an Aboriginal people distinct from Indian and Inuit;
- descendants of the historic Métis who evolved in what is now Western Canada as a people with a common political will; and
- descendants of those Aboriginal peoples who have been absorbed by the historic Métis.

Accordingly, estimates of the number of Métis range from less than 500 000 to more than 1 000 000, depending upon the source. The lack of accurate information resulted, as far back as 1941, from the actual deletion of "Métis" from the census. By 1980, 40 years later, government statistics (Canada, 1980) revealed the following figures:

- Métis and non-status Indian (core population)—300 000 to 435 000

- Métis and non-status Indian (self-identifying population)—400 000 to 600 000

- Métis and non-status Indian (non-core and non–self-identifying population)—1 to 2.5 million

After a lapse of several decades, the 1981 Census once again included Métis as a category of ethnic identification. The results were startling, since less than 100 000 people identified themselves as Métis. This would change again over the next 25 years.

According to the 2006 Census (Table 8.1), of persons who declared Aboriginal ancestry, 389 785 identified themselves as Métis, with a further 26 000 status Indians identifying themselves as Métis. Some of these are frustrated individuals who feel they are "Indian" but since they cannot obtain status, they settle for calling themselves Métis. Confusion over identity continues, as the next section of the chapter discusses.

TABLE 8.1	Size and Growth of the Métis Population, Canada, Provinces and Territories, 1996 and 2006		
	Métis Population		
Provinces and Territories	Number (2006)	Percentage Distribution (2006)	Percentage Change from 1996 to 2006
Canada	389 785	100	91
Atlantic region	18 805	5	192
Newfoundland and Labrador	6470	2	42
Prince Edward Island	385	0.1	250
Nova Scotia	7680	2	831
New Brunswick	4270	1	347
Quebec	27 980	7	80
Ontario	73 605	19	242
Manitoba	71 805	18	58
Saskatchewan	48 115	12	34
Alberta	85 500	22	73
British Columbia	59 445	15	132
Territories	4515	1	5
Yukon Territory	805	0.2	46
Northwest Territories	3580	0.9	-2
Nunavut	130	0	63

Source: Statistics Canada publication *Aboriginal Peoples, 2006 Census*, Cat. no. 97-558-XIE2006001, Table 13: "Size and growth of the Métis population, Canada, provinces and territories, 1996 and 2006." www12.statcan.ca/census-recensement/2006/as-sa/97-558/table/t13-eng.cfm.

| Box 8.1 | Métis Settlements in Alberta |

By the turn of the 20th century, the Métis of Alberta had begun organizing, and two decades later they were recognized by the provincial government. In Alberta, the provincial government's *Métis Betterment Act*, 1938, outlines its relationships with the Métis. The Alberta government does not acknowledge the legal existence of Métis off what were then called the colonies. Therefore, all Métis individuals who do not reside on a colony/settlement are considered regular Albertans with no Aboriginal or special rights. While most provinces argued that mixed ancestry individuals with Aboriginal backgrounds should be reinstated to Indian, Alberta took an alternative approach. During the Ewing Commission hearings, they took the position that Half-breeds/Métis were really Indians and took as a definition of Half-breed/Métis "a person of mixed blood, White and Indian, who lives the life of the ordinary Indian . . . " This definition was used in the 1938 *Métis Betterment Act*, which eventually established Métis settlements. Later, Alberta would revert to a blood-quantum theory— e.g., a person had to have at least one-quarter Indian blood to reside on the colonies. This blood requirement remained in the Act until 1990.

Métis settlements located across the northern part of Alberta include the settlements of Paddle Prairie, Peavine, Gift Lake, East Prairie, Buffalo Lake, Kikino, Elizabeth, and Fishing Lake (see Figure 8.2). These eight settlements form the only constitutionally protected Métis land base in Canada. They consist of 505 102 hectares, much of it covered by forest, pasture, and farmland.

The Métis are the descendants of European fur traders and Indian women who emerged as a distinct group on the Prairies toward the early part of the 19th century. Following the Northwest Rebellion of 1885, many Métis moved to the north and west. After a period of political activism among landless Métis in Alberta during the Depression, the provincial government passed the original *Métis Population Betterment Act* in 1938. Lands were set aside for Métis Settlement Associations, though four of the original settlements (Touchwood, Marlboro, Cold Lake, and Wolf Lake) were later rescinded by order of the Alberta government.

A distinct Métis culture, combining Indian and Euro-Canadian values and modes of expression, is practised in the Métis settlements. For example, jigging, a favourite form of dance, mixes the reels of Scotland and France with the chicken dance of the Cree. A distinct Métis language called Michif (combining Cree, French, and some English words) is still spoken alongside English. Most residents of Métis settlements retain Indian spiritual beliefs and customs.

The later 1955 and 1970 *Métis Betterment Acts* provided for settlement associations for each of the eight communities and laid the foundation for self-government. In each settlement, councils of five members are elected by settlement members to deal with matters affecting the settlements. In 1975 the Alberta Federation of Métis Settlement Associations was officially established to act as the political voice of the settlements and to pursue such goals as land security, local self-government, and long-term economic self-reliance. In 1985 the Alberta government passed what was known as Motion 18, a resolution committing the province to transfer title of the settlements to the Métis people and to provide provincial constitutional protection of the lands by means of an amendment to the *Alberta Act*. This paved the way for the historic 1989 Alberta Settlements Accord, which passed into legislation with the 1990 *Métis Settlements Act*. Replacing the previous *Métis Betterment Acts*, the *Métis Settlements Act* provides for the legal transfer of land title to the Métis people, as well as local municipal and traditional style self-government, and establishes eight settlement corporations and the Métis Settlements General Council as legal entities. The new Act establishes the Métis Settlements Appeals Tribunal, which provides a dispute resolution mechanism dealing with membership, land use, and resource matters on settlements. Also part of the Act is the Subsurface Resources Co-Management Agreement, an agreement whereby the settlements and the province jointly manage oil, gas, and other subsurface resources on the settlements. Significantly, the constitution of Alberta was itself amended in 1990 to recognize and protect the Métis settlements' interest in their land and resources.

Source: René R. Gadacz, *The Canadian Encyclopedia 2000*, World Edition. Toronto: McClelland and Stewart. Reproduced with permission.

THE QUEST FOR IDENTITY

The *Indian Act* and the Métis People

In the past, changes to the definition of the term "Indian" in the *Indian Act* have affected Métis identity. Because of these changes, "non-status" Indians (individuals who have, for one reason or another, lost their registration under the *Indian Act*) are often identified as Métis even if they have no connection to Métis societies that arose out of the fur-trade and evolved into a distinct Métis culture. In so identifying, such individuals are usually relating solely to their mixed genetic ancestry rather than to a cultural association with a Métis collectivity. Prior to the creation of reserves, Indians and Métis generally shared territory, usually peacefully.

Although their cultures were distinct, they shared harvesting areas and family ties. After treaties were entered into, some Métis individuals moved onto the new Indian reserves and became part of the Indian culture. Many maintained their identity as Métis despite being legally registered as Indians. At some subsequent point these families were removed from the reserves and lost their status under the *Indian Act*. They often returned to the off-reserve Métis society that persisted in the vicinity. Historically, Métis individuals

FIGURE 8.2	Alberta, Canada, Métis Settlements

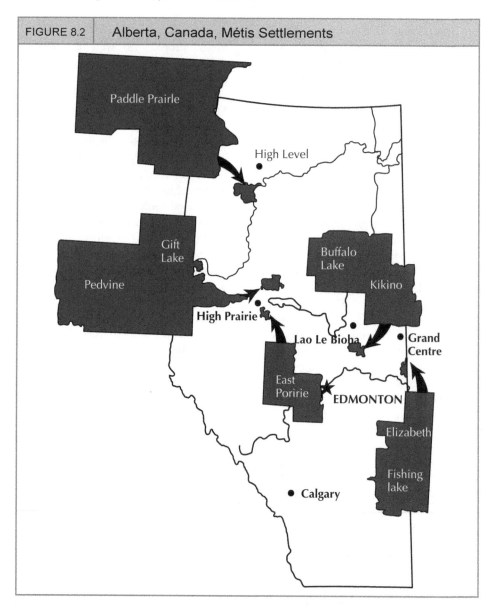

could choose to take treaty or not. Under the 1886 *Indian Act* a Métis individual who not to take treaty might have been considered a "non-treaty Indian," which the Act defined as a person of Indian blood who either belonged to an irregular band or followed the Indian mode of life, even if only temporarily resident in Canada. If a Métis individual chose to take scrip, he or she was not legally an Indian. If a Métis individual chose to take treaty, he or she would be entered on the band pay list and, after the creation of the *Indian Act* Registry in 1951, all such individuals were henceforth considered in law to be "status Indians."

The *Indian Act* is a statutory enactment of the federal government pursuant to its powers under s. 91(24) of the *Constitution Act, 1867*, which provides that the federal government has jurisdiction with respect to "Indians, and Lands reserved for the Indians." In addition, the terms of the *Indian Act*, including the definition of who is an "Indian," are subject to change from time to time. It is important to understand that the *Indian Act* is not to be confused with cultural identity. "Indian" in the Act is a legal, cover-all term that includes over 50 First Nations and Inuit and many if not all Métis. The changes to the definition of "Indian" in the Act over time have been inconsistent with respect to the inclusion of all Aboriginal peoples.

There is one historical fact worth mentioning—Métis have not always been excluded from the *Indian Act*. Prior to 1927, Métis (then still referred to as Half-breed) were included in the definition of "Indian" in the *Indian Act*. The 1927 Act contained the express exclusion of some Métis: It excluded a "half-breed in Manitoba who has shared in the distribution of half-breed lands" from being defined as an "Indian" but did not exclude those same Half-breeds from being defined as a "non-treaty Indian." It also did not exclude Half-breeds who did not "share" in the land distribution in Manitoba or Half-breeds in other provinces (whether or not they shared in Half-breed land distribution). As a result, in the 1927 Act, there were Métis who were "Indians" under the *Indian Act* and Métis who were not. That version of the *Indian Act* remained unchanged until 1951. In the 1951 *Indian Act,* many more Métis than those covered by the 1927 Act were expressly excluded. The 1951 Act added, as now excluded from the definition of "Indian," Métis scrip recipients and their descendents from other provinces.

With the addition of "Eskimo" to the definition of "Indian" in the Act following a Supreme Court of Canada decision in 1939, until 1951 the Act could be said to have included Indians, Inuit, and Métis. When this is added to the fact that many individuals who self-identify as Métis are today registered as "Indians" under the Act, the logical conclusion is that the definition is simply arbitrary and ambiguous. It has had to be repeatedly amended to bring it in line with human rights and constitutional principles. The *Indian Act* also reflects the assumption that men were the heads of the household and that the legal status of the women was determined by the status of the male. In practice, women and their children lost their "Indian" status when they married Métis or non-Aboriginal men (Indian men did not lose their status when they married non-Indian women).

From discussions in earlier chapters, we know that in the early 1970s Aboriginal women's organizations began to campaign to change the law. In 1974, the Supreme Court of Canada upheld the "marrying out" provisions in the *Indian Act* in *Lavell* v. *Canada*. Sandra Lovelace joined the campaign in 1977 and took her case to the Human Rights Committee of the United Nations. In 1981, the UN Human Rights Committee found Canada in breach of the International Covenant on Civil and Political Rights. In 1985, the *Indian Act* was amended by *Bill C-31*, discussed in an earlier chapter, so that Indian women who married non-Indians would no longer lose their status, nor would their children. Incidentally, this also brought the amended *Indian Act* in line with the new *Charter of Rights and Freedoms*, which is Part 1 of the Canadian Constitution (1982). Recently the British Columbia Court of Appeal ruled in *McIvor* (2009) that under *Bill C-31* men who married non-Indian women were treated better because they could pass on their status to their children, whereas women who married non-Indian men could not. The court held that this was clearly discrimination based on sex because *Bill C-31* enhanced the status of men who married non-Indian women and their descendants while it perpetuated discrimination with respect to women who married non-Indian men by limiting their ability to transmit status to their children. In addition to this confusion, many mixed ancestry individuals who had previously identified as "Métis" sought registration as "Indians" under the new *Bill C-31*. The Bill had a profound effect on the identity of both Indians and Métis in Canada. At least for the first generation, it substantially increased the numbers of status Indians. Statistics show that over 100 000 individuals obtained status cards.

The issue also had repercussions for the Alberta Métis settlements, where some members are registered as Indians under the *Indian Act*. Recently the Alberta Court of Appeal, in *Cunningham* (2009), held that individuals who identify as Métis and are registered as Indians under the *Indian Act* cannot be removed from membership or refused membership. The evidence seems to indicate that Métis rarely take on Indian status in order to become "Indians" culturally. Rather, they choose to adhere to the legal status of "Indian" in order to take advantage of the benefits that are available to those recognized as such. In *Sinclair* (2001) and in *Cunningham*, Indian status was chosen to obtain health benefits. In *Powley* (2003), Olaf Bjornaa gave a poignant illustration of this choice. When asked why he finally chose *Bill C-31* status when he had said he would identify as Métis until the day he died, Mr. Bjornaa told the court that he had been a commercial fisherman all his life but he had an accident on his boat and he could not fish anymore. He could no longer make a living from his fishing. Unfortunately, while he retained his commercial fishing licences he was denied welfare. Since fishing licences can be inherited, he did not want to give them up. Mr. Bjornaa was raising his grandchildren and now required over $300 a month in medicine. Taking *Bill C-31* was a pragmatic necessity. Mr. Bjornaa needed access to the health benefits available to status Indians but denied to Métis.

What are we to make of all this? The confusion between Indians and Métis has led some to ask whether one can claim to be both Métis and Indian. For example, if one had a Métis mother and an Indian father, one might, with some justification, claim to be both Métis and Indian. For some purposes an individual claim to dual heritage might be relatively insignificant. For instance, dual heritage would not mean double harvesting. After all, one individual still consumes the same amount of deer meat, whether that person identifies as Métis, Indian, or both. However, when one looks to political rights or access to programs and services, it becomes a more complex story. While one might be able to claim dual ancestral heritage, Indian and Métis, one would likely be prohibited from exercising rights in both societies concurrently. Such an individual would likely have to choose to exercise political rights and benefits under one entity. It should be possible to switch, but the rule, certainly as we have seen it develop in land claims agreements, is one enrolment at a time. This has substantially changed with the ruling of the Alberta Court of Appeal in *Cunningham*, where it seems that an individual can get health benefits as an "Indian" under the *Indian Act* and also obtain the benefits of membership in the Alberta Métis settlements. The issue of Métis identity has always been complicated. Identity is sensitive, complex, and personal. Identity can also mean different things in different contexts. Regardless of the purpose of the identification, being a member of a distinct Métis people—the Métis Nation—cannot be reduced to the issue of blood-quantum.

There is something else to consider as well. There is no single exclusive Métis people in Canada. Eastern Canadian Métis are different from Red River or Northwest Métis. At a provincial level, the issue of who is or is not Métis varies. In Alberta, changes to the *Métis Settlement Act* and the criteria set out by the Alberta Métis Nation Association have clarified the definition of a Métis. Both the government and the Association agree that a Métis is someone who declares himself or herself as a Métis, has traditionally held him or herself as Métis, and is accepted by the Métis community as Métis. In Manitoba, the federation definition of a Métis remains a racial one that enables non-status Indians to join. The Saskatchewan Association of Métis and non-status Indians split in 1987, so the Métis Society of Saskatchewan defines a Métis in a manner similar to Alberta.

Today the term "Metis" has widespread usage. Two different meanings have been given to the term. As the Métis National Council (1984) pointed out, written with a small *m,* "métis" is a racial term for anyone of mixed Indian and European ancestry. Nevertheless, the Council has objected to this distinction and argues that the acceptance of the latter (racial) definition undermines the rights of Métis people. Today there is a distinction made between the historical Métis and the pan-Métis. "Pan-Métis" is a more inclusive term that includes historic Métis, people of mixed Indian-European ancestry, as well as non-status Indians. As Lussier (1979) points out, they gain their identity from a multitude of national roots.

The federal government has taken the position that Métis are a provincial responsibility, even though there are federal departments that provide funding for them—Heritage Canada is a current example. The recent name change of Aboriginal Affairs and Northern Development reflects the more formalized inclusion of Métis and Inuit affairs within the department. This position is based on the argument that Métis are not included in Section 91(24) of the *Constitution Act, 1867.* Provinces (except Alberta) contend that Métis are included under Section 91(24). The Métis National Council also maintains that Métis are a federal responsibility. Chartier (1988) claims that in 1984 the federal minister argued that, even if the Supreme Court ruled that Métis were a federal responsibility, the government could refuse to exercise its responsibility. Nevertheless, Chartier argues that Métis are covered within the term "Indian" (as are the Inuit) in Section 91(24). Others, such as Schwartz (1986; see also Sawchuck, 1998), view Métis as a people distinct from Indians and thus side with the federal government. However, he does offer a compromise in suggesting that small-*m* métis would be covered by Section 91(24) while capital-*M* Métis would not. What is suggested is that Métis may be entitled to be governed by some federal laws. However, even if this were the case, substantial cooperation among all the provinces would be needed to generate a uniform regime of Métis control.

While the federal government regards the Métis as a provincial responsibility, certain interpretations of general programs provided to Canadians have allowed the Métis to benefit. In other areas of concern (e.g., constitutional negotiations), an informal agreement has been made whereby the minister of Justice is to act in a way that ensures that Métis interests are addressed and that the Métis have someone to listen to their concerns. Clearly, the inclusion of the Métis in Sections 35(1) and 35(2) of the Constitution is accorded legal significance. The recognition of the Métis as an Aboriginal people provides a constitutional base upon which negotiations for the recognition and compensation of their rights can fully begin. Finally, Section 25 also incorporates, by definition, a fiduciary relationship between the federal government and the Métis (Bell, 1991).

In 2002, the Métis Nation organization adopted a national definition of Métis and has since been ratifying this national definition in the provincial jurisdictions. Their definition is that the Métis have a shared history, a common culture (song, dance, dress, national symbols), a unique language (Michif, with various regional dialects), extensive kinship connections from Ontario westward, a distinct way of life, a traditional territory, and a collective consciousness. The Métis Nation is represented through province-wide governance structures from Ontario westward; namely the Métis Nation of Ontario, the Manitoba Métis Federation, the Métis Nation-Saskatchewan, the Métis Nation of Alberta, and the Métis Provincial Council of British Columbia.

It is reasonable to conclude that is the definition of a Métis will continue to be an issue as the boundary of inclusion and exclusion continues to shift. Aboriginal people define themselves inconsistently and shift categories depending upon the situation and the changing definition of who is an Indian (Giokas and Chartrand, 2002). It is clear that the designation cannot be a biological one, nor can it be dependent on kinship. The changing definition has clearly demonstrated that blood-quantum is a fruitless strategy for defining the boundaries of a people. An equally fruitless strategy is kinship, since out-marriage and enfranchisement have split families in many different ways. Self-identification is used by many Métis, but this strategy has not had any political or legal support. Nevertheless, it is the only real choice people of mixed ancestry have in developing boundaries and political power. As Giokas and Chartrand (2002) clearly noted, like much of our history, the basis for recognizing Aboriginal people is less a conscious policy and more of a shifting and haphazard strategy resulting from fiscal and political pressures over the years. As a result, no consistent basis for designating a person as Indian, Métis, or any other Aboriginal category has existed. As Peters, Rosenberg, and Halseth (1989) assert, the term Métis is widespread in usage. It appears to have a well-accepted general meaning, reflecting the social aspect of Métis identity, and a reality that cannot be denied.

Membership in the Métis Community

Any individual in Canada who can demonstrate any Aboriginal ancestry can self-identify as Métis and, in the absence of other reliable processes, self-identification may be sufficient for access to programs and services and educational facilities. However, mere self-identification is not sufficient for the purposes of claiming Section 35 constitutional rights. This is because the recognition and affirmation of Aboriginal rights under Section 35 of the *Constitution Act, 1982* is reserved for the "Aboriginal peoples of Canada." This implies that while an individual may self-identify as Métis, unless he or she can also prove membership in a Métis collective, such an individual will not likely be able to claim Section 35 protection. This line of reasoning was affirmed by the Supreme Court of Canada in *Powley* (2003) (see Box 8.2).

The term "Métis" in Section 35 therefore does not encompass all individuals with mixed Indian and European heritage; rather, it refers to distinctive peoples who, in addition to their mixed ancestry, developed their own customs, way of life, and recognizable group identity separate from their Indian or Inuit and European forebears. Métis communities evolved and flourished prior to the entrenchment of European control, when the

Box 8.2	Establishing Métis Rights

To confirm their rights, Métis have taken their case to the courts. In the case of *R. v. Powley*, the Supreme Court of Canada made its first contemporary ruling about Métis and their Aboriginal rights. In 1993, the Powleys (father and son) killed a moose and tagged it. One week later they were charged with hunting without a licence and unlawful possession of moose contrary to Ontario's *Game and Fish Act*. Five years later, the trial judge ruled that the Powleys had the "Métis right" to hunt, which is protected by Section 35 of the *Constitution Act, 1982*, and the charges were dismissed. The Crown appealed the decision, and in 2000 the Ontario Superior Court of Justice confirmed the trial decision and dismissed the Crown's appeal. The Ontario Court of Appeal heard the case in 2001 and upheld the earlier decisions. Nevertheless, the Crown appealed to the Supreme Court of Canada. On September 19, 2003, the Supreme Court of Canada, in a unanimous judgment, upheld the lower court decisions and said that the Powleys can exercise the Métis right to hunt as protected by Section 35. In summary, the court confirmed the existence of Métis communities in Canada and the constitutional protection of their existing Aboriginal rights.

The reader should note that the Supreme Court did not define who the Métis people are. The court set out three broad factors—self-identification, ancestral connection, and community acceptance—to be used in identifying who can exercise a Métis community's Section 35 right to hunt. This case is only about the Métis right to hunt and does not reflect on other rights Métis might have.

influence of European settlers and political institutions became dominant. A Métis community is defined as a group of Métis with a distinctive collective identity, living together in the same geographic area and sharing a common way of life (defined in the Powley case, 2003). One needs simply be a "group" or a "community" of Métis with a collective identity, living together in the same geographic area and sharing a common way of life. In fact, the *Report of the Royal Commission on Aboriginal Peoples* noted that at least one of the Métis "peoples" in Canada is the Métis Nation, which arose in the 1700s across central northwestern North America. On the face of it, this definition and view of what constitutes a Métis community seems reasonable.

Since *Powley*, however, identification of what constitutes a Métis community has become a major issue and an additional source of confusion (and grounds for litigation) in law. The Supreme Court of Canada in *Powley* said that it was necessary to determine if a Métis community existed and whether the harvesting took place in a location that was within that community's traditional territory. For the purposes of any given case, it is not necessary to define the limits of the traditional territory of a particular Métis settlement. Nor is it necessary to determine the outer parameters of a larger Métis community. Métis settlement is understood to be part of a larger political "nation" or "people." However, the case law to date indicates that there must be strong evidence to prove an historical Métis community in any given area as a prerequisite for rights claims.

Since 1982, when Aboriginal and treaty rights were given constitutional protection, the Supreme Court of Canada has heard many dozens of Aboriginal and treaty rights cases. With the exception of *Powley* and a few others, most of these cases concerned the Aboriginal and treaty rights of First Nations. For First Nations pursuing their claims in court, defining who, or what, is the rights-bearing entity has largely been a non-issue. The cases were by and large brought by an individual status Indian as a representative of a band within the meaning of the *Indian Act*. While the court routinely acknowledged the existence of an Aboriginal people, the final determination was restricted in its application to the band. In applying these Supreme Court of Canada decisions, for the most part, governments across the country have recognized that, for Indians, the rights reside in the larger group. Thus, when Sparrow won a food fishing right for the Musqueam in *R. v. Sparrow,* it was recognized by government that the right was applicable to the Coast Salish peoples.

In fact, the principles were generally applied throughout Canada to all Indians recognized under the *Indian Act*, whether or not their bands had treaty rights. The decision was widely applied in policy. One might have expected the same application for the Métis following *Powley*. However, it appears that a liberal application of the *Powley* principles has been resisted. Instead, most provinces have insisted that the Métis must prove the existence of an individual Métis rights-bearing community in court before they will apply *Powley*. As it appears to turn out, the Supreme Court's definition of a local, stable, and continuous community as the applicable rights-bearing entity (as applied to the Métis) is at odds with the historic reality of almost all Aboriginal peoples in Canada. While many Indian reserves have been created, most Aboriginal peoples who are members of those communities do not live on reserves. Therefore, if a community is to be the rights-bearing entity, how is one to define it in a meaningful way that reflects both the Aboriginal and the Canadian perspective? Certainly bands living on reserves do not reflect the historic Indian perspective. The question is particularly pertinent now for the Métis, who are not Aboriginal bands, do not live on reserves, and are highly mobile over a vast territory.

Unfortunately, the Supreme Court's decision in *Powley* appears to be based on the assumption that the Métis lived in stable, continuous communities and hunted primarily in the immediate environs of those communities. The ***Powley* "test"** (discussed below) requires that the Métis must prove the prior existence and continuity of individual communities. These fictional, court-created Métis communities are incompatible with the nature of a real Métis community. Where an Aboriginal group shows that a particular practice, custom, or tradition taking place on the land was integral to the distinctive culture of that group, then even if they have not shown that their occupation and use of the land was sufficient to support a claim of title to the land, they will have demonstrated that they have an Aboriginal right to engage in that practice, custom, or tradition.

It seems odd that a highly mobile hunter/gatherer/trader society that never lived in small, stable, continuous, localized communities is now required to prove the existence of just such an entity in order to exercise harvesting rights. Instead of identifying "a practice that helps to define the distinctive way of life of the community as an Aboriginal community" (*R.* v. *Powley*, 2003: 9), the Métis must now invent a community that helps define the practice. Prior to *Powley*, the prevailing legal theory did not acknowledge that the Métis were an Aboriginal collective with existing Aboriginal rights. *Powley* is important because it establishes the legal recognition that the Métis are indeed a rights-bearing collective. Sadly, since *Powley*, the courts have minimized the Métis rights-bearing collective.

THE MÉTIS IN SOCIETY TODAY

Métis Rights Claims: Slow Progress

As seen in earlier chapters, law in relation to Aboriginal rights and Section 35 of the Constitution of Canada (part II of the Constitution) has been developed by the Supreme Court of Canada. To date, this body of law has largely been aimed at one of the three Aboriginal peoples of Canada. *Powley* was the first case before the Supreme Court that dealt with attempting to adapt this law for the Métis. In *Powley,* the Supreme Court of Canada followed the general interpretive principles that apply to the claims of Indians, with necessary modifications. The Court confirmed that Section 35 rights claimed by Métis, like other constitutional rights, are to be interpreted purposively. In other words, they are to be interpreted in light of the interests they are meant to protect. The inclusion of the Métis in Section 35 is based on a commitment to recognizing the Métis and enhancing their survival as distinctive communities. The purpose and the promise of Section 35 is to protect practices that were historically important features of these distinctive communities and that persist in the present day as integral elements of their Métis culture.

The Crown argued in *Powley* that the Aboriginal rights of the Métis are derivative of and dependent on the pre-contact practices of their Indian ancestors. The Métis to date have argued that they are a distinct Aboriginal people and that the practices and culture of the Métis people are the source of Métis rights. The Supreme Court of Canada has now confirmed that Métis rights do not originate with their Indian ancestors. Were it otherwise, this would deny the Métis their full status as distinctive rights-bearing peoples whose own integral practices are entitled to constitutional protection. Thus, the law now recognizes and affirms the Aboriginal rights of the Métis, who appeared after the time of first contact. But herein lies a source of debate and confusion.

In *Van der Peet*, for First Nations, the Supreme Court of Canada held that for a practice, custom, or tradition to be given the protection of Section. 35, it had to be practiced prior to "contact" with European peoples, but recognized that this criteria was not necessarily applicable to Métis claims. The Court said that this criteria (or test) had to be modified to reflect the constitutionally significant feature of the Métis as peoples who emerged between first contact and the effective imposition of European control. The pre-contact test in *Van der Peet* is based on the constitutional affirmation that Aboriginal communities are entitled to continue those practices, customs, and traditions that are integral to their distinctive existence or relationship to the land. Their unique history can most appropriately be accommodated by a post-contact, but pre-control, test that identifies the time when Europeans effectively established political and legal control in a particular area. The focus should be on the period *after* a particular Métis community arose and *before* it came under the effective control of European laws and customs. This pre-control test enables us to identify the practices, customs, and traditions that predate the imposition of European laws and customs on the Métis, which will be different across the country among different Métis communities.

The Supreme Court said that the appropriate way to define Métis rights in Section 35 of the Constitution is to modify the criteria used to define the Aboriginal rights of Indians (called the *Van der Peet* test). This Métis "test" can be called the *Powley* test, and consists of several parts:

(1) Characterization of the right: For hunting, fishing, and gathering rights, the term "characterization" refers to the ultimate use of the harvest, be it for food, exchange, or commercial purposes. It is a general right to hunt for and gather food in the traditional hunting grounds of the Métis community.

(2) Verification of membership in the contemporary Métis community: There must be an "objectively verifiable process" to identify members of the community. This means a process that is based on reasonable principles and historical fact that can be documented. There are three components to guide the identification of Métis rights-holders: self-identification, ancestral connection to the historic Métis community, and community acceptance.

(3) Identification of the historic rights bearing community: An historic Métis community was a group of Métis with a distinctive collective identity who lived together in the same geographic area and shared a common way of life. The historic Métis community must be shown to have existed as an identifiable Métis community prior to the time when Europeans effectively established political and legal control in a particular area.

(4) Identification of the contemporary rights-bearing community: Métis community identification requires two things. First, the community must self-identify as a Métis community. Second, there must be proof that the contemporary Métis community is a continuation of the historic Métis community.

(5) Identification of the relevant time: In order to identify whether a practice was "integral" to the historic Aboriginal community, the Court looks for a relevant time. Ideally, this is a time when the practice can be identified before it was forever changed by European influence. For Indians, this is a "pre-contact" time. The Court modified this for the Métis in recognition of the fact that Métis arose as an Aboriginal people after contact with Europeans.

(6) Continuity between the historic practice and the contemporary right: There must be some evidence to support the claim that the contemporary practice is in continuity with the historic practice. Aboriginal practices can evolve and develop over time.

(7) Extinguishment: The doctrine of extinguishment applies equally to Métis and First Nation claims. Extinguishment means that the Crown has eliminated the Aboriginal right. Before 1982, this could be done by the Constitution or legislation or by agreement with the Aboriginal people. A Métis individual who is ancestrally connected to the historic Métis community can claim Métis identity or rights even if he or she had ancestors who took treaty benefits in the past.

Since 2005, the federal government has applied its *Federal Interim Guidelines for Métis Harvesting*. The provincial governments are primarily responsible for the management and regulation of most natural resources within their boundaries. However, the Government of

Canada is responsible for the management and regulation of those natural resources under its control. Areas of federal jurisdiction include federal lands, national parks, and other federally protected areas, military bases and ranges, and migratory birds and coastal fish species.

Many federal departments already had policies to accommodate First Nation hunting and fishing. The new guidelines now include Métis within their many policies that previously recognized only First Nation harvesting on federal lands or harvesting of federal resources. For this purpose, the enforcement arm of the federal government will not apply federal harvesting rules and regulations to Métis who meet the identification criteria. The guidelines are intended to facilitate Métis subsistence by assisting in the identification of Métis hunters and fishers. The guidelines recognize certain Métis membership cards where the organization has genealogy requirements with evidence that is objectively verifiable. The guidelines note that there is an obligation on part of the federal government to take steps to accommodate the existence of Métis rights to hunt, fish, and gather.

With respect to Aboriginal land rights and title, the most definitive statement comes from the Supreme Court of Canada in *Delgamuukw* (also discussed in Chapter 7). The case began in the early 1980s and concerns the Aboriginal title and self-government rights of the Gitxsan and Wet'suwet'en peoples, who claim ownership and jurisdiction over 58 000 square kilometres in northwest British Columbia. The Supreme Court of Canada set out several important tests in the judgment, including the test for the admissibility of Aboriginal oral history as evidence, the nature of Aboriginal title, the test for proving Aboriginal title, and the test for proving infringement and extinguishment of Aboriginal title. In order to make out a claim for Aboriginal title, the Aboriginal group asserting title must satisfy the following criteria: (i) the land must have been occupied prior to sovereignty; (ii) there must be continuity between present and pre-sovereignty occupation; and (iii) at sovereignty, that occupation must have been exclusive.

Perhaps the principles established in *Delgamuukw* and more recently in *Marshall (#3)* and *R.* v. *Bernard* with respect to proof of Aboriginal title can be applied to Métis claims. The issues that will likely be important in Métis land claims will be similar to those in *Marshall (#3)*—the criteria of sufficiency of use and occupation, exclusive occupation, and continuity. In *Delgamuukw*, the Supreme Court of Canada held that in order to prove Aboriginal title, the Aboriginal group must prove that at sovereignty their occupation was exclusive. This was qualified somewhat when the Court said that exclusive occupation can be demonstrated even if other Aboriginal groups were present or frequented the claimed lands. However, it is doubtful that any Métis group will ever be able to meet a test of exclusive occupancy. It seems that the Métis would have to make out a claim not to exclusive occupation, but rather Aboriginal title based on joint occupancy. To date, such a claim has never before been made in a Canadian court. Joint occupancy would mean that all Aboriginal peoples would be holders of title, and does not necessarily mean that they have equal title. To establish Aboriginal title, Métis claimants would have to establish occupation that goes beyond "occasional entry" or seasonal use.

To date, only one significant Métis case before the courts has dealt with Métis claims to land: The **Manitoba Métis Federation** *(MMF)* sought a declaration that Métis were unjustly deprived of their lands—a declaration that some federal and provincial legislation that purported to amend provisions of the *Manitoba Act, 1870* are unconstitutional. On that basis, the MMF wanted to proceed with a claim for compensation for the losses the Métis suffered as a result of the unconstitutional activities of the government.

The MMF went to trial in 2006, though the case was originally launched in 1981. In his opening remarks, MMF legal counsel Thomas Berger stated that the action was on behalf of the Manitoba Métis community and was not an action brought by any individual to vindicate individual interests in land. In December 2007, a Manitoba Court of Queen's Bench judge handed down his decision. He denied all aspects of the MMF claim. The plaintiffs claimed that the Métis were to have received a land base under the *Manitoba Act, 1870*. They asserted that they had suffered an historic injustice in not receiving such land base and wanted to sue Canada and Manitoba. The plaintiffs did not claim any specific land. The MMF asked that certain enactments, both statutes and Orders in Council, were unconstitutional, that Canada failed to fulfill its obligations, properly or at all, to the Métis under Sections 31 and 32 of the *Manitoba Act*, and that there was a treaty made in 1870 between the Crown in Right of Canada and the Provisional Government and people of Red River.

The judge held that in 1870 the Métis did not hold or enjoy Aboriginal title to the land and were not Indians within the meaning of Section 91(24) of the *Constitution Act, 1867*. The judge ruled that the Métis were not looked upon by those in the community as Indians and did not want to be considered as Indians. Rather, they wanted to be full citizens of the province, as they previously had been of the Red River settlement, a status that Indians at the time did not (and could not) enjoy. The judge held that because Métis were not "Indians" and had no Aboriginal title, there could be no fiduciary relationship existing between Canada and the Métis. Rather, Canada owed a public law duty to those entitled under Sections 31 and 32 of the Act. The MMF case was subsequently appealed to the Manitoba Court of Appeal, was heard in February of 2009, and was lost. However, in February 2011, the Supreme Court of Canada agreed to hear the case. On a positive note, the Court of Appeal did overturn "the lower courts finding that Métis do not have Aboriginal title and it recognized that there is a fiduciary relationship between the Crown and Métis people" (Métis National Council, press release of July 7, 2010).

From the 17th century, Britain and Canada made treaties with Aboriginal peoples. The primary purpose of the treaties was to ensure peaceful European settlement while upholding the rights of Aboriginal people. In exchange for title, First Nations received benefits and/or land. Unfortunately, history has shown that treaties have not always been honoured, and often they have been completely disregarded. Thus, many First Nations have made land claims that are essentially legal declarations of a claim to ownership and control over property. Currently there are over 800 specific claims in progress. On average it takes approximately 13 years to process a specific claim. To deal with the enormous processing times, the Government of Canada introduced a plan called Justice At Last (2009), which proposes to restructure the old claims system with a new, more efficient process. The main features of the plan are: (1) an independent claims tribunal comprised of retired sitting judges that will take over when a claim is not accepted for negotiation by Canada, in cases where all parties agree that a claim that has already been accepted should be referred for a binding decision, or after three years of unsuccessful negotiations (this new claims tribunal has no jurisdiction to award lands); (2) procedural improvements including dedicated funding and faster processing; and (3) better access to mediation. Currently the Justice at Last program does not include the Métis. Canadians need to know that the program does not seem to provide justice for all. It is only justice for some.

In the late 1970s, Canada agreed to enter into land claim negotiations with the Dene people of the Northwest Territories. By 1980 the Northwest Territories Métis Association and the Dene Nation were engaged in joint negotiations. These negotiations continued until 1990. Although the Dene/Métis leadership initialed the final agreement in April 1990, in July the assembly did not ratify the agreement. The agreement being negotiated was called the *Dene Métis Comprehensive Land Claims Agreement* and included all of the Métis who could trace their ancestry back to the Northwest Territories as of 1921. When the negotiations broke off in 1990, the government began to negotiate regional claims. Other examples include the Sahtu Dene and Métis Comprehensive Land Claim Agreement (1993). The chiefs of four Dene bands, the presidents of three Métis locals, and the Sahtu Tribal Council signed the agreement. Its preamble states that the Dene and the Métis of the Sahtu region negotiated the agreement in order to give effect to certain rights of the Dene and Métis. The "Aboriginal community" in the agreement is defined as the Dene bands in particular towns and the Métis locals in Fort Good Hope, Norman Wells, and Fort Norman. The agreement contains definitions of Sahtu Dene, Sahtu Dene and Métis, and Sahtu Métis. While they are separately named, each is defined exactly the same way and refers to persons of Slavey, Hare, or Mountain ancestry who resided in or used and occupied the settlement area prior to December 1921, or is a descendant of such a person.

There are also the South Slave Métis Framework Agreement (1996) and the Northwest Territory Métis Nation Framework Agreement (2003). The government promised that all Aboriginal peoples in the Northwest Territories would be included in a land claims process. When the First Nations south of Great Slave Lake chose Treaty Land Entitlement (TLE), a process that excluded the South Slave Métis, the government agreed to enter into a South Slave Métis Framework Agreement. (TLE concerns regional claim negotiations as opposed to comprehensive land claims negotiations. TLEs exclude the Métis, which forces the government to negotiate separately with the Métis. However, comprehensive claims can include both Indians and Métis, but only if both are willing co-negotiators.) The South Slave Métis Framework Agreement was signed in 1996. The parties to the agreement were the Métis of Fort Smith, Hay River, and Fort Resolution and the governments of the Northwest Territories and Canada. The framework agreement sets out the parties' agreement to explore ways and means of addressing the concerns of Métis. The South Slave Métis Framework Agreement notes that the "Indigenous Métis of Fort Smith, Fort Resolution and Hay River in the Northwest Territories are one of the Aboriginal peoples of Canada." The agreement contemplates a two-stage negotiation process. The first stage is the negotiation of an agreement in principle that will lead to a final agreement. The second stage will be the negotiation of a self-government agreement. Subjects for negotiation include eligibility, land and water, and economic benefits. In July 2002, the South Slave Métis Tribal Council changed its name to the Northwest Territory Métis Nation. In February 2003, the South Slave Métis Framework Agreement and the interim measures agreement were amended to replace the South Slave Métis Tribal Council name with the "Northwest Territory Métis Nation."

In addition, there is the Deh Cho First Nations Framework Agreement & Interim Measures Agreement (2001). In May 2001, the Deh Cho First Nations entered into a framework agreement and an interim measures agreement with Canada and the Government of the Northwest Territories. The framework agreement sets out the framework for land claims and self-government negotiations between the parties. The preamble states that for the purposes of the negotiations the Deh Cho First Nations represent the Deh Cho Dene and the Métis of the Deh Cho territory. The interim measures agreement states that

Deh Cho First Nation includes, among other First Nation entities, Fort Simpson Métis Local 52, Fort Providence Métis Local 57, and Fort Liard Métis Local 67. The interim measures agreement sets up processes for land withdrawal and participation by the Deh Cho First Nations in land and water regulation. In addition it provides processes for consultation with respect to sales and leases of lands, issuance of prospecting permits, and oil and gas exploration licences. New forest management authorizations will be issued in accordance with the interim measures agreement. The Deh Cho First Nations can nominate a member for appointment to the Mackenzie Valley Environmental Impact Review Board. There are also provisions for trans-boundary and overlap issues.

In May 2005, the Métis National Council and Canada entered into a framework agreement, the objectives of which were to engage a new partnership; to build capacity; to develop and establish processes to address the Aboriginal and treaty rights of the Métis, including the inherent right of self-government; to resolve long outstanding issues; and to identify and implement initiatives that will help to improve the quality of life of Métis people in Canada. The Métis National Council Framework Agreement contained a list of subject matters, including addressing the implementation of the *Powley* decision; finding the place of Métis within federal policies; enhancing electoral and governance capacity; exploring options to resolve long outstanding Métis legal issues, as well as exploring options to fund Métis litigation; examine opportunities of programs and services that may be suitable for devolution; identification and registration of Métis people based on their national definition of Métis for membership within the Métis Nation; exploring economic development initiatives; and exploring options for honouring Louis Riel and the contributions of the Métis people to the development of Canada. The Métis National Council Framework Agreement was to be in effect for a five-year period.

While not a land claim agreement, the Métis Nation of British Columbia Relationship Accord was entered into between the Métis Nation British Columbia and the province of B.C. in 2006. The accord commits the parties to a relationship and achievable results on areas that include housing, health care, education, employment opportunities, Métis identification, and data collection. This accord is intended to complement and renew a previous 2003 agreement that addressed socio-economic challenges faced by the Métis. The province noted in its joint press release that it is building relationships with Aboriginal people on principles of mutual respect and reconciliation with a goal of ensuring that Aboriginal people share in the economic and social development of British Columbia.

In September 2008, the Métis National Council entered into a protocol agreement with the federal government. The Métis National Council and Canada agreed to establish a bilateral process to examine jurisdictional issues, Métis students of residential schools, access to benefits and settlements by Métis veterans, governance and institution building, economic development including community capacity, and Métis Aboriginal rights including land and harvesting rights. The protocol envisions the need to include the provinces on some topics and is in effect for five years or until superseded by a subsequent agreement.

The question of jurisdiction for the Métis is clearly an issue that affects almost every aspect of Métis life. All governments have consistently denied jurisdiction for Métis who live south of the 60th parallel. North of the 60th parallel, the federal government does assume jurisdiction and responsibility for the Métis. In Alberta, the provincial government has been working with the Métis since the 1930s, although without claiming jurisdiction. While there are very large departments and ministries at the federal and provincial levels for Indians (AAND), no such permanent institutions of government are accessible by the Métis. A Federal Interlocutor was appointed, who is a federal minister in charge of the Métis and non-status Indian portfolio. Tellingly, the fact that this minister has the responsibility for both Métis and non-status Indians shows the federal tendency to lump Métis issues and non-status Indian issues together. It also seems to reflect the federal government's previous position that Métis are not a distinct Aboriginal people.

Recently, the Minister of Aboriginal Affairs has taken on the responsibility for Métis and non-status Indians. Whether this will result in Métis south of the 60th parallel being permitted to partake in any of the systems set up to deal with Aboriginal issues, such as the Indian Claims Commission, the Comprehensive Claims Process, the Specific Claims Process, or test case funding, remains to be seen. The decision of the Supreme Court of Canada in *Powley* did not seem to settle these matters.

Interestingly, Alberta is unique in the Métis Nation homeland in that it currently has the only legislated regime that recognizes and gives effect to Métis land and local governance. This has been accomplished through the *Métis Settlements Accord Implementation Act,* the *Métis Settlements Land Protection Act,* the *Métis Settlements Act*, and the *Constitution of Alberta Amendment Act.* These are collectively referred to as the Métis settlements legislation (1990), mentioned earlier in the chapter. The Métis settlements legislation is delegated authority from the provincial government. It provides a framework within which Métis settlement institutions can develop laws concerning membership, land, financial accounting, resource development, and other issues pursuant to settlement council bylaws, General Council policies, and ministerial regulations. The Métis settlements in Alberta comprise 1.25 million acres of land, most of which is affected by substantial oil and gas activity. An important issue for the General Council is to balance development and traditional lifestyles—for example, how to balance the economic value of oil and gas development while assessing the impact on subsistence activities such as berry picking, hunting, trapping, and fishing.

In 2009 in *Cunningham,* the Alberta Court of Appeal struck Sections 75 and 90 from the *Métis Settlements Act.* These sections dealt with registration and termination of members. The court found that these sections discriminated against members who identify as Métis and who are registered as Indians under the *Indian Act.* The general rule is therefore that provincial laws continue to apply to the Métis settlements. One exception is in the area of hunting, fishing, trapping, and gathering.

The Year of the Métis Nation and the Recognition of Louis Riel

On November 27, 2009, the Métis National Council meeting in Vancouver, British Columbia, passed several resolutions, one of which was to proclaim 2010 the "Year of the Métis Nation." That year marked the 125th anniversary of the Northwest Rebellion and the execution of Louis Riel. The Métis National Council proposed celebrations across Canada, on behalf of the almost 400 000 Métis Nation citizens—almost a quarter of all Aboriginal peoples in the country.

The politics of identity continues. To this day the name Louis Riel invokes intense emotional debate in Canada and has generated quite a bit of research (and popular) literature to this effect. To some, Riel is a hero and a great Métis leader. To others he is a martyr, a rebel, and a traitor. Louis Riel is revered by the Métis, by Quebeçois, and by many Canadians as a great political leader, a father of Confederation, and the founder of the province of Manitoba. Over time, more than 25 bills have been introduced in Parliament seeking the exoneration of Riel. Resolutions recognizing his contributions were passed in the Manitoba Legislative Assembly, in the House of Commons, and in the Senate. The movement has engaged the general public, the media, the Riel family, Métis leaders, and elected politicians. On September 23, 1983, Conservative member William Yurko tabled *Bill C-691, An Act to Grant a Pardon to Riel*, tabling it twice again in 1984 (*Bills C-228 and C-257*).

On December 13, 1984, NDP member Les Benjamin introduced a bill (*Bill C-217*) that called for the guilty sentence against Riel to be overturned. On November 28, 1985, Liberal member Sheila Copps asked the House for a posthumous pardon for Riel. On September 16, 1987, NDP member Nelson Riis introduced *Bill C-265*. On November 16, 1994, Suzanne Tremblay of the Bloc Quebeçois introduced *Bill C-288* requesting the revocation of the conviction of Riel. She tried again on June 4, 1996 (*Bill C-297*). *Bill C-380* was introduced on March 5, 1997. On June 3, 1998, Mr. Coderre (Liberal from Quebec) introduced *Bill C-417, An Act Respecting Louis Riel*, which sought to reverse the conviction and recognize and commemorate Riel's role in the advancement of Canadian Confederation and the rights and interests of the Métis people. On November 7, 2001, five members representing all parties in the House introduced *Bill C-411, Act Respecting Louis Riel*. The bill proposed to establish July 15 as Louis Riel Day and to revoke his conviction of August 1, 1885, for high treason. *Bill S-35*, a Senate bill, was introduced in 2001 (*Act to Honour Louis Riel and the Métis People*) and originally proposed to "vacate" the conviction of high treason.

In October 2002, the Senate bill was re-introduced but amended. It no longer proposed to vacate Riel's conviction, but now took the form of a bill to honour Louis Riel and the Métis people. *Bill S-9,* another Senate bill, was introduced in 2004 and proposed to honour Louis Riel as a Métis patriot and Canadian hero and to establish May 12 as Louis Riel Day. It also proposed to acknowledge the arrowhead *sash* as the recognized symbol of the Métis people. However, that bill contained no proposal to exonerate Riel or to pardon him. Finally, *Bill C-258* was introduced in 2006 (*An Act Respecting Louis Riel*) "to reverse the conviction of Louis Riel for high treason and to formally recognize and commemorate his role in the advancement of the Canadian Confederation and the rights and interests of the Métis people and the people of Western Canada."

Summary

- The question of who is Métis has generated considerable debate, research, and controversy.
- The *Manitoba Act* was crucial in the development of Métis identity.
- The provision of scrip to Métis has been a long standing issue for Métis in Canada.
- Court decisions have enabled Métis to further their quest for official recognition as well as Aboriginal rights.
- Métis have created pan-Canadian organizations to achieve their goals.

Key Terms

1990 *Métis Settlements Act* p. 256

Congress of Aboriginal Peoples p. 257

Dominion Lands Act p. 251

Manitoba Act p. 251

Manitoba Métis Federation p. 271

"Michif" p. 248

Powley "test" p. 268

Red River Métis p. 251

Scrip—Land scrip p. 255
—Money scrip p. 255

Questions for Further Discussion

1. What were the historical circumstances and conditions under which Métis identity emerged, and when in history was a Métis consciousness forged?

2. Were early Canadian governments accepting of the Métis as a separate Aboriginal group with claims for Aboriginal rights?

3. What factors operated to cast Métis out of the realm of federal Aboriginal policy?

4. In what ways has the Supreme Court of Canada applied more restrictive approaches to defining Métis rights compared to defining Indian rights?

5. Why are the Métis claiming fraud in the case of scrip allotments?

6. Why are the Métis settlements of Alberta considered a significant legal and political accomplishment?

7. What effect did *Bill C-31* have on the identity of Indians and Métis in Canada? Can a person be both Indian and Métis?

8. How is the *Powley* "test" different from the *Van der Peet* "test" in defining the Aboriginal rights of Indians and Métis?

9. Though *Powley* is a landmark Métis case, what issues relating to Métis rights has it left unresolved?

10. Should the conviction of Louis Riel be reversed and his role in advancing Canadian Confederation formally acknowledged?

The Inuit: Recognition in the 21st Century

INTRODUCTION

There are Inuit all across the northern region of Canada and they, like other ethnic groups, represent different cultures, languages, and people (see Figure 9.1). Contact with the outside world came at different times and in different ways in the history of each of these groups. An analysis of Canada's Inuit provides a revealing look at such issues as class formation, assimilation, the sources and uses of power, community building, and intergenerational differences. It also allows us to assess how Canadians have dealt with an ethnic group similar to but different from First Nations. Finally, it allows us to gain insight into the successes that Inuit have had in the past two decades over issues such as land claims—successes not shared by First Nations peoples (Brody, 2003). We begin with a brief history of how contact was made with the Inuit and then look at the social processes and change experienced by the group. We also look at the issue of identity and how it has changed over time.

In Inuktitut, the word *Inuit* means "the people." It replaces the previous term, *Eskimo,* which is an Indian word used to identify these Arctic people. As Euro-Canadians entered the North, they appropriated use of this term. It would not be until the 1970s that Inuit would ask others not to identify them as Eskimo. Nevertheless, today there are many Canadians who continue to do so, and, equally important, there are many residents of the Arctic who define themselves as Eskimo and continue to use the label first attached to them more than a century ago. Many Canadians view and treat Inuit as a homogeneous population and fail to recognize the different ethnic groupings of Inuit in the Arctic and the cultural differences between them. There are many recognized Inuit communities, language groups, and delineated cultural areas. Readers who are going on to specialize in

FIGURE 9.1	Approximate Location of Indian and Inuit Peoples in Northern Canada before A.D. 1500, by Language and Dialect Group

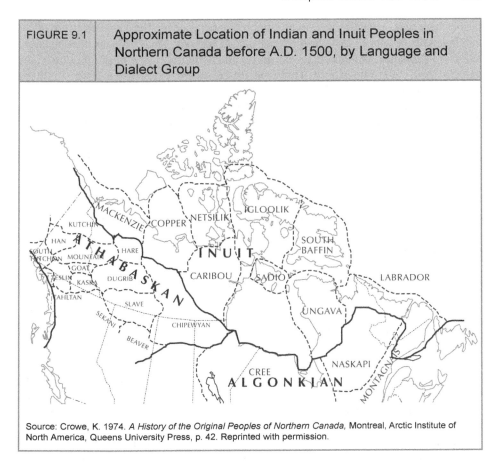

Source: Crowe, K. 1974. *A History of the Original Peoples of Northern Canada,* Montreal, Arctic Institute of North America, Queens University Press, p. 42. Reprinted with permission.

Aboriginal Studies will see that the level of generality in this introductory text requires refinement and specificity as they begin to look at the micro structures of communities and individuals. For example, the Caribou Inuit traditions and interaction patterns are quite different from those of the Baffin Island Inuit, which in turn are different from those of the Netsilik. Nevertheless, it is possible to discuss some common and fundamental aspects of Inuit society in an introductory text. Hence, a more macro perspective will be adopted as we develop a portrait of Inuit in Canada.

The origins of **Inuit** culture are rooted in the Neolithic cultures of northeastern Siberia (Wright, 2006). It is suggested that people resided in the region about 8500 years ago, living in small communities along the coastline of the Bering Land Bridge (Inuit Tapiriit Kanatami, nd). As these initial populations grew, they developed new settlements and moved into the northern coast area of Alaska. These early groups were called Sivullirmiut, and in less than a thousand years they migrated from Alaska to Greenland and settled on lands in between. Over time, regional groups developed, which remain today. Little is known about the culture and language of the Sivullirmiut but it is clear that they lived in small groups throughout the Arctic region. The Sivullirmiut people gave way to the **Thule** culture. The major distinction between the two cultures is that the Thule developed hunting weapons, boats and harvesting skills that allowed them to hunt large whales in the northern seas, a practice the Sivullirmiut did not engage in. The Thule also carried out hunting skills developed by their predecessors. As a result, Thule villages became larger and more permanent than those developed by the Sivullirmiut. Out of these cultures, the modern Inuit culture developed. However, as Europeans began to enter the Arctic in the 18th century, first as whalers and then as fur traders, Inuit culture changed rapidly. The introduction of new materials and technology affected all aspects of their life, and they were forced to accept new values imposed upon them by Canadian authorities.

Canadian Inuit have close ties with the **Inupiat** and **Yupik** of Russia and Alaska and with the Inuit of Greenland. Their links with the Alaskan Aleut are more tenuous. Inuit divide themselves into two groups based on language and cultural factors. The Yupik live in Russia and Alaska, and their cultural and language differences distinguish them from Inupiat and Inuit. There are about 27 000 Yupik in existence. The Inuit of Canada and Greenland and the Inupiat of Alaska and Russia make up the second common cultural group. These 152 000 Inuit are equally divided among Greenland, Alaska, and Canada, with a small population in Russia.

INUIT CULTURE: VALUES AND BEHAVIOUR

In traditional Inuit culture, the basis for social groups was the family unit, which included extended family members. We also know that the family was defined many different ways by the various Inuit cultural groups. Some saw family as defined by relationships on the male side, while others saw it as structured around an elder. In other cases it might be comprised of single adults, orphaned children, or multiple spouses. Family groups were not static, and families provided a fluid basis for social organization (Henderson, 2007). Given the importance of the family, however construed, it is no surprise that interpersonal relations were of the utmost importance in Inuit culture. In order to ensure harmonious relations, the distribution of resources became important. Hence, in traditional Inuit culture, the pre-eminent values focused on interpersonal relations, the distribution of resources, and clear strategies for ensuring compliance with these values.

Henderson (2007) argues that human relationships and the acquisition of resources were governed by utilitarianism. As such, the behaviour of traditional Inuit in their community focused on maximizing the efficiency of human and environmental resources. In doing so, sex roles were equitable and marked. Age status was important and the practice of "lending" individuals to other social units for a variety of purposes was an important component of their culture. In addition, cooperation was seen as an important value in Inuit society, although it existed alongside the value of self-reliance. Work was also considered an important value. As Briggs (1982) points out, "Inuit behave self sufficiently partly because they feel intensely dependent, and they are nurturant partly because they wish not to be" (p. 129). The concept of land ownership is not evident, and the idea of private property is even less clear. Although the practice of paying for services was nonexistent, if an individual needed to "borrow" something to carry out a needed function for the community, it would be expected that permission be given first. In this respect, sharing was viewed as an obligation to the social group. In traditional Inuit society, individual resources were always be shared with the collective if required.

Researchers have shown that Inuit society valued respect for authority, whether spiritual or temporal. In addition, children were to respect their elders and a strong vertical structure of power and authority over generations was evident in families and communities. Both leaders and elders were to be obeyed and respected for their wisdom and expertise. Henderson (2007) argues that Inuit possessed an enlightenment vision of the world. Just as the Europeans had in the 18th century, Inuit attempted to understand the world around them, although the methods by which they carried out their understanding differed. MacDonald (1998) clearly shows that Inuit followed a scientific process in their quest for knowledge. The difference between Inuit ways of knowing and Western ways of knowing was that Inuit used both spiritual and temporal explanations, including the belief in an animate universe that contained spirits. In turn, dealing with these spirits required that an elaborate system of taboos be followed, relating to such practices as at what point one could speak to someone whose relative had died or when women were deemed to be unapproachable. There were also many taboos related to hunting practices.

It is important to understand **Inuit cosmology**, which guides Inuit thinking and behaviour even today. While the following is a broad generalization for all Inuit, we believe the five central tenets of Inuit culture are:

1.   Everyone must contribute (the principle of communality).

2.   Life may have to be sacrificed in order for others to survive (the life principle).

3.   Every being contains its whole ancestry.

4.   There is no hierarchical classification of human and non-human creatures.

5.   Each form contains multitudes (no form is stable). (Dybbroe, 1996)

Inuit believe that human nature is fallible and that this is an innate attribute of people. Thus socialization and compliance need to be maintained so that those who engage in inappropriate behaviours can be controlled. Control is not achieved through punishment, however, but rather through "positive reinforcement," particularly for temporal mechanisms of social control. While this is an abbreviated discussion of Inuit culture, it provides an overview of some of its more important and salient aspects.

A Brief History

Few Canadians realize that the Arctic has been home to many different peoples over the past centuries. It is estimated that approximately 8500 years ago, the People of the Small Knife entered the valleys and plateaus of Alaska and the Yukon. They were replaced by the Long Spear People some 7000 years ago as they moved north into the lands vacated by the ice. This group was followed by the Denbigh People, who, about 5000 years ago, moved into the east shore of the Bering Strait. A fourth pre-historical group in the North was the People of the Old Rock. These residents of northern Quebec and Kivalliq remained in the North until about 3000 years ago, when the climate grew colder and pushed the people southward. This group was replaced by the People of the Arrowhead (3000 years ago) and the Harpoon People, who entered the region approximately 2000 years ago (Crowe, 1974; Richardson, 1993).

Modern-day Inuit emerged from recent groups living in the North. In about 1000 B.C., the Dorset People moved to Baffin Island and spread rapidly across the Arctic. They had moved down the Labrador coast and around the coast of Newfoundland by 500 A.D. Between 800 and 1300 A.D., new immigrants from the **western Arctic** migrated to the east. The new immigrants were better organized and equipped than the Dorset, and within a few years the Dorset People disappeared. The members of this new group (the Thule Inuit) are the direct ancestors of modern Canadian and other Arctic Inuit. It is thought that the original home of the Thule people was Alaska. The Inuit of Northern Labrador are the most southerly and easterly of Canada's Inuit. They are descendants of Thule Eskimo, and it is believed that they have lived in this area since the mid-15th century. They speak Inuktitut, but it is a unique dialect (Fossett, 2001).

Contact between Inuit and Europeans began around 1500 in the East and the late 1800s in the West. During the 1500s, various nations of Europe were exploring the world, wishing to conquer and spread the Christian faith to all. These European explorers first came into contact with Inuit on the eastern coast of Canada and later in the central Arctic as they made inroads into the archipelago. The explorer Frobisher kidnapped Inuit both to confirm his landings in a new country and to set up exhibitions for Queen Elizabeth I. The extent of contact is evident by the fact that, during the 17th and 18th centuries, major conflicts between the English and Inuit of southern Labrador were taking place.

The European invasion of the North occurred in four waves. First, the Norse and European explorers searched for the Northwest Passage. Although they spent little time living with Inuit, they began the process of cultural intervention by introducing new technology to the Inuit people. The fur traders constituted the second wave to enter the North. In order to effectively and efficiently exploit the fur trade, semi-permanent settlements were created, first along the coastlines and later inland. Trading posts, staffed by Europeans, established intermediary roles between the South and the Inuit. More important was the goal of the Europeans to change the lives of Inuit so that trapping and hunting were no longer matters of subsistence but instead economic activities in which they would engage in order to trade for tools, guns, and other European goods. The third wave (overlapping with the second wave of traders) consisted of the missionaries (Catholic and Anglican) whose sole goal was to convert the Inuit to Christianity. Thus, Inuit came into contact with white southern Canadians long before major economic and political interventions were implemented in the Arctic. The fourth and final wave saw Canadians entering the North in order to carry out their mandate of education, economic development, law enforcement, and political incorporation of the Inuit.

Ships began to hunt whales in the eastern Arctic in the 17th and 18th centuries. Most were Scottish and American, although whalers from around the world came to these fertile grounds. In the beginning, contact between whalers and Inuit on the east coast was peaceful and symbiotic. The Inuit were able to trade for goods not otherwise available to them, and the ships' captains were able to obtain information about whales held only by Inuit. There was a clear trade between information and material artefacts. By the early 20th century, whaling ships were carrying on a brisk trade with the eastern Inuit. However, the influence of the Euro-Canadians went beyond the material and social artefacts brought by the whalers; they also transmitted diseases that decimated many Inuit communities (e.g., scarlet fever and whooping cough) and introduced such goods as alcohol. Within a few years, most of the baleen whales in the eastern Arctic had been harvested, and land animals—e.g., caribou and muskox—were close to extinction as a result of the hunting efforts of the whalers and Inuit.

Inuit and outsiders in the western Arctic did not come in contact until later. American whalers entered the western Arctic waters through the Bering Strait around the mid-19th century. Many whaling ships leaving San Francisco in the spring didn't arrive in the

Arctic until summer, and had to "winter over" in order to complete their catch. During this period they remained in the western Arctic, bartering with local Inuit. Bartering was extensive, and the drawing power of the goods being offered by the whalers—e.g., guns and metal tools—was significant. The trade was so pervasive and lasted for so long that large numbers of Inuit migrated to the Beaufort Sea coast in order to participate in the exchange of goods.

The cultural impact of the American whalers was substantial, both in material arte-facts and way of life. Over time, many of the species in the area were reduced to the point that they would not support human habitation. In addition, the introduction of influenza and other epidemics decimated the Inuvialuit population, forcing the whalers to bring in Alaskan Inupiat to help them. So great was the social impact that, when the whale market collapsed in the western Arctic in the early 1900s, Inuit who were still alive were so inte-grated into the barter trade that they were unable to return to their former independent rural life (Alunik, 2003).

Following the fur trade, another major impact on the North was to be felt with the arrival of new agents of control from southern Canada. The first, in the 1600s, were the **Compagnie du Nord** and the free traders. These voyageurs had an important influence on Inuit as they developed the fur trade. The establishment of forts as the centres of trade along waterways and coastal areas encouraged Inuit to engage in the fur trade and remain in localized areas. The voyageurs also established the beginning of an unequal trade rela-tionship with the Inuit. Soon after, the Hudson's Bay Company began to dominate the fur trade and extend its sphere of influence into other domains of life.

On the Labrador coast, beginning in the 1750s, the Moravian missionaries and traders began to have sustained contact with Inuit, which was to last for over 200 years. Other missionaries from various religious denominations entered the North and attempted to convert Inuit to Christianity. Their impact on the social and cultural life of Inuit was sub-stantial. While their influence was directed toward religious activities, they struck at the basic norms and values of Inuit life. For example, religious groups destroyed the social solidarity of Inuit groups by insisting that sexual liaisons between men and women who were not yet married must stop.

Yet another group to have a deep influence on the Inuit was the Royal Canadian Mounted Police. This group was sent into the North to establish a Canadian presence as well as to enforce Canadian law. Any behaviour by Inuit that did not meet the minimum conditions of Canadian law was subject to immediate and harsh sanctions. The fur trad-ers, the missionaries, and the police would influence the lives of the Inuit across the Arctic for half a century (Crowe, 1974). As this triumvirate of Canadian institutions imposed its will, it was able to influence every institutional sphere and network of the Inuit. By the mid-20th century, much of the traditional Inuit way of life had changed (McGhee, 1996).

The traditional way of life of Inuit in the eastern Arctic underwent even more dra-matic changes following World War II. The collapse of the fur trade coincided with a decline in caribou and fox populations, which led to a greater dependency on imported goods (e.g., clothes and food) from the South. The collapse of the fur trade also meant that the productive activities of the Inuit, such as hunting and trapping, did not produce a wage or saleable goods. After World War II the federal government, in a continuation of its policy of centralization, aimed to "urbanize" the North by uprooting most of the Inuit population from the tundra, the sea, and the sea ice to live in small, serviced communities.

At the same time, improved educational and medical facilities in the small towns of the Arctic attracted Inuit. There was also the possibility of wage jobs in these settlements. As a result, for the next two decades there was a steady migration of Inuit from the tundra to the settlements. This movement was supported by government bureaucrats, since it meant that their charges would be in easy reach at all times. Thus, permanent residence in the settlements began, and social, economic, and transportation infrastructure was put in place in order to service these communities (Lu and Emerson, 1973).

For many years after Confederation, the federal government's concern with the North and its people was confined to establishing a physical presence and thus establishing sovereignty over the area. It is important to remember that the boundaries of the Northwest Territories have changed significantly over the past hundred years. In the early 1900s, Quebec, Ontario, and Manitoba were extended north at the expense of the Northwest Territories, while Alberta and Saskatchewan were carved out of their original boundaries, followed by the creation of the Yukon. More recently, Nunavut was established as a new territory out of land formerly belonging to the Northwest Territories.

It was believed that if Canada were to lay claim to the Arctic, it would have to demonstrate to the world that it had permanent residents upon the soil it claimed. While the placement of Royal Canadian Mounted Police stations in various parts of the North went some way toward establishing sovereignty, there was also a belief that "other" Canadians would have to be physically present. Moreover, there was a belief that the Canadian government would have to provide support to these residents. Thus, effective occupation was the primary goal of the government as the 20th century began. It was also incumbent upon the Canadian government to make sure that Canadians were living in the Arctic on a year-round basis. As such, relocation programs were invented in order to move Inuit to areas not previously inhabited. For example, families from Inukjuak would be relocated to high Arctic areas such as Grise Fiord (in 1953), and later Inuit would be moved to Resolute Bay. Other Inuit relocations were put in place throughout the 1950s. The placement of Inuit into permanent residences also demonstrates the push by government to urbanize the Arctic. The creation of communities in the Arctic was also justified on the basis that they would afford Inuit an opportunity to pursue their traditional lifestyle (Tester and Kulchyski, 1994; Henderson, 2007).

When, in the 1960s, the potential of natural resource development was recognized, Canadians once again looked to the North to solve their problems. By the end of the 1960s, Inuit were dominated economically, politically, and ideologically. The influence of the traders, missionaries, and police had been supplanted by the presence of the state and multinational corporations. Social programs were extended to Inuit, and housing and medical programs were expanded as the government took a lead in the economic and social development of the North. D'Anglure (1984) argues that the 1960s marked the end of the traditional culture of Inuit and the emergence of the modern economy in the North.

If there is a lesson to be learned from this short history of the Arctic, it is that the entry of southern Canadians has always created a crisis for Inuit. As Moss (1995) points out, their presence has always been so intrusive that it displaced and disrupted Inuit culture. Thus, it should not come as a surprise that Inuit are less than enthusiastic about any plans that southern Canadians have about the North, and that they wish to achieve some level of self-government that aligns with Inuit culture and cosmology.

Change in Inuit Culture

As Dybbroe (1996) points out, the significance of urbanization on Inuit culture may take more time to make itself felt. The relations among Inuit take place within the confines of the family. Although the family is affected by urban life, the family context mitigates its impact and allows Inuit to maintain a semblance of control over their lives. Nevertheless, Inuit recognize that change is occurring and accept that they must adapt their beliefs and behaviours to the new way of life.

LIVING IN INUIT NUNAAT

Four political regions encompass most Inuit living in northern Canada (see Figure 9.2). Within the **Inuvialuit** region, about 5000 Inuit live in the six communities. In Nunavut, the population is more than 23 000 and comprises 26 communities, most of which have a population of less than 1000. This political unit is further subdivided into three regions: Qikiqtaalu (Baffin), Kivalliq (Keewating), and Kitikmeot. The region of Nunavik has nearly 8000 Inuit who reside in 14 communities. Finally, Nunatsiavut counts 4500 Inuit residents (Inuit Tapiriit Kantami, nd). While Inuit living in the Inuit Nunaat region of Canada share a number of common culture and traditions, they also reveal considerable linguistic and geographic diversity (Gionet, 2008). Of the 52 communities in the Inuit

FIGURE 9.2	Four Regions of Inuit Nunavut

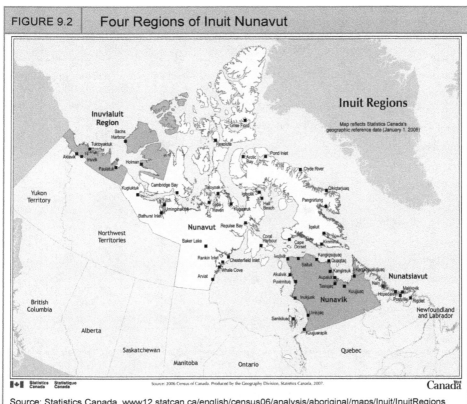

Source: 2006 Census of Canada. Produced by the Geography Division, Statistics Canada, 2007.

Source: Statistics Canada, www12.statcan.ca/english/census06/analysis/aboriginal/maps/Inuit/InuitRegions Aboriginal_Reference_ec.pdf.

Nunaat, many are remote communities that can only be accessed by air year-round or by sea in the summer months. These communities are small, with nearly 40 percent having fewer than 500 people. An additional 29 percent have between 500–999 people and the remainder have populations of 1000 or more.

Each of the four regions has a distinctive political structure and organization by which they carry out their business. In Inuvialuit, Inuvik is the administrative centre, although locally elected community councils deal with the administration and delivery of the many services provided to residents. In Nunavut, Iqualuit is the territorial capital, with regional administrative centres in Cambridge Bay and Rankin Inlet. In Nunavik, each community has its local administration provided by municipal councils as established by the Northern Village Corporation. Each Northern Village is part of the Kativik Regional Authority that oversees the administration of the region (Inuit Tapiriit Kanatami, nd.). Finally, in Nunatsiavut, Nain is the administrative centre, although locally elected community councils also provide services to its various villages.

POPULATION AND SOCIO-DEMOGRAPHIC PROFILE

Nearly 80 percent of Inuit live in one of the four regions that comprise the Inuit Nunaat (Inuit homeland). Table 9.1 illustrates the size, placement, and growth of the Inuit population between 1996 and 2006. The data show that nearly half of the Inuit reside in

TABLE 9.1	Size and Growth of the Inuit Population, Canada and Regions, 1996 and 2006		
Regions	2006	Percent	Percentage change from 1996 to 2006
Canada	50 485	100	26
Total – Inuit Nunaat	39 475	78	18
Nunatsiavut	2160	4	3
Nunavik	9565	19	25
Nunavut	24 635	49	20
Inuvialuit region	3115	6	−3
Total – Outside Inuit Nunaat	11 005	22	62
Rural	2610	5	67
Total urban	8395	17	60
Census metropolitan area[1]	4220		97
Urban non-census metropolitan area	4175		35

Note:
1. A CMA, or census metropolitan area, has a total population of at least 100,000 of which 50,000 or more live in the urban core.

Source: Adapted from Statistics Canada *Aboriginal Peoples, 2006 Census*, Catalogue 97-558-XIE2006001, www12.statcan .ca/census-recensement/2006/as-sa/97-558/table/t8-eng.cfm

Nunavut, although a sizeable number also reside in Nunavik. In all cases but one, there has been an increase in the population. The exception is a 3 percent decrease in the Inuvialuit region. Other areas have seen sizeable increases, such as outside Inuit Nunaat, where there has been a 60 percent increase in both rural and urban populations, and in census metropolitan areas, where there has been nearly a 100 percent increase. Overall, 22 percent of Inuit live outside of their homeland, up from 17 percent in 1996, revealing the continuing process of urbanization and migration away from the North. For Inuit living outside of Inuit Nunaat, nearly half live in one of five major centres in southern Canada. The mobility status of Inuit shows that over 50 percent of Inuit residing in Nunavut did not live at the same address five years ago.

In terms of religion, 80 percent of Inuit are Protestant, with only 18 percent Catholic. The remainder are "other" or have no religious affiliation.

Perhaps what is even more important than the small numbers and isolated villages is the linkages that the Inuit have established with other Arctic groups—e.g., Chukotka (Russia), Alaska (United States), and Greenland (Denmark). These groups have formed an international alliance and have become politically active over the past quarter-century.

Of all people who claim to be Aboriginal, about 4 percent (50 500) self-identified as Inuit in 2006. Compared to the numbers obtained in 1996, this represents an increase of over 25 percent. This is an astonishing rate of increase when compared to the overall Canadian population increase of 8 percent for the decade. As such, the Inuit population is very young (median age = 22) compared to the general Canadian population (median age = 40). Twelve percent of the Inuit population is less than five years of age—twice the proportion of non-Aboriginal people. An additional 11 percent are between 5–9 years of age, and over half (56 percent) of Inuit are under the age of 24.

Table 9.2 shows the age distribution and the median age for the various regions in Inuit Nunaat. These figures demonstrate that Inuit women have a high fertility rate. While it has decreased over the past two decades, it remains over twice as high as the Canadian fertility rate as a whole (3.2/1.56). Less than 4 percent of the Inuit population is 65 or older, while over 13 percent of the Canadian population is in this age group. The birth rate for Inuit is one of the highest in the world. If this rate were to continue, we could expect the population to double every 18 years. The high birth rate means that Inuit

TABLE 9.2	Inuit Age Distribution, 1996, 2001, 2006					
	2001		1996		2006	
	Number	Percent	Number	Percent	Number	Percent
Age Group						
0–14	17 460	38.7	16 510	41.0	17 705	35
15–24	8 260	18.3	7 605	18.9	10 555	21
25–64	17 950	39.8	15 095	37.5	20 370	40
65 and over	1 405	3.1	1 015	2.5	1 845	4

Source: "Population Reporting an Inuit Identity, and Age Groups, 1996 and 2001." Adapted from the Statistics Canada publication *Aboriginal Peoples of Canada, A Demographic Profile*, Catalogue 96F0030, January 2003; Inuit Tapirlit Kanatami, *Determining the Inuit Population*, December 2006, INAC 2006, Statistics Canada, 2005.

communities are "young" and will continue to exert pressure to integrate into the labour force for some years to come. Nevertheless, Inuit life expectancy is the lowest in Canada, at 67.7 years for males and 70.2 years for females. In summary, the Inuit population has grown rapidly over the past decade and estimates suggest that, if the present trends continue, there will be nearly 75 000 Inuit in Canada by 2016.

Housing has always been an issue for northern peoples, and Inuit live in some of the most crowded conditions in Canada. The housing stock in the North is aging and of poor quality. It is estimated that today the Inuit of the Arctic need 3000 new homes, but the federal government has projected budgets for only about 300 per year. If the current population were to remain stable, it would take a decade to provide the necessary housing units. Because most of the housing is located in urban settings, nearly two-thirds are linked to a municipal water system. However, about one-quarter of the current dwellings obtain their water directly from surface water (e.g., streams or lakes).

Less than a third of Inuit own their home, in comparison to three-quarters of Canadians. This lack of home ownership contributes to the high cost of living, since housing is at a premium in the private rental market. At the same time, nearly one-third of all Inuit live in crowded homes. Compared to the rest of Canada, where only 3 percent live in crowded conditions, this represents a major issue for Inuit. These crowding conditions have not changed over the past two decades. Related to the issue of crowding, data from Statistics Canada reveals that nearly one-fifth of Inuit live in a household home to more than one family, compared to only 4 percent in the non-Inuit population. Only a small proportion (6 percent) of Inuit adults live alone, compared to 13 percent of non-Inuit adults. While it is true that Inuit have traditionally lived in extended family groupings, data today show that, increasingly, several different families share the same crowded accommodations (Pauktuutit Inuit Women of Canada, 2006). Over one-fourth of Inuit live in multiple-family households.

One-third of the housing in Inuit Nunaat is in need of repairs; representing an increase from 19 percent a decade earlier. When we examine the Canada rate, we find that only 7 percent of dwellings are in need of major repairs (Inuit Tapiriit Kanatami, 2004). If instead we focus on housing conditions for non-Inuit in the North, we find that the percentage of housing requiring repairs has decreased over the past decade in almost every region. Inadequate and poor housing are associated with a number of social and health issues, regardless of where they exist. In the North, crowded living conditions lead to the transmission of diseases such as hepatitis A and tuberculosis. The tuberculosis rate for Inuit is more than 23 times higher than that for the general Canadian population. Moreover, data show that the hospitalization rates for Inuit children with severe lower respiratory tract infections are the highest in the world (Kovesi et al., 2007). In addition, crowded conditions are linked to increased risks for injuries, mental health problems, family conflict, and violence.

In 2006, the number of children aged 14 and younger living with two parents was somewhat similar to that of the general Canadian population—72 versus 80 percent. Of children living in a single-parent family, about 20 percent lived with a female lone parent and 6 percent with a male lone parent, again similar to the rate in the general Canadian population. However, a small but significant number (4 percent) of Inuit children live with a relative who is not a parent, while less than 1 percent of non-Inuit children live with a relative who is not a parent (Statistics Canada, 2006).

TABLE 9.3	Inuit Occupational Distribution by Sex (%) in Nunavut, 2005	
	Experienced Labour Force	
	Male	Female
Total	6 025	5 200
Management	12.9	7.9
Business, finance and admin.	7.5	23.3
Natural and applied sciences and health	6.6	6.8
Sales and service	22.2	30.8
Art, culture, recreation	6.4	5.6
Social science, education, government	7.9	21.8
Trades, transport, equipment operators	31.7	1.8
Other/not stated	4.5	1.8

Sources: Statistics Canada, 2005; INAC, 2006; INAC, 2000; Champagne, Torjesen and Steiner, 2005; Statistics Canada, 2004.

Table 9.3 identifies Inuit placement in the occupational structure for 2005. The data show that most of the Inuit in the labour force were employed in semi-skilled and manual-labour types of jobs (52 percent). There were some skilled craftspeople and semi-professionals (29 percent), but these were limited. Even fewer were in positions of power and decision-making. It is also important to note that, regardless of the field, many of the jobs in the Arctic are in government (federal, territorial, and municipal) as opposed to the private sector. In Nunavut alone, nearly one-third of the government positions have remained unfilled for the past three years due to the lack of residents holding the necessary technical expertise.

While standard measures of employment and income may not be as appropriate for Inuit living in the North as for other Canadians, the data show that over the past two decades labour force participation has increased for both Inuit men and women. At the same time, the unemployment gap between Inuit and non-Inuit increased. What is problematic is that the highest rate of unemployment is among the young people who are entering the labour market. Moreover, the data show that there has been no change in the percentage of Inuit moving from low-skilled occupations to more highly skilled jobs, with a concentration in tertiary industries—health and social services, trade and government services.

These rates varied among the four different regions, with Nunatsiavut having the highest rate of unemployment (34 percent) and Nunavut having the lowest (14 percent). These high unemployment rates are reflected in the median income for adults. The median income for Inuit adults was $9000 lower than that for all Canadians ($25 955), and the gap has remained consistent over the past decade. Compared to non-Aboriginal adults in the labour force in the North, Inuit median incomes are $43 378 less. Given the high cost of living in the North, the low income is even further reduced in terms of its purchasing power. For example, the total cost of a bag of potatoes, 1 litre of milk, 1 lb of ground beef, and 2.5kg of white flour is between $17.40 and $31.22, depending where you live in the North. The same items in Ottawa would cost $9.47, or in Montreal, $9.37.

As Inuit have become more involved in the wage economy, young people have redefined their involvement in subsistence activities. However, the change is not simple or straightforward. The cumulative changes have led to a reorientation of daily practices that has caused young Inuit to see subsistence activities not as desirable and valuable, but as recreations and something to be enjoyed once other more important demands—e.g., waged labour-force participation—are met (Stern, 2000). Young people see the town they live in as the "place they work and live" and the land as a "place to get away from it all." In addition, participation in the labour force acts as both a barrier and facilitator for individuals to engage in subsistence activities. For example, additional cash allows those who have high-status, high-paying jobs to purchase snowmobiles and other pieces of equipment that facilitate their "back to the land" activities. Those who are not able to afford this kind of equipment are not able to participate in subsistence activities.

Urbanization

Nearly one-fourth of the Inuit population lives in large southern urban areas. The numbers in Table 9.4 provide the reader with some sense of the size of Inuit populations in urban areas of southern Canada and the North. If northern towns are added to the list, nearly 90 percent of the Inuit population lives in non-rural areas. Today, in the five largest communities in Nunavut, with the exception of Iqaliut (which is the government centre for the Territory), over 80 percent of the population is Inuit.

The number of Inuit in large urban centres in the South has grown significantly since the 1960s to nearly 11 000. Kishigami (1999) found that Inuit living in the South comprised three major groupings: students, workers, and the unemployed. She also found that many residents of Montreal had moved from the North in order to escape alcohol and drug problems, sexual and physical violence, and other problems of human relations in the small towns. In short, she found that individuals' decisions to move to a southern urban centre were not mainly a function of urban resources and opportunities available to them, but were rather due to their desire to leave the North. Some Inuit city residents, such as students, found they were able to expand their job opportunities once they had

TABLE 9.4	Inuit Populations in Various Communities by Region, 2006		
South		**North**	
Toronto	1 500	Iqaluit	6 184
Edmonton	590	Arviat	2 060
Montreal	570	Rankin Inlet	2 358
Ottawa–Hull	725	Baker Lake	1 728
Calgary	350	Kuujjuaq	1 477
Vancouver	425	Yellowknife	640
Winnipeg	355		

Source: Statistics Canada, 2010. 2006 Aboriginal Population Profile, accessed June 15, 2011, at www12.statcan.ca/census-recensement/2006/dp-pd/prof/92-594/index.cfm?Lang=E.

completed their education and therefore postponed returning to the North. However, none of the Inuit living in urban centres were able to develop or create an Inuit urban culture and identity. The lack of a strong social network and the paucity of Inuit in any one locale prevents the development of Inuit organizations, the continuation of the Inuit language, and the maintenance of Inuit culture.

Education

At the end of World War II, only four schools existed in the Northwest Territories. Three were Catholic and the other was Anglican. When the federal government took over northern education in 1947, it assumed that Inuit were illiterate and "backward" because they had not been exposed to the southern Canadian educational system and did not speak English or French. Thus, without evaluating the type of education system that the North required, the entire southern educational structure was exported there. Two years later the government established a network of public schools for Inuit. However, because no southern non-Inuit teachers could speak Inuktitut (or any of the dialects), the sole language of instruction was English or French.

By 1951 a system of residential schools was established, with students from remote areas being relocated to schools for up to 10 months a year. While the government covered the cost of education, the schools were run by religious institutions. These residential schools isolated children from their parents, whose socialization efforts were limited to short visits. Parental control was replaced by the religious fervour exhibited by the Catholic or Anglican teachers, who felt that students would fare better once removed from the negative influences of home and parents.

Once communities grew to sufficient size, day schools were established. Nevertheless, the southern, Euro-Canadian curriculum in northern schools continued to be taught by non-Inuit, southern-trained teachers. It would not be until the 1960s that a curriculum was implemented that took into consideration Inuit language, culture, and values (Duffy, 1988). In 1970, administrative responsibility for northern schools was transferred to the Government of the Northwest Territories. The Inuit Tapirisat's lobbying efforts were a major factor in the government's decision to change its educational methods in the Arctic. The Tapirisat proposed that courses be taught with a strong northern orientation, and the Inuit Cultural Institute was created to protect Inuit language and culture. In addition, the establishment of Nunavut and Aurora Arctic College has afforded the opportunity for Inuit students to obtain selected degrees while remaining in the North. As a result, many teachers in Inuit communities have bachelor's and master's degrees in education and have taken on some administrative responsibility in the schools.

Table 9.5 illustrates the level of formal education of Inuit for the years 1981 to 2006, in percentages. It shows dramatic increases in the proportion of Inuit attending formal schooling since 1981. Comparing this data to that of non-Inuit, over twice the number of Inuit had less than a Grade 9 education. However, with regards to having completed a trades program or college, Inuit were similar to non-Inuit. The number who had completed a university program was three times less than their non-Inuit counterparts.

Over half of the adult Inuit population had less than a high school diploma in 2006. However, more than one-third had a postsecondary diploma or degree. In comparison, just over 60 percent of the non-Aboriginal population had completed a post-secondary

TABLE 9.5	Highest Level of Education of Inuit Aged 15 and Over, Canada, 1981–2006 (in Percentages)		
	YEAR		
Level of Education	1981	2001	2006
Less than grade 12	60.5	53.5	51.1
Some high school	20.1	8.5	–
High school certificate	3.2	7.3	13.0
Some post-secondary	6.3	15.6	17.2
Trades certificate	8.0	11.4	13.5
University graduation	1.6	3.3	4.2

Source: Adapted from: Inuit Tapiriit Kanatami and Research and Analysis Directorate, *Gains Made by Inuit in Formal Education and School Attendance, 1981–2001*, Strategic Research and Analysis Directorate, Indian and Northern Affairs Canada, December, 2006; Statistics Canada, 2004, 2005; Inuit Tapiriit Kanatami, 2008.

education program. The unemployment rate for men was 23 percent and for women 15 percent (compared to non-Inuit, with 5 percent unemployment in 2006). As such, the unemployment rate was almost four times higher for Inuit adults than for their non-Inuit counterparts. The depressed economy of the Arctic is the major structural reason for its high unemployment, and this is not likely to change in the near future.

There has been, and continues to be, a high attrition rate of Inuit from the education system. Data show that about one-third of Inuit children reach Grade 9, compared to over 80 percent of the Canadian population. Less than 25 percent graduate from high school (the overall Canadian rate is about 76 percent), and less than 4 percent go on to university. In the North, post-secondary institutions exist in Whitehorse, Yellowknife, and Fort Smith that allow students to transfer to southern post-secondary institutions and continue their educational program to obtain a university degree. Today there are three post-secondary institutions in Nunavut—Iqaluit, Cambridge Bay, and Rankin Inlet. In other Inuit communities, there are "community learning centres" that provide post-secondary courses. Focusing on the adult population (ages 35–49), 34 percent have less than a high school education. Twenty percent claim to have a secondary education and 16 percent claim some post-secondary education (e.g., trades or college certificate). Just over 10 percent have a university certificate, diploma, or degree.

When we look at the younger population (ages 5–14), we find that 99 percent are currently attending school, with over three-quarters claiming to have an Aboriginal teacher. Eighty-one percent of students say that their teachers use English in the classroom. However, nearly three-quarters also report that an Aboriginal language is also used in classes. Grades 1 through 3 in Nunavut and other Inuit communities are taught in Inuktitut, even for non-Inuit students in the class. This suggests that today's classrooms are bilingual, perhaps explaining why Inuktitut is still a thriving language (Sarkadi, 1992; Dorais and Krupnik, 2005). Well over two-thirds of the Inuit population know and use Inuktitut regularly. Furthermore, almost 70 percent of Inuit children claim an ability to carry on a conversation in Inuktitut.

Language

While there are five distinct Inuit language dialects spoken in the Inuit Nunaat region, they are collectively referred to as Inuktitut. Research has shown that Inuktitut is one of the three major Aboriginal languages that have been designated as having long-term survival. However, as recent data shows, while the language remains strong overall, knowledge and use are declining. In 2006, just under two-thirds of the total Inuit adult population indicated Inuktitut as their mother tongue, down from 68 percent in 1996. In addition, the percentage of Inuit adults who speak their mother tongue at home is 50 percent, down from 58 percent in 1996. Nearly 70 percent of Inuit claimed that they spoke Inuktitut well enough to carry on a conversation, and this was true for almost all age groups. However, if we examine Inuit who live in urban areas, we find they are much less able to speak Inuktitut. For example, for Inuit living in urban centres, only 15 percent could converse in Inuktitut compared with 84 percent of people living in Inuit Nunaat. Moreover, the overall picture does not reveal the regional differences in language competency. Inuktitut language use and competency is strongest in the regions of Nunavik (99 percent) and Nunavut (91 percent), while in Nunatsiavut just over one-quarter could hold a conversation in Inuktitut (Statistics Canada, 2006; INAC, 2007).

Less than one-quarter of Inuit children report reading Aboriginal language newspapers, newsletters, or magazines. Three-quarters of adults claim to speak Inuktitut. Three-quarters of the Inuit population report speaking Inuktitut in the home, while only one-third speak it at work and only 10 percent in school. Two-thirds of Inuit adults are able to read Inuktitut, and nearly half of them claim to read Inuktitut newspapers and magazines. Sixty percent claim that they are able to write in Inuktitut (Taqralik, 1984; Patrick, 2005).

Health

Settlements with populations of over 200 usually have nursing stations, which are the backbone of the health care system of the North. They are staffed by registered nurses and are open 24 hours a day. Although health clinics have been established in the larger communities, the existence of hospitals in the North is not extensive. During the 1970s and 1980s the federal government carried out an evaluation of the efficiency and effectiveness of maintaining hospitals in the North. It concluded that, except in the largest urban areas, the existence of hospitals was inefficient, ineffective, and posed both staffing and financial hardships. For example, it found that, while funds could be allocated for the construction of a hospital, staffing was most problematic. As such, even the best and most up-to-date equipment was useless if qualified staff were not in residence. It was agreed that clinics would be the standard providers of health care in the North, although for serious medical cases patients would be airlifted to nearby northern hospitals or the nearest hospital in the South. Nevertheless, many culturally-relevant health services are provided in the existing hospitals—for example, in Iqaluit local healers are allowed to provide care for patients. In other cases, local medicinal remedies are provided.

For the first half of the 20th century, the most prevalent disease afflicting Inuit was tuberculosis. In 1944 the tuberculosis rate was 568 per 100 000. In an effort to combat the disease, the federal government promoted extensive relocation and regimentation of the Inuit population. Large Inuit communities were created in southern Canada through the establishment of TB sanatoriums, and it has been estimated that at one time the largest Inuit community was in Ontario. Today the rate is less than 50 cases per 100 000, but this is still considerably higher than the overall Canadian rate.

The infant mortality rate in Inuit communities is 20 per 100 000, while for the general Canadian population it is less than 5 (Inuit Tapiriit Kanatami, 2008). This high mortality rate is partially determined by the low birth rate of newborns. Low birth weight infants are at a greater risk of disability and diseases. At present, the rate of low birth weight is 1.3 times higher than in Canada as a whole, and it has increased over the past decade.

We also find that among adult Inuit, more than 30 percent suffer from one or more long-term health conditions. Specifically, respiratory problems, e.g., asthma, emphysema, high blood pressure, and heart problems are the most pronounced. Among Inuit children, one third suffer from one or more long-term health conditions of which allergies and ear infections are the most pronounced. Because Inuit are heavy smokers, their lung cancer death rate is one of the highest in the world. Today, the lung cancer death rate is about 150 per 100 000 people.

The age standardized mortality rate (per 100 000) for Canada overall is 197 (a decrease from 221 in 1994), while for the Inuit Nunaat region, it is 537.1 and has increased in the past decade. Age standardized mortality rates for specific causes are identified in Table 9.6. The table reveals that in all cases, the Inuit mortality rate is much higher than the overall Canadian rate. Moreover, it shows that while there has been a decrease for Canadians, some increases are shown for Inuit. Life expectancy for Inuit is very different than for the general Canadian population. In 2006, the estimated life expectancy for Inuit was 72 years for women and 63 for men; in the general Canadian population this rate stood at 82 and 77 percent. Put another way, in 2004 the potential years of life lost (see Chapter 1) for Canada overall was 4130. For Inuit, the number was 16 022. In short, the number of years of life not lived because a person dies prematurely is four times higher for Inuit than for other Canadians.

In summary, when health rates of Inuit are compared to those for the rest of Canada, the disparity between the two groups is very clear. Infant mortality is nearly three times higher in Inuit communities. The average Inuit can expect to live a decade less than other Canadians, and a newborn Inuit child is 20 percent more likely to be born underweight

TABLE 9.6	Age Standardized Mortality Rates by Selected causes			
	1994		2004	
	Inuit Nunaat	Canada Overall	Inuit Nunaat	Canada Overall
Suicide/self-inflicted injury	73.7	10.0	107.3	9.7
Unintentional injury	95.1	21.8	85.2	19.8
Respiratory disease	58.9	13.4	54.1	11.1
Cancers	110.6	65	119.3	60.9

Source: Adapted from Inuit Tapiriit Kanatami, 2008, *Inuit Statistical Profile*, Ottawa, 2010; *Health Indicators of Inuit Nunangat within the Canadian Context 1994–1998 and 1999–2003*. Ottawa. Accessed June 15, 2011, at www.itk.ca/sites/default/files/20100706Health-Indicators-Inuit-Nunangat-EN.pdf. Used with the permission of Inuit Tapiriit Kanatami (www.itk.ca).

(Inuit Tapiriit Kanatami, 2010). Regarding mental health, the suicide rate for Inuit is more than 11 times higher than the overall Canadian rate (135/11.8 per 100 000).

Another health issue for Inuit is the infant mortality rate. In 1958, the rate for Inuit was among the highest in the world, at 151 per 1000 live births (compared to 30 per 1000 for the rest of Canada). Again, due to improved health care, this figure has dropped dramatically over time. In 2004, the infant mortality rate was 16 per 1000, still three times the national average.

Inuit health has been influenced by ecological, social, and nutritional changes. For example, creating urban zones in permafrost areas has created major environmental and health problems for residents. Poor nutrition also has contributed to a general decline in the health of Inuit in all areas of the North. Increasing consumption of imported foods with little or no nutritional value characterizes the Inuit's current eating habits. Over time, Inuit have come to rely more and more on imported foods, of whose nutritional content they are not aware. Thus, the standard of health for Inuit has steadily deteriorated.

During the 1960s and 1970s, the mortality rate and causes of death changed dramatically for Inuit. As the incidence of tuberculosis decreased, pneumonia became the leading cause of death. By the 1960s, pneumonia accounted for over one-fifth of Inuit deaths. Today, injuries, violence, and accidents are the leading causes of mortality for Inuit. Drug and alcohol addictions also have become major problems. In addition, new health hazards appeared in the late 20th and early 21st centuries, and sexually-transmitted diseases such as gonorrhoea and AIDS have attained near-crisis levels (Gombay, 2005; Martin, 2005).

Law and Justice

As Canada began to impose its cultural and administrative structures on northerners, the implementation of southern law and justice prevailed. Today, most police services are provided by the RCMP with little input from Inuit residents. However, in some areas, such as Kativik, Quebec, a regional police force composed of many Inuit officers operates in Inuit communities (Burkhardt, 2004).

With regard to involvement in the justice system, many Inuit are serving sentences in federal and territorial prisons. Faulkner (1992) carried out a study of over 50 Inuit men and women currently serving time in correctional institutions. She found that, with few exceptions, the major cause for imprisonment was substance abuse. She also found that in most federal jails workers are not sensitive to the cultural needs of Inuit prisoners. Recent data confirms that this remains the case. Although many correctional personnel have obtained cross-cultural training, much of it is geared to the cultural needs of First Nations and not Inuit. In an attempt to address this concern, Corrections Canada is contracting out many of the activities dealing with Inuit inmates (Burkhardt, 2004).

ECONOMIC DEVELOPMENT OF THE NORTH

Under current arrangements, the North is completely dependent upon the federal government. Over 90 percent of territorial government revenue is derived from federal transfer payments. All natural resource royalty payments in the North flow directly to the South, and government spending accounts for about two-thirds of the territory's economy.

When the federal government began to actively intervene in ongoing activities in the Northwest Territories during the 1950s, solutions to the economic plight of Inuit had a high priority. While co-ops in the rest of Canada were given lukewarm reception by the federal government, in the North they were supported and heavily subsidized. Although this was a departure from the usual stance taken by government, it was felt that the end justified the means. The co-ops of the North were specifically ethnic and were not integrated into the mainstream co-op movement in southern Canada. As such, they did not pose an economic threat to private industry. By 1966, 22 Arctic co-ops had been established, and by 1982 the annual level of business exceeded $30 million. Today there are over 40 active Inuit co-operatives, each belonging to one of two administrative bodies. There are 12 Arctic Quebec co-ops under the Montreal-based Fédération des Cooperatives du Nouveau-Québec, with the remainder being members of Arctic Co-operatives Limited (based in Winnipeg). Today the major activity of the co-ops is in the production and marketing of handicrafts.

As noted, co-ops were the federal government's economic structure of choice for integrating Inuit into Canadian society. But although they have had some success, particularly in the production of handicrafts, overall they have not allowed Inuit to integrate economically and have not provided a linkage with other Canadian economic institutions. The inability of co-ops to increase their membership and assets meant that Inuit were forced to look for new ways to develop sustainable economic ventures. But with no large amounts of money, little human capital relevant to the industrial economy, and limited backing by the federal government, this proved to be an impossible task. However, the settlement of comprehensive land claims has provided some hope as new forms of economic structures have emerged. When the new "development corporations" were established, their first act was to hire qualified individuals. Because co-ops had provided training for Inuit, they were the first place to look. And with offerings of higher status and salaries, it was not difficult to produce a "brain drain" in the co-op management. The impact of this action has been to further decrease the effectiveness of co-ops as independent economic institutions.

Most of these new development corporations have focused their efforts on megaprojects, requiring skilled workers and considerable up-front, sunken costs. The end result has been the hiring of large numbers of non-Inuit and a reliance on capital from outside the region. For example, Makivik lost over $10 million in its first four years of operation. While it is making a small profit today, many of its subsidiary companies are losing money or have been terminated (e.g., Air Inuit and Kigiak Builders Inc.). Nevertheless, other Inuit-owned-and-operated businesses are slowly developing into sustainable operations. Many northerners do not wish to work for government or may not have the skills to participate. Thus, many of the public service jobs created remain unfilled.

A recent federal report on the economic health of Arctic communities shows that only seven communities in the Northwest Territories were rated as being "developed," which means that they have good transportation systems, a significant private sector, and the potential to provide residents with jobs. Six other communities had some "potential," but the majority were classified as "underdeveloped," with no real economic potential. However, when areas do have economic potential, Inuit involvement is challenged. For example, the discovery of copper, cobalt, and nickel in Voisey's Bay (50 kilometres north of Davis Inlet–Utshimassits) prompted the Inuit and Innu to more forcefully make their land claim case, since Voisey's Bay is within a currently contested land area. However, neither the federal nor provincial government has suggested that land rights might take precedence over outside exploitation of natural resources. In a recent move, the Province of Newfoundland and Labrador placed restrictions on the development of the potential nickel mine, with the result that the developers chose to shelve their plans for the immediate future and move their development efforts to other areas in the world that are "more friendly" to the exploitation of natural resources.

During the late 1980s and early 1990s, non-renewable resource development was touted as an alternative supply of work. However, mining has never employed more than 1.5 percent of the Native labour force in the Northwest Territories, and oil development has involved even fewer. Moreover, the boom and bust nature of such activities creates a volatile and transient labour force. Myers (2001) argues that the traditional economy is an important component of local life, and asserts that, in the 1980s, an average of $11 000 (which today would equal $28 000) was an imputed value per Native household for country food and domestic production. He goes on to claim that more than 90 percent of Inuit households consume country food, and more than 70 percent hunt or fish. Today a boom is being contemplated once again. The major gas fields in the Mackenzie Delta area of the Northwest Territories and the proposed Mackenzie Pipeline are being touted as economic development projects that can involve local Aboriginal people. However, many note that the local people do not have the necessary skills to participate in long-term jobs associated with the development of the gas field and pipeline.

The North remains significantly unexplored, but there is considerable evidence that it is a rich storehouse of oil, gas, gold, copper, zinc, uranium, diamonds, and other minerals. In 2006, mining was the largest sectoral contributor to the gross domestic product (20 percent). In that year, $110 million worth of mineral exploration activity was under way just in Nunavut. Towns such as Yellowknife and Inuvik clearly have developed markets in the retail and wholesale business sector and could expand their scope. Communities such as Kugluktuk and Cape Dorset could expand their roles as regional supply centres and broaden the local range of goods and services. Other smaller communities have the potential for developing their arts and crafts and various forms of human and natural resource development. For example, one in five individuals in the Nunavut region sold crafts in 2005.

The traditional economy of the Inuit is no longer the main support structure for the development of an Arctic economy. The existing structures remain isolated from both the Canadian and the global industrialized economies. Even the new development corporations that have been created are marginal in their ability to become "engines" of growth in the Arctic. As a result, there is a clear ethnic stratification that segregates Inuit from non-Inuit southerners. This inequality is maintained through unequal access to jobs, services, and goods. Individual and structural discrimination has further divided the Indigenous population from other Arctic residents. For example, when the shrimp quota for Canada was increased because of new sources in the North, only 51 percent of the increase was allocated to northern companies, with the remainder being allocated to southern interests. These kind of structural inequalities make it difficult for local businesses such as Pangrirung Fisheries (which employs 100 people and processes 1.5 million pounds of fish per year) to succeed.

Today there is recognition that development in the North until the present has been southern-driven, with only short-term benefits for northern residents. As a result, the traditional-based economy has survived and reaffirmed Inuit cultural and social values. There is acknowledgement that if the Inuit do not want to lose young people from the North to the South, they will need to develop and create community-based economic opportunities that meet the needs of northern residents. As such, four factors will need to be taken into consideration for economic development: physical capital (e.g., housing, commercial space, transportation, telecommunications), human capital (e.g., individual skill sets), natural capital (e.g., natural resources), and social and organization capital (e.g., community cohesion).

The utilization of "country foods" also supports Inuit culture in that it involves the sharing of resources with roles and responsibilities for each member based on age, sex, and experience with the kinship affiliate. Tait (2006) points out that the sharing of food is an important Inuit tradition that serves to keep family and community ties strong. This tradition has remained alive and well in all regions across the North, as nearly all Inuit households shared harvested food with others outside of their home in the year 2000 (Burch, 2004). Today the size of the land-based economy is estimated at about $60 million per year (Canadian Arctic Resources Committee, 2004). Its contribution to the social fabric of Inuit society is invaluable. Nunavut's wage economy is estimated to be about $800 million. Nevertheless, it is clear that Nunavut's four forms of capital will need to be supported if true development is to take place in the region.

A TIME FOR CHANGE

As the Cold War intensified in the 1950s, the Distant Early Warning system was put in place throughout the Canadian Arctic. Small, isolated military installations brought southerners to the Arctic on a permanent basis. Infrastructure had to be put in place in order to ensure that these installations could be accessed at any time. It also meant that existing communities in the North had to be modernized so that they could act as a secondary stage to access these installations. In short, the modern industrial economy began to make its presence felt in the Arctic. At the same time, social programs were being made available to Inuit.

In the early 1960s, the federal government implemented a policy to develop the natural resources of the North. The government's "Roads for Resources" program, which gave direction to the development of the natural resources of the North, had introduced multinationals and their associated technology to the region. It was at this time that Inuit communities became more actively involved in policy and programs directed toward the North, even though they themselves were not able to participate due to a lack of education and technical skill (Jull, 1982).

Inuit have long been interested in integrating into the larger economic institutions of Canada and have expressed concerns for Aboriginal rights, but it has only been in the past few years that they have been able to forcefully act on those beliefs. They have been facilitated by external and internal forces. For example, environmental concerns, linkages with other national Indigenous groups, land settlements in Alaska and Greenland, and less demand for developing petroleum resources in the North have reduced southern intrusion into the Arctic and have given Inuit an opportunity to organize and clearly articulate their concerns and goals as Canadians. At the same time, Inuit participation in domestic governmental structures (both federal and territorial) has produced an awareness of Inuit concerns and helped them to develop political and economic strategies to deal with those issues.

The process of decolonization has begun for Inuit as self-government negotiations have taken place in all Arctic regions, and it has come to fruition in Nunavut. Inuit have always argued that they do not want to achieve self-determination through racially segregated structures or secession. They consider themselves Canadian, yet they want an explicit recognition of their place in Canadian society.

LAND CLAIMS AND POLITICS

Aboriginal land claims are as old as Canada, and while many land claims were settled through treaty, there are virtually no treaty settlements involving the North. A review of government documents clearly demonstrates that the federal government did not want to treat Inuit as they did Indians and insisted they did not have any specific responsibilities toward them. Federal officials were adamant that Inuit were not Indians (although the Supreme Court decided differently in 1939) and they therefore refused to establish treaties with them. As a result, until the 1970s, most of the land in the Yukon and Northwest Territories was under contested ownership. The *Alaska Native Claims Settlement Act* (1971) in the United States was the first modern Aboriginal land settlement in North America and became the precursor to modern Aboriginal land claims in Canada. It set the stage and served as a model for Canadian legal settlements. It should be made clear that the impetus for settling land claims was not generated by Inuit but by the federal government. The government's interest emerged out of the potential difficulties it foresaw in developing the natural resources of the North. Land claims were entered into because the government saw them as a legal obstacle that needed to be dealt with as quickly as possible.

The first major, modern-day land claims settlement occurred in 1975 with the James Bay Cree and Inuit of Quebec, who reside north of the 55th parallel. Government interest was piqued only once the Inuit and Indians had objected to development and obtained a court injunction against it. The end result, the James Bay and Northern Quebec Agreement (1975), dealt with Aboriginal land claims and compensation. The Inuit communities of this region became public municipal governments under Quebec's municipality legislation (Purich, 1992). The Kativik regional government in northern Quebec is the administrative structure now used to govern the region. This structure, like others advocated by Inuit, is not racially based. Because of their majority status, the Inuit are able to control their regional government; however, their efforts are limited by their financial dependence on the federal government. Other organizational and administrative structures were also put in place, such as the Makivik Corporation. Its role is to receive compensation and invest it in such a way that it will improve the quality of life of Inuit. The Kativik School Board was also established under the provisions of the James Bay Agreement.

Inuvialuit Agreement: Western Arctic

In the western Arctic, the Inuvialuit founded the Committee for the Original People's Entitlement and formed an alliance with eastern Inuit. First put forward in 1976 by the Inuit Tapirisat of Canada, a proposal for establishing Nunavut as a politically distinct federal territory extracted from the Northwest Territories was presented to the federal government. Later that year the proposal was withdrawn, and a new land claim was submitted a year later by the Committee for Original People's Entitlement, focusing only on the western Arctic. In 1984 the Inuvialuit Final Agreement was signed, providing a guarantee that Inuvialuit would not be treated any less favourably than any other group in the western Arctic. Under this agreement, the Inuvialuit surrendered their rights to

344 000 square kilometres of land. In return they were guaranteed title to 91 000 square kilometres and mineral rights in one-seventh of that zone, the **Inuvialuit Settlement Region** (see Figure 9.3). In addition, they received $152 million compensation payable over a 13-year period. Several wildlife-management structures were also put into place, along with an income support program (Alunik, 2003).

FIGURE 9.3	Inuvialuit Settlement Region

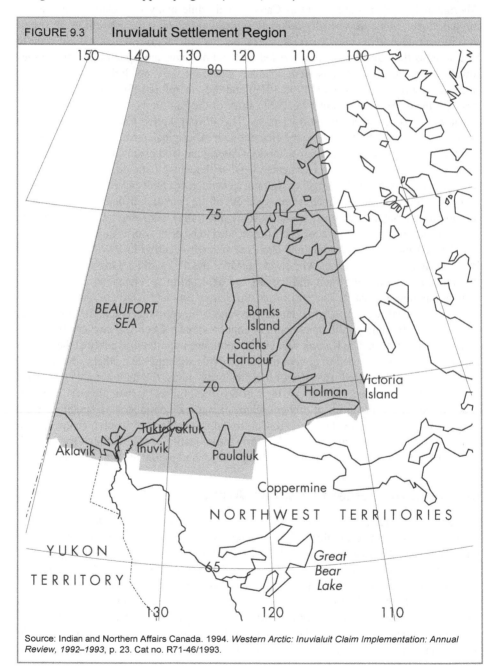

Source: Indian and Northern Affairs Canada. 1994. *Western Arctic: Inuvialuit Claim Implementation: Annual Review, 1992–1993*, p. 23. Cat no. R71-46/1993.

Nunatsiavut (Labrador)

As the Moravians entered the eastern coast of Labrador, they were able to acquire land upon which to base their operations. Labrador Inuit subsequently tried for some time, unsuccessfully, to get that land back. In 1974 the Labrador Inuit Association outlined its land claims against the federal government. However, it would take more than 10 years before a comprehensive framework agreement to cover Labrador Inuit claims was initialled by the interested parties. By 1978 the federal government had accepted the claim by 3500 Inuit of Labrador. One year later the province of Newfoundland agreed to enter into the negotiations. It would not be until 1990, however, that the two governments signed a framework agreement outlining the scope, process, topics, and parameters for negotiation (Purich, 1992). It then took until 2005 before the Labrador Inuit land claim agreement was ratified.

The Labrador Inuit Association, the regional organization that has spearheaded the struggle for recognition by the Inuit of Labrador, represents about 5000 people, and is recognized by the Government of Canada and the province of Newfoundland and Labrador. As Haysom (1992) notes, the Labrador Inuit Association also has been influential outside the claims arena. Specifically, the association has sponsored at least nine other organizations that are influential in the provision of social, health, and economic benefits to Inuit—e.g., the Torngat Regional Housing Association, the Labrador Inuit Health Commission, the Labrador Inuit Development Corporation, and the Labrador Inuit Alcohol and Drug Abuse Program.

Inuit Corporate Structure

As noted earlier, the economic development of the North and its function has been a concern for both northerners and government for some time. As a result, when governments have negotiated with Inuit people and land settlements were resolved, part of the agreements has been the creation of an overarching organization that will manage the financial dimension. These corporate structures are entrusted with ensuring that due diligence is given before development is undertaken, and that accountability is maintained for both the communities and the government.

For example, the Inuvialuit Petroleum Corporation, an oil and gas exploration and production business, is owned by the Inuvialuit. With current assets of over $35 million, it has returned financial benefits to the community and provided training and opportunity for academic achievement. It has interests in over 100 oil wells and nearly as many gas wells.

As the Inuit have tried to develop these new ethnic economic structures, they have realized that they must develop links with other national and multinational companies. Thus, their primary activity today is constructing linkages that will provide them with the necessary capital and technology, while at the same time allowing them to receive a fair return on their investment and keep the development within their scope of control. The Inuit want their ventures to provide long-term opportunities for employment and training. Their overall goal is to nurture a more stable economy through recycling profits and wages, and to allow the Inuvialuit to contribute to, and gain from, the successful growth.

NEW FORMS OF GOVERNMENT: THE QUEST FOR SELF-GOVERNMENT

Until the creation of **Nunavut** (see the section "Nunavut, Our Land" below) the bulk of the Inuit population in Canada resided in the Northwest Territories (see Figure 9.4). The government structure in the Northwest Territories consisted (and still consists) of three levels: territorial, regional, and local. Local governments generally represent communities and are

FIGURE 9.4	Nunavut

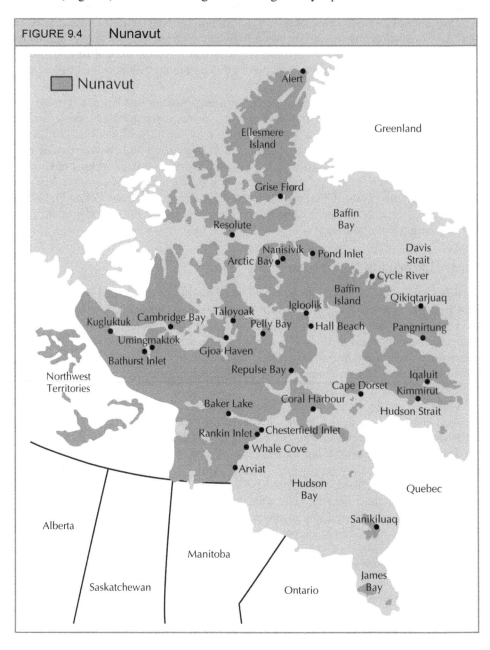

elected by local residents. Regional councils are made up of municipal officials chosen by local councils. They are responsible to local government councils. Regional councils are unique to the Northwest Territories and are funded by the territorial government. Aboriginal people are interested in obtaining more authority in running programs of the territorial government within their regions via the regional governments being proposed. Without taking over ministerial responsibility, they want more program responsibility for setting policy and standards (Dickerson, 1993). This was clearly a foundational principle when the Nunavut territory was established, as was the principle of decentralization.

The question regarding the political structure of the North has been reviewed by the federal government many times in the past half-century. One of the first to investigate the issue of self-government was the Carrothers Commission, struck in 1966. The Commission's report (1967) concluded that the Northwest Territories should be self-governing and that Yellowknife should be its capital. More recently, the *Drury Report* once again addressed the issue of self-government and division of the Northwest Territories. While the report did not reject the idea of division, it suggested that Inuit land claims and the setting aside of land for Inuit were the priority issues. The question of self-government and division could come later. The Inuit Tapirisat of Canada rejected this conclusion.

Ten years later, the Inuit Tapirisat of Canada presented a case for settlement of its land claim along with the creation of Nunavut. In 1979 the Inuit Tapirisat of Canada adopted the contents of the document entitled *Political Development in Nunavut.* By that time, a territorial assembly had been put in place. The election that year brought about a change in the ethnic composition of the assembly in that a majority of the members were now of Aboriginal ancestry (Duhaime, 1992).

As Inuit continued to press their concerns, the federal government agreed to hold a plebiscite. In 1982 the first plebiscite for division of the North was held, with 56 percent casting their ballots in favour. It was then agreed that two forums be established to discuss the separation issue: the Nunavut Constitutional Forum (in the eastern Arctic) and the Western Constitutional Forum (in the western North). By 1984 Inuvialuit of the western Arctic independently signed an agreement with the federal government and settled their land claims. The activities of the Western Constitutional Forum were further supplanted by the Dene/Métis land claims negotiations.

Provincial governments have their own constitutional existence without a formal reporting relationship to the federal government. Most of the provincial government structures are set through either constitutions or conventions. However, this is not the case for the territorial governments. Much of the power they wield is not provided for by statute, but is in place as a result of discussions between political leaders in the North and the federal minister of Aboriginal Affairs and Northern Development. In some cases, this power is given formal recognition in letters of instruction, while in others it is instituted through unwritten understandings between the federal and territorial governments (Indian and Northern Affairs Canada, 1995).

Nunavut, "Our Land"

The push for Nunavut began in the 1960s, when international demand for energy products, mining, and hydroelectric resources sparked a heightened interest in resource development. Canadians and other major resource users felt that new, stable sources of these commodities would need to be found if they were to ensure their access to these products. The

North held vast amounts of these potential resources, and there was a rush to exploit them. As well, the Cold War was in full operation and the Arctic and its strategic military importance did not escape notice.

By the 1970s, the *Alaska Native Claims Settlement Act* (1971) had been passed by U.S. Congress and set the framework for other settlements that would follow. The Act demonstrated to Canadians that agreements could be made that would simultaneously address the concerns of government, private industry, and Indigenous people while allowing for the development of natural resources. The international Copenhagen Conference in 1971 was also influential in giving legitimacy to the claims of Indigenous peoples. Early attempts to create Nunavut did not express the realities of Inuit life and culture. As Gombay (2000) and Dahl (1997) argue, the Aboriginal populations of the North exhibit a communitarian nationalism rather than regional nationalism. Accordingly, their form of nationalism is not aligned with the politics of Canada. Gombay contends that regional identities are superimposed on a people where no such identity has traditionally existed. Inuit therefore had a difficult time in attempting to accommodate self-government through public government.

Another global event impacting the claims laid by Inuit was the Danish parliament's agreement to grant home rule for Greenland (1979). This agreement is unique among modern settlements in that it was the first to provide for wide-ranging Aboriginal self-government. Moreover, the agreement made no provisions for monetary compensation, nor did it require the Aboriginal people to give up their ancestral Indigenous rights. During this time, the Inuit Committee on National Issues was created (1979) and, until it disbanded in 1987, developed national positions on constitutional reform for the Inuit.

Through their various organizations (e.g., Inuit Tapirisat of Canada, the Nunavut Constitutional Forum, and the Tungavik Federation of Nunavut), the Inuit struggled to achieve Inuit rights and the establishment of Nunavut. It was first proposed in 1976, supported through a referendum in the Northwest Territories in 1982, and eventually came into existence under the *Nunavut Act* (1993). The *Nunavut Act* ensures the cultural survival of Inuit through control of a non–racially-based democratic government.

Fenge (1992) points out that the Inuit used every method available to them through the 1980s in order to achieve the creation of Nunavut. The distance between eastern communities and Yellowknife (the capital of the Northwest Territories since 1967) was a key argument presented to justify the existence of Nunavut. Other issues, such as the relative lack of east–west air traffic compared to north–south air traffic, revealed that the North was, in reality, divided into two separate entities. Minority rights and group rights were also cited as important factors in the need to create Nunavut. To work out the terms with their respective constituents, the federal government created the Western Constitutional Forum and the Nunavut Constitutional Forum, Inuit-dominated organizations established for the specific purpose of achieving Nunavut. The forums were a particularly suitable method for facilitating claim negotiations, environmental and social impact assessments of oil and gas development in the Arctic, national constitutional discussions, and advocacy.

In 1983 the Nunavut Constitutional Forum presented a proposal on how the government of the new territory would operate. The document, *Building Nunavut,* was widely circulated among Inuit communities. By 1985, the revised version, *Building Nunavut: Today and Tomorrow,* was required reading for all Inuit. When the Iqaluit Agreement was signed two years later with the federal government, the principles in this document were agreed upon by both the Western and Nunavut Constitutional Forums. In 1987 the

Western Constitutional Forum agreed on the splitting of the Northwest Territories and by 1990 an agreement in principle was signed between government and the Inuit, giving support to the creation of a division of the existing Northwest Territories.

In 1991, the federal government released a comprehensive package of proposals for the Arctic, called *Shaping Canada's Future Together.* Both the federal government and the Inuit (through the Inuit Tapirisat of Canada) conducted hearings across the country; the results of these consultations formed the Pangnirtung Accord, which was adopted unanimously by the Inuit Assembly on the Constitution. The Inuit outlined three of their major concerns in this accord. They wanted recognition of the inherent right of self-government, equal participation in the political reform process, and recognition of Inuit as a distinct society with cultural and language rights. The Inuit Tapirisat of Canada presented a brief to the then minister of Constitutional Affairs, entitled *Inuit in Canada: Striving for Equality,* which expanded upon the three fundamental objectives of the Pangnirtung Accord. In 1992 a non-binding vote was held, establishing a boundary line that would separate Nunavut from the remainder of the Northwest Territories. Fifty-four percent voted in favour of the proposal.

The Nunavut Territory came into existence in 1999 through a political process that had taken over a quarter of a century. After years of negotiation, the federal government gave its commitment to creating Nunavut and signed a political accord and land claims agreement in 1992. One year later the *Nunavut Act* was signed and work on the details of how the new government would operate began. In 1999, the Nunavut government was created and given responsibility to operate as a territorial government. Budgets were allocated to the new government and the transfer of power gave it authority to provide service delivery, to carry out economic and resource development, and to enact legislation for the territory. The agreement gives Inuit title to more than 350 000 square kilometres of land, including nearly 40 000 square kilometres for which they have sole mineral rights. As with Indian treaties, the Inuit agree to cede, release, and surrender all their Aboriginal rights and claims to the land and water.

The agreement allows for land titles to be held in two forms: fee simple including mineral rights, or fee simple excluding mineral rights. Finally, access to and across Inuit-owned lands is granted only with the consent of Inuit. Compensation of $1.14 billion is being paid over 14 years. Additional royalties from natural resource development are paid to Inuit—a sharing of royalties that the government receives from natural resource development on Crown land. Specifically, Inuit annually receive 50 percent of the first $2 million of resource royalties received by government, and 5 percent of additional resource royalties within the newly created territory of Nunavut. In addition, a $13-million training trust fund has been established. There are also specific measures to increase Inuit employment within government in the Nunavut settlement area, and to increase access to government contracts.

Nunavut has three official languages: **Inuktitut**, English, and French. In anticipation of the split occurring, in mid-1990 the Inuit formed the Nunavut Wildlife Advisory Board in opposition to the existing territorial Wildlife Advisory Board. The Nunavut Tungavik Incorporation will administer the land claim. This organization is responsible for making sure that the terms of the Nunavut Political Accord signed by the federal government are honoured. Members of the organization meet in different Inuit villages to listen to the wishes of the people and to make decisions on implementing the content of the Nunavut Land Claims Agreement.

The Inuit also created the Nunavut Trust, an organization that receives the cash compensation under the land claims settlement. The Nunavut Agreement identifies five new institutions: a Nunavut Wildlife Management Board, a Nunavut Impact Review Board (which screens project proposals to determine whether there is a need for a review of environmental, social, or economic impacts), a Nunavut Planning Commission (which develops land use plans and monitors compliance with land use plans), a Nunavut Water Board, and a Surface Rights Tribunal. This last organization has jurisdiction across all of the pre-1999 Northwest Territories, whereas the others are limited to Nunavut. An advisory group called the Nunavut Implementation Commission was established to advise the government on the setting up of the government. Like Quebec, Nunavut is to be a "distinct" society, although it is structured so as to operate like any province. Since 85 percent of the population is Inuit, it is highly unlikely that the elected government would represent anything other than Inuit needs and goals. However, Nunavut does not hold title to any land or non-renewable resources. The land is owned either by Nunavut Tungavik Inc. or by the federal government.

Constitutionally, Nunavut has the same territorial powers afforded the Northwest Territories and Yukon. However, because of the Inuit majority, it is truly a form of Inuit self-government. As such, the Inuit will be in charge of education, health and social services, justice, and other social and economic programs. The legislative assembly (19 members) runs on a non-partisan basis and operates in a consensus style.

The dominant power structure in Nunavut is that of a coarchy (where all actors are in positions of power) (Legare, 1996). Legare notes that this mode is unstable and can be easily broken if a higher political status actor (policy maker) tries to impose its own solutions to Inuit demands. The question now remains as to whether Inuit can change the power structure to that of a stratarchy (where most, but not all, actors are in authority), which would allow them to take on positions of authority while other actors (e.g., transnational companies) have less power. Nevertheless, the planned Nunavut government will have a premier, cabinet, legislature, and 10 ministries.

The Nunavut Agreement is not without critics. Many believe that the Inuit gave away too much in return for the small amount of land, rights, and cash received. For example, the per capita cash payout is less than that received in the James Bay settlement. Others claim that there is no real power for the new territory. Still others feel that, since the Inuit owned all the land, they gave away much of what was really theirs to begin with. Moreover, there are many groups who opposed the creation of Nunavut. The Dene Nation vehemently opposed the proposed boundaries for Nunavut and called upon its members to vote against it. Likewise, First Nations from Keewatin and the northern regions of Saskatchewan and Manitoba, as well as the Assembly of First Nations, were urged to vote against the proposal. Non-Natives have also been critical of the creation of Nunavut.

The issue of the western boundary between Nunavut and the remainder of the Northwest Territories has long been contentious. During the early years, the Western and Nunavut Constitutional Forums, along with the Constitutional Alliance, met to negotiate the exact boundaries. Later, the Tungavik Federation of Nunavut and the Dene/Métis Joint Negotiating Secretariat took over. After many years of negotiating, the two parties have not yet come to an agreement as to where the exact boundaries will be.

Residents of the "rump" Northwest Territories, and particularly those in the Mackenzie Valley, were given assurances that the federal government would provide additional funds to stabilize the level of services in the remainder of the Northwest Territories after the creation of Nunavut. Moreover, other residents of the Northwest Territories would not be asked to cover the cost of the establishment of Nunavut. A vote was taken over the boundary proposed by the proponents of Nunavut; it passed (56–44 percent). The closeness of the vote reflects a divisiveness that stems from ethnic origin (Kulchyski, 1994).

RESISTANCE: CONFRONTATION AND POLITICAL ACTIONS

The Inuit did not historically view themselves as a distinct ethnic group. It was only through contact with outsiders that a clear demarcation between "us" and "them" emerged. Mitchell (1996) claims that the birth of the pan-Inuit movement occurred with the development of co-ops. She goes on to argue that the 1980 co-op conference was referred to as the Pan-Arctic Conference, and that the relationship between Inuit and other Canadians was the central issue discussed. It was agreed by Inuit that co-ops would best serve their goal of achieving both economic and cultural independence.

Over the years, Inuit have learned from other Aboriginal groups that ethnic organizations can be powerful tools in achieving community goals. The Inuit Tapirisat of Canada (created in 1971) grew out of a meeting of Inuit leaders in Coppermine and has become the major organization speaking on behalf of Inuit in Canada. One of its first actions was to begin the preparation of what would become the 1976 proposal, *Nunavut.* The Labrador Inuit Association was established in 1973 as an affiliate member of the Inuit Tapirisat of Canada. In 1979 the latter created the Inuit Committee on National Issues, which was given sole responsibility to advance the Inuit case in constitutional negotiations. The Inuit Committee on National Issues has been active since the 1980s, when it formally stated that Canada had not respected Inuit nation status and had failed to recognize the constitutional status of Inuit people.

Mitchell (1996) argues that Inuit have used non-confrontational techniques in dealing with the dominant society. The total domination by the South did not mean that Inuit simply accepted each new value and artefact as it was introduced. Both passive and active resistance has been exhibited over time. Back-to-the-land movements have been extensively used since the 1970s and have given Inuit the feeling of independence as well as lent credence to their traditional culture. Both elders and young Inuit have embraced this movement, which has also given legitimacy to the current land claims now being negotiated. Linked to this movement are the Inuit cultural associations that have sprung up over the past quarter-century. Language has been the focus of many of these associations, and is now viewed as an important indicator of cultural preservation. Other cultural associations (created in the 1970s) have taken on the larger task of revitalizing Inuit culture. For example, the Inuit Cultural Institute is obtaining knowledge from elders in an attempt to preserve it as a basis for teaching new generations. The Inuit Tapirisat of Canada has created a language commission to standardize the two writing systems for Inuit: the roman orthography system developed by the then Department of Indian and Northern Development and the syllabic system taught by the missionaries. Other organizations, such as the Torngasok Cultural Association in Labrador and the Avataq Cultural Institute (Northern Quebec), have similar objectives (Mitchell, 1996).

Other Inuit have taken on more direct confrontational strategies in dealing with social change. For example, the Kitikmeot and Keewatin Inuit Association, along with other

Aboriginal organizations, opposed the Polar Gas pipeline proposal. Similarly, the Inuit Tapirisat of Canada protested the International Whaling Commission's ban on beluga and narwhal hunting. More recently, the Quebec Inuit presented a strong campaign for compensation for those Inuit who were forcibly relocated in the 1950s. Lobbying efforts have been made to challenge the European Union's ban on sealskins and to enforce environmental guidelines for economic development projects.

In the early 1970s, Inuit from Alaska, Canada, and Greenland met in Copenhagen to discuss the back-to-the-land movement. This unity movement was first tested in 1975 when the Alaska Eskimo were asked to support the Inuvialuit fight against the Canadian government's decision to allow offshore drilling in the Beaufort Sea. In 1977, Canadian Inuit joined forces with other Aboriginal peoples from Alaska, Greenland, and Russia. This pan-Eskimo movement sponsored a yearly Inuit Circumpolar Conference at which issues common to all are discussed. In 1983 the conference was accepted by the United Nations as a non-governmental agency. It was also at this time that the conference joined with the World Council of Indigenous Peoples, which established the Alaska Native Review Commission and in turn hired Justice Thomas Berger as the commissioner. Its overall goal has been to establish some control over the development of Arctic policy (e.g., natural resources, land, and environment). However, as Hamilton (1984) points out, this is not a radical movement that uses political rhetoric or public demonstrations, but rather one that has carefully thought out the steps it will need to take if Inuit culture is to survive.

The Inuit of today are caught in a complex web of institutional networks that hinders their attempts to overcome their marginality in Canadian society. First, they have been burdened with a history of exploitation and neglect. Second, the opportunities for economic development have not been extensive. Today, even marginal activities such as fur production have been devastated by European interest groups. Other forms of economic development, such as natural resource development, require large "up front" and "sunken" capital that Inuit communities are unable to raise. Third, the ecology of the area makes it difficult for Inuit to develop cohesive organizational structures. Until recently, communication links were so tenuous that most Inuit communities acted in isolation. Fourth, the colonization of the Arctic by Euro-Canadian southerners has intruded into almost every institutional sphere of the Inuit.

The development of communication linkages among Inuit communities has provided the basis for organizational cohesion. Since television was introduced in the North in 1978, it has had both a positive and negative impact on the culture of Inuit. It was not until 1982 that the Inuit Broadcasting Corporation aired its first program, and not until a decade later that it provided a dedicated channel. Its broadcasts are solely in Inuktitut and reach nearly 100 communities in the Northwest Territories, Yukon, Quebec, and Labrador.

Out of these linkages have come political and interest group organizations, such as the Inuit Tapirisat of Canada, that have provided the basis for political mobilization. As the organizations become more stable and influential, Inuit become better able to exert their sphere of influence on the decisions that affect their lives. During the constitutional debate in 1992, Aboriginal people crashed the meeting at Harrington Lake. While the Inuit did not participate in this public confrontation, they did attempt to negotiate with other government (federal and provincial) officials to be included in the process. Although the Inuit overwhelming supported the Charlottetown Accord, it was defeated in a national referendum.

Inuit of the North are facing the issues of modernity and identity, as are other colonized peoples. Inuit are slowly being incorporated into the contemporary mainstream society of Canada. As Dorais (1997) points out, this inclusion brought with it the economic, political, and cultural institutions developed by Western capitalist societies. In many respects, these values and organizations do not reflect Aboriginal values and attitudes. The forces of modernity, such as delinking space and time, are evident in Inuit communities, and the intrusion of individualism and specialization are seen in the behaviour of individuals as well as in communities. These changes have brought about major changes in the way communities are organized, the way Inuit think about themselves, and the identity of the group. How Inuit will creatively deal with these forces and still remain Inuit is a major task set before them.

Summary

- Northern development is seen as the purview of southern outsiders.
- Public service organizations established in the North are replicas of those in the South.
- Urban settlement has been the major policy in developing the North.
- Natural resource extraction is the largest activity in the North and benefits transnational corporations.
- Development in the North has not involved northerners and has not resulted in true development for the region.
- Inuit are struggling to develop economic, political, and social infrastructure.

Key Terms

Alaska Native Claims
  Settlement Act p. 299
Compagnie du Nord
  p. 283
Inupiat p. 280
Inuit p. 279

Inuit cosmology p. 281
Inuit health p. 295
Inuktitut p. 305
Inuvialuit p. 285
Inuvialuit Settlement
  Region p. 300

Nunavut p. 302
Thule p. 279
western Arctic p. 281
Yupik p. 280

Questions for Further Discussion

1. Was the contact between Inuit and southern Canadians both beneficial and harmful? Why or why not?
2. What are the five tenets of Inuit culture?
3. How is Inuit health influenced by ecological, social, and nutritional changes?
4. What types of Inuit values will need to be taken into consideration when developing a course for Inuit economic development?
5. Why do many public service jobs remain unfilled in the North? What are the implications?
6. Why do Inuit people strive for self-government?

CHAPTER 10

Self-Determination and Self-Government: The Rights of Peoples

LEARNING OBJECTIVES

After reading this chapter you should be able to:

1. Explain the significance of the constitutional patriation.

2. Define self-determination.

3. Know the benefits of community-based self-government.

4. Identify the general principles of Indian government.

5. Understand the significance of the *Sechelt Act*.

6. Discuss the implications of an Aboriginal municipal government for self-government.

7. Discuss the major problems confronting Aboriginal groups in attempting to establish self-government.

INTRODUCTION

The quest of the Aboriginal people for self-determination and self-government has persisted since the first treaties were signed. For just as long, government policies have focused on assimilating Aboriginal peoples into the larger society (Wherrett, 1999; Hurley, 2009), and it would not be until late in the 20th century that Aboriginal people exercised limited federally delegated powers. However, the 1973 *Calder* case ruled that Aboriginal title existed prior to Confederation, heralding a new era of discussions between Aboriginal groups and the government (Dyck, 1996) and placing self-government back onto the negotiation table. During the late 1980s, there was a "three track" approach to **Aboriginal self-government**. On one track were the constitutional negotiations; at the same time, a second track of concurrent negotiations were taking place within communities. A third track was to introduce self-government within the comprehensive land claims settlements that were taking place.

Aboriginal peoples continue to make choices that maximize economic and social activities while struggling to maintain their group identity and political self-sufficiency. Aboriginal groups across Canada agree that the right to self-determination requires control over one's life both individually and collectively (Fontaine, 1998). Yet this struggle for self-determination takes place in a society that exhibits the ethos that Aboriginal cultures are doomed to extinction. This philosophy was in evidence throughout the past two centuries as vigorous measures were designed to undermine tribal authority and extinguish tribal ways of life (Laselva, 1998–99). Moreover, the approach of the federal government has been to unilaterally dictate the scope and content of "permissible" Aboriginal law-making.

That Aboriginal people are victims of colonialism and have, in their own homeland, been treated as inferior beings is unquestionable. As Laselva points out, the offer of equality has always been contingent upon the renunciation of their identity. First Nations peoples have rejected assimilation, exhibited the will to survive, and insisted on their right to self-government (Bell, 1998). Aboriginal people argue there needs to be a bilateral review process of issues such as the rule of law, a comprehensive claims policy, and land and resource rights because federal policy has not kept pace with the changing jurisprudence. Before delving into the issue of self-government, we must address the issue of a "right" and then place the issues of sovereignty and self-government in the Canadian historical context. We will then review the legal status of self-government for Aboriginal people. Finally we will provide some examples of how self-government is currently manifested in Canada.

THE CONCEPT OF RIGHT

As Doerr (1997) points out, the recognition of an inherent right is central to Aboriginal ideas of self-government and self-determination. The word "right" means that one person has an affirmative claim against another—that is, the other person has a legal duty to respect that right. Thus, the concepts of right and duty go hand in hand. However, the concept of right is not to be confused with that of privilege. The difference seems to lie in the fact that it is the absence of duty that identifies a privilege. The privilege to engage in a certain act arises where the privileged person has no duty to refrain from the privileged act. When people assert that they have a right, it means that they are confirming that they have a legal interest in an object, such as land. But whether someone else can change the nature of that legal interest depends on the powers and the immunities associated with that object. Powers are created by statute and involve the ability to change the nature of the interest. Anyone who tries to deny another's interest in an object but does not have the power to do so can be accused of acting *ultra vires*—that is, beyond the scope of the powers granted them by law (Henderson, 1978; Barsh and Henderson, 1982; Dupuis and McNeil, 1995).

The *St. Catharines Milling* case, decided in the late 19th century, was regarded as the precedent-setting case with respect to Aboriginal rights until 1973. The general import of the decision was that the source of Indian rights in Canada was the ***Royal Proclamation of 1763***. However, in 1973, the *Calder* case in British Columbia tentatively ruled that Indian rights were not dependent upon the *Royal Proclamation* but could be viewed as independent rights—that is, as rights independent from anyone's ruling or document. It was not until 1984, with the *Guerin* case, that the Supreme Court ruled that Aboriginal rights were derived from the original possession of the North American continent—in other words, that Indian interest in the land was a pre-existing legal right not created by the *Royal Proclamation,* by statute, or by executive order. This important ruling set the stage for the federal government's willingness to begin discussions with Aboriginal people with regard to self-government (Canada, 1983).

With the patriation of the Constitution in 1982, Aboriginal peoples finally had their Aboriginal and treaty rights recognized and affirmed. Section 32 of the Constitution explicitly states that all laws and policies in Canada must be consistent with these rights. While the federal government has accepted these guidelines in principle, in practice it continues to develop policy and programs that often run counter to the Constitution. Despite some progress, this opposition is most clearly seen in the area of land rights. Aboriginal people feel that their land rights should be recognized and that actions should be taken to reaffirm those rights. The government has taken the stance that it would like to extinguish the "burden" of Aboriginal rights (ONWA, 1983).

Needless to say, the government's position was found wanting by Aboriginal people and was finally called into question by the courts with the 1973 *Calder* v. *Attorney General of British Columbia* and the 1974 *Cardinal* v. *The Queen* rulings. Ten years later, *Nowegijick* v. *The Queen* (1983) and *Guerin* v. *The Queen* (1984) would reaffirm these earlier decisions and fundamentally alter the relationship between Aboriginal people and the government (both federal and provincial) (Anaya, Falk, and Pharand, 1995). Since these rulings, both parties have continued to try to resolve the question of rights and responsibilities, but by the beginning of the 21st century the underlying premises were to change yet again (Belanger, 2008).

During the 1980s and 1990s, because of international pressure and domestic priorities, the Canadian government tried to deal directly with the issue of Aboriginal rights. Specifically, the patriation of the Constitution led to a sense of urgency in resolving outstanding problems and issues. In the end, the government entrenched Aboriginal rights in the Constitution without really knowing or specifying what they entailed. The inclusion of the phrase "existing rights" has done little to clarify the meaning of the concept, although as Flanagan (1983a; 1985) points out, this may at some point provide a legitimate (legal) basis for excluding Métis Aboriginal rights claims—or certainly making it more difficult for the Métis to claim their rights.

The existence of Aboriginal rights in Canada must be understood in the context in which these rights are presented. On the one hand, there are a number of academics, historians, and legal advisors who are convinced of their existence based upon their assessments of the law and of history (Wilkins, 1999; Davies, 1985). On the other hand, when one considers case law, it appears that many trial judges are not of the same opinion. Past and current court decisions suggest that, if Aboriginal rights do exist, they take the form of personal usufruct—the right of an individual to occupy and use a piece of land—not collective, group rights. The *Baker Lake* decision (1980) is one notable exception to this rule.

The *Hamlet of Baker Lake* v. *Minister of Indian Affairs and Northern Development* decision arose out of a dispute between the Inuit around Baker Lake and the private corporations that were attempting to exploit the mineral potential in the area. In this case, Justice Mahoney ruled that the original Inuit had an organized society. He stated that they did not have a very elaborate system of institutions but that theirs was a society organized to exploit the resources available in the area. He also recognized the existence of Aboriginal land use rights *and* that these rights belonged to the Aboriginal **collectivity**. It follows that, if the collectivity has rights, it must also have the right to determine how it will exercise those rights.

An Aboriginal tribe, however, has no status as a legal entity under international law. It is generally accepted that, even though Indians were "sovereign and independent" societies before Europeans entered North America, this status was lost through the operation of European international law. The British and American claims tribunals have stated that an Indian tribe is not subject to international law and is a legal unit only insofar as the law of the country in which it lives recognizes it as such (Bennett, 1978; Gibbins, 1986b; Anaya, 2000).

However, international law has a more direct influence on how Canada deals with its Aboriginal people through the international treaties that have been signed and ratified by Canada. Breach of these treaties could bring international censure, judgment by the International Court of Justice, or an arbitration tribunal. Again, however, Aboriginal people have no international standing and thus cannot sue Canada for breach of its obligations toward them. It should also be noted that Canada is not legally bound by many international treaties because it has not signed them. The rationale for not signing them has two bases: (1) many of the matters involved are not under federal jurisdiction but are provincial, and (2) a concept of written codes of human rights seems to be contrary to common law and to the doctrine of parliamentary sovereignty (Culhane, 1998).

What legal or political conditions would be necessary for Aboriginal peoples to convince others that they have Aboriginal rights? Elliott (1991) has noted different ways it could be argued that such rights exist. One of the most easily recognized ways is through reference to royal prerogatives. These are statements issued by a government in the name of the sovereign with regard to a particular issue. They have the force of statutes. In Canada, the *Royal Proclamation* (1763) is an example of a royal prerogative. The *Royal Proclamation* was issued by King George III of Britain, and one section of it concerns Indian people: It suggests that Indians had a pre-existing title to lands. Some would argue, therefore, that it supports Aboriginal claims to Aboriginal rights. The section that deals with Indian people has never been repealed and thus still remains part of our legal system (Henderson, 1985). We now turn to the issue of jurisdiction and self-government.

JURISDICTION: WHERE FROM AND HOW MUCH?

The issue of self-government requires that we first determine what jurisdiction is being established. For example, are we talking about territorial or personal jurisdiction? Are we talking about exclusive or concurrent jurisdiction? And are we talking about legislative, executive, or judicial jurisdiction? (McNeil, 2007) Where does the right of jurisdiction come from? To answer this question requires an examination of whether the jurisdiction is inherent or delegated. All of these issues are important in the discussion of Aboriginal self-government and self-determination.

What do Aboriginal people expect when they claim they have the right to achieve self-government? Beginning with the source of jurisdiction, Aboriginal people are very clear that they see their right of self-government as an inherent right. Moreover, they view their political authority as emerging from a spiritual, not a secular, basis. As the Royal Commission on Aboriginal Peoples Report (1993) noted, "**Sovereignty**, . . . is the original freedom conferred to our people by the Creator rather than a temporal power. As a gift from the Creator, sovereignty can neither be given not taken away" (p.109).

The source of inherent jurisdiction is, for Aboriginal people, the Creator, with whom Aboriginal people have a special relationship. However, from a non-Aboriginal perspective, the source of jurisdiction of Aboriginal governments is viewed in more secular terms. For example, the Supreme Court has ruled that jurisdictional rights of Aboriginal

people emerge from the fact they occupied lands as a people long before European settlers took over the country. For most Canadians, the jurisdictional rights emerge from
a pre-existing sovereignty of Aboriginal nations or have been delegated by the federal
government. In short, the origins of jurisdiction take on a factual or historical basis, not a
spiritual one (McNeil, 2010).

Canadians view their legal system as more secular and as derived from the legal
structure of European thinking. Moreover, Canadians argue that if Aboriginal people are
to be given self-government rights, they must arise from the premise that the federal/
provincial/territorial governments delegate those rights. As such, while there is some
sympathy toward Aboriginal people and an inclination to give them some control over
their lives, considerable resistance to Aboriginal claims of inherent rights is evident in
Canadian society. In short, most Canadians would argue that self-government must come
about through delegation from the federal or provincial government.

We now turn to the issue of scope. Just how much authority do Aboriginal people
have? Is it all-encompassing or is the inherent authority limited to specfic matters such as
land and/or water? Aboriginal people argue that if the Creator had not given Aboriginal
people authority over a particular matter, it had then been retained by the Creator and
thus settlers could not come in and claim an interest in that matter. As McNeil (2007)
points out, even if there were limitations on the authority given to Aboriginal people by
the Creator, it would not produce a jurisdictional vacuum that could be filled by the colonizer. In short, the relationship between the Creator and Aboriginal people covers the
general understanding that the place of humans in the natural world is equal to other
aspects of the natural world. Accordingly, humans have a responsibility to ensure that all
elements of the natural world are respected

From the Aboriginal perspective, the scope of jurisdiction is total. It includes Mother
Earth, water, plants, animals (including humans), and all that exists. As such, there is no
void that allows Canadians to claim jurisdiction over issues that are not covered by the
totality of scope envisioned by Aboriginal people. From a non-Aboriginal perspective,
there is little agreement as to the source of Aboriginal rights or the scope of jurisdiction.
After a century of court decisions, two different perspectives have emerged regarding the
scope of Aboriginal jurisdiction. The first is exemplified by the *R* v. *Pamajewan* decision
in 1996. This decision basically stated that Aboriginal people do not have "general"
rights but rather have specific rights and thus are forced to demonstrate before the courts
that a specific right existed before European settlement. For example, in the Pamajewan
case, the court decided that gambling was not an integral activity in Aboriginal culture
before European settlement and thus their claim that they had a right to govern gambling
(casinos) was not acknowledged. Subsequent Canadian courts have concluded that in
order to claim jurisdiction over an activity, the Aboriginal community must meet the
"integral to the distinctive culture" test. In practical terms this means that each time
Aboriginal people want to claim a right, they will have to demonstrate it was an integral
component of their culture prior to European settlement.

A different approach to the issue of jurisdiction is to say that since Aboriginal people
were independent sovereign nations at the time of contact, they held the rights of all
encompassing activities. In this perspective, the onus is on the government to show how
certain rights were diminished or extinguished; through legislation, executive decree, or
negotiations. Thus, in this scenario, the "box" is full and those issues that have not been

diminished still remain in the box. Parties are now discussing what issues are to be placed in the self-government box and which issues will remain outside. However, to date, there has been little agreement as to what issues would be within the purview of Aboriginal government.

Finally, the issue of exclusive versus concurrent jurisdiction needs to be determined. Who has jurisdiction? Is the jurisdiction shared? Aboriginal people have argued that some aspects of self-government that deal with language, culture, and other internal community issues should be under the sole purview of Aboriginal people. At the same time, they are respectful that some issues, such as immigration, may be outside their scope of interest. However, with other matters, such as environmental protection, resource use and natural resource development, it is less clear as to whether they are should be Aboriginal or federal/provincial jurisdiction. In some cases, the issue has been solved by claiming there is "concurrent" jurisdiction. Again, there is considerable disagreement between government and Aboriginal people as to who has exclusive rights over certain issues. Government officials tend, in the first instance, to push for exclusive jurisdiction in which only they have control over various aspects of life. A fallback position is to argue for concurrent jurisdiction since it is the model they know best and would allow them to interfere with jurisdictional issues at any time or place (Graham, 2007).

CONSTITUTIONAL PATRIATION

Before we begin discussing sovereignty and self-determination, we need to place these ideas in their philosophical and political context. The federal government's desire to patriate the Constitution facilitated the efforts of Aboriginal people to bring their concerns to the fore and even raised several new issues. The discussion of constitutional issues provided a national and international forum for Aboriginal people to air their concerns about their inability to participate in Canadian society. The average Canadian could no longer claim to be ignorant of these issues, nor could elected representatives hide behind such a facade. The issues became public and were forcefully articulated by Aboriginal leaders, who also managed to convey a sense of urgency (Morse, 1991).

Until the late 1970s, the federal government's attempts to patriate our Constitution were vague and episodic. Eventually, however, constitutional reform won national attention because of (1) Quebec's threats to secede from Confederation, (2) the increasing alienation of the West, and (3) conflict between the federal and provincial governments (Gibbins, 1986b). Constitutional reform did not come about as a result of the concerns of Aboriginal people or lobbying efforts exerted by Aboriginal organizations. Nevertheless, Aboriginal people had become interested in the constitutional issue and had been active in the arena since the mid-1970s, when northern Aboriginal people developed and presented the *Dene Declaration*. This was followed by the Inuit's *Nunavut Proposal* and the Federation of Saskatchewan Indians' *Indian Government* proposal. In line with these new political philosophies, Indian organizations adapted to the new realities of the time; for example, the National Indian Brotherhood reorganized during the 1980–82 period and became the **Assembly of First Nations**. These political activities by Aboriginal groups were made possible through increased government funding and by the 1973 Supreme Court ruling in the Nisga'a land-claims case, which acknowledged (albeit indirectly) the existence of Aboriginal rights.

When the first constitutional amendment bill was introduced in 1978, only vague references were made to Aboriginal issues. This suggested that federal and provincial governments did not consider Aboriginal people to be an important element in Canadian society. It also seemed to imply that the 1969 *White Paper* (which would have done away with the legal concept of "Indian") was being implemented through the back door. Late in 1979, the Continuing Committee for Ministers on the Constitution (CCMC) met to decide how to handle further challenges and protests from Aboriginal people. They created a steering committee to meet formally with the three Aboriginal organizations representing status Indians, Inuit, and non-status Indians and Métis—the National Indian Brotherhood (NIB), the Inuit Committee on National Issues (ICNI), and the Native Council of Canada (NCC). The Federal–Provincial Relations Office (the federal body dealing with Aboriginal people on this issue) met both formally and informally with Aboriginal groups through the remaining months of 1979 (Bartlett, 1984).

When the 1980 First Ministers' Conference was held, specific "Aboriginal" concerns were not on the agenda, and Aboriginal peoples were invited only as observers. However, many matters under discussion directly affected Aboriginal peoples even though they were not distinctly "Aboriginal" issues; for example, provincial versus federal jurisdiction. Feeling completely excluded from the process, Aboriginal people chose to act in a more visible political manner, not just nationally but internationally as well (Sanders, 1983b). This resulted in increased international activity on the part of Aboriginal people and produced some coalitions among the three major Aboriginal groups as well as among non-Aboriginal organizations. In early 1981, the federal government relented and added two sections to the constitutional proposals that (1) protected the rights of Aboriginal peoples, and (2) required that future first ministers' meetings be held to deal with Aboriginal issues. Further amendments were introduced by the government that would have permitted it and any provincial government to come to a bilateral agreement nullifying the protection of Aboriginal peoples (Zlotkin, 1983). As a result, Aboriginal people, with the exception of the Inuit, withdrew their short-lived support of the first constitutional conference.

In late 1981, the Supreme Court ruled that a unilateral request by the federal government to the parliament of the United Kingdom to amend the Constitution was legal but not in keeping with tradition. But since the federal government wanted the provinces' support, it agreed to delete the clause affording protection to Aboriginal people from the final form of the November Accord of 1982. When it was announced, the Accord did not contain any clause recognizing or affirming Aboriginal or treaty rights. The Aboriginal groups strongly objected and created the Aboriginal Rights Coalition in protest. In addition, they began to intensify their international lobbying (Sanders, 1983a). It was also at this time that media support began to materialize on behalf of the Aboriginal people; for example, the *Globe and Mail* supported the entrenchment of Aboriginal rights. As a result of both domestic and international concern, the premiers agreed to reinstate the Aboriginal-rights clause with one change: "rights" was changed to "existing rights."

Aboriginal rights were finally entrenched in Section 35, which is Part II of the *Constitution Act,* and came into effect April 17, 1982. In addition, Section 25 of this Act (**Section 25 of the *Charter of Rights and Freedoms***) ensures that Aboriginal rights are not adversely affected by the *Charter of Rights and Freedoms* and recognizes the *Royal Proclamation* of 1763. Finally, Section 32 requires that the federal government convene

additional constitutional conferences to deal with Aboriginal peoples. The first conference, held in 1983, resulted in minor changes to Sections 25(b), 35, and 37 of the Constitution. Three additional first ministers' meetings were held to deal with Aboriginal issues.
However, none of these meetings produced any substantive results. (For a thorough review
of the first two conferences, see Schwartz, 1986.)

Between the first conference in 1983 and the last one in 1987, the *Penner Report* was
released, *Bill C-31* was passed, and the task force reviewing comprehensive claims policy
released its report. A new political climate was evident as the participants prepared for
the last conference, but internal discord emerged on the Aboriginal side, and a lack of
political will was apparent in the preliminary statements released by the premiers. The
talks, therefore, were doomed to failure before they began. Moreover, provincial officials
had quietly agreed among themselves to take a stand against the form of Indian self-
government being promoted by the Assembly of First Nations. The premiers were not
prepared to be innovative in their approach to Aboriginal issues, nor were they in any
mood to propose new policy directions themselves. In short, their chief concern was to
maintain the status quo while still fulfilling the requirement to hold this conference, as
was set out in the Charter in 1982 (Assembly of Manitoba Chiefs, 1994).

Aboriginal involvement in the constitutional patriation process had been based on
several premises. First, Aboriginal people saw the Constitution as a symbolic statement
about what is important in Canadian society. They also viewed the document as a potential lever for use in future political action. As Gibbins (1986a) pointed out, the inclusion
of Aboriginal people and their concerns in such important documents as a country's constitution legitimizes the group's interests and claims. In short, Aboriginal people felt that,
if they could be recognized as an important group in Canadian society, they could use this
as a stepping stone to further such aspirations as settling land claims and achieving sovereignty. They also wanted to influence the government with regard to Aboriginal and
treaty rights. Finally, they hoped that through their involvement in the patriation of the
Constitution, they would be able to exert pressure on the federal government to discuss
issues of sovereignty and self-government.

The initial involvement by Aboriginal groups in the constitutional talks was minimal
because of a lack of organization and funds. They did not offer any stance of their own in
regard to Aboriginal rights, but merely reacted to the federal and provincial governments'
vague pronouncements. It was only after debate had been initiated that Aboriginal groups
put forth more specific proposals with regard to Aboriginal, treaty, and land rights.
Federal and provincial officials reacted to these proposals by asking for more information
and clarification. The governments did not put forth any new proposals, but simply used
this strategy of stalling to maintain a benevolent image by never having to say no
(Schwartz, 1986). It also was during this time that Aboriginal people began to discuss the
issues of sovereignty and self-government. Although their concerns were initially dismissed by government officials, their persistence paid off. Slowly these issues entered the
public arena of discussion, and when the *Constitution Act, 1982,* was finally enacted,
Aboriginal rights had been entrenched.

The preamble to the *Constitution Act, 1982,* makes a significant statement on the
nature of Canadian culture: "Canada is founded upon principles that recognize the
supremacy of God and the rule of law." This assumption is implicitly insensitive to cultural differences and inappropriate for Aboriginal groups (e.g., the rule of law is not an

integral component of Aboriginal culture). Furthermore, the Charter does not support a collectivist idea of rights for culturally distinct (non-European) peoples. Turpel (1990) notes that the Charter largely expresses the values of a liberal democracy on the European model. With the exception of sections dealing with language and education rights, gender, multiculturalism, and Aboriginal rights, the Charter arguably favours individualism and assumes a highly organized and impersonal industrial society. The paradigm of individual rights is antithetical to the understanding of the individual's relationship to society widely shared by First Nations peoples.

In 1995, the Department of Aboriginal Affairs and Northern Development (then INAC), with the blessing of the federal government, accepted the inherent right of Aboriginal peoples to govern themselves. This is quite different from "delegated" jurisdiction or rights. In the case of the federal/provincial governments, they exercise legislative jurisdiction that was delegated to them through the *Constitution Act, 1867* from British parliament. Municipal legislation has been delegated through provincial delegation. However, Aboriginal people regard jurisdiction to be inherent and as such reject any delegated jurisdiction from the federal government. Moreover, Aboriginal people argue that this inherent jurisdiction is an Aboriginal right and thus built into the Canadian Constitution, which states that the existing Aboriginal and treaty rights of Aboriginal people are recognized and affirmed.

SOVEREIGNTY AND ABORIGINAL RIGHTS

The concept of sovereignty as defined by Aboriginal people implies the right of self-determination. This right, they argue, arises not only out of the various treaties, the *Constitution Act, 1867,* the *Royal Proclamation* of 1763, and assorted other federal acts, but also (and perhaps more importantly) as a gift from the Creator. This gift has never been, nor can it ever be, surrendered (Nadeau, 1979). Aboriginal people also argue that there are certain federal statutes (or documents that have the force of statutes) that specify that the federal government has a special trust relationship with them and is responsible for providing the resources that will enable them to achieve their goal of self-sufficiency. Aboriginal sovereignty and governance exist because they had their own government and economies prior to the arrival of the settlers. As such, Aboriginal sovereignty and governance exist independently of British constitutional law (Henderson, 2008).

Aboriginal organizations formally established their positions on this issue, but, partially because the various Aboriginal groups could agree and partially because the issue had not been fully analyzed, no precise statement on sovereignty, self-determination, or self-government had ever been articulated by Aboriginal groups or organizations. This changed with the publication of the the Royal Commission on Aboriginal Peoples and later with the Assembly of First Nations. Here, for the first time, alternative options were presented, though it was concluded that the specific form would vary from one First Nation to the next (Fleras and Elliott, 1992).

For ideological and practical reasons, governments have always argued against Aboriginal self-determination. From an ideological perspective, Canadians argue that all legal authority had been delegated to either the federal or provincial government and that there was nothing left to delegate (from the point of view of the *British North American Act*, for example). Furthermore, there is a belief by policy makers and government officials (evidenced by their support of the ***Indian Act***) that Aboriginal people have not yet become sufficiently "developed" to make major political and economic decisions. Finally, it is argued that Aboriginal people, as Canadian citizens, are subject to the federal and provincial levels of government. From a practical standpoint, few people could envisage over 600 (band) mini-governments—even the Royal Commission on Aboriginal Peoples suggested there might be as many as 60 First Nations governments. The economic implications of such an arrangement alone were mind-boggling (Mickenberg, 1971).

Aboriginal people began to demand the right to be recognized as distinct cultures with all the rights afforded to sovereign nations. They argued that when the existing Constitution was put in place, Aboriginal people were excluded and treated as a racial minority, rather than as a political community with full collective rights (Chartrand, 1993). They demanded that the two levels of government recognize them as a collective, "distinct society" with political rights (Deloria and Lytle, 1984). Aboriginal people began to demand policies and programs that would support Indigenous institutions and wanted the freedom to adopt (or not!) whatever non-Aboriginal institutions they thought were compatible with Aboriginal values. Aboriginal people have not merely asserted their rights or claimed that their goal was to "oust" the colonizers, but have pushed for what they see as their legitimate entitlement of self-government (Monture-Angus, 1999).

Aboriginal people want a new order of government that would be set within the Canadian Constitution and would guarantee the inherent right of Aboriginal people to be self-determining and self-governing (Bell, 1998). This new order of government would have the right to opt out of parts of the Canadian *Charter of Rights and Freedoms* under certain conditions. Aboriginal people want to be assured that they have the authority to make their own choices as to how they are governed (Hutchins, Hilling, and Schulze, 1999). For example, *Bill C-49* (Statutes of Canada, 1999—*First Nations Land Management Act*) gives signatory bands the power to expropriate land for community use and draft land codes. Aboriginal people argue that the Supreme Court has supported their basic objective of self-government. In the *Delgamuukw* case, the chief justice (of the Supreme Court of Canada) noted that the Crown is under a moral, if not a legal, duty to enter negotiations with Aboriginal people in good faith with the objective to achieve reconciliation of the pre-existence of Aboriginal societies with the sovereignty of the Crown (Laselva, 1998–99).

Cultural resurgence and the defence of territory are but two overt expressions of Aboriginal self-determination. The concept of self-determination was born during the French Revolution, though it has roots in earlier times. Our (and the Aboriginals') use of the term refers to the right of Aboriginal people to determine their political future and to freely pursue their cultural and economic development (Umozurike, 1972). Politically, this idea is expressed through independence, self-government, local autonomy, or some other defined form of increased participation in the governing process. In Canada, federalism and minority rights are fundamental constitutional principles and have acquired increased importance over the past several decades. Aboriginal people seek independence in order to ensure their self-determination and limit the extent of external domination.

Unfortunately, the concept of self-determination has been variously defined and interpreted. This has made cross-cultural communication between Aboriginal people and those non-Aboriginal people who discuss the issue rather problematic. Whatever unifying factors are used to define a people—for example, ethnicity, nationality, class, or race—are in the end simply arbitrary symbols, though profoundly meaningful for the people using them. The basis for unifying people may change over time or may contain more than one of these factors. It may also lead to different strategies being employed by different Aboriginal people to achieve the common goal of self-determination (Miller, 1991).

The existence of Aboriginal rights can be argued in Canada by reference to the decisions of the courts—that is, common law. As Elliott (1991) points out, two conflicting notions about Aboriginal rights have emerged out of common law. One was that the *Royal Proclamation* of 1763 gave Indians Aboriginal title, and the other was that Aboriginal title was derived from their use and occupancy of the land from time immemorial. As noted earlier, in 1973, Canadian common law on the issue of Aboriginal rights would change from an exclusive basis in royal prerogative to include a possible basis in use and occupancy. This new interpretation was based on the *Calder* v. *Attorney General of British Columbia* (1973) case. In this case, the Nisga'a Indians (represented by Calder) lost their land claims but won judicial recognition of the crucial issue that their claim to the land was based on their ancestors' occupation and use of it from time immemorial (Gibbins and Ponting, 1986).

Today, both arguments are used to support Aboriginal claims of Aboriginal rights. However, the question remains as to whether the *Calder* case stands as a general legal recognition of the validity of occupancy-based claims. The answer, unfortunately, is both yes and no. Some courts have recognized and accepted this argument, while others have not. A review of court decisions would suggest that lower Canadian courts have accepted occupancy-based title as a legitimate argument, while higher courts have not always given clear legal recognition to it (Elliott, 1991: 81; Federation of Saskatchewan Indian Nations, 1985; Green, 1983).

The third support for Aboriginal rights comes from the constitutional framework of a country (Henderson, Benson, and Findlay, 2000). While there has been no general legislation passed by the Canadian parliament that explicitly recognizes Aboriginal title, there are some pieces of legislation that implicitly apply to Aboriginal rights—for example, the *Manitoba Act, 1870*; the *Dominion Lands Act,* from 1872 to 1908; land cession treaties; and, of course, Sections 35 and 37(1) and (2) of the *Constitution Act, 1982.*

Then there is the issue of changing or extinguishing Aboriginal rights. Here the question is whether these rights can be legally terminated or otherwise changed so that they are not as comprehensive as previously thought. The law has provided for this possibility. Again, using Elliott's example of land title, one can point to treaties that were negotiated for the express purpose of obtaining land rights from Indians. The issue becomes more problematic, however, when actions taken by the government seem to extinguish Aboriginal rights (land title) while not explicitly saying so. This was one of the reasons the Supreme Court justices differed in their decisions with regard to the Nisga'a in the *Calder* case.

Finally, there is the question of compensation for Aboriginal rights. As Elliott (1991) noted, although many statutes provide for compensation when property is expropriated, there is no constitutional right to compensation. Even though the Canadian *Charter of Rights and Freedoms* provides for the right of the individual to life, liberty, and security of person, and the right not to be deprived of any of these except by due process of law, it does not address the matter of compensation when these rights are infringed upon or taken away. In other words, if private property is expropriated, there is no legal statute that forces the government to compensate for it (see Manville, 2001).

Aboriginal rights in Canadian law are still defined as work in progress, but two basic points are now clear. First, these rights are collective rights, which derive legal force from common-law recognition of the legitimacy of the prior occupancy and use of certain territories. Second, the essence of the common-law view of these rights is that they protect whatever it was that the organized society of Aboriginal peoples did before coming into contact with Europeans. To date this has focused Aboriginal concerns mainly on land use and occupancy (usufruct), but, logically speaking, Aboriginal rights could include many other social activities, such as the determination of descent, family and kinship matters, and ceremonial practices. This, of course, is what is now being discussed under the rubric of self-government.

Regardless of how tentative and vague the above issues may appear, the *Constitution Act, 1982*, Section 35(1), recognizes and affirms *existing* Aboriginal rights. What these rights are has been the subject of intense debate. Aboriginal people argue that they include a number of general concerns, such as education, self-government, and housing. But others feel that the list needs to be more specific. The task before the courts and politicians is to define and outline exactly what "existing" Aboriginal rights are.

If the evidence overwhelmingly points to the existence of Aboriginal rights, why have they not been acted upon? First, for a number of years government officials simply refused to acknowledge that Aboriginal people had specific claims or rights beyond that of ordinary Canadian citizens. Government officials also acted in a unilateral fashion to suspend certain rights through a variety of procedures. For example, it would not be until the second half of the 20th century that Aboriginal persons had federal voting rights. In other cases, historical documents were not released, were kept hidden, or were ignored as not relevant to the case at hand. Still other procedures were implemented to keep Aboriginal groups from pursuing various claims—for example, preventing lawyers from accepting monies to act on behalf of Indian peoples. The end result was that Aboriginal claims, whatever they were, were defined by Canadians as not of sufficient importance for federal or provincial officials to pursue; Aboriginal rights were considered to be a myth perpetuated by Aboriginal people.

After the 1973 *Calder* Supreme Court decision, both levels of government had to face the legitimacy of Aboriginal claims. The government's initial reaction was to claim that rights had been repealed, rendered inoperative, or extinguished. Others believed Aboriginal rights had been "superseded" by federal and/or provincial legislation. As Clark (1994: 149) pointed out, this might have been appropriate if Aboriginal self-government had been constituted as domestic common law instead of being confirmed by imperial legislation. In other cases, provincial governments claimed that the 1763 *Royal Proclamation* did not apply to them; other rulings suggested that the *Quebec Act, 1774*, repealed the *Royal Proclamation* and as such it was not operative. And so on. Whatever the basis, the government argued that Aboriginal claims had been extinguished, or at least derogated, from the constitutional character of the protection identified by the *Royal Proclamation*. However, it soon became clear enough that the number of court rulings in favour of Aboriginal peoples' claims increasingly supported the Aboriginal position. As a result of these court decisions and a concurrent change in the public's attitude toward the rights of Aboriginal people, the federal government embarked upon a new policy for Indian affairs.

One might ask why Aboriginal people didn't pursue their claim of Aboriginal rights more vigorously. In other words, if the case is clear that Aboriginal people have certain rights (e.g., land and self-government), why did they not directly challenge the federal government? The answer lies in the practical realities of implementing these rights. The federal government has to anticipate the administrative and financial costs involved in attempting to implement many different Aboriginal governments; for example, assuming that each band achieved self-government, there would be over 600 different Aboriginal governments (Ponting and Gibbins, 1980). Government officials would be concerned with the cost of operating such a structure. There would also be the cost of reparation to Aboriginal peoples by the Canadian government—that is, if the federal government accepted the inherent right to self-government, then under the rulings outlined in many recent court cases, compensation would have to be made to those bands that expressed a desire to achieve self-government in the past but were thwarted by the federal government. As a result, government officials have steadfastly rejected the idea of Aboriginal rights, irrespective of court decisions. Nevertheless, as legal decisions continue to uphold and reinforce Aboriginal claims—claims to self-government, to land, and to the government's fiduciary responsibility to Aboriginal people—the federal government has been held accountable to deal publicly with these ideals.

The question still remains as to why Aboriginal people have not "forced the hand" of government to recognize their specific claims. This would mean pursuing additional court cases and running the risk of not having their cases upheld. The *Delgamuukw* v. *British Columbia* case, for example, supported their suspicions. Even though that decision was later reversed by a higher court, the claims of Aboriginal groups remained in suspension until a higher court ruled. Aboriginal people have always viewed the courts as foreign institutions that they do not fully understand and trust. Perhaps even more important is the issue of money. It is all very well to force the government, through the courts, to admit to the existence of such rights as self-government. However, even if such rights were publicly recognized, the government is not obligated to bear the cost of the resulting administrative structures—it would be a pyrrhic victory for Aboriginal people.

Because of these issues, Aboriginal people and the federal government have tried to establish a common ground for dealing with Aboriginal rights claims from which a compromise acceptable to both parties would result. The federal government developed its first strategy to deal with this problem in the 1973 *Indian Affairs Policy Statement*. This document noted that the government was determined to find the most effective way of giving Aboriginal peoples control over their affairs. It clearly stated that the government was aware of the problem of Aboriginal claims and was prepared to do something about it. However, the statement was equally clear in developing a policy that preserved the government's view of its reality. For example, while the federal government acknowledges the Aboriginal right of self-government, the only form of self-government defined as acceptable in the initial stages of discussion was the delegated-municipal style. This position was buttressed by the federal government's concurrent policy that self-government would be dealt with in all comprehensive land claims. This strategy for enticing Aboriginal people to accept self-government under these conditions focused on providing Aboriginal people with funds if they were willing participants in the process of negotiating their claims, whatever they were. The acceptance of negotiation as a mode of decision making meant that the government would not have to relinquish decision making to an independent third party—e.g., the courts. And, by not allowing the courts the right to make decisions, the government avoided the possibility of any (in its view) unacceptable decision confirming Aboriginal rights—such as inherent traditional self-government. Aboriginal people caught between the confirmation of rights and the lack of funds to implement them then sought to enter the negotiation process in the belief that they could achieve both goals. They did so on the basis of past actions they had undertaken with regard to the federal government and the belief that they could replicate the results. For example, the gains Quebec Cree achieved when they dropped their court case—a guaranteed annual income, a land base, and funds to operate Aboriginal businesses—gave some support to this view. In other cases, bands were able to negotiate specific claims that they felt were in their favour, instead of taking the long, expensive route through the courts.

THE CONCEPT OF SELF-GOVERNMENT

As Clark (1994) points out, the concept of self-government must be distinguished from self-management and administration. These latter terms refer to managing or administering laws that have been created and put in place by other legal entities. The history of the Aboriginal claim to self-government is long, although for over a century government officials simply denied its existence. It would not be recognized until the *Calder* (1973) decision, when the Supreme Court of Canada ruled that Aboriginal title is a legal right. Ten years later the *Constitution Act* established that Aboriginal rights and treaty rights both exist and may be acquired, recognized, and affirmed. In 1990, the Supreme Court (*Sparrow*) ruled that in order to extinguish Aboriginal rights, there had to be "clear and plain intention," and if not, then those rights continued. In *Delgamuukw* (1997), the courts confirmed that Aboriginal title exists and is a right to the land as well as to hunting, fishing, and gathering rights. In 2005, the B.C. Supreme Court ruled that self-government is an Aboriginal right, thereby solidifying the 1995 announcement by the Government of Canada that Aboriginal self-government is inherent (Morellato, 2003). Moreover, legal experts suggest that not only should Canadian jurisprudence achieve reconciliation with Aboriginal peoples, but also that this accommodation or adaptation protects Aboriginal governance rights and provides opportunities for their expression. Nevertheless, the notion of "inherent rights" and sovereignty independent of a particular form of government is foreign to Canadian thinking—that is to say, Canada has always followed a European political tradition in which sovereignty is tied to a particular form of government (Bish, 1990).

As noted, until the late 1970s, the federal and provincial governments' response to demands for Indian self-government was an adamant no. They took the position that they could not recognize Indian sovereignty because the only sovereignty that existed in Canada was vested in the Crown. Therefore, if any group claimed sovereignty on any other basis—such as use and occupancy from time immemorial—governments were not prepared to discuss or even consider it. It was not until the constitutional debates of the early 1980s and the First Ministers' Conferences in the mid-1980s that the federal government agreed to act on the issue. The Supreme Court's ruling in the *Musqueam* case (1985) persuaded the two levels of government to rethink their position. In that case, the Supreme Court recognized that Indian sovereignty and Indian rights are independent and apart from the Crown. The court ruled that these rights flow from Indian title and Indian occupation and from no other source (Cardinal, 1986). Nevertheless, provincial governments remain highly skeptical of such a change, although they did not overtly challenge the issue. Their concerns about Aboriginal self-government and their willingness to discuss the issues emerged out of their growing recognition of the increased role they might play in Aboriginal affairs. They were also acutely aware of the federal government's thinking. For example, Indian Affairs published its *Directional Plan of the 1980s,* in which it argued that Indians, instead of using so many federal programs and resources, should take advantage of more provincial programs and resources. Other federal documents, such as the *Nielsen Study Team Report* (1986) and the *Indian and Native Sector* (1986), reiterated these strategies (Harvey, 1996).

The federal government has taken the position that given the different circumstances of Aboriginal peoples across the country, self-government may not be the same from one region of the country to the next. Moreover, Indian, Inuit, and Métis peoples have different needs, and these differences must be respected as self-government programs are developed. In addition, the government takes the position that the implementation of self-government may occur through a variety of mechanisms such as treaties, legislation, contracts, and memoranda of understanding. The federal government argues that the cost of self-government is to be shared among the federal, provincial, territorial, and Aboriginal governments. And, to that end, the government requires that an agreement on cost-sharing among the various parties be established before the beginning of negotiations (Hurley, 2009).

In addition, the central objective of the federal government is to reach an agreement with Aboriginal peoples regarding self-government as opposed to legal definitions of the "inherent right." Thus far, the government is prepared to give Aboriginal jurisdiction to matters that are internal to Aboriginal people, integral to its distinct Aboriginal culture, and essential to its operation as a government or institution. At the same time, the government argues that there are matters for which there is no compelling reason for Aboriginal governments to have authority (e.g., defence, immigration).

Although these federal policies have only selectively been implemented, they certainly influenced the provinces' perception of how the federal government planned to act in the future and have forced them to develop strategies to deal with the possible changes in policy. Because there are significant differences in political philosophies among provinces, there would be both constitutional and practical implications to consider. As a result, there are several different stances evident among individual provinces: Alberta insists that Indians are a federal responsibility, while Quebec's position is more ambiguous (Calder, 1986; Gadacz and McBlane, 1999).

From the other side, there has never really been a single position among Aboriginal groups as to what self-government means or how it is to be implemented (Cardinal, 1986). Aboriginal people have argued that there is an inherent right of citizens to create and control their own governments. As such, citizens will create different governments for different purposes, and there may be more than one form of government applicable to different groups of people.

In summary, there is, from an Aboriginal perspective, no single model of governance but rather there are different models for different peoples and for different functions (Bish, 1990). First Nations people have insisted that their inherent sovereignty defines and formalizes them as a fourth level of government. Inuit, on the other hand, prefer to develop a provincial-type government because they occupy a large land base and make up nearly all of the population of that area. Finally, non-status Indians and Métis have publicly accepted the fact that any government for them will have to be delegated by the provincial or the federal government. Clearly, because of different historical experiences, the evolution of Aboriginal–non-Aboriginal relationships has not been the same for the three major Aboriginal groups (Hawkes, 1985).

Nevertheless, there is some agreement on what is embodied in the concept of self-government. In general terms, Aboriginal people agree that self-government (or autonomy) implies that important national issues will remain within the territorial jurisdiction of the provincial or federal government, but First Nations will enjoy the freedom to regulate certain of their own affairs without interference (Kulchynski, 1994; Hylton, 1994). While no list of issues has been drafted, general principles of democracy, justice, and equality would be supported. Other rights, such as freedom of speech, the right to be judged by one's peers, and equal access to educational and economic institutions, would also be supported. By granting autonomy to Aboriginal peoples, the government would acknowledge that certain rights are to be given to a specific segment of the country's population, which needs protection in view of the way that many of its characteristics differ from those of the majority of the population. Autonomy would also allow the people inhabiting a local area to exercise direct control over important affairs of special concern to them, while allowing the larger entity, which retains certain powers over the local area and other areas, to exercise those powers that are in the common interest of both Aboriginal and non-Aboriginal people (Umozurike, 1972). In order to preserve Aboriginal culture, language, and religion, Aboriginal people would prefer to have complete control over their own schools, and would prevent the federal and provincial governments from interfering with their traditional way of life. Because they perceive that they are different from the majority of Canadians, they insist on different rights to maintain their uniqueness (Englestad and Bird, 1993).

Aboriginal leaders would like to have a fourth order of government—one that fits with their notion of sovereignty. They see self-government as a means of allowing them to achieve three central goals: (1) to increase local control and decision making; (2) to recognize and respond to the diverse needs and cultures of Aboriginal peoples throughout Canada; and, (3) to provide accountability to local electors rather than to a federal bureaucracy. This new order of government would have powers similar to those of the federal and provincial governments. It would, for example, have full jurisdiction over such areas as resources, education, social development, and taxation (McMahon and Martin, 1985).

LEGAL AND POLITICAL ISSUES

Within the federal system there are different levels of government. As Rieber (1977) pointed out, each level relates directly to the immediately superior level from which it receives its enabling organizational act. However, when Aboriginal government is introduced, a potential new structure emerges. In this organizational structure, Aboriginal people would not only relate to the federal government (in its trust relationship) but also to lower levels of government.

The major problems confronting Aboriginal groups in attempting to establish self-government are diverse and extensive (see the papers in Hylton, 1994). For example, as noted earlier, the issue of jurisdiction and subrogation must be resolved before the process can continue. This latter issue is the process whereby, as a consequence of a change of territorial sovereignty, there is a legal transfer of liabilities or of rights and duties arising from treaties and other international agreements. Added to this problem is the level of government with which Aboriginal people have to deal on any specific issue. For example, Aboriginal people are part of the tripartite (Aboriginal–federal–provincial) structure in which jurisdictional issues can arise in any one of the three relationships: Aboriginal–federal, Aboriginal–provincial, and provincial–federal. In some cases, issues fall clearly along one of the arms of this triangle. For example, reserves are clearly in the Aboriginal–federal arm of the triangle, except under certain circumstances. Other issues of relevance to Aboriginal people are domain (jurisdictional specification over property), fishing and hunting rights, law enforcement, financing, economic development, community development, and off-reserve Indian rights (Paton, 1982). Are these Aboriginal–federal or Aboriginal–provincial?

According to the *Indian Act*, neither the band nor the band council can be incorporated for the purpose of establishing a band government. Since Aboriginal peoples are pressuring the federal government for local self-government, this problem must be resolved. Any solution must include both the legal and political issues at stake. For example, a municipal government might act in a fashion appropriate to a province, or it might act in a fashion appropriate to itself as a municipality. This means that, in part through social necessity, even though municipalities are created by the province, they are able to control their own affairs (e.g., pass bylaws, levy taxes, and create policy and programs). The federal government would like Aboriginal self-government to be modelled on municipal government. Aboriginal people, on the other hand, reject this proposal, wishing to establish their own form of government that would not be dependent on the provincial governments for some issues and on the federal government for others (Cassidy and Bish, 1989; Ponting, 1997).

Poelzer (nd.) argues that self government is the primary means by which Aboriginal people can formalize their relationship to their lands and resources as well as preserve their culture. And, in doing so, they will have the necessary autonomy to make decisions about their future. The road to self-government began with the *Calder* (1973) Supreme Court decision that found that if there is an Aboriginal historic presence on the land, Aboriginal title could be recognized as common law without the support of federal or provincial government. This decision was followed in 1982 by the creation of **Section 35 of the *Constitution Act*,** which states Aboriginal and treaty rights are affirmed. Eight years later the Supreme Court in the *Sparrow* (1990) and *Sioui* (1990) cases ruled that these Aboriginal rights would remain in place unless there was clear and explicit evidence they were extinguished. By 1997 (*Delgumuukw*), the Supreme Court confirmed that Aboriginal title exists and that when dealing with Crown land, the government must consult with Aboriginal people. More recently, in 2001 the B.C. Supreme Court ruled that self-government is an Aboriginal right and is one of the underlying values of the Constitution that remains outside the powers that were distributed to parliament and/or the provincial legislatures. Thus, from a legal perspective, there is considerable evidence that Aboriginal people have the right of self-government.

A Historical Précis: The Federal Government's Position

After the *Calder* decision, Ottawa introduced its community-based self-government policy and began negotiating with specific Aboriginal communities. Aboriginal people have long argued that they require an authority base that would allow them, collectively, to advance their own interests, and they vigorously resisted the early efforts of the federal government to implement this policy. Aboriginal people held that this authority had to derive from their Aboriginal title and not from parliament (Tennant, 1984). They claimed that they originally had a system of self-government that regulated their internal and external relations (Boldt, Long, and Little Bear, 1985). As Aboriginal organizations lobbied for self-government during the 1970s, DIAND developed a policy (without consulting Aboriginal people) to create "band" governments within the structure of the *Indian Act.* This devolutionary process was to lead to an entirely new relationship between Aboriginal people and the government. Each band would be given the opportunity to choose the form and structure of a type of self-government that it saw fit for itself. This policy was rejected by Aboriginal people because it failed to recognize the Aboriginal source of authority (Tennant, 1984).

The rejection of DIAND's proposed self-government policy led to the creation of a special federal committee that was charged with reviewing all legal and related institutional factors affecting the status, development, and responsibilities of band government on Indian reserves. The **Penner Report**, produced by the special committee, listed 58 recommendations designed to integrate Aboriginal people into Canadian society. The most relevant for our purposes are the recommendations that Aboriginal people should have self-government and that this should be recognized as an Aboriginal right. As Tennant (1984) observed, the committee recommended that the Indian governments should derive their existence and legitimacy not from parliament or legislation, nor even from the Constitution, but from a pre-existing (inherent) right. The committee proposed legislation that would have the federal and provincial governments recognize Indian governments, author federal–Indian agreements, and allow Indians to govern themselves (Tennant, 1984). Finally, the committee recommended that the Indian band-government legislation proposed by DIAND be rejected and that new legislation be implemented to clear the way for a different form of Indian self-government. In summary, the *Penner Report* called for a new order of government to be established in order to incorporate Aboriginal people into Canadian society. The primary unit of self-government would be the band. Thus each Indian governing body would then be related to the two higher levels of government through the band government.

DIAND and the Assembly of First Nations (AFN) quickly responded to the recommendations of the committee. At the end of 1983, a draft policy, *Indian Nations Recognition and Validating Act,* was completed by DIAND officials. This proposed act formally recognized Indian First Nations and allowed each nation to enact legislation independently of Canada as long as it did not conflict with the laws of parliament. The federal government responded in early 1984. It refused to accept self-government as an *Aboriginal right.* Nevertheless, it agreed to drop the band-government legislation and began investigating the possibility of implementing the spirit of the *Penner Report.*

The result was the creation of a new committee consisting of a number of people from the constitutional unit of the then DIAND and the public-law unit of the Ministry of Justice. Their job was to draft new legislation that would incorporate the recommendations of the *Penner Report* but would also be palatable to parliament. The first draft was rejected by the Priorities and Planning Committee of the cabinet. New officials were then added to the committee drafting the legislation. In June 1984, *Bill C-52, An Act Relating to Self-Government for Indian Nations,* was introduced. While some of the recommendations of the *Penner Report* were part of this bill, it was little more than a reformulation of the old band-government legislation. As parliament dissolved, so did the bill and the policy alliance that had formed between AFN and the government in the workings of the special committee.

To reiterate, self-government for Aboriginals means that they, as First Nations, will govern their own people and their own affairs, including land and its use. Self-government flows from Aboriginal rights, which provide for the right of a people's cultural survival and self-determination (Leonard, 1995). Specifically, this would exempt them (or at least protect them) from the application of laws of another jurisdiction (Ahenakew, 1985; Plain, 1985). Aboriginal proposals for self-government call for a new order of government with powers similar to those of a province. In fact, some proposals have even suggested that the Indian First Nations would have the right to sign international treaties and to issue valid passports (Dalon, 1985). These proposals have been summarily rejected by both levels of government. There was a great fear that until all the implications of self-government were clear, it could not be entrenched in the Constitution or given even tentative support (Dalon, 1985; Long, Boldt, and Little Bear, 1983).

Nevertheless, the federal government's proposal did not suggest that each band's authority would come from its status as a sovereign entity. Rather, the authority was seen to exist because the federal government chose to delegate it to the band. Aboriginal people have objected vociferously to this stance. They are adamant that self-government is an inherent right, not a contingent right (i.e., "at the pleasure of the Crown"). They pointed out that an all-party committee (the Special Committee on Indian Self-Government, 1983) endorsed their constituency's right to self-government. At the same time, as Dyck (1991) asserted, there must be no illusion about the difficulties that would be encountered in trying to implement the process. Anderson, Benson, and Flanagan (2006) note that, over time, Aboriginal people have become more adept at resisting authority than exercising it, and this will have to change if self-government is to succeed.

Aboriginal people wanted to entrench their rights in the Constitution by establishing a form of Aboriginal government outside the framework of the *Indian Act* (Weaver, 1984; Tennant, 1984). One year after *Bill C-52* was introduced, the Mulroney Conservatives replaced the Turner Liberals in office, and the government presented new legislation in parliament to allow for the recognition of Indian government—*Bill C-93*. The proposed legislation was not meant to displace (or act as a substitute for) constitutional processes and initiatives. It was explicitly noted that it would not detract from existing Aboriginal and treaty rights affirmed in the Constitution (Long, Boldt, and Little Bear, 1982).

This proposed legislation was not really what Indian people had in mind when they raised the matter of self-government. (See, for example, the Assembly of First Nations' *Proposed 1985 Constitutional Accord Relating to the Aboriginal Peoples of Canada*, First Ministers' Conference on Aboriginal Constitutional Matters, 1985.) Aboriginal peoples believe that, in order to survive as a cultural entity, they must have a land base and self-government. The government, although agreeing in principle, would first like to see the broad parameters as it maps out its response. For example, are they land-based? If so, this might be an appropriate model for Indians and Inuit but not necessarily for Métis. In addition, neither the provincial governments nor the federal government are prepared to include in the concept of self-government the notions of full independence or sovereignty. Although Aboriginal people do view self-government as an inherent right, they have always pictured its expression as taking place within the Canadian political system (Hawkes, 1985). They also believe that self-government could be attained even without a land base if there were guaranteed representation for Aboriginal peoples in the House of Commons, the provincial legislatures, and the senate.

The First Nations Position: The Point of Departure

Cornell and Kalt (2001) point out that at the heart of nation building is sovereignty—in other words, who is in charge of making decisions? While this has been sought by Aboriginal peoples for nearly a century, the federal and provincial governments have resisted such a change. The governments continue to argue that their definition of treaty rights, Aboriginal rights, funding obligations, and fiduciary duties are correct, while those of Aboriginal people are wrong. Rather than seek a resolution to the differences, the governments refuse to negotiate issues such as self-government. As the Auditor General (2006) pointed out in her assessment of the B.C. negotiations with Aboriginal people, after more than 10 years of negotiations, at a cost of $726 million dollars, there were no treaties, no resolution on self-government, and no settlement of a comprehensive land claim. This inflexibility shown by provincial and federal governments has not led to good governance structures in Aboriginal communities, nor has this approach led to a better quality of life for Aboriginal people.

How did Aboriginal people react to the legislation and initiatives concerning Aboriginal self-government proposed early on by the federal government and the then DIAND? And what is their overall position (despite the fact there has never been a single position among all Aboriginal groups) as to what self-government means or entails? In 1975, the National Indian Brotherhood passed a resolution that in part stated a need for a phased approach to the revision of the *Indian Act*. It also put forth the principle of optional adoption by bands of any revised provisions of the Act (Hawkes, 1985). However, Aboriginal people today argue that, because the political scene is radically different than in 1975, this resolution is no longer applicable; they consider it obsolete. They further argue that if the federal government had consulted with them, they would have long ago realized that this was no longer a viable position for Aboriginal people to hold.

The general principles of Aboriginal government might be summarized as follows. These principles may not be fully endorsed by all Aboriginal people, but they would seem to be those that are most consistently advocated. Aboriginal people argue that *sovereignty exists in and of its own right.* It is a gift from their Creator, which has never been and can never be surrendered. In pre-contact times, Aboriginal people formed a variety of political units, with their own governments and other institutions. They claim that, with colonization, their right to exercise their sovereignty was unjustly abrogated and ignored, and their political institutions were systematically dismantled. But, as in the past, they continue to assert their sovereignty and the right to create their own unique institutions of self-government.

In accordance with the principle of self-determination, Aboriginal people want to exercise their right to make and administer decisions on all matters pertaining to themselves and their lands. Aboriginal government is the expression of this inherent right of sovereign nations to self-determination. First Nations claim to have exclusive legislative, executive, and administrative jurisdiction over their lands and resources and over the people within their territories. First Nations territory would have three components: (1) land and territory as presently recognized; (2) territory to which there is a valid claim; and (3) those hunting, fishing, trapping, and gathering territories not included in the first two components. First Nation governments would have jurisdiction over all persons on First Nations land and exclusive jurisdiction in determining First Nations citizenship. They would be responsible for peace, order, and good government within Indian territory and for the maintenance and well-being of First Nations people. First Nations jurisdiction would not be limited to First Nations territory when matters of social and cultural responsibility for its citizens extend beyond it (Hodgins, Heard, and Milloy, 1992). In point of fact, where First Nations have successfully negotiated comprehensive land claims agreements, there has also been the successful establishment of Aboriginal governments with wide-ranging jurisdictions and powers (see Box 10.1).

Indian people would continue to develop their own constitutions. They themselves would determine whether they choose to be single units or to amalgamate to pursue common goals as Indian nations. The actual form that these political units take would be based on the needs and aspirations of the Indian people involved. Aboriginal people feel that the rights confirmed by the *Royal Proclamation,* the *British North America Act,* the treaties, and the trust relationship between Indians and the federal government mean that the Government of Canada is responsible for providing the resources, including land, that would enable Aboriginal governments to attain their goal of economic self-sufficiency. Of course, self-government *in practice* might end up looking quite different.

Box 10.1	Self-Government in 2010

In 1984, the Mi'kmaq of Miawpukek were recognized by the federal government as a band under the *Indian Act*. Since then, band members have expanded their jurisdiction over lands and resources. Today the band exercises local control over band administration, membership, elections, schools, and on-reserve lands. In 2008 it began to develop a community-based constitution for the entrenchment of its rights of self-determination. The community began with the belief that self-government is about Aboriginal government passing and making decisions on matters:

- internal to their communities;
- integral to their unique culture, traditions, and language;

- connected to their special relationship to the land and its resources.

The Mi'kmaq constitution is designed to establish a future that will see Aboriginal people in control of their destiny. The goal is to restore legitimate and accountable Aboriginal government and a sense of ownership and responsibility for what happens in the community. It will create the foundation for a renewed relationship and an improved quality of life for Aboriginal people in the community, which in turn will attract economic development and foster self-sufficiency.

The preamble incorporates the shared values and provisions for a

Miawpukek constitution that are based on Mi'kmaq customs and traditions and will establish rules governing the Miawpukek First Nation with regard to law-making, leadership, accountability, conflict of interest, rights of appeal, and redress. In addition, this agreement outlines how individual and collective rights will be respected and how Miawpukek laws and federal laws will coexist.

The framework agreement defines the relationship between all governments and establishes the guidelines for the negotiation of sub-agreements, including jurisdiction and/or authority to be exercised by the Miawpukek First Nation. This process includes specific rules for resolving conflicts between laws and for identifying those *Indian Act* provisions that will no longer apply, as well as ratification procedures.

SELF-GOVERNMENT IN THE NEW MILLENNIUM

There are a number of models by which Aboriginal people can achieve self-governance. Some of the models proposed by Aboriginal people suggest a high degree of political separation from Canada such that they would become "states" in their own right. In other cases, Aboriginal people have not argued such extreme positions but maintain they are "a nation within," and as such have both sovereignty and control over a number of jurisdictional activities. This latter model is most representative of the political position that most Aboriginal people have taken in their negotiations with the federal government. Their position is not to fully secede from Canada and establish a new "state," but rather to dismantle that part of the political and economic structure that denies them their rightful place as original occupants of Canada (Maaka and Fleras, 2008). Maaka and Fleras compared the different models shown in Table 10.1

In 1995, the federal government established a policy and process by which it would be able to accept the principles of Aboriginal self-government. In developing the policy, the government consulted widely with Aboriginal people from across the country, including

TABLE 10.1	Typology of Different Models of Self-Government	
Statehood	**Nationhood**
de jure sovereignty	de facto sovereignty
full (internal and external) autonomy	some autonomy and control
complete independence	"a nation within"
community	institutional
functional sovereignty	nominal sovereignty
community-based autonomy	institutional decision making
limited jurisdiction	creation of parallel structures

Source: Adapted from Maaka and Fleras (2008).

provincial and territorial governments in the discussions. Today the government's position is that it recognizes the inherent right of self-government as an existing right within Section 35(1) of the *Constitution Act, 1982*. As such, it reasons that negotiations with Aboriginal peoples are the preferable approach, and litigation is a last resort. In addition, because self-government may take many different forms, the federal government feels that their provincial counterparts are necessary parties to the negotiations. However, there are limits to the recognition of Aboriginal self-government: Aboriginal self-government does not include a right of sovereignty in the realm of international law, nor will it result in sovereign independent Aboriginal nation states. As such, any agreement and form of self-government stipulates that the *Charter of Rights and Freedoms* will apply to Aboriginal governments and institutions. Negotiations with Aboriginal groups will include a wide array of issues, including membership, marriage, education, social services, policing, property rights, taxation, hunting, housing, local transportation, and a host of others. Any arrangement will have to be harmonized with existing Canadian laws (Daugherty, Wayne, and Magill, 1980).

How will these agreements be implemented? There are a number of ways. For example, new treaties and agreements, parts of comprehensive land claims, and addenda to existing treaties continue to be the favoured strategies. However, other mechanisms have been identified by which self-governing arrangements will be implemented. These include actual legislation, contracts, and non-binding memoranda of understanding (MOU) or memoranda of agreement (MOA). There also is recognition that the form and process of achieving self-government may be different for the various Aboriginal groups, and these have been identified. For example, in the policy paper, there is an explicit recognition of the different groups—First Nations, Inuit communities, Métis and Indian groups without a land base, Métis with a land base, and Aboriginal groups in the western Northwest Territories. The policy recognizes that Aboriginal self-government may have an impact upon third parties. As such, the process of negotiating self-government has become public, with provinces, municipalities, and other interest groups becoming party to the negotiations. The 1999 Sechelt treaty is a good example of how the community can be part of the overall process, but it is not the only one.

It is probably difficult to ascertain the specifics of what is involved in the notion of Aboriginal self-determination or Aboriginal rights. Here is a summary of the central tenets of self-government from the perspective of Aboriginal peoples. The following four factors are key to Aboriginal thinking on self-government:

1. *Greater self-determination and social justice.* Protection of and control over one's own destiny, rather than subordination to political and bureaucratic authorities based outside the group.

2. *Economic development to end dependency, poverty, and unemployment.* Economic justice, in the sense of a fair distribution of wealth between the Aboriginal and non-Aboriginal populations.

3. *Protection and retention of Aboriginal culture.*

4. *Social vitality and development* that will overcome such existing social problems as ill health, the housing crisis, irrelevant and demeaning education, and alienation.

In order to achieve these aspirations, Aboriginal self-governments would need (1) political institutions that would be accountable to the Aboriginal electorate, (2) a territorial base, (3) control over group membership, and (4) continuing fiscal support. This would mean control over a number of areas that concern Aboriginal people—for example, citizenship, land, water, forestry, minerals, conservation, environment, economic development, education, health, cultural development, and law enforcement (Peters, 1987).

If Aboriginal people object to what is being proposed by the federal government, what have they offered instead? Over the years, various Aboriginal groups have developed a framework to deal with Canada with regard to the recognition and implementation of Aboriginal self-government. Unfortunately, the media has not presented their perspective, and thus most Canadians have little knowledge of counter proposals presented by Aboriginal people by which self-government could be achieved within the existing constitutional framework. Moreover, the current Conservative government does not exhibit the political will for "transformative change" in Aboriginal quality of life. For example, the AFN proposed a new framework in their report *Our Nations, Our Government: Choosing our Own Paths.* Their recommendations began with the premise that they wished to enable the political, social, economic, and cultural development of First Nations peoples to exist, continue, and prosper consistent with treaties and inherent rights. They proposed development of a political level accord that addresses the Supreme Courts' identification of the need for reconciliation and the request that Canada embark upon a process of transformative change with regard to Aboriginal people. They also noted the need to acknowledge shared interests between government and Aboriginal people, to address the issue of "government to government" relationships, and to affirm key principles in a manner acceptable to both parties (not a unilateral process). The report recommended the establishment of a process to discuss and implement a framework for recognition of First Nations governments and Aboriginal treaties and claims, as well as a basis for review of federal policies and laws to conform with the framework.

To achieve the above, federal government would need to create a *First Nations Government Recognition Act*, which has been recommended by numerous commissions and federal reports over the past three decades. A new Ministry of First Nations—Crown Relations would be created, as would a new Aboriginal and Treaty Rights Tribunal. At the same time, AAND would be limited to the delivery of programs and administration of the *Indian Act*. In short, the new organizational structure would see the ministry responsible for the following activities, with each of these departments acting independently but reporting to the Ministry of First Nations—Crown Relations.

The AFN Proposal: Ministry of First Nations—Crown Relations

— Specific Claims Secretariat
— Office of Fiscal Relations
— Office of First Nations Auditor
— Office of First Nations Ombudsman
— Office of the Treaty Commission
— First Nations Recognition and Implementation Secretariat

The document (AFN, 2005a) goes on to identify the specific function and activities that each of the offices reporting to the ministry would carry out, as well as their limitations. In addition to the above proposed structure, a new Aboriginal and Treaty Rights Tribunal would be established. This was recommended by the *Penner Report*, the Royal Commission on Aboriginal Peoples, and the Supreme Court of Canada. The powers of this tribunal, and the rules under which it would operate are very clear.

Aboriginal people are aware that these changes would not take place overnight. They understand that achieving the full recognition and implementation of Aboriginal self-government is a long-term and complex process. Capacity building is identified as a priority and requires strategies by which Aboriginal peoples could develop in areas such as accountability, capital management, management and administration, and judicial and program governance. However, they await movement on the part of the government toward a transformative Aboriginal self-government, one that would involve a new political accord between Aboriginal people and the Government of Canada and provide the political foundations upon which to base Aboriginal control, authority, and responsibility.

MODELS OF SELF-GOVERNMENT

After the 1973 *Calder* decision, the federal government attempted to implement some degree of Aboriginal self-government across the country. However, for the next 25 years, their efforts were limited in number and scope (e.g., Sechelt, Yukon). None of these self-government agreements were covered by Section 35 of the Charter, and none have any real Constitutional protection. As such, many Aboriginal groups found this process wanting and much of the federal government's efforts were not fruitful.

The Royal Commission on Aboriginal Peoples presented its ideas on self-government in 1996 when it recommended that there be created an *Aboriginal Nations Recognition and Government Act.* Furthermore, it recommended the elimination of the Department of Indian Affairs and the creation of a new Department of Aboriginal Relations. Along with this, they wanted the passage of the *Aboriginal Parliament Act* to establish a representative body of Aboriginal peoples that would evolve into a House of First Peoples and become part of parliament. One year later, the federal government responded with the publication of the document *Gathering Strength*. In this document, the government agreed to "strength Aboriginal governance" and to work with First Nations to achieve self-government within the context of the treaty relationship.

The federal government argued for years that First Nations people could achieve self-government through the *Indian Act* and that it was just a matter of "tweaking" the Act to accomplish this. Community-based government was one of the first approaches, although few Aboriginal communities utilized it. Early in 1982, the Optional Indian Band Government Legislation was introduced and was incorporated into federal legislation. Those bands that did not want to participate (either then or in the future) could remain under the *Indian Act.* However, the *Indian Act* would be revised and new alternative funding arrangements would be implemented for bands remaining under its jurisdiction. This new alternative allowed Aboriginal groups to apply to the federal government in order to assume greater control over various facets of reserve life, including management of lands and monies, and definition of who is defined as a member of the band. If, at some future time, the "less advanced" bands wanted to further develop their own form of self-government, they would have had the experience of exercising control over financial matters and other concerns (DIAND, 1982d).

In 1985, the federal cabinet began to discuss constitutional and non-constitutional initiatives that would enable Aboriginal peoples to directly take on some form of self-government. In 1986, the federal government publicly announced its community-based self-government policy. This new policy was intended to circumvent parts of the *Indian Act.* Under this policy, a community could be composed of individual bands, groups of bands, tribal councils, treaty groupings, or other regional entities. The government recognized that not all bands are the same and that a great diversity of Aboriginal communities exists. As a result, the policy of self-government could be achieved through a number of avenues, each to be negotiated by the local community

The first attempt to achieve self-government outside the rubric of the *Indian Act* was through the *Cree-Naskapi Act* of 1984 as part of the James Bay Settlement Agreement. Out of this experience, the **Sechelt Indian Band Self-Government Act** (1986) was passed as part of the government's plan to redefine Aboriginal governments as municipal governments. In this Act, the Sechelt took on a form of municipal government in which the province delegated powers to the Sechelt Aboriginal community. Through this legislation, under which the Sechelt assumed the rights of self-government, the Sechelt band was established as a legal entity. A written band constitution was put in place under the Act, and the band council became the governing body of the band. According to these legal conditions, the band could enter into contracts and agreements, acquire and hold property, and spend, borrow, and invest money. The council also had additional powers under the *Sechelt Act.* Not only was it to enjoy all the powers identified under the *Indian Act,* it could also carry out actions that were previously entrusted to the minister—for example, the construction of roads, the granting of access to and residence on Sechelt lands, and the zoning of land.

Under the *Sechelt Act,* both federal and provincial laws of general application would be in effect with regard to the band and its members, except those laws that were inconsistent with the *Indian Act* (Peters, 1987). The financing arrangements under the *Sechelt Act* are quite different from those of the *Indian Act.* Under the Act, the band has powers to tax local residents and businesses for maintaining the local infrastructure. Furthermore, the band may seek external financing with regard to any projects it wishes to take on. In addition, the band received a single lump sum of money to be held in trust for its own use.

In 1999, the Sechelt First Nation signed an agreement with the federal and provincial governments (a tripartite process) after five years of negotiation. This agreement was the first signed by the B.C. Treaty Commission, which was then negotiating with 50 other Aboriginal groups. The new treaty gave the Sechelt $42 million in cash, 933 hectares of provincial Crown land, and an additional 288 hectares of non-Crown land. Other resources included commercial fishing licences, management of forest resources, and additional property within the coastal community. Band members lost their tax-exempt status and began paying provincial goods and services taxes eight years after the treaty came into effect, and then income tax after 12 years. The treaty incorporated self-government into the language and allowed the communities to develop self-sufficiency.

The Nunavut settlement is another model of self-government for Aboriginal people. (See Chapter 9 for more detail.) This model entails a form of public government where the Inuit are the majority but the government is inclusive of all groups. The new government has an elected legislative assembly, a cabinet, and a territorial court. Over time it assumes the responsibilities exercised by the Government of the Northwest Territories. In the

Yukon Territory, the Council of Yukon Indians has taken on self-government through its comprehensive land claims that began in the early 1970s. In both cases, the process has focused on constitutional development and comprehensive land claims for which a holistic approach could be taken in addressing the issues of self-government (Doerr, 1997).

More recently, the Nisga'a Final Agreement (1998) served as another form of self-government. However, this agreement is first and foremost about treaty settlement. Within the treaty there is a self-government provision. Moreover, any amendment to the agreement requires the consensus of all three parties, meaning that the agreement cannot be unilaterally revoked. In addition, it clearly spells out the continuing obligations, rights, and responsibilities of each of the governments to the agreement.

The first 21st century treaty, concluded with the Nisga'a Nation, demonstrates that the province of B.C. agrees that the Nisga'a Nation has the inherent right of self-government. In the treaty, the government outlines the jurisdictional boundaries of the Nisga'a government. The B.C. government challenged this treaty in the courts, arguing that the Canadian Constitution did not allow for Aboriginal governments because all the legislative powers had been divided between the provincial and federal governments under the *Constitution Act, 1867*. In *Campbell* v. *British Columbia* (2005), the B.C. Supreme Court disagreed and noted that legislative powers had not been exhaustively distributed; thus, if the province and the Nisga'a want to define the inherent jurisdiction of the Nisga'a, they are welcome to do so.

In the Nisga'a Agreement, there are 14 areas included under Nisga'a law. For example, citizenship in the Nisga'a community, language, and licensing of Aboriginal healers all fall exclusively within Nisga'a law. However, other areas of jurisdiction have implications for non-Nisga'a people and nearby communities, such as issues of education and forestry. In these cases, the Nisga'a jurisdiction must meet or exceed federal/provincial standards and thus is concurrent with existing government requirements. At the same time, there are many issues over which Nisga'a law has no say, including criminal law and immigration. Nevertheless, the Nisga'a constitute a third order of government alongside the federal and provincial, possessing control over jurisdictions that transcend certain federal and provincial laws without deviating from the Canadian Constitution. It is a hybrid of state and self-determination and is embodied in provincial-like powers. At the same time, the governance structures remain embedded within the framework of the larger Canadian society (Maaka and Fleras, 2008). In July 2000, Westbank First Nation (WFN) in the central Okanagan Valley in B.C. concluded a self-government agreement with the federal government, the fifth self-government agreement for a Native community in Canada. The WFN agreement covers all aspects of band management and accountability; introduces special land, resource, and development codes; and removes the community from the jurisdiction of the *Indian Act*. The agreement was ratified in May 2003 and received royal assent in May 2004.

In summary, over the past number of years there have been four different models of self-government developed and implemented. Abele and Prince (2006) identify them as "mini-municipalities," federalism, third order, and "nation to nation" forms of government. As of today, only the latter two are serious contenders in the negotiations between Aboriginal people and the federal government. Table 10.2 identifies the various features of each of the models as well as the power relations embodied in them. It helps identifiy why Aboriginal people are reluctant to adapt either a mini-municipality or adapted federalism as the governing structure for themselves.

TABLE 10.2	Features of Four Models of Self-Government.			
Attributes of Model	Mini	Federalism	Third Order	Nation to Nation
Sovereignty	Federal government	Federal government	Shared levels of government	Parallel set of two among three sovereign nations
Origin of law-making powers	Canadian Constitution	Canadian Constitution	Canadian Constitution	Co-equal sets of Canadians and Aboriginal rules
Basis of Aboriginal-Canadian relations	*Constitution Act, 1867*; other federal laws	*Constitution Act, 1867*; other federal laws	*Constitution Act, 1867*; treaties, inherent rights	*Royal Proclamation*, 1763; treaties; Constitution 1982
Nature of the relationship	Assimilate neo-colonial	Integrate	Integrate, 2-way process; semi-sovereign yet cooperative	Co-exist, distinct
Source, scope, and nature	Delegated limited	Negotiated	Negotiated	Inherent and negotiated, shared powers
Concurrency of power	None	Modest	Relatively more	Not formally
Asymmetry in relationships	None	Small	Some	Substantial
Power status for Aboriginal governments	None	Within Federation	More power within federation	Power alongside the Canadian federation

Source: Abele, F., and M. Prince. "Political Spaces for Aboriginal Communities in Canada," in I. Peach (Ed.) *Constructing Tomorrow's Federalism*. Winnipeg: University of Manitoba Press, 2006, p. 584. Courtesy of the University of Manitoba Press.

Over the years, a number of Aboriginal groups have taken on (de-facto) inherent self-government. In so doing, they do not act in isolation but rather work within a network of federal, provincial, territorial, and municipal governments and share jurisdictional issues. The question now is: Who has the ultimate decision-making powers (paramount decision making) and when are the decision-making processes concurrent (both have some decision making rights)? McNeil (2010) argues that in cases where Aboriginal jurisdiction conflicts with federal or provincial jurisdiction in core areas, Aboriginal jurisdiction will be paramount. In cases where Aboriginal people choose not to invoke jurisdiction, federal or provincial jurisdiction will assume paramountcy. As one can see, there is an extensive set of Aboriginal self-government models currently in operation. In some cases they are imbedded in land claims agreements, while in others they are in self-government accords or agreements-in-principle. Whatever the basis, the agreements set out a framework for governance, outlining powers and responsibilities that a specific Aboriginal government may control.

There is considerable evidence that self-government is a necessary condition for communities and nations in order to make progress in improving the well-being of its citizens (Graham, 2007). Aboriginal people themselves agree that self-government is necessary if they are to prosper (Ekos, 2001). Thus, it would seem that government and Aboriginal people agree that self-government is vital to the establishment of good governance and economic success in Aboriginal communities. *The Charlottetown Accord*, had it passed, would have "constitutionalized" the right of Aboriginal people to self-government.

Nonetheless, there have been major difficulties in reaching self-government agreements over the past three decades. The current process of negotiating self-government is time consuming and is being resisted by the federal and provincial governments. Moreover, the governments want to establish a single template that will provide a "universal formula" or nationwide approach as to how Aboriginal self-government is created and implemented. There is considerable resistance to allowing communities to create and shape their own paths and structures of self-government. Government still wishes to impose its definition of self-government upon Aboriginal people and fails to appreciate that no outside agency can impose good governance. Instead, strong political commitment must come from within the community. Good self-government reflects a structure that has a balanced system in which the various components have appropriate roles to play. For example, the government sector should be balanced with an independent media and an active participation of voluntary organizations. Finally, it should be noted that there are a number of regulatory voids facing Aboriginal communities. While some of these are being addressed, it has taken the government half a century to implement legislation to do so. For example, because provincial law relating to land does not apply to reserves, there is little federal legislation to do with land development, Aboriginal communities do not enjoy the legislative protection of neighbouring non-Aboriginal communities in areas such as water, waste, and natural resource management. However, in 2010 the federal government passed the *First Nations Certainty of Land Title Act*, which closes the gaps between federal and provincial legislation so that industrial and commercial development projects on reserve lands can now take place. This legislation represents a step in the right direction, but it is interesting that the government knew about this void for the past 50 years.

Aboriginal people once again find themselves at the crossroads of their destiny. Despite great strides, they are cognizant that they will remain, for some time, economically dependent upon government for the implementation of various programs and services. At the same time, they are determined to develop greater self-control and self-reliance. Their task is to develop one or several workable systems within the context of the Canadian federal system by which they can achieve this goal—unfortunately, there can be no "one size fits all" solution.

Summary

- A policy watershed took place in 1973, when self-government was officially sanctioned by the federal government.
- The nature and structure of self-government vary from region to region.

- The Royal Commission on Aboriginal Peoples advanced the notion of self-government.
- Self-government has been a technique to transfer operations from AAND to Aboriginal communities.
- The policy of self-government has allowed Aboriginal communities to advance their status from "management" to "authority."

Key Terms

Aboriginal self-government p. 310

Assembly of First Nations p. 315

Calder v. *Attorney General of British Columbia* pp. 312

Collectivity p. 312

Indian Act p. 319

Penner Report p. 327

Royal Proclamation of 1763 p. 311

Sechelt Indian Band Self-Government Act p. 335

Section 25 of the *Charter of Rights and Freedoms* p. 316

Section 35 of the *Constitution Act* p. 326

Sovereignty p. 313

Questions for Further Discussion

1. How did the constitutional patriation allow Aboriginals to voice their concerns about their participation in Canadian society?

2. By having the right of self-determination, what do Aboriginals have the right to?

3. When an Aboriginal government is introduced, what potential new structure emerges? Explain the structural changes.

4. What three goals could self-government allow Indians to achieve?

5. Discuss the four focal points of Aboriginal self-government and the required action to ensure success.

Economic Involvement of Aboriginal Peoples

INTRODUCTION

Prior to this point, we have profiled the socio-economic positions of Aboriginal individuals and of Aboriginal communities across Canada. In both cases we have shown that there is a high incidence of social pathology such as substance abuse, family violence, a heavy dependency on social assistance, poorly functioning government services including housing, a run-down infrastructure, a dysfunctional governance system, and little vision for the future. There are some Aboriginal communities that have tackled these issues, but the majority have not been able to end this downward spiral and enhance the quality of life of their people. While government continually focuses on developing the economic potential of Aboriginal communities, it fails to make a distinction between economic growth and economic development. As a result, government tends to focus on indicators that reveal an increase in economic growth and thus use this indicator as a measure of success of programs supported by the government. In truth, the structure and productivity of the community has not changed, and prospects for the future remain as dim and dismal as they were before the period of increased growth.

We will begin with an attempt to explain how Aboriginal people find themselves in an underdeveloped position today. We will identify the conditions that placed this people into a marginal position within the larger Canadian economy. Both external and internal forces have created a political and economic environment that has led to the current economic state of Aboriginal people. How the government of Canada has dealt with this issue will also be discussed. Finally, we will focus on what contemporary research has to say about Aboriginal economic development and how it fits into current government programs. We will begin by discussing the difference between growth and development and then offer a tentative explanation for the lack of economic development in Aboriginal communities across Canada.

ECONOMIC GROWTH VERSUS ECONOMIC DEVELOPMENT

Economic growth is a concept that is measured by positive or negative change in the level of production of goods and services by a country over a certain period of time. Nominal growth is defined as economic growth including inflation, while real growth is nominal growth minus inflation. The most widely-used measure of economic growth is the real rate of growth in a political unit's total output of goods and services (gauged by the gross domestic product adjusted for inflation, or "real GDP"). Other measures, such as national income per capita and consumption per capita, are also used. The rate of economic growth is influenced by natural resources, human resources, capital resources, and technological development in the economy along with institutional structure and stability. Other factors include the level of world economic activity and the terms of trade.

On the other hand, **economic development** is the evolution of an economy dependent on agriculture or resource extraction into a prosperous economy with diversified industrial activities. Economic development typically involves large capital investments in infrastructure (roads, irrigation networks), industry, education, and financial institutions. Economic development is usually brought about by technological innovation and positive external forces. It is indicative of a changing institutional order as well as changes in the nature and type of work carried out by the people. It includes the expansion of new technology and methods of production in order to eliminate the gap between the most advanced sectors of the economy and those that lag behind. However, for most of us, economic growth is usually reflective of an interest in jobs and income, while economic development is reflected in the concern of nation building.

These two concepts refer to very different economic activities. Moreover, economic growth can occur without economic development, which is exactly what is happening in most Aboriginal communities. An increase in the rate of the production of oil from an Aboriginal community will in turn increase the per-capita income of residents in that community. The expansion of a mine and the resulting exports will increase the per-capita of the residents. Or, if the population of a community has increased, there will be an increase in expenditures. Treaty settlements with a community will also increase the per-capita income for members and may be utilized as an indicator of economic growth. And, in still other communities, payments for residential school traumatization will increase the per-capita income of members, with a resulting increase in economic growth. Another example is the Paix des Braves agreement that was signed between the Province of Quebec and the Quebec Cree in 2002. This agreement provided the 15 000 Cree of northern Quebec with $3.5 billion over the next 50 years, as well as a share of the profits from future natural resources development on their land. In return, the Cree dropped their lawsuit against Quebec. More recently (2011), the Innu signed an agreement with Hydro-Quebec that will provide them with $125 million over the next 40 years in exchange for dropping a lawsuit against the province. However, in none of these examples has the structure of the economy or the institutional order changed—that is, there has been no economic development.

Graham and Levesque (2010) outlined the key features of the two approaches (see Figure 11.1) and identified some of the main differences between them. They show that there are major differences in developing projects, depending on the perspective taken.

FIGURE 11.1	Attributes of Economic Growth versus Economic Development Approaches.

Economic Growth	Nation Building (Economic Development)
Responds to anyone's agenda	Community builds own agenda
Focus on short-term benefits	Focus on long-term benefits
Focus on creation of businesses	Create an environment for sustainable businesses
Measure success through income/jobs	Measure success through cultural, social, and economic impact
Elite of community dictate economic activities	Leaders liaise with community to develop appropriate development strategies
Solution is increased financial support by government	Solution is development of sound institutions to support economic ventures

Source: Stephen Cornell and Joseph Kalt. 2003. "Sovereignty and Nation-Building: The Development Challenges in Indian Country Today." *Joint Occasional Papers on Native Affairs*, no. 2003-03. © 2003 Harvard Project on American Indian Economic Development. Accessed June 2, 2011, at www.jopna.net/pubs/jopna_2003-03_Sovereignty.pdf.

Their study also reveals that, in engaging in economic development strategies, the community must take charge and look at long-term projects rather than seek quick solutions to endemic issues.

THEORIES OF ECONOMIC DEVELOPMENT

Early Explanations for Lack of Economic Development

Two traditional explanations for the persistent poverty and lack of economic development in many Aboriginal communities are:

(1) Aboriginal people lack objects such as natural resources or capital goods conducive to economic development; and

(2) Economic development is inimical to Aboriginal culture.

With regard to the first explanation, there are many examples of peoples around the world (as well as Aboriginal communities) having little of either resources or capital and still able to establish economic development. Something else must be involved. Increasingly, emphasis is shifting to the notion that it is ideas, not objects, that poor communities lack. The second explanation is that there is something about Aboriginal culture that stymies economic development. For example, people argue that the "communal" nature of Aboriginal culture is the antithesis of capitalism. Others claim that Aboriginal "ways of knowing," such as believing in spirits and respecting them, do not allow capitalism to take hold in the community. However, this argument has been discredited over time given the many Aboriginal communities that have engaged in economic development while maintaining their Aboriginal culture. As such, there must be other reasons why Aboriginal communities have not participated in the "modern" economy, engaged in economic development, and integrated into the larger global economy.

Dos Santos (1971) and Frank (1967) point out that earlier theorists have argued that undeveloped peoples have to pass through a series of stages in order to reach the developed stage. They propose that traditional societies have to establish some "preconditions" to begin the process of development, then move into the "take off" stage before driving to maturity as a developed economy. Their explanation as to why Aboriginal communities have not become economically developed is that they have not met the "preconditions" for economic development. For example, these authors would argue that because the human and social capital in a community is low or because there is a lack of natural resources, the community cannot meet the minimal conditions necessary to develop into a modern society.

Others have been suspicious of such claims and have argued instead that Aboriginal communities are not "undeveloped" but are "underdeveloped." This argument challenges the assumption that Aboriginal communities are lacking the necessary human and social capital required to enter the industrial world. While they would agree that these communities are not rich in different forms of capital, they nonetheless have access to capital necessary to meet the "preconditions" of economic development. Government programs and funds generated in Aboriginal communities are sufficient to begin the process of economic development from traditional to modern. Expertise lacking in the community can be brought in through a variety of grants and contracts. Accordingly, the arguments that the preconditions cannot be met are invalid.

The **neoclassical theory**—sometimes called "neo-conservatism" (which was popular in the 1980s when many governments throughout the industrialized world were governed by conservative political parties)—argues that economic stagnation in Aboriginal communities is a result of poorly designed economic policies and excessive state interference in the economy. Neoclassical theorists dismiss structural economic and neo-Marxist theory as flawed and unrealistic. They reject claims that the problems of developing regions are due to structural impediments in the international economy and that domestic structural flaws require significant state intervention. They argue instead that to stimulate the domestic economy and promote an efficient market requires the privatization of government-owned enterprises, the promotion of free trade, the elimination of restrictions on foreign investment, and the elimination of government regulations regarding the market. In summary, this position argues that market forces, not government intervention, will bring about economic development in stagnating economies. This policy was in evidence during the last two decades of the 20th century as Canada introduced new policies and regulations regarding economic activities, such as deregulation, NAFTA (North American Free Trade Agreement), and the privatization of many services, to the continued detriment of Aboriginal communities. Since these new policies were put into place, Aboriginal people have not seen an enhanced quality of life or an increase in their human or social capital.

If the above positions have been discredited, we are still left with the question as to why Aboriginal communities have not experienced economic development and integrated into the larger national and global economy. The answer would seem to lie in the historical conditions experienced by Aboriginal peoples as well as how local Aboriginal economies are linked to the larger national and international economic structure. This requires us to understand how "underdeveloped" economies transform from a traditional subsistence agricultural base into a modern economy. A modern economy is defined as one in which most of the population is urban and the bulk of the output is in the form of manufactured products or services. The development model used in the previous chapters incorporates the basic tenets of three major theoretical perspectives: colonialism, political economy, and settler society. The first two perspectives were fully articulated in Chapters 1 and 2 (Cumming, 1967; Carstens, 1971; Patterson, 1972).

The concept of "**settler society**" has been invoked to explain ethnic relations in colonial situations. These are societies that have been settled by Europeans, who have retained their political dominance over Indigenous peoples. They are typified by a system in which land, resources, and labour are controlled by European settlers (Stasiulis and Yuval-Davis, 1995; Alfred, 2005). Settler societies generally have established social boundaries between the indigenous population and the European settlers. These boundaries determine the actions deemed to be legitimate and legal for all members of society. In most settler societies, the dominant culture reflects the "mother" country's values and culture, and is constantly reinforced through immigration and importation of "mother" country institutions, values, ideologies, and economic practices. What worked in the mother country is reproduced in the colony.

Non-Aboriginal Canadians developed a strategy in their relationship with Aboriginals prior to the patriation of the Constitution in 1982: the myth of equality (Willhelm, 1969). This myth's basic premise is that all humans are equal no matter how diverse they appear to be. This, however, acted as a rationale for denying special privileges and affirmative action programs to various minority groups. The federal government's 1969 *White Paper*, which recommended that reserves be terminated and special status revoked, exemplified this myth. Contemporary legislation continues to reflect this view of equality somewhat, though not as prominently. Proponents argue that the laws that express the equality of ethnic groups ought to be sufficient, regardless of the impact of centuries of entrenched discrimination.

New Modes of Explanation: Dependency and World Systems Theory

For government, the ultimate question becomes how to expand the modern economy while weakening the Indigenous traditional economy of the region. The object of economic development is the structural transformation of underdeveloped economies so as to permit a process of self-sustained economic growth. This may only be achieved by eliminating the underdeveloped economy's reliance on "foreign" demand for its primary exports (raw materials) as the backbone fueling economic growth. Moreover, economic development must be sustained through an expansion of the internal industrial sector within the Aboriginal community.

As a result, in the globalized economy, high-income countries control the development of low-income countries to the extent that they cause a continuation of underdevelopment of the low-income countries while at the same time enriching the highly developed countries. The argument is that poor regions (e.g., reserves) export primary commodities to the rich economies (the Canadian private sector), which then manufacture products out of these commodities and in turn sell them back to the poor regions. Because of the price differential between the raw material and the "value added" material, the poor regions can never earn enough to become a "rich" region, and thus remain poor in perpetuity. In fact, some argue that rich economies arranged this inequity so that they would continue to benefit while poor regions would not. There are two types of regions— centre and periphery. World systems theorists go even further to argue that poverty is a direct consequence of the evolution of the international political economy (globalization) into a rigid division of labour that favours the rich and penalizes the poor. As Dos Santos (1971) contends:

> Dependency is an historical condition that shapes a certain structure of the world economy such that it favours some countries to the detriment of others and limits the development possibilities of the subordinate economics . . . a situation in which the economy of a certain group of countries is conditioned by the development and expansion of another economy, to which their own is subjected. (p 226)

This perspective accepts the premise that external forces (outside the community) are important in the economic activities of any centre or peripheral region. These external forces can be multinational corporations, international commodity markets, or agencies such as the World Bank, which ensure that the interests of the centre regions are protected. There also is acknowledgement that the relationship between the periphery and the centre is steeped in history and evolves over time as the two parties continue to link with each other.

We take the theoretical underpinnings of such an argument and apply it to the relationship between Aboriginal communities and the larger economic market of Canada (and transnational corporations working in Canada). Our task is to see whether the empirical basis of Canada's relationship with Aboriginal people meets the criteria of dependency theory. Clearly, Canada has had a long history of involvement with Aboriginal people. Moreover, this involvement has been based on the principles of assimilation and control. And, as Abele (2004) noted, it is impossible to look at the economic conditions of Aboriginal peoples without taking into consideration the history of their relationship to the state. Aboriginal peoples are engaged in legal and political struggles challenging the legitimacy of Canada's claim of sovereignty over the land. It should also be noted that there has been a long history of policies denying the relevance of Aboriginal cultures. This has weakened the cohesiveness and social sustainability of Aboriginal communities with the resultant high level of dependency on the Government of Canada.

As such, the Aboriginal peoples' history of colonialism in Canada has been the basis for their underdevelopment and not a result of their culture. This systematic colonist exploitation has resulted in a state of underdevelopment. Evidence of this can be found in the manner by which resources such as minerals, forestry, oil, and gas have been extracted by the dominant economic and political forces in Canada from the Aboriginal communities and their lands to sustain the economic growth and wealth of the elite. In short, the very success of the major corporations in Canada is the cause of the underdevelopment of the reserves. This has come about because of the historical and continued coercive and exploitative manner by which the Aboriginal people have been integrated into the larger economy. In short, the global economy is characterized by a relationship between the major corporations, which, using political, military, and economic power, extract a surplus from Aboriginal lands. Any attempt by the Aboriginal people to resist the influences of dependency results in economic and social sanctions and control by either or both the government and corporations.

Dependency theory argues that international capitalism has created a rigid division of labour that is responsible for the underdevelopment of Aboriginal peoples. In turn, the Aboriginal lands supply cheap minerals, agricultural commodities, and cheap labour. Moreover, these people also serve as the repositories of surplus capital, obsolescent technologies, and manufactured goods. As such, existing Aboriginal economies are oriented toward the outside. Money, goods, and services do flow into Aboriginal communities, but the allocation of these resources is determined by the economic interest of the major corporations and the government and not by the interests of the Aboriginal communities. Thus, Aboriginal communities are not simply lagging behind the rest of Canada; they are poor because they were coercively integrated into the larger Western capitalistic economic system. However, not only is the exploitation maintained by the government and the elite of the private sector, but also by the elite of the Aboriginal communities. When the private interests of the Aboriginal elite coincide with the interests of the government and corporations, further underdevelopment is ensured.

Since the end of the 19th century, Aboriginal people have been unable to participate fully in the Canadian economy. Even before our economy moved to an agricultural base and then on to one of modern technology, Aboriginal people were restricted in their involvement and, as a result, fell further behind in their ability to integrate. Aboriginal people still find themselves operating in a subsistence or welfare economy parallel to that of the more modern economy. In other words, there are two economies in our society. This dual system emerged over time as changes in institutional structures, technology, and industrial work practices took place. Aboriginal people were prevented from participating in the modern economy through a variety of policies and programs established by government and supported by the private sector. For example, Aboriginal people were prohibited from using resources in direct competition with non-Aboriginal users. Before the 20th century, Aboriginals were not allowed to take homestead lands, as these lands were available only to immigrants. Indigenous people were refused licences to act as commercial big-game hunting outfitters in areas where non-Aboriginal people had established commercial enterprises. And when inland commercial fisheries were created in the Canadian northwest, regulations were put in place so that Aboriginals could not compete with non-Aboriginals.

As Euro-Canadian society moved more quickly into an industrial–technological economy in the early 20th century, Aboriginal people found themselves without the skills and resources necessary to participate. As a result, two almost separate economies emerged: a modern, dynamic sector (industrially and technologically based) and a traditional, land-based subsistence sector. The former creates change, which in turn promotes further change, while the latter tends to resists change, may cling to traditional ways, and might see little need to adopt new technology except when it is expedient to do so (Wien, 1986). Aboriginal people have discovered that, without the necessary skills, they are able to participate only at the fringes of the industrial economy. A contemporary example of this dynamic is the request by Aboriginal communities for the past half-century to amend the *Indian Act* so that Indian lands would be more attractive to investors. It would not be until 2005 that the *First Nations Commercial and Industrial Development Act* was passed by parliament allowing First Nations to pursue a large-scale commercial or industrial on-reserve project. It took another five years to implement changes (*First Nations Certainty of Land Title Act*) to this Act when it was discovered that the first version fell short of achieving its stated goal.

THE EVOLUTION OF ABORIGINAL DEVELOPMENT

An underlying assumption held by many Canadians is that First Nations contribute little economic product to the Canadian economy. Non-Aboriginal people believe that the larger dominant economy supports the Aboriginal economy through governmental subsidies and through the creation of, and payment for, a variety of health, economic, and social services. For example, many people point out that governmental transfers provide between 80 and 100 percent of Aboriginal salaries and non-earned income. If Aboriginal communities did not receive government subsidies, their local economies would collapse.

However, as Salisbury (1986) notes, this perspective and its underlying assumption represents a fundamental misunderstanding of the relation between Aboriginal people and the federal government (and, indeed, the people of Canada). For example, the flow of money stems specifically from a "contract" agreed upon by the two parties (the fiduciary relation between the Crown and Aboriginal peoples) and cannot be revised or amended unilaterally over time. The contents of the agreement were agreed to by both parties at the time of signing and were deemed to be in the best interests of both parties. *The Royal Proclamation* of 1763 is the best and earliest example of an agreement between the two parties that is still legally binding and recognized in the Canadian Constitution. Under this agreement, it was understood that, in return for the Aboriginal peoples' recognition of the sovereignty of the monarch, the monarch would protect them and preserve the Aboriginal way of life. While some specifics of the agreement have been modified (in favour of Euro-Canadians), the courts have forced the federal government to accept the spirit of the original agreement. Hence, the "subsidization" of services to Aboriginal people has been and continues to be paid for by Aboriginal people through their original transferring of land and allegiance in 1763. Many will argue that contracts and treaties can be changed. And while we acknowledge this, they cannot be abrogated unilaterally. Over time, the Crown has tried to withdraw from the commitments made, and, in some cases, the courts have allowed this to happen.

As the settler economy developed, Aboriginal economies were disrupted and put in disarray. Some of the more isolated reserves were less affected than those close to urban centres, but as external controls gradually became institutionalized, further Indigenous community disruption occurred. While government wanted Aboriginal people to enter agricultural pursuits, these efforts were not successful because government refused to provide sufficient resources such as land, equipment, and capital (Carter, 1990). In fact, there is considerable evidence that the federal government of the time (late 19th and early 20th centuries) purposely undermined Aboriginal successes and efforts in agricultural pursuits (Miller, 2000). Thus, the transition from a traditional to a modern economy was very difficult for many Aboriginal people, and their participation was marginal. Continuous debates about who was responsible for Aboriginal people further reduced their ability to secure support. As the Royal Commission on Aboriginal Peoples commented, prior to the 1960s, Aboriginal economic development was not a priority for the federal government, and, as time went on, Aboriginal dependency on federal assistance grew.

After World War II, Aboriginal people began to shed their passivity and to demand a much more active role in Canadian society (Miller, 2000). The government (both provincial and federal), having experienced the atrocities of the war, began to implement policies that would forever change its ideological position toward Aboriginal people. Human rights acts were passed, social assistance programs were put in place, and specific actions were taken regarding Aboriginal people—e.g., the *Indian Act* underwent its first major revision in almost a century. In the 1960s the federal government made public its report, *A Survey of the Contemporary Indians of Canada: Economic, Political, Educational Needs and Policies*. The report identified the poor quality of life experienced by Aboriginal people and concluded by suggesting extensive changes in government policy and programs. The government did act on the recommendation to set up programs for community development. The strategy consisted of two stages. First, the community would define its own problems and devise ways to achieve its goals. Second, the community would be given resources to implement the program. While phase one was implemented, phase two was never sufficiently funded, and by the late 1960s the concept of community development had died.

After refusing to give local communities the necessary resources to achieve their goals, Indian Affairs implemented the National Indian Advisory Board. However, its ineffectiveness led to its abandonment in the 1970s. By this time the federal government had settled on a more traditional and orthodox plan for integrating Aboriginal people into the economy—modernization. The new approach embodied the principle of assimilation, yet it was hidden behind more opaque beliefs. Modernization meant that, if an individual wanted to enhance his or her quality of life, then he or she had to move from traditional beliefs, values, and behaviours to adopt more modern ones. This meant that science would be the basis for action, creative rationality would be the underlying mode of operation, and new ways of thinking would be embraced. There was (and continues to be) a belief that change and "progress" is inevitable and preferable. Furthermore, it signifies a belief that the direction of that change, along with its impact, can be controlled.

The federal government felt that Aboriginal peoples' traditional ways of life would have to end and a cultural replacement would have to be found. Specifically, individual values and goals needed to supersede those of groups or communities. Many Aboriginal groups rejected this approach. They began to suggest that economic integration of Aboriginal people would require more than individual initiative and effort. They began to see the structure of our society as responsible for the poor quality of life experienced by Aboriginal people. For example, the Métis Women's Association of Manitoba saw Aboriginal problems as a symptom of larger social and cultural problems, including patriarchy. It argued that, as long as development initiatives were handled solely by outsiders and men, the structural problems would remain.

The federal government, in its attempt to implement its modernization policy, established the **Indian Economic Development Fund** in 1970. This fund continued the policy of funding only legal (registered, status) Indians. It provided direct loans, loan guarantees, and other forms of credit only to on-reserve projects. The National Indian Brotherhood publicly noted its objection to the way the fund was being operated by Ottawa. Aboriginal people felt that if economic development was to occur, they must have control, and that this in turn implied political autonomy (P. Elias, 1991).

In the mid-1970s the federal government began to develop community and regional plans for Aboriginal economic development. A joint effort of the National Indian Brotherhood and DIAND produced its first report in 1976. This report made it clear that Aboriginal people were not prepared to sacrifice their culture, land, or identity in order to develop economically. They wanted to develop in such a way that development and culture were complementary. Aboriginal people felt that local self-government could be the structure wherein both economic development and cultural maintenance could coexist. It was under these conditions that Aboriginal organizations became involved in economic development. As P. Elias (1991) pointed out, by the late 1970s models of change advocated a more multidisciplinary approach. Social and cultural issues became more important, and new models of socio-economic change sought to integrate them. The underlying assumption was that economic changes included cultural revitalization as much as possible.

By the mid-1980s Aboriginal organizations had accepted economic proposals on a project-by-project basis as the major thrust of advancement. At the same time, however, they tried to develop new ideologies through different channels. The ideas of self-government, sovereignty, and Indian rights began to surface and were pursued through other Canadian institutions, especially the courts. Nevertheless, they had now accepted a blended (Aboriginal/non-Aboriginal) course of action through which they would pursue their economic development. Meanwhile, the federal government continued to view its own definition of development as the only acceptable one. The Indian Economic Development Fund was later replaced by the **Canadian Aboriginal Economic Development Strategy**, and then in 1989, the Aboriginal Economic Development Strategy was created. Essentially all development programs established over the years by the federal government have been top-down economic initiatives that explicitly favour individual entrepreneurship and enterprise over any strategies based on community control (P. Elias, 1991; Armstrong, 1999).

In 1989 the federal government earmarked nearly $900 million (over five years) for Aboriginal economic development. It also suggested that more Aboriginal control would be given with respect to financial resources and decision making. The design of the plan was such that Indian Affairs's role in program delivery would be phased out as local Aboriginal control took over. As Gadacz (1991) noted, the then DIAND's old focus on control, structure, rules, and procedures was to be replaced by collaboration, learning, networking, and innovation. In short, Indian Affairs would switch roles from a direct supplier of services to an assistant and facilitator for Aboriginal communities. By the 1990s, funding policies once again began to change. An increased emphasis on providing training and education for all ages of Aboriginal people was the order of the day.

ABORIGINAL ECONOMIC PROGRAMS AND AAND

While community-based development was the overall paradigm used by government to encourage economic development in the 1960s (La Rusic, 1968), by the 1990s this perspective had disappeared. AAND's current economic policy attempts to use an integrated, holistic approach that combines such dimensions as governance, culture, spirituality, and education. In short, the economic strategy of today is to strengthen Aboriginal culture as Aboriginal nations develop. The current philosophy recognizes that problems of economic development are not solvable by a single approach, and that policy and programs must reflect community desires, needs, and control. There is also an understanding that Aboriginal economic development cannot take place in isolation from the rest of the country—its very context. However, given the shortage of land and resource allocation for Aboriginal communities, this approach also recognizes that economic development must be long term.

FIGURE 11.2	Twenty-First Century Socio-Economic Policy Mandate of Indian Affairs
	• Improving access to capital
	• Facilitating access to markets
	• Supportive business economic climate
	• Developing/improving infrastructure
	• Partnership building
	• Improving access to lands and resources
	• Enhancing access to the rkforce
	• Skills and experience development

Today the Economic Development Sector of AAND is responsible for community planning, development, and access to resources. Two units (the Socio-Economic Policy Unit and the Programs and Economic Development and Special Initiatives Unit) have been created to deal with economic issues. The goal of this sector is to strengthen the economic base of First Nations communities, to remove obstacles to economic development, and to facilitate economic opportunities (see Figure 11.2). Most of the work of this sector is focused on developing and supporting the implementation of the Canadian Aboriginal Economic Development Strategy established by the government to help Aboriginal peoples achieve their goal of economic self-reliance. This partnership among AAND, Industry, Science and Technology, and Human Resources Development/Employment and Immigration Canada has spent over $100 million over the past decade to ensure achievement of its goal. This approach is different from past attempts at providing economic development services directly to Aboriginal people. The new strategy offers support for Aboriginal economic development decision making, priority setting, and delivery of economic development services through community-based organizations.

In order to implement this program, the government has fostered linkages between Aboriginal communities, the private sector, and government (federal, provincial, and territorial) agencies in order to promote greater participation by First Nations in the mainstream economy. The Canadian Aboriginal Economic Development Strategy comprises eight programs, including Business Development, Joint Ventures, and Skills Development. These economic programs have evolved over time but represent the major efforts undertaken by the federal government to create economic development on the reserves and to help individual Aboriginals integrate into the mainstream economy.

The overall strategy is to develop an Aboriginal economic development program for the long term, which will be designed to support control by Aboriginal communities i.e., community-based decision making, priority setting, and delivery of services. AAND's Community Economic Development Program has been the key component of this strategy. This component is designed to assist Aboriginal people, through community economic development organizations, to create, maintain, or strengthen local organizational, advisory, and development capacities, which will help Aboriginal community members more clearly define and achieve their economic goals.

The Commercial Development Program handles business development activities. Because of the creation of the Canada Aboriginal Economic Development Strategy, direct contributions to Aboriginal businesses have ceased. Instead, in 2001–02, the department budgeted nearly $140 million for economic development. An additional $900 million was set aside for capital facilities and maintenance. In addition to the above initiatives, Aboriginal Affairs has created a number of other programs and strategies to enhance First Nations economic development. Programs such as the Resource Partnerships Program, the Major Business Projects Program, Procurement Strategy for Aboriginal Businesses, and the Aboriginal Fisheries Strategy Allocation Transfer Program are just a few initiatives that add support to the economic development thrust initiated by Aboriginal Affairs. Others—for example, the Aboriginal Business Development Initiative—were launched in 1999 with $21 million designed to improve business development opportunities for Aboriginal communities. The Aboriginal Business Development Initiative strengthens the capacity of First Nations financial organizations (such as the Aboriginal Capital Corporations and Aboriginal Community Futures Development Corporations) to access capital and to network with other organizations, thus gaining access to new technologies and expanding the markets and outreach for Aboriginal entrepreneurs.

ABORIGINAL DEVELOPMENT: THEORETICAL UNDERPINNINGS

Cornell and Kalt (1992) and the Royal Commission are clear in terms of what is needed for Aboriginal economic development and have noted that at whatever level, it is complex and difficult. They argue that the specific situation and historical time period will profoundly influence the nature of the economic development, the extent of government support, and the probability of success of the project. For example, on the basis of many case studies, they concluded that one of the most important factors in developing a successful economic project is to understand the political, economic, and geographic environment of the Aboriginal community. They identify eight major considerations in assessing the level of success of any project:

1. the degree to which Aboriginal people have the ability to make decisions;

2. the extent to which the project fills a unique economic niche or opportunity;

3. the degree to which the Aboriginal community has access to financial capital on a long-term basis;

4. the distance from the Aboriginal community to the market;

5. the amount of natural resources available to the community;

6. the level of human capital;

7. the organizational structure of the Aboriginal community; and

8. the level of integration of the Aboriginal community with the dominant society.

More recently, Simeone (2007) concluded that economic development for Aboriginal people requires three necessary and two subsidiary conditions. The necessary conditions are:

1. **Jurisdiction**. There has been a long-held assumption on the part of the government that it knew best with regard to diagnosing a problem and devising a plan to solve that problem with regard to Aboriginal people. As Simeone (2007) points out, the Harvard project found that First Nations must be allowed to make their own decisions about economic projects. The government's ignorance regarding the needs and aspirations of Aboriginal people over the years did great social and economic damage. As such, Aboriginal people must be able to make their own decisions about the design, development strategy, and resource allocations of the project (Cornell, 2002b). It means that the economic agenda and control of the necessary resources is placed within the Aboriginal community's purview. The leaders are then accountable to the community and cannot claim that the decisions are made by outside third parties. In summary, they need to have established a level of self-government with regard to economic activities that will allow the decisions of the leaders and community members to be linked to the resulting consequences.

2. **Institutions**. If true economic development is to occur, the ability to make decisions must be supplemented by capable institutions of governance. In this regard, the decision rules regarding economic activities must be fair and independent from the politics of the community. Moreover, the governing institutions in the community must be stable (e.g., the rules of economic decisions must be clearly spelled out and supported by the community; there must be a firewall between economic and political decisions so that businesses are protected from political interference). In addition, there must be effective and non-politicized resolution of disputes. Finally, there must be the creation of a structure in the community that is large enough to reflect the community wishes but small enough that it is nimble and can make the necessary decisions to operate an economic venture (Cornell, 2002b).

3. **Culture**. Successful economic ventures must be based upon Aboriginal culture and include a governing structure, an economic system, and policies and procedures that fit within the local culture. In short, there must be a "fit" between the economic venture and the culture of the community in such a way that the community would see the institutional structures supporting the economic development as appropriate. It does not mean that Aboriginal communities must necessarily develop institutions or governments that are capable of operating effectively in the contemporary world. For example, Dowling (2005) argues that in some respects, traditional First Nations are essentially opposed to the very conditions of industrial development, the accumulation of wealth, and Westernized notions of progress. However, this does not obviate Aboriginal people from engaging in Western economic ventures. Rather, the structure and the organization of the economic venture need to fit into the values, norms, and ethos of the Aboriginal culture.

In addition to the above three conditions, it has been noted that leadership and strategic thinking should be part of the overall economic vision. This means that economic development requires leaders who introduce new knowledge and experiences will be able to convince other members of the community that things can be different. Finally, to be economically successful, Aboriginal communities must move away from crisis manage-ment and opportunistic projects to those that reflect long-term, sustainable development. While these five criteria will not guarantee economic success, they are characteristic of communities that have established sustainable economic development. Moreover, once these key factors are in place, other human and social capital such as education, natural resources, and access to capital will be integrated into the development plan and bring about successful economic ventures.

This new model reflects five principle dimensions related to effective institutions. First, it reflects stable institutions and policies. This means that everyone needs to know the "rules of the game" and that they will not change as leadership in the community changes. In other words, the rules are not dependent upon specific individuals and do not change when the individuals leave but rather are of an enduring nature. This also includes rules regarding fair and consistent dispute resolution. Second, there has to be a separation of politics from day-to-day business decisions. This does not mean that the Aboriginal community and leadership have no linkages with business decisions. Quite the contrary. Aboriginal leaders and the community must be involved in the setting of directions and policy formation for economic projects taking place in the community. However, the leadership and community must not be involved in the decisions regarding the day-to-day activities of the business such as hiring, firing, purchasing, operating hours, and rates of remuneration. Third, the business must operate within a competent bureaucracy. That is, the community must attract, develop, and retain skilled personnel and abide by the open and transparent rules outlined for good governance. Fourth, there has to be a "match" between the prevailing ideas in the community and the governing institutions. Only if there is a match will the economic activities be supported by the community and its lead-ership. Finally, the community must have some form of "de facto" sovereignty. This means that the community must be in charge of realizing it economic development activi-ties. When the community takes responsibility for what happens and has the practical power and capacity to act on its own behalf, it will begin to approach economic develop-ment and sustainability (Cornell and Kalt, 2001: 29–30).

A number of alternatives have been suggested as ways Aboriginal people could more fully integrate into the political economy of Canadian society. These recommendations for ending Aboriginal economic dependence have been around for a long time. For example, Heilbrun and Wellisz (1969) have suggested that the federal government pro-vide funds for Aboriginal communities, as is done with the International Bank for Recon-struction and Development or the International Finance Corporation. These organizations make loans to underdeveloped countries based on long-term projects. These loans are not subject to an annual review, and thus financing is assured for five to seven years. These projects can be reviewed and revised during the financing period so as to keep up with global changes. And qualified staff would be attracted to projects because of the long-term stability and assured financing of the projects (Daugherty, 1978).

Others, such as Sorenson and Wolfson (1969), have suggested that, in addition to long-term financing of economic projects in Aboriginal communities, other structural rearrangements need to be made. For example, they claim that the unbalanced, single-industry approach taken by government is unsustainable. They also maintain that secon-dary and tertiary industries must be planned for Aboriginal communities (Deprez and Sigurdson, 1969; Banner, 2005). On this basis, it is clear that not all Aboriginal communities will benefit equally over time with similar types of development. Any proposed development should be tailor-made for a community and implemented only when internal and external conditions are appropriate. Economic development for Aboriginal peoples also means that they must regain control over decisions, both at the planning and the operational stages. Moreover, this means that developmental policies and programs must be designed and delivered by Aboriginal institutions. As the Royal Commission on Aboriginal Peoples noted, instead of Aboriginal communities having to adjust to the criteria and procedures of distant bureaucracies, the process needs to be reversed. The communities need to define priorities and the instruments best suited to meet them. As such, the transformation of Aboriginal economies is a large-scale undertaking that will require resources as well as a concerted, comprehensive effort over an extended period (Canada, 1996a).

As Peters (1968) stated long ago, new industries and the upgrading of Aboriginal skills are the key to economic development. The creation of new jobs for Aboriginal people would also boost reserve profits, upgrade individual income standards, and provide invaluable work experience for the development of Aboriginal leaders in community and business affairs. However, the federal government long argued against the creation of industries and jobs within Aboriginal communities. It steadfastly held that the reserve is basically a residential area and cannot be converted to industrial or commercial use. For example, 50 years ago, Recommendation 3 of the Hawthorn Report (1966–67: 13) stated:

> The main emphasis on economic development should be on education, vocational training, and techniques of mobility to enable Indians to take employment in wage and salaried jobs. Development of locally available resources should be viewed as playing a secondary role for those who do not choose to seek outside employment.

NEW POLICIES FOR ABORIGINAL DEVELOPMENT

Presently, Aboriginal people own or control over 15 million hectares of land, while Inuit have control over 47 million hectares. First Nations reserves account for 3.3 million hectares and are expected to increase by a further 1.1 million hectares as a result of treaty land entitlements and other claim settlements. On this land, over $315 billion in major resource projects have taken place. Overall, the Government of Canada spends more than $10 billion annually on programs directed to Aboriginal people. All this demonstrates that there is a potential growing economic base for First Nations. In addition, given that nearly half the Aboriginal population is under the age of 25, there will be a growing potential labour force while at the same time there is a continuing decrease in the number of young non-Aboriginal Canadians. Moreover, it is estimated that from 2010–2026, the cumulative impact of various development projects on Aboriginal people could be well in excess of $400 billion. Aboriginal businesses have grown over the past decade, with a 20 percent increase in self-employed Aboriginal workers from 2000–2006.

The last major policy framework for Aboriginal economic development was implemented over 20 years ago. In the interim period, structural and political conditions have changed—both on and off the reserves. An assessment of the impact of the 1989 policy reveals that the economic development of Aboriginal people has not progressed in a positive fashion. For example, the unemployment rate for Aboriginal people was 15 percent (compared to 6 percent for non-Aboriginal people) in 2006; income generation lags far behind non-Aboriginal people and investments in Aboriginal peoples projects have stagnated. As such, in 2008, the federal government developed new policies with regard to Aboriginal economic development. Its new program was aligned with its overall economic policy (Advantage Canada: Building a Strong Economy for Canadians). One year later, the federal government's Canada's Economic Action Plan was introduced, and nearly $1.5 billion were set aside over the next two years to meet specific needs of Aboriginal people and communities. However, at the end of 2011, this funding will cease to exist; and, as usual, new pilot programs will likely be initiated. This lack of continuity and interconnectedness means that new projects do not build upon completed ones nor do they integrate into future programs. Each of the programs is simply a "stand alone" project that does not leverage other funding or fit into a larger vision.

The new economic program (2009) established by what was then INAC begins with six basic assumptions regarding the barriers to Aboriginal economic development:

- **Legal and Regulatory Environment**: Revise *the Indian Act* and replace outdated regulations that impede economic development;
- **Lands and Resource Access**: Process land claims in a fairer and timelier manner;
- **Skilled Labour:** Address the lack of education and skill development.
- **Deficits in Infrastructure**: Upgrade and modernize existing infrastructure and improve communications and transportations systems to Aboriginal communities.
- **Deficits in Capacity**: Enhance both human and social capital.
- **Limited Financing**: Improve funding access of Aboriginal people/communities for various economic development projects.

In summary, AAND (formerly INAC) has concluded that Aboriginal people find themselves subject to untargeted business opportunities due to the control of funds by the government. Thus, rather than building upon needs and opportunities of Aboriginal people, regulations prevent targeted business developments. Because of their marginalized status, Aboriginal people have few links with the private sector and the links that exist are mostly conflict based. Aboriginal people also find that their ability to engage in economic development projects is limited by the rules and regulations of the *Indian Act* or other policies established by AAND. For example, the use of Indian monies is restricted and controlled by AAND. Many Aboriginal development projects cannot be supported by local individuals since they do not have the human capital by which a project can be sustained. It should be noted that the over 30 different departments deal that with Aboriginal people act independently and do not coordinate their activities nor leverage their combined activities for the betterment of Aboriginal people. In summary, there is now recognition by AAND that there are major barriers created by the actions of the federal government that continue to prevent Aboriginal people from engaging in economic development.

The current federal policy has four pillars upon which it plans to use as its basic strategy for Aboriginal economic development (see Figure 11.3). AAND argues that such a framework will help as a decision-making tool, an assessment tool, and a communication tool. Used in combination, the strategic process will enhance the economic development of First Nations and enhance their quality of life.

FIGURE 11.3	Aboriginal Economic Development Strategic Priorities		
Strengthening Aboriginal Entrepreneurship	Developing Aboriginal Human Capital	Enhancing the Value of Aboriginal Assets	Forging New and Effective Partnerships
A more business-friendly climate on reserve and outside and improved access to capital and other business opportunities will strengthen entrepreneurship.	Supporting demand driven labour market development will build human capital.	Aligning federal investments with viable economic opportunities, better management of business and community assets, and a modern lands/resource management regime will help enhance the value of assets.	Promoting partnerships with provinces and territories and the private sector will ensure longterm sustainable economic development.

Source: Indian and Northern Affairs Canada, 2009. *Federal Framework for Aboriginal Economic Development.* Cat. number: R3-75/2009E-PDF. Retrieved May 9, 2011, from www.publications.gc.ca/site/eng/ccl/copyrightClearance/apply.html?execution=e7s14.

As such, the federal government has specified that it will engage in a number of actions to strengthen the success of the four pillars (see Box 11.1).

Box 11.1	Aboriginal Business Success

An innovative partnership will see Taku River Tlingit First Nation gain an equity stake in the running of a river hyrdo project in northern British Columbia. Along with renewable energy, the project will also produce employment opportunities and reliable revenue streams. The project emerges from a $7 million First Nation Regeneration fund, created by Tale'awtow Aboriginal Capital corporation, Tribal Resources Investment Corporation, Ecotrust Canada, and the Government of Canada. The fund helps Aboriginal businesses and communities in British Columbia participate in renewable energy projects by extending loans to acquire equity in generation facilities. The First Nations will repay the loans with royalties and dividends they earn from the project. Designed and developed to meet the needs of First Nations in the region, the fund demonstrates the valuable role the partnerships can play in effective sustainable economic development. Funding from the Government of Canada was provided through the Major Resource and Energy Development pilot project, which leverages financial participation from other levels of government, the private sector, and Aboriginal partners. This increases the availability of equity funding to medium and large Aboriginal businesses in order for them to participate in major development projects and be active partners in joint ventures.

Source: Indian and Northern Affairs Canada, 2009. *Federal Framework for Aboriginal Economic Development,* Ottawa, p. 16. Catalogue No. R3-75/2009E-PDF. Retrieved May 9, 2011, from http://www.publications.gc.ca/site/eng/ccl/copyrightClearance/apply.html?execution=e7s14. Reproduced with the permission of the Minister of Public Works and Government Services, 2011.

TABLE 11.1	Programs to Support Aboriginal Economic Development

Business Development Program

• Aboriginal Business Development Program

• Access to Capital Program

• Financial Institutions Program

• Loan Loss Reserve Program

• Major Resource and Energy Development Investments Initiative

Community Economic Development

• Aboriginal Workforce Participation Initiative

• Community Economic Development Program

• Community Economic Opportunities Program

• Community Support Services Program

• Procurement Strategy for Aboriginal Business

Lands and Environmental Management

• Commercial Leasing

• Contaminated Sites Management Program

• First Nations Land Management Regime

• Reserve Land and Environment Management Program

Source: INAC. 2009. Backgrounder: Renovating Programs in Support of Lands and Economic Development. Retrieved May 9, 2011, from www.ainc-inac.gc.ca/ai/mr/nr/m-a2010/23367bg-eng.asp.

To implement the federal framework for Aboriginal economic development, the government has created three major branches of support. One deals with business development, the second with community economic development, and the third focuses on lands and environmental management. Table 11.1 identifies the specific programs.

Some programs, such as the Community Economic Development Program, provide the core funding for Aboriginal economic development services to their community. Others, such as the Loan Loss Reserve Program, are specific to First Nations. The Loan Loss Reserve Program provides some support for commercial financial institutions to debt finance various businesses that have an asset on a reserve. The First Nations Land Management Regime is a First Nations–led initiative that provides First Nations with law-making powers to govern their own reserve lands, resources, and environment.

As a new "key" driver of change, the government has implemented a new Treasury Board Policy that relates to the delivery of transfer payment programs. Under the new policy, all federal departments linked with First Nations have to adopt a risk-based approach, engage recipients, establish service standards, and pursue opportunities for harmonization and standardization. This translates into new relations with First Nations people. It rejects the "one size fits all" approach that has been so traditionally used by AAND, allows for multi-year funding agreements that must engage the recipients of the program.

The federal government has implemented two major legislative changes that will support Aboriginal economic development. First, they amended the *Indian Oil and Gas*

TABLE 11.2	Percentage of Small- and Medium-Sized Enterprises owned by Aboriginal People by Sector, 2009					
3.5%	1.6	1.7	1.3	1.1	2.7	2.8
Agriculture/ Primary	Manufacturing	Wholesale and Retail	Professional Services	Knowledge- Based Industries	Accomodation and Food Services	Other

Source: Government of Canada, 2009. *Renovating Programs in Support of Lands and Economic Development*, Ottawa: Indian and Northern Affairs Canada, p. 17. Retrieved May 9, 2011, from www.ainc-inac.gc.ca/ecd/prg_reno-eng.pdf.

Act, which addresses the regulatory gap between on- and off-reserve resource development and could, with some stimulation, increase economic development on reserves in this capacity. Second, it amended the *First Nations Commercial and Industrial Development Act*, which will allow First Nations communities to create commercial real estate developments on reserve land.

The extent to which Aboriginal people are involved in the economic domain has increased over the past three decades. In 2006, there were more than 34 000 self-employed Aboriginal people, of which 40 percent were women. Nearly 3 percent of small and medium enterprises in Canada are owned by Aboriginal people. To support these entrepreneurs, 60 Aboriginal financial institutions provide advice and financial support. Table 11.2 shows the proportion of Aboriginal involvement in various sectors of the economy. At present, Indigenous peoples make up 3.5 percent of agricultural/primary businesses and around 2.7 percent in accommodation and food services and "other" activities.

Impact on Aboriginal Peoples

Several basic assumptions (which the federal government had been slow to accept over the years) underline the need for community development and control. First, all people fundamentally desire to better themselves. When their attempts to do so are blocked, the social and psychological damage is considerable. Second, the major obstacle to improvement is a lack of such resources as human and social capital. Third, given resources and opportunity, people find their own effective ways to meet their needs and improve their lives. In the past, Aboriginal people were forced to try to solve problems through the solutions provided for them by government agencies; procedures not part of the dominant capitalist culture were criticized and rejected. Fourth, a change in only one aspect of a group's behaviour seldom produces meaningful, lasting results. A simple influx of money does not solve very much given that the social behaviour of humanity has many facets; each component of behaviour stands in relationship to other components. This interrelationship must be considered when any attempts at change are made (Belanger, 2006; Aberle, 1970; 2004).

If Aboriginal economic development is to occur, several structural changes need to take place. These changes will not happen overnight, nor will they occur without an impact on Aboriginal people. The effects of industrialization on a population are well known and have been extensively documented. Industrialization has had a traumatic impact on people in virtually every society that has made the transition from agrarianism, let alone hunting-and-gathering. The disruptions of social relationships and related customs and practices are particularly severe. These disruptions were evident when Aboriginal peoples changed from a nomadic to a sedentary society. In short, the transition to an industrial economy and a more sedentary lifestyle has always exacted a great toll in terms of human suffering.

Nonetheless, it does not necessarily follow that Aboriginal people must experience the same level of disruption that others have had to undergo. Some structural changes could be introduced to bring about cultural and economic change with minimal impact. For example, movement into the city, a traditionally frustrating and tension-producing activity, can be facilitated through the proper institutional help. The removal of barriers to jobs can be implemented. The settlement of Aboriginal title and the integration of development plans can also be undertaken. In addition, development needs to proceed under local control—that is, only after plans have been developed that meet local needs and priorities rather than those of the national government or multinational corporations. Finally, there must be more integration. Modern and traditional activities need to be developed together, rather than allowing one to develop at the expense of the other. The various institutional sectors of Aboriginal society also need to be "synchronized" with the dominant society. For example, educational needs have to be integrated with economic needs, and health-care facilities need to be related to the work world (Wien, 1986).

This structural approach to social change clearly requires an understanding of the institutional structures that influence Aboriginal life. Rather than focusing on the individual as the unit of analysis, such an approach examines the socio-economic role of internal Aboriginal institutions and their external relationships (Girvan, 1973). For too long, theorists have viewed Aboriginal–Euro-Canadian relations as an "Aboriginal problem" rather than as a "white problem," and have failed to take external factors into account (Skarlicki, n.d.).

Clearly, the "Aboriginal problem" has been created by the economic, cultural, and political structures of Canada, as much of this book has tried to demonstrate. The position of Aboriginal people in Canada is certainly not the result of cultural isolation or their particular psychological tendencies. Nor does individual racial and cultural discrimination provide a sufficient explanation for the historically low socio-economic position of Aboriginal people in Canada. While individual discrimination may have slowed upward socio-economic mobility, it has not eliminated it. Sunkel has shown that a totally marginal group is "deprived of all means of access to a source of income of reasonable level and stability" (1973: 141); clearly this is not the case for Aboriginal people in Canada.

The marginal position of Aboriginal people can only be explained when institutional and systemic discrimination against them are considered along with their limited sources of income, their lack of control over the means of production, and the historical conditions that were imposed upon them. The manner in which resources are deployed, whether human, capital, or technological, determines the level of employment, the extent of industrialization, and the distribution of income. As Mariategui (1934) pointed out in the early part of the last century, the roots of the Aboriginal problem are economic and historical and lie in the system of land ownership. This clearly implies that the economy is not embedded in social relations, but rather that social relations are structures within society's economic institutions (Polanyi, 1974).

In the course of Aboriginal–Euro-Canadian relations, traditional systems have been replaced with foreign, imposed ones, or have been eroded to the point where they are in danger of being lost altogether. Aboriginal political structures, languages, and systems of religious beliefs and practices—including the family and kinship structure—have suffered oppression as well as transformation. Part of the revitalization process may involve reconstructing and reviving traditional ways of doing things, or, at the very least, the process can involve gaining control over, modifying, or imbuing existing imposed structures with a sense of local ownership and local values.

Holistic Aboriginal Economic Development

The key to successful revitalization and development lies in a unified (holistic) and dynamic approach that must take into account the social, cultural, political, and environmental/ecological aspects of Aboriginal community life—not just the "economic" aspect. One of the characteristics that distinguishes Aboriginal development from mainstream community development (as the concept is usually defined in the literature) is the equal significance of a non-market or subsistence orientation (Coffey and Polese, 1985; Hanson, 1985; Four Worlds Development Project, 1985; Robinson and Ghostkeeper, 1987, 1988; Usher, 1989). This unified approach thus includes local authority over economic decisions; the revival of traditional community structures; the creation of an economic mix that may include a combination of a subsistence, industrial, and retail orientation; and even the promotion of greater ecological harmony.

The idea of **holistic development** further includes all elements of human life that contribute to human welfare, such as nutrition, health, shelter, work and employment, the physical environment, and the socio-cultural environment. Participation in decision-making processes, a sense of human dignity and belonging—anything pertaining to the "style" or pattern of development that is appropriate to Aboriginal peoples' values and circumstances—must likewise be part of a development strategy. In short, a holistic and unified approach to community development, or revitalization, calls for a renewed focus on people, not solely on the "product" or "project."

There is a growing sense among a number of political and economic theorists, as well as among Aboriginal people and environmentalists, that there are alternative forms of economic development that can be undertaken outside the capitalist mode. Moreover, there is a serious questioning of why an industrial and market-based economy that is the basis for development should entail environmental degradation, the squandering of non-renewable resources, the diminution of human dignity, and the alienation of the individual from social and cultural life among some of its consequences. Thomas Berger (1977; 1985), for example, has dealt in detail with the effects of industrial development on Aboriginal cultures with strong continuing ties to the land-based or bush economy. Berger (1977) argues that:

> It is self-deception to believe that large-scale industrial development would end unemployment and underemployment of Native people in the North. In the first place, we have always overestimated the extent to which Native people are unemployed and underemployed by understating their continued reliance on the land. Secondly, we have never fully recognized that industrial development has, in itself, contributed to social, economic, and geographic dislocation among Native people. (p. 123)

Community revitalization and development could, realistically, be considered in the context of both a hinterland economic adaptation and a so-called multi-sectoral approach. In place of the dependency that accompanies external cash transfers to local Aboriginal (and even non-Aboriginal) economies, for example, options for development should be balanced, pragmatic, and locally controlled. One flexible and adaptable option may be a revitalized domestic economy, involving home or local production and household self-reliance, in combination with occupations that are based on the rhythm of a seasonal lifestyle. Unfortunately, "mainstream" socio-economic development has always regarded these factors as barriers; yet it might be precisely this option that could be the most viable for many Aboriginal communities in the face of their continued marginalization from metropolitan centres and relative geographical (and social) isolation (Usher, 1989).

Another option, in combination with the previous one, might be a mixed and multi-sectoral economic base. Such an economic base might consist of mixing primary resource extraction, cultural industries, light manufacturing, and service industries into one sustainable economy. Such a "mixture" would include the features of a subsistence/bush economy as well as an industrial/market-based economy. Going further, Robinson and Ghostkeeper (1987; 1988) have argued that there may even be emerging structural parallels between a traditional bush economy and a post-industrial, or "next," economy (one that focuses on information and services). Features shared by both types of economy might be exploited by Aboriginal entrepreneurs and become the basis for community development that does not have to depend upon specialization, competition, hierarchy, or environmental degradation for success and viability (Indian Minerals Directorate, 1981a; 1981b).

It is clear from the current thrust of federal government policy making and band/tribal council development initiatives that the emphasis is increasingly being placed on self-reliance, self-government, and the use and development of local resources. On the one hand, AAND's openness towards the promotion of Aboriginal self-government may be seen as an implicit recognition of the need for a bottom-up approach to Aboriginal development. On the other hand, there is growing evidence that many First Nations communities are adopting a more entrepreneurial perspective on their common future. The creation, for example, of numerous Aboriginal-based development corporations and businesses is testimony to this trend (e.g., Canadian Indian Resource Corporation). Many communities, however, are still inclined to pursue more traditional paths of development.

An Aboriginal community's value system is part of the total resources of the community that must be considered during the actual course of economic revitalization and development. To generate a truly Aboriginal-value–based list of indicators requires the identification of those aspects of the community and community life that residents desire to maintain, enhance, or even remove. Validating a list of indicators provides an opportunity to ascertain how ready community residents are for changes; which changes they feel are most desirable, urgent, or wholly unacceptable; and which values they anticipate might be compromised as a result of development. The formulation and assessment of the effectiveness of holistic development strategies should be enhanced by the use of an indicator system. Some "baseline" data are necessary in order to detect the effects of changes brought about by development in Aboriginal communities, and provide the foundation for helping the direction of that change. Indicators and an **indicator system** are a means of building this kind of a database. An indicator system could be incorporated into more comprehensive First Nations development studies (Gadacz, 1991; Armstrong and Rogers, 1996).

ECONOMIC STRATEGIES AND APPROACHES

We will now turn to a discussion about ways in which Aboriginal people could develop their economic base: the concession, the joint venture, co-management, the service contract, the management agreement, the community development corporation, and local producers' cooperatives. Even though all these activities point to active participation by Aboriginal people in development, the question of the extent of their involvement remains. How deeply do the bands want to be involved, for instance, in projects where the risk factors might be high? Recently, the then INAC commissioned a study looking at 65 reserves that are economically prospering in an attempt to ascertain the causes of their success. It turned out that nearly all of these successful reserves are near urban areas and have access to a larger infrastructure and transportation routes and have, over the years, established economic relationships with nearby municipal governments.

The Concession

Concession has been the traditional strategy whereby Aboriginals (through the federal government) grant a company production rights. The company makes a direct equity investment for the sole purpose of extracting a resource (Bankes, 1983). As Asante (1979) pointed out, in many cases the concession amounts to a virtual assumption of sovereignty over the host country's or nation's resources by transnational corporations. Under these conditions, the corporation asserts ownership not only of the fixed assets but also of the natural resource itself (Bankes, 1983). During the mid-20th century, it was probably the most widely employed development strategy used by Aboriginal people.

Under a concession agreement, there is very little direct "up-front" cost for the band. Nor are there any operating costs. In addition, these agreements are easy to administer, since the need for supervision, auditing, and training is minimal. All of this is provided by the company that agrees to exploit the resource. In short, the cost to the band is minimal, but the return is also minimal. Aboriginal people have found that this type of agreement does not encourage the training of local residents in order to assume jobs in the industry, thereby introducing them into the wage economy. While this type of business arrangement was popular in the mid-20th century, Aboriginal communities and businesses have not used it in recent years.

The Joint Venture

Joint ventures normally involve an entity formed between two or more parties to undertake business activity together. In this type of venture, the parties agree to create a new entity and ultimately share in the revenues, expenses, and control of the enterprise. There are two major types of joint ventures: equity joint ventures and non-equity joint ventures. Equity joint ventures involve two or more parties, one of which provides most of the capital involved with undertaking the project. This type of partnership offers companies that lack the monetary resources the means to finance the project. On the other hand, non-equity ventures usually involve one partner gaining technical and management skills from a larger partner. The smaller partner can still provide resources such as labour and land to the other partner, but these are often limited. Non-equity joint ventures are the most common business arrangement between Aboriginal communities and non-Aboriginal companies (Canadian Council for Aboriginal Business, 2010). An example is the Bigstone Forestry Inc. joint venture. In this case, the start-up capital was acquired with a substantial equity investment by Bigstone Cree Nation of about a third of the capital while Al-Pac provided additional funds and a guarantee for the loan Bigstone had to take out to get the business up and running. Once it was in operation, it established five-year contracts with Al-Pac and Weyerhaeuser to provide timber.

The joint venture type of agreement requires that Aboriginal people (1) already possess the technical expertise, and (2) have some "interest" that is considered valuable by the other party, such as land or mineral rights. There is both a direct and indirect cost involved with this type of development. The joint venture generally presents an opportunity for the local people to increase their control over the development. It can increase revenues for Aboriginal people and it allows for a flexible method of collecting revenues (Bankes, 1983; Asante, 1979). For example, the Mississauga of the New Credit First Nation recently purchased a 70 percent interest in a company that is involved in a casino-supply business and is now operating on the reserve. The government has also entered into joint ventures though loaning money to Aboriginal companies and has guaranteed its backing. But since the government allows for no control or ownership of the natural resources, it is unlikely that these types of joint ventures are a viable long-term economic strategy (Dyck and Waldram, 1993).

For Aboriginal businesses, there appear to be numerous benefits to partnership, including enabling Aboriginal businesses to qualify for contracts that they would not otherwise be able to qualify for; providing access to partner resources, new opportunities, new markets, capital, and technology; employment, job creation, knowledge transfer, role modelling, and mentorship; capacity and skills development; revenue generation; sharing of responsibility and risk; training; de-bunking myths and stereotypes about Aboriginal people; demonstrating the capacity and potential of Aboriginal people and communities; supporting the growth of Aboriginal business and business expertise; diversity; providing authenticity, legitimacy, and credibility; and adding value and strengthening ties.

Historically, joint ventures between Aboriginal and non-Aboriginal companies were relatively rare. However, since the early 1980s, joint ventures and Aboriginal–non-Aboriginal partnerships have been on the rise. In 1985, the Department of Indian Affairs estimated that approximately 1.3 percent of all Aboriginal-owned businesses were joint ventures. However, by 2008, nearly 10 percent of Aboriginal businesses based on reserves and 18 percent off reserves were joint ventures with other companies. This increase has come about through changes in social policies and the global environment. Factors such as the following have led to the increased interest in joint venture agreements:

- a change in the global competitive environment
- a broadening and deepening of society's expectations about what constitutes socially responsible corporate behaviour in general and toward Aboriginal people in particular
- the large and growing number of legal and regulatory mechanisms that impose requirements and restrictions on business ventures affecting Aboriginal lands and people

- the large and growing Aboriginal population, its increasing affluence, and its increasing level of education
- the already enormous and rapidly-growing pool of natural and financial resources (in addition to human resources) that Aboriginal people control or will control in the near future

On the non-Aboriginal business side, joint ventures can result in a new customer base, a new source of labour, tax benefits, access to new opportunities through government procurement contracts, improved access to natural resources, a new labour force, the creation of new suppliers and new markets, supporting companies in achieving their employment equity goals, and business growth.

The Co-Management Partnership

Partnerships involve two or more parties, whereby Aboriginal people would have a say in determining the rate and nature of development. Economic linkages with other organizations must be evaluated and "costed out" as to the benefits and costs for Aboriginal communities. Aboriginal people have generally opted for co-management strategies when renewable resources are involved. Ownership of the resources is not necessary, but all parties must recognize that each has a legitimate interest in them. Aboriginal people use co-management strategies based on the belief that the orderly use of resources will facilitate the survival and health of their environment. Pinkerton (1989) has argued that Aboriginal people will continue to pursue co-management agreements between themselves and non-Aboriginal people. There are several reasons for this preference:

1. Co-management creates cooperation among individual workers.

2. Co-management creates a commitment among local workers to share the costs and benefits of their efforts toward enhancement and conservation.

3. Co-management creates a higher degree of organization and mutual commitment among Aboriginal workers, which translates into a better bargaining relationship with external agents.

Co-management arrangements represent a transfer of decision-making power to Aboriginal people, and are therefore difficult to negotiate with non-Aboriginal people. However, the view that Aboriginal people have a legitimate interest in natural resources is one that is slowly being recognized by government and business. The 1990 *Sparrow* decision by the Supreme Court, which noted that Aboriginal people have a legal and legitimate interest in renewable resources, went far in alerting government and businesses to accept this perspective and consider co-management initiatives.

The Service Contract

Under agreements of this type, the status of Aboriginal ownership over a natural resource is reaffirmed. Thus, rather than transferring the title of the resource (as in a concession) to the developing company, the band simply hires the corporation as a contractor or business partner to perform a specific task for a specified amount of money. The disadvantage in using this type of strategy is that bands must have a substantial cash flow in order to pay for the up-front cost of the development, which can be quite high. Both Zakariya (1976) and Bankes (1983) pointed out that under this type of agreement, the band has no internal control over the project, and there are few opportunities for Aboriginal people to gain employment or technical and administrative skills. Also, the project must to be carefully monitored by the band to ensure that its members receive the maximum benefits from it. The advantage of such an arrangement is Aboriginal ownership and jurisdiction over the natural resource. In addition, other firms supply the technology (and risk capital) to explore, develop, and market the resources. Western Micro Systems Ltd. (an Aboriginal-owned company) recently formed a partnership with IBM through their program PartnerWorld that allows Western Micro Systems to supply access to other markets while receiving education, supplies, and various products and services.

The Management Agreement

The management agreement is a strategy whereby Aboriginal people purchase expertise for a specified period of time. The contracted consultants can either act as advisors while the Aboriginal management retains sole control of the company, or the Aboriginal people can choose to relinquish control to the consultants. The Savanna Energy Services Corporation is a good example of a management agreement. This oil rig construction and drilling company has half of its rigs owned by an Aboriginal community (Alexis Nakota Sioux Nation, Blood Tribe). However, Savanna oversees the hiring, administration, and activities such as tax filing. In short, Savanna oversees much of the day-to-day management of the rigs and the Aboriginal partners are fully engaged and aware of the business activity.

The Community Development Corporation

A band or a First Nation can form a corporation and explore for minerals on its reserve. The corporation is granted permits and leases according to terms set by the federal government. These corporations are created to help plan and implement the business development goals of a community or region, and they can be involved either in risking capital or acting as an advisory body. A variation of this strategy is called a local producer's cartel, which involves the formation of a syndicate or trust that is able to take over a business venture from the original developer and carry on all negotiations with developers. In the mid-1960s, when 25 American Indian tribes created the Council of Energy Resource Tribes (CERT) in order to control all mineral development on their reserves, they established a cartel.

Some bands and larger Aboriginal groups that have taken this course have chosen either to remain independent or to enter into joint ventures with other non-Aboriginal companies. Two major problems have beset those Aboriginal groups that have created corporations. First, the corporations tend to benefit from the development more than the band does, and may become more powerful than the band. This problem has been somewhat alleviated by making all members of the band (including newborns) members of the corporation. The second problem centres on the risk factor and the need for a considerable amount of money up front before the development starts. These difficulties are not insurmountable, as evidenced by the numerous success stories throughout Canada. A notable one is Makivik Corporation, created in 1978 pursuant to the signing of the James Bay and Northern Québec Agreement (1975). The corporation, headquartered in Kuujjuaq (Nunavik, Quebec), has the mandate to implement the agreement and to administer the funds accorded to the Inuit.

The Local Producers' Cooperative

These are usually voluntary, non-profit societies incorporated to run a business. The members of the cooperative own shares of the business and have one vote at each general meeting. A board of directors is elected to operate the business and carry out day-to-day activities. In effect, a cooperative is a business owned by its customers (see Box 11.2 for an example).

A history of the cooperatives shows that until the 1950s most of the Aboriginal trade in Canada (particularly in isolated regions) was carried out through the Hudson's Bay

Box 11.2	First Nations and Business Liaison Group of New Brunswick Inc.

On June 2, 2007, the New Brunswick Chiefs passed a resolution to create the First Nations and Business Liaison Group of New Brunswick Inc. A steering committee was thereafter established with clear terms of reference on November 15, 2007.

The group was created as a result of recognition that the First Nations of New Brunswick can benefit economically from a direct and continuing dialogue with the business sector and that there is significant potential regarding employment opportunities and business development projects for the mutual benefit of both First Nations and the business community.

Thus, the First Nations and Business Liaison Group of New Brunswick Inc. formed as a partnership of all the First Nations in New Brunswick in order to identify business opportunities that First Nations and businesses could develop as partners. The Liaison Group works to support partnership development for New Brunswick First Nations but also supports individual communities and Aboriginal entrepreneurs.

The head office of the First Nations and Business Liaison Group of New Brunswick Inc. is situated at Eel Ground First Nation. There is also a satellite office in Fredericton at St. Mary's First Nation. An executive director, whose primary role is to facilitate job opportunities and business relationships, oversees daily operations. A steering committee of six guides the process. There is also a board of directors comprised of the 15 First Nations in the province and 15 business representatives.

The vision of the First Nations and Business Liaison Group of New Brunswick Inc. is to facilitate communications between First Nations and the business community in New Brunswick, to foster the building of economic relationships and business activities between the two communities, including those that create employment opportunities for Aboriginal people, all in accordance with the interests and aspirations of both parties.

The First Nations and Business Liaison Group of New Brunswick Inc. has a mandate to foster business partnerships throughout the province between Aboriginal people and non-Aboriginal businesses. Because it is a relatively new undertaking, it has spent the bulk of its time thus far promoting collaborative and business partnership opportunities with New Brunswick First Nations. Two partnerships that were recently initiated are between Indian Island First Nation and Ocean Spray and the Imperial Manufacturing Group.

Ocean Spray, a leading producer of canned and bottled juice drinks, contacted the First Nations and Business Liaison Group of New Brunswick Inc. in an effort to reach out to First Nations for a potential partnership. In turn, the First Nations and Business Liaison Group of New Brunswick Inc. referred the company to the Indian Island First Nation, which then dealt with Ocean Spray

directly. A partnership has been formalized with a formal agreement.

Imperial Manufacturing Group is a leading producer of air distribution and building products for residential and light commercial applications and a producer of indoor air quality equipment for the North American heating, ventilation, and air-conditioning industry. The company has expressed an interest in working with the Elsipogtog First Nation and is in discussions to introduce a pilot program that would help train and employ members of the First Nation at the Richibucto, New Brunswick, plant. A partnership has been formalized through a legal agreement.

Company. In 1959 the government began to encourage and support a number of locally-owned-and-operated cooperatives. This idea seemed to fit particularly well with one of the elements of Aboriginal culture—sharing. The first Aboriginal cooperatives were producer-oriented and involved such activities as art, crafts, or fishing. Then consumer cooperatives emerged, where importing and exporting activities were carried out. In many communities, cooperatives and other private enterprise businesses, such as the Hudson's Bay Company, existed side by side, selling and buying many of the same products.

In the past, Aboriginal cooperatives encountered two major problems in their operations. First, they lacked skilled managers. Second, they found it difficult to engage in direct competition with integrated, multinational companies. Nevertheless, they have succeeded in providing employment for Aboriginal people. Today they are the largest employer of Aboriginal people in the North and elsewhere, and register annual sales in excess of $30 million. There are currently well over 50 cooperatives nationwide, employing more than 600 people and generating between $10 and $20 million in income annually. However, an infusion of government monies is still required for some co-ops to survive; various government departments continue to contribute to their development. Much of this money is put toward training directors, managers, and staff. Additional federal monies are set aside to help with new production techniques and business marketing strategies.

NEW FORMS OF ECONOMIC RELATIONS

New forms of business relations between Aboriginal and non-Aboriginal units are emerging. For example, there are procurement for goods and service policies that give preference to local Aboriginal businesses. Sodexo Canada has developed a "teaming agreement" with local Aboriginal communities with regard to procurement policies. It has established preferred contract proposals whereby a community that has already nego-tiated an impact benefit agreement is offered a service contract or given preferential treatment in the bidding process. Cameco Corporation is another good example in that 70 percent of its service purchase orders come from Aboriginal sources. Diavik Diamond Mines Inc. has implanted a reliable "supply chain" process with Aboriginal peoples in the region that helps build local business capabilities that can service the organization. It created a socio-economic monitoring agreement that evaluates the benefits to the local region. In turn, Diavik affirms its actions in providing training, employment, and business development to the neighbouring Aboriginal communities. In other cases, non-Aboriginal corporations are developing participation agreements and impact benefit agreements with various Aboriginal communities. These agreements allow the individual community to specify what it wants to get out of the project in terms of the economic and social benefits and, in return, will assure its support for the project. The nature of the participation can range from employment training to human capacity development and business participa-tion that will create the business space for Aboriginal communities.

Other forms of linking business opportunities between Aboriginal communities and businesses and non-Aboriginal businesses have taken hold. Below are just a few of the ways in which these new linkages have emerged:

Franchising When an individual or community acquires a branch of a larger company, the franchisee benefits from the "parent" company by being able to access expertise and government and operations practices modelling the corporate structure.

Spin-off partnerships When a business evolves as a result of another business or partnership but eventually separates into a separate initiative.

Client–corporation partnerships When an Aboriginal business partners with a client to acquire expertise and develop its human resources potential.

Business-to-business partnerships When two or more businesses come together to partner for mutual benefit.

Public–private relationships When government engages with a privately owned business.

The economic impact of these different agreements has been substantial. For exam-ple, Syncrude has awarded contracts to Aboriginal businesses in the fields of welding, fabricating, environmental monitoring, and waste management over the past 20 years that have exceeded $1.2 billion. Sodexo Canada currently has contracts with Aboriginal-owned companies that exceeded $14 million in 2009, and Diavik granted $1.2 billion in contracts with Aboriginal businesses over the past decade. These examples demonstrate that there are a variety of linkages between Aboriginal communities and non-Aboriginal businesses that have increased the community's economic growth and can potentially lead to economic development.

Each of the strategies identified, including international ventures, points to the quest by Aboriginal people to gain control over their resources and to manage them. The variety of strategies reflects the differing situations in which Aboriginal people find themselves. Nevertheless, the ultimate goal for Aboriginal people is to control their land and resources. Establishing the proper administrative structures is only the beginning. Once control has been established, structures have to be devised to manage economic development and to foster an enhancement of quality of life. This requires the necessary skills to operate businesses and to participate in what is already a global economy.

Each of the development strategies discussed above has benefits as well as costs. For this reason the type of agreement that an Aboriginal group might wish to make is ultimately determined by the group's goals. For example, if the Aboriginal group wants to maintain a subsistence way of life, like the Cree of James Bay, and still allow development of natural resources, the concession type of agreement might be appropriate. On the other hand, if it wants to become directly involved in a particular project, then a joint venture would seem more appropriate. For example, a joint venture called Shehtah Drilling was formed between Esso (50 percent), the Dene (25 percent), and the Métis (25 percent) development corporations in 1983 to conduct drilling and service-rig operations in the Northwest Territories. The ATCO/EQUTAK drilling venture organized between Atco-Mustang Drilling and the Inuvialuit Development Corporation (with the assistance of Petro Canada), and Beaufort Food Services, a joint venture between Beau-Tuk Marine Services and the Inuvialuit Development Corporation, are two other examples of joint ventures that have been relatively successful. Aboriginal international joint ventures of different kinds in this age of globalization and international capitalism are surely expected to increase in the decades to come.

Where successful agreements have been made to develop band natural resources, what do Aboriginal people do with their increased income? The number of cases is relatively small, but the Hobbema reserve in Alberta is one good example. There, the Samson Band's energy revenue exceeded $60 million even in 1980. The band used some of its profits to build and operate a 283-hectare grain operation. But the band has also made investments beyond the agricultural domain. In the early 1980s, the Samson business manager bought the charter of the Edmonton Canadian Insurance Company for slightly more than $1 million. Other Samson Band investments now include rental properties in Edmonton, shares for subdivisions in three nearby towns, shares in a Vancouver condominium project, and shares in a housing development in Cold Lake, Alberta. Other bands, like Samson, are also investing in land purchases, housing projects, and banks.

A DISTINCTLY INDIGENOUS APPROACH TO ENTREPRENEURSHIP

The results of this research project suggest that Aboriginal–non-Aboriginal business partnerships share many of the same elements that other partnerships share. However, there seem to be specific factors that are unique to Aboriginal–non-Aboriginal partnerships and indeed to Indigenous entrepreneurship in general. Indigenous approaches to business tend to have a strong cultural element. Moreover, obligations tend to extend beyond those to the individual and his/her immediate family to the extended family, the local Aboriginal community, and the larger Aboriginal community. There is a strong tie to the community and an expectation and obligation to "give back," with the goal of setting the stage for a more solid future for future Aboriginal generations. Thus, it appears that this alternative way of conducting business is infused with culture and something distinctly "Indigenous" that differentiates the Aboriginal approach significantly from conventional business approaches. This might suggest that there is a distinct way of conducting business between Aboriginal and non-Aboriginal partners, one that differs from models upon which conventional business approaches are currently based. This new model moves well beyond the "bottom line" mentality toward a new paradigm that incorporates Aboriginal principles to guide partnerships without sacrificing profit. It also incorporates Aboriginal tenets of cultural respect, cultural sensitivity, and trust.

DEVELOPMENT AND LIABILITIES

Although economic development is seen as a positive step in Aboriginal self-governance, it must not be totally controlled by the corporate sector of Canadian society. The federal government must not allow the corporate sector to interfere with or influence the development of Aboriginal communities, since economic development of the Aboriginal community is not in the corporations' interests. So far, through close ties with the political elite, corporations have successfully blocked the federal financing that would permit Aboriginal economic development. For example, Saskatchewan First Nations hold $170 million in government-backed mortgages and pay over $1 million a month to mortgage companies in interest alone. If Aboriginal people started paying interest to their own institutions, the profit could be used to build up their own communities. If Aboriginal people were allowed to develop and control the reserves, they could eliminate corporate contracts for reserve projects and drain off the unskilled labour surplus for primary sector industries (Dyck, 1996).

If the corporate sector were allowed to initiate economic development on reserves unencumbered, franchising would result. Under a franchise system, a corporation advances money to an individual Aboriginal person, who then manages a store that sells the corporation's product exclusively. The corporation also provides certain services and trains staff to ensure proper marketing techniques. In return for setting up the store, providing the loan, and training the staff, the company reaps several benefits, including a large percentage of the profits and access to the reserve and nearby communities. Franchising is an efficient and inexpensive way to guarantee non-Aboriginal corporate control of the reserve. Again, the presence of an Aboriginal staff defuses anti–non-Aboriginal sentiments and prevents the organization of a cohesive revolt. Moreover, the development of the reserve by outsiders allows for external control over the speed, extent, and nature of that development (Tabb, 1970: 58).

Although non-Aboriginal institutions are promoting individual entrepreneurship, many Aboriginal people have begun to recognize that the result of this policy will be continued subordination. Increasingly, cogent arguments such as the following are put forward in support of Aboriginal community control and development and propose four sets of recommendations:

(i) The establishment of economically viable reserves controlled by the Indians with sufficient natural resources to ensure adequate incomes for the residents. The key element in this recommendation is that the natural resources of expanded Indian lands should be firmly placed in the control of the community and its representative leaders.

(ii) The establishment of an Indian corporation which can receive direct grants and long-term low-interest loans to promote economic development on the reserve, to improve and initiate village services, and to in other ways enable Indians to better utilize their natural and economic resources.

(iii) A major revamping of the educational system so as to reduce discontinuities in learning, sustain effective ties with parents, strengthen the student's self-image as Indian, and maintain his self-esteem, as well as prepare him to be economically and socially competent in dealing with the institutions of the larger Canadian society.

(iv) The establishment of an Indian social development program, funded by the federal and/or provincial governments, which can assist in providing the mechanism for the emergence of new Indian leaders, increase communication with other Indian and non-Indian groups, and promote local and regional community, social, and political infrastructures. (Chance, 1970: 33–35)

But just as there are different kinds of development strategies, as outlined above, and a whole range of potential projects and activities, communities must remain alert to possible negative or unintended consequences. Even more, bands and communities must resist the temptation to "make a fast buck" by being drawn into "lucrative" enterprises in the name of "tradition" that are potentially damaging to their people and culture. Economic benefits may come with potential social costs.

An example is the October 2006 official opening of the River Cree Resort and Casino on the Enoch reserve near Edmonton, Alberta. The Enoch Cree were one of the first to submit an application for a casino after the Alberta government announced in 2002 that it was prepared to accept proposals from provincial First Nations. In April, 2004, the Alberta Gaming and Liquor Commission approved the band's application to construct an on-reserve casino. After wrangling with the City of Edmonton concerning access to municipal utilities and services, the Enoch Cree offered to pay the city $1.4 million for water, sewer, and firefighting services for its proposed casino.

Touted as Alberta's first Native-run casino, it claims to be one of the largest employers of Aboriginal people in the province. The $178-million casino includes restaurants, bars, grills, two ice rinks (including an NHL-size hockey rink), and a nine-story, 255-room hotel with pool and fitness centre. The casino itself has 600 slot machines and 40 gaming tables in the gaming rooms, with plans to double the number of slot machines in the future. The Enoch band's business partner is a corporation based in Las Vegas. The Alberta government made some rules about how First Nations spend the revenues: money will go toward addictions treatment, cultural events, elder and senior care, reserve infrastructure, community safety projects, and life-skills training. However the $25 million profit realized the first year more than pays for these and many other initiatives for the community (Belanger, 2006).

Summary

- Economic growth is different from economic development.
- Reallocation of institutional structures is necessary to achieve economic development.

- Aboriginal communities must develop "firewalls" between political activities and economic decisions.
- Government needs to take steps to allow for Aboriginal economic development.
- A changing role for Aboriginal people in the economic institutional order may bring about tension and conflict.

Key Terms

Canadian Aboriginal
   Economic Develop-
   ment Strategy p. 349

dependency theory
   pg. 346

economic develop-
   ment   pg. 341

economic growth
   pg. 341

holistic development
   pg. 360

Indian Economic Devel-
   opment Fund p. 348

indicator system p. 361

neoclassical theory
   pg. 343

settler society p. 344

Questions for Further Discussion

1. How has settler society impacted Aboriginal economic development?
2. Explain why economic development is a necessary strategy for Aboriginal communities.
3. What is the evidence to argue that Aboriginal communities are underdeveloped as opposed to undeveloped?
4. What is new about AAND's approach to development compared to previous approaches?
5. What constitutes successful holistic economic develement?
6. Are the seven economic strategies discussed in pages 362-367 compatible with holistic economic development?
7. Might new forms of business relations between Aboriginals and non-Aboriginals come at a social cost?

CHAPTER 12

Conclusions: Canadian Aboriginal Peoples in Global Context

This book has been an effort to describe the Canadian Aboriginal experience both from an historical and a contemporary social science perspective. It is important to recognize that Canada's Indian, Inuit, and Métis peoples continue to face problems shared by the world's Aboriginal peoples. Under colonialism in the past and inner colonialism in the present, the relentless pace of modernization and development has seen Aboriginal traditional cultures erode and their territories taken or signed away as part of the economic coercion to which they have been subjected. Whether as hunters and gatherers or urban dwellers, Aboriginal peoples who, willingly or not, are part of national societies face discrimination and exploitation in social service delivery, housing, education, and employment opportunities.

Most if not all Aboriginal societies today find themselves in a world that demands of them a choice between forging a new and hybridized set of social and cultural values and assimilation. For most of the world's Indigenous peoples—Canada's included—their traditional ways of life now exist only in the collective memory of surviving elders. Contact with dominant societies has eroded the need for many traditional aspects of life, rendering them redundant. No Aboriginal society has been immune to the effects of change, sometimes violently imposed, upon its traditional life-world. No Aboriginal society has retained the entirety of its traditional way of life into the present, nor does any traditional economy of Aboriginal people exist that is viable by itself. Without a complete set of new perceptual and conceptual tools, Aboriginal peoples cannot interpret the reality of the present.

Faced with a fractured and often violent past, Indigenous peoples have had to come to terms with an ill-understood present. This presents a doubly difficult challenge. While members of the dominant society have had many generations to internalize the necessary accommodations that so-called modern society requires, Aboriginal peoples have not. Achieving success requires the forging of a new set of values and outlooks, and places historical and cultural traditions at great risk (Cultural Survival, 1993).

For the dominant society, whose core values have developed to correspond to the demands of the economic system within which they live, success within that system does not require contradictory compromises. For Aboriginal peoples, it does—the demands of the industrialized economy run directly counter to their traditional values and beliefs. The present industrial world economy is not their system; it remains an externally imposed reality, not yet fully internalized.

Aboriginal peoples thus find themselves marginalized and isolated in an alien environment where racism and discrimination prevent them from becoming full participants in the mainstream. They are caught between competing versions of separate worlds.

All cultures experience continual change. Rapid, imposed, and sometimes violent change, however, can threaten the very heart of a culture and its continued existence.

Some Aboriginal cultures and societies will—and have—disappeared. Some will survive and thrive. Resiliency in the face of change is a hallmark of cultural strength. Many have begun the process of creating new cultural identities by preserving core values from the past and adapting them to the present in order to meet the demands of the future.

For there to be a future for Aboriginal peoples, there must be a need for them to continue to exist. There must be a cultural coherence that is able to adapt to the new world and meet its demands. The challenge is for Aboriginal people, as individuals and as collectivities, is that they must make choices without full knowledge of the consequences, and without full knowledge of their impact or repercussions.

All Aboriginal societies today have been irrevocably altered by contact with a dominant world economy based on capitalist industrial exploitation and its associated underpinnings. All have faced, and continue to face, challenges and choices in the quest to absorb what they perceive to be the best of what this new world has to offer, while struggling to retain that which they value from their traditional ways of life. These emergent life-worlds are not "traditional" cultures, nor are they truly part of the new world order—and most will never be. These hybrid cultures are being tested and refined in the present. Experimentation in this "real" world characterizes Aboriginal life-worlds, as their readjustments are melded into the cultures that will carry Aboriginal peoples into the future. What will this future hold? What is it that Aboriginal peoples want from the dominant societies? What are the basic demands these Aboriginal entities are articulating (and have been for a long time)?

Above all, all Aboriginal peoples desire the opportunity to survive. At the very basic level, Aboriginals value the things they share as a culture, the commonalities that set them apart from all other peoples. All Aboriginal societies want, at a minimum, a chance to hand down those core identifying values they hold dear to succeeding generations, in their own ways and without interference. Across the planet, the dominant perceptions of reality are being challenged by a rebirth of Aboriginal pride to accommodate to modern society. New concepts and philosophical constructs are being incorporated into the Aboriginal tool box of ideas. They are trying to find solutions that work, with varying results. At the local, national, and international levels, a host of new Aboriginal organizations dedicated to rekindling cultural pride have emerged in recent years.

Non-governmental organizations such as Aboriginal Survival International, the World Council of Aboriginal Peoples, the Grand Council of the Cree (Quebec), the Indian Council of South America, the International Indian Treaty Council, and the International Organization of Indigenous Resources Development, to name but a few (most of which are based in North America), have secured consultative status with the United Nations Economic and Social Council (ECOSOC) and are attempting to coordinate efforts on a global level. Pan-Inuit associations such as the Inuit Circumpolar Conference (also with the ECOSOC) are actively involved in many facets of international cooperation. National groups of Aboriginal populations are emerging in most nations and are beginning to have an effect on government policy in some jurisdictions. A variety of non-governmental organizations, such as the Workgroup for Aboriginal Peoples (based in the Netherlands), are organizing to support these efforts (Venne, 1998).

On a world level, these efforts can be seen as a movement. This movement represents a profound realization in Aboriginal peoples that their traditional life-worlds are in grave danger of disappearing. The choice is clear: They must consolidate what they value now, or face total assimilation. The growth of Aboriginal organizations dedicated to cultural survival in the face of serious challenges has come to characterize the Aboriginal experience in the 21st century. Most of their communities have proven to be remarkably resilient in the face of external threats to their continued existence. They have learned to cope with massive and unrelenting change as a constant fact of life. The world over, many Aboriginal societies have moved from the "Stone Age" to the "Atomic age" to the "Digital Age," literally within the span of a single human lifetime, and have had to internalize and incorporate ideals of new realities—both economic and technological. They have not always had the benefit of generations of adaptive time.

Despite the changes that have engulfed them, all Aboriginal societies have managed to retain the core values central to their existence. Outward accommodation has in many ways been accomplished without the alteration of the essentials that constitute what it means to be Aboriginal. Most are building upon their core values in an effort to reformulate their collective identities as distinct peoples and to translate these into a single resolution: to adapt tradition and custom in a modern world of change. Often, this involves reinventing tradition. New versions of older traditional societies are emerging everywhere.

In the contemporary setting, two forms of accommodation have to be reached. All Aboriginal societies have to accommodate to new and altered patterns of existence. On this score, they are restructuring their lives accordingly, though it is not a painless process. The internal strength they are developing, the cultural pride that is emerging, and the empowerment that is evident are the necessary series of constructs needed to ensure continued cultural survival. Not only must Aboriginal peoples accommodate themselves to the larger society—i.e., the international world "out there,"—but they must, through organizational identities, find acceptable ways to ensure that the dominant society will accept them.

This is a difficult task. To even secure a voice with which to articulate their demands for accommodation within the power structures of the dominant society, they will have to learn new ways of speaking. Then they must convincingly articulate their need and desire for a social space in which they can live, prosper, and continue to develop as separate cultural entities. It seems a cruel twist of logic that Aboriginal people must first compromise and accommodate to the dominant system before they can begin to argue that the system should accommodate them. Accommodation is also achieved by demanding inherent rights in the name of international justice and human rights (Ignatieff, 2000).

Broadly speaking, there are three basic Aboriginal demands. First is a secure and tenured land base, approximating as far as possible the extent of the territories that historically have been alienated from them. Aboriginal peoples are connected to the land in spiritual ways that are difficult for non-Aboriginal peoples to appreciate. Without such lands on which to live and secure a livelihood, assimilation is inevitable. All Aboriginal groups accept the fact that there are competing interests in the lands they claim; most are willing to negotiate. The second need is the desire for a viable and culturally relevant economy based on a mixture of traditional and sustainable renewable resources with non-traditional developments of their own choosing, and incorporating a community-oriented and participative approach to economic development. Aboriginal societies are opposed only to development that is destructive to their cultures. Sharing resources with the dominant society is not a problem, so long as there are benefits for both sides. Third is the right to a measure of political self-determination and self-government as distinct peoples, the ability to organize to preserve valued cultural traditions, the ability to say no to outside forces, and the ability to make their own mistakes in all relevant aspects of life. Other pressing and more immediate concerns include systemic and daily discrimination in health care delivery, education, and employment.

There has been progress, but the learning curve has been exceedingly steep. The Aboriginal 4 percent of the world's population—most of whom belong to the most disadvantaged groups in the world—has found the will to voice their concerns loudly and has demanded, in the name of justice and humanity, a meaningful place as nations in their own right on the national and international stages. Globally, there are an estimated 300 million Aboriginal peoples living in more than 70 countries, half of whom are included in the populations of China and India alone. Fifty million inhabit the world's tropical rainforests. At least 5000 Aboriginal groups can be distinguished by language and cultural differences. It is no exaggeration to suggest that some Aboriginal peoples live under the threat of extinction—if not physical threat, then certainly cultural (see Box 12.1). At the same time, Aboriginal people currently occupy lands endowed with nearly half of the world's natural resources and thus have become a target of development activities not always in their best interests.

Fortunately, the recognition of Aboriginal issues such as language loss, poor health and shortened life expectancy, economic exploitation, and loss of livelihood has been gathering momentum in the United Nations system and within the international legal community for quite some time. The International Labour Organization (ILO) was among the first to take steps to promote the rights of Aboriginal peoples in its Convention No. 107 in 1957 by establishing international standards with respect to government and state responsibilities. ILO Convention 169, a revision of the earlier convention, was ratified in 1996 but by only 10 countries; Canada was not one of the 10.

Other positive and noteworthy initiatives include the UN's Draft Declaration on the Rights of Indigenous Peoples (1993), which included parts or sections pertaining to the collective rights of Aboriginal people, the rights to self-determination, the rights to practice cultural traditions and customs, the rights to develop their own political and economic systems, and, importantly, the obligation and duty of governments and states to allow Aboriginal people access to funding and technical assistance so they can pursue their goals. Other parts of the declaration spoke to issues of access to, and use of, land and resources, intellectual property rights, and so forth.

Aboriginal peoples worked to promote the acceptance and passage of the Draft Declaration by the General Assembly of the United Nations. This work was conducted by the UN Working Group on Indigenous Populations, the centre of Indigenous rights activities. However serious the attempt is at setting international norms (and international customary law), a final General Assembly resolution even in the form of an actual declaration (like the Universal Declaration of Human Rights, 1948) is not legally binding and so cannot be enforced (for a complete treatment of the evolution of the Draft Declaration, see Venne, 1998). Opposition was brought forth by such colonizer states as Canada and the United States, particularly to the inclusion of anything related to self-determination or land rights. In the spirit of the attempt, the United Nations proclaimed 1993 the International Year for the World's Indigenous People to promote awareness and understanding of the Draft Declaration within the international community and the importance of the Draft's goals.

Box 12.1	Dozens of Aboriginal Languages Near Death: UNESCO

It may be spoken by thousands, but a United Nations agency says Micmac [sic], an Atlantic Canadian language, could go the way of Latin and die, only to be studied through books by historians and no longer spoken among people.

And it's just one of many endangered languages, according to UNESCO, an agency dedicated to education and culture. A new report from the agency lists 88 of Canada's Aboriginal languages as critically close to becoming extinct, and predicts they won't be around in the next century.

Canada has the fifth highest number of endangered languages in the world. Only India, Indonesia, China, and the U.S. have more.

Often, Aboriginal languages serve as modern day links to the history and culture of the peoples that speak them. Cultural rituals like performing arts and crafts depend on language to be passed down from generation to generation, and when a language is lost, parts of the traditions associated with that language are also wiped out, the report says.

A Statistics Canada report published two years ago says that irreversible damage has already been done to 10 once-flourishing Aboriginal languages that have become extinct over the past 100 years. Most of the endangered languages on the list are in B.C. and Ontario and the number of speakers are dangerously low. Only 55 people speak Southern Haida in B.C. Their average age is 62 years old. In Ontario, Munsee only has 10 speakers left with an average of 52 years old.

Languages or dialects start to disappear when the number of native speakers plummets, often because they switch to a more dominant language in their region. In Canada this means any First Nations people switched to English and started speaking it to their children instead of an Aboriginal language. Canada's residential school history has had a damaging effect on Aboriginal languages today

Source: CTV.ca News Staff, Bell Media, Nov. 8, 2009. Accessed June 7, 2011, at www.ctv.ca/CTVNews/Canada/20091106/dying_languages_091108.

In 1994, the UN General Assembly proclaimed 1994–2004 to be the International Decade of the World's Indigenous People, with the goal to extend the work of the previous year toward international cooperation—including Aboriginal organizations and NGOs—in the attempt to find solutions for problems in such areas as human rights, development, health, and education. The initiatives of the decade were numerous: to encourage partnerships among Aboriginal peoples, states, and the UN; to finally adopt a declaration on the rights of Indigenous peoples; to create a permanent forum for Aboriginal peoples in the UN system; and to involve more UN agencies such as UNESCO and the WHO in education, training, and other collaborative projects. The General Assembly also declared August 9 the International Day of the World's Indigenous People.

But despite Canada's optimistic involvement, Canada initially saw fit to vote against the UN Declaration when it was finally tabled at the UN's General Assembly on September 13, 2007 (Resolution 61/295). The Declaration (now no longer merely a draft) passed 143 for and 4 against (11 countries abstained), with Canada standing with Australia, New Zealand, and the United States against (the colonizer states!). This prompted was anger and surprise from Aboriginal leaders, human rights groups, and opposition parties—even Amnesty International weighed in. Canada's ambassador to the UN (John McNee) as well as the then Indian Affairs minister (Chuck Strahl) defended the vote, claiming that the wording of the Declaration was inconsistent with the Canadian Constitution, the *Charter of Rights and Freedoms*, existing treaties, and several acts of parliament. The government also claimed that sections of the Declaration pertaining to maintaining distinct political, legal, and economic systems were "unworkable" and "inconsistent with the Canadian reality" (The Canadian Press, 2007). Then Australian prime minister John Howard lost his election over his government's decision; the new government subsequently adopted the Declaration.

UN officials maintained that the non-binding Declaration merely emphasizes the rights of Indigenous peoples to maintain and strengthen their own institutions, cultures, and traditions and to pursue their development in keeping with their own needs and aspirations. The text also prohibits discrimination against Aboriginal peoples and promotes their participation in matters that concern them, as well as their right to remain distinct and to pursue their own visions of social development. In a turn-around decision, Canada formally endorsed the Declaration on November 12, 2010, showing renewed leadership. And there was also progress on the domestic front: In what is truly a shift in Canada's relationship with its Aboriginal peoples, the government apologized to former students of residential schools, created the Truth and Reconciliation Commission, apologized for the relocation of Inuit to the high Arctic in the 1950s, and honoured Métis veterans of World War II.

Throughout Canada's history, little attention was paid to developing an Aboriginal policy that has significant Aboriginal input. Now the courts have become a major force in ensuring that government change its perspective about Aboriginal issues. Judicial decisions since 1982, which form the basis of Aboriginal law in Canada, have grown increasingly more flexible and liberal in their interpretation of Aboriginal rights. As Isaac (2001) points out, restrictive, narrow views of these rights are being replaced by flexible and accommodating interpretations. These new interpretations have forced the federal government to make accommodations to existing programs and policies and to bring old attitudes and views about Aboriginal people into line with the courts' new decisions.

The federal government has tried to involve provincial governments in Aboriginal affairs, but it has not had much success except in the area of treaty and land claims. Provincial governments, with much different agendas and priorities, have rejected the notion that they should become directly involved in Aboriginal issues. They resist involvement on the grounds that this is not their responsibility, and that becoming involved would cause their commitments and their associated costs to snowball. For their part, Aboriginals have found out over the years that the Government of Canada does not always favour Aboriginal interests when making decisions. As a result, Aboriginal people have tended to distrust government in general. In particular, they are suspicious of the participation of provincial governments, fearing a lessening of federal responsibility with an overall decrease in services. Aboriginal Canadians are convinced that the federal government must continue to honour its historical agreements with them, and that any transfer of these agreements is unlikely to be in their best interests. However, recently the federal government undertook a new strategy in approaching Aboriginal issues by developing an accountability framework. This strategy is designed to provide clear articulation of the goals and objectives of Aboriginal Affairs and Northern Development.

Currently, Aboriginal people are isolated from non-Aboriginal society and continue to be confronted by discrimination on a daily basis. To counter this position, they have embarked upon the long, arduous task of defining their group identity and clarifying their future goals. The growth of Aboriginal organizations domestically and internationally shows that Aboriginal people have strengthened their political and cultural position. And, as Boldt (1980b) has shown, they are increasingly willing to engage in "extra-legal" politics:

> Enlightened Indian leaders reject white society's comfortable notions of slow and steady progress toward the achievement of basic human rights for their people and most are inclined not only to approve of extra-legal activity as a justifiable means for achieving their conception of the "good society," but are also willing to participate and, if necessary, suffer the consequences of such actions for their cause. (p. 33)

Aboriginal people have learned over time that externally directed conflict tends to enhance group solidarity. Group boundaries come into sharp focus as in-group members are differentiated from out-group members. As conflict emerges, the group is also forced to explicitly define its aims and goals. As grievances are defined, adversaries emerge and are identified. In the case of Aboriginal groups, the adversaries are non-Aboriginal. Relations between the two become a zero-sum game.

In a zero-sum game, one player always gains precisely what the other player loses, and vice versa. In other words, relations between the two sides are always competitive and antagonistic. Identification with one's "side" pervades the daily life of each group member. Each participant finds a particular role in the collective action and receives internal and social rewards for behaviour that reinforces group aims. Identification with the group grows, as do linkages with other members. As Pettigrew (1964) described:

> Recruits willingly and eagerly devote themselves to the group's goals. And they find themselves systematically rewarded [by the group]. . . . They are expected to evince strong radical pride, to assert their full rights as citizens, to face jail and police brutality unhesitatingly for the cause. Note that these expected and rewarded actions all publicly commit the member to the group and its aim. (pp. 195–96)

And, as Himes (1966) stated, out of organized group conflict grows a strong group identity:

> In the interactive process of organized group conflict, self-involvement is the opposite side of the coin of overt action. Actors become absorbed by ego and emotion into the group and the group is projected through their actions. This linkage of individual and group in ego and action is the substance of identity. (p. 10)

With the emergence of a strong pan-Aboriginal identity, the sense of alienation experienced by many has been dispelled by a new sense of significance and purpose, especially in light of international developments. The personal ethnic identity of Aboriginal people is stronger now than it has been for many decades, as leaders of national and provincial Aboriginal organizations have successfully developed a national cohesiveness. As Pitts (1974) pointed out, ethnic identity is a social product, a result of actions and interpretations in a social context.

Aboriginal identification is a mixture of internal dynamics and external pressures. At present, that identification is being translated into what Enloe (1981) called ethnic mobilization—the mobilization of an ethnic group's resources and manpower to better its position. Hopefully, non-Aboriginal Canada will no longer respond with such demobilization techniques as the 1969 *White Paper* in order to remain in a controlling position. In response to such techniques, Aboriginal mobilization in turn would increase, and the accelerating spiral of conflict that could be set in motion would be counterproductive. In light of the new UN Declaration, such attempts would be seen as retrograde, even if Canada was not a signator.

Aboriginal people are, as always, prepared to negotiate within the existing socio-legal system. In fact, Aboriginal people, private industry, and governments are prepared to negotiate within certain boundaries. The boundaries generally determine the status quo, and all parties are accustomed to operating within it. The Oldman River (Alberta) conflict, the Oka (Quebec) conflict, the current continuing violence at Caledonia (Ontario), and other Aboriginal–non-Aboriginal conflicts generally reflect a long history of Aboriginal peoples negotiating for social change that the other party is unwilling to accept. Constitutional talks and conferences since 1982 (over a quarter of a century ago!) show that the government is slow to change the status quo when it deals with First Nations and Aboriginal peoples as a whole. While it has been in favour of establishing conditions for a "distinct Quebec society" in the Constitution, the government has, sadly, been very slow to give Aboriginal peoples similar consideration.

Even as we experience the second decade of the 21st century, more meaningful changes are still needed to enhance the political, socio-cultural, and economic position of Aboriginal people in Canada. As Canadians, we would be poorer as a nation if Aboriginal leaders and youth abandoned the legal and political means to effect those changes, or to direct their frustration and helplessness inward. It is clear that we have a collective responsibility to ensure the prosperity and self-determination of this land's first inhabitants.

Bibliography

Abbott, K. 2003 *Urban Aboriginal Women in British Columbia and the Impacts of the Matrimonial Real Property Regime*, Report prepared for Indian and Northern Affairs Canada.

Abele, F. 2004 *Urgent Need, Serious Opportunity: Towards a New Social Model for Canadas Aboriginal Peoples*, CPRN Research Report 39, Ottawa: Canadian Policy Research Networks.

Abele, F. and M. Prince 2006 "Political Spaces for Aboriginal Communities in Canada." In *Constructing Tomorrows Federalism*, I. Peach (ed.). Winnipeg: University of Manitoba Press.

Aberle, D. 1970 "A Plan for Navaho Economic Development." In *American Indians: Facts and Future, Toward Economic Development for Native American Communities*, Joint Economic Committee. New York: Arno Press.

Ablon, Joan 1965 "American Indian Relocation: Problems of Dependency and Management in the City." *Phylon*, 26 (Winter): 362–371.

Adelson, N. 2005 "The Embodiment of Inequality Health Disparities in Aboriginal Canada." *Canadian Journal of Public Health*, 92: S45–S61.

Aggamaway-Pierre, M. 1983 "Native Women and the State." In *Perspectives on Women in the 1980's*, J. Turner, and L. Emery (eds.). Winnipeg: University of Manitoba Press, pp. 66–73.

Ahenakew, D. 1985 "Aboriginal Title and Aboriginal Rights. The Impossible and Unnecessary Task of Identification and Definition." In *The Quest for Justice*, M. Boldt, J. Long, and L. Little Bear (eds.). Toronto: University of Toronto Press.

Alfred, T. 2005 *Wasase: Indigenous Pathways of Action and Freedom*. Peterborough: Broadview Press.

_____ 2009 "Colonialism and State Dependency." *Journal of Aboriginal Health*, 5: 42–58.

Allan, D.J. 1943 "Indian Land Problems in Canada." In *The North American Indian Today*, C.T. Loram and T.F. McIlwraith (eds.). Toronto: University of Toronto Press.

Allen, P.G. 1992 *The Sacred Hoop: Recovering the Feminine in American Indian Traditions*. Boston, Beacon Press.

Altman, J. and J. Nieuwenhuysen 1979 *The Economic Status of Australian Aborigines*. Cambridge: Cambridge University Press.

Anand, S., S. Yusuf, R. Jacobs, A. Davis, Q. Yi et al. 2001 "Risk Factors, Atherosclerosis, and Cardiovascular Disease among Aboriginal People in Canada." *The Lancet*, 358: 1147–1152.

Anaya, S. James 2000 *Indigenous Peoples in International Law*. New York: Oxford University Press.

Anaya, S., R. Falk and D. Pharand 1995 *Canada's Fiduciary Obligation to Aboriginal Peoples in the Context of Accession to Sovereignty by Quebec*, Vol. 1. Ottawa: Minister of Supply and Services.

Anderson, T., B. Benson and T. Flanagan 2006 *Self-Determination*. Stanford CA: Stanford University Press.

Anderson, C. and C. Denis 2003 "Urban Natives and the Nation: Before and After the Royal Commission on Aboriginal Peoples." *Canadian Review of Sociology and Anthropology*, 40, 4: 373–390.

Anderson, T. and D. Parker. 2006 "The Wealth of Indian Nations: Economic Performance and Institutions on Reservations." In *Self Determination: The Other Path for Native Americans*. T. Anderson, B. Benson, and T. Flanagan (eds.), Stanford CA: Stanford University Press.

Andrist, Ralph 1964 *The Long Death.*
New York: Macmillan.

Armstrong, R. 1999 "Mapping the Conditions
of First Nations Communities." *Canadian
Social Trends,* Winter: 14–18.

Armstrong, R. and T. Rogers 1996 *A First
Nations Typology: Patterns of Socio-
Economic Well-Being.* Ottawa: Research
and Analysis Directorate, Policy and Stra-
tegic Direction, Department of Indian
Affairs and Northern Development.

Asante, S. 1979 "Restructuring Transnational
Mineral Agreements." *American Journal of
International Law,* 73(3): 355–371.

Asch, Michael 1993 *Home and Native Land:
Aboriginal Rights and the Canadian Con-
stitution.* Vancouver: University of British
Columbia Press.

_____ **1997** *Aboriginal and Treaty Rights
in Canada: Essays on Law, Equality, and
Respect for Difference.* Vancouver: University of British Columbia Press.

Assembly of First Nations 1990a *Assembly of
First Nations' Critique of Federal Gov-
ernment Land Claims Policy,* August 21,
Summerstown, Ontario.

_____ **1990b** *Doublespeak of the 90s: A
Comparison of Federal Government and
First Nation Perception of Land Claims
Proces,.* August. Mimeo.

_____ **2005** *Our Nations, Our Governments:
Choosing our own paths,* Ottawa.

_____ **2005a** *A Treaty among Ourselves.*
Ottawa: AFN Renewal Commission.

_____ **2006** *Royal Commission on Aboriginal People at 10 Years: A Report Card,*
Ottawa: Assembly of First Nations.

_____ **2007** *Leadership Action Plan.* Ottawa.

_____ **2007** *The Relationship Between
Domestic Violence and HIV Infection.*
Ottawa, Health and Social Secretariat.

**Assembly of Manitoba Chiefs/Indian and
Northern Affairs Canada 1994** *Towards
First Nations Governments in Manitoba—
Work Plan.* November 22, 1994.

Atleo, E. 2004 *Tsawalk.* Vancouver: University of British Columbia Press.

Auditor General 2006 *Status Report of the
Auditor General of Canada,* Ottawa:
House of Commons.

_____ **2004** *Report of the Auditor General.* Ottawa: House of Commons.

_____ **2004** *Report of the Auditor General,* Ottawa: House of Commons.

_____ **2000** *Report of the Auditor General,* Ottawa: House of Commons.

Axtell, J. 1981 *The European and the Indian.*
New York: Oxford University Press.

Bakker, P. 1997 *A Language of Our Own: The
Genesis of Michif, the Mixed Cree-French
Language of the Canadian Métis.* New
York, Oxford University Press.

Bankes, N. 1983 *Resource Leasing Options
and the Settlement of Aboriginal Claims.*
Ottawa: Canadian Arctic Resources.

**Barkwell, L., N. Chartrand, D. Gray, L.
Longclaws, and R. Richard 1989** "Deval-
ued People: The Status of the Métis in the
Justice System." *The Canadian Journal of
Native Studies,* 9.1: 121–150.

Barnhardt, R. 2001 *Domestication of the
Ivory Tower Institutional Adaptation to
Cultural Distance.* Unpublished paper.

Barreto, M. and N. Ellemers 2009 "Multiple Identities and the Paradox
of Social Inclusion." In *Coping with Minority Status.* F. Butera and J. Levine
(eds.). New York: Cambridge University
Press, pp. 269–292.

Barsh, R. and J. Henderson 1982 "Aboriginal
Rights, Treaty Rights and Human Rights:
Tribe and Constitutional Renewal." *Jour-
nal of Canadian Studies,* 2: 55–81.

Bartlett, Richard 1980 *Indian Act of Canada.*
Saskatoon: Native Law Centre, University
of Saskatchewan.

_____ **1984** "Aboriginal Land Claims at
Common Law." *Canadian Native Law
Reporter,* 1: 1–63.

Bastien, B. 2004 *Blackfoot Ways of Knowing:
The World View of Siksikaitsitapi.* Calgary:
University of Calgary Press.

Battiste, M. and J. Barman (eds.) 1995 *First
Nations Education in Canada: The Circle
Unfolds.* Vancouver: University of British
Columbia Press.

Beattie, K. 2005 "Adult Correctional Services
in Canada, 2003/2004" *Juristat.* Canadian
Centre for Justice Statistics. Ottawa:
Statistics Canada.

_____ **2006** "Adult Correctional Services in Canada, 2004/2005." *Juristat,* Canadian Centre for Justice Statistics, Catalogue no. 85-002-XIE, 26,5. Ottawa: Statistics Canada.

Belanger, Y. 2006 *Gambling with the Future.* Saskatoon: Purich Publishing.

_____ **2008** *Aboriginal Self-Government in Canada,* Saskatoon, Purich Publishing Ltd.

Bell, C. 1991 "Who Are the Métis in Section 35(2)?" *Alberta Law Review,* 24 (2): 351–381.

_____ **1995** "Métis Constitutional Rights in Section 35(1)." *Alberta Law Review,* 36(1): 180–217.

_____ **1998** "New Directions in the Law of Aboriginal Rights." *Canadian Bar Review,* 77, 1 & 2: 36–72.

_____ **1999** Métis Settlements Appeal Tribunal, Contemporary Métis Justice: The Settlement Way. Native Law Center, University of Saskatchewan: Saskatoon.

_____ **2003** "Towards an Understanding of Metis Aboriginal Rights: Reflections on the Reasoning in R. vs. Powley." In *Aboriginal Rights Litigation,* J. Magnet and D. Dorey (eds.). Ch. 13. Markham, Ontario: Butterworths.

Bennett, G. 1978 "Aboriginal Rights in International Law." *Royal Anthropological Institute of Great Britain and Ireland,* Occasional Paper No. 37.

_____ **1978a** "Aboriginal Title in the Common Law: A Stoney Path through Feudal Doctrine." *Buffalo Law Review,* 17: 601–623.

Berger, Thomas 1977 *Northern Frontier, Northern Homeland—The Report of the Mackenzie Valley Pipeline Inquiry,* Vol. 1. Ottawa: Minister of Supply and Services Canada.

_____ **1981** *Fragile Freedoms: Human Rights and Dissent in Canada.* Toronto: Clarke, Irwin and Co. Ltd.

Berry, J. 2001 "A Psychology of Immigration." *Journal of Social Issues,* 57:615-631.

_____ **1999** *Cultures in Contact: Acculturation and Change,* Allahabad, Pant Social Science Institute.

Berry, J. and U. Kim. 1988 "Acculturation and Mental Health." In *Health and Cross-Cultural Psychology: Towards Applications,* P. Dasen, J. Berry, and N. Sartorius (eds.). London, Sage, pp. 207–236.

Bish, R. 1990 *Community Models of Indian Government,* National Indian Government Conference, Osgoode Hall Law School, Toronto, October 3–5.

Blair, P. 2005 *Rights of Aboriginal Women On-and Off-Reserve,* Toronto, The Scow Institute.

_____ **1985** *Village Journey.* New York: Hill and Wang Co.

Blauner, Robert 1969 "Internal Colonialism and Ghetto Revolt." *Social Problems,* 16 (Spring): 393–408.

Blaut, J. 1993 *The Colonizer's Model of the World: Geographical Diffusionism and Eurocentric History,* New York, Guilford Press.

Bobet, E. 1997 *Diabetes among First Nations People.* Ottawa: Statistics Canada, Medical Services Branch, Health Canada.

Boe, R. 2000 Aboriginal Inmates: Demographic Trends and Projections. *Forum,.* 12 (1): 4–17.

Bol, M. (ed.). 2003 *Stars Above, Earth Below.* Colorado: Roberts Rinehard.

Bolaria, S. 1979 "Self-Care and Lifestyles: Ideological and Policy Implications." In *Economy, Class and Social Reality,* J.A. Fry (ed.). Toronto: Butterworths, pp. 350–363.

Boldt, M. 1980a "Canadian Native Leadership: Context and Composition." *Canadian Ethnic Studies,* 12 (1): 15–33.

_____ **1980b** "Indian Leaders in Canada: Attitudes toward Extra-Legal Action." *Journal of Ethnic Studies,* 8 (1): 71–83.

_____ **1993** *Surviving as Indians: The Challenge of Self Government.* Toronto: University of Toronto Press.

Boldt, M., and J. Long 1983 *Tribal Traditions and the Canadian Charter of Rights and Freedoms.* Lethbridge AB: University of Lethbridge. Mimeo.

_____ **1985a** "Tribal Traditions and European–Western Political Ideologies: The Dilemma of Canada's Native Indians."

In *The Quest for Justice*, M. Boldt, J. Long and L. Little Bear (eds.). Toronto: University of Toronto Press.

_____ **1985b** "Tribal Philosophies and the Canadian Charter of Rights and Freedoms." In *The Quest for Justice*, M. Boldt, J. Long and L. Little Bear (eds.). Toronto: University of Toronto Press.

Boldt, M., J.A. Long and L. Little Bear (eds.). 1985 *The Quest for Justice*. Toronto: University of Toronto Press.

Bougie, E. 2010 "Family, Community and Aboriginal Language Among young First Naations Children Living off-reserve in Canada." *Canadian Social Trends*. 90:73–82.

Bourhis, R., L Moise, S. Perreault and S. Senecal. 1997 "Towards an Interactive Acculturation Model: A Social Psychological Approach." *International Journal of Psychology*, 32: 369–386.

Breton, R. 1964 "Institutional completeness of ethnic communities and the personal relations of immigrants." *Canadian Review of Sociology and Anthropology*, 4 (1):41–53.

Briggs, J. 1982 "Living Dangerously: The Contradictory Foundations of Value in Canadian Inuit Society." In *Politics and History in Band Societies*, E. Leacock and R. Lee (eds.). Cambridge: Cambridge University Press, pp.109–132.

Brody, Hugh 1987 *Living Arctic.* Vancouver: Douglas and McIntyre.

_____ **2003** *Inuits, Indiens, chasseurs-cueilleurs: les exiles de l'Eden.* Monaco: Editions du Rocher.

Brown, Dee 1971 *Bury My Heart at Wounded Knee*. New York: Holt, Rinehart and Winston.

Brown, J. 1980 *Stronger in Blood: Fur Trade Company Families in Indian Country.* Vancouver, University of British Columbia Press.

Brown, J. and E. Vibert (eds.). 2003 *Reading beyond Words: Contexts for Native History.* Peterborough ON: Broadview Books.

Browne, A., H. McDonald, and D. Elliot 2009 *First Nations Urban Aboriginal Health Research Discussion Paper.* Ottawa, National Aboriginal Health Organization.

Bruhn, J. 2009 In Search of Common Ground: Reconciling the IOG Governance Principles and First Nations Governance Traditions, Ottawa, Institute on Governance, Policy Brief No. 33.

Brunnen, B. 2003 *Achieving Potential: Towards Improved Labour Market Outcomes for Aboriginal People*, Report # 19. Calgary: Canada West Foundation.

Brzozowski, J., A. Taylor-Butts and S. Johnson 2006 "Victimization and Offending among the Aboriginal Population in Canada." *Juristat*, 26 (3). Ottawa: Statistics Canada.

Buckley, H. 1992 *From Wooden Ploughs to Welfare*. Montreal and Kingston: McGill-Queens University Press.

Burch, E. 2004 "The Caribou Inuit." In *Native Peoples,* B. Morrison and R. Wilson (eds.). Toronto: Oxford University Press, pp. 74–95.

Burkhardt, K. 2004 *Crime, Cultural Reintegration and Community Healing: Narratives of an Inuit Community.* Ph.D. dissertation, University of Windsor.

Butera, F. and J. Levine (eds.) 2009 *Coping with Minority Status:Responses to Exclusion and Inclusion.* Cambridge: Cambridge University Press.

Butera, F., J. Levine and J-P. Vernet 2009 "Influence without Credit: How Successful Minorities Respond to Social Cryptomnesia." In *Coping with Minority Status: Responses to Exclusion and Inclusion,* F. Butera and J. Levine (eds.). New York: Cambridge University Press, pp. 311–332.

Brzozowski, J., A. Taylor-Butts and S. Johnson 2006 "Victimization and Offending Among the Aboriginal Population in Canada." *Juristat*, 26, no. 3. Statistics Canada catalogue 85-002-XIE.

Cairns, Alan C. 2000 *Citizens Plus: Aboriginal People and the Canadian State*. Vancouver: University of British Columbia Press.

Cairns, A. 2005 *First Nations and the Canadian State.* Queens University, Institute of Intergovernmental Relations.

Cajete, G. 2000 *Native Science: Natural Laws of Interdependence.* Santa Fe, NM: Clear Light Publishers.

Calder, W. 1986 "The Provinces and Indian Self Government in the Constitutional Forum." In *Indian–Provincial Government Relationship*, M. Boldt, J. Long, and L. Little Bear (eds.). Lethbridge AB: University of Lethbridge.

Canada, Government of 1966–70 A*nnual Reports: 1966–67; 1968–69; 1969–70.* Department of Indian Affairs and Northern Development. Ottawa: Queen's Printer.

_____ **1969** *Statement of the Government of Canada on Policy, 1969* (White Paper). Ottawa: Queen's Printer.

_____ **1973** *Report of Task Force: Policing on Reserves.* Edmonton: Department of Indian and Northern Affairs.

_____ **1974** *Perspective Canada I.* Ottawa: Information Canada.

_____ **1977** *Perspective Canada II.* Ottawa: Statistics Canada, Supply and Services.

_____ **1978a** *A Recommended Plan for Evaluation in Indian Education.* Ottawa: IIAP, Department of Indian Affairs and Northern Development, Program Evaluation Branch.

_____ **1978b** *Evaluation of the RCMP Indian Special Constable Program (Option 3B).* Ottawa: IIAP, Evaluation Branch, Department of Indian Affairs and Northern Development, March 1978b.

_____ **1978c** *Indian Affairs and Northern Development Business Loan Fund: Indian Economic Development Direct Loan Order Policy and Guidelines.* Ottawa: Department of Indian Affairs and Northern Development, Loan Fund Division.

_____ **1979a** *Perspective Canada III.* Ottawa: Statistics Canada, Supply and Services.

_____ **1979b** *Social Assistance and Related Social Development Programs of the Department of Indian and Northern Affairs.* Ottawa: IIAP, Department of Indian Affairs and Northern Development.

_____ **1980** *Indian Conditions, A Survey.* Ottawa: Department of Indian Affairs and Northern Development.

_____ **1981** *In All Fairness: A Native Claims Policy.* Ottawa: Minister of Supply and Services.

_____ **1982** *Population, Repartition geographique—Terre-Neuve.* Recensement du Canada, 1981. Ottawa: Statistique Canada (Catalogue 93–901).

_____ **1983** *The Report of the House of Commons Special Committee on Indian Self-Government* (The Penner Report). Ottawa: Minister of Supply and Services Canada.

_____ **1984** *Response of the Government to the Report of the Special Committee on Indian Self-Government* (reply to the Penner Report). Ottawa.

_____ **1985a** *Living Treaties: Lasting Agreements.* Report of the Task Force to Review Comprehensive Claims Policy. Ottawa: DIAND.

_____ **1985b** *Indian and Native Programs.* A Study Team Report to the Task Force on Program Review. Ottawa: Minister of Supply and Services.

_____ **1988** *Census Metropolitan Areas, Dimensions,* Ottawa: Supply and Services.

_____ **1989** *The Canadian Aboriginal Economic Development Strategy.* Ottawa: Indian and Northern Affairs Canada.

_____ **1990** *Annual Report, 1989–90,* Department of Indian Affairs and Northern Development. Ottawa: Minister of Supply and Services.

_____ **1991** *Language, Tradition, Health, Lifestyle and Social Issues.* Ottawa: Statistics Canada (Catalogue 89-533), (1991): 52,102.

_____ **1996a** *Looking Forward, Looking Back. Royal Commission on Aboriginal Peoples.* Ottawa: Minister of Supply and Services.

_____ **1996b** *Restructuring the Relationship.* Royal Commission on Aboriginal Peoples. Ottawa: Minister of Supply and Services.

_____ **1996c** *Soliloquy and Dialogue: Overview of Major Trends in Public Policy relating to Aboriginal Peoples.* From the series "Public Policy and Aboriginal Peoples" 1965–1992, Volume 1. Royal

Commission on Aboriginal Peoples, Canada Communication Group: Ottawa.

_____ **1996d** *Report of the Royal Commission on Aboriginal Peoples*, Ottawa: Canada Communications Group-Publishing.

_____ **1998** *Gathering Strength: Canada Aboriginal Action Plan.* Ottawa: Ministry of Supply and Services.

_____ **1999a** *From Restorative Justice to Transformative Justice.* Ottawa: Law Commission of Canada.

_____ **1999b** *A Second Diagnostic on the Health of First Nations and Inuit People in Canada*, November. Ottawa: Health Canada.

_____ **2000** *Diabetes Among First Nations People.* Ottawa: Statistics Canada, Medical Services Branch, Health Canada.

_____ **2001** *Statistical Profile on the Health of First Nations in Canada.* Ottawa: Health Canada.

_____ **2003** *Registered Indian Population by Sex and Residence 2002.* Ottawa: Indian Affairs and Northern Development, Public Works and Government Services Canada.

_____ **2007.** *Basic Departmental Data, 2007.* Ottawa. Indian and Northern Affairs Canada.

_____ **2010** A Progress Report on Aboriginal Initiatives from the Government of Canada, 2009–2010. Ottawa, Indian Affairs and Northern Development.

_____ **n.d.** *Indian Claims in Canada/ Revendications des Indiens au Canada.* Toronto: Clarke, Irwin and Co. Ltd.

Canadian Arctic Resources Committee 1989 "An Inuit Response: Tungevik Federation of Nunavut." Retrieved June 15, 2011 (www.carc.org/index.php?option=com_wrapper&view=wrapper&Itemid=174).

Canadian Council for Aboriginal Business 2010 *Partnerships and Prosperity: Key Findings from CCAB,* Progressive Aboriginal Relations Research Series. Issue #2.

Canadian Council on Learning 2009 *The State of Aboriginal Learning In Canada,* Ottawa. Canadian Council on Learning.

Canadian Press 2007 Bell, Inc. "Canada Votes Against UN Aboriginal Declaration", 14/09/077 news release. Retrieved June 15, 2011 (www.ctv.ca/CTVNews/Canada/20070913/aboriginal_rights_070913).

Cantryn, M. n.d. "Evaluation—Native Women's Program." Ottawa: Secretary of State.

Cardinal, H. 1969 *The Unjust Society.* Edmonton: Hurtig Publishers

_____ **1979** "Native Women and the Indian Act." In *Two Nations, Many Cultures,* J. Elliott (ed.). Scarborough: Prentice Hall Canada, pp. 44–50.

_____ **1986** "Constitutional Change and the Treaty 8 Renovation." In *Indian–Provincial Relations*, M. Boldt, J.A. Long, and L. Little Bear (eds.). Lethbridge: The University of Lethbridge.

Carstens, P. 1991 *The Queen's People.* Toronto: University of Toronto Press.

Carter, S. 1990 *Lost Harvests.* Montreal and Kingston: McGill-Queen's University Press.

_____ **1999** *Aboriginal People and Colonizers of Western Canada to 1900.* Toronto: University of Toronto Press.

Cassidy, F. and R. Bish 1989 *Indian Government: Its Meaning and Practice.* Halifax: Institute for Research on Public Policy.

Castellano, Marlene 1970 "Vocation or Identity: The Dilemma of Indian Youth." In *The Only Good Indian*, Waubageshig (ed.). Toronto: New Press.

Catellani, E. 1901 Le droit international au commencement du XXE siècle, VIIIm Paris, Revue Generale de Droit International Public.

Chance, Norman 1970 *Development Change among the Cree Indians of Quebec.* Summary Report, ARDA Project 34002 (Reprint 1970), Ottawa: Department of Regional Economic Expansion.

Chandler M. and C. Lalonde 2006 (Transferring Whose Knowledge?) Exchanging Whose Best Practices?: On Knowing About Indigenous Knowledge and Aboriginal Suicide." In *Aboriginal Policy Research*. D. Beavan & J. White (eds.). London, ON: Althouse Press.

Chapman, L. 1972 *Women's Rights and Special Status for Indians: Some Implications of the* Lavell Case. Ottawa: Carleton University, n.p.

Chartier, C. 1988 *In the Best Interest of the Métis Child.* Saskatoon, Saskatchewan: Native Law Centre.

Chartrand, P. 1993 "Aboriginal Rights: The Dispossession of the Métis." *Osgoode Hall Law Journal*, 29: 425–467.

Chartrand, P. and S. Giokas 2002 "Defining 'The Metis People': The Hard Case of Canadian Aboriginal Law." In P. Chartrand (ed.). *Who are Canada's Aboriginal Peoples?* Saskatoon, Purich Publishing, pp 157–186.

Chartrand, P. (ed.). 2002 *Who are Canada's Aboriginal Peoples?: Recognition, Definition, and Jurisdiction*, Saskatoon, Purich Publishing.

Cheda, S. 1977 "Indian Women: An Historical Example and a Contemporary View." In *Women in Canada,* M. Stephenson (ed.). Don Mills: General Publishing, pp. 195–208.

Cherubini, L. 2008 "Aboriginal Identity, Misrepresentation, and Dependence: A Survey of the Literature." *The Canadian Journal of Native Studies*, 28:221–240.

Churchill, W. 1999 *Struggle for the Land.* Winnipeg: Arbeiter Ring.

Clark, T. 1994 *Lonewolf vs. Hitchcock: Treaty Rights and Indian Law at the End of the Nineteenth Century.* Lincoln: University of Nebraska Press.

_____ **2003** "Impacts of the 1985 Amendments to the Indian Act on First Nations Populations." In *Aboriginal Conditions: Research as a Foundation for Public Policy,* J. White, P. Maxim and D. Beavon (eds.).Vancouver: UBC Press.

Clatworthy, S. 2001 *Re-assessing the Population Impacts of Bill C-31* Gatineau, Quebec: Indian and Northern Affairs Canada.

_____ **S. 2003** *Factors Contributing to Unstated Paternity*, Ottawa: Strategic Research and Analysis Directorate, Indian and Northern Affairs Canada.

_____ **2007** *Aboriginal Housing Conditions and Needs on-reserve*, Ottawa: Research and Analysis Directorate, INAC.

_____ **2009** "Mobility and Migration Patterns of Aboriginal Populations in Canada: 2001–2006." *Diversity*, 7:43–51.

_____ **2010.** *Estimating the Population Impacts of the E-Dbendaagzijig Naaknigwwin-Excerpts*, Winnipeg, Four Directions Project Consulting.

Coates, K. 1991 *Best Left as Indians: Native–White Relations in the Yukon Territory, 1840–1973.* Montreal and Kingston: McGill-Queen's University Press.

_____ **2000** *The Marshall Decision and Native Rights.* Montreal and Kingston: McGill-Queen's University Press.

Coates, K. and W. Morrison 1986 "More Than a Matter of Blood: The Federal Government, The Churches and the Mixed Blood Populations of the Yukon and the Mackenzie River Valley, 1890–1950." In *1885 and After,* F. Barron and J. Waldham (eds.). Regina: Canadian Plains Research Centre pp. 253–277.

Coffey, W. and M. Polese 1985 "Local Development: Conceptual Bases and Policy Implications." *Regional Studies* 19 (2): 85–93.

Cohen, F. 1960 "Indian Wardship: The Twilight of a Myth." In *The Legal Conscience: Selected Papers of Felix S. Cohen,* L. Cohen (ed.). New Haven: Yale University Press.

Connelly, M. 2008 *Fatal Misconception:The Struggle to Control World Population.* Cambridge: Harvard University Press.

Cornell, S. 1988 *The Return of the Native.* New York: Oxford University Press.

_____ **2000** Evidence presented to the Standing Committee on Aboriginal Affairs and Northern Development, June 6.

_____ **2002a** *Speaking Truth to Power.* Vancouver: BC Treaty Commission.

_____ **2002b** *The Harvard Project Findings on Good Governance*, Vancouver: B.C. Treaty Commission.

_____ **2005** "Indigenous Peoples, Poverty and Self-Determination in Australia, New Zealand, Canada and the United

States." In *Indigenous Peoples and Poverty*, R. Eversole, J.A. Mcneish, and A. Cimadamore (eds.). London: Zed Books, pp. 199–226.

Cornell, S. and J. Kalt 1992 "Reloading the Dice: Improving the Economic Development on American Indian Reservations." In *What Can Tribes Do? Strategies and Institutions in American Indian Economic Development.* Los Angeles:University of California.

_____ 2000 "Where's the Glue? Institutional and Cultural foundations of American Indian Economic Development." *Journal of Socio-Economics*, 29(5): 443–470.

_____ 2001 *Sovereignty and Nation Building: The Development Challenges in Indian Country To-day*, Boston: Harvard project on American Indian Economic Development. Retrieved June 15, 2011 (http://hpaied.org).

Cornell, S., M. Jorgenson and J. Kalt 2002 *The First Nations Governance Act: Implications of Research Findings from the United States and Canada*, Native Nations Institute, Tuscon, Udall Center for Studies in Public Policy.

Courchene, T. and L. Powell 1992 *A First Nations Province.* Kingston ON: Queen's University Institute of Intergovernmental Relations.

Crowe, K. and Kingston 1974 *A History of the Original Peoples of Northern Canada.* Arctic Institute of North America. Montreal: McGill-Queen's University Press.

Culhane, Dara 1998 *The Pleasure of the Crown: Anthropology, Law and First Nations.* Vancouver: Talonbooks.

Cultural Survival 1993, *State of Peoples: A Global Human Rights Report on Societies in Danger.* Beacon Press: Boston.

Cumming, P. 1967 "Public Lands, Native Land Claims and Land Use." In *Canadian Public Land Use in Perspective*, J. Nelson, R. Scace, and R. Kouri (eds.). Proceedings of a symposium sponsored by the Social Science Research Council of Canada, Ottawa, pp. 206–238.

Cumming, P., and N. Mickenberg 1972 *Native Rights in Canada*, 2nd ed. Toronto: Indian–Eskimo Association of Canada.

Cunningham. 2009 ABCA 239 (Can LII) – 2009-06-26 Alberta Court of Appeal.

Dahl, J. 1997 "Gender Parity in Nunavut." *Indigenous Affairs*, 3–4: 42–47.

Dalon, R. 1985 "An Alberta Perspective on Aboriginal Peoples and The Constitution." In *The Quest for Justice*, M. Boldt, J.A. Long, and L. Little Bear (eds.). Toronto: University of Toronto Press.

D'Anglure, B. 1984 "Inuit of Quebec." *Handbook of North American Indians, v*ol. 5, *Arctic*, D. Damas (ed.). Washington: Smithsonian Institute, pp. 476–507.

_____ 2005 "The 'Third Gender' of the Inuit", *Diogenes*, 52:134–144.

Daniel, R. 1980 *A History of Native Claims Processes in Canada, 1867–1979.* Ottawa: Research Branch, Department of Indian Affairs and Northern Development.

Daniels, H. 1998 *Abocide : Bill C-31,* Speaking notes of Harry W. Daniels' presentation to The Native Women's Association of Canada March 23, 1998 CAP Online-. www.abo-peoples.org/programs/C-31/spknts.html

Daughtery, W. 1978 *Discussion Report on Indian Taxation.* Ottawa: Department of Indian and Northern Affairs, Treaties and Historical Research Centre.

_____ 1982 *A Guide to Native Political Associations in Canada.* Treaties and Historical Research, Research Branch, Corporate Policy. Ottawa: Department of Indian and Northern Affairs.

Daugherty, Wayne and Dennis Magill 1980 *Indian Government under Indian Act Legislation, 1868–1951.* Ottawa: Research Branch, Department of Indian and Northern Affairs.

Davies, M. 1985 "Aspects of Aboriginal Rights in International Law." In *Aboriginal Peoples and the Law,* B. Morse (ed.). Ottawa: Carleton University Press, pp. 16–47.

Delgamuukw vs. Her Majesty the Queen in Right of the Province of British Columbia 1997 Supreme Court of Canada Decision, File No. 23799, December 11.

Deloria, V. and C. Lytle **1984** *The Nations Within: The Past and Future of American Indian Sovereignty.* New York: Pantheon Books.

Deprez, Paul and Glen Sigurdson **1969** *Economic Status of the Canadian Indian: A Re-Examination.* Winnipeg: Centre for Settlement Studies, University of Manitoba.

DIAND (Department of Indian Affairs and Northern Development) **1969** *Statement of the Government of Canada on Indian Policy.* Ottawa: Queen's Printer.

_____ **1978** *Native Claims: Policy, Processes and Perspectives.* Ottawa: Queen's Printer.

_____ **1980** *Indian Conditions. A Survey.* Ottawa: Minister of Supply and Services.

_____ **1980–81** *Annual Report.* Ottawa: Minister of Supply and Services.

_____ **1981** *In All Fairness: A Native Claims Policy.* Ottawa: Queen's Printer.

_____ **1982a** *Outstanding Business: A Native Claims Policy.* Ottawa: Minister of Supply and Services.

_____ **1982b** *James Bay and Northern Quebec Agreement Implementation Review.* Ottawa: Minister of Supply and Services.

_____ **1982c** *Strengthening Indian Band Government in Canada.* Ottawa: Minister of Indian Affairs and Northern Development. Ottawa, c. 1982c.

_____ **1982d** *An Optional System of Indian Band Government.* Ottawa: Minister of Indian Affairs and Northern Development. Ottawa, d, 1982d.

_____ **1982e** "The Legislation Proposals." *Annex I.* Ottawa: Minister of Supply and Services, c. 1982e.

_____ **1982f** "Financial Considerations—The Funding System." *Annex II.* Ottawa: Minister of Supply and Services, c. 1982f.

_____ **1982g** "Appendix VI: Pick up of Provincial Program Costs." Ottawa: Mimeographed, c. 1982g.

_____ **1982h** *The Alternative of Optional Indian Band Government Legislation.* Ottawa: Minister of Indian Affairs and Northern Development.

_____ **1984** *House of Commons. Indian Self-Government in Canada: Report of the Special Committee,* Ottawa.

_____ **1985** *Living Treaties: Lasting Agreements. Report of the Task Force to Review Comprehensive Claims Policy.* Ottawa: Department of Indian Affairs and Northern Development.

_____ **1986** *Coolican Report.* Ottawa: Department of Indian Affairs and Northern Development.

_____ **2006** *Registered Indian Population by Sex and Residence, 2005.* First Nations and Northern Statistics Section. Ottawa: Public Works and Government Services Canada.

Dickason, Olive **1992** *Canada's First Nations: A History of Founding Peoples from Earliest Times.* Norman: University of Oklahoma Press.

_____ **2002** *Canada's First Nations.* Don Mills, ON: Oxford University Press.

Dickson, O. and W. Newbigging **2010** *A Concise History of Canada First Nation* (2nd ed.) Toronto, Oxford University Press.

Dickerson, M. **1993** *Whose North?* Calgary and Vancouver: The Arctic Institute of North America and the University of British Columbia Press.

Dockstator, M. **2005** "Aboriginal Representation of History and the Royal Commission on Aboriginal Peoples." In *Walking a Tightrope: Aboriginal People and Their Representation*, U. Lischke and D. McNab (eds.). Waterloo ON: Wilfrid Laurier University Press.

Doerr, A.D. **1974** "Indian Policy." In *Issues in Canadian Public Policy*, G.S. Doern and V.S. Wilson (eds.). Toronto: Macmillan.

Doerr, A. **1997** "Building New Orders of Government—The Future of Aboriginal Self-Government." *Canadian Public Administration*, 40:274–289.

Dorais, Louis-Jacques **1997** *Quaqtaq: Modernity and Identity in an Inuit Community.* Toronto: University of Toronto Press.

Dos Santos, T. **1971** "The Structure of Dependence." In K. Fann and D. Hodges (eds.) *Readings in U.S. Imperialism,* Boston, Porter Sargent.

Dowling, C. 2005 "The Applied Theory of First nations Economic Development: A Critique." *Journal of Aboriginal Economic Development*, 4:120–128.

Driben, Paul 1975 *We Are Métis*. Ph.D. dissertation. Minneapolis: University of Minnesota.

_____**1983** "The Nature of Métis Claims." *The Canadian Journal of Native Studies*, 3 (1): 183–196.

Duff R. 1997 *The Indian History of British Columbia*. Revised ed. Victoria: Royal British Columbia Museum.

Duffy, R.Q. 1988 *The Road to Nunavut*. Kingston and Montreal: McGill-Queen's University Press.

Duhaime, G. 1992 "Le chasseur et le minotaure: Itineraire de l'autonomie politique au Nunavut." *Etudes/Inuit/ Studies*, 16 (1–2): 149–177.

_____ **1993** *The Governing of Nunavut: Who Pays for What?* Universite Laval, Groupe d'etudes Inuit et circumpolaires.

Duhaime, G., E. Searles, P. Usher, H. Myers, and P. Frechette 2003 "Social Cohesion and Living Conditions in the Canadian Arctic: From Theory to Measurement." *Social Indicators Research*, 61: 1–23.

Dunning, R. 1972 "The Indian Situation: A Canadian Government Dilemma." *International Journal of Comparative Sociology*, 12 (June): 128–134.

Dupuis, R. and K. McNeil 1995 *Canada's Fiduciary Obligation to Aboriginal Peoples in the Context of Accession to Sovereignty by Quebec*, Vol. 2, Ottawa: Minister of Supply and Services.

Dybbroe, S. 1996 "Questions of Identity and Issues of Self-Determination." *Etudes/ Inuit/Studies*, 20 (2): 39–53.

Dyck, Noel 1990 "Cultures, Communities and Claims: Anthropology and Native Studies in Canada." *Canadian Ethnic Studies*, 22 (3), 40–55.

_____ **1996** "Tutelage, Resistance and Co-optation in Canadian Indian Administration." *Canadian Review of Sociology and Anthropology*, 34 (3): 333–348.

Eberts, M. 1985 In *Minorities and the Canadian State*, N. Nevitte and

A. Kornberg (eds.) *Minorities and the Canadian State*. Oakville ON: Mosaic Press, pp. 53–70.

Ekos. 2001 Highlights of First Nations Survey on-Reserve. Retrieved June 15, 2011 (www.ekos.com/admin/articles/INACe.pdf).

Elias, P. 1991 *Development of Aboriginal People's Communities*. Toronto: York University, Captus Press.

Elliott, D. 1991 "Aboriginal Title." In *Aboriginal Peoples and the Law*, B. Morse (ed.). Ottawa: Carleton University Press, pp. 48–121.

Emberley, J. 2001 ('The Bourgeois Family, Aboriginal Women, and Colonial Governance in Canada: A Study in Feminist Historical and Cultural Materialism,') *Signs* 27:59–85.

Englestad D. and J. Bird 1993 *Nation-To-Nation: Aboriginal Sovereignty and the Future of Canada*. Toronto: Anansi Press.

Enloe, C. 1981 "The Growth of the State and Ethnic Mobilization: The American Experience." *Ethnic and Racial Studies*, 4 (2): 123–136.

Ens, Gerhard 1996 *Homeland to Hinterland: The Changing Worlds of the Red River Métis in the Nineteenth Century*. Toronto: University of Toronto Press.

Environics. 2010 *Urban Aboriginal Peoples Study*, Toronto, Environics Institute.

Erasmus, George 2010 Aboriginal Healing Foundation Media Advisory, "No funds committed to AHF in Canada's 2010 budget." March 5, 2010.

Ewing Commission Report 1935 *Royal Commission on the Conditions of the Halfbreed Population of the Province of Alberta Report, 1935*. Sessional Paper No. 72.

Faulkner, C. 1992 "Inuit Offenders. In *Aboriginal Peoples and Canadian Criminal Justice*, R. Silverman and M. Nielsen (eds.). Toronto: Butterworths.

Fenge, T. 1992 "Political Development and Environmental Management in Northern Canada: The Case of the Nunavut Agreement." *Etudes/Inuit/Studies*, 16 (1–2): 115–141.

First Nations Centre National Aboriginal Health Organization 2004 *Preliminary*

Findings of the First Nations Regional Longitudinal Health Survey. Ottawa: National Aboriginal Health Organization.

First Nations Resource Council 1990 *Socio-Economic/Quality of Life Indicators Symposium,* May 31 Report. 13 pp. Edmonton.

Flanagan, T. 1983a "The Case against Métis Aboriginal Rights." *Canadian Public Policy,* 9: 314–315.

_____ **1985** "Métis Aboriginal Rights: Some Historical and Contemporary Problems." In *The Quest for Justice,* M. Boldt, J. Long and L. Little Bear (eds.). Toronto: University of Toronto Press.

_____ **1990** "The History of Métis Aboriginal Rights: Politics, Principle and Policy." *Canadian Journal of Law and Society,* 5, 71–94.

_____ **2000** *First Nations? Second Thoughts.* Montreal–Kingston: McGill-Queens University Press.

Flanagan, T., C. Alcantara and A. Dressay 2010 *Beyond the Indian Act,* Montreal–Kingston, McGill-Queens University Press.

Fleras, A. and J. L. Elliott 1992 *The Nations Within: Aboriginal–State Relations in Canada, United States, and New Zealand.* Don Mills, ON: Oxford University Press.

Fleras, A. and R. Maaka 2000 "Reconstitutionalizing Indigeneity: Restoring the Sovereigns Within." *Canadian Review of Studies in Nationalism,* 27: 34–49.

Fontaine, P. 1998 "Aboriginal Peoples Making Giant Strides on Long Journey to Better Lives." *Canadian Speeches: Issues of the Day,* September, 32–34.

Fossett, R. 2001 *In Order to Live Untroubled: Inuit of the Central Arctic.* Winnipeg: University of Manitoba Press.

Foster, H. 1998–99 "Honouring the Queen: A Legal and Historical Perspective on the Nisga'a Treaty." *B.C. Studies,* 120: 5–11.

Foster, J. E. 1978 "The Métis, the People and the Term." *Prairie Forum,* 3 (1 - Spring): 3(1): 79–91.

Four Worlds Development Project 1985 *Towards the Year 2000.* Lethbridge AB: University of Lethbridge.

Francis, D. 1983 *A History of the Native Peoples of Quebec, 1760–1867.* Ottawa: Indian Affairs and Northern Development.

French, B.F. 1851 *Historical Collections of Louisiana.* Dublin: Arbers Annals.

Frank, A. G. 1967. *Capitalism and Underdevelopment in Latin America,* New York, Monthly Review Press.

Frideres, J.S. 1972 "Indians and Education: A Canadian Failure." *Manitoba Journal of Education,* 7 (June): 7: 27–30.

_____ **1974** *Canada's Indians: Contemporary Conflicts.* Scarborough ON: Prentice Hall Canada.

_____ **1986** "Native Claims and Settlement in Yukon." In *Arduous Journey,* J.R. Ponting (ed.). Toronto: McClelland and Stewart, pp. 284–301.

Frideres, J. and W. Reeves 1981 "Government Policy and Indian Urbanization: The Alberta Case." *Canadian Public Policy,* 7 (4): 584–595.

Frohlich, L., N. Ross and C. Richmond. 2006 "Health Disparities in Canada today: Some Evidence and a Theoretical Framework." *Health Policy,* 79, 132–143.

Fuchs, Estelle 1970 "Time to Redeem an Old Promise." *Saturday Review* (January 24): 53–58.

Furniss, E. 2000 *Victims of Benevolence.* Vancouver: Arsenal Pulp Press.

Gadacz, René 1991 "Community Socio-Economic Development from a Plains Indian Perspective: A Proposed Social Indicator System and Planning Tool." *Native Studies Review,* 7 (1): 53–80.

Gadacz, René and N. McBlane 1999 "Aboriginal Peoples and National Rights Issues in Quebec." Special Issue of the *Native Studies Review,* 12 (2): 1–4, Saskatoon: University of Saskatchewan.

Galley, V. 2009 "An Aboriginal Languages Act: Reconsidering Equality on the 40th Anniversary of Canada's *Official Languages Act.*" *Diversity,* 7:35-41.

George, M., S. Loh, R. Verma and E. Shin 2001 *Population Projections for Canada, Provinces and Territories, 2000–2026.* Ottawa: Statistics Canada.

Gibbins, R. 1986b "Citizenship, Political and Intergovernmental Problems with Indian Self Government." In *Arduous Journey*, J.R. Ponting (ed.). Toronto: McClelland and Stewart.

Gibbins, R. and R. Ponting 1986 "An Assessment of the Probable Impact of Aboriginal Self Government in Canada." In *The Politics of Gender, Ethnicity and Language in Canada*, A. Cairns and C. Williams (eds.). Vol. 34. Research Studies of the Royal Commission on the Economic Union and Development Prospects for Canada. Toronto: University of Toronto Press.

Gibson, G. 1998–99 "Comments on the Draft Nisga'a Treaty." *B.C. Studies,* 120: 55–72.

Giokas, J. and P. Chartrand 2002 "Who Are the Métis? A Review of the Law and Policy." In *Who are Canada's Aboriginal People?* P. Chartrand (ed.). Saskatoon: Purich Publishing. pp. 73–97.

Giokas, J. and R. Groves 2002 "Collective and Individual Recognition in Canada." In *Who are Canada's Aboriginal People?* P. Chartrand (ed.). Saskatoon: Purich Publishing, pp. 41–82.

Gionet, L. 2008 Inuit in Canada, *Canadian Social Trends*, November 26:59-64.

Girvan, N. 1973 "The Development of Dependency Economics in the Caribbean and Latin America." *Social and Economic Studies*, 22: 1–33.

Gombay, N. 2000 "The Politics of Culture: Gender Parity in the Legislative Assembly of Nunavut." *Etudes/Inuit/Studies*, 24 (1): 125–148.

_____ **2005** "Shifting Identities in a Shifting World: Food, Place, Community and the Politics of Scale in an Inuit Settlement." *Environment and Planning Society and Space*, 23 (3): 415–433.

Gordon, I. 2009 *A People on the Move: The Métis of the Western Plains.* Victoria, B.C.: Heritage House.

Graham, J. 2010 *The First Nation Governance System*, Ottawa, Institute on Governance.

_____ **2007** *Rethinking Self-government: Developing a More Balanced Evolutionary Approach*, Ottawa, Institute on Governance.

Graham, J. and F. Levesque. 2010 *First Nation Communities in Distress: Dealing with Causes, not Symptoms*. Ottawa: Institute on Governance.

Grand Council of the Crees 1998 *Never Without Consent: James Bay Crees' Stand against Forcible Inclusion into an Independent Quebec.*

Grant, A. 1996 *No End of Grief: Indian Residential Schools in Canada.* Winnipeg: Pemmican Publications.

Green, L. 1983 "Aboriginal Peoples, International Law and the Canadian Charter of Rights and Freedoms." *The Canadian Bar Review*, 61: 339–353.

Guimond, E. and N. Robitaille 2009 "Aboriginal Populations in Canadian Cities: Why are they Growing so Fast?" *Canadian Issues*, June, 11–18.

Gunder Frank, André 1967 *Capitalism and Underdevelopment in Latin America.* New York: Monthly Review Press.

Hall, T. 1991 "Aboriginal Futures— Awakening Our Imagination." *Canadian Dimension*, July/August, 15–17.

Halvorson, K. 2005 *Indian Residential School Abuse Claims.* Toronto: Thomson Carswell.

Hamilton, E. 1984 "Rosing Wins Second Term—Arctic Policy Delayed." *Inuit Today*, Special edition. Iqaluit: Inuit Circumpolar Conference, (February): 6–7.

Hampton, E. 1993 "Toward a Redefinition of American Indian/Alaskan Native Education." *Canadian Journal of Native Education*, 20 (2): 14–23.

Hanselmann, C. 2001 *Urban Aboriginal People in Western Canada: Realities and Policies.* Calgary: Canada West Foundation.

Hanselmann, C. and R. Gibbins 2002 *Another Voice Is Needed: Intergovernmentalism in the Urban Aboriginal Context.* Paper presented at the Reconfiguring Aboriginal–State Relations in Canada Conference, Queens University, November.

Hanson, B., 1985 *Dual Realities—Dual Strategies: The Future Paths of the Aboriginal People's Development.* Saskatoon, privately printed.

Harris, S., B. Zinman, A. Hanley, J. Gittelsohn, R. Hegele, P. Connely, B. Shah and J. Hux **2002** "The Impact of Diabetes on Cardiovascular Risk Factors and Outcomes in a Native Canadian Population." *Diabetes Research and Clinical Practice*, 55: 165–173.

Harvey, S. **1996** "Two Models to Sovereignty: A Comparative History of the Mashantucket Pequot Tribal Nation and the Navajo Nation." *American Indian Culture and Research Journal*, 20 (1): 147–194.

Hatt, Fred K. **1972** "The Canadian Métis: Recent Interpretations." *Canadian Ethnic Studies*, 3 (1): 23–26.

_____ **1982** "On Hold: A Review of *In All Fairness: A Native Claims Policy*." *The Canadian Journal of Native Studies*, 2 (2): 352–355.

Hawkes, D. **1985** *Aboriginal Self-Government*. Kingston, Ontario: Queen's University, Institute of Intergovernmental Relations.

Hawley, D. **1990** *1990 Indian Act*, Toronto: Carswell.

Hawthorn, H.B. **1966–67** *A Survey of the Contemporary Indians of Canada* ("Hawthorn Report"), 2 Vols. Indian Affairs Branch. Ottawa: Queen's Printer. Excerpts reproduced by permission of Information Canada.

Health Canada **2000** Diabetes *Among Aboriginal People in Canada: The Evidence.* Ottawa: Minister of Public Works and Government Services Canada.

_____ **2003** *Health Policy Research Bulletin*, 1, 5.

_____ **2005** *First Nations, Inuit and Aboriginal Health.* (www.hc-sc.gc.ca/fniah-spnia/diseases-maladies/2005-01_health-sante_indicat-eng.php)

_____ **2006** *Healthy Canadians-A Federal Report on Comparable Health Indicators*, Ottawa, Minister of Health.

_____ **2009** *A Statistical Profile on the Health of First Nations in Canada.* Ottawa, Minister of Health.

Hedican, E. **1991** "On the Ethno-Politics of Canadian Native Leadership and Identity." *Ethnic Groups*, 9: 1–15.

_____ **1995** *Applied Anthropology in Canada: Understanding Aboriginal Issues.* Toronto: University of Toronto Press.

Heilbrun, James and Stanislaw Wellisz **1969** "An Economic Program for the Ghetto. " In *Urban Riots*, Robert Conner (ed.). New York: Random House.

Henderson, A. **2007** *Nunavut: Rethinking Political Culture*, Vancouver: UBC Press.

Henderson, J. **2008** "Treaty Governance." In *Aboriginal Self-Government in Canada*, Y. Belanger (ed), Saskatoon, Purish Publishers, pp. 20–38.

Henderson, J., M. Benson and I. Findlay **2000** *Aboriginal Tenure in the Constitution of Canada.* Scarborough ON: Carswell.

Henderson, J.Y. **1985** "The Doctrine of Aboriginal Rights in Western Legal Tradition." In *The Quest for Justice*, M. Boldt, J. Long and L. Little Bear (eds.). Toronto: University of Toronto Press.

Henderson, J. **2008** *Indigenous Diplomacy and the Rights of Peoples.* Saskatoon: Purich Publishing Limted.

Henderson, W. **1983** "Canadian Legal and Judicial Philosophies on the Doctrine of Aboriginal Rights." In *Aboriginal Rights: Toward an Understanding*, J. Long, M. Boldt and L. Little Bear, (eds.). Lethbridge, Alberta: University of Lethbridge.

Henerson, W. **1978** *Land Tenure in Indian Reserves*, Ottawa: DIAND Report.

Himes, J. **1966** "The Functions of Racial Conflict." *Social Forces*, 45: 1–10.

Hodgins, B., S. Heard and J. Milloy **1992** *Co-Existence? Studies in Ontario–First Nations Relations.* Peterborough ON: Frost Centre for Canadian Heritage and Development Studies, Trent University.

Holmes, J. **1987** *Bill C-31, Equality or Disparity? The Effects of the New Indian Act on Native Women*, Canadian Advisory Council on the Status of Women, Ottawa.

Hornsey, M. and M. Hogg **2000** "Assimilation and Diversity: An Integrative Model of Subgroup Relations." *Personality and Social Psychology Review*, 4: 143–156.

Howard, J. 1951 "Notes on the Dakota Grass Dance." *Southwestern Journal of Anthropology*, 7: 82–85.

Howard, Joseph Kinsey 1952 *Strange Empire:A Narrative of the Northwest*. Toronto: Swan Publishing Co. Ltd.

Hull, J. 2005 *Aboriginal Post-Secondary Education and Labour Market Outcomes, Canada, 2001*. Ottawa: Research and Analysis Directorate, INAC.

_____ **2006** *Aboriginal Women: A Profile from the 2001 Census*. Ottawa: Indian and Northern Affairs Canada.

_____ **2005** *Post Secondary Education and Labour Market Outcomes*. Ottawa: Strategic Research and Analysis, INAC.

Hurley, M. 2009 *Aboriginal Self-Governanment*. PRB 09-23-E, Ottawa: Library of Parliament, Parliamentary Information and Research Services.

Hurley, M. 2009a *The Indian Act*. Ottawa: Library of Parliament, Social Affairs Division.

Huo, Y. 2003 "Procedural Justice and Social Regulation Across Group Boundaries: Does Subgroup Identity Undermine Relationship based Governance?" *Personality and Social Psychology Bulletin*, 29: 336–348.

Huo, Y. and L. Molina. 2006 "Is Pluralism a viable Model of Diversity? The Benefits and Limits of Subgroup Respect." *Group Processes and Intergroup Relations*, 9: 359–376.

Hutchins, P., C. Hilling, and D. Schulze 1999 "The Aboriginal Right to Self-Government and the Canadian Constitution: The Ghost in the Machine" *UBC Law Review*, 29(2):251–287.

Hylton, John (ed.) 1994 *Aboriginal Self-Government in Canada: Current Trends and Issues*. Saskatoon: Purich Publishers.

Ignatieff, Michael, 2000 *The Rights Revolution*. House of Anansi Press: Toronto.

Imai, Shin and Donna Hawley 1995 *The Annotated Indian Act*. Toronto: Carswell.

Indian and Northern Affairs Canada 1977 *Arctic Women's Workshop*. Ottawa: DIAND.

_____ **1982** *The Elimination of Sex Discrimination from the Indian Act*. Ottawa: DIAND.

_____ **1983** *A Demographic Profile of Registered Indian Women*. Ottawa: DIAND.

_____ **1984** *Western Arctic Claim Agreement (Inuvialuit Final Agreement)*. Ottawa: Minister of Supply and Services.

_____ **1988** *Basic Departmental Data*. Ottawa: Minister of Supply and Services.

_____ **1990** *Basic Departmental Data*. Ottawa: Minister of Supply and Services.

_____ **1993** *Basic Departmental Data*. Ottawa: Minister of Supply and Services.

_____ **2000** *Registered Indian Population Projections, 1998–2008*. Ottawa: Minister of Supply and Services.

_____ **2002a** *Basic Departmental Data*. Ottawa: Minister of Supply and Services.

_____ **2002b** *Highlights of Aboriginal Conditions 1981–2001, Part 1, Demographic Trends*. Ottawa: Minister of Supply and Services.

_____ **2003** *Basic Departmental Data*. Ottawa: Minister of Supply and Services.

_____ **2006** *Aboriginal People in Canada*. Ottawa: Strategic Research and Analysis Directorate, Ministry of Industry.

_____ 2008 Departmental Planned Spending and Full-Time Equivalents.

_____ **2010** *Explanatory Paper: Proposed Amendments to the Indian Act Affecting Indian Registration*, Ottawa: Minister of Public Works and Government Services Canada.

_____ **2010** *Education Facilities*, Ottawa. Infrastructure Operations Directorate.

_____ **2010** *Explanatory Paper: Proposed Amendments to the Indian Act Affecting Indian Registration McIvor v. Canada*, Ottawa.

INAC 1995 *Aboriginal Self-Government*, Ottawa: Public Works and Government Services Canada.

Indian and Northern Affairs Canada, News Releases 2011, Ref. #2-3429. Canada Endorses the United Nations Declaration on the Rights of Indigenous Peoples. www.ainc-inac.gc.ca/mr/nr/s-d2010/23429-eng.asp

Indian and Northern Affairs Canada www.ainc-inac.gc.ca/ai/mr/is/info123-eng.asp. The International Decade of the

World's Indigenous People – November 1998.

Indian Association of Alberta 1971 *The Native People*. Edmonton.

Indian Claims Commission 2005 *Charting the Claim Inquiry Process: How the ICC's System Works* 10 (4).

Indian Minerals Directorate 1981a Personal Communication, Reserves and Trust Branch, Department of Indian and Northern Development, Ottawa.

Innis, Harold A. 1970 *The Fur Trade in Canada*. Toronto and Buffalo: University of Toronto Press.

International Labour Organization 1989 Convention on Indigenous Populations No. 169, 27 June 1989. Geneva.

International Labour Office 1994 A Guide to ILO Convention No. 169 on Indigenous and Tribal Peoples. Geneva.

Inuit Tapiriitt Kanatami 2004 Backgrounder on Inuit and Housing, Housing Sectoral Meeting, Nov. 24–25, Ottawa: p. 5.

_____ **2006** *Determining the Inuit Population*. Ottawa: INAC.

_____ **2007** *Knowledge and Use of Inuktitut Among Inuit in Canada, 1981*–2001. Ottawa: INAC.

_____ **2008** *Inuit Statistical Profile*. (www.itk.ca)

_____ **nd.** *Inuit History and Heritage*. (www.itk.ca)

_____ **2010** Health Indicators of Inuit Nunangat within the Canadian Context, July 13.

Isaac, T. 1995 *Aboriginal Law: Cases, Materials, and Commentary*. Saskatoon: Purich Publishing.

_____**2001** *Aboriginal Law: Cases, Materials, and Commentary* (2nd edition). Saskatoon: Purich Publishing.

_____**2004** *Aboriginal Law: Cases, Materials, and Commentary* (3rd edition). Saskatoon: Purich Publishing.

Iverson, P. 1990 "Plains Indians and Australian Aborigines in the Twentieth Century." In *The Struggle for the Land*, P. Olson (ed.). Lincoln NB: University of Nebraska Press, pp. 171–188.

Jaenen, C. 1986 "*French Sovereignty and Native Nationhood during the French Regime*." Native Studies Review, 2: 83–113.

Jamieson, K. 1978 *Indian Women and the Law in Canada: A Citizens Minus*. Ottawa: Minister of Supply and Services Canada.

_____ **1979** "Multiple Jeopardy: The Evolution of a Native Women's Movement." *Atlantis* (part 2), 4 (2), 157–178.

Jantzen, L. 2003 "Reporting Métis in Urban Centres on the 1996 Census." *Canadian Ethnic Studies*, 35 (1): 149–170.

Jarvis, G. and T. Heaton 1989 "Language Shift among Those of Aboriginal Mother Tongue in Canada." *Canadian Studies in Population*, 16 (1), 25–42.

Jenness, D. 1967 *Indians of Canada*, 7th ed. Ottawa: Queen's Printer.

Johnson, S. 2005 "Returning to Correctional Services after Release: A Profile of Aboriginal and non-Aboriginal Adults Involved in Saskatchewan Corrections from 1999/00 to 2003/04." *Juristat*, Canadian Centre for Justice Statistics, Cat. No. 85-002-XIE. 25.2. Ottawa: Statistics Canada.

Justice at Last 2009 www.ainc-inac.gc.ca/al/ldc/spc/pubs/pamp/pamp-eng.asp.

Kay, F. and R. Johnston 2007 *Social Capital, Diversity and the Welfare State*. Vancouver: University of British Columbia Press.

Kaye, L. 1981 "I Think I'm Indian . . . But Others Aren't Sure." *Ontario Indian*, 4 (5), 8 and 34.

Kennedy, Raymond 1945 The Colonial Crisis and the Future." In *The Science of Man in the World Crisis*, Ralph Linton (ed.). New York: Columbia University Press.

Kerr, S. 1975 *Women's Rights and Two National Native Organizations: The Native Council of Canada and the National Indian Brotherhood*. Ottawa: Carleton University, n.p.

King, Cecil 1972 "Sociological Implications of the Jeannette Corbiere Lavell Case." *The Northian*, 8 (March): 44–45.

Kirmayer, L. and G. Valaskakis. 2009 *Healing Traditions: the Mental Health of Aboriginal Peoples in Canada*, Vancouver: University of British Columbia Press.

Kishigami, N. 1999 "Why Do Inuit Move to Montreal? A Research Note on Urban Inuit." *Etudes/Inuit/Studies*, 23 (1): 221–227.

Kllunaxa/Kinbasket Tribal Council. Nd. *The Self Government landscape*, Vancouver.

Kovesi, T., N. Gilbert, C. Stocco, D. Fugler, R. Dales, M. Guay, J. Miller. 2007 "Indoor air quality and the risk of lower respiratory tract infections in young Canadian Inuit Children." *Canadian Medical Association Journal.* 177 (2): 1451464.

Krosenbrink-Gelissen, L. 1983 *Native Women of Manitoba, Canada: Feminism or Ethnicity?* Nijmegen, the Netherlands: Catholic University of Nijmegen, n.p.

_____ **1984** *No Indian Women, No Indian Nation: Canadian Native Women in Search of Their Identity.* Nijmegen: the Netherlands: Catholic University of Nijmegen, n.p.

_____ **1989** "The Métis National Council: Continuity and Change among the Canadian Métis." *Native American Studies*, 3 (1), 33–41.

_____ **1991** *Sexual Equality as an Aboriginal Right.* Saarbrucken, Germany: Verlagbreitenbach.

Kulchyski, P. (ed.). 1994 *Unjust Relations: Aboriginal Rights in Canadian Courts.* Toronto: Oxford University Press.

_____ **2005** *Like the Sound of a Drum.* Winnipeg: University of Manitoba Press.

Laing, A. 1967 *Indians and the Law.* Ottawa: Queen's Printer.

Lalonde, C. 2005 "Creating an Index of Healthy Aboriginal communities." *Developing a Healthy Communities Index*, Ottawa: Canadian Institute for Health Information.

Lambertus, Sandra 2004 *Wartime Images, Peacetime Wounds: The Media and the Gustafsen Lake Standoff.* Vancouver: University of British Columbia Press.

LaRocque, E. 2010 *When the Other is me: Native Resistance Discourse 1850–1990*, Winnipeg, University of Manitoba Press.

La Rusic, Ignatius 1968 *Hunter to Proletarian.* Research paper for Cree Development Change Project.

Laselva, S. 1998–99 "Aboriginal Self-Government and the Foundations of Canadian Nationhood." *B.C. Studies,* 120: 41–55.

Laurie, N. 2008 *The Cost of Poverty*, Toronto: Ontario Association of Food Banks.

Le Clercq, C. 1691 *First Establishment of the Faith in New France*, Paris.

Legare, A. 1996 "The Process Leading to a Land Claims Agreement and Its Implementation: The Case of Nunavut Land Claims Settlement." *Canadian Journal of Native Studies*, 16 (1): 139–163.

Leigh, D. 2009 "Colonialism, Gender and the Family in North America: for a Gendered Analysis of Indigenous Struggles." *Studies in Ethnicity and Nationalism*, 9:70-88.

Leonard, D. 1995 "Indigenous Nature of Water." *The DLA Financial*, 2 (3): 15–27.

Leslie, J. and R. Maguire 1978 *The Historical Development of the Indian Act, Treaties, and Historical Research Centres.* Ottawa: Department of Indian Affairs and Northern Development, PRE Group.

Levesque, C. 2003 "The Presence of Aboriginal Peoples in Quebec's Cities: Multiple Movements, Diverse Issues." In *Not Strangers in These Parts*, D. Newhouse and E. Peters (eds.). Ottawa: Policy Research Institute, pp. 23–34.

Levine, S. 1970 "The Survival of Indian Identity." In *The American Indian Today*, S. Levine and N. Lurie (eds.). Hardmondsworth, UK: Pelican.

Little Bear, L. 2000 "Jagged Worldviews Colliding." In *Reclaiming Indigenous Voice and Vision*, M. Baaataaatise (ed). Vancouver: University of British Columbia Press.

Long, D. and O. Dickason 2011 *Visions of the Heart* (3rd ed.) Toronto: Oxford University Press.

Long, J.A., M. Boldt, and L. Little Bear 1982 "Federal Indian Policy and Indian Self-Government in Canada: An Analysis of a Current Proposal." *Canadian Public Policy*, 8 (2): 189–199.

_____ **1983 (eds.).** *Alberta Law Foundation.* Lethbridge AB: Law Foundation.

Longboat, D. 1987 "First Nations Control of Education: The Path to Our Survival as Nations." In *Indian Education in Canada*,

Vol. 2, J. Barman, Y. Hebert and D. McCaskill (eds.). Vancouver: University of British Columbia Press.

Lower, A. 1957 *Colony to Nation: A History of Canada.* Toronto: Longman, Green.

Lussier, A. 1979 *Louis Riel and the Métis: Riel Mini Conference Papers.* Winnipeg: Pemmican Publishers.

Maaka, R. and A. Fleras. 2008 "Contesting Indigenous Peoples Governance." In *Aboriginal Self-Government in Canada,* Y. Belanger (ed.), Saskatoon: Purich Publishing, pp. 69-104.

MacDonald, J. 1998 *The Arctic Sky: Inuit Astronomy, Star Lore, and Legend.* Toronto, Royal Ontario Museum and Nunavut Research Institute.

Macdougall, B 2010 *One of the Family: Métis Culture in 19th Century Northwest Saskatchewan.* UBC Press: Vancouver.

Macklem, Patrick 2001 *Indigenous Differences and the Constitution of Canada.* Toronto: University of Toronto Press.

Mainville, Robert 2001 *An Overview of Aboriginal and Treaty Rights and Compensation for Their Breach.* Saskatoon: Purich Publishers.

Mallea, R. 1994 *Aboriginal Law: Apartheid in Canada.* Brandon MB: Bearpaw Publishing.

Manitoba Métis Federation Inc. v. Attorney General of Canada, 2007 MBQB 293 (Can LII) – 2007-12-07 Manitoba Court of Queen's Bench.

Mann, M. 2005 *Aboriginal Women: An Issues Backgrounder*, prepared for Status of Women Canada.

_____ **2005a** *Indian registration: Unrecognized and Unstated Paternity*, Ottawa, Research Directorate, Status of Women Canada.

Mariategui, J.C. 1934 *Siete ensayos de interpretación de la sealidad peruana*, 2nd ed. Lima: Editorial Librariá Peruana.

Marshall #3; R. v. Bernard 2005 S.C.J. No. 44 http://scc.lexum.org/en/2005/2005scc43/2005scc43.html

Martin, S. 2005 *Determinants of Well-Being in Inupiat and Yuplit Eskimos: Do Communities Matter?* Ph.D. dissertation, University of Texas at Dallas.

Marule, M.S. 1977 "The Canadian Government's Termination Policy: From 1969 to the Present Day." In *One Century Later*, J. Getty and D. Smith (eds.). Vancouver: University of British Columbia Press.

Maxim, P. and J. White 2003 "Toward an Index of Community Capacity: Predicting Community Potential for Successful Program Transfer." In *Aboriginal Conditions*, J. White, P. Maxim and D. Beavon (eds.). Vancouver: University of British Columbia Press, pp. 248–263.

Maybury-Lewis, D., T. Macdonald and B. Maybury-Lewis (eds.) 2009 *Manifest Destinies and Indigenous Peoples*, Harvard University: Harvard University Press.

McCaskill, D. 1981 "The Urbanization of Indians in Winnipeg, Toronto, Edmonton, and Vancouver: A Comparative Analysis." *Culture*, 1: 82–89.

McCullum, H. and K. McCullum 1975 *This Land Is Not for Sale.* Toronto: Anglican Book Centre.

McGhee, R. 1996 *Ancient People of the Arctic.* Vancouver: University of British Columbia Press.

McInnis, E. 1959 *Canada: A Political and Social History.* New York: Holt, Rinehart and Winston.

McMahon, D. and F. Martin 1995 *Aboriginal Self-Government: Legal and Constitutional Issues.* Ottawa: Minister of Supply and Services.

McNab, David 1999 *Circles of Time: Aboriginal Land Rights and Resistance in Ontario.* Waterloo: Wilfred Laurier University Press.

McNeil, K. 2010 "Reconciliation and Third Party Interest." *Indigenous Law Journal*, 8:6-26.

_____ **2007** *The Jurisdiction of Inherent Right Aboriginal Governments*, Ottawa: National Centre for First Nations Governance.

Melville, B. 1981 *Indian Reserves and Indian Treaty Problems in Northeastern B.C.* Vancouver: B.C. Hydro and Power Authority.

Mendelson, M. 2006 "Improving Primary and Secondary Education on Reserves in Canada." *Caledon Commentary*, October, 1–7.

_____ **2008** *Improving Education on Reserves: A First Nations Education Authority Act*, Ottawa: Caledon Institute of Social Policy.

_____ **2009** *Why We Need a First Nations Act*. Ottawa: Caledon Institute of Social Policy.

_____ **2006** *Aboriginal Peoples and Postsecondary Education in Canada*, Ottawa:Caledon Institute of Social Policy.

Mendelson, M. and K. Battle 1999 *Aboriginal People in Canada's Labour Market*. Ottawa: Caledon Institute of Social Policy, June.

Mendes, E. and P. Bendin n.d. "The New Canadian Charter of Rights and International Law and Aboriginal Self-Determination: A Proposal for a New Direction." Saskatoon SK: mimeograph.

Métis National Council 1984 *The Métis Natives.* Toronto: Métis National Council.

Mickenberg, Neil 1971 "Aboriginal Rights in Canada and the United States." *Osgoode Hall Law Journal*, 9: 154.

Miller, J. B. 1986. *Toward a New Psychology of Women*, 2nd edition. Boston: Beacon Press.

Miller, J.R. 1991 *Sweet Promises*. Toronto: University of Toronto Press.

_____ **2000** *Skyscrapers Hide the Heavens: A History of Indian–White Relations in Canada.* Toronto: University of Toronto Press.

_____ **2009** *Compact, Contract, Covenant: Aboriginal Treaty-Making in Canada.* Toronto, University of Toronto Press.

Mitchell, M. 1996 *From Talking Chiefs to a Native Corporate Elite*. Montreal and Kingston: McGill-Queen's University Press.

Monture-Angus, P. 1995 *Thunder in My Soul: A Mohawk Woman Speaks*, Halifax: Fernwood Publishing.

_____ **1999** Journeying Forward: Dreaming First Nations' Independence, Halifax: Fernwood Publishing.

Moore, M. 2010 "Indigenous Peoples and Political Legitimacy." In *Between Consenting Peoples*, J. Webber and C.M. Macleod (eds.). Vancouver: University of British Columbia Press, pp. 143-163.

Morellato, M. 2003 The Existence of Aboriginal Governance Rights within the Canadian Legal System, mimeo.

Morris, Alexander 1880 *The Treaties of Canada with the Indians of Manitoba and the North West Territories*. Toronto: Belfords, Clark.

Morrison, Bruce and C. Roderick Wilson (eds.) 2004 *Native Peoples: The Canadian Experience.* Toronto: McClelland & Stewart.

Morse, B. (ed.) 1991 *Aboriginal Peoples and the Law: Indian, Métis and Inuit Rights in Canada*. Ottawa: Carleton University Press.

_____**1999** "The Inherent Right of Aboriginal Governance." In *Aboriginal Self-Government in Canada*, J. Hylton (ed.). Saskatoon: Purich Publishers.

Morton, W.L. 1963 *The Kingdom of Canada: A General History from Earliest Times*. Toronto: McClelland and Stewart.

Moss, W. 1995 "Inuit Perspectives on Treaty Rights and Governance Issues." In *Aboriginal Self-Government*, P. Macklem, D. Reaume and M. Levin (eds.). Ottawa: Royal Commission on Aboriginal Peoples, pp. 55–139.

Moss, W. and P. Niemczak 1991 *Aboriginal Land Claims Issues*. Ottawa: Library of Parliament.

Murphy, M. 2001 "Culture and the Courts: A New Direction in Canadian Jurisprudence on Aboriginal Rights?" *Canadian Journal of Political Science*, 34 (1): 109–129.

Nabokov, P. 1999 *Native American Testimony*, rev. edition. New York: Penguin.

Nadeau, Ron 1979 *Indian Local Government*. Ottawa: Department of Indian Affairs and Northern Development. Policy Research and Evaluation.

Nagy, M. (ed.) Population and Migration, *Etudes/Inuit/Studies*, Vol 26 (1 and 2): 1-5.

National Centre for First Nations Governance, 2009 *Rebuilding Nations*, West Vancouver.

National Council of Welfare. 2007 First Nations, Metis and Inuit Children and Youth: Time to Act. Ottawa, Volume #127.

Native Women's Association of Canada. 2007 Aboriginal Women and the Legal Justice System in Canada, Presented at the National Aboriginal Women's Summit, June 20-22, Corner Brook, Newfoundland.

Native Women's Association of Canada. 2007a) *Social Determinants of Health and Canada's Aboriginal Women.* Submission to the World Health Organization's Commission on the social Determinants of Health, Ottawa.

Naumann, D. 2008 "Aboriginal Women in Canada: On the Choice to Renounce or Reclaim Aborginal Identity." *The Canadian Journal of Native Studies,* 28:343–362.

Nesdalel, D. and A. Mak 2003 "Ethnic Identification, Self Esteem and Immigrant Psychological Health." *International Journal of Intercultural Relations,* 27: 23–40.

Newell, D. 1993 *Tangled Webs of History: Indians and the Law in Canada's Pacific Coast Fisheries,* Toronto, University of Toronto press.

Newman, D. 2009 *The Duty to Consult,* Saskatoon, Purich Publishing.

Newhouse, D. 2003 "The Invisible Infrastructure: Urban Aboriginal Institutions and Organizations." In *Not Strangers in These Parts: Urban Aboriginal Peoples*, D. Newhouse and E. Peters (eds.). Ottawa: Policy Research Institute, pp. 243–254.

Newhouse, D. and E. Peters (eds.) 2003 *Not Strangers in These Parts: Urban Aboriginal Peoples.* Ottawa: Policy Research Initiative.

Nichols, R. 1998 *Indians in the United States and Canada.* Lincoln NB and London ON: University of Nebraska Press.

_____ **2009** "National Expansion and Native Peoples of the United States and Canada." In *Manifest Destinies and Indigenous Peoples*, D. Maybury-Lewis, T. Macdonald and B. Maybury-Lewis (eds.). Harvard University: Harvard University Press, pp, 145–171.

Nielsen, M. 1991 "Balance and Strategy: Native Criminal Justice Organizations, Native Communities and the Canadian State." Kingston ON: Paper presented at the Annual Meeting of the Canadian Sociology and Anthropology Association.

Nisga'a Lisims Government. Nd. Self Government: *The Five Realities,* Vancouver.

Norris, M.J. 1998 "Canada's Aboriginal Languages." *Canadian Social Trends,* Winter, 8–16.

_____ **2000** "Aboriginal Peoples in Canada: Demographic and Linguistic Perspectives." In *Visions of the Heart: Canadian Aboriginal Issues,* D. Long and O. Dickason (eds.). Toronto: Harcourt Brace Canada.

Norris, M. 2009 "Linguistic Classifications of Aboriginal Languages in Canada: Implications for Assessing Language Diversity, Endangerment and Revitalization." *Diversity,* 7:21-34.

_____ **2007** Aboriginal Languages in Canada: emerging Trends and Perspectives on Second Language Acquisition." *Canadian Social Trends,* 83:19-27.

_____ **2006** "Aboriginal Languages in Canada. In *Aboriginal Policy Research,* J. White, S. Wingert, D. Beavon, and P. Maxim (eds.). Toronto: Thompson Educational Publishers.

Norris, M., D. Beavon, E. Guimond and M. Cooke 2001 *Migration and Residential Mobility of Canada's Aboriginal Groups.* Ottawa: Indian and Northern Affairs Canada.

Norris, M.J., M. Cooke, and S. Clatworthy 2004 "Aboriginal Mobility and Migration Patterns and Policy Implications." In *Population Mobility and Indigenous Peoples in Australasia and North America,* J. Taylor and M. Bell (eds.). London: Routledge Press.

Norris, M.J. and L. Jantzen 2003 "Aboriginal Languages in Canada's Urban Areas." In *Not Strangers in These Parts,* D. Newhouse and E. Peters (eds.). Ottawa: Policy Research Initiative, pp. 93–118.

Nuttall R. 1982 "The Development of Indian Boards of Health in Alberta." *Canadian Journal of Public Health,* 73: 300–303.

O'Donnell, V. and H. Tait 2004 "Well-being of the Non-Reserve Aboriginal Population." *Canadian Social Trends,* Spring, 19–23.

Oliver, C. 1990 "Determinants of Interorganizational Relationships: Integrative and Future Directions." *Academy of Management Review,* 15 (2): 241–265.

Omi, M. and H. Winant 2008 "Once More with Feeling; Reflections on Racial Formation." *Comparative Racialization*, 123, Number 5.

ONWA 1983 *Nations within a Nation: An Aboriginal Right?* A Report of the Conference Proceedings, November 12, 13 and 14, 1982. Thunder Bay: ONWA.

Organization for Economic Co-Operation and Development (OECD) 1973 *List of Social Concerns Common to Most OECD Countries, Paris: OECD.*

Papillon, M. and G. Cosentino 2004 *Lessons from Abroad: Towards a New Social Model for Canada's Aboriginal Peoples*, Ottawa: Canadian Policy Research Newtowks, Research Report F/40.

Paton, R. 1982 *New Policies and Old Organizations: Can Indian Affairs Change?* Centre for Policy and Program Assessment, School of Public Administration. Ottawa: Carleton University.

Patrick, D. 2005 "Language Rights in Indigenous Communities: The Case of the Inuit of Northern Quebec." *Journal of Sociolinguistics*, 9 (3): 369–389.

Patterson, E. Palmer 1972 *The Canadian Indians: A History Since 1500*. Toronto: Collier-Macmillan Canada.

Pauktuutit Inuit Women of Canada 2006 *The Inuit Way: A Guide to Inuit Culture.* (www.pauktuutit.ca/pdf/publications/paukt uutit/InuitWay_e.pdf)

Peeling, A. and P. Chartrand 2004 "Exploring the Origins of Métis Rights of Self-Government in the Context of s. 35, *Constitution Act*, 1982" *Saskatchewan Law Review*, 67 (1): 339–357.

Paxton, S. 2002 "The Paradox of Public HIV Disclosure", *AIDS-CARE*, 14: 559-567.

Pelletier, Emile 1974 *A Social History of the Manitoba Métis*. Winnipeg: Manitoba Métis Federation Press.

_____ **1975** *Exploitation of Métis Lands.* Winnipeg: Manitoba Métis Federation Press.

Pelletier, W. 1970 *Two Articles.* Toronto: Neewin Publishing.

Pendakur K. and R. Pendakur. 2008 *Aboriginal Income Disparity in Canada*, Working Paper Series, Metropolis British Columbia, No. 08-15.

Pennekeok, F. 1976 "The Anglican Church and the Disintegration of Red River Society, 1818–1870." In *The West and the Nation*, C. Berger and R. Cook (eds.). Toronto: McClelland and Stewart.

Penner, K., 1983 *Indian Self-Government in Canada: Report of the Special Committee* (The Penner Report). Ottawa: Minister of Supply and Services.

Peters, E. 1987 *Aboriginal Self Government Arrangements in Canada: An Overview.* Kingston ON: Queen's University, Institute of Intergovernmental Relations.

_____ **2000** "Aboriginal Peoples in Urban Areas." In *Visions of the Heart: Contemporary Aboriginal Issues*, D. Long and O. Dickason (eds.). Toronto: Harcourt Brace, 238–333.

_____ **2001** "Developing Federal Policy for First Nations People in Urban Areas." *Canadian Journal of Native Studies*, 21 (1): 57–96.

_____ **2002** "Our City Indians: Negotiating the Meaning of First Nations Urbanization in Canada, 1945–1975." *Historical Geography*, 30: 69–84.

_____ **2004** Three Myths about Aboriginals in Cities, paper.

Peters, E., M. Rosenberg, and G. Halseth 1989 "The Ontario Métis: A People without an Identity." Mimeographed.

Peters, Omar 1968 "Canada's Indians and Eskimos and Human Rights." Paper presented to the Thinkers' Conference on Cultural Rights. Mimeographed.

Peterson, Jacqueline and Jennifer S.H. Brown (eds.) 1985 *The New Peoples: Being and Becoming Métis in North America.* Winnipeg: University of Manitoba Press.

Pettigrew, T. 1964 *A Profile of the Negro American*. Princeton: D. Van Nostrand Co.

Pfeiffer, J. and G. Salanchik 1978 *The External Control of Organizations: A Resource Dependence Perspective*. New York: Harper and Row.

Phinney, J. 1990 "Ethnic Identity in Adolescence and Adults: Review of Research." *Psychological Bulletin*, 108: 499-514.

Phipps, S. 2004 *The Impact of Poverty on Health: A Scan of Research Literature,*

Ottawa: Canadian Institute for Health Information.

Piche, Victor and M.V. George 1973 "Estimates of Vital Rates for the Canadian Indians, 1960–1970." *Demography*, 10: 367–382.

Pinkerton, E 1989 *Co-operative Management of Local Fisheries: New Directions for Improved Management and Community Development*, Vancouver: University of British Columbia Press.

Pitts, J. 1974 "The Study of Race Consciousness: Comments on New Directions." *American Journal of Sociology*, 80: 665–687.

Plain, F. 1985 "A Treaty on the Rights of the Aboriginal Peoples of the Continent of North America." In *The Quest for Justice*, M. Boldt, J. Long, and L. Little Bear (eds.). Toronto: University of Toronto Press.

Poelzer, G. n.d. *Inherent* vs. *Delegated Models of Governance*, University of Northern British Columbia.

Polanyi, Karl 1974 *The Great Transformation*. Boston: Beacon Press.

Ponting, J.R. 1986 *Arduous Journey: Canadian Indians and Decolonization.* Toronto: McClelland and Stewart.

_____ **1987** *Profiles of Public Opinion on Canadian Natives and Native Issues: Special Status and Self Government.* Calgary: Research Unit for Public Policy Studies, University of Calgary.

_____ **1997** *First Nations in Canada: Perspectives on Opportunity, Empowerment, and Self-Determination.* Toronto: McGraw-Hill Ryerson.

Ponting, J.R. and R. Gibbins 1980 *Out of Irrelevance: A Socio-Political Introduction to Indian Affairs of Canada.* Toronto: Butterworth and Co. (Canada.)

Portes, A. and L. Hao. 2002 "The Price of Uniformity: Language, Family and Personality Adjustment in the Immigrant Second Generation." *Ethnic and Racial Studies*, 25:889–912.

Portes, A. and P. Landolt 1996 "The Downside of Social Capital." *The American Prospect*, 16: 18–21.

Postl, B. 2005 *British Columbia First Nations Schools Funding Analysis: 2003-04 School Year.* Report submitted to Indian and Northern Affairs Canada.

Prentice, J. and J. Bellegarde 2001 *Report to the House of Commons Standing Committee on Aboriginal Affairs*, Ottawa: Indian Claims Commission Annual Report 1999–2000.

Price, R. (ed.) 1979 *The Spirit of the Alberta Indian Treaties*. Montreal: Institute for Research on Public Policy.

_____ **1981** "The Viability of Indian Languages in Canada" *Canadian Journal of Native Studies,* 1 (2): 349–361.

Price, Richard, 2009 "The British Columbia Treaty Process: An Evolving Institution", *Native Studies Review* 18 (1): 139-169.

Pross, P. (ed.) 1975 *Pressure Group Behaviour in Canadian Politics.* Scarborough ON: McGraw-Hill Ryerson.

_____ **1981** "Pressure Groups: Talking Chameleons." In *Canadian Politics in the 1980s,* M. Whitington and G. Williams (eds.), Toronto, Methuen.

Public Health Agency of Canada. 2004 HIV/AIDS Among Aboriginal Peoples in Canada: A Continuing Concern. (www.phac-aspc.gc.ca/publicat/ epiu-aepi/epi_update_may_04/9-eng.php)

Purich, D. 1988 *The Métis.* Toronto: James Lorimer.

_____ **1992** *The Inuit and Their Land.* Toronto: James Lorimer.

Quebec Native Women Inc. 2010 Position Paper: Bill C-3. Presented to House of Commons Standing committee on Aboriginal Affairs and Northern Development, Kahnawake, April 20.

QED Information Systems 2004 *Funding for First Nations Schools: A Comparison of INAC and Provincial Funding Regimes in Saskatchewan.* Report submitted to Indian and Northern Affairs Canada.

Quesnel, J. 2010 *Respecting the Seventh Generation: A Voluntary Plan for Relocating Non-Viable Native Reserves*, Winnipeg, Frontier Centre for Public Policy.

Raunet, D. 1984 *Without Surrender without Consent.* Vancouver: Douglas & McIntyre.

Ray, Arthur J. 1974 *Indians in the Fur Trade.* Toronto and Buffalo: University of Toronto Press.

_____ 1996 *I Have Lived Here Since the World Began.* Toronto: Key Porter Books.

Red Horse, J. G., R. Lewis, M. Feit and J. Decker 1978 "Family Behavior of Urban American Indians." *Social Casework,* February: 67–72.

Red Horse, J. G. 1980 "Family Structure and Value Orientation in American Indians." *Social Casework,* October:462–467.

Reeves, W. and J. Frideres 1981 "Government Policy and Indian Urbanization: The Alberta Case." *Canadian Public Policy,* 7 4 (Autumn): 7 (4) 584–595.

Report of the Affairs of the Indians in Canada 1844 "History of the Relations between the Government and the Indians." *Journals,* Section 1. Ottawa: Queen's Printer.

Richards, J. and M. Scott. 2009 *Aboriginal Education: Strengthening the Foundations.* Ottawa: Canadian Policy Research Network.

Richards, J. J. Hove and K. Afolabi 2008 *Understanding the Aboriginal/Non-Aboriginal Gap in Student Performance.* Ottawa: C.D. Howe Institute.

Richards, J. 2008 *Closing the Aboriginal/Non-Aboriginal Education Gaps,* Ottawa: C.D. Howe Institute Backgrounder 116.

Richardson, B. 1993 *People of Terra Nullius.* Vancouver: Douglas & McIntyre.

Rieber, J. 1977 *Fundamental Concerns Regarding Indian Local Government: A Discussion Paper of Potential Problem and Research Areas.* Ottawa: Department of Indian Affairs and Northern Development.

Robinson, M. and E. Ghostkeeper 1987 "Native and Local Economies: A Consideration of Economic Evolution and the Next Economy." *Arctic,* 40 (2): 138–144.

_____ 1988 "Implementing the Next Economy in a Unified Context: A Case Study of the Paddle Prairie Mall Corporation." *Arctic,* 41 (3): 173–182.

Romaniuc, A 2003 "Aboriginal Population of Canada: Growth Dynamics under Conditions of Encounter of Civilizations." *Canadian Studies in Population,* 30(1): 75–115.

Romaniuc, A. and V. Piche 1972 "Natality Estimates for the Canadian Indians by Stable Population Models, 1900–1969." *The Canadian Review of Sociology and Anthropology,* 9 (1): 1–20.

Roness, A. and M. Collier 2010 Examining Partnership Arrangements Between Aboriginal and non-Aboriginal Businesses, Halifax, Atlantic Policy Congress.

Rotman, Leonard I. 1996 *Parallel Paths: Fiduciary Doctrine and the Crown–Native Relationship in Canada.* Toronto: University of Toronto Press.

_____ 1997 "Symposium on Aboriginal Legal Issues." Special Issue of *Alberta Law Review,* 36 (1). University of Alberta.

Salisbury, R. 1986 *A Homeland for the Cree.* Kingston and Montreal: McGill-Queen's University Press.

Sanders, D. 1979 "Métis Rights in the Prairie Provinces and the Northwest Territories: A Legal Interpretation." In *The Forgotten People: Métis and Non-Status Indian Land Claims,* H. Daniels (ed.). Native Council of Canada: Ottawa.

_____ 1983a "The Rights of the Aboriginal Peoples of Canada." *Canadian Bar Review,* 6 (1): 314–338.

_____ 1983b "Prior Claims: Aboriginal People in the Constitution of Canada." In *Canada and the New Constitution: The Unfinished Business,* S. Beck and I. Bernier (eds.). Montreal: Institute for Research on Public Policy.

_____ 1983c "The Indian Lobby." In *And No One Cheered,* K. Banting and R. Simeon (eds.). Toronto: Methuen.

_____ 1985a "The Indian Lobby and the Canadian Constitution, 1978–1982." In *Indigenous Peoples and the Nation-State: 'Fourth World' Politics in Canada, Australia and Norway,* N. Dyck (ed.). St. John's: Memorial University of Newfoundland, Institute of Social and Economic Research, pp. 151–189.

_____ **1985b** "Aboriginal Rights: The Search for Recognition in International Law." In *The Quest for Justice*, M. Boldt, J. Long, and L. Little Bear (eds.). Toronto: University of Toronto Press.

_____ **1990** "The Supreme Court of Canada and the 'Legal and Political Struggle' Over Indigenous Rights." *Canadian Ethnic Studies*, 22 (3): 122–129.

Satzewich, V. And N. Liodakis, 2010 *'Race' & Ethnicity in Canada.* Toronto: Oxford University Press.

Sawchuk, Joe 1978 *The Métis of Manitoba: Reformulation of an Ethnic Identity.* Toronto: Peter Martin Associates.

_____ **1998** *The Dynamics of Native Politics: The Alberta Métis Experience.* Saskatoon: Purich Publishing.

Sawchuk, J., P. Sawchuk and T. Ferguson 1981 *Métis Land Rights in Alberta: A Political History.* Edmonton: The Métis Association of Alberta.

Schwartz, B. 1986 *First Principle: Constitutional Reform with Respect to the Aboriginal Peoples of Canada, 1982–84.* Kingston: Institute of Intergovernmental Relations, Queen's University.

Sealey, D. Bruce 1975 "One Plus One Equals One." In *The Other Natives: The Métis.* Antoine S. Lussier and D. Bruce Sealey (eds.). Winnipeg: Manitoba Métis Federation Press.

Sealey, D. Bruce and Antoine S. Lussier 1975 *The Métis—Canada's Forgotten People.* Winnipeg: Manitoba Métis Federation Press.

Sharpe, A., J. Arsenault and S. Lapointe 2007 *The Potential Contribution of Aboriginal Canadians to Labour Force, Employment, Productivity and Output Growth in Canada*, 2001-2017. Ottawa: Centre for the Study of Living Standards, report No. 2007-04.

Shea, I.G. 1879 *Charlevoix's History of New France.* New York: Colonial Documents, Vol. 2, 1879.

Siggner, A. 1980 "A Socio-demographic Profile of Indians in Canada." In *Out of Irrelevance*, J.R. Ponting and R. Gibbins (eds.). Toronto: Butterworth (Canada).

_____ **1986** "The Socio-demographic Conditions of Registered Indians." *Canadian Social Trends,* (Winter): 2–9.

_____ **2001** *Profile of the Urban Aboriginal Population, Canada, 1996.* Ottawa.

_____ **2003a** "Urban Aboriginal Populations: An Update Using the 2001 Census Results." In *Not Strangers in These Parts: Urban Aboriginal Peoples*, D. Newhouse and E. Peters (eds.). Ottawa: Policy Research Initiative.

_____ **2003b** "Impact of 'Ethnic Mobility' on Socio-economic Conditions of Aboriginal Peoples." *Canadian Studies in Population*, 31 (2): 137–158.

Siggner, A. and R. Costa 2005 *Aboriginal Conditions in Census Metropolitan Areas, 1981-2001.* Ottawa: Indian and Northern Affairs Canada.

Siggner, A. and C. Locatelli 1980 *Regional Population Projections by Age, Sex, and Residence for Canada's Registered Indian Population, 1976–1991.* Ottawa: Research Branch, Department of Indian Affairs and Northern Development.

Silvey, L. E. 1997 *Ordinal Position and Role Development of the Firstborn Daughter Within Her Family of Origin.* Dissertation. Lansing: Department of Family and Child Ecology, Michigan State University.

Simeone, T. 2007 *The Harvard Project on American Indian Economic Development*, Boston: Harvard University.

Simon, B. and B. Klandermans 2001 "Politicized Collective Identity: A Social Psychological Analysis." *American Psychologist*, 56: 319–331.

Skarlicki, D. n.d. *Socio-Economic Planning Model: Tools for Native Community Economic Planning.* Edmonton: First Nations Resource Council.

Smith, A. 1981 *The Ethnic Revival.* New York: Cambridge University Press.

Smylie, J. 2000 *A Guide for Health Professionals Working with Aboriginal Peoples*, Ottawa, Society of Obstetricians and Gynaecologist of Canada.

Sorenson, Gary and Murray Wolfson 1969 "Black Economic Independence: Some

Preliminary Thoughts." *The Annals of Regional Science*, 3 (December): 168–178.

Speck, D. C. 1989 "The Indian Health Transfer Policy: A Step in the Right Direction, A Revenge of the Hidden Policy?" *Native Studies Review*, 5 (1): 187–214.

Stanbury, R., and J. Fields 1975 *Success and Failure: Indians in Urban Society.* Vancouver: University of British Columbia Press.

Stanley, George 1952 "The Indian Background of Canadian History." *Canadian Historical Association Annual Report.* Canadian Historical Society.

_____ 1961 *The Birth of Western Canada: A History of the Riel Rebellions.* New York: Longman, Green.

Stasiulis, D. and N. Yuval-Davis (eds.) 1995 *Unsettling Settler Societies*, Vol. 11. London: Sage Publications.

Statistics Canada 1986 *Canadian Metropolitan Areas.* Dimensions Series. Ottawa.

_____ 2001a *Aboriginal Peoples Survey.* Ottawa: Indian and Northern Affairs Canada

_____ 2001b *Aboriginal Peoples of Canada: Demographic Profile.* Ottawa: Ministry of Industry.

_____ 2003 *Aboriginal Peoples Survey.* Ottawa.

_____ 2004 *Aboriginal Network*, Winter. Ottawa.

_____ 2005 *Projections of the Aboriginal Populations, Canada, Provinces and Territories: 2001–2017.* Ottawa: Ministry of Industry.

_____ 2003 *Aboriginal Peoples Survey 2001 Initial Findings: Wellbeing of the Non-Reserve Aboriginal Population."* Ottawa, Minister of Industry.

_____ 2006 Living Arrangements of Inuit and Non-Aboriginal Children Aged 14 Years and Under, Canada and Inuit Region, 2001 and 2006.

_____ 2009 Incarceration of Aboriginal people in Adult Correctional Services, The Daily, July 212. Catalogue no. 11001-XIE.

_____ Canadian Centre for Justice Statistics Profile, Religious Groups, Ottawa.

Stern, P. 2000 "Subsistence: Work and Leisure." *Etudes/Inuit/Studies*, 24 (1): 9–24.

Sterritt, N. 1998–99 "The Nisga'a Treaty: Competing Claims Ignored!" *B.C. Studies,* 120: 73–98.

Sunkel, Oswaldo 1973 "Transitional Capitalism and National Disintegration in Latin America." *Social and Economic Studies,* 22: 132–176.

Surtees, R.J. 1969 "The Development of an Indian Reserve Policy in Canada." *Ontario History*, LCI, 2 (June): 87–98.

Swain, H. 1988 "Comprehensive Claims." *Transition*, 1 (6): 7–9.

Tabb, William 1970 *The Political Economy of the Black Ghetto.* New York: W.W. Norton.

Tait, H. 2006 *Harvesting and Community Well-being among Inuit in the Canadian Arctic.* Ottawa: Ministry of Industry, Statistics Canada.

Tanner, A. (ed.) 1983 *The Politics of Indianness.* St. John's NF: Institute of Social and Economic Research, Memorial University of Newfoundland.

Taqralik 1984 *Native Women's Association Offers Help to Inuit Women.* Mimeograph.

Taylor, D. 1997 "The Quest for Collective Identity: The Plight of Disadvantaged Ethnic Minorities." *Canadian Psychologist,* 38:174–190.

Taylor, J. 1983 "An Historical Introduction to Métis Claims in Canada." *The Canadian Journal of Native Studies*, 3: 151–181.

Taylor, J. and M. Bell (eds.) 2004 *Population Mobility and Indigenous People in Australasia and North America.* London: Routledge.

Teillet, J. 2009, 2010 Métis Law Summary. www.pstlaw.ca

Tennant, P. 1984 "Indian Self Government: Progress or Stalemate." *Canadian Public Policy*, 10 (2): 211–215.

Terrell, J. and D. Terrell 1976 *Indian Women of the Western Morning: Their Life in Early America.* New York: Anchor Press.

Terry, D., C. Carey and V Callan. 2001 "Employee Adjustment to an Organizational Merger: An Intergroup Perspective." *Personality and Social Psychology Bulletin*, 27: 267–280.

Tester, F. and P. Kulchyski 1994 *Tammarniit: Inuit Relocation in the Eastern Arctic,*

1939-63. Vancouver: University of British Columbia Press.

Thomas, D.H. 1972 "Western Shoshoni Ecology Settlement Patterns and Beyond." In *Great Basin Cultural Ecology: A Symposium,* D.D. Fowler (ed.). Desert Research Institute, Publications in the Social Sciences, 8.

Thompson, R. 1982 "Aboriginal Title and Mining Legislation in the Northwest Territories." *Studies in Aboriginal Rights No. 6.* Saskatoon: University of Saskatchewan Native Law Centre.

Thornton, R. 1987 *American Indian Holocaust and Survival.* Norman: University of Oklahoma Press.

Titley, B. 1983 "W.M. Graham: Indian Agent Extraordinaire." *Prairie Forum,* 8: 26–28.

_____ **1986** *A Narrow Vision.* Vancouver: University of British Columbia Press.

Tjepkema, M. 2002 "The Health of the Off-Reserve Aboriginal Population." *Supplement to Health Reports,* Vol. 13. Ottawa: Statistics Canada, Cat. No. 82-003.

Tobias, J. 1976 "Protection, Civilization, Assimilation: An Outline of Canada's Indian Policy." *Western Canadian Journal of Anthropology,* 6 (2): 13–30.

Tran, K., J. Kaddatz and P. Allard 2005 "South Asians in Canada: Unity through Diversity." *Canadian Social Trends,* Autumn, 20–25.

Treaty 7 Elders and Tribal Council 1996 *The True Spirit and Original Intent of Treaty.* Montreal and Kingston: McGill-Queen's University Press.

Trigger, B. 1965 "The Jesuits and the Fur Trade." *Ethnohistory,* 12 (Winter): 30–53.

_____ **1985** *Natives and Newcomers.* Kingston and Montreal: McGill-Queen's University Press.

Tropp, L. and R. Bianchi 2006 "Valuing Diversity and Interest Group Contact." *Journal of Social Issues,* 62 (3): 533–551.

Trudel, Marcel and Genevieve Jain 1970 "Canadian History Textbooks." *Studies of the Royal Commission on Bilingualism and Biculturalism,* No. 5. Ottawa: Queen's Printer.

Turcotte, M. and J. Zhao 2004 "Well-being of off-Reserve Aboriginal Children." *Canadian Social Trends,* Winter, 22–27.

Turpel, Mary 1990 "Aboriginal Peoples and the Canadian Charter: Interpretive Monopolies, Cultural Differences." *Canadian Human Rights Year Book,* 1989–90. Ottawa: University of Ottawa, Human Rights Research and Education Centre, pp. 3–45.

Umorzurike, U 1972 *Self-Determination in International Law.* Hamden CT: Anchor Books.

United Nations, Department of Public Information. 1992. "The Internatioal Year for the World's Indigenous People." Retrieved June 13, 2011 (www.ciesin.org/docs/010-000a/Year_Worlds_Indig.html).

University of Saskatchewan 2010 Aboriginal Urbanization in Canada: challenges in Measurement and Interpretation, (http://gismap.usask.ca/website/Web_atlas/AOUAP/)

Usher, P. 1989 *Towards a Strategy for Supporting the Domestic Economy of the Northwest Territories.* Ottawa.

Usher, P., G. Duhaime, and E. Searles 2003 "The Household as an Economic Unit in Arctic Aboriginal Communities and its Measurement by Means of a Comprehensive Survey." *Social Indicators Research,* 61: 175–202.

Uslaner, E. 2002 *The Moral Foundations of Trust.* Cambridge: Cambridge University Press.

Venne, Sharon Helen 1998 *Our Elders Understand Our Rights: Evolving International Law Regarding Indigenous Peoples.* Penticton BC: Theytus Books.

Verkuyten, M. 2005 "Ethnic Group Identification and Group Evaluation Among Minority and Majority Groups: Testing the Multiculturalism Hypothesis." *Journal of Personality and Social Psychology,* 88: 121–138.

Walker, James 1971 "The Indian in Canadian Historical Writing." *Canadian Historical Association, Historical Papers,* 1971: 21–47.

Walters, D., J. White and P. Maxim 2004 "Does Postsecondary Education Benefit Aboriginal Canadians? An Examination of Earnings and Employment Outcomes for

Recent Aboriginal Graduates." *Canadian Public Policy/Analyse de politiques*, 30 (3): 283–301.

Warry, W. 2007 *Ending Denial.* Peterborough, ON: Broadview Press.

Washburn, W. 1957 "A Moral History of Indian White Relations." *Ethnohistory*, 4:47–61.

Waters, A. (ed.) 2004 *American Indian Thought.* Malden, MA: Blackwell Publishing.

Waubageshig 1970 *The Only Good Indian.* Toronto: New Press.

Weaver, S. 1978 *Indian Women, Marriage and Legal Status.* Waterloo, ON: University of Waterloo, n.p.

_____ **1980** *The Hidden Agenda: Indian Policy and the Trudeau Government.* Waterloo, ON: University of Waterloo, mimeo.

_____ **1981** *Making Canadian Indian Policy: The Hidden Agenda 1968–1970.* Toronto: University of Toronto Press.

_____ **1983** "Federal Difficulties with Aboriginal Rights Demands." In *Aboriginal Rights: Towards an Understanding*, J.A. Long, M. Boldt, and L. Little Bear (eds.). Lethbridge, AB: University of Lethbridge.

_____ **1984** "A Commentary on the Penner Report." *Canadian Public Policy*, 10 (2): 215–221.

_____ **1986** "Indian Policy in the New Conservative Government, Part II: The Nielsen Task Force in the Context of Recent Policy Initiatives." *Native Studies Review*, 2 (2): 1–47.

Webber, J. and C. Macleod (eds.). 2010 *Between Consenting Peoples*, Vancouver, University of British Columbia Press.

Weinstein, J. 2007 *Quiet Revolution West: The Rebirth of Métis Nationalism.* Calgary: Fifth House Ltd.

Wertman, P. 1983 "Planning and Development after the James Bay Agreement." *Canadian Journal of Native Studies*, 2 (3): 48–56.

Wherrett, J. 1999 *Aboriginal Self-Government*, 96-2E, Ottawa, Library of Parliament, Parliamentary Information and Research Services.

Whitehead, S., B. Henning, J. Johnston and A. Devlin 1996 *Developing an Injury Morbidity and Mortality Profile in the Sioux Lookout Zone: 1992–1995.* Ottawa: Canadian Hospitals Injury Reporting and Prevention Program.

Whiteside, D. 1972 *A Good Blanket Has Four Corners: An Initial Comparison of the Colonial Administration of Aboriginals in Canada and the United States.* Paper presented at the Western Association of Sociology and Anthropology, Calgary.

_____ **1980** *Bullets, Bibles, Bureaucrats, and Businessmen: Indian Administration in Upper Canada, 1746–1980.* Address to the Indian Historical Conference, Walpole Island Reserve, November 15, 1980.

White, J., P. Maxim and D. Beavon. 2003. *Aboriginal Conditions: Research as a Foundation for Public Policy*, Vancouver, University of British Columbia Press.

Wien, F. 1986 *Rebuilding the Economic Base of Indian Communities: The Micmac in Nova Scotia.* Montreal: Institute for Research on Public Policy.

Wildsmith, B. 1985 "Pre Confederation Treaties." In *Aboriginal Peoples and the Law*, B. Morse (ed.). Ottawa: Carleton University Press, pp. 122–271.

Wilkins, K. 1999 ". . . But We Need the Eggs: The Royal Commission, the Charter of Rights and the Inherent Right of Aboriginal Self-Government." *University of Toronto Law Journal*, 44 (1): 53–121.

Willhelm, Sidney M. 1969 "Red Man, Black Man, and White America: The Constitutional Approach to Genocide." *Catalyst*, 4 (Spring): 3–4.

Williams, A. 1997 "Canadian Urban Aboriginals: A focus on Aboriginal Women in Toronto." *The Canadian Journal of Native Studies*, 17:75–101.

Williams, K. and A. Carter-Sowell 2009 "Marginalization Through Social Ostracism: Effects of Being Ignored and Excluded." In F. Butera and J. Levine. *Coping with Minority Status*, Cambridge: Cambridge University Press, pp. 104–124.

Wilmont, S. 2003 "Urban reserves." *New Socialist Magazine* (www.newsocialist.org/magazine/44/article5.html

Wilson, D. and D. Macdonald 2010 *The Income Gap Between Aboriginal Peoples and the Rest of Canada*, Ottawa: Canadian Centre for Policy Alternatives.

Wong, D. 2002 *Cities at the Crossroads: Addressing Intergovernmental Structures for Western Canada's Cities.* Calgary: Canada West Foundation.

Wood, D. and C. Griffiths 2000 "Patterns of Aboriginal Crime." In *Crime in Canadian Society.* Toronto: Harcourt Brace Canada.

Woodward, J. 1989. *Native Law*, Toronto, Carswell.

Wotherspoon, T. 2003 "Prospects for a New Middle Class among Urban Aboriginal People." In *Not Strangers in These Parts*, D. Newhouse and E. Peters (eds.). Ottawa: Policy Research Institute, pp. 147–166.

Wotherspoon, T. and V. Satzewich 1993 *First Nations: Race, Class and Gender Relations.* Scarborough: Nelson Canada.

Wright, C. 1995 "Diversions are a Bright Light." *Native Issues Monthly*, special issue, 61–63.

Wright, J. 2006 *A History of the Native People of Canada: 10,000-1,000 BC*, Ottawa, Mercury Series, Archaeological paper 152, Canadian Museum of Civilization.

Wright, R. 2003 *Stolen Continents: Conquest and Resistance in the Americas.* Toronto: Penguin Canada.

Wuttunee, W. 1972 *Ruffled Feathers: Indians in Canadian Society.* Calgary: Bell Books.

Young, K. 1984 "Indian Health Services in Canada: A Sociohistorical Perspective." *Social Science and Medicine*, 18(3): 257–264.

Young, T., J. O'Neill and B. Elias, J. Reading, and G. McDonald 1998 (First National and Inuit Regional Health Survey National Steering Committees and Technical Committees), "Chronic Diseases Among Aboriginal People in Canada." Conference of the National Aboriginal Information and Research. Ottawa.

Zakariya, H. 1976 "New Directions in the Search for and Development of Petroleum Resources in the Developing Countries." *Vanderbilt Journal of Transnational Law*, 9 (Summer): 545–577.

Zlotkin, N, 1983 *Unfinished Business: Aboriginal Peoples and the 1983 Constitutional Conference.* Kingston ON: Institute of Intergovernmental Relations, Queen's University.

Index